S0-AXJ-968

DATE DUE

Studies in Decision Making

edited by Martin Irle

Studies in Decision Making

Social Psychological and Socio-Economic Analyses

edited by
Martin Irle
in collaboration with Lawrence B. Katz

Walter de Gruyter · Berlin · New York 1982

HM
73
S87
C·1

#8194514
DLC

12-9-82 JH

This book is edited on behalf of the Sonderforschungsbereich 24 'Sozialwissenschaftliche Entscheidungsforschung' of the Univerität Mannheim, Federal Republic of Germany.

Dr. Martin Irle
o. Professor, Director of the Institut f. Sozialwissenschaften, Universität Mannheim.

Cip-Kurztitelaufnahme der Deutschen Bibliothek

Studies in decision making:
social psycholog. and socio-econom. analyses/
ed. by Martin Irle in collab. with Lawrence B. Katz
(This book is ed. on behalf of the Sonderforschungsbereich 24
"Sozialwissenschaftl. Entscheidungsforschung" of the Univ.
Mannheim, Federal Republic of Germany). – Berlin; New York :
de Gruyter, 1982.
ISBN 3-11-008087-7
NE: Irle, Martin (Hrsg.)

Library of Congress Cataloging in Publication Data

Main entry under title:
Studies in decision making.

Monographs in English by members of the Sonderforschungsbereich 24 "Sozialwissenschaftliche Entscheidungsforschung," University of Mannheim, describing research
done on nineteen of their projects, from 1968-1977/78.
"Publications originating from studies conducted in the
SFB 24, University of Mannheim": p.
Includes bibliographical references and indexes.
1. Decision-making--Addresses, essays, lectures.
2. Decision-making, Group--Addresses, essays, lectures.
3. Decision-making--Research--Addresses, essays, lectures.
4. Consumption (Economics)--Addresses, essays, lectures.
I. Irle, Martin. II. Katz, Lawrence B. III. Sonderforschungsbereich 24
"Sozialwissenschaftliche Entscheidungsforschung."
HM73.S87   302.3   82-1506
ISBN 3-11-008087-7   AACR2

© Copyright 1982 by Walter de Gruyter & Co., Berlin 30
All rights reserved, including those of translation into foreign languages. No part of this book may be reproduced in any form – by photoprint, microfilm or any other means nor transmitted nor translated into a machine language without written permission from publisher. Printing: Karl Gerike, Berlin. – Binding: Dieter Mikolai, Berlin. – Printed in Germany.

Preface

"The German Journal of Psychology" provides up-to-date information of the progress and current state of psychological science
in German-speaking countries since 1977. In addition to abstracts covering German language publications, the journal
publishes review articles on selected topics of current research. During my term as president of the "Deutsche Gesellschaft für Psychologie", the editors of the journal invited me
to write an article on "The state of psychology in the Federal
Republic of Germany" for publication in Vol. 1, No. 1 (Irle,
1977). In the journal's second number, Dieter Frey wrote a review article entitled "Social psychology and decision-making
processes: The interdisciplinary research institute of SFB 24
at the University of Mannheim" (Frey, 1977), though the space
that he was allotted only allowed for a short and rough overview. We at the SFB shared the journal editors' view that a
communication gap existed with respect to German psychology
and accessibility to non-German speaking psychologists: To
quote from the journal's introductory editorial (1977, p. 1):

> "For quite some time psychologists in the German-speaking
> countries have been aware of a communication gap since,
> for psychologists from non-anglophonic countries, cross-
> language communication in psychology is typically asymmetri-
> cal. Colleagues from abroad frequently substantiate that
> there is comparatively less awareness of - and, consequent-
> ly, less scientific response to - psychological research
> work published originally in the German language than
> there is in the reverse direction."

During its first ten years (1968 to 1977), members of our research institute have published several hundred articles scattered over numerous journals, as well as a few books and chapters
of books, most of them published in German language.

This present book contains research monographs from nineteen of
our projects from 1968 to 1977/78, describing for the first
time the research of these projects in totality. Thereby these

470132

ALUMNI MEMORIAL LIBRARY
Creighton University
Omaha, Nebraska 68178

nineteen chapters contain also many new research results, not published elsewhere before. The aim of this book is twofold, first to present our research in decision making in a more unique form, and second to present it in English language, hopefully to improve communication within the international scientific community. A third aim is to support our readers with informations about where they can find reports of our former studies in more detail.

To make understandable the origin of this ongoing, large scale research effort, a few words should be said about the granting policy of the "Deutsche Forschungsgemeinschaft - DFG" (the German National Science Foundation). As elsewhere, most grants are awarded to individual researchers; in Germany, these grants cannot exceed three years. A few years ago, however, a second type of grant, the so-called "Forschungsschwerpunkte", has been instituted, it being awarded to groups of scientists from different universities who coordinate their research efforts within a single field. In psychology, "Forschungsschwerpunkte" have been awarded for topics like behavior modification, psycholinguistic, psychological ecology, psychology of thinking and, very recently, social attitudes and behavior (with Arnold Upmeyer of the Technical University of Berlin, and managing editor of the European Journal of Social Psychology, as coordinator). A third granting strategy centers on the "Forschergruppe", grants being awarded to research groups whose members are all from one university. These groups are interdisciplinary in most cases; the one closest to psychology has been related to "social indicators" and "quality of life".

There is as well a fourth granting strategy, one based on the idea of the "Sonderforschungsbereich" (SFB). These university research institutes are comparable to the institutes of the "Max Planck Gesellschaft" (which operate outside of the universities), and they cover fields neglected by the Max Planck institutes. SFB grants were first given in 1968. Since then, there are more than 120 of these institutes distributed over

nearly all universities in the Federal Republic of Germany and
Berlin (West). A couple of them contribute to research in social science at large, and one of them - the SFB 24 "Sozialwissenschaftliche Entscheidungsforschung" - is primarily devoted to social psychological and related research on decision-
making processes. This SFB 24 is one of the few SFB of the
'first hour'; that is, founded in 1968 and still in existence.
We do, however, have to face the sad fact that the DFG will not
grant any SFB forever and that this special granting ("Sonderförderung") might cease at the end of the year 1984, as it will
cease for the few other SFB of the 'first hour' which are still
in existence today. The greater the response that we receive
from the international scientific community for the present
work, the more we shall aspire to publish a second volume summarizing our research from 1978 to 1984/85.

A "Sonderforschungsbereich" does not have a president or a
director. I have been the elected outside speaker and inside
chairman from 1968 to 1978, and again this is my duty for the
last phase of the SFB 24 in 1982 to 1984. For most of these
former years, the above-mentioned Arnold Upmeyer has been my
partner in this task, and I am deeply devoted to this friend
and former co-worker. It is a great honor and pleasure to me
that the assembly of the institute members asked me to edit
our book. Lawrence B. Katz, a student of William J. McGuire,
improved our English language, chapter by chapter, and, moreover, made a lot of suggestions in order to improve the book's
form and contents. Though he is a true co-editor, he is in no
way responsible for any shortcomings still existing, this
responsibility resting solely with myself. On behalf of our
institute and even more on my own, I am grateful to have him
as a co-editor and friend.

We - the authors and the editor - would like to thank Ekkehard
Rosch and Claudius Sauer, who, besides their duties as authors,
managed the whole organizational task of preparing this book
for publication. We would also like to thank our staff of

secretaries, headed by Mrs. Irmgard Becker, who were responsible
for preparing the book's final manuscript. Our thanks go as
well, of course, to the "Deutsche Forschungsgemeinschaft" for
all the good will it showed us and for its readiness to apply
this fourth type granting strategy to our group. Last but not
least, we are grateful to our publishing company, especially
to Mr. Werner Schuder, who did not fear the risks involved in
publishing this volume.

This book is dedicated to Leon Festinger, doctor honoris causa
of the Universität Mannheim. Chairman, at the time, of the
Committee on Transnational Social Psychology of the Social
Science Research Council, it was he who provided the key encouragement for this research program when we were together
at an international conference at Frascati, Italy, in 1964.

Martin Irle

Contributors

Numbers in parentheses indicate the pages in which the authors'
contributions begin

Aschenbrenner, Karl-Michael; Dipl.-Psych., Dr. phil.,
   Research Associate, Psychologisches Institut, Universität
   Heidelberg (675)

Bandilla, Wolfgang; Dipl.-Soz., Research Associate, SFB 24,
   Universität Mannheim (89)

Beeskow, Werner; Dipl.-Wi.-Ing., Research Associate, SFB 24,
   Universität Mannheim (549)

Bollinger, Günter; Dipl.-Psych., Dr. phil., Research Associate,
   Fakultät für Sozialwissenschaften, Universität Mannheim
   (15)

Bollinger-Hellingrath, Christa; Dipl.-Psych., Dr. phil.,
   Clinical Psychologist, Lebenshilfe e.V., Bad Dürkheim (15)

Borcherding, Katrin; Dipl.-Psych., Dr. phil., Research Associate,
   SFB 24, Universität Mannheim (627)

Burger, Christine; Dipl.-Psych., Research Associate, SFB 24,
   Universität Mannheim (167)

Dichtl, Erwin; Dipl.-Kfm., Dr. oec. publ., Professor of Marketing, Institut für Marketing, Universität Mannheim (549)

Dickenberger, Dorothee; Dipl.-Soz., Dr. phil., Research
   Associate, Lehrstuhl für Sozialpsychologie, Universität
   Mannheim (311)

Etzel, Gerhard; Dipl.-Psych., Dr. phil., Siemens AG - Unter-
   nehmensbereich Datentechnik, Betriebspsychologisches
   Zentrum, München (115)

Finck, Gerhard; Dipl.-Kfm., Research Associate, SFB 24,
   Universität Mannheim (549)

Frey, Dieter; Dipl.-Soz., Dr. phil., Professor of Social Psychology, Institut für Psychologie, Christian-Albrechts-Universität Kiel (281, 343)

Füchsle, Traudl; Dipl.-Psych., Dr. phil., Research Associate, SFB 24, Universität Mannheim (167)

Gniech, Gisla; Dipl.-Psych., Dr. phil., Professor of Psychology, Universität Bremen (311)

Grabicke, Klaus; Dipl.-Psych., Research Associate, SFB 24, Universität Mannheim (489)

Grabitz, Hans-Joachim; Dipl.-Psych., Dr. phil., Professor of General and Social Psychology, Psychologisches Institut Universität Düsseldorf (235)

Groffmann, Karl-Josef; Dipl.-Psych., Dr. phil., Professor of Psychology, Lehrstuhl für Psychologie I, Universität Mannheim (195)

Haisch, Jochen; Dipl.-Soz., Dr. phil., Research Associate, Psychologisches Institut, Universität Düsseldorf (235)

Hefner, Margarete; Dipl.-Kfm., Industrie- und Handelskammer, Mannheim (489)

Irle, Martin; Dipl.-Psych., Dr. rer. nat., Professor of Social Psychology, Lehrstuhl für Sozialpsychologie, Universität Mannheim (281)

Iseler, Albrecht; Dipl.-Psych., Dr. phil., Professor of Psychology, Institut für Psychologie im Fachbereich Erziehungswissenschaften, Freie Universität Berlin (15)

Jeromin, Sabine; Dipl.-Psych., Mannheim (737)

Kayser, Egon; Dipl.-Psych., Dr. phil., Research Associate, SFB 24, Universität Mannheim (359)

Kirsch, Werner; Dipl.-Kfm., Dr. rer. pol., Professor of Organizational Science, Universität München (443)

Klump, Hans; Dipl.-Soz., Mannheim (89)

Kroh-Püschel, Edith; Dipl.-Psych., Counselling Psychologist,
    Psychologische Beratung für Studenten, Freie Universität
    Berlin (195, 737)

Krolage, Josef; Dipl.-Soz., Research Associate, SFB 24,
    Universität Mannheim (89)

Ksiensik, M. Isis; Dipl.-Psych., Research Associate, SFB 24,
    Universität Mannheim (675)

Kumpf, Martin; Dipl.-Psych., Dr. phil., Research Associate,
    Lehrstuhl für Sozialpsychologie, Universität Mannheim (281,
    343)

Kutschker, Manfred; Dipl.-Kfm., Dr. rer. pol., Osram AG,
    München (443)

Lamm, Helmut; Ph.D., Professor of Psychology, Fakultät für
    Erziehungswissenschaften, Universität Köln (359)

Lilli, Waldemar; Dipl.-Kfm., Dr. rer. pol., Professor of
    Social Psychology, SFB 24, Universität Mannheim (89)

Mai, Norbert; Dipl.-Psych., Dr. phil., Max-Planck-Institut,
    München (675)

Möntmann, Volker; Dipl.-Soz., FHS der Bundesanstalt für Arbeit,
    Nürnberg (281)

Müller, Günter F.; Dipl.-Psych., Dr. phil., Institut für
    Psychologie, Universität Oldenburg (411)

Müller, Stefan; Dipl.-Psych., Research Associate, SFB 24,
    Universität Mannheim (549)

Ochsmann, Randolph; Dipl.-Soz., Dr. phil., Research Associate,
    Fachbereich 3 Psychologie, Universität Osnabrück (281,343)

Raffée, Hans; Dipl.-Kfm., Dr. rer. pol., Professor of Marke-
    ting, Universität Mannheim (489)

Rosch, Ekkehard; Dipl.-Soz., Research Associate, SFB 24, Universität Mannheim (69, 89)

Sauer, Claudius; Dipl.-Soz., Research Associate, SFB 24, Universität Mannheim (281, 343)

Schaefer, Ralf E.; Dipl.-Psych., Dr. phil., Professor of Psychology, Universität Mannheim (627)

Schätzle, Thomas; Dipl.-Kfm., Research Associate, SFB 24, Universität Mannheim (489)

Schellhammer, Edith; Dipl.-Soz., Research Associate, SFB 24, Universität Mannheim (115)

Schöler, Manfred; Dipl.-Kfm., Deutscher Sparkassen- und Giroverband, Bonn (489)

Schwinger, Thomas; Dr. phil., Research Associate, SFB 24, Universität Mannheim (359)

Trommsdorff, Gisela; Dipl.-Soz., Dr. phil., Professor of Social Psychology, Institut für Erziehungswissenschaft der Technischen Hochschule Aachen (145, 167)

Wender, Ingeborg; Dipl.-Psych., Dr. phil., Fachbereich V, Technische Universität Braunschweig (195)

Zaus, Michael; Dipl.-Psych., Dr. phil., Institut für Psychologie, Universität Oldenburg (675)

Contents

Introduction

Martin Irle

It is usually the case that theory and research on decision
making limits itself to choices of actions under incomplete
knowledge and/or with uncertain preferences. States of world,
alternative choices of action, and resulting outcomes are defined; they describe a situation for decision.

We do not intend to propose a more comprehensive, descriptive
theory of decision nor to trace out a theory of action. On the
contrary, we have reason to assume that middle and smaller-
range theories achieve greater explanatory power in circum-
scribed empirical fields. But the task still remains of explaining more complex decisional behavior - outside of the
lab - usig a set of overlapping theories.

Flow charts of decision making customarily start with (1) identification of a problem, followed by (2) search of information
relevant to the problem, (3) production of possible solutions,
(4) evaluative comparison of solutions, (5) choice of one solution, (6) execution of this solution by action and finally,
(7) an evaluative comparison of predicted and actual consequences of action (Brim et al., 1962). Of course, such flow charts
only define sub-classes of decision-oriented behavior that can
be at least partly overlapping in space and time and that can
sometimes occur to some degree in the reverse order. Eberhard
Witte has demonstrated this with his study of written reports
of vendors and buyers of computer equipment in West Germany
during the sixties (Witte, 1968). As 'phase' 7 may initiate a
new or repeated decision-making process, and as each 'phase'
may contain the whole process from phase 1 to phase 7 in a
nut-shell, even Festinger's classification of pre- and post-
decisional periods or pre- and post-choice situations may be
a bit arbitrary (Festinger, 1964). It seems to be nothing else
than a question of research perspective whether we consider
our subjects to be in a pre-decisional, a post-decisional, or
between-decisional state or phase.

We have been particularly struck by the fact that recent decision theory and research has been restricted to establishing
boundary conditions (as part of the "explanans") of given states
of the world and of given levels of information usable in chos-
ing between given alternatives of action. We have also remarked that in this recent research 'choice' has been the dominant
dependent variable, or the main "explanandum".

At the same time, we learned from Hans Albert (1968) that there
is no principal difference between epistemological decisions
(i.e., decisions to believe in the truth of knowledge) and technological ones (i.e., decisions to intervene in a world, or to
create a new world, with expectancy of success). Those who love
flow charts are invited to introduce an intermediate stage between steps 6 and 7 that they might call the "implementation"
of the chosen alternative, this holding true especially within
collective and organized decision-making processes.

As far as its broad aims, our program of research centered on
the two following points. First, we tried to broaden our perspective of individual and of collective decision-making to
include the seeking and evaluation of information, as well as
the possible distortion of information during judgmental processes. That is, we tried to find out how the results of information seeking (step 2 in the "typical" decision flow chart)
may change the identification of problems (step 1) or how
control of a decision (step 7) may change the actual choice of
action, and so on. Second, we tried to take the dichotomy between "cognitivism" versus "behaviorism" seriously by assuming
that all decisions can fruitfully be looked on from a perspective of psychological epistemology.

The founders of the SFB 24, the majority of whom have now mov-
ed to other universities, adapted their ongoing research activities to fit within these guidelines. This fresh look and the
recognition of the necessity of coordinating ones own research
interests with others has been and still is our answer to the
demands of the "Deutsche Forschungsgemeinschaft" with regard

to the "Sonderförderung" granting strategy. The danger with such programs, of course, is that coordinating or even more integrating specific research programs into a unified whole - even when defined under the broadest perspectives - runs the risk of conflicting with the particular research goals of about 15 to 20 small research teams involved in their own, very specific projects. Evidence that the individual research teams did manage to preserve a considerable degree of autonomy abounds in their respective chapters. As editor, I must confess that the task of writing an individual introduction for each, explaining the research project's position in the context of the institute as a whole, exceeded my capacity for "leveling."

At the least, this book can be considered as a collection of monographs summarizing the activities of a group of loosely coordinated research projects. In the early morning, when the sun is rising, everyone is full of hope and faith that he will reach his main goal for the day before twilight sets in. By early (or late?) afternoon, he becomes wise and modest. We have reached this latter point!

The idea behind the sequence of chapters is twofold: Chapters 1 to 13 are loosely ordered according to the steps of the decision flow chart outlined above. Chapters 14 to 19 are less oriented towards empirically testing theories than they are towards examining the usefulness of theories in explaining empirical problems that are not yet well understood. Chapters 14 to 16 apply social psychological theories to problems of marketing research, while chapters 17 to 19 apply prescriptive decision theory as a decision aid in several different fields. Two early projects in organizational decision making are not reported in this book; new projects in organizational and juridical decision making that started in 1978/79 are not included either.

Again, we believe in the usefulness of flow charts only as a pragmatic device for rough analytical classification. In this sense, chapter 1 addresses the question of how decisional tasks emerge. Very often the problems in need of solution are ill defined when the individual or collective decisional processes begin. Whenever the problem does not admit to a single "correct" solution that need only be retrieved from memory or some external data source, the influence of divergent thinking and its antecedents should be taken into account. Chapter 1 implicitly adheres to the fact that the majority of decisional problems are of a probabilistic, not deterministic, type. Ideation in this chapter is analyzed as a type of cognitive behavior aimed at redefining problems and thereby leading to different alternative paths in solving a decisional task. The question of imitation of ideation within groups is of special interest. The authors do not mention "group think" (Janis, 1972), but they do provide evidence for a tendency, under certain conditions, to reproduce the ideas of others even when there is no pressure to conform. Since ideation or divergent thinking takes place in settings in which the individual or a group has no firm assumptions or hypotheses about the problem matter that they are faced with (in dissonance theory terms, their hypotheses' resistance to change is low), such situations should be characterized by a high degree of uncertainty among individuals and, hence, a readiness to mold one's own opinion to other's.

Chapter 2, 3, and 4 are devoted to processes and consequences of social judgment. We confess that our research (chapter 2) testing models of information integration and summation ended in a blind alley. Mainly, evaluation of diagnostic information is not a reactive or even passive calculation: Lay people as intuitive scientists do not use incoming information in an inductive manner; they actively test the truth of their hypotheses by a sort of deductive reasoning. This theoretical perspective should include theories able to explain cases in which lay hypotheses are changed to fit to empirical facts: The problem is to make clear that circumstances under which theories are "dictated" by facts instead of vice versa. This problem is not unique to lay epistemology. Diagnostic, cognitive behavior is also the central topic of research summarized in chapter 3.

Stereotyping of information seems to be a preferred alley for
reducing ideation or divergent thinking to reproductive thinking. Using Krechevsky's (1932) terms, people cognitively change
information to fit to their hypotheses when the hypotheses are
strong. Implicitly, strength of a hypothesis refers to its resistance to change, and high resistance to change of a (lay)
hypothesis might lead to stereotypic distortions of information.

Chapter 4 gives an overview on research which is partly reported in more detail in Volume 14 of "Advances in Experimental
Social Psychology", edited by Len Berkowitz (Arnold Upmeyer:
"Perceptual and Judgmental Processes in Social Contexts").
Applying signal detection (SDT) theory and comparable models
to social judgment seems far removed from decision-making. But
on the contrary, SDT is a convincing example of the importance
of perceptual (!) information processing relating to decisions
of knowledge; i.e., decisions as to the truthfulness of received information. This chapter (and Upmeyer's contribution to
AESPs) offers some empirical evidence that distortion or defor-
mation of information by the receiver, as compared to properties of the stimulus delivered by a transmitter, has to be located in response biases. Social contexts as response sets
(converted into subjective hypotheses) "distort" within the
second step of information processing (output), but may nevertheless improve the first step, that of perceptual performance
(input). Research reported in chapters 2 to 4 and several later
chapters (especially chapters 8 and 9) strengthened our suspicion that Festinger (1964, p. 8 f. and 152) is wrong in assuming that pre-decisional gathering and evaluation of information
is unbiased, impartial, and objective in comparison to post-
decisional information processing (cf. post-decisional selective exposure to information).

Chapters 5, 6, and 7 deal with much more complex cognitive behavior within social contexts than the preceding chapters. They
center on situations in which no direct tests of reality or
of the truth of judgments are possible. Chapters 5 and 6 deal

with orientations toward the future. Expectations about public events in the middle and long-ranged future are dependent on beliefs about triggering conditions, consequences, and the desirability of such events, as well as on influences stemming from group-discussion that affect extremization, certainty and the balance of optimism and pessimism concerning those events (chapter 5). Future orientation is part of time perspective; that is, of the psychological presentation of past, present, and future within the life space of a person at a given place in time and space. Limitations of future orientation are analyzed theoretically and studied empirically as a function of social class, social roles, patterns of child-rearing, and delinquency, with special attention on delay of reward (chapter 6).

The research described in chapter 7 revisits social learning theory and deals with behavioral changes that may or may not result from decisions.[1]

The authors ask to what extent behavioral change follows not so much from decisions to act in different ways than before but just a consequence of observations of other persons' behavior in comparable situations. Within developmental psychology and/or socialization theory, children are not viewed at as decision-makers but as imitators. The extent to which the actions of individual adults (or more or less organized groups of them) are consequences of modeling processes has been neglected in decision research. That is, even in cases of objective probabilistic problems with no best solution, people apply those solutions (decisions) they have observed in similar appearing cases.

---

[1] Closely related to this project, another research group at our institute studied diverging and contradicting theoretical assumptions from Piaget and Bandura concerning the development of competence through social learning. This latter project is not reported here but is subject of a separate monograph (Waller, 1978).

There is a field still open for the SFB 24 in studying the garbage can theory of decision making by March & Olson (1976) in more detail: Problems and solutions are mixed by chance within one universe; tasks and instruments may join by chance.

Chapter 8 to 11 tackle decisional processes by applying balance theory approaches. Chapter 8 especially makes it more than doubtful that pre-decisional information-processing is as unbiased, impartial, and objective as Festinger (1964, p. 8 f., p. 152) believed.

The experimental studies presented in chapter 8 deal with information search, comparison of different solutions for a given problem, and final choice. The earlier a hypothesis about a correct or best solution of a problem is arrived at, the more, later on, incoming information is distorted to fit as evidence for the hypothesis. This occurs, furthermore, even when the refuting information is unequivocal or the corroborating information ambiguous.

Such series of decisions about the diagnostic value of incoming information might be viewed at as micro choices preceding final choice of a macro decisional process. At least two different mechanisms seem to operate in these experimental situations, one being directed by a need for consistency (consonance or balance) and the other by a need for validity (or fear of invalidity). A third mechanism, directed by a need for reaching a preferred or positively evaluated goal, could also be involved.[1]

The research summarized in chapter 8 stimulated another program within the SFB 24 in order to reconsider the theory of cognitive

---

[1] Arie Kruglanski in a personal communication to the author, interpreting the results of these studies in terms of his theory of lay epistemology.

dissonance, mainly in its relation to post-decisional dissonance and selective exposure to information.[1]

This research, summarized in chapter 9, encouraged the author of this introduction to propose a revised theory of cognitive dissonance, using concepts which can be traced back to Krechevsky (1932) and Postman (1963; see also the excellent presentation of the "hypothesis" theory of perception by Allport, 1955, p. 375 - 406). This revised theory of cognitive dissonance which is still in the process of being tested in lab and field settings, is presented as appendix to this chapter.[2]

Chapter 10 deals with the theory of psychological reactance. This theory of freedom of choice is of special interest in explaining pre- and post-choice consequences; that is, steps (4) (evaluative comparisons of solutions) (5) (choice) and (7) (evaluative comparison of consequences) of the decision flow chart.

The empirical research carried out at Mannheim led to a revision of this theory too, these revisions centering mainly on identifying the conditions under which no reactance will occur (given threatened freedom of choice) as well as developing the distinction between 'freedom to' and 'freedom from'. A futural goal is to logically reduce a revised theory of reactance to dissonance theory terms, it being our opinion that what contradictions remain between the two theories are due to ambiguities in the theories' original forms.

---

[1] Part of the research on "selective exposure to information" has been done without grants to the SFB 24 and will be published elsewhere (Frey, 1982).

[2] It should be noted that these assumptions within cognitive psychology can be traced back also to the "Würzburger Schule", especially to Selz (1922) and even to the philosopher Immanuel Kant. This theoretical stream is non-positivistic and fundamentally analyzed and substantiated by Popper (1935), who calls it "critical rationalism."

At a first glance, social deviancy does not seem to have anything to do with decisional behavior. It is, however, the topic
of one of our newest projects, whose results are summarized in
chapter 11. This research concentrates on the consequences of
choices, especially for those cases where discrepancies between
predicted and actual results (cf. step 7) are extreme and chro-
nical. We are still in an early and preliminary state in trying to explain chronic violation of social norms in social
aggregations in terms of faulty decision making. The notion of
"learned helplessness" is strongly connected to this approach,
as is the theory of the cognitive balance.

The approach to decision making described in chapter 12 and
13 has its roots in game theory and is directed primarily toward step 5 (choice) in the decision flow chart.

Equity theory, as recently proposed by Walster et al. (1978)[1],
does not explicitly take in account social norms about what is
equitable or just and what is less (or not at all) just. Nor
does it take into account conflicts between subjective but
still normative standards of equity and normative standards
imposed from the exterior.

Equity and justice may differ. In chapter 12 two negotiation
paradigms concerning allocations in cases of justice and of
equity are theoretically and empirically compared. This research is related especially to decisions that are the result
of restricting conditions in negotiations and bargaining. Since
these conditions are typical of most social negotiation contexts, this research constitutes an important part of the
SFB 24 program.

Chapter 13 presents research on bargaining and its consequences. Our studies try to clarify what happens motivationally
in mixed motive or mixed sum games. Level of experience in

---

[1]This book was completed when two of the authors were guest
research professors at the SFB 24, Mannheim.

bargaining, aspiration level, degree of pay-off information, social power and other independent variables are applied to test a motivational theory of conflict resolution similar to the viewpoint developed by Morton Deutsch (1973). Chapter 13, using the same paradigm as chapter 12, is directed more to intra-individual than to inter-individual differences in nego- tiation behavior.

Though empirical scientific research is usually classified as being either basic or applied, we prefer a more refined, three- level classification (Irle, 1975). While "basic" research is research aimed at empirically testing the truth or worth of a theory in explaining facts, it is also "applied" in so far as the theory is used to explain and forecast real phenomena. The difference is one of emphasis, the basic researcher being more interested in the explanatory power of a theory than in the specific facts that he/she uses to test the theory's work.

The applied researcher, on the other hand, takes the theory's explanatory power as a given; either alone or in combination with others, the theory provides the applied researcher with a framework for analyzing and, hopefully, clarifying the parti- cular phenomenon with which the researcher is concerned. Yet it can also happen that applied research leads to modifications in the theory or theories that guided it.

A third type of empirical research can be referred to as "tech- nological" research, its motive being to steer or to control ("Steuerung", see Albert, 1976) by applying techniques that either modify existing conditions or create new ones (e.g. psychotherapy could be placed in this category). Social and/or behavioral techniques, like those of engineering, are not at all pure transformations of theory into practice but rather are a mixture of theory-guided applications with pre-scientific lay knowledge about how to solve practical problems (Bunge, 1967). Technological devices may be tested by simulations - in a laboratory situation - before being applied. This type of empirical research too may lead to revisions of the theory or theories underlying it.

The first 13 chapters of this book deal with basic research, testing and revising theories that are directed at explanating decisional behavior and its boundary conditions. Chapters 14 through 19 on the other hand, deal with applied and, in some cases, technological research, their aim being to clarify and/ or modify problematic real-world situations.

While chapters 1 to 13 report more theory-oriented research, chapters 14 to 16 are more oriented to clarification and ex- planation of problems, and chapters 17 to 19 deal with empi- rical research on prescriptive decision theories and with transformations of such theories in social technologies or more specific: in decision aids.

Chapter 14 reports a study of joint decision processes that occur during negotiations between sellers and buyers of in- dustrial investment goods. Data on actual transactions were collected in a survey and then analyzed in terms of a causal model featuring various endogenous (episode) and exogenous (surround) variables. The authors make a point of stating that the particular model that they employed could probably be re- placed with other models without any loss of precision. Never- theless, they are able to achieve an impressive degree of correspondence between a complex reality and a complex theo- retical frame of reference.

Chapter 15 reports several studies that center on the first two stages of our decision flow chart (identifying the problem, and seeking out relevant information), the central problem being one of understanding how consumer decisions are made in private households. Information requirements, search of in- formation, information needs as a function of product type and consumer segment, language barriers of foreign workers as consumers, and other topics are studied using social psycho- logical theories as interpretive tools. The research of this program is explicitly consumer oriented.[1]

A third research program touching on socio-economics is reported in chapter 16. First steps are undertaken to support public
consumer policy with information from consumers about their
needs and satisfaction with supply of daily necessities within
their area of residence. It is hoped that such information
could provide the basis for better reglementation of local
supplies of consumer goods, especially where this would alle-
viate the problems of immobile consumer segments.

This program makes use of theoretical, empirical, and methodological analyses that rely not only on information about objective states of supply but also on information about subjective states of consumer households. As part of social indicators, results of such a strategy might become more than a descriptive clarification of a supply segment of life quality,
namely an aid for improved decisions in regional and community
policy.

Chapter 17 through 19 deal with decision aids, presenting methodological and empirical analyses on issues concerning steps 4
(evaluative comparisons of alternative solutions) and 5 (choice
of one solution) in the decision flow chart. The research reported in each chapter makes use of multi-attribute utility
models.

While chapter 17 emphasizes the comparing, testing, and developing such models, chapter 18 is directed more towards the application of these models as practical tools for decision aid
(though several methodological and theoretical points are made
as well).

Chapter 19 is exclusively devoted to a specific real world
problem, that of occupational choice and job decisions for young

---

[1] A follow-up program, independent from the SFB 24 and sponsored
by the federal government, has been recently been established
under the name "research group - consumer information."

people. It is hoped that the tools developed by this project
will be of use in redressing the current deficiencies in public
occupational counselling in the Federal Republic of Germany.

Yet at this point, basic research and its funding finds its
limit in our country. Applied research as technological research is very seldom part of granted and mostly part of research commissioned by public or private institutions.

Chapter 1 Ideation in Individual and Group Settings
G. Bollinger, C. Bollinger-Hellingrath and A. Iseler

1. Introduction

The analysis of decision making usually starts by assuming
several well-defined sets of marginal conditions (e.g. the
desirability of the consequences of the various decision alternatives, the possible states of nature and ways of gathering
information about them) that determine whatever final decision
is made. Whereas these sets are sometimes clearly specified by
the characteristics of the decision situation itself, the
salience and extent of their contents are in most cases affected by ideational processes that occur before, during and after
the decision process.

A sharp distinction between "reproductive" and "creative" ideation has been made obsolete by the more active views of human
memory put forward by the cognitive psychology of the last
decade. For this reason it does not seem advisable to regard
decision processes as beginning at a precise point in time
between the cessation of "creative" ideation and the start of
"reproductive". Rather, it seems more natural to regard those
ideational processes that lead to the awareness of marginal
conditions as being part of, or at least integrated with, the
decision process itself.

Nevertheless, it would be worthwhile to investigate ideation in
situations where the subjects do not have to make decisions.
Though, at first glance, there seems to be a close resemblance
between this aspect of decision research and research on creativity or divergent thinking, the latter is oriented primarily

towards identifying the factors (individual difference, situational or process-centered) that determine the production of ideas that fulfill some more or less arbitrarily established criterion of goodness that as a rule, touches upon originality, flexibility or fluency. Though decision making can be greatly improved by creative ideational input, the effects of creativity on decision making are often masked by other aspects of ideation whose influence on the final decision may be even stronger.

Our investigation started with a set of tests representing the factors of semantic divergent production according to Guilford's (1967) well-known structure of intellect model. As our research interests broadened, we felt it adviseable to extend our scoring techniques to cover previously unconsidered dimensions of ideational output, the nature of our efforts in this direction being described in the report's second section. This second section also deals with the problem of clustering in ideational production; i.e. the tendency to generate ideas in sequences, where the probability that a given idea will be generated varies positively with the similarity of the preceding data. Clustering should not only provide a means for gaining insight into the cognitive processes involved in creative thinking but also have obvious close connections to more applied problems like the lack of flexibility or the channeling of ideas during decision making.

The third section of this report deals with individual differences in ideation. Such differences have a double interest in connection with decision making: On the one hand, they can lead to differences in the speed or even in the result of decision making (e.g. as when there are differences in the awareness of relevant marginal conditions); on the other hand, the dimensional analysis of these differences and their relations to other personality variables can suggest hypotheses about the mechanisms and structures underlying ideational production and how they affect decision making.

Ideational production in groups has been investigated by a
considerable number of studies. In most, the production of an
entire group of subjects working together (a "real group") was
compared with the combined output of an equal number of subjects working separately (a "nominal group"). In our experiments, which are reported in section 4, we took a different
approach: We analyzed the ideational production of individuals,
introducing various aspects of a group situation (presence of a
listener, variations in ideational production of group partners,
etc.) as experimentally manipulated, independent variables.
This method has the advantage of enabling us to more precisely
pin down the conditions and mechanisms that lead to an altered
ideational production in the group situation and to draw
tentative generalizations concerning ideational production in
decision making groups.

2.   Method development

2.1. Scoring of ideas and sequences of ideas

In research on problem solving, the primary criterion for
scoring responses is 'true-false'. In our own research, however,
we are not interested in problems that have only one clear-cut
solution - so called convergent problems. Instead, we are
interested in problems having numerous "correct" solutions,
where "to be correct" means that there is a perceivable reference to the question asked.

Similarly, practicality will not enter into our evaluation of
subjects' responses. In fact, problems in divergent thinking
often purposefully lack in clear correspondence to reality in
order to minimize the role that subjects' prior experiences
have in determining their performance. The "originality" of
responses is what is of interest to us. Though we cannot here
enter into the theoretical details, there are two approaches to

operationalizing "originality", one involving having judges
rate subjects' responses in terms of "cleverness" or "remote-
ness", the other the calculation of the statistical rarity of a
response with reference to the responses made by a specified
subject population.

Subjects' responses will also be content analyzed in terms of
pre-established content categories and assessed in terms of such
formal criteria as concreteness and elaboration. Based on his/
her multiple responses to the series of test items, each subject will receive the following overall scores:
- a fluency score based on the overall number of correct
  responses
- an originality score based on the weighted or unweighted sum
  of the originality ratings for the subjects responses
- an elaboration score based on the weighted or unweighted sum
  of the elaboration ratings;
- a flexibility score based on the number of different content
  categories represented in the subject's responses or the
  number of between category shifts (both are highly correlated).

In having subjects generate many ideas to a problem, one can
assume that the reporting of later ideas is not independent of
the earlier ones; the earlier ideas may guide the thinking process into a certain direction and thus make the "discovery" of
a new idea possible. On the other hand, however, a fixation of
the thinking process in a certain direction may also occur, so
that later ideas are only unimportant variations on the previous ones. The relative prevalence of stimulating or inhibiting influences cannot be determined with the measures described
above, the number of categories or shifts providing only a very
rough measure of response chaining. We will develop statistical indices to measure this response characteristic in the
section that follows and will refer to them as indices of
"resonance". Though cognitive psychologists have used the term
"clustering" to refer to similar phenomena, their main interest
has tended to center on subjects' response patterns themselves

and not on the underlying mental processes. It is to emphasize our concern with process that we employ the different term.

2.2. Process-centered analysis of response sequences

An important characteristic of ideation, as opposed to problem solving, is that a single, correct solution is not called for. Rather, the only requirement is that the subjects' responses bear a relevance to the question posed. Though one way of scoring an individual subject's performance is to calculate totals on the basis of all his/her responses to a given problem, such a method does not enable one to easily investigate the processes underlying ideation. A more effective way of studying such processes is to examine the sequence of separate ideas generated in response to the problem in question.

The first study of sequential patterns in ideation was conducted by Bousfield and Sedgewick (1944) who graphed the course of ideation with cumulative reaction curves. The course of the curve could be well approximated by the equation

$$u = f(t) = c(1-e^{-mt}),$$

the variables u (number of ideas named until t) and t (time) being empirically determined, while c (maximum amount of stored information) and m (retrieval speed) are estimated from the data.

In the free recall of a list of elements belonging to distinguishable, different sized classes, one can observe that elements of the same class frequently tend to follow one another, a phenomenon known as "grouping". As a measure of grouping Bousfield (1953) proposed a coefficient RR - the "ratio of repetition" - that relates the number of sequential elements belonging to the same class to the total number of pairs of responses. With r sequential elements from the same class and a total of n items recalled, the ratio is calculated as follows:

$$RR = \frac{r}{n-1}$$

This coefficient is dependent on the number of responses as well as recall stimuli's class make-up. A more suitable measure of clustering, however, would be one that, instead of being based on the number of responses and class make-up, gave some idea of how much the observed clustering deviates from that expected on solely a random basis. Bousfield and Bousfield (1966), Frender and Doubilet (1974) and Hubert and Levin (1976, 1977) discuss other measures that relate the observed RR to its expected value, while Tulving (1962) proposes comparing the observed RR to the maximum value attainable. Though both alternatives still reflect the number of responses and the stimuli's class make-up, they do so to a lesser degree than the RR used alone.

Indication of resonance in ideation

One indicator of resonance is the presence of a high degree of semantic similarity between adjacent or nearly adjacent responses. The more distant two semantically similar items are from each other in the response sequence, the less likely it is that the appearance of the second is due to resonance from the first, since resonance should decrease over time. An adequate operationalization of resonance will therefore require the integration of semantic similarity and temporal distance in a single, quantitative index.

To determine the semantic similarity, the most obvious method would be to compare each idea with each of the others and thus arrive at an index of relative similarity. This method, however, is not practical, as it generally requires that far too many judgments be made. For a single subject giving 20 responses to a problem 190 judgments would have to be made. A less precise but more efficient method makes use of semantic categories, with all ideas falling into a given category being assumed to be more similar with each other than with ideas of other categories. Similarity, with this latter technique, can be treated

as a dichotomous or continuous variable. In the former case,
there is only the within group maximum similarity and the between group minimum similarity. In the continuous case, the
similarity between category-pairs can be rated and these
ratings attached to the pairs of ideas in question.

There are also several ways of operationalizing temporal proximity. Measures of clustering in free recall are dichotomous
in that they assume that inter-item dependencies are operant
only when the items appear adjacently to one another in the
response sequence. Such an assumption, however, seems rather
arbitrary. Why should an idea's influence be limited to immediately afterwards? A more plausible first assumption would be
that inter-item influence decreases with the time separating
the two items in question. Figures 1 and 2 present two different models of the decline of stimulation. In the first, influence is seen to be reduced by a constant decrement each time
a further item is generated. If we assume, for example, that
this decrement is 1/2, then figure 1 shows that the influence
of idea i on idea j is reduced by $(1/2)^2$ - from what it would
be if the two ideas were given consecutively.

Figure 1. Strength of the aftereffect of idea i on idea j
          according to the discrete method

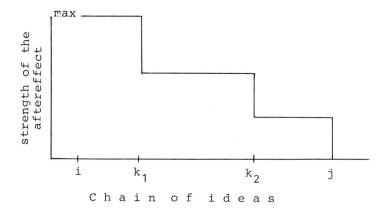

Figure 2. Strength of the aftereffect of idea i and idea j
         according to the continuous method

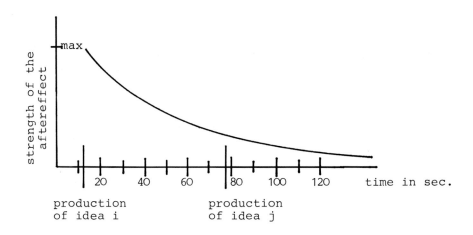

production   production
of idea i   of idea j

It should be noted that this method does not take into account
the actual length of time separating the two items in the recall sequence.

The model presented in Figure 2 considers one idea's influence
on another to be a negative, negatively accelerated function of
the amount of time that separates them, the exponential form of
the curve closely resembling those of habituation functions in
psychophysiology. Preliminary investigations with different
types of divergent thinking problems have established the
following function as a good empirical approximation of the
relation between aftereffect and temporal distance:

$$F(t) = \exp(-0.03t)$$

where $F(t)$ is the residual of the after-effect after t seconds.

Calculating raw scores for resonance

A coefficient combining the two parameters "semantic similarity"
and "temporal proximity" should have the following properties:

1. The maximum value should be attained whenever there is a maximum degree of similarity between two ideas separated by the smallest temporal distance possible.

2. The minimum value should occur whenever the semantic similarity between two ideas is the smallest. Low similarity may not be compensated by temporal proximity.

3. The coefficient should decrease with growing temporal distance between two ideas.

In order to fulfill all the requirements, a multiplicative index is needed in which "similarity" is weighted by "proximity". As in the building of sums for scales or tests, the index can then be used to calculate a total score for a sequence of ideas, the form of this calculation being as follows:

$$S_{raw} = \frac{\sum\limits_{i=1}^{n-1} \sum\limits_{j=i+1}^{n} s_{ij} \cdot c_{ij}}{\sum\limits_{i=1}^{n-1} \sum\limits_{j=i+1}^{n} c_{ij}} \qquad (1)$$

n   = number of ideas in the sequence
i   = index of all ideas whose aftereffects are observed
j   = index of all ideas which follow an idea i
s_{ij} = similarity between i and j
c_{ij} = proximity between i and j.

When proximity is scaled dichotomously ($c_{ij}=0$ for "no proximity" $c_{ij}=1$ for "proximity"), the formula reduces to:

$$S_{raw} = \frac{\sum\limits_{i=1}^{n-1} s_{i,i+1}}{n-1} , \qquad (2)$$

Under these simplified assumptions the formula is identical with the one developed by Bousfield (1953). If, as in the model presented in Figure 1, an idea's aftereffect is thought to decline at a fixed increment with each subsequent response, the following expression results:

$$S_{raw} = \frac{\sum\limits_{i=1}^{n-1} \sum\limits_{j=i+1}^{n} s_{ij} \frac{1}{k^{(j-i)}}}{\sum\limits_{i=1}^{n-1} \sum\limits_{j=i+1}^{n} \frac{1}{k^{(j-i)}}} \quad (3)$$

k = constant of decline

If, on the other hand, the item's aftereffect is thought to decline continuously as a function of temporal distance (Figure 2), the formula reads:

$$S_{raw} = \frac{\sum\limits_{i=1}^{n-1} \sum\limits_{j=i+1}^{n} s_{ij} \cdot e^{(-pt_{ij})}}{\sum\limits_{i=1}^{n-1} \sum\limits_{j+1}^{n} e^{(-pt_{ij})}} \quad (4)$$

p = parameter of decline

t_{ij} = time interval between i-th and j-th idea

If one considers that "proximity" may also be scaled either dichotomously or in multiple gradations there are six possible ways of operationalizing the stimulating content of a sequence of ideas:

RRW_1 dichotomous proximity scaling, dichotomous similarity rating (calculation according to formula (2))

RRW_2 dichotomous proximity scaling, multigrade similarity rating (calculation according to formula (2))

RRW_3 multigrade proximity scaling, dichotomous similarity rating (calculation according to formula (3))

RRW_4 multigrade proximity scaling, multigrade similarity rating (calculation according to formula (3))

RRW_5 continuous proximity scaling, dichotomous similarity
rating (calculation according to formula (4))

RRW_6 continuous proximity-scaling, multigrade similarity
rating (calculation according to formula (4))

The most complex of these operationalizations is RRW_6, as it
posits that an idea's influence decreases continuously with
time. As it stands, however, RRW_6 is inadequate. Even with a
completely random sequence of ideas in which no idea stimulates
the occurrence of another, the above version of RRW_6 would
result in a positive value. In the experiments on "influence of
other peoples' ideas" (section 4.6.), a refined version of RRW_6
was used to measure the aftereffect of ideas.

Resonance scores

Let us assume that a person has a capacity for storing say 30
ideas concerning a particular problem. Assume further that not
every idea belongs to a separate semantic class. It then
follows that even if the person in question generates the
ideas randomly, there is a certain probability that similar
ideas will be generated one after another. Furthermore, as our
operationalization allows for aftereffects even in those cases
where there are intervening dissimilar ideas, each randomly
generated response sequence will present fallacious evidence
that resonance had occurred. The extent of this "random" resonance depends on the ratio of ideas and to semantic classes: it
will be zero if there is only one idea for each class of ideas,
and it will be one if all the ideas belonged to the same class.

Since we choose to operationalize resonance in terms of a model
that posits a continuous decline of resonance with time (Figure
2), the occurrence of this "random resonance" cannot be analyt-
ically determined. Instead, however, a Monte-Carlo-simulation
study could be performed in which the resonance scores are
calculated for a large number of randomly generated response
sequences and these scores then compared to real resonance

scores obtained with the same number of ideas, classes, and ideas per class and with the same response times.

The distribution of random resonance scores could then provide a metric for evaluating the amount of real resonance that occurred in a given response sequence. For example, if a given raw score was greater than 91 of 100 random resonance scores generated under the same marginal conditions (i.e. number of ideas, classes, response times etc.), we could assign it a score of 91 and thus have some idea of how much the observed resonance could be attributed to chance alone.

As the Monte-Carlo-simulation would involve all sequences possible under the given marginal conditions, the problem of stability of the subsequently calculated coefficients has to be taken into account. The size of the simulated sample is, of course, an essential factor. Since the coefficient is a percentage of critical events over independent trials, its sampling error is $100 \sqrt{p(1-p)/N}$ (with p = probability of a random permutation with lower resonance score, and N = number of permutations). This means that 100 simulations are necessary to reduce the standard error to 3 points on our scale, when the "true score" is 90. Although the expenditure of computer time was considerable for the simulation, this degree of accuracy seemed necessary. Therefore, 100 random sequences were generated for each true sequence to assure stability of the coefficients in the empirical studies reported later on.

Without risking too many details at this point, there are two final points that should be taken into account when analyzing chains of ideas. If we talk of an idea's aftereffect, this does not mean necessarily that it makes the occurrence of certain later ideas more probable; an idea can also act in an inhibitory manner. Both types of effects can be measured: In the first case, the resulting coefficient is greater than the average random resonance, while in the latter case it is less. Secondly, when studying resonance that occurs in groups, it is important to distinguish between the resonance

to the subjects own ideas and the resonance due to ideas generated by the other group members.

2.3. Critical evaluation of measures of resonance or clustering

The measures of resonance mentioned above take into account
temporal proximity and similarity of ideas in varying degrees.
The comparison with randomized sequences gives information
about the significance of deviation from a random expectation
and hence has a function similar to the normalization of index
"Γ" in the framework of Hubert and Levin (1976, 1977) to be
discussed later.

Limitations of this kind of approach have been shown elsewhere
(Iseler, 1978), and only a global sketch of this line of argument can be given here. It is well known from the general
theory of significance tests that the percentage of samples in
which a certain amount of deviation from random expectation is
exceeded under random conditions (i.e. the level of significance associated with this deviation from random expectation)
is a function not only of the data generating system's deviation
from randomness but also of sample size. This implies that
this percentage is useful as a measure of the true amount of
deviation from randomness only for samples of equal size.

The same is true if we do not draw independent samples but
randomizations of one empirical set of data. Thus, we could
take random permutations of the empirical values of y (the
values of x being fixed) and compute a correlation coefficient
for each random permutation. For constant true correlation
(≠ 0), the expected percentage of random permutations yielding
a correlation coefficient higher than the empirical one would
be negatively related both to the departure of the true correlation from a zero correlation and to sample size.

We can transfer this to our index of resonance in the following way: The percentage of random permutations giving a lower

resonance raw score than the empirical data does not reflect
the "true" resonance tendency alone but depends also on the
"sample size" (i.e. the number of ideas in the protocol). Unfortunately, it depends also on other factors (like number of
categories and distribution of ideas over categories), and
these effects are more difficult to control than those of
sample size.

Hubert and Levin (1976) and other authors (quoted in their
paper) try to compensate these effects by a normalization procedure, taking into account both size and categorial composition of the sample. Briefly, their normalized clustering index
Z is based on the number of category repetitions, for which
these authors use the letter Γ. The difference between the
empirical value of Γ and its random expectation is divided by
the standard deviation of its probability distribution under
random conditions.

Again - as has been proven elsewhere (Iseler, 1978) - Hubert
and Levin's formula does not give a measure of amount but rather
of significance of departure from random expectation. This can
be demonstrated by a simple example. For the sequence
AAAA BBB AA BBBB
containing items from only two categories A and B, we get a
normalized clustering coefficient of Z = 2,018 according to
Hubert and Levin's equations. If we repeat this sequence giving
AAAA BBB AA BBBB AAAA BBB AA BBBB
the actual degree of clustering would be no higher but the
resulting normalized clustering coefficient would be Z = 2,386.

The larger coefficient in the second case does not reflect an
increase in the amount of clustering but only that the degree
of clustering could be better confirmed with the larger set of
data.

In summary, this index is also a measure of significance of
departure from a random sequence. A high value of the index
indicates either the presence of a strong tendency for cluster-

clustering or small or moderate clustering well confirmed by a
large set of data.

2.4. The stochastic structure of ideational production

In the preceding paragraph, we referred to a "true resonance
tendency" that a useful index should reflect. We will now make
this concept more explicit. This can be done by considering
ideational production as a stochastic process. In this frame
of reference, resonance can be defined as an increase in the
probability that an idea will be produced in some time interval
t to t+d, where this increase is due to the facilitating influence of preceding ideas.

For a more precise definition, we make use of the concept
"intensity" drawn from the theory of stochastic processes in
continuous time. We define the conditional intensity of an idea
a at time t given some sequence of ideas until t as

$$h_a(t/V_t) = \lim_{\substack{d \to 0 \\ d > 0}} \frac{p(t < t_a \le t+d/V_t)}{d}$$

with

V_t = sequence of ideational production until t

$h_a(t/V_t)$ = conditional intensity of idea a at time t, given
               V_t, and

$t < t_a \le t+d$ = "There is a point of time t_a, in which idea a is
               uttered and for which the inequality is true".

Roughly speaking, the conditional intensity $h_a (t/V_t)$ is the
probability that idea a is produced in an infinitesimally small
time interval after t, divided by the width of this time interval. This probability is conditional upon V_t, which is a
sequence of pairs of data, each pair consisting of an idea and
the time of its observable production.

Mathematical models can be formulated much more comfortably in the language of intensities than on the basis of conventional probabilities or probability density functions. A calculus translating intensity-orientated formulations into probabilities or probability density functions has, however, been developed (Iseler, 1974).

In this conceptual framework, resonance is represented by an increase of the conditional intensity of an idea at time t due to the presence of similar ideas in V_t and their temporal proximity to t. If we work with multiplicative models (the reason for which will be discussed later), we assume that the conditional intensity of an idea immediately after the production of another highly similar idea differs from what it would be without such facilitation by some factor η, which is called the resonance parameter.

There are several advantages of conceptualizing resonance in this language of intensities. One of them is concerned with the evaluation of measurement techniques. For this purpose we might formulate a criterion like the following one: If for two subjects (or for two measurements under different conditions) the "true resonance" (understood as something like a latent trait) is identical, the measures should differ only by the random variation inherent in any psychological measure. On the other hand, an increase in true resonance should be reflected by an increase of the statistic under discussion. Criteria of this kind make sense only if there is a well defined concept of "true clustering tendency" or "true tendency of resonance". It seems most natural to define this concept as a parameter in a data generating probability distribution.

Following this line of argument, Iseler (1978) performed a Monte-Carlo-simulation study. To eliminate other distorting factors (especially lack of knowledge about the entire set of available ideas), a free recall experiment was simulated instead of one dealing with ideation. It was assumed that a subject has learned a set of items belonging to 2 categories A and

B (without any serial aspect) and has to recall the items in
arbitrary order. All items are learned equally well. Therefore,
they have the same basic intensity ϑ as long as no facilitating
effects are present. If, however, at some point in time t, the
last item reproduced before t belongs to the same category as
some item in a, then the intensity of a at this point of time
is $\vartheta.\eta$.

Naturally, an item that has already been recalled has zero
intensity (i.e. the simulated subject avoids repetitions).
Observation of the subject was assumed to be continued until
all items had been recalled.

In the simulation study, three factors were varied: the number
of items (20 or 30), the proportion of items belonging to the
more frequent category (.5, .6, .7 or .8) and the value of the
resonance parameter η (1, 1.5, 2, 2.5 or 3). For each simulation, the normalized clustering measure Z explained above was
computed. Comparison of the cell means led to the following
results:

a) with increasing value of η, the average value of Z increased.
This means, that this index reflects variations in "true clustering".

b) For identical values of $\eta > 1$, a higher average Z was obtained with a list of 30 items than with the 20-item-list. If
we accept that identical values of η mean an identical "true
tendency of resonance", this result indicates that the same
resonance leads to a higher Z-value when better confirmed by a
longer sequence.

  For identical values of η and identical relative frequencies
  of the categories, the ratio of the average Z-values for
  sequences of 30 and 20 items varies from 1.24 to 1.34 with
  a median of 1.28 (and without any consistent relation to η
  or to proportions of the categories). This means that the
  effect of sample size is slightly stronger than would be
  expected by the $\sqrt{N}$-law (the ratio of sample size being 1.5
  and $\sqrt{1.5} = 1.22$). Nevertheless, this sample size effect could
  roughly be compensated for by defining a new index, based on

Z divided by the square root of the number of items reproduced.

c) For identical values of $\eta > 1$, the average value of Z is a
monotonically decreasing function of p (the proportion of the
more frequent category).

> The meaning of this result will become clearer if we con-
> sider the definition of Z: It is the difference between the
> empirical number of category repetitions and the expectation
> of its probability distribution under the assumption of no
> true clustering, this difference being divided by the stand-
> ard deviation of the same probability distribution. Return-
> ing to the basic measure Γ (the number of category repeti-
> tions), we can formulate the following result: The expecta-
> tion of Γ under the assumption of no true clustering shows
> a considerable increase (from 9.0 to 12.6 for 20 items and
> from 14.0 to 19.4 for 30 items) if p is varied from .5 to
> .8. In our simulation study, the same was true for the aver-
> age of Γ, but the effect was much smaller for $\eta > 1$ (e.g.
> for $\eta = 3.0$ an increase from 13.3 to 14.9 for 20 items and
> from 20.7 to 22.9 for 30 items). In other words, the effect
> of clustering on η becomes much smaller as p increases. The
> standard deviation of η under the assumption of no true
> clustering decreases with increasing p, too, but its de-
> crease is weaker. Therefore dividing the difference between
> η and its expectation by this standard deviation compensates
> for the effects of relative category frequency only under
> the assumption of no true clustering (e.g., for the demon-
> stration that actual data are scarcely compatible with the
> assumption of no true clustering) but not for describing the
> amount of a deviation from this assumption.

In summary, the Monte-Carlo study confirmed the expectation
that the standardized clustering measure Z is not only affected
by the amount of true clustering but also by the size of the
set of items reproduced and by the relative frequencies of
categories. The standardization compensates for these effects
only under the assumption of no true clustering. The Z-statistic is useful to quantify the significance of deviation from
random clustering. However, like a t-ratio or other statistics
whose distribution is based on H_o-premisses, it should not be
used to measure the amount of deviation from random clustering
as long as the other variables affecting the statistic cannot
be held constant. This seems nearly always to be the case with
ideation.

Apart from this information about the properties of Hubert and
Levin's (1976) standardized clustering statistic Z, the simulation study demonstrates the use of a stochastic model in evaluating measurement techniques for properties of processes like
clustering in ideation or free recall: The question of whether
Z is a good index of resonance or clustering has much more
meaning if the "true clustering tendency" is defined as a property of a data generating system, rather than on the basis of
Z itself.

Until now, we have not discussed the multiplicative assumption
that underlies our model. We assumed that an idea's intensity
when facilitated by another idea belonging to the same category
is given by the product of its "basic intensity" ϑ (i.e. its
intensity without facilitating effects) and some parameter η
(which we identified as the resonance parameter). We will now
demonstrate that this multiplicative assumption is implicit in
the usual concept of clustering.

Let us assume that two subjects S_1 and S_2 have produced the
same ideas in a divergent thinking task (or in free recall) and
that the production times of one subject are equal to those of
the other multiplied by some constant c. It would seem sensible
that all concepts of resonance or clustering should imply that
the data of these subjects do not differ in resonance but only
in speed of production (or fluency). This same requirement can
be stated for data generating systems: If the stochastic properties of two data generating systems are identical except for a
multiplication of all times by a constant, then both systems
have identical clustering tendency.

We should first apply this principle to the rather simple
stochastic process of our simulation-study. We should note that
an additive model exists which makes exactly the same predictions as the assumed multiplication by a resonance parameter
η (see above p. 31): If we define $\vartheta^* = \vartheta (\eta -1)$, the conditional intensity of an item is $\vartheta+\vartheta^*$ if the preceding item belongs

to the same category. ϑ^* is thus an additive parameter of clustering. It can, however, be shown that the stochastic properties of two data generating systems of this kind are identical except for a multiplication of all times by a constant, if and only if the ratios of intensities are identical. (For subjects with differing values of ϑ this would be given, if ϑ is multiplied by the same value, if the last preceding item belongs to the same category.) Therefore, identical values of η in the multiplicative formulation of our model are indicators of identical resonance according to our postulate, whereas this is not true for identical values of ϑ^* in the additive model. Therefore, the multiplicative model is in better accordance with the above stated requirement.

In this model, additivity or multiplicativity turned out to be a question of formulation without empirical consequences. This stems from the assumption that the basic intensity is identical for all items. If we introduce variation in basic intensities and keep the assumption that resonance is given by multiplication of the basic intensities by a constant η, no simple additive equivalent of this multiplicative model could be formulated. In this case, it is an empirical question whether multiplicative or additive models show a better fit with empirical data. If the former turns out to be better, the multiplicative implications inherent in the usual concept of "identical clustering" would be corroborated. If the latter proved better, on the other hand, it would require a revision of the clustering concept.

Model tests can be carried out using methods developed in this project. Since these methods have not yet been tried out extensively enough to produce notable results, only a sketch of them will be given here (cf. Iseler, 1974, for a detailed discussion). The model (or alternative models) to be tested must be formulated in terms of functions allocating a conditional intensity $h_a(t/v_t)$ to idea a as a function of time t, ideational production before t(i.e. v_t) and of parameters associated

with ideas and/or subjects. An example of such a function would
be:

$$h_a(t/v_t) = \vartheta_a \left[\frac{n+c \cdot \tau}{1+c \cdot \tau}\right]^{dav_t}$$

with

ϑ_a = basic intensity of idea a (which may be split into one
         parameter for idea a and one for the subject)

n = resonance parameter for the subject

c = parameter corresponding to rate of decay of resonance

τ = time elapsed since last production of an idea before t

dav_t = index of relation of idea a to production sequence v_t:
         dav_t = $-\infty$ if a is already contained in v_t (giving an
         intensity of zero); otherwise dav_t is 1, if the last
         idea belongs to the same category as a, and zero other-
         wise.

The above model equation can be verbally formulated in the
following way: If idea a has not yet been produced, and the
last idea before t does not belong to the same category as a,
dav_t is zero and a's conditional intensity is therefore identical with its basic intensity ϑ_a. If however, dav_t is 1 (i.e.
the preceding idea is from the same category), the basic intensity is multiplied by the fraction in brackets, which
depends on τ (the time elapsed since the preceding idea). Immediately after the preceding idea (τ = 0), the fraction has the
value n, and for increasing values of τ it converges towards 1,
the speed of this convergence depending on c. In other words,
resonance consists of an initial multiplication of the basic
intensity by a parameter of initial resonance (n); with elap-
sing time, the intensity returns continuously to the basic
value ϑ_a. The speed of this decay is indicated by parameter c.

It is possible to derive likelihood functions for empirical
data for practically all models formulated in this way. For a

theorem making this possible under very mild restrictions, see
Iseler (1974). A comparison of different models could consist
of maximizing these likelihood functions by optimal choice of
parameters and then comparing these maxima (taking into account
variables like different numbers of parameters etc. as is
necessary for all maximum likelihood tests).

This leads us to a third use of the intensity approach: The
parameter values maximizing the likelihood function can be used
as maximum-likelihood-estimators for the parameters. For instance, an estimator of our parameter η would be a useful
measure of clustering. Obviously, it would be worthwhile to
know that the intensity of an item is multiplied by a factor of
about 2 after the production of another item belonging to the
same category. And this would be more informative than the
statement that the number of category repetitions is 1.6 standard deviations above its random expectation. In addition, the
statistical properties of these estimators seem to be better
than for other statistics (Iseler, 1978).

Future work will be devoted to the solution of technical problems of parameter estimation in order to render this a routine
technique for measuring resonance and other properties of
ideational production.

In summary, the theoretical and empirical analysis of ideation
by means of intensity models is useful in that it gives a more
precise meaning to theoretical concepts and provides a background for evaluating the properties of statistics developed as
empirical indicators of these concepts. By the same approach,
general techniques for model tests are suggested together with
parameter estimations that are more intelligible and have
better statistical properties than other statistics developed
for the description of similar aspects of ideation. As soon as
the technical problems associated with the maximum-likelihood-
techniques (which have been developed simultaneously with the
empirical studies reported in section 3 and 4) have been solved,
this approach could be useful for the formulation of models of

ideation in individual and group settings.

3.   The differential approach

3.1. Discussion of existing structural models

The starting point of the present investigation was the examination of existing structural models that underly, either implicitly or explicitly, tests of creative thinking. The most
well known among these are:
a) tests developed and presented in numerous research reports
by Guilford and his collaborators (cf. the survey by Guilford
and Hoepfner, 1971).
b) Tests developed by Torrance and collaborators (cf. Torrance,
1966) - Torrance Tests of Creative Thinking (TTCT, sometimes
also called Minnesota Tests of Creative Thinking).
c) The test battery developed by Wallach and Kogan (1965).
d) The test battery "Der Verbale Kreativitätstest" developed
by Schoppe (1977), the first and so far only creativity test
published in German speaking countries.

Though all the tests consist entirely of divergent thinking
problems, they differ with regard to scoring techniques and
mode of application. These differences have to be taken into
consideration when discussing the structural models that underly the tests. For example, with respect to the question of
what these tests measure, answers range from Guilford's posit-
ing of 24 factors of divergent thinking to Wallach and Kogan's
and Schoppe's single factor views. Torrance has not explicitly
expressed himself as to the question of dimensionality. He does,
however, compute separate scores for "fluency", "flexibility"
and "originality" with respect to both semantical and figural
problems, thus - implicitly, at least - making reference to
six factors.

Though Torrance posits that the three dimensions of fluency (operationalized as the number of ideas generated), flexibility (the number of distinct classes of ideas) and originality (the unusualness of the generated ideas) are mutually independent, the results from virtually all empirical studies on this question suggest otherwise. If one takes all three measures for a given problem and then performs a factor analysis, one does not obtain three independent factors. Taking a look at the within - and between - item correlations shows why this happens, as the mean correlation between the three measures on any problem is always considerably higher than the mean correlation of a single measure across different problems. (Hargreaves & Bolton, 1972; Harvey et al., 1970; Kreft, 1976; Plass et al., 1974 and Seiffge-Krenke, 1974.) The high intercorrelation between the different measures for single problems is essentially due to the statistical dependence of the flexibility and originality measures on the number of ideas. As the number of generated ideas increases, so does the probability that a greater number of content classes will be represented. On the other hand, if originality is operationalized in terms of statistical rarity, the originality score will also increase with the number of ideas.

The model proposed by Wallach and Kogan (1965) can be regarded as the most prominent of the single - dimensional approaches to divergent thinking. There have, however, been doubts raised as to the model's adequacy. For example:

a) Wallach and Kogan's tests are administered without time limitation. Results by Christensen et al. (1957) make clear, however, that tests of divergent thinking measure different things with different time limits. Responses to the same problem at different time intervals can show different factor loadings. With no time limit, performance at the end of a problem solving session may be greatly influenced by extraneous non-ability factors, such as concentration and level of aspiration, and this in turn will influence between test homogenity.

b) All the subtests, even those with figural stimuli, require
verbal responses. In comparison with the Guilford tests, their
contents are much more homogeneous. The limited variation in
problem contents may alone be responsible for the high intercorrelations obtained.

This last objection can also be applied to the test developed
by Schoppe (1977).

Guilford's structure, or facet model is based on his statements
concerning the dimensionality underlying abilities. It, too,
has been subject to criticism, which we will deal with below.
Yet in response to his critics, Guilford has shown an impressive ability to devise new problem types, the problem contents
being extremely varied. Unlike Torrance, he avoids using different methods of evaluation on single problems claiming that the
results of such measures will be highly dependent upon one
another. He also calls for standardized conditions of administration so that different investigations will be comparable.
Considering these three aspects, it can be said that his
approach is the only one of all the ones discussed here that
cannot be rejected solely on the basis of bothersome methodological deficiencies.

Guilford developed a classification scheme in which he distinguishes cognitive abilities on the basis of the operations
involved, the contents dealt with, and the complexity of the
result. He posits five classes of operations, four content
classes and six levels of product complexity, these together
constituting his structure of intellect model (SI-model), the
latter being plotted in the shape of a die with (5x4x6=) 120
cells (Guilford, 1959a,b; Guilford & Höpfner, 1971).

Divergent thinking is one of the five classes of operations in
Guilford's model. Considering this class alone, the model can
be simplified and be represented as the matrix shown in
Figure 3.

Figure 3. Section of the SI-Model for the operation, "divergent
thinking"*

	content			
	figural	symbolic	semantic	behavioral
units	DFU	DSU	DMU	DBU
classes	DFC	DSC	DMC	DBC
relations	DFR	DSR	DMR	DBR
systems	DFS	DSS	DMS	DBS
transformations	DFT	DST	DMT	DBT
implications	DFI	DSI	DMI	DBI

(product, vertical label on left)

*
  Each cell entry consists of three initials, the first
  referring to the operation involved (in all cells of the
  above matrix, divergent thinking), the second to the content class, and the third to the complexity of the product.

If all the cells are completely occupied, the SI-model, as far
as divergent thinking is concerned, consists of 24 factors.
Since, however, adequate subtests could not be developed for 8
of the factors, the test for divergent thinking is limited to
16 factors. In the following, we will refer to the SI-model
presented above as "Model 1".

3.2. Alternative models

Before discussing the alternative models, several terminological matters need be clarified. With respect to our present
problem, a "general factor" will be one that shows significant
loadings for *all* variables. A "group factor", on the other
hand, will have at least seven, and a "specific factor" not
more than six such loadings. Finally, a "pure factor" is one
that has a significant loading for only one variable.

Altogether four other models will be tested against Guilford's.
The first has 9 factors and represents a more economical alternative of the "structure of intellect"-model. Like the SI-model,
it contains the categories "content" and "product", these being
subdivided into four and six known dimensions, respectively.
Instead, however, of the specific factors that result from the
cross classification of "content" and "product" in the SI-model,
the alternative model posits three content factors (semantic,
figural, behavioral) and six product factors (units, classes,
relations, systems, transformations). Hence, each variable gets
two marks and the concept of "pure factor" is given up.

The second alternative model takes into consideration criticisms made by Cronbach (1971) based on his empirical tests of
three hypotheses derived from the SI-model.

1) Divergent thinking tests that, according to Guilford's
   classification, belong to the same content and product-
   categories should be more highly correlated than other
   tests having only one category in common.

2) Tests pertaining to the same "content"-category should show
   a higher correlation than tests pertaining to different con-
   tent-categories.

3) Tests for the same product category should correlate more
   highly than tests for different product categories.

His findings supported the second hypothesis only, thus leading
him to conclude that the SI-model has more factors than are
needed for capturing the systematic variance. The second alternative model, therefore, consists of only five factors, three
of which pertain to content (semantic, figural and behavioral),
and two referring to the neutral processes needed for solving
the test problems (memory search, inference).

The third alternative model has 13 specific factors and, with
one minor exception (there is no distinction drawn between
symbolic and semantic units), corresponds to the SI-model. In
addition, the "semantic", "figural" and "behavioral" dimensions

are included as wider group factors. The model thus contains a
total of 16 factors, each variable being marked by one wide
group factor and one specific factor.

The fourth alternative model is identical with the previous
except for one additional general (divergent thinking) factor,
so that each variable is marked by three factors - the general
factor, the relatively wide group factor, and the specific
factor.

3.3. The factor analytic evaluation of models

Factor analysis (FA) has always been the preferred method for
demonstrating that observed behavior is the resultant of a
relatively few replicating, basic functions (Pawlik, 1968).
Though most often used for detecting latent structures in extensive quantities of data, factor analysis can also serve as
a means for testing of hypotheses (Jäger, 1967). The logic
behind this procedure is the following: From a given psychological theory, assumptions are drawn as to what a model of a
factor matrix should look like. This model is then compared
with a matrix based on empirical data using measures of factorial congruence or distance after the empirical matrix has been
adapted as closely as possible to the theoretical (target)
matrix by means of target rotation.[1]

The quality of adaptation of a target-rotated factor matrix
can be determined by a chi-squared test so long as Maximum
Likelihood Methods are used. The Maximum Likelihood approach
assumes that the data conforms to a multivariate normal distribution, something that is seldom to be found in practice. In

---

[1] This method of analysing data using target rotations has been
criticized by several investigators on the grounds that it
could be used to fit data to virtually any theoretical structure. (Greif, 1972; Horn, 1967; 1972; Horn & Knapp, 1974). It
has somewhat disparagingly been called the "procrustes
method".

addition, programs for estimating coefficients following this approach are limited for large sets of variables because of the huge amount of space they require even on big calculating machines. One way to circumvent this last problem is by simulating random data for every single case. Through simulation a random distribution of similarity coefficients can be gotten by rotating the empirical factor matrix to each of the n random matrices. The resulting distribution can then serve as a basis for assigning z-scores to the coefficients stemming from the comparison of the empirical and target matrices.

In order to trace differences in the results back to influences represented in the target matrix, all conditions that may have an influence on the quality of adaptation must be identical in the random and model matrices. That is, the matrices must
a) feature the same number of variables and factors,
b) have the same number of target loadings per variable and
   per factor.

To solve this problem, an already existing program (Fcomp) for similarity rotation from the OSIRIS-3 package has proven useful. It is based on a procedure described by Ahmavaara (1954) of adapting one structure to another, its advantage compared to other programs for similarity rotation being that it enables a selection of orthogonal or oblique rotation. Furthermore, the program has been amended so as to allow the generation that fulfill specified marginal conditions. These marginal conditions are:
- the number of variables,
- the number of factors,
- the number of marking loadings per factor,
- the number of marking loadings per variable,
- the information whether certain factors shall be uncoupled
  from the random process.

It is randomly decided on which of the factors the variables get their marking loading.

The rundown of the total calculating program includes the following steps:

1) The empirical factor matrix is rotated to the hypothetical matrix.

2) The similarity of the rotated matrix and the model matrix is calculated for the total configuration and for each factor in particular.

3) The empirical factor matrix is rotated to the first random matrix.

4) The similarity of the empirical factor matrix and the first random matrix is calculated for the total configuration and for each factor in particular.

Steps 3 and 4 are repeated as often as random matrices are generated, the remainder procedure being the same as is usually followed in significance testing. It is determined in how many cases the rotation to random matrices leads to higher similarity coefficients than the rotation to the theoretically based model matrix. At a rate of significance of 5%, for instance, not more than 5 of 100 rotations to random matrices should yield coefficients higher than those from the rotation to the model matrix.

For calculating the similarity between matrices there are, in principle, several methods at ones disposal. For our present purposes, we selected the "root-mean-square coefficient" (RMS), this having been designated as the most sensible of the methods available (cf. Joereskog, 1963). This method is based on the sum of squared deviations between corresponding elements of the rotated factor matrix and the target matrix. If there is a complete correspondence, the RMS-score is zero, whereas its value under maximum deviation depends on the number of variables and factors.

3.4. Testing the models

Data was collected from 204 high school students, a detailed description of the test problems, the composition of the sample, the methods and scoring being beyond the range of our present discussion. For a detailed presentation of these points, the reader is referred to Bollinger (1978).

Eighty-seven divergent thinking problems were selected on the basis of the following two criteria:
1) They must have contributed to the identification of a factor in former investigations (marking variables).
2) They were solvable within time limits imposed by group testing.

In spite of the extensive number and the high variety of the problems, we were unable to find at least one test for each cell of the Guilford model, three of the 24 cells remaining unrepresented.

A model's adaptability to data is not the only criterion of quality; just as important is the question of what portion of the total variance the extracted variance represents. Table 1 presents the proportion of variance accounted for by each of the models tested.

A usual standard for tests of intelligence is that factor solutions account for at least 50% of the data's variance. By this criterion, alternative 2, with its five dimensions, must be rejected even though it might provide a good structural fit of the data.

Non-parametric tests were performed for the models and their factors by determining the number of random matrices and

Table 1. Proportion of the variance accounted for by the differ-
        ent models

name of the model	number of factors	number of factors per variable	number of variables	proportion of variance in y
Guilford-Model	14	1	87	39.11
Alternative 1	9	1	87	48.77
Alternative 2	5	1	87	38.29
Alternative 3	16	2	87	62.62
Alternative 4	17	3	87	64.41

factors that allowed a better adaptation to the data. In addition, parametric tests using the z-statistic were also performed though, in case of doubt, the decision to discount a model
or factor was made on the basis of the non-parametric tests
alone. The non-parametric procedure gives exact information as
to the random probability of the appearance of a certain structure. The accuracy of the z-statistic, on the other hand,
depends on the quality of the approximation of the RMS-values
to the normal distribution, and this can vary greatly, especially with a small number of units of observation.

For determining significance levels up to $p < .01$ using a non-
parametric test, at least 100 random models had to be generated.
During the course of the analyses it appeared that generating
random matrices for models 4, 5 and 6 was excessively time consuming. For each of these three models, therefore, only 20
random models were generated. The non-parametric testing of
these models, therefore, was carried out at the .05 level, the
rest being tested at .01. The results of these tests are summarized in Table 2.

The SI-model and the three alternatives all appeared to represent the structure underlying the data far better than the
random models did: not one of the 100 (or 20) random models

Table 2. Global model control

name of the model	number of random matrices	z-value for model RMS	number of random matrices better than model matrix
Guilford-Model	100	23.17	O
Alternative 1	100	15.38	O
Alternative 3	20	59.60	O
Alternative 4	20	51.40	O

compared to each theoretically based model proved more adapt-
able to the data. The main finding of the study is therefore
that, contrary to the claims of numerous critics, it is not
true that target rotation can adapt empirical factor matrices
to any matrix equally well. Our results indicate that the
theoretically based matrices constitute far better "targets"
than the matrices generated at random.

The z-values in Table 2 provide additional information concerning the adaptation of the data to the theoretical and random
matrices. According to the z-values, alternative 5, a model
with three broad group factors and the specific factors of the
SI-model, was the most effective, coming off much better than
the SI-model or any other of its alternatives. It thus seems
that a model with general group factors better represents the
ability structure in divergent thinking than do models consisting exclusively of specific group factors. Furthermore, a two
level model appears to be optimal in terms of adaptation; including a third level in the form of a general factor (as in
model 4) does not result in an improvement with regard to adaptation.

The analysis of the model's inner structures follows the same
principle as the global tests. Instead of comparing the "target"
quality of the theoretical and random matrices, the comparison
was made for each individual factor. The analysis reveals that

all of the models, including Model 3, contain factors that cannot be distinguished from random factors. This result qualifies the importance attached to the global tests implying that the latter are so powerful that even a minimal similarity of data and model structure will lead to significant results.

4. Ideational production in group settings

Results of studies comparing performance in nominal and real groups provide little evidence that individuals' ideational production is either quantitatively or qualitatively as high in groups as it is in individual test situations. A question remains, however, as to what factors produce this inferior performance in group settings.

In the series of experiments described below, we tried to identify situational, process-centered, and individual difference factors that could have inhibiting influences on any of several aspects of ideational production. Production measures were fluency, flexibility, originality and a measure of resonance (imitation) developed in section 2.

4.1. Design problems of group experiments

A review of the relevant literature provides little insight, as confounded effects often prevent unequivocal conclusions from being drawn concerning the nominal/real group differences. A study by Collaros and Anderson (1969) provides an example of this problem. This study examined the influence of social inhibitions on group members' production of ideas. 240 subjects participated in the experiment in groups of 4, their task being to generate ideas concerning the question, "How can a person of average ability achieve fame and immortality though he does not possess any specific talents?"

The subjects were randomly assigned to one of three experimental conditions: They were either (a) told that all other members of their group were brainstorming experts, (b) told that
one of the group members was a brainstorming expert, or (c)
told nothing about the group members. The significant increase
in performance under condition *c* compared to condition *a* was
attributed to the social inhibitions stimulated by the perceived high competence of the supposed brainstorming experts.
Although this interpretation seems reasonable, there is at
least one other that should be considered. While generating
ideas, subjects could perceive how many ideas the other group
members were producing, an output that varied, as prediced,
between experimental conditions. The lower production rate by
subjects in condition *a* may thus have been the result of adaption to the other group members' low output. According to this
alternative explanation, the presence of real experts in these
groups (and, consequently, a higher than average rate of production) would have led to a different pattern of findings.

The problem with designs such as Collaros and Anderson's is,
of course, that the independent variables manipulated to influence the group settings have multiple, confounding effects.
Steiner (1972) found a solution to this problem in the use of
"synthetic" groups. In this tactic's original form, subjects
were separated from each other in accoustically-sealed cabins
and were led to believe that, via their headphones, they could
hear the ideas that the other subjects produced. In fact, however, the ideas that they heard were from tapes programmed by
the experimenter according to experimental condition. Sometimes,
a confederate was used instead of the tapes in order to avoid,
or at least decrease, the occurrence of overly artificial or
inappropriate response patterns.

4.2. Effects of the anticipated evaluation of other persons

One possible factor influencing the production of ideas in a

group situation is the fact that other people are present or
are supposed to be present who can hear and possibly evaluate
one's own production of ideas. Numerous studies have shown
that the presence of others influences performance. Although
all these studies were based on the hypothesis that the presence of others has a positive influence on performance - see,
for example, Allport's (1924) "social facilitation" hypotheses - their findings allow no systematic conclusions to be
drawn. In going back over this literature, however, Zajonc
(1965) came to the conclusion that the influence of the presence
of others depends on the kind of behavior to be performed, its
effect being positive in the case of already well-learned behaviors but negative if learning or innovation was involved.
Having derived this new hypothesis from the basic assumptions
on learning and performance formulated by Hull (1943) and
Spence (1956), Zajonc proposed that "arousal" served as an intervening variable, the presence of others increasing the level
of arousal and with it the probability of the occurrence of
dominant (i.e. well-learned) reactions.

Zajonc's claim that the mere presence of others suffices to enhance or inhibit performance has not, however, received unequivocal empirical support from subsequent research (cf. Lück,
1969, Cohen & Davis, 1973). Cottrell (1968) modified the hypothesis by restricting it to such situations in which the people
present seem likely to evaluate the subject's performance.
Zajonc's and Cottrell's explanations are not necessarily in
conflict, a point already made by Cottrell. A study by Cohen
and Davis (1973) supports this position, showing that "an audience which has been labeled neutral produces the predicted
(Zajonc, 1965) facilitating effects, and that giving it an
alleged evaluation role increases the intensity of those effects" (p. 83). When applied to divergent thinking, theoretical
work by Maltzman (1955) suggests further modification of
Zajonc's position. Maltzman distinguishes responses (ideas)
according to their degree of "reactional potential" in relation
to the given problem.

Responses with low reactional potential have a low probability
of occurrence and are therefore, in Zajonc's terms, "non-do-
minant." In ideation, original responses will belong to this
class. Combining Cottrell's and Maltzman's position, it thus
follows that the assumed presence of others who are in a position to evaluate one's own performance leads to a decrease in
the proportion of original ideas.

We conducted an experiment to investigate these matters. The
participants were 88 volunteers (44 femals, 44 males) from high
schools in the Mannheim-Ludwigshafen area. Sessions were held
in the linguistic laboratory of the University of Mannheim.
The subjects were run ten at a time, each being placed in an
individual soundproof cabin.

Tapes were prepared for each experimental condition and were
transmitted to subjects via headphone. Each type had one track
that contained general instructions, the text of the problems,
the signals for the beginning and end of the working period,
and the independent variable manipulations. A second track on
each tape used to record the ideas generated by the subject.
Each subject worked on six problems, these dealing with "unusual uses" and "consequences" (see appendix - for example of
the problems used). The time allowed for each problem was four
minutes. The "presence" of others was induced by including the
following message in the·taped instructions for subjects assigned to the experimental condition:

> "From the tape on which you are to record your ideas, you
> will hear a buzz once in a while. It is of no importance. In
> addition, we have connected two of the cabins so that any-
> thing that is said in one can be heard in the other, but not
> vice-versa. We have marked the cabins on the front side. If
> your window has an *A* on it, this means that all you say can
> be heard by a subject in another cabin."

Performance in ideation can be differentiated into three components labeled "ideational fluency", "flexibility" and "originality." The first refers to the ease with which stored information can be recalled, the second to the ability to gene-

rate a large number of different ideas with different contents, and the third to the ability to generate ideas that, though rare, are nevertheless appropriate to the problem at issue. With the exception of the first, which was used solely in the warm-up phase of the experiment, these three aspects were measured for each test problem. A system of content categories was devised for each problem and served as a means for determining the distribution of ideas over content categories. In addition, each idea was rated for originality: Two judges first had to decide whether the response was adequate to the problem and, if so, then classified it according to whether it was "usual" or "remote."

An analysis of covariance was performed on fluency and flexibility data using subjects' responses to the warm-up problem as the co-variate. As the distribution of the data concerning originality showed an extreme positive skew, it was decided to analyze this variable using the non-parametric Wilcoxon U.

The adjusted means for the fluency and flexibility data are presented in Table 3.

Table 3. Fluency and flexibility

Problem	Fluency		Flexibility	
	presence (simulated)	no presence	presence (simulated)	no presence
Unusual uses (NEWSPAPER) *	18.15	21.98	8.81	9.77
Unusual uses (CHAIR)	13.78	17.41	7.16	8.12
Consequences (COLOR-BLIND)	15.21	19.20	7.10	8.09
Consequences (90% Girls)	13.03	16.72	6.30	7.52

*Problems are described in the appendix.

A first glance at the table indicates that, for all four problems, fewer and less varied ideas were produced in the experimental, "simulated presence" condition. The results of the corresponding analysis of covariance are presented in table 4. For
both, fluency and flexibility, the corresponding F-values prove
statistically significant.

Table 4. The influence of presence on fluency and flexibility

Problem		MS	MS$_{error}$	$F_{1,55}$
unusual uses (newspaper)	F L U E N C Y	215.67	36.04	5.98*
unusual uses (chair)		194.75	18.33	10.62**
consequences (color-blind)		233.98	36.20	6.46*
consequences (90% girls)		200.20	22.94	8.73**
unusual uses (newspaper)	F L E X I B I L I T Y	14.48	2.63	5.50*
unusual uses (chair)		14.61	2.47	5.93*
unusual uses (color-blind)		15.34	2.96	5.18*
unusual uses (90% girls)		28.17	3.51	8.03*

*   p<.05
** p<.01

The originality scores were analyzed by calculating for each
problem, under each condition, the percentage of generated ideas
that were judged as being original. The resulting Wilcoxon

U was significant at the 5% level, thus confirming our hypothesis concerning the negative influence that the perception of
the presence of others has on the appearance of original ideas.

These results can be regarded as providing further support for
the "social facilitation" approach formulated by Cottrell.
Across the different problems used in the study, subjects produced fewer, less varied, and less original ideas if the experimental instructions led them to believe that other subjects
could hear and possibly evaluate their responses. Applying
these findings to natural group settings, they help explain the
reduction in ideational output that groups have been found to
elicit, since each group member is faced with having others
present who can hear and evaluate their remarks. In real groups,
this effect may be even stronger as a result of the greater
potential for communication (both verbal and nonverbal) between
group members than was possible in the present experiment's
"synthetic" group situation.

4.3. The influence of others' ideas (imitation)

In real groups, the individual is confronted with the presence
of others as well as with what those others say (e.g. their
arguments, ideas,etc.). The previous experiment analyzed the
effect of evaluation apprehension induced by a simulated audience. In the following two experiments, we investigate the
influence of ideas generated by others on subjects' own fluency,
flexibility and originality.

The hypotheses were based on the consideration that, as a behavior, ideation is less well-learned than the strategies typically involved in everyday problem solving and thus occasions
considerable insecurity on the part of subjects asked to perform our test problems. Given this insecurity, it seems likely
that subjects will be especially open to influence by the behavior of others performing the same task. Studies by Zimmermann and Dialessi (1973) and Belcher (1975) show that children

presented with a model demonstrating high ideational fluency
had more ideas with a similar problem than did children whose
models had produced few ideas. Belcher also found that the number of original ideas generated by subjects increased with the
model's originality.

Proceeding from these results, we wanted to see whether similar
imitation effects would occur in situations that are more realistic with respect to interaction processes. Subjects responded in Belcher's experiment only after having observed the model's behavior (presented in film) in its entirety. In our experiment, on the other hand, subjects interacted with the model
and made their responses at the same time the model made his/
hers.

The subjects in our first experiment (cf. Hellingrath & Bollinger, 1976) were 40 high school students run in groups of three,
each subject being separated in a sound-proof cabin equipped
with a headphone-microphone combination. The subjects were told
that they could address whichever partner they wanted and at
the same time hear that partner's own ideas. Actually each
subject heard pre-programmed ideas on tape, the fellow subject
being simulated.

The subjects began with a warm-up problem that was not considered in the scoring. Next, they were given five problems, comparable to those used in the previous study (cf. appendix),
with eight minutes allotted for each problem. While they worked,
subjects received the simulated partner's responses via the
headphones. In "high ideational fluency" condition, the "partner" generated 33 ideas for each problem, while in the "low
ideational fluency" condition, the partner's output per problem was 13. In order to keep the number of interruptions constant for both of the experimental conditions, a buzz was sound-
ed in the low fluency condition as a sign that talking was not
allowed at that moment. The dependent variable was the mean
number of ideas generated by subjects in the low and high fluency condition. In all five cases, subjects' own fluency was

greater when the model's fluency was high. A simultaneous comparison of the two fluency groups over the five test problems
using Hotelling's T^2 revealed an effect for fluency significant
at the .05 level.

Table 5. Ideational output as a function of interacting with a
         low or high production model

Problem	Means low	high	t-value
Ideational fluency (fluids)	20.65	25.8	1.8*
New uses (pencil)	16.6	23.3	2.43**
Job symbols (sun)	12.9	18.9	2.21*
Planning (organize a trip)	20.0	27.3	2.14*
Ideational fluency (Things round)	32,9	43.6	2.44*

* p<.05
**p<.01

In the second study, the subjects were 38 high school students.
This experiment differed from the first in that the originality
of partner's ideation was manipulated and its effect on the
originality of the subjects' responses monitored. Also, in this
second study, a live "confederate" was used instead of the pre-
programmed tape, the confederate being instructed, however, to
give specific ideas at specified times during the work period.
The confederate had a list of ideas consisting of different
content categories from which he randomly chose items to "generate" during the work period. As there were a considerable

number of ideas for each category, the confederate could avoid
giving ideas already generated by the subject. The subject and
confederate were separated by a folding screen so that the subject was not able to see that the confederate had a list of
ideas in front of him.

Subjects' originality was consistently greater when the model
expressed original ideas then when he/she did not; this held
true not only when the results were averaged over test problems (9.95 vs. 8.12,· t = 2.91, p<.01,) but also for 7 of the 8
test problems considered individually.

The results of the two investigations demonstrate that, even in
ideation, people tend to model their own behavior on the behavior of other people in the same situation. It is important to
point out, that we have no direct evidence that "insecurity"
and/or "arousal" produced the effects we obtained. That is,
subjects may imitate models, regardless of whether they are insecure or aroused. Taking part in an experiment is, in itself,
an insecurity-producing situation that could promote the tendency to imitate other people. Future experiments might therefore measure whether the tendency to imitate declines at the
experimental session progresses; i.e. as the subject becomes
accustomed to the task and task setting.

4.4. Effects of group relevant personality factors

The studies discussed above show that insecurity may produce
differences in imitative behavior but that these effects may
be modulated by social inhibition. It therefore follows directly that the magnitude of imitation effects may be influenced
by more general, individual differences in social insecurity.
Although personality variables have been studied in many different fields of research - for example, attitude change, group
dynamics, social perception - the results indicate that the
majority of personality effects can be traced to a few key
variables. Among these is "self-esteem." Cohen (1959, p. 103)

writes: " Self-esteem concerns the amount of value an individual attributes to various facets of his person and may be said
to be affected by the successes and failures has has experienced in satisfying central needs. It may be viewed as a function
of the coincidence between an individual's aspirations and his
achievement of these aspirations." People with high self-esteem
should therefore be less bothered by situational pressure than
are those low in self-esteem. With respect to imitation and
ideation, it follows that high self-esteem subjects should
show less imitation of a "partner's" ideation than should low
self-esteem subjects.

The subjects in the present study were 79 female students in
the last three grades of high school. The subjects first worked on a personality questionnaire for 45 minutes and then a
few days later participated in the main experiment which also
lasted 45 minutes.

Self-esteem was measured by 4 sub-scales from the "Freiburger
Persönlichkeitsinventar" (Fahrenberg & Selg, 1970). In particular, the depression, shyness, social insecurity, and social
inhibition scales were used. In the second session, each subject was taken into a room alone and was acquainted with the
ideation task by performing a practice problem. Afterwards,
subjects worked on another ideation problem together with a
confederate, the latter having a list of ideas consisting of
16 different content categories from which he randomly chose
items to "generate" during the work period. The procedure was
similar to that reported previously. Each subject performed
two test problems, the dependent variable operationalized in
terms of the measure S_6 (cf. section 2.2). The data were analyzed by multiple regression. The results, presented in Table 6
(see next page), support the hypothesis for both test problems.

For the unusual uses problem, a stepwise regression indicated
that "social inhibition" did not account for much variance in
the imitation scores: this variable was therefore omitted in
the calculation of the multiple correlation. The same applies
for "social insecurity" in the consequences problem.

Table 6. Multiple correlation between the self-esteem variables
         and imitation

unusual uses
(newspaper)   *Predictors:* Depression
Multiple R: 0.42   shyness, social insecurity
        p: < 0.01

Consequences
(90% girls)   *Predictors:* Depression
Multiple R: 0.33   shyness, social inhibition
        p: < 0.05

4.5. Effects of perceived competence

An essential aspect of group situations that has been neglected in most of the experiments on ad-hoc groups concerns the
cognitions that the members of a group develop with regard to
the other group members. These cognitions may be developed as
a result of common experiences in groups working continuously
together or as a result of information concerning, for example,
the other members' social status. In problem-centered groups,
the performance of the individual participant is of particular
importance for the others, and the development of such expectancies should therefore be especially pronounced.

With regard to imitation, we propose that the perceived competence of a group partner plays an important role in determining
how much attention a subject devotes to him/her and thus the
extent to which the subject imitates the partner's behavior.
Relevant here are findings by Rosenbaum (1963) and Horowitz
(1966) that show, beside some significant effects for model
competence, significant negative correlations between the number of imitating reactions by observers and measures of the
estimations of the observer's competence in relation to the competence of the model. Horowitz states that "...factors that
lead the subject to believe that he is incompetent, or that

others are more competent that he, are associated with highten-
ed susceptibility to social influence" (p. 235).

Our present hypotheses are, therefore, as follows:
- subjects' ideation will be influenced more by the ideas of
  others whom they recognize as being more competent than by
  the ideas of others at their own competence level.
- subjects' ideation will be less influenced by the ideas of
  others whom they perceive as being less competent than they
  are themselves than by others who share their competence
  level.

35 male students and 34 female students from four different
high schools participated in the experiment, the subjects'
average age being 18 years.

The subjects were given six divergent thinking problems to
work on, three that involved generating consequences to hypothetical events (e.g. what would happen if sleep became unnecessary?) and three that involved thinking up novel uses for
ordinary objects (e.g. a pencil is usually used for writing.
What else could it be used for?).

The procedure required two sessions, the first serving only to
set the stage for the manipulations. At the first session, subjects worked individually on four problems. The layout for the
second session was exactly as it had been for the studies described above. Perceived competence was manipulated by varying
the contents of the instructions given at the start of the
session: subjects were given their own (fictitious) test results from the previous session (for all subjects 'average')
together with those of the "partner" with whom they would be
working, the partner's score being either lower than, equal to,
or higher than the subject's own. While working on the problems
in the second session, subjects heard 20 ideas per problem,
ostensibly generated by their partner. In fact, those responses
were pre-recorded on a master tape piped into the sound-proof
cabins.

For measuring the imitation of the partner's ideation the resonance score based on RRWG (cf. Section 2.2) was calculated.[2]

To test the hypothesis concerning perceived competence, planned
comparisons were carried out, the results of which are summarized in Table 7. As readily can be seen, the predicted effects
did obtain for the consequence generation tasks ("color blind",

Table 7. Planned comparisons for task-type "consequences"

Task	Comparison	F-Value	df	p
Consequences	A1-A2	3.675	1/48	<.06
(color-blind)	A1-A3	12.801	1/48	**
Consequences	A1-A2	<1.000	1/48	n.s.
(90% girls)	A1-A3	4.336	1/48	*

*   p<0.05

** p<0.01

A1: equal to
A2: lower than   } partner's score
A3: higher than

girl"), subjects showing more imitation of the highly competent
partner's ideation than they did for the partner who was as
equally competent as themselves. The second hypothesis was not,
however, confirmed, the competence manipulation having had no
effects on subjects' performance on the problems involving the
generation of novel uses.

---

[2] The experimental design contained two other factors: Order in
which the problems were presented and sex. We were not able
to vary systematically the sex composition of the subject-
partner pairs and so made them homogenous, female subjects
having female partners and male subjects, male partners. Analysis of the data revealed that the overall level of imitation
was higher in the female pairs than in the male.

5. Concluding remarks

The methodological and empirical studies reported in the previous sections can be viewed under two aspects: As contribution
to the analysis of ideation and of decision making. Under the
first perspective, the implications of our findings for the
results of other authors were treated in the individual sections. A discussion of possible conclusions for the psychology
of decision making should, however, refrain from a naive belief
in transferability of results. Nevertheless, several questions
about decision making were suggested. We can only give a few
examples here.

The methods of analyzing clustering, for instance. could be
used as a tool for studying the emergence and advancement of
new arguments in group discussions. Describing processes of
this kind by relating them to ordered points between the two
extremes of a randomized and a fully ordered sequence of ideas
would give important information about the decision making
process in groups.

Individual differences in the ideation about the "marginal
conditions" of a decision will undoubtedly be influenced by
prior information and attitudes towards these conditions. The
results to the factor analyses reported in section 3 suggest
that cognitive functions, which can be differentiated according to their content and the cognitive complexity of their
products, should be taken into account as additional sources
of individual differences and that their relative contribution
to ideation in decision making be investigated.

Although it is tempting to translate the results about improvements, deteriorations and other changes of ideation in a group
setting (reported in section 4) into hypotheses concerning
ideation in group decisions, one should keep in mind that the
evaluation of ideas in this latter situation is generally done
according to the degree to which they contribute to a good decision rather than in terms of their originality or other

aspects that we may have emphasized in our research. But even if our findings cannot be simply generalized, similar questions can be asked and investigated using similar methods in decision making groups.

Appendix

The following presents a brief description of each of the divergent thinking problems used in the study discussed in section 3.2. Some of these problems were used in other experiments as well.

Word fluency (WF/DSU)[*]
In this test, words have to be named which contain certain letters.
Example: ;Write words which contain the letter 'E'."

Prefixes (VS/DSU)
This test involves generating German words, beginning with a certain prefix at as fast a rate as possible.
Example: "Write words with the prefix 'wahr'..."

Ideational fluency (IF/DMU)
In this test, things have to be named that possess a certain attribute or set of attributes.
Examples: "Fluids that burn"; "things that are round."

Consequences (CQ/DMU, DMT)
The task is to name as many consequences as possible that would follow from certain hypothetical situations.
Example: "What would happen if sleep became unnecessary?"

---

[*]The first set of initials within the parenthesis are an abbreviation of the test's name, and the second is the classification of the test in terms of Guilford's SI-model.

Unusual uses (UV/DMC)

As many as possible uses for familiar objects, or parts of them, have to be named. The uses should not be in accordance with the usual use for the object and they should be different from each other.

Example: "A newspaper is used for reading. List other uses for which it or parts of it could serve.

Groupings (GR/DMC)

Given words have to be attached to different classes of concepts according to their content.

Example: a) arrow b) bee c) crocodile d) kite e) fish f) sail-boat g) sparrow. Possible classes include air (a,b,d,g) or 'animals' (b,c,e,g) and so on.

New uses (NU/DMU; DMC)

In this test, possible uses for familiar objects had to be generated.

Example: "Name as many as possible uses for a brick as you can."

To find headings (ÜF/DMU; DMT)

The test involves finding appropriate headings for short stories, the headings being as original as possible.

Associational fluency (AF/DMR)

The generation of synonyms for specified "target" words.

Example: "Write words that mean the same as 'hard'."

Comparisons (VG/DMR)

In this test, words or expressions have to be found which can be meaningfully inserted into incomplete comparisons.

Example: "A thief is as ..... as a cat."

Expressional fluency (EF/DMS)

This test involves the construction of four word sentences, each word beginning with a specified letter.

Example: "E... Z... G... W..."

Similar interpretations (GI/DMS)

This test involves the generating of rationales underlying simi-les and metaphors.

Example: "A stockbroker is like an acrobat because ..."

Job symbols (BS/DMI)
To given symbols, up to six jobs have to be named that match
the symbol concerned.

Planning (PL/DMI)
The task is to name the preparations necessary for a given
project.
Example: "You have to organize a trip to Paris. What has to be
prepared and clarified before the trip can be embarked on?"

Sketches (EW/DFU)
The test involves drawing as many different sketches as possible
with the help of a basic pattern.

Match problem (SP/DFT)
In this test patterns of matches are to be seen. The matches
are arranged in squares. Some of the matches have to be crossed
out in a way that the remaining matches build new patterns in
the shape of squares.

Making objects (GZ/DFT)
The task is to arrange simple figures in a way that certain
objects result. The following rules have to be observed.
1. Only the given figures can be used.
2. The size or position of a figure can be changed but not its
   shape.
3. A given figure can be used repeatedly in order to construct
   the certain object.
4. Not all of the figures have to be used, but at least two of
   them.

Decorations (DV/DFI)
Objects shown only in outline have to be decorated. In doing so
it is important that different decorations are chosen.
Example: "The furniture of a room is shown in outline. The containing pieces of furniture have to be decorated with different
patterns."

Expression of feelings (GA/DBU)

In this test the subjects have to imagine what a person who has a certain feeling may express.

Example: "What could a person say who is angry?"

Ambiguous social situations (DK/DBU)

The subject has to generate possible explanations of ambiguous social situations.

Example: "Person A is a student of your age. In a trolley he has a seat face to face with an older couple. The two of them keep staring at him continually. What might be the reason for this?"

Relations between three persons (DP/DBS)

Based on a short characterization of the three persons, as many as possible different situations have to be named in which the persons could relate to each other.

Example: Person A - an anxious woman

        Person B - an angry man

        Person C - an unhappy child

Developing a situation (GG/DBT)

A situation is described in which three persons take part. Subjects are here to describe possible further developments of this situation.

Example: "Two sisters A and B have fallen in love with the same young man. One day he visits them at home unexpectedly. How could this situation develop?"

Family problems (FF/DBI)

In this test the task is to imagine problems that can arise among the members of a typical family.

Example: "Which personal problems may a brother and sister have with each other?" The problems may contain feelings, thoughts and attitudes of the participating persons.

Conflict situations(KS/DBI)

A social conflict situation is described. As many as possible solutions to this conflict have to be named.

Example: "Imagine you have made a weekend trip to the country

with a group of friends. Your friends would like to hike with
you on Sunday. Your intention, however, is to visit the museum
nearby. What could you do in order to convince your friends
to give up their hiking plans and to go to the museum with
you?"

Interpretations (IT/DBI)
Different possible explanations for certain behavior or facts
have to be generated.
Example: "Person A is proud of his clothes. What might be
the reason for this?"

Chapter 2   Impression Formation and Social Judgment
E. Rosch

1. Introduction

The present paper summarizes work on social *impression formation* conducted in two different research projects. The first
of these projects ran from 1970 to 1974 and was based on the
principles of *integration theory* (cf. Anderson, 1974) together
with the results of some previous work in this area reported by
Schümer[1] (1976). The second project ran from 1975 to 1977 and
followed a *social judgment* approach to impression formation.
The two projects together addressed the following problems:

(1) What relation do *global impressions* bear to judgments concerning the individual pieces of information upon which
they are based?

(2) Does the *context* in which information is received determine
the manner in which it is judged?

(3) Do people in impression formation settings *infer* other,
non-specified facts about the judgment object from the
pieces of information that they are given?

---

[1] Several abridged passages of this report by R. Schümer have
been integrated in this chapter. Schümer himself, however, was
not consulted during the chapter's preparation and should
therefore not be held responsible for its possible shortcomings.

2. Theoretical framework

Ash has argued on the basis of several experiments (e.g. Asch, 1946) that the impression that subjects form of a target person depends upon the entirety of traits ascribed to him/her, each individual trait acquiring an important part of its meaning from the set of other traits that are presented along with it. Predicting an overall impression on the basis of subjects' judgments concerning each of the component traits taken singly would, according to Asch, be impossible.

Several other authors, (e.g. Anderson, 1962, 1972, 1974; Fishbein, 1963; Manis et al., 1966; Osgood & Tannenbaum, 1955), however, have drawn the opposite conclusion, each working towards developing *quantitative models* that predict global impressions from subjects' judgments of isolated component traits. The two models that have received the most attention are Anderson's *averaging model* (Anderson, 1967, 1972) and the *additive model* (Fishbein, 1963; Fishbein & Hunter, 1964a,b). Since both of these models yield only approximate quantitative predictions, critical tests between them have centered on the following issue:

The *additive model* implies that the global impression will be more extreme than the judgment concerning any one of the traits upon which it is based, while the *averaging model* implies that the global impression will be more moderate than the judgments concerning its most extreme components.

The paradigmatic procedure for testing these models is simple and straightforward. First, ratings are obtained for individual traits on relevant dimensions of judgment, the dimension most often used being the evaluative "like-dislike". These component traits are then combined in lists and presented to subjects as describing a single target person. The subjects are asked to form an impression of this person and to rate him/her on the same dimension(s) that the component traits were judged. This latter rating is, of course, the global impression, which can then be compared to the ratings of the component traits upon which it is based.

3.   Empirical Research

3.1.   Relation between single elements and the overall impression

3.1.1. Scaling of traits in regard to their likeability rating and the measurement of their underlying similarities (Busz, Cohen, Poser, Schümer-Kohrs, Schümer & Sonnenfeld, 1972a)

Busz et al. first tested the suitability of various *scale types* for measuring *likeability*, finally choosing a 21-point rating scale ranging from -10 (highly unlikeable) through 0 (neither likeable nor unlikeable) to +10 (highly likeable). This scale was then used to obtain likeability ratings for 880 *personality descriptors* taken from the Dornseif dictionary (1954) and from scales used in the experiments of Cohen (1969), the descriptors being broken down into 5 sets of 176 items each, each set being rated by a different group of subjects (n for each group = 50) drawn from the male and female students at the University of Mannheim.

Contingency estimations for these ratings showed satisfactory results ($r_{tt} > .9$). A comparison with the ratings of the English equivalents from the list of 550 terms published by Anderson (1968) resulted in r of .85, this being high enough to assure a good basis of comparison for the results of experiments using terms from these two lists.

As a further analysis, the pattern of *similarities* between more than 100 terms selected from the list was tested. Subjects rated these terms on 48 bipolar scales, their ratings then being put through a Q-analysis. The results indicated that 60

of the terms could be described by three factors marked with
more or less equal frequency (see Busz et al., 1972a, Table 7,
pp. 302-304):

Factor I: intellectual passive vs. intellectual active
              (e.g. dependent - independent; intelligent -
              untalented)

Factor II: negative vs. positive "character"
              (e.g. modest - haughty; motivated by interest -
              motivated by reward)

Factor III: schizothymic vs. zyclothymic
              (e.g. cranky - affable; ill-humored - cheerful)

3.1.2. Influence of the average likeability rating, its simi-
       larity and the amount of information on the overall
       judgment

Schümer (1971) reports two experiments testing the effects
that the *amount and homogeneity of information* have on the
forming of global impressions. Subjects in both experiments
were first to judge the likeability of fictitious target persons described by specific *combinations of traits* and then
to rate how certain they were concerning each of their likeability judgments. The number of traits per target person
(2 vs. 4 in experiment 1; $2 \leq n \leq 6$ in five steps in experiment 2)
and the average likeability of the trait combinations (4 levels, 2 positive and 2 negative, in each experiment) were
varied orthogonally. Furthermore, the second experiment varied
the variance of the components' scale ratings within each of
the trait combinations, these combinations consisting either
of traits that were relatively homogeneous in their likeability ratings, or traits whose likeability ratings were relatively heterogeneous.

Results:

(1) The effect of varying the evaluative extremity of Indivi-
    dual traits

Target persons described by trait combinations whose component
traits had extreme likeability ratings were themselves more
extremely liked (or disliked) than those described by more
moderate combinations. At the same time, subjects' confidence
in their global judgments of the target person also increased.
The former result was, of course, expected both on the basis
of common sense and from the derivations of all the major judgment models. The positive correspondence between evaluative
extremity and subjective certainty was, on the other hand, less
expected, though it seems consistent with earlier findings
(e.g. Hofstätter, 1963, p. 170) that indicate a positive
relationship between commitment and attitudinal extremity.

(2) The effect of varying the amount of information

Holding their mean evaluative extremity constant, increasing
the number of traits in a given combination resulted in increasingly extreme global impressions being formed. A similar
"set size effect" was found for subjective certainty, subjects'
confidence in their global judgments increasing with the number
of traits they received for each target person. It should be
noted that the relation between the amount of information and
the extremity of the global likeability judgments is contrary
to what one would expect on the basis of an averaging formulation. Though the averaging model can be extended (by introducing the notion of the evaluatively neutral, initial impression, cf. Anderson, 1972) to account for such set size effects,
the role that changes in subjective certainty might play in
mediating these effects has not yet been sufficiently clarified.

(3) The joint effects of varying the amount of information
    and its mean evaluative extremity

The results from experiment 2 indicated that the influence of

set size on the global likeability judgment was more pronounced when the traits presented were evaluatively extreme than
when they were evaluatively moderate.

According to Anderson (personal communication to R. Schümer,
1971), such an interaction is to be expected. If we simplify
by assuming equal scale values and weights for the component
traits as well as postulate the existence of an initial impression, M_o , with the corresponding weight, β_o , the following
inferences can be drawn.

The theoretical expression for n traits with an extreme average scale-value, M_h , is:

$$(n\beta M_h + \beta_o M_o) / (n\beta + \beta_o)$$

The corresponding expression for n traits with a more moderate
average scale value, M_1, is:

$$(n\beta M_1 + \beta_o M_o) / (n\beta + \beta_o)$$

Hence it follows - by a simplifying transformation -

$$n\beta \ (M_h - M_1) / (n\beta + \beta_o)$$

The influence of the *amount of information* on the global judgments thus increases to the same degree as the difference between the average scale values of traits in a combination.

(4) The effects of varying information homogeneity-heterogeneity

The information *homogeneity-heterogeneity* variable permits the
pitting of Anderson's *integration-averaging model* against the
congruency model of Osgood and Tannenbaum (1955), the former
predicting that the variable should have no effect on global
impressions, while the latter predicts that impressions based
on heterogeneous trait combinations (the amount and mean evaluative extremity being held equal) should be more extreme
than those based on more homogeneous trait sets. The rationale
underlying this latter prediction is based on the assumption

that the more extreme a given trait is, the heavier it will be
weighted in the forming of the global impression. Since the
heterogeneous trait combinations have a greater number of
these heavily weighted, evaluatively extreme components than
do the homogeneous trait sets, the global impressions based
upon them should be more extreme as well.

The results support the congruity model, target persons described by heterogeneous trait combinations being more extremely liked or disliked than those described by more homogeneous
trait sets. The heterogeneity-homogeneity variable was also
found to effect subjects' confidence in their global impressions, this confidence being greater for impressions formed
from heterogeneous sets.

There is however, a great deal of controversy in the literature concerning the effects of information heterogeneity (e.g.
Levy, 1964; Manis et al., 1966; Podell & Podell, 1963; Willis,
1960). Despite the consistency of the present findings the
effects of this variable on impression formation should still
be considered as being rather unsystematic.

3.1.3. Restrictive conditions for impression formation models: averaging and adding

A study by Rosch (1977) followed up Schümer's work on trait
heterogeneity and also attempted to determine the conditions
under which *averaging or adding* models best describe the forming of global impressions from trait combinations. A further
aim in this experiment was to determine whether the *"discounting effect"* reported by Anderson and Jacobson (1965) occurs
even in situations when subjects are not explicitly instructed
to disregard discrepant pieces of information.

Two factors thought likely to determine whether averaging or
adding models provide the best description of the impression
formation process are
(a) whether the trait combinations judged are evaluatively

homogeneous or heterogeneous, and

(b) whether the traits convey positively or negatively valenc-
ed information.

These two factors were therefore varied orthogonally in a
standard impression formation paradigm, with 50 male and female students aged 17-19 judging approximately 200 combinations of three traits attributed to a fictitious target person.

The data on 72 specific combinations of three were analyzed
for goodness of fit by a splitting procedure (Sutcliffe, 1957).
The results are presented in Table 1.

Table 1. Frequency of applicability of the integration principles

| | | Models | |
		averaging	adding
positive	homogeneous	14	4
	heterogeneous	17	1
Information			
negative	homogeneous	0	18
	heterogeneous	15	3

The frequency values in Table 1 clearly show that the averaging model is the more applicable in the case of heterogeneous
information (chi-square = 6.22; df = p<.02). The case for
homogeneous information is, however, less clear; when the information is negative, the *additive* model is the most applicable but, when the information is positive, the averaging
model is again preferable.

With regard to the occurrence of "discounting", analyses revealed that for "positive, positive, negative" trait combinations, discounting was found in only one of thirty cases
(p<.001, one-tailed, by a McNemar-test). For "negative, negative, positive" combinations, on the other hand, discounting

was found to be more frequent (in fourteen of thirty cases),
thus suggesting that a discrepant positive trait is more readily discounted than a discrepant negative one is. In the ++-
condition there were fifteen cases in which the judgment was
"biased" toward the scale of the negative adjective; in the
--+ condition there were thirteen cases in which the overall
judgment was more negative than the most extreme component.
This, of course, is consistent with certain theoretical developments in *attribution theory* (cf. Kanouse & Hanson, 1972)
and numerous empirical results (e.g. Anderson, 1965; Labbie,
1972; Wyer, 1974) that indicate that negative information is
weighted more heavily than positive information in impression
and attitude formation.

3.1.4. Conclusion

The experiments discussed so far conform to the standard,
linear model paradigm, person perception being analyzed in
terms of combinations of discrete personality traits (and
nothing else) in order to test derivations from various, competing quantitative models. The limitations of this approach
are, however, evident. Most importantly, the models discussed
in this section are of limited value as bases for generating
precise, quantitative predictions concerning impression formation. At their best they serve as *ex post facto* rationali-
zations of impression formation phenomena, often requiring
the addition of auxiliary assumptions before their "predictions" fall in line with obtained empirical results. This
state of affairs is clearly unsatisfactory and has resulted in
a fragmentary, disjointed understanding of impression formation processes (cf. Irle, 1975, p. 129). One remedy may be to
develop hypotheses stating the various conditions under which
each of the models best applies. The experiment by Rosch (1977)
discussed above may represent a first step in this direction.

3.2. Experiments concerning context effects

Asch (1946) was of the opinion that the meaning that subjects
attach to a given trait is strongly influenced by the *context*
in which the trait is examined. Contrary to this, the *quanti-*
tative models for impression formation discussed above assume
traits' meanings to be essentially invariable. It should be
possible, according to these models, to predict subjects'
judgments of trait combinations from their "context-free"
judgments of each of the component traits taken singly. The
best example of this latter approach to contextual influences
(or the lack of them) is Anderson (1966, 1971) who proposed a
relatively simple model in which the judgment of a trait received in the context of others corresponds to the weighted
average of its judgment when context-free and the overall
judgment (I) of the trait combination of which it is a part.

3.2.1. Experiments by Balzer et al. (1974) and Schümer
(1973a,b)

Balzer et al. tested how subjects' judgments of certain target traits were influenced by variations in both the evaluative context and number of traits presented along with them.
In addition, the study checked the effects of various instructions designed to vary the immediacy of the relation
between target and context traits and hence change the relative weight of the overall impression in determining how the
target component is judged. Trait combinations were formed in
such a way as to systematically vary the number of context
traits (over two levels) and the average scale value of the
target trait (over three levels).

The relative accentuation of the *relation between context and*
target traits was varied by using four different instructions,
with subjects in the "low" or "high" accentuation conditions
being told that each trait in a given combination referred to

either the same person or different people, respectively. Subjects were first asked to indicate how likeable they thought
the person (or group of persons) described by the trait combination would be and then to rate the target trait alone as a
"partial aspect" of the person (or group).

The results provided only partial support for Anderson's context model: the more positive the average rating of the *context
traits*, the more positively the test trait was judged. Judgments of the target trait were, however, unaffected bv variations in the number of context traits that appeared along with
it, even though this manipulation did have the expected,
strong effect on the global impression.

Varying the instructions also had no effect: the influence of
the context was equally strong regardless of whether the instruction accentuates the fact that all traits in a combination refer to different persons or to one single person. It
thus seems that the explicit accentuation of the fact that all
traits in a combination refer to a single person is not necessary for judgments of the target trait to be displaced towards the context's average scale value.

A study by Schümer (1973a,b) followed up earlier work by Kaplan
(1971) and Wyer and Watson (1969). These latter authors argued that trait adjectives differ in the range over which their
meanings can vary and attempted to manipulate this meaning
variability by selecting adjectives whose pretest scale values
showed different levels of variance. Schümer, however, argued
that variability in the judgments of a trait may mean only
that the judgments themselves are unstable and does not necessarily imply the trait is ambiguous. He selected, therefore,
another, more direct operationalization of trait ambiguity,
having pilot study subjects rate trait adjectives on a 7-point
(1= unequivocal to 7= ambiguous) "ambiguity"-scale and then
using in the main experiment trait combinations that varied
with regard to four independent factors:

(a) Context: The average likeability rating of the context
                traits varied over four levels
(b) Number of context traits: n = 2 or 6
(c) Valence of the test traits: positive vs. negative
(d) Ambiguity of the test traits: weak vs. strong

The dependent variables were the global impression and the
judgment of the component test trait, both made on a likeability scale. Once again, however, the amount of context information affected only the global impressions and not the component judgments. Although ambiguous traits were found to
change more as a result of context than less ambiguous traits,
the corresponding context x ambiguity interaction was not
significant. The results of this experiment thus support
neither Asch's nor Anderson's formulation of context effects.

3.2.2. Cohen and Schümer (1972)

The context experiment by Cohen and Schümer (1972) dealt with
the influence of *contradictions* between context and test information on component judgments. Previous work (e.g. Cohen,
1967; Cohen & Schümer, 1968, 1969; Haire & Grunes, 1950; Pepitone & Hayden, 1955) had shown that the reception of *contradictory information* stimulates judges to search for higher
level, encompassing concepts that "neutralize" the contradiction. The question addressed here was whether similar processes
occur when contradictions occur between single test traits and
their contexts.

From previous work on the *similarity structure of traits* (Busz
et al., 1972, cf. also Section 3.1.1.), trait combinations
were formed whose test and context components were either highly similar (high positive Q-correlation), independent (Q-correlation almost 0) or contradictory (negative Q-correlation).
Subjects were once again instructed to indicate both their overall impression and their judgment of the test trait, this time
using a series of bipolar rating scales. The results indicated

that, when test traits were in contradiction to their context
they were judged far more extreme with respect to other judgmental dimensions besides "liking" than they were when they
were not in contradiction. Integration theory cannot account
for this spread of context effects to multiple judgmental dimensions.

3.2.3. Conclusions

Neither Asch's theoretical reflections nor Anderson's quantitative model can adequately account for the results of the context effect studies described above. One problem in empirically testing either of these approaches, however, lies in the
difficulty of adequately registering change of meaning; the
change of the meaning of a trait in context with one or several
other traits is surely not registerable on a simple likeability
scale alone. Also, the study of context effects is concerned,
among other things, with linguistic processes and cannot be reduced to terms appropriate for. a simple quantitative model without sacrificing much of the phenomenon's necessary complexity.

It should be pointed out that the studies discussed above each
conceive of context as consisting of other personality traits,
a conception that excludes factors that would ordinarily be
considered under the heading "context" and seem likely to
exert a great influence on the organization and formation of
impression; e.g., the general features of the situation in
which a given behavior takes place.

The *script-theory* by Abelson (1976; Schank & Abelson, 1977)
may be seen as a useful approach in studying these more general
context effects, scripts being schemata of situations and behavior that underly naive *inference processes* (see Schneider
et al., 1979, p. 268).

3.3. Impression formation and social judgment

By having subjects express their global impressions or judgments of component traits in terms of likeability, we are able to directly compare the results of the experiments just discussed to the initial data of Busz et al. (1972) in order to test Anderson's averaging model. A further aim of our research, however, was to learn, firstly, whether subjects draw inferences from information that they are given about a target person to other, non-specified characteristics concerning him/her, and, secondly, the effect that salient information (e.g. information on the target person's group affiliation) has on the impression that is finally formed.

In the following experiments, comparisons between likeability ratings are not drawn; instead subjects are asked to make inferences from the given information. These inferences regarding further traits are indeed calculated as if they were likeability ratings, but this calculation was done indirectly by taking the pre-rated values of the inferred traits.

3.3.1. Inferences from physiognomical traits to personality characteristics

An experiment by Rosch and Klump (1975) tested whether subjects infer personality traits from physiognomic descriptions. In a pilot study, the likeability of 110 personality traits (from Busz et al., 1972) and 40 physiognomic descriptors were rated by 30 high school students. The personality traits were then formed into lists, each list having six positive, six negative and six neutral traits. The physiognomic descriptors were used to construct a positive, neutral, and negative stimulus person (e.g. positive person: fair hair, high forehead, big eyes; negative person: bulbous eyes, prominent ears, low forehead; neutral person: thin lips, straight hair, long nose).

Each stimulus person was, in addition, described as belonging
to one of two different social groups (high school student vs.
trade apprentice) in order to see how information about group
affiliation influenced trait assignation.

The subjects in the main experiment were pupils aged between
16 and 19. They were instructed to mark those three traits in
the corresponding list which in their opinion fitted the stimulus person. The average likeability rating for the three
traits selected formed the dependent variable.

Table 2. Averaged likeability rating of the three chosen traits

		Initial Description			
		positive	neutral	negative	total
	pupils	2.20	1.61	.01	1.27
group affiliation	apprentice	2.86	.46	-.71	.87
	total	2.53	1.04	-.35	

The results indicated that the traits that subjects inferred
for each of the target persons were comparable in their likeability ratings to the target person's physiognomic characteristics, the average likeability of the assigned traits increasing as a positive function of physiognomic likeability
$(F_{2,92} = 41,16;\ p<.001)$.

Group affiliation also affected the likeability of the assigned traits; in the neutral condition, the high school student
was perceived as more likeable than the apprentice $(F_{simple} =
6.12;\ df = 1,138;\ p<.05)$ and, over all conditions, subjects
tended to judge the high school student (the subjects were
themselves high school students, it will be recalled) less
extremely than they did the apprentice $(F_{2,92} = 4.47;\ p<.05)$.

3.3.2. Influence of group affiliation on judgments concerning a target person (Rosch et al., 1976)

Group affiliation was selected from the Rosch and Klump (1975) experiment for further investigation, this time, however, varied in such a way that subjects would not identify with any of the groups used. The assignation of personality traits was only of secondary importance, the primary aim being to determine whether an *inconsistent description* (e.g., positive description - negative group affiliation and vice versa) of the stimulus person would cause a distortion of the judgment toward the group *label* as compared to an initial description solely of personality traits.

Method

In a pilot study, 49 occupations were classified in a 21-point likeability scale. During the main experiment, the subjects (30 male and female high school students aged between 17 and 19) were given a number of person descriptions whose mean likeability varied over 5 levels: very positive (5.00<x<6.50), positive (2.50<x<4.00), neutral (1.50>x>-1.50), negative (-2.50>x>-4.00), very negative (-5.00>x>-6.50).

These descriptions consisted of three traits supplemented by an additional piece of information: Another trait vs. the occupational identification of the target person as an unskilled laborer/docker (negative occupation) or editor/engineer (positive occupation). As the dependent variable, subjects were to choose four traits from a list of 64 traits that in their opinion best described the stimulus person.

Results

The likeability ratings for the four traits that subjects chose to describe the stimulus person presented the same clear picture as in Rosch's and Klump's experiment: The more likeable the initial description, the more likeable the further traits ascribed to the stimulus person.

Table 3. Averaged likeability ratings for the four chosen
traits

Valence of the initial description

	very positive		positive		neutral		negative		very negative	
	Additional information									
	occ.	adj.	occ.	adj.	occ.	adj.	occ.	adj.	occ.	adj.
pos.	3.2	2.8	2.1	2.4	-.3	.4	-1.3	-1.1	-2.2	-2.0
neg.	3.0	2.8	1.0	.5	-1.0	-.9	-1.4	-1.6	-2.0	-2.3
	2.95		1.50		-.45		-1.35		-2.13	

(left axis label: Valence of the additional information)

The results show that there is no effect of the kind of additional information (occupation vs. trait adjective; $F<1$). The
effect of the valence of the additional information (positive
vs. negative) was, however, as expected ($F_{1,28} = 6.40$; $p<.05$).

Table 4. Averaged likeability ratings when inconsistent information is added to the initial description

		initial description	
		positive	negative
Additional information	inconsistent occupation	1.98	-1.75
	inconsistent adjective	1.63	-1.56

A further prediction was, that, in the case of inconsistency
between the additional information and the initial description,
the overall judgment would be influenced more when the additional information referred to occupation than when it was an
additional trait. Thus, in terms of Table 4, evaluations in the
upper row should be less extreme than those in the bottom row.

The results, however, pointed in the opposite direction, indicating that the inconsistency may be reduced by *discounting* occupational information and integrating trait information.

3.3.3. Conclusion

Neither of the two experiments discussed in this section showed evidence of the "negativity bias" often found in impression formation research (e.g. Kanouse & Hanson, 1972). On the contrary, a rather abstract hint as to the target person's occupation was sufficient to reverse the influence of negative trait adjectives and confer a rather positive judgment on the target person. It can be assumed that this tendency toward a *"positivity bias"* should increase when the anonymity of the person to be judged is reduced; for example, when familiar instead of unknown stimulus persons are to be judged (also see Carver et al., 1977). With regard to the possibility of a "labeling effect" occurring when subjects are informed of the target person's occupation, the negative results of the experiment by Rosch et al. (1976) lead to the conclusion that a label can only be effective when the "pattern" it implies fits that created by the other information known about the target person (e.g. Gollin, 1954; Higgins & Rholes, 1976; Higgins et al., 1977; Markus, 1977).

The indirect measure of likeability used in these last two experiments render integration theory useless as a basis for generating quantitative predictions. That subjects' likeability judgments were evaluatively consistent with the initial descriptions is a finding derivable from any number of other theoretical formulations, though, in the present case, the work concerning implicit theories of personality (cf. Hastorf et al., 1970; Wegner & Vallacher, 1977; Schneider et al., 1979) semm especially pertinent.

4. Concluding discussion

In my opinion, the experiments on social impression formation
conducted within the linear model paradigm have led to a blind
alley, even though the amount of research done in this area
would seem to disprove this. The various points for which
linear models can be criticized are the following:

(1) The quantitative models of impression formation are limited
    to predicting judgments made along single evaluative di-
    mensions. While the models are most often tested in terms
    of the evaluative dimension, their applicability is not
    restricted to evaluative information (see Schneider et al.,
    1979, p. 176). For an adequate test of linear models,
    other dimensions should also be used.
(2) The models seem applicable only as long as the target per-
    son remains "anonymous"; i.e. outside any well-developed
    connotative framework.
(3) The models are only capable of yielding ex post facto
    descriptions of data; they do not explain.
(4) There is no rule or theory specifying which quantitative
    model is applicable under which condition.
(5) The *cognitive processes* that mediate impression formation
    are not considered.
(6) Inadequate attention is paid to the *semantic content* of
    impression formation material.

Due to these shortcomings, only limited progress has so far
been made in advancing our theoretical understanding of impression formation processes within integration theory. A
symposium held at the APA convention in 1975 revealed, however,
that research on impression formation is beginning to break
out of the narrow channels in which the preoccupation with
linear models has held it. The research discussed in this symposium (e.g. Ebbesen et al., 1975; Hamilton & Katz, 1975;
Lingle et al., 1975) as well as other, more recent articles
(e.g. Cantor & Mischel, 1977, 1979; Higgins & Rholes, 1976;

Higgins et al., 1977; Ostrom & Lingle, 1977; Srull & Wyer, 1979; Wyer & Carlston, 1979) clearly show the narrowness and theoretical barrenness of the integration approach. It is interesting to note that many of these new approaches return for their inspiration to ideas originally presented by Asch in 1946 and stress the dynamic character of the impression formation processes. It has been said, for example, that in "an organized impression, qualities are not merely passively or linguistically related. Often they are related more dynamically" (Schneider et al., 1979, p. 267). Scripts, schemata, or *prototypes* - all refer to organizing principles which "will help us to a better understanding of how perceivers process, organize, and store information and all these models presuppose an active information processor as perceiver..." (ibidem, p. 269). Concomitant with this concern for process, there is also a move towards extending considerations to stimulus materials other than trait adjectives (see Schneider et al., 1979 for an overview).

Within our own research project, we have recently initiated experiments concerning these active perceptual processes, the theoretical background being provided by Abelson's script-theory (Abelson, 1976; Schank & Abelson, 1977) and the prototype approach (Cantor & Mischel, 1977, 1979). Behaviors, situations and traits are our materials for describing stimulus persons. One of our first experiments was concerned with an examination of the mediating processes underlying attribute inference judgments (Semin & Rosch, 1980). The findings of this study demonstrate that subjects activate the prototypes of categories associated with the stimulus attributes and do not make inferences on the basis of the semantic similarity between stimulus attributes and response attributes. These findings suggest that categorical processes are involved in attribute inference judgments.

Chapter 3 Social Judgment, Stereotyping and Polarization Effect

W. Bandilla, H. Klump, J. Krolage, W. Lilli and E. Rosch

1. Introduction

The topic of this paper is social judgment, the aim being to contribute to the development of some concepts in this research area as well as to point out conditions restricting their applicability concerning the judgment of persons and objects. Our discussion focuses upon judgmental distortion, which we interpret as being the product of cognitive processes stimulated by social variables such as schemata, values, cognitive dispositions, etc.. Our analyses are based on the following theoretical concepts:

Accentuation: Ideas developed by Tajfel (1957) and Holzkamp and his colleagues (Holzkamp et al., 1968) are especially useful in generating cognitive explanations of judgmental phenomena. Tajfel's stimulus classification theory (Tajfel, 1963; Tajfel & Wilkes, 1963), for example, serves as a basis in the present report for an analysis of stereotyping.

Value connotations: Our analysis of polarization effects is based on the empirical research of Sherif and Hovland (1961) and others and on theoretical work by Eiser and Stroebe (1972) and Naatz and Hümmelink (1971). Our aim is to develop more precise explanations of polarization phenomena, a central assumption being that social stimuli are associated with value connotations that determine the strength and direction of distortions.

2. Empirical and theoretical research

In the following chapters we discuss each of the focal points
of our empirical and theoretical research; Accentuation (section 1), Stereotyping (section 2) and Polarization (section 3).
In the final section we attempt to develop an overall theoretical synthesis of our research results.

2.1. Accentuation

Research on accentuation has, to a certain extent, undergone a
two-sided development, with accentuation being treated as
either a perceptual or a cognitive phenomenon. The two approaches do, however, have a common starting point in that they both
seek to account for the occurrence of shifts and biases in the
judgment of social stimuli. For a detailed discussion of the
various perceptual and cognitive accentuation theories see
Lilli (1975b).

2.1.1. Perceptual accentuation

The concept of perceptual accentuation originated with the "new
look in perception" (Allport, 1955) and to a substantial degree
dates back to Bruner and Postman (e.g. 1949a). Bruner and
Goodman (1947, p. 36) give the following description of perceptual accentuation: "Perceptual objects which are habitually
selected become more vivid, have greater clarity or greater
brightness or greater apparent size." These authors differentiated between autochtoneous (i.e. innate) and behavioral (e.g.
needs, tensions, past experience) determinants of perception
and ascribe the dominant role in social perception to the
latter.

The classic experiments on perceptual accentuation (e.g.
Bruner & Goodman, 1947; Bruner & Postman, 1947, 1948) tested
whether behavioral determinants have a direct influence on perception, the specific hypothesis being that subjects' percep-

tion of desired objects are distorted in such a way as to make
these objects appear larger than they actually are. The overall
evidence from these experiments does not, however, support the
"directive-state" hypothesis; although numerous studies (e.g.
Carter & Schooler, 1949; Klein et al., 1951) report distortions
as regards stimulus reproduction, no evidence of direct effects
on subjects' perceptions was reported.

2.1.2. Cognitive accentuation

This unsatisfactory situation led to the formulation of new,
more cognitively oriented approaches. Bruner and Rodrigues
(1953), for example, introduced the notion of "relative accentuation", pointing out that the magnitude of the distortion
depended on the correlation of value and size of the judgment
objects.

McCurdy (1956), on the other hand, assumed that, when subjects
judge valuable objects (e.g. coins), memory schemata operate
that are resistant even to direct perceptual contact with the
judgment object. According to this conception, distortions in
stimulus reproduction could be reduced to the interaction of
"emotional states" and the "need for adjustment" to the objective reality.

Tajfel's concept of the accentuation of differences (e.g.
Tajfel, 1957) and the cognitive-absolute approach of Holzkamp
and his colleagues (Holzkamp, 1965; Holzkamp et al., 1968;
Naatz & Hümmelink, 1971) are also of central importance here.
As these two approaches were dealt with in detail in another
article (Lilli, 1975a), we shall concentrate here on discussing
the differences between the two approaches.

2.1.2.1. Absolute vs. relative accentuation

The controversy whether accentuation is relative or absolute
arises from the different ways of interpreting accentuation

phenomena. Tajfel (1957), for example, interprets accentuation effects as changes in the perceived differences between two or more stimuli (relative accentuation). According to Tajfel, such effects can occur only if the stimuli occur in series whose quantitative (e.g. stimulus size) and qualitative (e.g. stimulus value) aspects covary. Holzkamp (e.g. Holzkamp et al., 1968), on the other hand, considers accentuation independently from stimulus series, arguing that accentuation can occur for any isolated stimulus as long as its underlying quantitative and qualitative aspects have become associated through past experience (absolute accentuation).

In several tests of his position (Holzkamp & Perlwitz, 1966; Holzkamp & Keiler, 1967; Holzkamp et al., 1968), Holzkamp found it unnecessary that test stimuli be related in series for accentuation effects to occur. Lilli (1972), however, criticizes these findings, contending that Tajfel's concept of the accentuation of differences is not falsified by Holzkamp's arguments. Lilli offers the following two arguments in support of his own position:

1) The relation between quantitative and qualitative stimulus dimensions is best learned when the stimuli are presented in a series, as also can be seen in the Holzkamp studies themselves. 2) If two dimensions covary, the repercussions extend to every object for which the two dimensions are relevant. It is therefore of little importance whether, in an actual judgment situation, an individual stimulus or a stimulus series is presented.

The second of these arguments implies that if a rule of correspondence responsible for the occurrence of accentuation effects had been learned in a series context, then the direction (i.e. under- or overestimation) of subsequent accentuation can be predicted for both serial and non-serial stimulus constellations. The following experiment by Lilli and Winkler (1973) tested this point.

Method: Subjects were 36 students between 19 and 23 years of age. They were distributed over four experimental conditions

created by the factorial combination of two independent variables: "serial vs. non-serial context" and "stimulus object with
vs. without value". Stimulus object was a grey disc presented
by projector and described as being either "a metal disc" or
"a disc made of a precious metal called Rhodium, its estimated
value being DM 260,50." The disc was presented either as the
middle item in a series of three, or by itself. Subjects were
simply asked to estimate the disc's diameter.

Results: According to the rule of correspondence valid for precious metals (the more precious, the smaller), informing the
subjects that the disc consisted of precious metal should have
resulted in their underestimating the disc's diameter. This
indeed happened. The underestimation occurred regardless of
whether the disc was presented separately or in a series.
Lilli's second argument thus stands confirmed.

2.1.3. Conclusions: Convergence of the concepts of Tajfel and Holzkamp

Subsequent for further experiments by Holzkamp and his colleagues (Naatz & Hümmelink, 1971; Naatz & Dickhoff, 1975), we tried
to bridge the primarily terminological gap between the absolute
and relative approach and establish a common basis between
them (Lilli, 1975a). This later research, in conjunction with
the studies described above, led us to the following conclusions:

1) Both approaches concur that accentuation effects are the
result of rules of covariation between judgmental dimensions
underlying the stimulus object(s).
2) The serial conditions discussed by Tajfel and the dimensional conditions of Holzkamp's cognitive-absolute approach
are compatible; in both cases, it is the value (in the non-
qualitative sense) of variables and their systematic relation
to the values of other variables that influence the judgment.

2.2.   Stereotyping

2.2.1. Theory of stimulus classification

The theory of stimulus classification developed by Tajfel and his colleagues (Tajfel, 1959, 1963; Tajfel & Wilkes, 1963) serves as a basis for several experiments aimed at elaborating the central features of an approach to stereotyping. The theory of stimulus classification deals with the effect that categorical dimensions have on subjects' judgment of stimulus series.

This theory complements the theory of the accentuation of differences discussed above in that it rests on the same two premises:

1) Forming judgments involves comparing stimuli:
a stimulus judged on a certain dimension will always be considered in relation to other stimuli along that same dimension.
2) The covariation between the classification and the judgmental dimension is the result of learning.

Lilli and Lehner (1971, 1972) have presented Tajfel's theory of stimulus classification in detail:
1) A classification added to a series of physically defined stimuli has an effect on the judgments of these stimuli only under the condition that a direct and consistent relationship exists between the classification and the stimuli to be judged.

2) The existence of such a relation leads to an increase of between-class differences (inter-class-effect) and a decrease of within-class differences (intra-class-effect) in the judgments (see Figure 1 on page 95).
3) The effects in 1 and 2 appear more frequently if the classification is emphasized.
4) The perceived between-class differences and within-class similarities become more pronounced as subjects become more experienced with the stimuli and the classificatory schema.

Figure 1. Stereotyping. Interclass-effects (1) and intraclass-
effects (2) in the judgment of classified stimuli.

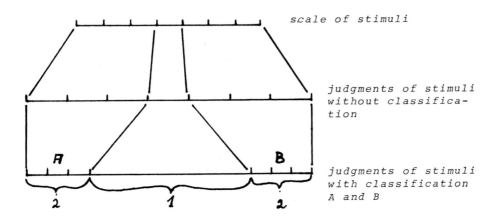

scale of stimuli

*judgments of stimuli
without classifica-
tion*

*judgments of stimuli
with classification
A and B*

5) As complexity of stimulus material increases, the differences between classes also increase, whereas the within-class differences decrease.

The first empirical tests of this theory were made by Tajfel
and Wilkes (1963), who presented their subjects 8 lines of different lengths to be estimated. In one experimental condition,
the four shorter lines were always marked with an A, and the
four longer with a B. In a second condition, the A's and B's
were assigned randomly and, in a third condition, the lines
were presented without additional symbol.

The condition with the systematic covariation of classification
and judgmental dimension (lengths of lines) showed a significantly greater "interclass-effect" than did the other two. Moreover, the "interclass-effect" was strongest when repeated measure were taken within the experimental session; in such
cases, a comparison of the first and second measure revealed
an "intraclass-effect" as well. A second session held one week

after the first showed no further increase of the effects.

The main result of this experiment is that the "inter-class-effect" was significantly greater if the stimulus series was systematically classified. The postulated simultaneous occurrence of "inter-" and "intra-class-effects" was, on the whole, not confirmed, though it could, however, be observed as subjects became more experienced with the classificatory schema and stimuli during a single session. It thus seems possible that increasing experience enhances these effects. The experiment did succeed, however, in demonstrating that judgmental distortions can occur in abstract judgment tasks.

2.2.2. Degree of covariation between a classification and a series of stimuli

The study by Lilli (1970), following up Tajfel and Wilkes (1963), tested whether the degree of judgmental distortion is a function of the covariation of the classification and the judgment dimension. Tajfel and Wilkes' systematic and random correspondence conditions represent two extremes in the possible degrees of correspondence between a classification schema and a series of stimuli. In the Lilli experiment, the probability of correspondence between classification and stimulus-series was varied over several levels. It was hypothesized that judgmental distortion would increase with increasing correspondence between the classificatory schema and the series of stimuli.

Method: The stimuli used were Tajfel and Wilkes' eight lines as well as the labels A and B.

Degree of correspondence was operationalized as the probability with which the shorter distances (lines No. 1 to 4) were labelled A, and the longer (lines No. 5 to 8), B. It was manipulated over five levels (p = 1,0; p = 0.92; p = 0,83; p = 0.67; p = 0,5).

Each line was presented for estimation individually. In addition, two extreme lines (10cm and 30cm) were presented at the beginning of the main experiment to anchor subjects' judgments. In order to get precise estimations, subjects were asked to make their responses to the millimeter.

Results: The judgmental distortion (inter-class-difference) was measured by the difference in estimations for lines No. 5 and No. 4, that is, the shortest of the four longer lines minus the longest of the four shorter ones.

The prediction that judgmental distortion (inter-class-effect) would decrease with decreasing correspondence between classification and stimulus series was confirmed ($F_{4,60} = 7.52$; $p<.01$). Further analysis, however, showed that the conditions $p = 1.0$ and $p = 0.92$ differed from all the others. This seems to indicate that systematic judgmental distortion appears only if the classification schema and stimulus series show a clear and precise relation to each other. Finally, presenting the stimuli twice did not result in judgmental distortions, thus contradicting the hypothesis that distortion increases with increasing familiarity with the stimuli and classification schema.

2.2.3. Stimulus complexity and value of the classification

Previous experiments have shown that stereotyping occurs even in the context of a simple length estimation task so long as subjects regard the abstract classificatory schema as judgment-relevant information. In another experiment, Lilli (1970) investigated whether the degree of judgmental distortion varies as a positive function of both the complexity of the stimulus series and the emotional significance of the classificatory schema. There would seem to be a difference between the relatively abstract, impersonal task of estimating distances and the more emotionally charged task of classifying people according to nationality, race or any other real-life group affiliation. According to Tajfel (1963, 1969), the degree of stereotyping should increase in such emotionally charged situations.

Method: Two series of 8 faces were shown, the height of the foreheads varying within each series. The two series differed in complexity; one consisted of simple, schematically drawn faces, while the other series consisted of faces that were more complex, with realistic eyes, nose, mouth, etc.. Subjects' estimates of forehead heights was the main dependent variable.

Emotionality was varied by using the letters "A" and "B" as labels in one case (low emotionality) and "blue collar worker" and "official" in the other (high emotionality), with "A" (blue collar worker) always being used for the four lower foreheads and "B" (official) for the four higher foreheads. Control groups were shown the faces without classificatory labels. The height of the highest and lowest foreheads were given to all subjects as anchors.

Results: The hypothesis that judgmental distortion would increase with increasing stimulus complexity was not confirmed. The emotionality of the classificatory scheme was, however, found to influence judgmental distortion ($F_{2,72} = 6.4$; $p<.01$).

An experiment by Marchand (1970) also tested the effect of emotionally significant classifications on judgmental distortion. Marchand had pupils (aged 12 - 15 years) estimate the sides of eight squares that had been labelled by colors and letters (A, green = small; B, blue = large). The emotional value of the classification was determined by a gambling game played before the estimation took place in which, for example, the smallest square meant a loss and the biggest a profit etc., or where profit and loss were distributed randomly. It was shown that augmenting emotional significance of the classification leads to an increase of the estimated differences between stimulus classes (inter-class-differences) ($F_{1,44} = 7.12$ and 9.42; $p<.05$). In discussing this result, Irle (1975), concluded that the degree of stereotyping increases to the extent to which the respective classes are each associated with an emotional value.

In order to test the emotionality-variable, Upmeyer et al.
(1976) made use of a pre-existing classificatory schema, drawing their subjects from two local soccer clubs that competed
in the same league and between whom a strong rivalry could be
assumed to exist. Using a signal detection paradigm (cf. Banks,
1970), Upmeyer et al. presented negative attributes paired with
the names of both competing clubs as well as with the names of
two comparable clubs from outside the league. After subjects had
been exposed to all the attribute-club pairs, they were presented with the list of attributes and had to designate the
club with which the attribute had been previously paired. The
subjects were also to indicate their confidence in each of their
responses. The results indicate that memory performance is
better than to outside clubs ($F_{1,30}$ = 109.23; p<.001). Furthermore, in the case of the competing local clubs, a judgmental
distortion (bias) appeared, with subjects tending to over-
attribute the negative traits to their local competitor
($\bar{x}_{diff}$ = 1.51; t = 2.00; df = 30; p<.027).

2.2.4. Interaction between Inter- and Intra-class differences, and consistency of stereotyping effects

Lilli and Lehner (1971) dealt with two problems that had not
received previous empirical attention but that are of primary
importance in developing a conceptual framework for the study
of stereotyping: the interaction between the magnitude of inter-
and intra-class differences in a social stimulus situation,
and the resistance to change of classificatory judgments.

Stereotyping can be regarded as the product of a highly economical method of information processing: a wide variety of stimuli
are categorized according to a relatively small number of focal
criteria, with all members of a given category being treated as
equivalent. As a result, responses to individual stimuli are
supplanted by resonses to stimulus categories, and judgments
concerning complex situations are reduced to judgments about

focal criteria, thus, in effect, reducing the number of separate situations to which the subject has to respond. As proposed by Lilli and Lehner (1971), the mechanism underlying this
process is a form of generalization whereby subjects' responses
to individual stimulus situations are transferred from other
situations falling in the same category (see also Ferguson,
1954, 1956). The greater the correspondence between the stimulus series and the category schema, the more pronounced this
transfer process should be.

It should also be noted that this way of accounting for stereotyping suggests that stereotyped judgments should be particularly resistant to change by experience: Since stimuli are perceived only in terms of a classification, other, possibly contradictory features that they possess are not likely to be
considered. Thus, a second issue addressed by Lilli and Lehner
was the extent to which previously acquired stereotyping habits
will be modified in response to contradictory social stimuli.

Method: Subjects were male and female students. The stimulus
series were six faces that differed in the height of their
foreheads. The variation of the relation between the classification schema and stimulus series was achieved, as in Lilli
(1970), by changing the probabilities of correspondence of labels A and B with lower or higher foreheads. This variable varied over six levels, with the probability of correspondence
equalling 1.0, 0.96, 0.83, 0.75, 0.67 and p = 0.50.

In a training phase, subjects were shown series of faces that
either increased or decreased with respect to forehead height
in order to enable subjects to realize that the relation between classification and height of forehead could be learned.
In the experiment itself, however, the faces were presented
individually and in a random order, the estimate of forehead
height being the main dependent variable. During the estimation phase, the pairing of labels A and B with the high and
low foreheads was reversed so that the relation between clas-

sification scheme and foreheads was the opposite of what it
was during the training phase.

The size of the inter-class differences was measured by taking
the difference between the size estimates for foreheads three
and four. The intra-class difference was determined as the
average difference of the highest and the lowest forehead in
both classes.

Results: The relation between the inter- and intra-class difference was checked by a correlation analysis and, as expected,
the inter- and the intra-class difference was found to be negatively related ($r = .7678$; $n = 60$; $p < .01$). Here too, however,
it was seen that the intra-class difference was influenced much
less by classification than the inter-class difference. The
transfer hypothesis was also confirmed ($F_{1,19} = 7.22$; $p < .025$);
the relationship that subjects discovered in the training phase
evidently prevented them from applying the reversed relationship in the main experiment. This result is remarkable, particularly in view of the two test groups with their visibly close
connections ($p = 1.0$ and $p = 0.96$). The confirmation of this
transfer hypothesis was regarded as an indication that classification judgments are resistant to alterations.

Rosch and Müller (1978) argued that the simultaneous occurrence
of inter- and intra-class effects is unlikely in situations
with a low number of judgment stimuli. Though between-class
differences are likely in such cases, the relatively small
number of stimuli falling in each class permit them to be easily differentiated,and thus obviates the need to reduce within-
class stimulus distances. The authors argue that in most of
the experiments conducted so far the number of stimuli was too
small for a diminishing of within-class differences to occur.
Indeed, an experiment by M. Rosch (1975) showed that simultaneous inter- and intra-class effects do occur when the number and complexity of the stimuli used in such experiments
is increased.

In their experiment, Rosch and Müller (1978) demonstrated that
when subjects were asked to estimate the size of ten countries,
the smaller ones being marked "A" and the larger ones "B", the
resulting inter-class differences are significantly greater
than those found for a non-labelled control group ($F_{1,180}$ =
31.12; p<.001).

In another experiment, Rosch and Müller (1978) had subjects
make similarity judgments rather than absolute judgments, their
rationale being that since stereotype theory places emphasis on
the inter-relationship between stimuli, similarity judgments
are more appropriate. For each of 30 pairs of countries resulting from the combination of the 10 countries previously used,
the subjects had to mark the similarity in km^2-size on a 21-
point scale. Here, too, the size sequence of the countries as
well as the categories A = big and B = small were emphasized
in a preliminary phase. The results indicate that, once again,
the inter-class difference was significantly stronger (Mann-
Whitney-U = 64; p<.05) and the intra-class difference significantly weaker (U = 26; p<.001) in the classified than in the
non-classified condition.

These experiments show that the interrelation of inter- and
intra-class difference seems to occur only if *large* numbers of
complex stimuli are judged. Moreover, similarity judgments seem
better suited than the more frequently used absolute judgments
as a test of the underlying concepts.

2.2.5. Stimulus presentation as a determinant of stereotyping

Lilli and Krolage (1977) investigated whether the occurrence
of stereotype schemata depends on certain stimulus constellations. Their reasoning was based on the following two cases in
which shifts of judgments can occur:

1) Judgmental shifts as a result of stimulus differentiation.
In his theory on the accentuation of differences, Tajfel (1957)

points out that differences between stimuli are over-accentuated in order to facilitate a distinct coding of individual stimuli within memory schemata (cf. McCurdy, 1956).

2) Judgmental shifts as a result of stimulus classification. The stimulus classification theory (Tajfel, 1963; Tajfel & Wilkes, 1963) accounts for situations in which a stimulus differentiation strategy no longer guarantees efficient information processing. Reduction of stimulus-complexity in such situations can only be successful if memory schemata in terms of categories are formed. In such cases over-accentuation of differences between *individual stimuli* is substituted by over-accentuation of differences between *classes of stimuli*. Thus it follows that classifying stimulus conditions should result in a greater judgmental bias - but a smaller judgmental variability - than differentiating stimulus conditions.

Besides these types of stimulus presentation (classifying vs. differentiating), Lilli and Krolage manipulated two further independent variables, namely the amount of information (high vs. low) and the emphasis of stimulus similarity versus dissimilarity. An increase in the amount of information should increase the effect of the various kinds of stimulus presentation. Likewise, emphasizing stimulus similarities should increase stereotyping in the classifying stimulus condition, whereas emphasizing stimulus dissimilarities should increase stereotyping in the differentiating stimulus condition.

Method: Subjects were female high-school students between 15 and 17 years of age. The task was to estimate the intelligence of the presented faces on a 21-point-scale. The three independent variables were operationalized as follows:

Classifying vs. differentiating stimulus conditions: 4 faces with different forehead heights were either divided into two classes by adding the labels "white collar worker" vs. "blue collar worker" (classifying stimulus condition), or were each assigned a different occupational label (construction worker, automechanic, teacher, professor) (differentiating stimulus condition). The two levels of amount of information were varied by presenting either just information about the occupation or information concerning both occupation and income. Stimulus similarity-dissimilarity was indicated by instructing the subjects that the presented faces were either similar to one another or each different.

In line with the hypotheses, there were two dependent variables, one measuring judgmental distortion and the other judgmental variability. Judgmental distortion was calculated for each subject as a ratio comparing the differences between the estimates of the faces No. 2 and No. 3 (the lowest forehead of the high class minus the highest forehead of the low class) and the total range of the subject's estimation. The standard deviation of the estimations per subject was the measure for judgment variability.

As the authors had reasoned, judgmental distortion was stronger under classifying stimulus conditions than under differentiating stimulus conditions ($F_{1,56}$ = 21,63; p<.01). The hypothesis concerning judgmental variability was, however, not statistically confirmed, although the mean values all lay in the predicted direction. Increasing the amount of information had only a slight effect on the magnitude of judgmental distortion but led, as predicted, to a substantial reduction in judgment variability ($F_{1,56}$ = 7.23; p<.01). Both predictions concerning stimulus similarity-dissimilarity were confirmed ($F_{1,56}$ = 4.47 and 6.03; p<.05).

Altogether the experiment successfully demonstrated that the occurrence of stereotype schemata depends on the kind of stimuli and their presentation.

2.2.6. Cognitive complexity as a codeterminant of judgmental behavior

People differ in the way they observe their social surroundings

and cope with available information. Concepts of cognitive
structure (Harvey et al., 1961; Schroder et al., 1967; Schroder
& Suedfeld, 1971) and cognitive complexity (Kelly, 1955; Bieri
et al., 1966) provide a theoretical basis for this assumption.
Measures have been developed for determining 1) the number of
dimensions a person is capable of differentiating and 2) the
degree to which persons are capable of integrating different
stimuli into unifying concepts (Werner, 1957; Zajonc, 1960;
MacNeill, 1974). The "role construct repertory" (rep) method
developed by Bieri et al. (1966) on the basis of Kelly's (1955)
"personal construct theory" (Bonarius, 1965; Bannister & Fransella, 1957) is particularly useful for the study of cognitive
complexity. Subjects taking the "rep" test are confronted with
a 10 x 10 matrix consisting of persons (e.g. father, boss, etc.)
and bi-polar adjective pairs (e.g. interesting - dull) and are
asked to judge each person on each adjective pair using a six-
point scale. The degree of cognitive complexity is determined
by comparing all 10 judgments for each person. More detailed
descriptions of this method are given by Lilli (1973) and
Rosch (1975).

Our present aims with respect to the rep test are two-fold:
1) To empirically examine whether the rep-variable accurately
   predicts differences in judgmental behavior.
2) To investigate whether the rep test adequately measures
   cognitive complexity.

With respect to the first of these issues, Lilli and Rosch
(1977) tested whether high cognitive complexity subjects are
more reactive to changes in the amount of information than low
cognitive complexity subjects. 32 female students between the
ages of 17 and 19 had to classify faces according to intelligence and indicate their confidence in their judgments. The
amount of information was manipulated by whether or not additional information (personality characteristics) was presented with the faces. The results indicate that high cognitive
complexity subjects increased both the range and the confidence

of their judgments as the amount of information increased,
while low cognitive complexity subjects did not $F_{1,18} = 8.45$;
p<.01). A further study by Lilli (1973) showed that cognitive
complexity as measured by the rep test varies directly with an
active preference, and indirectly with a passive preference, for
complex stimuli. These studies thus show the rep variable to be
a sufficiently reliable predictor of differences in judgmental
behavior.

Concerning the second issue mentioned above, factor analysis of
the 10 x 10 rep matrices of 110 subjects (Winkler, Rosch &
Lilli, 1973) revealed, as already shown by Ickert et al. (1972),
that the distinction between the various degrees of cognitive
complexity is insufficient, with adequate differentiation occurring only when extreme groups are compared.

Rosch (1975), too, thoroughly investigated the validity of the
rep test as a measure for cognitive complexity and found it to
be issue-specific. On the whole, it seems that the rep test
shows serious deficiencies in measuring cognitive complexity.

2.2.7. Stereotyping in a social context: the effects of a cognitive schema in the judgment of persons

In addition to our research concerning the cognitive basis of
stereotyping, we thought it advisable to examine stereotyping
in more naturalistic social contexts. Forming impressions of
people often involves inferring non-observable traits and
characteristics from whatever observable information happens to
be available. For example, we might infer a person's intelligence from the height of his forehead, so that (as long as
no further contradictory information is received) people with
high foreheads are perceived as being more intelligent than
people with low foreheads. Lilli and Krolage (1975, 1976) empirically investigated whether this relation between forehead
height and perceived intelligence mediates a further relation

between forehead height and liking. They reasoned that since in everyday life intelligence is a central trait, a high intelligence rating would result in positive ratings on other traits as well and thus lead to the formation of a favorable overall impression.

Method: The subjects were 60 men and women from 20 to 65 years of age. Their task was to ascribe various positive and negative traits to one of two faces that differed as to the height (high or low) of their foreheads. Besides forehead height, one independent variable was "mode of presentation", with faces being either shown visually or merely described verbally. Another independent variable was trait ambiguity, with one half of the positive and negative traits being "ambiguous" as to their precise meaning and the other half being unambiguous. With respect to this last variable, it was predicted that the tendency to assign likeable traits to the face with high forehead would be most pronounced when the traits were ambiguous.

Results: The dependent variable was the number of hits in the sense of "high forehead = likeable, low forehead = not likeable". With one exception, faces with high foreheads were assigned more positive traits than were those with low foreheads ($t_{min} = 3.30$; n = 30; p<.01). As expected, this pattern was more pronounced among ambiguous traits than it was among unambiguous ones ($F_{1,58} = 36.53$; p<.01). Visual stimulus presentation proved less effective than verbal stimulus presentation in eliciting the high forehead-high likeability schema ($F_{1,58} = 6.30$; p<.05).

2.2.8. Further evidence of stereotyping effects in a social context

Lilli, Krolage and Rosch (1977, 1978) investigated the influence of political party stereotypes on judgments concerning the two West German parties, the Social Democratic Party (SPD) and the Christian Democratic Union (CDU), as well as their top candidates, Helmut Schmidt and Helmut Kohl, during the 1976 election. ·It was predicted that subjects intending to vote for one of the two parties would judge both the two parties and their top candidates as being less similar than would subjects not intending to vote for either party. It was also predicted that the magnitude of this stereotyping effect would progressively increase during the elections.

Method: The subjects were high-school students between 18 and 20 years of age. Their task was to rate the CDU, SPD, Kohl and Schmidt twice, once at the beginning and once at the end of the election campaign, on a series of bi-polar scales. There were three independent variables: 1) preference for one of the two parties vs. no preference, 2) objects of judgment e.g. parties vs. candidates and 3) judgment at the beginning vs. judgment at the end of the election campaign. The dependent variable was the sum of the differences on the trait scales per judgment object (parties and candidates) and per subject.

Results: As predicted, subjects preferring one of the two parties regarded the differences between the parties and between the candidates as being more enhanced than did subjects with no preference ($F_{1,96}$ = 21.52 and 10.18; p<.001 and <.01). At the end of the election campaign, the subjects with a preference regarded the parties and their candidates as being significantly less similar than they did at the beginning of the campaign ($F_{1,96}$ = 7.47 and 5.20; p<.01 and <.05).

2.3. Polarization as a stereotyping effect

In this section we intend to demonstrate that the accentuation and stereotyping effects discussed above are capable of explaining judgmental distortions in the judging of attitude items by persons with extremely positive or negative attitudes concerning the attitude object.

2.3.1. Problem

Numerous experiments have shown a connection between a person's
attitude concerning an attitude object and his/her judgmental
behavior (comp. Hovland & Sherif, 1952; Upshaw, 1962; Selltitz
et al., 1965; Zavalloni & Cook, 1965): Persons with extreme
attitudes show a greater tendency to differentiate between positive and negative statements concerning the attitude object
than do persons whose attitudes are more neutral. This effect
is called polarization. Close analysis of the results of these
experiments has shown, however, that polarization effects are
mainly produced in the case of extremely positive attitudes;
persons with extremely negative attitudes often do not differ
in their judgmental behavior from those with neutral positions.
Numerous attempts have been made to explain this effect, the
best of which seems to be the assimilation-contrast model
(Sherif & Hovland, 1961). One objection to this model is that
it describes the effect without explaining it (cf. Eiser &
Stroebe, 1972). In his "variable series model", Upshaw (1962)
starts from a definite theoretical position but fails to explain the asymmetry with respect to positive and negative attitudes.

2.3.2. Theoretical approach

These polarization effects are the target of some recent theoretical work by Eiser and Stroebe (1972), who use Tajfel's
work on stimulus classification (1959; Tajfel and Wilkes, 1963)
as a starting point for their theorizing.

2.3.2.1. The judgmental model

The judgmental model underlying Eiser and Stroebe's (1972)
approach distinguishes between focal and peripheral stimulus
dimensions. Focal dimensions are those dimensions to which the
judgment task refers, whereas peripheral dimensions are other

dimensions underlying the stimulus series. The conditions under which a peripheral dimension exerts its effects are determined by the nature of the connection between the peripheral and focal dimensions within the stimulus series.

According to Eiser and Stroebe, the focal dimension is established by the degree to which the items about the attitude object do or do not favor this object. The extent of acceptance or rejection of these items by the subject constitutes the peripheral dimension which, in the case of subjects with extreme attitudes,stands in a monotonic relation to the focal dimension. Since this monotonicity is lacking in the case of subjects with non-extreme attitudes, these subjects will be less likely than the extremists to draw marked distinctions between positive and negative statements concerning the attitude object.

2.3.2.2. Value connotations

In order to account for the empirical data on polarization, Eiser and Stroebe extend this model by adding another peripheral dimension called "value connotation". In short, this means the "social desirability" of an attitude concerning a socially relevant attitude object. The connection of this dimension to the focal dimension may be in the same direction as that of the other peripheral dimension and thus enhance the latter's directive effect. In other cases, however, the two connections may be negatively correlated and the dimensions' directive effect diminished. Thus, for example, a person with an extremely positive attitude toward a socially desirable attitude object should show strong polarization, accepting statements he considers as positive and rejecting those he considers as negative.

On the other hand, a person with an extremely negative attitude toward a socially desirable attitude object will, as a consequence of his own socially undesirable attitude, not be able to agree as strongly to items considered positive (statements

against the attitude object) nor reject as strongly items considered negative (statements in favor of the attitude object),
thus showing less polarization.

At first sight this model offers a reasonable explanation of
the polarization effects. One of its shortcomings, though, concerns the mutually neutralizing effects of incongruent connections, since the model cannot in all cases yield clear predictions concerning the directions of the subsequent judgment
shifts. In order to improve this, Klump and Bandilla (Klump &
Bandilla, 1978; Bandilla et al., 1973) propose that the multi-
dimensionality concept of Eiser and Stroebe be joined to the
accentuation theories of Holzkamp and colleagues (Holzkamp et
al., 1968), thus yielding a system that allows to predict the
direction of judgment shifts on the basis of the sign of the
dimension connections. Holzkamp's theory was initially developed to account only for values as a peripheral dimension, but
was later extended to cover cases with other peripheral dimensions as well. It is based on the following hypothesis: "subjects with a previously established associative link between
the evaluative and some other, peripheral dimension will, when
confronted with an evaluative stimulus that is to be judged on
the peripheral dimension, be more tolerant of judgmental distortions that are in the same direction as the link and be in-
tolerant of those that are not (Naatz & Hümmelink, 1971, p.
364)[1]". This means that in the case of a *positive* monotonic relation between the focal and peripheral dimensions, subjects
will overestimate (relative to subjects for whom this relation
does not exist) the magnitude or intensity of a given stimulus,
while in the case of a *negative* relation, a corresponding underestimation will occur.

If this theory, which so far has only been tested with physically defined stimulus material, is applied to account for

_____

[1] Translated by the authors of this paper.

polarization differences in the scaling of attitude items, the
assumption is that agreement/rejection of statements by the
judging subject and the degree of social desirability of the
attitude expressed by the statements constitute *two* peripheral
dimensions. If both dimensions relate positively to the focal
dimension, the overestimation effects in the positive and negative statement classes will be maximal, and strong polarization
will occur. If, on the other hand, the first peripheral dimension is connected to the focal dimension negatively, and the
second positively, the over- and underestimation effects will
neutralize each other, resulting in weaker polarization effects.

2.3.2.3. Experimental test

The following experiment tested two hypotheses:
The polarization effect shown by subjects with extreme attitudes is a result of the *over*estimation of positive and negative items.

The tendency for overestimation increases if the congruity of
the connection between peripheral and focal dimensions increases.

Method: The experimental design included the following independent variables: "attitude towards the attitude object" (pro,
neutral, contra), "valence of the attitude statements" (positive, negative) and "scale label" (scale I: congruity for pro-
judgments, incongruity for contra-judgments; scale II: incongruity for pro-judgments, congruity for contra-judgments; scale
III: no explicit value connotations), the two latter variables
being manipulated within subjects. The N per cell was 20.

The attitude object was the introduction of no-lead petrol. The
advocates of this law stressed mainly the environmental benefits
resulting from the introduction of no-lead petrol, the opponents pointed out its economical disadvantages (increased petrol prices, etc.). The subjects judged a total of 16 statements
on three 15-point (-7 to +7) scales, eight of the statements

being in favor of no-lead fuel, and eight opposed. Two of the
scales, "good vs. bad for the environment" and "economically
wise vs. unwise" had explicit value connotations, while the
third "in favor vs. not in favor of the law", was without value
relevance. For the first scale, connections between the focal
and the two peripheral dimensions should have been congruent to
a person with a positive attitude but incongruent to someone
with a negative attitude. The second scale should have presented the reverse situation.

Results and discussion: The mean of each subject's judgments of
the eight positive and eight negative statements was used as a
measure for the dependent variable. The predictions concerning
overestimation effects by subjects with extreme attitudes was
significantly confirmed (individual comparisons of means according to Scheffé; $p<.01$): the extremity of positive statements was overestimated on all three scales by subjects in favor of no-lead fuel and on the second scale by those opposed
to it, while the extremity of negative statements was overestimated on the first and third scale by the pro-subjects and on
the second and third scale by the contra-subjects. The distribution pattern of the overestimation effects over the three
scales conforms to our prediction concerning the dependency
of these effects on the congruency/incongruency of the focal-
peripheral connections.

3. Concluding remarks

The theoretical approach followed here started from a multidimensional judgment model whose fundamental assumption is that
"peripheral" stimulus dimensions that are not directly involved in a judgment situation can, under certain conditions, influence subjects' judgments along the relevant dimension.
Depending on the "peripheral" scale's characteristics, such
indirect influences can result in an over-accentuation of

similarities and differences within a stimulus series or the over- or underestimation of stimulus properties, the sole pre- condition being that the peripheral dimension be positively or negatively correlated with the dimension along which judg- ments are to be made. Research with simple physical stimuli has shown the usefulness of this approach with respect to the accentuation of differences, absolute accentuation and stimulus classification. When extended to include judgments on social stimuli, the model was able to clarify certain aspects of stereotyping as well as polarization effects.

Extending our analysis to more complex stimulus material re- vealed, however, some of its deficiencies, since social stimuli probably vary in many more dimensions than was assumed in our earlier experiments. An initial attempt at a more complex analy- sis was made in our research on polarization, when we extended our consideration to the normative aspects of social judgments. Further progress in this direction will require the develop- ment of means to improve the prediction of the influences of multiple peripheral dimensions on judgments in complex settings.

Chapter 4 Two Judgmental Processes: An Approach to Perception, Memory and Response in Social Context

G. Etzel and E. Schellhammer

1. Introduction

Everyday observations and systematic research both indicate
that physically identical stimuli are often judged differently
depending upon the perceiver him-/herself and the context in
which the stimuli are presented. When they occur between different perceivers, such judgmental differences often take the
form of systematic biases and persist even when the stimuli
in question can be more or less objectively characterized.

The interaction between the stimulus' physical parameters, the
quality of the perceptual apparatus, and the perceiver's information processing capacity must certainly be regarded as one
source of this judgmental variance. In most cases, however,
judgmental variance cannot be explained in reference to these
three factors alone, but requires that the stimulus context
also be taken into account. By "context", we here refer to (1)
stimuli or information existing in addition to the stimulus to
be judged, and (2) the information that the observer brings
into the judgmental situation.

The first problem that arises with respect to contextual influences is to determine at which point in information processing contextual factors operate. It seems reasonable to assume
that they influence the perception, analysis and storing of stimuli, and that, as a result, they influence how stimuli are subjectively represented. Moreover, it seems likely that context
variables somehow affect the verbal or behavioral responses
involved in making stimulus judgments. That both classes of
effects occur jointly also seems likely.

At present, there is no general theory of social judgment that,
while taking into account all the essential factors, can clarify the nature of the influence that context variables have on
internal representations and/or judgmental responses. As a
first step towards answering this need, we conducted a series
of experiments based on the assumption that the analysis of
stimuli and the making of judgmental responses (response
behavior) are two distinct psychological processes influenced
by different sets of variables.

2. Stimulus analysis and judgmental response

Our experiments were based on Guilford's 2-level judgment model
(Guilford, 1954). Guilford postulates that stimuli are first
represented on an internal continuum that the individual forms
from subjective units suited to the specific judgment problem.
This representation subsequently forms the basis for a second
representation on a verbally or behaviorally structured response dimension. In actual situations there is usually only
one or a limited number of response dimensions, the connection
with the underlying, internal continuum being determined by
two factors: a) the response scale's origin and b) the response
scale's standard interval. When estimating the stimulus magnitude, for example, the numerical value of the smallest stimulus
is determined by the scale's origin, whereas the relations
between the other stimuli are quantified in terms of the response scale's standard interval.

Breaking as it does from the view that there is a one-to-one
correspondence between perceptions and judgmental responses,
the two level model gives rise to several unique methodological
problems. Since the two stages - (a) "stimulus analysis", the
result of which is the internal representation of the stimulus
and (b) "transformation of the internal representation into
response language" - are in a sense independent of one another,

each can be differently influenced by any given context variable. In order to clearly determine the variable's effect, we
therefore needed a method that enabled us to measure the outcome of the stimulus analysis process independently of the response behavior.

2.1. Methods for separating stimulus-analysis and judgmental response

Our methods for separating stimulus analysis and judgmental
response fall into two categories. For judgmental processing
involving binary decisions (e.g. Yes-No decisions), we used a
method provided by signal-detection theory (SDT), while for
those involving graduated decisions concerning subjective quantities, we used a regression model similar to Upshaw's personal
reference scale (Upshaw, 1969). The following two subsections
give a brief description and background of each method.

2.1.1. The Signal-Detection-Theory

In the simplest SDT paradigm, the observer must decide on the
presence or absence of a specific, target stimulus - for example, whether or not a sound of a specific frequency was emitted
by noisy speaker system. The basic assumption of SDT in such
cases is that the individual's observation is internally represented on a continuum that can be simply conceived of as
being a bipolar, subjective confidence scale, the central point
of which represents a state of uncertainty and the two end-
points certainty concerning the sound's absence and presence.
It is furthermore assumed that repeated observations of the
target stimuli and background noise do not result in constant
internal representations but rather are normally distributed
in the internal continuum, these being two distributions according to whether the target stimulus was present or absent. The
variation of these representations are caused by fluctuations

of the signal strength of the target stimulus and noise and by
fluctuations in the individual's own physiological apparatus.

If the signal to noise ratio is large, the two distributions
will show no overlap, while for decreasing signal strength,
there will be more representations falling in the same points
of the internal continuum regardless of whether they are a result of the perception of the target stimulus or just noise,
thus bringing about an overlap of the two distributions. The
extent to which the two distributions overlap constitutes a
metric for assessing what workers in SDT refer to as "sensitivity."

In cases of overlap, the observer's decision as to whether the
target stimulus was present or absent depends on the likelihood
that the resulting representation belongs to either of the two
distributions. If this likelihood ratio exceeds a certain value in favor of the distribution for the stimulus, the decision
is "YES"; otherwise "NO". This critical value, called the
"decision criterion", can be chosen by the individual according
to situational circumstances. It is independent of sensitivity
and accounts for judgmental behavior (response behavior). Deviations of individuals' critical values from those prescribed when
the probability of stimulus occurrence is known (i.e. the optimal value) are called response-bias.

In our own research we measured sensitivity by the relative
frequency of correct decisions; i.e. ratio of the sum of "YES"
-judgments if a stimulus was present and "NO"-judgment if there
was only noise, to the overall number of decisions, or the relative range of overlap of the two subjective distributions
(called: ROC, i.e., Receiver Operating Characteristic).

As a measure for response-bias, we used the relative frequency
with which a response alternative was decided on regardless
of whether it was correct or not. In the realization, SDT can
be applied to any binary decision situation.

2.1.2. The Reference-Scale-Model

Upshaw's reference-scale model (1969), as operationalized by
Etzel (1978), makes it possible to describe the results of
stimulus analysis (i.e., the internal representation of stimuli)
and response behavior in cases where people have to estimate
stimuli on continuous judgmental dimensions. The model is based
directly on Guilford's approach (1954), postulating an internal
continuum on which the stimuli are represented and a transformation of these representations onto a response dimension. The
model's applicability is based on the assumption that the transformation is linear.

We can thus formulate one essential statement about differences
in the internal representation of multiple judged stimuli. If
there is a high correlation between 2 judgmental series about
identical stimuli, the internal representations of these stimuli, too, are of great similarity. The extent to which the linear correlation between two response series about similar
stimuli is decreasing indicates the difference between the respective internal representations. It is, however, of little
importance whether the judgmental series are from two individuals or whether the series are judged twice/two times by the
same individual.

Before discussing the problem of measuring the quality of stimulus analysis (i.e., the precision of the internal representation), we shall give reasons for postulating that the transformation of the internal representation onto the response
scale is linear.

As mentioned earlier in connection with Guilford's judgment model, we suppose that the internal continuum does not consist of
units corresponding to those of the response scale. Upshaw (1969)
speaks of the internal continuum as being one of "subjective
quantity" and argues that it is at the outset dimensionless,
and that it is only when representations are being transformed
onto the response scale that an attribution equilibrating units

on the subjective continuum and response scale is made. Thus, the *relations* between stimuli on the response scale and stimuli on the internal continuum are always the same regardless of the value ascribed to X during the attribution process. Furthermore, there is no absolute origin on the internal continuum, since each stimulus, if perceived at all, is represented in form of subjective quantities.

The observer can, therefore, freely decide how to transform subjective quantities into units on the response scale and can also freely choose the scale unit that he/she attributes to the stimulus with the lowest subjective standing, thus determining the response scale's origin.

The problem of measuring the quality of the stimuli's internal representation can be solved if it is possible to define the stimuli objectively, which generally means that it should be possible to measure them in physical units.

Since we postulate a linear transformation of internal representations into the response dimension, it follows that physically measured stimuli and their internal representations have the same functional relation as the stimuli and the resulting judgmental responses. It should thus be possible to establish a linear relation between stimuli and their internal representation by replacing the original, physically defined stimulus scale by a scale that is a linear transformation of the internal continuum according to the relation between stimuli and judgmental responses.

When stimuli are measured on a scale that is linear to the response scale (e.g., tones measured on a musical scale rather than in terms of Hertz), the objective stimulus value can be assumed to bear a linear correspondence to the stimulus' internal representations. The quality of the internal representation can thus be measured by the linear correlation between the objective stimulus values and the subsequent judgmental responses. The square of the linear correlation shows to what

extent the variance within a series of judgments can be explained by objective variations in the stimuli; i.e., the degree to
which the relations between different stimuli are reflected in
the relations between the corresponding responses. In accordance
with SDT, this is called the measurement of sensitivity.

The response behavior may be described in terms of the trans-
formation-paramenters of the internally represented stimuli on
the response scale; i.e. in terms of the additive (the shift
of the origin) and the multiplicative (the result of extending
or reducing the response scale) constants of the linear regression equation.

We assumed, as shown, that judgmental processes can be described by two levels; i.e. by stimulus analysis resulting in an
internal representation of the stimuli, and by the judgmental
responses (response behavior); i.e. the transformation of the
internally represented stimuli onto a response scale. It is,
of course, possible to interpret the process of the stimulus
analysis as a process which itself represents several stages.
Assuming that the human system of information processing consists of several actively interacting subsystems (such as the
sensoric registers, and the short- and long-term memory (cf.
Erdelyi, 1974), it is possible to conclude that stimuli are
subjectively represented in each of these subsystems. When
transforming these representations from one subsystem into
another the internal representations are expected to change
with some probability.

In order to understand our theoretical concept, it is necessary
to realize that the measurements of the internal representations mentioned above - i.e., the sensitivity measurements -
refer basically and exclusively to the internal representation
of stimuli, which finally are converted into responses without
regard to the kind of intermediary steps through which they
might have passed. In memory tests, for example, sensitivity
statements refer to the internal representations that are recalled from the appropriate subsystem and that in the end
transformed into judgmental responses.

2.2. Stimulus analysis and judgmental response in a social context

Previous research on social perception and social judgment has largely neglected the distinction between the internal representation of stimuli and the selection of the overt judgmental response. Either the distinction was not regarded as interesting and thus not included in the guiding theoretical conceptions (cf. Upmeyer & Layer, 1973), or it was dismissed as an unsolvable methodological difficulty or "semantic artifact" (Erdelyi, 1974). Whether they were in fact due to stimulus analysis or response behavior, results in this earlier research were nearly universally interpreted in terms of motivational factors such as those operant in social comparison processes (Festinger, 1954) and vigilance (Levine & Murphy, 1943).

2.2.1. The quality of stimulus analysis

It can be assumed that an individual's attention to certain stimuli co-varies with his/her level of motivation to analyze these stimuli; so long as there is no extraneous variation in stimulus strength or the efficacy of the perceptual apparatus, increased attention leads to improved internal representations of stimuli. The individual's sensitivity should show a similar increase with attention.

2.2.2. Influences on response behavior

Though the above reasoning may at first appear trivial, the claim that any variable that increases attention should also increase sensitivity runs contrary to a series of previous empirical findings. For example, in Asch's (1951) classic study, naive subjects showed high levels of attention to the stimuli but nevertheless responded incorrectly in a way that varied systematically from reality. Similarly, Campbell (1967) argued that while individuals in a majority group tend to be especially

attentive to certain types of information concerning members
of minorities, their judgments of these minorities are systematically distorted so as to minimize the differences between the
various minority groups and exaggerate the differences between
these groups and one's own.

In light of these earlier findings, we postulate that people in
judgment settings strive to attain the greatest possible confidence that their responses describe the stimuli adequately or
correctly (cf. Irle, 1978, Chapter 2). Stimuli encountered
in social contexts are frequently difficult to discriminate,
and even when an increase in attention improves their internal
representations, the individual may be uncertain how to reproduce the internally represented stimuli on the response scale.
People in such settings will thus often search for additional
information that will enable them to judge with greater certainty. It is characteristic of social contexts that such information is generally available, either as a part of external environment or in the store of previous experience that the people bring with them into the judgment situation.

According to these arguments, the fact that the confederates
in Asch's (1951) experiment gave systematically biased responses both increased subjects' judgment uncertainty and provided
a means for reducing it - namely, by conforming to the group
judgment. Similarly, if people are provided with the hypothesis
that members of a certain group can in general be characterized
in a certain way, it will later be possible for them to use
this hypothesis as an additional piece of information when
passing judgment on a particular member of that group. In each
case, this additional information may influence the final
response to so great an extent that the effects of heightened
attention are no longer observable.

Using the methods described above, we tested this reasoning
in experiments that are described in the following sections.
One of our aims was to employ our techniques for separating
stimulus analysis and response behavior to determine the extent

to which judgmental contexts produce a response behavior which makes an underlying increase in sensitivity. We also investigated the role that subjective utility plays in the paradigm, our hypothesis being subjects avoid making judgmental responses that may result in sanctions and favor those that seem likely to bring rewards.

3. Empirical tests

In the experiments described below, an attempt was made to manipulate subjects' attention and the kinds of situational information available and thus produce systematic variations in their sensitivity and selection of judgmental responses, respectively.

Attention level was manipulated by rewarding subjects for accurate responses and varying the extent of agreement between the subjects' judgments and the programmed judgments of confederates, it being assumed that, as in the Asch paradigm, subjects' attention would increase with heightened disagreement. A third means of manipulating attention level was to vary the extent to which the stimuli were categorizeable, our assumption being that stimuli referring to persons, objects or incidents that the judge can relate to definite concepts will receive more attention than stimuli without such a grounding. We assumed furthermore that a categorized stimulus would receive more attention the more the category was emotionally or evaluatively charged.

Two sets of variables were used to manipulate judgments. The first consisted of variables that the experimenter manipulated himself during the course of the experiment and that were independent of the content of the subjects' memory; e.g. reward, feedback, group pressure. In the discussion that follows, these variables are referred to as "external context variables." The second set of variables, referred to below as "subjective

hypotheses", consisted of characteristics of subjects' cognitive system such as attitudes, stereotypes, etc. that were measured or defined by the experimenter during the course of the
experiment.

3.1. Variability of judgment processes due to external context variables

Among the external context variables influencing judgmental
processes, we were particularly interested in the role played
by reference groups in situations where a person tries to evaluate his/her own performance or the validity of his/her opinions. In line with Festinger's (1954) theory of social comparison, we assume that a person who realizes that his/her performance is lower or his/her opinions are different from those
of a reference person or group will be motivated to change his/
her performance or opinions in the direction of the group norm.
Furthermore, following from our discussion in the preceding
section, a negative evaluation of one's own performance or
disagreement with others should increase attention to task or
opinion relevant information as compared with positive evaluation or agreement and should thus result in an improved stimulus analysis. In the event that such an increase in attention
does not eventuate in a positive evaluation and/or agreement,
response confidence should decrease, since the motive underlying the heightening of attention was directed towards a reduction of judgment uncertainty.

Three experiments were conducted to clarify these issues. In
an experiment conducted by Upmeyer and Layer (1972), one subject and two confederates performed a recognition task, the
subject bearing given fictitious feedback concerning his performance relative to the two confederates. The task was run
over three different trials; in one trial, the subject was indirectly informed that his/her performance was superior to the
two confederates, in another he/she learned that his/her per-

formance was inferior to the two confederates, and in a third
the subject performed the task in isolation and had no basis
for comparison. The task was to remember geometrical figures
which afterwards had to be recognized among a set of similar
figures. Hence it was impossible for the subjects to have developed ideas about an optimal response strategy on the basis
of feedback or to have had experience with the stimulus or response situation.

The prediction that providing a basis for comparison would increase attention was confirmed, memory performance (measured
in terms of the SDT sensitivity parameter) being higher in
those trials in which the confederates were present than it was
when subjects were tested alone. As predicted, performance was
highest following negative feedback. The hypothesis about response confidence was also confirmed; following negative feedback, subjects' confidence regarding response correctness was
significantly lower than it was following positive feedback.
This effect accurred in spite of the fact that performance was
actually better following negative feedback. A post hoc analysis
of response confidence - separating ratings made for objectively
correct and false responses - showed that the effect of feedback was only significant in the case of false responses.

The last result suggests that subjects had cognitions about the
adequacy or inadequacy of their stimulus analyses and that it
was only in the case of decisions that gave rise to a certain
degree of internal uncertainty that the subjects allowed their
confidence ratings to be influenced by external factors (i.e.,
their standing relative to the confederates). Assuming that
the probability of a correct response is a direct function of
the quality of the stimulus' internal representation, it can
be concluded that objectively incorrect responses are based on
internal representations of lower quality than are objectively
correct responses. Thus assumption is supported by the fact
that the subjects were significantly more confident with respect to correct than with false decisions.

An experiment by Upmeyer and Schreiber (1972) featured the same
recognition task but, instead of manipulating subjects' attention by means of feedback about their performance relative to
the confederates', attention was manipulated by having the confederates make pre-programmed responses that either supported
or contradicted the subjects'. In line with Festinger's theory
of social comparison (1954), it was predicted that if predominantly contradicting responses were given by the confederates,
the naive subjects would become uncertain would hence be more
motivated to increase their attention to the stimuli than they
would have been had the confederates responded in a predominantly confirmative manner.

The results were analogous to Upmeyer and Layer (1972). Increased attention due to the confederates' contradicting responses resulted in a better memory performance. This effect,
however, occurred only - as Festinger's theory would lead one
to expect - if the disagreement was not extreme. At the same
time, the subjects' confidence concerning their responses decreased if there was disagreement concerning responses, this
effect being most pronounced for responses that were actually
incorrect.

In a third experiment, Upmeyer (1971) simultaneously investigated the changes in sensitivity brought about by changes in
attention and the response bias caused by heightened attention
to available, external information. Demonstrating that these
two effects can co-occur would enable us to account for the
results of Asch's experiment (1951) that stand in ostensible
contradiction to our "attention-hypothesis."

As will be recalled from the discussion above, our own interpretation of what took place in Asch's study, is that the confederates' contradictory responses made subjects uncertain as
to whether their own responses were correct. In order to reduce this uncertainty, subjects became more attentive, and
thus more sensitive as well, to the test stimuli. In light,
however, of the confederates' continued disagreement, this

strategy did not succeed in reducing uncertainty, and so subjects made use of the confederates' regular - if puzzling -
response pattern as an additional piece of uncertainty-reducing
information. By following the lead of majority, the subjects
were able to reduce their own uncertainty, this despite the
fact that their perceptions of the test stimuli were actually
sharpened.

Upmeyer's study was similar to Asch's, subjects being asked to
decide whether given stimuli were identical or different while
being exposed to systematically dissenting responses of confederates. The task was to decide whether two successively presented light-stimuli were equally bright or whether the first
stimulus was brighter than the second. The subjects were given
a 4-point-rating scale ranging from "definitely equal" to
"first stimulus was definitely brighter." From the objective
stimulus situation ("equal" or "brighter") and subjects' responses on this scale, the SDT-parameters sensitivity and response bias could be obtained by establishing subjective distributions on the basis of the scale ratings under the "same"
and "different" conditions. The overlap of these distributions
constituted the sensitivity measure, while response bias was
measured by the average value of all responses made when the
two lights were in fact equal.

The results supported Upmeyer's predictions, subjects who had
been exposed to the judgments of the dissenting confederates
showing greater sensitivity and response bias (in the direction
of conformity) than did control subjects who were not confronted with the confederates' judgments. Furthermore, it could be
confirmed that the extent of increase in sensitivity and the
shift of the response bias did not correlate.

All three experiments referred to in this chapter support the
applicability of our two-stage judgmental model to situations
where people's responses are evaluated by other in their environment. This evaluation, if experienced as being negative,
results in an increase of attention and thus in an improved

stimulus analysis. At the same time, however, the person's subjective confidence decreases. If external information about the
test stimuli is available, subjects will use it in order to reduce the uncertainty concerning their judgmental responses.

3.2. Variability of judgmental processes under the influence of subjective hypotheses

In addition to environmental influences, it has been observed
that in certain situations judgmental processes are influenced
by variables specific to the individual. These variables are
generally of the nature of subjective experiences or hypotheses
of the stimuli's appearance, their value on certain dimensions,
their relation to other stimuli on these dimensions, etc.

Research dealing with these hypotheses and their effects on
judgment has been carried out under the rubrics "accentuation"
(e.g. Bruner & Goodman, 1947) "stereotyping" (e.g. Tajfel,
Sheikh & Gardner, 1964), "ethnic identification" (e.g. Upmeyer,
1976) and "attitudes and memory" (e.g. Upmeyer & Layer, 1973).
The research deals, for example, with problems such as: how
hunches as to a coin's value affect peoples' judgments of its
size, or how an earlier established opinion about individuals,
objects or incidents affects the memorization of later information concerning them, and what happens if later information
supports and/or contradicts the earlier established opinion.

Our two-stage judgment model leads us to expect two kinds of
effects to occur in this kind of stimulus situation. If the
stimuli refer to persons, objects or incidents about which
subjects maintain concrete ideas, the subjects can be expected to pay more attention to these stimuli than to others that
are represented less concretely. This difference should be even
more pronounced if the stimuli call for evaluation. In those
cases in which subjects are uncertain how to respond, they are
likely to use the additional information provided by their previous experiences and hypotheses as guides. Our project in-

vestigated these general propositions with respect to accentuation and stereotyping, attitudes and memory and ethnic identification.

3.2.1. Accentuation and stereotyping

The central hypothesis of accentuation research states that the greater the value attached to a given object, the greater the tendency to overestimate that object's size. Early theoretical work in this area seems to interpret accentuation effects as being the product of processes operant during stimulus analyses; i.e. that the valued object's internal representation becoming more vivid, clear and large (cf. Bruner & Goodman, 1947).

Later work by Tajfel (1957) modified the accentuation hypothesis, holding that accentuation effects occur only in those cases where there is a systematic covariation between the judgmental and "peripheral" dimensions; a coin is overestimated because the size of coins covary with their values. According to Tajfel, the peripheral dimension does not have to refer to value but can be any dimension that correlates with the dimension upon which the judgment is to be made. Tajfel himself does not address, however, the problem of whether such effects are the result of stimulus analyses or response behavior, his main concern being specifying the conditions under which such accentuation effects occur.

Our own analyses of accentuation effects in terms of our two-stage judgment model is based on the assumption that an individual with subjective hypotheses concerning the correlation of peripheral and response dimensions should be particularly attentive during stimulus analyses and thus achieve better internal representations of the stimuli. At the same time, however, the hypothesized correlation constitutes an additional piece of information that can serve as a means for reducing uncertainty during the transformation of the internally represented stimulus onto the response dimension. This, in turn,

would result in a modification of the response scale's interval
and, possibly, a shift of the scale's origin.

Upmeyer and Cleary (1975) investigated the role that stimulus
analyses and response behavior play in mediating accentuation
effects, having subjects estimate the sizes of coins and circles. When the data were analyzed according to Rule, Curtis
and Markley's (1970) input-output transformation model, no firm
conclusions could be drawn. Etzel (1977a) however, reanalyzed
the data according to Upshaw's (1969) reference scale model and
found support for the two hypotheses. Subjects were more sensitive when judging coins than when judging circles, a greater
part of the overall judgmental variance being attributable to
the stimuli in the set of coins than in the set of circles.
At the same time, the well-known response effects were observed, the judgment scale being stretched to a greater degree for
judgments concerning coins than for those concerning circles.

Tajfel and Wilkes' "classification" concept (1963) is closely
related to accentuation, it applying to those cases in which a
dimension consisting of discrete categories correlates with a
continuous dimension on which the actual judgments are to be
made. The effect observed in such cases is that the differences
between stimuli belonging to different categories are overestimated whereas the differences between stimuli belonging to the
same category are underestimated. This classification concept
is also used to explain stereotype judgments and to describe
certain judgment processes caused by attitudes. Upmeyer and
Layer (1974) believed the accentuation and classification processes may occur during stimulus analyses as well as in response behavior.

Such systematic correlations between categorial and continuous
judgmental dimensions are generally due to the individual's
previous experience and/or subjective hypotheses. Hypotheses
in this case can be in the form of either stereotypes ("aca-
demics are more intelligent than workers") or attitudes ("I
don't like black people because they are aggressive"). Stimuli

labeled in terms of a familiar classificatory scheme should attract more attention than those that are not and should therefore give rise to more precise internal representations. In addition, it seems likely that attention would increase with increasing relevance of the stimuli and/or labels, especially when the label elicits evaluative reactions from the person judging.

Classification effects can also operate at the level of response behavior. For example, if racially prejudiced subjects are required to recognize from memory whether a certain behavior was described as being performed by a black or a white, they might use their negative attitude towards black people as a basis for attributing to blacks a disproportionate number of negative behaviors. The more uncertain the subjects are concerning the correct response, the more they should rely on such support.

An experiment by Upmeyer and Layer (1974) was conducted to test classification effects with respect to both stimulus analysis and response behavior. The subjects, who were believed to have a positive attitude towards the West German politician Willy Brandt and a negative attitude towards another West German politician named Rainer Barzel, were presented with a set of statements labeled "Brandt", "Barzel", "person X" and "person Y", it being predicted that the subjects would remember the statement about "Brandt" and "Barzel" better than those about the insignificant persons X and Y. This prediction was significantly confirmed. It was also predicted that subjects would show a predilection for using the label "Brandt" when recognizing positive statements and "Barzel" when the statements were negative. This prediction was not confirmed. Apparently, simple correspondence between the evaluations of labels and the valence of statements is not sufficient to influence the response behavior.

In a later replication of this experiment, the label "Barzel" was replaced by the label "Strauß" (referring to another West

German politician viewed negatively by the subject sample), because the statements adequately characterized the person Strauß.
In this case, a significant effect on response behavior was
obtained, subjects making use of a correspondence between
their attitudes toward the politicians and the favorability
of the statements in performing the recognition task.

Upmeyer, Krolage, Etzel, Lilli and Klump (1976) tested the same
hypothesis in another experiment. The members of two Mannheim
soccer teams were presented with negative statements that per-
tained either to one of their two teams or to two teams from
Northern Germany, the assumption being that the relevant local
labels would attract more attention than the northern ones.
The results indeed indicated that subjects recognition performance was far better for statements paired with the local labels than it was for those pertaining to either of the northern
teams. It was also predicted that members of the local teams
would consider the negative statements more characteristic of
their rivals than of themselves and would consequently favor
the rival team as a response alternative.

This prediction was confirmed for the members of one team only;
no response bias was observed as regards the members of the
other team. A post-experimental inquiry revealed that the
latter actually did consider the statements as characteristic
for both the rival team and their own.

Etzel (1977b, 1978) performed two experiments with the intention of replicating these findings within the context of the
original classification paradigm; i.e., having subjects judge
the magnitude of physical stimuli. He hypothesized that stimuli varying on a physical dimension correlated with a classification scheme are observed with more attention and receive
better internal representation than would be the case if no
such correlation obtained. At the same time, responses in the
case of uncertainty were expected to be influenced by the additional information provided by the systematic correlation.

In Etzel's first experiment (Etzel, 1977b), subjects were required to judge the lengths of 8 different lines. In the experimental group, the four shorter lines were labelled "A", and the
four longer ones "B", whereas in a control group no labels were
given. Subjects in the experimental group performed only slightly better than the control subjects with respect to estimate
the lines' lengths, though this weak finding may have been due
to a ceiling effect, members of both groups responding almost
perfectly. As expected, however, subjects in the experimental
group seemed to allow the classification scheme to influence
their judgments of lengths, overestimating the difference between the lines in class A and those in class B.

In Etzel's second study (Etzel, 1978) the attempt was made to
directly manipulate need for certainty. Subjects had to judge
a series of eight stimuli that were presented either without
classification, with a classification scheme that placed the
four smallest stimuli in one class in 80% of the cases and in
the other class the rest of the time while doing the opposite
for the four longest stimuli, or a classification that was
entirely unambiguous, the four smallest stimuli always belonging to one category and the four longest to the other. The
need for certainty was operationalized by whether or not a
reward was offered for very good responses.

The performance of subjects in the two "classification groups"
was slightly better than that of the control group.[1] Rewarding
subjects resulted in an increase in attention, i.e., in the
reward conditions, sensitivity increased. The hypotheses concerning response effects tested by Etzel (1977b) were also supported. The members of both experimental groups used the addi-

---

[1] It is not clear, however, whether the method based on the reference scale model which was used in this test is suited to
examine hypotheses concerning the various qualities of internal
representations. The stimulus series would have to be made so
complicated that a ceiling effect can be definitely excluded.
In that case, however, a statistically verifiable linear correlation between stimuli and responses could not be established.

tional information provided by the classification scheme when
making their responses, and rewarding subjects increased the
extent of their rise when the scheme was unambiguous.

The findings of the studies discussed in this section thus seem
to support the general hypotheses derived from our two-level
judgment model. Labelling stimuli was found to increase the
attention paid to them and to thus result in an improvement of
their internal representation. The amount of improvement depends upon the initial quality of the internal representation
and the relevance, to the judge, of the stimuli and/or labels.

With respect to response behavior, if a person holds a hypothesis concerning systematic correlations between the labels
and the stimuli's standing on the dimension on which the judgments are to be made, he/she will use this additional information to avoid or reduce potential uncertainties concerning the
correctness of his/her response. The extent of this effect
depends on the extent of the uncertainty, on the strength of
the subjectively assumed correlation and on the importance
attached to the response.

3.2.2. Attitudes and memory

In experiments concerning attitudes' influence on the storing
and retrieval of information, the hypothesis most often tested
has been that people more effectively store information that
supports their own attitudes than they do information that is
not attitude supportive. This selectivity hypothesis has been
supported by several experiments (Edwards, 1942; Levine & Murphy, 1953; Jones and Aneshansel, 1956; Jones & Kohler, 1958;
Kanungo & Dutta, 1966), only partially supported by others
(Alper & Korchin, 1952; Taft, 1954; Kanungo & Das, 1960; Malpass, 1969) and rejected by still others (Garber, 1955; Waly
& Cook, 1966; Greenwald & Sakumura, 1967; Brigham & Cook, 1969).

There are several different theoretical approaches to the selectivity hypothesis and its inconsistent empirical support,

and they have been thoroughly discussed by Upmeyer and Layer (1973). These authors center their criticism on the conceptions about basic judgment processes that have guided previous research in this area as well as on the methods that have been employed, their basic point being that workers in this area have not considered the possibility that attitudes could have different influences on stimulus analysis and response behavior and/ or have not used methods that would enable the separation of effects at these two mediating stages.

According to Upmeyer and Layer's analysis, the extent to which a given piece of information is subject to stimulus analysis (i.e., the extent to which it is represented internally) is chiefly determined by its relevance - pro or con - to one or several of the person's attitudes. Upmeyer, Layer and Schreiber (1972) discuss this greater concern for attitude relevant information in terms of Asch's (1946) approach to impression formation, arguing that people strive to develop more fully integrated impressions of the attitude relevant material, developing associations between it and other elements in the cognitive system that can aid in the eventual recall. In short, the person's attitudes give rise to selective attention which in turn results in the selective memorization of attitude relevant material. It should be noted that, contrary to many of the earlier studies that had predicted superior memorization of attitude-supporting information only (e.g. Levine & Murphy, 1943), this line of analysis developed by Upmeyer and his colleagues indicates that both supporting and contradicting information should be equally well memorized and that the valence of the information's source should also have little if any effect.

Upmeyer and Layer (1974) stipulate a direct influence of the attitude on the response behavior of an individual while processing attitude-relevant material. They postulate that if there exist rules of correspondence between attitudes and the information to be memorized, these might result in response biases (preference for a given response alternative). So it is

possible to establish rules of correspondence by regarding the
presented stimulus material as being characteristic (or plausible) for the attitude object and/or if the valence of the attitude corresponds to the valence of the material.

Experiments conducted so far to test Upmeyer and Layer's approach have demonstrated that attitudes affect stimulus analysis and response behavior in different ways. In these experiments the two processes covaried; i.e. a high performance in
discrimination covaried with a response bias: If there were
no biases, discrimination was poor. Since significance and presence of a correspondence between information and classification (labels) existed only for attitude-relevant stimulus material, it could be argued that the independence of stimulus
analysis and response behavior does not exist as far as attitudes are concerned. Schellhammer (1977), therefore, in her
experiment made the attempt to demonstrate that the stimulus
analysis can vary if the response behavior is kept constant.
As regards the attitude context this means an attempt to demonstrate that discrimination performance improves with an increasing significance (attitude relevance) of the information
material. However, since for both levels of relevance, provisions
were made for establishing rules of correspondence, response
biases were expected in both cases. In Schellhammer's experiment, subjects were presented with essays about "restricted ad-
mission to the university (RA)", it being assumed that a relatively homogenous attitude against RA prevailed within the
subject population. Accordingly, arguments against RA were defined as attitude supporting, while those in favor of RA were
considered to be attitude contradicting. The essays were attributed to four different authors, it being expected that these
authors would differ in relevance, two being highly relevant
and two being less relevant. Each essay contained an equal
amount of RA supporting and RA contradicting information. At the
same time, however, the authors were described as being either
in favor of or opposed to RA, this factor being varied orthogonally with their relevance. Each subject read all four essays,

with source, relevance and order of presentation being fully counterbalanced over the entire sample.

The chief dependent variables - discrimination performance and response behavior - were administered in the form of an unannounced memory test and involved the matching of arguments from the essays with the corresponding source. For each argument, subjects had two sources to choose from, it being varied, between subjects, whether the two sources were of equal valence or equal relevance.

The results indicated no significant effect to discrimination performance for source relevance, though there was a trend in the predicted direction for source relevance. Several explanations seem plausible for this finding; the instructions may have produced maximally high attention in all the conditions and thus masked the effects of the source relevance by a ceiling effect, or the stimulus material may have been too complicated (each subject had 80 sentences to memorize). Because subjects' attitudes towards RA have not been uniform as we had expected, the influence of the valence of the information and the valence of the sources of information to discrimination performance could actually not be tested. One minor prediction that was supported, however, was that subjects showed a response bias towards attributing statements favorable to RA to sources in favor of RA, and those opposed to RA to opposed to RA sources.

This last finding suggests, as Schellhammer sought to demonstrate at the outset, that response biases can occur independently of stimulus analysis, but, due to weak results concerning the "relevance hypothesis", the findings must be taken as a weak confirmation of Schellhammer's argument. Another experiment by Etzel, Lang and Upmeyer (unpublished) further examined this issue, seeking to avoid the problems encountered by Schellhammer by using different independent variable manipulations. Instead of a relatively complex, political issue, the attitude objects in this second study were individuals - the subject him/herself, a person that he/she liked, and a person that he/she disliked. It was assumed that subjects' attitudes would be

positive towards the self and the liked other and would be negative towards the disliked other, and that subjects would be
more involved when judging themselves than when judging others.

From a list containing an equal number of positive and negative
adjectives, the subjects were asked to select an equal number
of positive and negative adjectives that best described each of
the three attitude objects, it being assumed that for the self
and the liked other, the positive adjectives would be attitude-
consistent and the negative adjectives attitude-inconsistent,
with the reverse holding for the disliked other. In a subsequent
memory test, subjects were again presented with all the adjectives and had to indicate which they had chosen as characteristic of each attitude object.

The results of this experiment clearly confirm our hypotheses.
The subjects were able to recognize the adjectives they had
chosen for themselves better than those they had chosen for the
other two individuals. Positive and negative adjectives were
remembered equally well regardless of the attitude object; i.e.,
there was no difference between attitude supporting and attitude contradicting information.

An analysis of subjects' errors reveals, however, that response
behavior was influenced by a tendency for subjects to assume a
correspondence between the valence attached to the attitude
object and the valence of the information. In cases, where subjects were unsure of their responses, there was a marked tendency to report having used positive adjectives as descriptors
of liked attitude objects (i.e., the self and the liked other)
and negative adjectives as descriptors of the disliked attitude
object. The results thus support the hypotheses that all attitude-relevant information is memorized equally well regardless
of whether it is attitude-inconsistent. In other words, stimulus analysis is unaffected by considerations of attitude consistency. With respect to response behavior, however, there is
a tendency for a person to respond consistently with his/her
attitudes when he/she is otherwise uncertain of the correct
response.

3.2.3. Ethnic identification

Ethnic identification refers to people's association with their
respective ethnic groups (Upmeyer, 1976). In a sense, the psychological processes involved in this identification are the
reverse of those involved in social stereotyping. Whereas the
latter involves the inferring of personal characteristics on
the basis of an individual's group membership, the former involves inferring the individual's group membership on the basis
of his/her personal characteristic.

The question most frequently examined with respect to ethnic
identification is what factors are the most influential in the
assignation of ethnic labels. In terms of SDT this refers to the
problem of sensitivity. In a typical experiment in this area,
Savitz and Tomasson (1959), first presented subjects with silent stimulus persons, then added language and mimicry, and
finally gave the persons individual names, the subjects' task
being to identify who among the stimulus persons were Jews.
Upmeyer's reanalysis of the data in terms of SDT (1976) revealed an increase in sensitivity as greater numbers of individual
characteristics were presented.

Other factors that may influence subjects' sensitivity in such
situations.are whether the subjects themselves belong to the
groups whose members they are to identify (Savitz & Tomasson,
1959; Scodel & Austrin, 1957) or whether they are prejudiced
against these groups((Allport & Kramer, 1946; Lindzey & Rogolsky, 1950). Whereas being a member of one of the groups usually
tends to improve the identification performance (sensitivity),
this has been found not to be the case with people who are prejudiced. Upmeyer (1976) assumed that identification performance
improves in relation to the range of different characteristics
available and the subjects' familiarity with these characteristics. This would explain, on one hand, the findings of Savitz
and Tomasson (1959) as well as the fact that the members of
one ethnic group recognize members of their own group particularly well.

Upmeyer (1976) also proposed that skill at identification is generally well developed when individuals take interest in *and* have had experience with members of the to-be-identified group, and that such interest can be motivated by prejudice. According to Upmeyer, however, prejudice operates primarily at the level of response behavior. As prejudice towards a group is related to a feeling of being threatened by it, prejudiced people tend to overestimate the group's size and thus identify people as belonging to the group more often than is warranted. Personal advantage can also, of course, exert an effect here. To a "faithful civil servant", it is more important to identify an "enemy of the constitution" than to correctly identify a "friend of the constitution." When in doubt, therefore he/she will prefer the former alternative to the latter.

Lang (1976) conducted an experiment intended to test the effect that feeling threatened by a given ethnic group has on stimulus analysis and response behavior during the making of ethnic identifications concerning it. Lang's subjects were presented with photos of people whom they had to identify as either Germans or foreign workers. Lang assumed that because of the competition of finding jobs, unemployed German workers would be more threatened by foreign workers than employed workers and students would be. For half the subjects in each of these groups, Lang emphasized this threat in his wording of the experimental instructions, while the rest of the subjects received instructions that were favorable to the foreign workers. Lang predicted that effects of threat would be manifest at the level of response bias, the response alternative "foreign worker" being preferred most by unemployed subjects and with the "high threat" instructions.

None of the hypotheses were significantly confirmed. This absence of significant findings may mean either that the foreign workers were not perceived as threatening by any of the subject groups or that threat alone is insufficient to produce a response bias. Both interpretations are plausible and can be valid simultaneously. Additional experiments in which the initial conditions are better controlled and/or manipulated are needed in order to resolve this ambiguity.

4. Summary

The experiments described in this paper constitute a representative sample of all the experiments that we conducted during a period of ten years to test our two-stage judgment model. We did not discuss some experiments that can be regarded as replications of experiments mentioned here nor those dealing with details of marginal relevance to the model itself. Furthermore, we did not discuss experiments in the process of being run at the time of our writing.

On the whole, the research described here supports our view that the separate consideration of stimulus analysis and response behavior results in more detailed knowledge of the influence that situational variables exert on stimulus processing. It was possible to demonstrate that the sensitivity of individuals during stimulus processing reflects not only the stimulus strength and the quality of the individual's physiological apparatus, but also to a large extent the contextual and individual difference factors influencing attention. Among the former are performance feedback and group pressure, while the latter include the individual's previous experience as well as the subjective hypotheses that he/she holds concerning the stimuli to be processed or the persons, objects and situations to which the stimuli refer. With regard to these latter, individual difference factors, we were able to show that an individual's attention is directed in a relatively unspecific way at all stimuli related to his/her experiences or hypotheses regardless of whether the stimuli confirm or contradict them.

With respect to situational influences on response behavior, our analysis rests on the assumption that individuals are moti-

vated to avoid or reduce response uncertainty. The greater the
individual's uncertainty as to sufficiency or correctness of a
response, the greater the tendency to seek additional information - in the form of others' judgments concerning the same or
comparable stimuli, the individual's own previous experience,
etc. - about the stimulus to be judged. We were also able to
demonstrate that stimulus analysis and response behavior, though
independent of one another, can vary simultaneously in the same
context and that the effects on response behavior are often so
strong that those on stimulus analysis (in most cases improvements) cannot be determined without applying a suitable experimental technique.

Chapter 5   Group Influences on Judgments Concerning the Future

G. Trommsdorff

1. Introduction

Decision making and judgment under group conditions has often
been shown to differ from that which occurs in individual settings, and research on such group phenomena frequently follows
the assumption that the principles governing group behavior
differ qualitatively from those governing the behavior of individuals. The present work deals with the question of whether
this assumption is justified. It may be, for example, that the
group situation is no more than a special condition under
which individual action occurs, so that the behavior that takes
place in either setting can be accounted for by a common set
of behavioral principles.

In this paper, groups and individuals will be compared with
respect to their judgments concerning the future. Since the
criteria for such judgments are highly subjective, one can
assume that judges will feel rather uncertain about their
judgments' correctness and will be open to re-evaluation and
possible change. Of special interest will be the comparison
of the conditions under which group and individual judgments
are most subject to subsequent alteration.

Part 2 deals with this problem in terms of group extremization
and polarization, while part 3 is devoted to a discussion of
some information processing approaches to judgmental change. In
part 4, several experiments on judgments in groups and under
individual conditions are presented, the empirical findings of
these experiments being discussed in part 5, along with some
characteristics for a general theory of judgmental change.

2. Group influences on decision making and judgments

Group situations provide especially interesting settings for
studying the determinants of decision making and the formation
of judgments. Besides enabling the study of group processes,
such situations allow us to examine general psychological principles under special, easily definable conditions.

2.1. Development of research on group influences

Interestingly, research on group-induced change in decisions
and judgments has focused primarily on group processes and has
often neglected the study of individual psychological processes. This has been the case, for example, in research on the
risky shift (e.g. Stoner, 1961; Kogan & Wallach, 1967) and on
group-induced extremization and polarization (e.g. Moscovici
& Zavalloni, 1969). Since the classic studies on attitude
change of individuals in groups (Lewin, 1948) and the studies
on the improved problem-solving ability of groups as compared
to individuals (Shaw, 1932), further experiments on these topics have been directed towards specifying the conditions that
have to be met in order for these group effects to arise (cf.
Kelley & Thibaut, 1969; Lamm & Trommsdorff, 1973).

Recent interest on group-induced risky shift and attitude/
judgment polarization and extremization has stimulated extensive research on the group processes underlying these phenomena (cf. Pruitt, 1971a,b; Lamm & Myers, 1978). Though individual processes have been taken into account (such as need for
social approval - cf. Lamm, Schaude & Trommsdorff, 1971; Lamm,
Trommsdorff & Rost-Schaude, 1972 - or individual decision making
and information seeking - cf. Myers, 1973; Vinokur & Burnstein,
1974; Lamm, Rost-Schaude & Trommsdorff, 1978), such change in
decisions, judgments and attitudes following group discussion
had been considered as being a group-specific phenomenon.

2.2. Some theoretical explanations of group influences on decision and judgment change

It has been found that the polarizing effects of group discussion extend beyond decisions in hypothetical risk-taking situations, affecting attitudes, judgments, interpersonal impressions, risk-taking decisions, pro- and antisocial behavior, conflict resolution in Prisoner's Dilemma games and negotiations (cf. Lamm & Myers, 1978). The present study is concerned with the effect of group discussions on judgments concerning possible desirable or undesirable future developments dealing with private and public aspects of life.

Of the various theoretical explanations for group effects, only a subset seems relevant here. We can exclude, for example, explanations based on the notions of the diffusion and "infusion" of responsibility and concentrate instead on those having to do with: (a) commitment, (b) influence of the majority, (c) influence of the group leader, and (d) social comparison and value theory (cf. Trommsdorff, 1975, 1978).

(a) According to Moscovici and Zavalloni (1969), group discussion increases individuals' *commitment* and involvement in their original positions, thus causing these positions to become more extreme and bringing about an increase in the certainty with which they are held. According to the commitment approach, the degree of judgment and/or decision change should depend on the individual's initial position and reflect (1) group extremization (i.e., movement away from the neutral point, measured in terms of the absolute difference between the group mean and the scale midpoint) (cf. Doise, 1969; Moscovici & Zavalloni, 1969); (2) individual extremization (i.e., the mean distance of the individual positions from the scale mid-point) (cf. Kogan & Wallach, 1964); and (3) polarization (i.e., the strengthening of the dominant response, as reflected by the shift of the group mean to one end of the scale) (cf. Lamm & Myers, 1978).

Though the empirical support for these assumptions has been
inconsistent (cf. Kogan & Wallach, 1964), a good part of the
problem may lie in the techniques used to measure the various
types of change. Measuring changes in *group* extremization by
taking the difference between two mean group extremity values
seems to yield no more than a statistical index of group-induced change. In the same way, the index for the *individual* extremization (which takes into account the individual positions
of the group members) yields no direct information concerning
individual deviations from the scale mid-point and neglects
to take into account the direction of change. This creates
problems when judgments change value while their absolute extremity remains the same, as when a person makes a more optimistic judgment in the first place and, later, a more pessimistic judgment - in each case with equal distance from the
scale mid-point. In such cases, of course, the real judgmental
shift is much greater than would be shown by the index of individual extremization (cf. more detailed comments in Trommsdorff, 1978, p. 200f.).

Despite these reservations about the validity of the group extremization measure, we will, in the following, use both the
group and individual extremization indices in line with the
traditional studies on group-induced judgmental change.

That commitment results in an increase in group extremization
has been verified by several empirical studies (cf. Moscovici &
Zavalloni, 1969; Moscovici & Lecuyer, 1972; Moscovici, Doise &
Dulong, 1972; Rost-Schaude, 1975). The influence of commitment
on decision stability has also been demonstrated for risk-taking
decisions, more risky shift occurring when subjects are less
committed to their original positions (cf. Trommsdorff, 1971).

(b) According to the *majority-influence* explanation, group
extremization occurs as a result of the minority's conformity
with the majority. This implies that, whenever extremization
occurs, the mean original positions and the mean extremization
scores should correlate, something that has not as yet been

empirically demonstrated (cf. Myers & Lamm, 1976). In fact, the
contrary often seems to occur, the minority influencing the
majority to change their original position following group
discussion (cf. Lamm, Trommsdorff & Rost-Schaude, 1973; Moscovici, 1976). In order to test the influence of a majority or
minority, some variance of group positions must be given. In
dyads where skewedness of positions cannot occur, the operation of majority or minority decision rules cannot be used to
explain the dyadic shift.

(c) The *leader-influence* explanation assumes that persons with
extreme positions can present their options and judgments
much more convincingly and with higher certainty than those
with more moderate positions, thus having greater influence on
the other group members in the direction of their more extreme
positions. According to this assumption, one would predict a
positive correlation between extremity and status among members of any given group. In addition, the leader's extreme
judgment should not change during the course of the group discussion. Empirical results are contrdictory: those of Stroebe
and Fraser (1971) partly supported this explanation, while
those of Lamm and Sauer (1974) did not.

(d) According to the *social comparison and value* theory, group
interaction should produce judgment change whenever it leads
group members to perceive that their original position's relied
on incorrect or incomplete information or did not conform to
the group's values. This position - as presented by Brown
(1965) and Pruitt (1971a,b) - derives from Festinger's theory
of social comparison processes (1954). The general assumption
is that individuals strive to validate their opinions and
judgments by orienting themselves to a reference group. Accordingly, group members should change their decisions and/or
judgments towards what group discussion reveals as being the
group's preferred position. Though the essential features of
social comparison theory have received empirical support in
the group discussion setting (cf. Codol, 1976; Lamm & Myers,

1978), an experiment by Lamm, Trommsdorff & Rost-Schaude (1972) has shown that the perceived difference between oneself and one's fellow group members does not correlate with the individual shift following group discussion, and that the amount of shift shown by groups strongly underestimating peer positions does not differ from that occurring in groups whose estimates are realistic.

An experiment by Lamm, Schaude and Trommsdorff (1971) shows that personal ideals also play a role in mediating group discussion effects, with people who perceive their initial positions as being largely discrepant from their ideals showing a greater tendency to shift towards the ideal position following group discussion than did those whose initial positions were in greater conformity with their ideals. According to social comparison theory, one might reason that mere knowledge of the group's favorite position is sufficient to induce a shift toward this ideal (Levinger & Schneider, 1969). One could also say that learning that a group member has a position close to one's ideal induces a shift toward greater extremity as a result of a modeling effect. Alternatively, it might be argued that other group members "release" the subject from the constraints of an assumed social norm towards conservatism. The group leader, too, may serve as a releaser and/or model. Somewhat inconsistent with these release and modelling explanations, however, are findings from experiments by Pruitt (1971a,b) and Myers and Kaplan (1976) indicating that merely informing subjects of the average group response was sufficient to induce a polarization of judgments.

Summary. All of the above stated theoretical approaches to group-induced judgment change assume that the conditions that give rise to the judgment change are unique to group settings. Furthermore, the above stated theoretical approaches all contain the implicit assumption that changes of judgments following group discussion occur as a result of cognitive processes induced by certain informational influences stemming from the

group discussion. According to the commitment theory, the crucial factor is the individual group member informing other
members about his/her preference. According to the majority,
minority, leadership-influence, social comparison, value and
release theories, it is the reception of information about the
position of the other group members that induces the subject
to change to a more extreme position.

In the following, some general cognitive principles concerning
informational selectivity are discussed with respect to their
explanatory value for judgment and decision change.

3. Information selection and processing when positions in group or individual situations are changed

If judgmental changes following group discussion are due to
informational influences, it should be asked whether such influences are effective only in group situations or whether
they are based on fundamental psychological processes that
can also occur in individual settings.

3.1.   Information processing in groups

3.1.1. Judgment change following presentation of new arguments

Group discussion, as a kind of social influence, affects individual judgment and decision making by means of information
transmission. Information, for example, concerning the other
group members' preferences may help validate one's own judgment in terms of accuracy, adequacy, or social desirability.
In addition, one may simply be interested in hearing further
relevant arguments favoring or questioning one's position, and
such novel arguments alone - without information concerning
the other group members' positions - are often enough to induce judgment change (cf. Vinokur & Burnstein, 1978). In this

latter case, the judgment changes seem to be the product of purely individualistic information processing.

The kind and degree of judgment change after learning about new arguments depend on the arguments' direction, persuasiveness and subjective novelty (Vinokur & Burnstein, 1974; Vinokur, Trope & Burnstein, 1975). A further important characteristic is the degree to which the arguments are consistent with pre-existing cognitive schemata, people tending to prefer arguments that are consistent with what they already believe, while inconsistent arguments are likely to be rejected (Janis, 1972).

Such inconsistent information, however, is not necessarily rejected, disregarded, or devalued. If certain arguments imply that the person's position is wrong or in conflict with the generally accepted judgment, the likelihood of change is high as long as the situation evokes a strong need for accuracy or for conforming with the majority. Under such conditions, the person would expect greater disadvantage should he/she disregard the discrepant information and not make the called-for changes in his/her own judgment.

3.1.2. Judgment change as a result of receiving critical arguments on the probability of future social or personal events

This section concerns the process that mediate changes in probability judgments concerning uncertain future events. Since no objective criteria exist for assessing these judgments' validity, they should be especially analysed with regard to situational influences. The typical experimental task is to have the person judge the probability that a given future event will, in fact, occur, the judgment being recorded on a probability scale on which the middle range represents high uncertainty and the two ends either optimism or pessimism, depending on the event's desirability.

Empirical studies dealing with the influence of group discussion on such probability judgments indicate that groups tend to produce arguments that emphasize the possible failure of desirable future developments, thus inducing group members to change their original judgments in the direction of greater pessimism. For example, Kogan and Wallach (1964) report that subjects judged desirable developments in American society as being less likely to occur after having participated in a group discussion than they did prior to the discussion session. Similarly, Madaras and Bem (1968) showed that attractive but risky decision alternatives were judged as being less likely to succeed after a group discussion than they were before. Lamm, Trommsdorff and Kogan (1970) replicated the Madaras and Bem findings with an added control group that indicated that a similar shift towards pessimism does not occur when individual subjects are asked to reconsider their original probability judgments.

The above cited studies deal with probability judgments concerning the success or failure of hypothetical persons or social developments but do not deal with personal success or failure. For this latter type of judgment, it seems plausible that the person him/herself would be better acquainted with the relevant arguments than would the other group members whom he/she had met for the first time in the laboratory. But it might nevertheless be important in such cases for the person to learn more about the arguments of other group members, especially when they disagree with the person's own point of view and/or convey previously unconsidered information. Such arguments may pertain either to facts or values, the latter becoming important if, for example, the person's optimistic expectations are taken to reflect arrogance and immodesty. In such cases, the need to present oneself as a modest but successful person may dictate a tempering of optimism in one's judgments concerning the likelihood of future success.

Experimental data bear out this reasoning. Frey, Götz and
Götz-Marchand (1975) demonstrated that subjects who expected
feedback on their achievements avoided optimistic estimates
since, if their judgments had turned out to be false later on,
they would have had to face criticism for an arrogant self-
presentation. Results reported by Schneider (1969) can be interpreted in a similar way, subjects' self-presentation being
less favorable when the subjects expected feedback on their
real achievements. Schneider found that this tendency was especially marked with subjects who had no previous experience of
success or failure that they could use as a basis for estimating the probability of future success.

These findings support the general hypothesis that people refrain from positive judgments on their future outcomes when
they have reason to believe that these judgments could be interpreted by others as being presumptuous and arrogant; in
order to avoid possible negative sanctions, people revise
their self-estimates so as to reflect lower optimism. The social comparison processes that occur in groups can convey information about the adequacy of a person's judgments and serve
as a basis for these judgments' revision. Since the information generated in group discussions tends to be critical and
to emphasize the possibilities of failure for desired future
outcomes (cf. Kogan & Wallach, 1964; Lamm, Trommsdorff & Kogan,
1970), it follows that judgments following group discussion
should shift primarily in the direction of greater pessimism.

3.1.3. Judgment change in individual settings

We return here to the previously raised question of whether
the group setting gives rise to special processes that do not
occur in individual settings and which render judgment changes in the two situations incomparable. Individuals must often
judge alone, apart from a social group; so long as they cannot
rely on external criteria for validating their judgments, they

have to refer to internal criteria based on individual experiences, opinions, and cognitive schemata. In the following,
two theoretical approaches are presented that allow predictions
of judgment change in such situations.

"Socratic thinking". As the individual reflects on these internal criteria, his/her original, spontaneous judgment may
appear to be the result of insufficient reasoning, being inconsistent with previous experiences, one-sided, or inadequately
based on empirical facts. Such reflections could, of course,
serve as grounds for the person's revision of his/her original judgment. Thus, prolonged thinking and reflection - as a
process of internal argumentation - may help discover inconsistencies in the original judgment's premises or possible implications, these, in turn, bringing about the judgment's revision.

According to McGuire (1960; 1968), spontaneous judgments often
reflect a wishful-thinking component, such that, all else being
equal, desirable events are judged as more likely to occur
than undesirable events. McGuire demonstrated, however, that
inducing people to reflect upon the premises underlying their
original judgments can lead them to discover and correct for
the logical inconsistencies that result from the wishful-
thinking tendency, thus resulting in a revision of their original, overly-optimistic judgments.

Cognitive schemata. Since the studies of Heider (1958) and
Jones, Kanouse, Kelley, Nisbett, Valins & Weiner (1972), it has
been recognized that judgments on social objects are based on
subjective, causal schemata characterizable as quasi-logical,
cognitive structures. Though attribution theory has been largely
directed towards understanding how people explain events that
have already occurred, recent work by Ross and his colleagues
(e.g. Ross, 1977; Ross, Lepper, Strack & Steinmetz, 1977) has
studied the effect of these causal schemata on the expectation
of *future* events.

Ross et al. (1977) assume that persons tend to expect higher probabilities of success for those events that are believed to be the logical consequence of certain causal "scenarios". Information that enables the person to construct such scenarios thus leads to an increase in the subjective probability with which the event is expected to occur. These scenarios, furthermore, are remarkably resistant to revision in the face of subsequently received, disproving information; even when shown to bear no correspondence to actual reality, the scenarios still serve as a basis for the person's future expectations (cf. Ross, Lepper & Hubbard, 1975).

Though Ross's work with causal schemata deals exclusively with information and cognitions dealing with events' causal antecedents, information on possible consequences of and obstacles to a future event's occurrence should also be relevant for structuring the cognitive schemata that underlie explanations and predictions. Since information on an event's consequences is necessarily consistent with the expectation that the event in question will occur, such information should support pre-existing cognitive schemata concerning the event and result in an increase in its subjective probability of occurrence. Information on obstacles, on the other hand, would contradict pre-existing causal schemata and, as a result, lead to a decrease in the event's subjective probability.

Another shortcoming of previous work on causal schemata has been that it does not account for the effect of needs and motives on judgment stability or change. If a positivity bias influences a person's judgments, information concerning causal predictions should have a different impact on the subsequent judgments depending on whether the event in question is desirable or undesirable.

3.1.4. Conclusion

The discussion above implies that judgments can be changed not

only in group but also in individual settings, the magnitude
and direction of the change depending on the way information
processing is directed. As far as the processes that mediate
this change are concerned, it should be irrelevant whether
such information stems from internal or from external sources.
Studies concerning these assumptions will be reported in the
next section.

4.   Some experimental studies on judgment change: A compari-
      son of group versus individual settings and directed ver-
      sus nondirected information processing

4.1. Hypotheses

Though derived from assumptions typical to research on group-
influenced judgment change, the hypotheses tested in the first
three studies reported below are novel in that they concern
judgments on the likelihood of occurrence of future, personal
and public events and yield differential predictions depending
on these events' desirability. The group discussions in all
three studies were *undirected*. It was predicted that commitment, influences from the group leader and social comparison
processes would all operate to change judgments in the direction of (a) extremization, (b) increased certainty, and (c)
decreased optimism.

The second group of experiments discussed below (Experiments
IV, V and VI) all concern the general hypothesis that judgment
change in group and individual settings does not differ so
long as subjects' information processing is *directed*. It was
predicted that directing information processing in a way consistent with subjects' cognitive schemata would result in
judgment change in the direction of (a) extremization, (b) increased certainty, and (c) increased optimism.

4.2 Summary of methods

Experimental design. Two main independent variables were manipulated: group versus individual settings (in all experiments),
and different ways of directing information (in Experiments
IV - VI).

In all experiments, a "before-after" strategy was used to measure judgment change, the first measure being taken at the
start of the session and the second at the end, after the subjects had either taken part in a group discussion concerning
the future likelihood of the events in question or simply individually listed arguments concerning the likelihood of each
event. Experiment I featured an additional, control group in
which subjects were not assigned any activity between the two
judgment measures.

In the *undirected information processing* treatment, subjects
were free to discuss (in the group condition) or write down
(in the individual condition) arguments concerning the probability that the given future events would occur before the
year 2000. In the *directed information processing* condition,
subjects were to discuss or write down arguments on (a) the
events' preconditions and consequences (Experiment VI), (b)
obstacles (Experiment V) to the occurrence of desirable events,
and (c) negative consequences of, and obstacles to, the occurrence of undesirable future events (Experiment VI).

The future events that subjects had to make judgments about
were either desirable or undesirable and dealt with either
personal matters or matters of larger, public concern. Some
examples are: Arabs and Israelis living peacefully together;
strikes preventing the production of basic goods and services;
I travel around the world; I do not find satisfaction in my
work. A major reason for choosing such judgmental material
was to make sure that objective criteria for evaluating the
correctness of responses were not available and that all subjects would be in a similar position of uncertainty when making
their judgments.

Sample. Subjects were recruited from the university and high schools in Mannheim. They participated voluntarily and received a small honorarium. The subjects were:

Experiment I, 46 male college students; Experiment II, 40 female college students; Experiment III, 50 female high school pupils; Experiment IV, 64 female college students; Experiment V, 38 female college students; Experiment VI, 96 female high school pupils.

Dependent variables. With regard to the probability estimates and judgments of certainty, subjects first estimated the probability of occurrence of the future events on an 11-point scale (0 = not at all probable; 10 = definite) and then indicated how certain they were about this estimate on a 7-point scale (1 = extremely uncertain; 7 = extremely certain). Extremity scores were computed from the probability judgments in the following way: (a) for *individual extremity,* the absolute difference between each subject's probability score and the middle point of the scale (50) was computed (cf. Kogan & Wallach, 1966); (b) for *group extremity,* the absolute difference between the group mean and the middle point of the scale was computed (cf. Moscovici & Zavalloni, 1969). The group extremity score does not, of course, take into account the variance of judgments in the group and involves further difficulties more extensively discussed by Trommsdorff (1978).

Group interaction analyses. In order to analyse the process and content of the group interactions, several of the experiments monitored the following indicators: discussion time, frequency of verbal utterances for the various group members (the relation between these first two scores providing an indicator of the relative verbal intensity); frequency of interruptions; frequency of opening a discussion; persuasiveness and attractiveness of each group member as determined by ratings made by other members of his/her group.

The arguments discussed in the groups and noted by subjects in the individual condition were rated by means of content analyses by two independent raters according to the following categories: optimism, pessimism, neutral definitions. These categories were further differentiated according to whether they dealt with preconditions, consequences, or obstacles.

4.3. Results

Nondirected information processing. The most interesting results of Experiment I (in which subjects judged the likelihood of 14 desirable, public events) were as follows (cf. Lamm & Trommsdorff, 1974): (a) the group and individual conditions differed significantly with respect to the degree and kind of judgmental change, with group discussions resulting in group but not individual extremization and having no effect on either certainty or pessimism, while in the individual condition, judgments became less extreme and less certain; (b) group extremization did not correlate with discussion intensity; and (c) group members favoring extreme positions were more certain than their fellow group members and caused the others' (individual) extremization to increase.

The main findings of Experiment II (in which subjects judged the likelihood of 10 undesirable, public events) were: (a) in general, judgmental shifts differed between the group and individual conditions: in the group condition, extremization was found on both the group and individual levels, subjects' judgmental certainty was found to increase, but no shift towards pessimism occurred; (b) positive correlations were found for the group condition between judgment extremity and group persuasiveness and certainty.

The primary results from Experiment III (in which subjects judged the likelihood of 6 desirable and 6 undesirable personal events) were as follows: (a) judgmental shifts differed between individual and group conditions: group and individual

extremization and a shift towards pessimism for desired events
were found in the group condition; (b) arguments generated
during the group discussions were biased towards pessimism.

Directed information processing. The main findings of Experiment IV (in which subjects had to generate preconditions or
desirable consequences for 10 desirable, public events) (cf.
Trommsdorff & Lamm, 1972) were: (a) there were no differences
found in judgmental shifts between the group and individual
conditions, judgments in both cases becoming more optimistic
and more certain; (b) extremization only occurred when information processing was directed towards consequences; (c) subjects in both conditions produced greater numbers of optimistic than pessimistic arguments.

The main results of Experiment V (in which subjects had to
generate obstacles to the occurrence of 10 desirable public
events) were: (a) there were again no differences found between
the judgment shifts in the group, both conditions showing an
increase in extremization (increased distance from the scale
mid-point for probability estimates) and certainty, but no
change with regard to optimism/pessimism; (b) subjects in both
conditions produced greater numbers of pessimistic than optimistic arguments.

In Experiment VI (in which subjects generated negative consequences of or obstacles to the occurrence of undesirable public events) there were again no differences in judgment shifts
between individual conditions, (a) subjects in both conditions
showing greater optimism, less extremity in their probability
estimates, and less certainty in their judgments after having
generated the negative consequences and (b) greater extremity
after having generated obstacles to the events' occurrence.

4.4. Discussion

The results from the Experiments (I-III) that featured *undirected information processing* showed that while group discussion resulted in judgments becoming more extreme and certain,

having individuals simply list arguments about the events did
not. After *directed information processing,* (Experiments IV-
VI), however, the direction and extent of the judgment change
following the group and individual treatments were similar.
This seems to indicate that the results of Experiments I - III
reflect the operation of processes unique to group interactions, while those of Experiments IV - VI are due to processes
common to both groups and individuals.

(1) Experiments I - III on undirected information processing.
The leader-influence and commitment theories (cf. Stroebe &
Fraser, 1971; Moscovici & Zavalloni, 1969; respectively) have
not been falsified by our data. The leader-influence theory
was supported in so far as extreme and very certain group
members were regarded by their groups as being persuasive;
these "leaders" tended not to change their position, serving
rather as the focus towards which the other group members
shifted, the judgment of the group in general (Experiment I)
and/or the individual group members themselves (Experiments II
and III) becoming more extreme. The extremization following
group discussion in Experiments I - III also supports the
view that committing a group member to a given position leads
him/her to defend that position by moving towards greater
extremity.

Thus, the first three experiments can be interpreted in the
same way as traditional experiments on judgmental shift following group discussion; i.e. as primarily favoring the leadership and commitment approach. It should be noted that both
of these two latter approaches assume general processes of
social comparison to be operant in group situations.

Experiment III gives further interesting information about the
function of such social comparison processes when groups discuss problems concerning their members' personal future, as
it supports the claim that the information generated by groups
tends to be oriented more towards the possibility of failure
than of success (cf. Kogan & Wallach, 1964; Lamm, Trommsdorff

& Kogan, 1970). A shift in judgments towards pessimism occurred, however, only after desirable future events had been discussed, not after the discussion of undesirable events. The
discussion of such personal developments presumably activates
a need for positive self representation such that an overestimation of one's future success is regarded as socially undesirable and arrogant. The group situation seems to activate
group members' fears of being trapped by presumptuousness;
thus, the group members try to avoid arguments favoring the
probability of success but rather concentrate on arguments
describing possible obstacles blocking the attainment of the
desired goals. Content analyses showed that arguments were
indeed biased towards pessimism. These findings closely parallel those reported by Lamm, Trommsdorff, Burger & Füchsle
(1980) in an experiment using a different set of stimulus events.

(2) Experiments IV - VI on directed information processing.
These studies clearly show that group influences are only one
possible precondition for judgmental change. When subjects'
information processing is directed in a certain way, judgment
change can occur in individual settings as well.

Emphasizing desirable events' positive aspects (preconditions
and desirable consequences) resulted in an increase in both
the optimism concerning the likelihood of their occurrence and
the certainty with which these likelihood judgments were made.
This positivity bias may have been due to the fact that the
events' desirable aspects were accentuated to such a degree
that subjects forgot about the one-sided line of argumentation (cf. Trommsdorff, 1978). Alternatively it may be that -
regardless of an event's desirability - merely making its
antecedents and consequences salient in subjects' minds suffices to bring about increases in judgments concerning the
event's likelihood of occurrence (cf. Ross et al., 1977). Such
an analysis, however, could not account for the findings of
Experiment VI, where having subjects generate causal information (negative consequences of undesirable future events) resulted in a decrease in probability judgments.

The present experimental studies were not designed to systematically analyse the "causal schemata theory". Further studies
should investigate the effect of evaluative factors (e.g. positive and negative antecedents and consequences for desirable
and undesirable future events) on the change of probability
estimates. It would be especially interesting to analyse the
effect on judgments of causal schemata representing possible
obstacles to the occurrence of future events. Despite the
results of Experiments V and VI, the consideration of such obstacles has been found to lead to greater realism in the estimation of the chances for success (cf. Heckhausen, 1977) and,
in decision situations, may result in the choice of a subjectively costly but eventually more successful alternative.

5. Final comments

The assumption that group processes are characterized by unique
psychological processes is questioned by our findings on directed information processing. Since the judgmental changes
that occurred in the group and individual settings were similar both in form and degree, it seems likely that they were
the result of the same underlying processes. The findings thus
call for a general theory of judgment change that would allow
one to readily establish parallels between processes that
occur on group and individual levels. Such a theory would
treat, for example, social influences (e.g. mediated by social
comparison processes or the influence of a leader) as being
the functional equivalent of certain cognitive and motivational processes that mediate an individual's response in directed task settings.

Until now, the primary focus in attribution and other cognitive theories has been on the cognitive processes in information selection, decision making and judgments, neglecting
affective and motivational factors (cf. Carroll & Payne, 1976).

However, the evaluation of information, its processing and integration (as a basis of subsequent behavior) relies on subjective criteria that are not at all consistent in a logical sense, and that are variable across different situations. These individual criteria are presumably based on subjective needs and motives.

Depending on the situation and the motives operant, a person trying to arrive at a judgment may either accept a one-sided body of information or reject it as being inadequate. As we have seen above, when a persuasive and attractive group member (leader) favors a certain position, or when group members emphasize arguments on obstacles to positive developments and thus favor modesty in self-presentation, one-sided information is likely to be readily accepted as a basis for revising judgments. Such one-sidedness can occur as well as a result of the wishful thinking tendency, especially when the person does not have an opportunity to compare his judgment with those of others. However, when one-sided information on negative aspects of the future conflicts with the positivity bias, or when the premium placed on veridical judgments is especially high, such one-sidedness is likely to be rejected. The precise form of this balancing and interplay of motives for one-sidedness and veridicality is to be studied by future research.

Chapter 6 Social and Psychological Aspects of Future Orientation

G. Trommsdorff, C. Burger and T. Füchsle

1. Introduction

Although the significance of time perspective for individual behavior has frequently been emphasized, there has as yet been no theory developed. The present study attempts to answer this need by addressing one aspect of time perspective - future orientation - seeking to gain both empirical and theoretical insight with respect to its development and its impact on individual action.

In part 2 we will discuss the concept and measurement of future orientation, while part 3 will cover some studies on future orientation's development and change. Data concerning the relation between future orientation and delinquency are described in section 3.6, while part 4 presents two laboratory experiments on the situational and dispositional factors affecting future orientation as well as two field studies concerning social influences on the development of delay of gratification.

2. Conceptualization and measurement of future orientation

2.1. Conceptualization

Future orientation (FO) is an aspect of time perspective which - according to Lewin (1948) - comprises plans, aspirations, expectations and fears concerning events and actions realisti-

cally possible in the near or distant future (Lewin, 1948).
It differs from time perspective in that the latter also en-
compasses the psychological present and past.

According to Heider (1958), persons try to understand and explain the world around them and, in so doing, develop subjective theories to systematize their experience. In this light,
FO can be understood as a kind of subjective theory for predicting and explaining the future (cf. Kelly, 1955). If such
a theory were to be analysed according to scientific criteria
(cf. Epstein, 1973), one would be interested in the differentiation, consistency and coherence of such a theory - the anticipation of events, the kind of anticipated causes for these
events and their consequences.

As is known from studies on human thinking, perception and information processing, such subjective theories do not, however,
conform to purely logical principles but are biased by subjective needs and preferences (cf. McGuire, 1960; Trommsdorff,
1978a). It is in recognition of this fact, for example, that
the various expectancy-value theories posit interactions between people's expectations on the one hand, and their values,
needs and desires, on the other (cf. Atkinson, 1964; Heckhausen, 1977). We will follow this practice in our present analysis by taking future orientation (FO) to be a complex of
cognitive and affective-motivational components; it is the
anticipation and evaluation of future events structured in a
time sequence. Previous discussions on FO have tended to center
on either one of these components at the exclusion of the
other, with the result that it has become increasingly difficult to draw comparisons between different experiments (cf.
Ruiz, Reivich & Krauss, 1967). The following conceptualiza-
tion takes into consideration the previous approaches in the
literature (cf. summary by Winnubst, 1975; Devolder, 1978)
and attempts to integrate some of these in terms of the framework proposed by Trommsdorff and Lamm, 1975).

Structure of time-related and other cognitions. The cognitive aspect of FO - the structuring of anticipations according to a future time sequence - can be analyzed in terms of a variety of thematically different criteria. What have been referred to as the "density" and "coherence" of the cognitive structure are typically measured by projective methods (Wallace, 1956; Kastenbaum, 1961). Since anticipations are not independent of their time-ordering in the near or distant future, the concept "extension" of anticipations has also been used as a measure of FO (Wallace, 1956).

The behavioral relevance of these cognitive aspects has been hypothesized to lie in the influence that they exert on the person's decision-making. For example, people with a relatively unstructured, non-extended FO are thought to make decisions without taking into account the possible consequences of their behavior, acting impulsively and preferring immediate rewards of small value to delayed but more valuable rewards. Such decision alternatives occur frequently in everyday life. In our Western culture, planning, delay of gratification and other future-oriented behaviors are highly valued and serve as means for social adjustment, success and upward mobility.

Motivational and affective structure. How anticipated events are structured does not in itself provide much information on their subjective importance. Some authors (e.g. Nuttin, 1964; Lessing, 1972; Nuttin & Grommen, 1975) have therefore emphasized the necessity of considering the motivational aspect of FO when seeking to explain individual behavior on the basis of the person's FO. Nuttin, for example, understands FO as the person's motivational structuring of the future in terms of his/her valued goals, these latter serving as foci towards which all the person's hopes, fears and plans are oriented.

In line with expectancy-value theories (cf. Atkinson, 1964), we assume here that the kind of goals a person strives for depends on his/her expectations of success in attaining these goals and the value that he/she attaches to them. This assump-

tion is part of the theoretical framework for the present study and is especially relevant for the study of future-oriented action, such as delay of gratification. More generally, we
assume that the structuring of anticipations concerning all
types of future events consists of two components-, a cognitive component corresponding to the subjective probabilities attached to the events' eventual occurrence, and a motivational
component that consists of the values that the events carry.
Thus, one may look into the future rather optimistically or
rather pessimistically, depending on the expected probability
of occurrence for desired and undesired future events. The
way in which one structures one's future can clearly determine one's decision making and behavior. According to Heckhausen (1963, 1977), for example, FO is an important factor
for achievement-motivated behavior, varying positively with
the degree to which the person is optimistic towards attaining valued outcomes. In addition, Raynor (1974) has shown
that success in achievement situations is more likely for persons who have a differentiated FO with respect to achievement-
related goals.

Attribution theory suggests that the way a person's anticipations are structured will depend on the cognitive schemata
that he/she has available for explaining the possible causes
of future events. For example, a person who thinks that he/she
exercises a high degree of control over the occurrence of future events might be expected to have a highly differentiated
and extended FO. Despite their apparent usefulness in this
respect, however, the various approaches to attribution theory
(e.g. Jones, Kanouse, Kelley, Nisbett, Valins & Weiner, 1972;
and Harvey, Ickes & Kidd, 1976) have had little influence on
FO research and, along with Rotter's (1966) theory of internal
and external locus of control, have been employed in only a
studies on time perspective (e.g. Platt & Eisenman, 1968;
Strickland, 1973).

Thematic structuring. Given that FO is a cognitive-motivational structuring of the future, it is necessary to take into account the possibility that the characteristics of this structuring will vary according to thematic content. For example, a person might be more concerned about his/her family life than he/she is about the political future and, having structured the former thematic area more complexly, show a greater tendency to engage in future-oriented activities touching on that domain of life. Though Lewin (1948) has already proposed this idea in his theorizing on time perspective, it has been largely neglected in the recent research literature. Roberts and Greene (1971) and Lessing (1972) have, however, empirically demonstrated that differences that people show in FO can be traced to underlying differences in thematic content. This thematic variation can be analyzed in terms of the structural criteria discussed above; for example, the extent that FO is differentiated according to thematic area, the degree to which the thematic areas differ in their evaluative content, salience, extension, etc.

Summary. FO is understood here to be a cognitive-motivational structuring of the future. It is thought not only to enable people to generate predictions and provisory explanations of events they anticipate in the future but also, by entering into people's decision processes, to exert a direct influence on individual's behavior. FO can be analyzed in terms of structural criteria like differentiation, extension, salience, etc. One important characteristic of FO is its variation with thematic content, its precise form being determined not only by the person in question but also by the specific region of the "life-space" (e.g. politics, family, etc.) under consideration.

2.2. Measurement of future orientation

In terms of the above discussion, the measurement of FO should focus on the following aspects: (a) differentiation, (b) exten-

sion, (c) attribution of anticipated causes, (d) probability
estimation, and (e) evaluation. Each of these dependent variables should, furthermore, be studied in relation to thematic
variations in FO. While some of these variables have received
previous study (cf. Winnubst, 1975; Devolder, 1978), the limited selection of the measurement devices used in these studies
are not derived theoretically and therefore cast some doubt on
the validity of the findings (Trommsdorff, Burger, Füchsle &
Lamm, 1978, p. 32ff.). In the following subsections, we will
present two of our own instruments for measuring FO; 1) The
"Future Orientation Questionnaire" (unstructured and structured questions used in the studies of Lamm, Schmidt and Trommsdorff (1976), Schmidt, Lamm and Trommsdorff (1978), Trommsdorff,
Lamm and Schmidt (1979), Burger (1975), Füchsle (1975) and
Trommsdorff et al. (1978)) and 2) The "Future Life Events
Inventory" (structured questions and scales developed on the
basis of data concerning the "hopes and fears" of various subject populations) (cf. Füchsle, Trommsdorff & Burger, 1980).

2.2.1. Future Orientation Questionnaire

In the majority of our experiments, we have measured FO by ad-
ministering either or both of two specially designed questionnaires. The first, questionnaire A, is unstructured and involves having subjects record their personal "hopes and fears",
while the second, questionnaire B, has subjects respond to
structured questions concerning various future developments.

In questionnaire A, the *differentiation* of FO was operationalized as the percentage of noted hopes/fears in relation to the
total number of responses that subjects listed. Responses were
categorized by two independent raters using a category system
similar to Cantril's (1965). The categories used fell into two
broad categories corresponding to the private and public domains of life.

Subjects indicated the year in which they expected each of the
listed events to occur, thus providing us with an index for
measuring extension. In order to measure the anticipated causal locus for each event (attribution), subjects were to indicate on a four-point scale the extent to which each event's
occurrence would depend on external, situational factors or on
internal factors emanating from the subjects themselves.

For questionnaire B, subjects were given two lists, each containing 10 areas of the private and public life, which, for
the purpose of data analysis, were grouped into the same categories as in questionnaire A. For each of the 10 areas, subjects indicated on eleven-point scales ("the ladder of life")
the perceived quality of life in that area for three time
periods: the present, the near and the distant future. These
ratings were used to measure *optimism for the future*. Subjects'
judgments on the desirability and probability of occurrence of
30 private and 30 public events were used as a further measure
of optimism. Finally, the causal locus of each event was measured on a seven-point internality-externality scale (cf.
Trommsdorff & Lamm, 1976 for all these indicators).

2.2.2. Future Life Events Inventory

Recently, we developed a method for measuring FO on a more
structured basis ("Future Life Events Inventory"). The item
pool for the "Future Life Events Inventory" is based on the
hopes and fears that were listed by young people from a variety of educational and social backgrounds in a series of earlier
studies (see 2.), the 100 "most important" items being selected for inclusion in the present questionnaire. These "hopes
and fears" extend over the following content areas: occupation,
family, self, material well-being. On the basis of these items,
five questionnaires were constructed which were intended to
measure the following components of FO:

(a) *Cognitive differentiation* - measured by the number of pre-requisites mentioned for the occurrence of given future events.

(b) *Causal attribution* (encompassing the variables "externali-ty/internality" and "variability/stability") - measured by the number of mentioned causes in each of the four categories "chance" (external/variable); "external circumstances" (ex-ternal/stable); "personal ability" (internal/stable) and "per-sonal effort" (internal/variable).

(c) *Optimism* - the extent to which desirable events were rat-ed (on a seven-point scale) as being likely to occur and un-desirable events unlikely (the inverse, of course, holding for *pessimism*).

(d) and (e) *Importance* and *desirability* - measured on separate, seven-point scales.

The questionnaire was first administered to a sample (n = 344) of university students, vocational school pupils, "Gymnasium" pupils and prisoners between the ages of 18 and 25 years. On the basis of this data, items were selected on the criteria "importance" (mean > 4.0 on the seven-point scale) and "desi-rability" (mean < 3.0 for undesired events and mean > 5.0 for desired events on the seven-point scale) and then factor ana-lyzed. The resulting factors were taken to represent the basic thematic areas of FO. Further analyses (discriminability of the items and inter-item consistency) were carried out and relationships among the separate components of FO computed. With the resulting instrument (cf. Füchsle et al., 1980), the different components of FO and its content can be described and measured more reliably. The construct validity of this instrument is presently being investigated.

3. Correlates of and conditions for future orientation

Given FO's assumed importance as a determinant of human action (cf. Lewin, 1948), differences in action between individuals should, in some cases at least, be traceable to corresponding differences in FO. Relationships have already been demonstrated, for example, between the extension and/or structure of FO and such broad social categories as class membership (LeShan, 1952), alcoholism, schizophrenia and deviant behavior (cf. Wallace, 1956; Roos & Albers, 1965; Landau, 1975). These studies were, however, primarily concerned with unspecific relations between FO and action. *Specific* relationships between characteristics of FO and individual actions have rarely been analyzed in the frame of a functional theory.

Cognitive social learning theory can serve as a theoretical starting point for deriving hypotheses concerning the influence that social factors have on the development (and change) of FO and its impact on individual action. As adaptation to one's environment is a learning process, it is likely that an individual's previous experiences steer the fashion in which he/she conceptualizes the future and the way he/she can deal with it, thus giving rise to a "subjective theory of the self in the future". Such a subjective theory will be more or less integrated, differentiated, coherent and extended depending on the way the previous experiences are cognitively structured. For example, stored experiences may be dispersed over several themes or concentrated on a relatively few and, depending on their content, will imply future success or failure and the ability to exert personal control over one's outcomes. They might also vary in the extent to which they convey information concerning the breadth of consequences of one's action for the near and distant future and, subsequently, of the degree of one's responsibility to others.

We pursued these ideas in a series of studies on the relationship between social factors and the structure of FO. If not indicated otherwise, the method used in the following studies is based on the instrument developed by Trommsdorff and Lamm (1976) (see 2.2.1., questionnaires A and B).

3.1. Impact of social class

In our search for a variable that would represent a broad
range of distinct, social experiences differentiable according
to several psychological criteria, we settled on the variable
of "social class". Assuming that experience in public spheres
and experiences of autonomy in occupational and private life
vary positively with class level (cf. Pearlin & Kohn, 1966;
Popitz, Bahrdt, Jüres & Kesting, 1967; Lepsius, 1979), we formulated several hypotheses on class-specific characteristics
of FO (cf. Lamm et al., 1976; Schmidt et al., 1978).

Method. The sample consisted of 100 teenagers (14-16 years of
age) and 100 adults (45-55 years of age). Social class was
conceptualized by selecting subjects with different educational background. Half of the subjects had (or were getting)
the grammar school certificate, while the other half had completed (or was about to complete) the "Gymnasium" or university. Future orientation was measured using the questionnaire
described in 2.2.1. (Form A and B of Trommsdorff & Lamm, 1976).

Results. On the whole, the hypotheses were confirmed, though
the strength of this confirmation varied depending upon the
thematic content of the future area. Grammar school students
mentioned fewer hopes and fears in the public sphere and more
in the occupational area than did the Gymnasium students and
had a less-extended FO in both public and private spheres.
While a similar difference in extension was found between
adults with low versus high education, there were no differences among the adults with respect to differentiation.

Grammar school students and adults with a grammar school degree believed less in their ability to exert personal influence on future events (particularly in the public sphere) than
did their more highly-educated counterparts. The education
variable also had a definite impact on optimism/pessimism in
the adult population: Adult subjects with a higher education
judged the distant future more optimistically than those with
only a grammar school education.

Discussion. The kind of education people receive influences a broad range of individual experiences and thus, too, the structure of their FO. The resulting differences between education classes are not only of a cognitive and intellectual nature; differences in optimism among adults and the fact that, for less educated teenagers, the occupational area is more differentiated than for those more highly educated, illustrate the motivational character of FO.

Those similarities in FO between adults and students with the same educational background suggest that the differences in experience-range induced during the years in school are subsequently reinforced by occupation. The class-specific variations of a differentiated FO are primarily visible in the extension of hopes and fears into the future, people with less education not looking as far into the future as people with higher education.

Since differences in class membership entail differences in past experience, we wanted to investigate the relationship between these experience-differences and the corresponding differences in FO.

3.2. Influence of social roles

Besides social class, social roles such as those connected with sex and age represent another potent determinant of a person's experiences and are therefore likely to influence the content and structure of FO.

Sex. As a result of traditional sex roles, females are more likely to acquire experiences in the family area than males are. On the other hand, though education and occupation are important for females' financial independence, they are not as closely tied to their self-fulfilment and competency as they are for males (cf. Lehr, 1972; Hoffman, 1977). As a result, females' life plans and FO should differ from males', being more structured in terms of family-related activities than for occupational ones. Females with a higher education, however, should see more chances for self-fulfilment in a career and thus show a FO more similar to those of males than are those of less-educated women.

These hypotheses were supported in studies by Burger (1975), Füchsle (1975), Lamm et al. (1976) and Trommsdorff et al. (1978). In a study of young students, Lamm et al. (1976) found that while males listed greater numbers of occupational hopes and fears than females did, the latter listed greater numbers of hopes and fears concerning private (including the family) matters. The expected sex differences in the extension of FO in the occupational sphere were found among grammar school students but not among those in the Gymnasium. In addition, females as compared to males at both educational levels, however, expected their future to be more dependent on external circumstances than on themselves.

In a second study, again with Gymnasium students ranging from 11 to 15 years of age, we obtained similar findings (cf. summary of Trommsdorff et al., 1978, p. 124). With respect to the family, females' FO was both more differentiated and more extended than the males' was, while the latter showed greater structuring of the occupational area and more future optimism concerning it. Females saw negative occupational developments as being more likely to depend on themselves than males did.

These and other, more detailed results indicate that adolescents' conception of the future essentially mirrors the traditional sex role framework that underlay their previous experience. This correspondence, furthermore, extends to both the structural and content characteristics of FO. Females orient themselves more towards family matters and males more towards occupational ones. With respect to their occupational future, females are rather pessimistic and unsure, expecting less satisfaction and success in this area than males do (cf. Trommsdorff, 1979; Trommsdorff, Burger & Füchsle, 1980).

Age and employment. Social role differentiation exists also
with respect to age, the social expectations bearing upon
teenagers, for example, being in many ways quite different
from those that bear on adults. When these role expectations
influence individual action and shape experience, it is to be
expected that they exert an influence on FO as well. Klineberg
(1967) and Lessing (1972) have demonstrated such age-specific
influences on the structure of FO.

One question for investigation, however, is whether these age-
specific influences interact with sex roles, so that the FO's
of males and females diverge in different ways at different
points of their life development. It might be, for example,
that those sex-specific differences in adolescents' FO with
respect to occupation diminish in adulthood as females develop
careers and acquire experience in a social environment more
similar to that of men (cf. Trommsdorff, 1979).

(a) Comparison of adolescents and adults (cf. Lamm et al.,
1976; Schmidt et al., 1978; Trommsdorff, 1978b). The studies
discussed in section 3.1. found that the FO of adults and teenagers from the same social class was very similar. The sex differences with respect to occupation found for the teenagers
did not, however, appear in the adult population. Working women structured the private sphere, especially the family area,
more complexly and with a longer extension than working men;
in structuring the occupational area, however, working women
did not differ from working men.

The teenagers' FO differed from adults' in that their expectations concerning political developments were less complex
and they expected to personally have less influence in this
sphere. Adults, on the other hand, expected to have less influence on their personal development than the teenagers did,
showing greater pessimism and a less extended FO in this area.

(b) Comparison of adolescents from different age groups: In
the study reported by Burger (1975), Füchsle (1975) and

Trommsdorff et al. (1978), samples of 11, 13, and 15 year old school pupils were compared as to their FO. It was found that 15-year olds structured their hopes regarding family matters more precisely than did the other two age groups. The 15-year olds also expected to have less personal influence over future developments in several different areas than the 11-year olds did.

(c) Longitudinal study of adolescents (cf. Trommsdorff et al. 1979). Teenagers drawn from a grammar school and Gymnasium were questioned at an interval of one year (n = 48), during which time the former had finished school and begun working (at the time of the second measurement they had worked for nine months). The working grammar school pupils listed a greater number of occupational hopes and fears than Gymnasium pupils did and also showed an increase in this respect compared to their own responses at the time of the first measure. It was also found that working girls structured their occupational future more precisely at the time of the second measurement than at the time of the first, and that both males and females in the grammar school sample increased in the extent to which they believed they were personally able to influence their future.

Discussion. These results show that social roles exert a profound influence on FO. Whether they act directly or in interaction with each other (as was found to be the case, for example, with occupational and sex roles), their influence on FO seems to stem from their shaping of individual experience. While changes in social role can often produce changes in the structure of FO, there are other influences that appear to remain constant through time. This is especially true for influences due to social class, the differences in FO between different social classes being far greater than, for example, the difference between various age groups within the same social class.

The process of personal maturation and development can be seen
as a series of experiences that indicate one's capabilities
and limitations for shaping the environment. Children's belief
in their personal ability to control their future was found,
for example, to decline between the ages of eleven and fifteen
as the children presumably became better acquainted with the
external factors that shape their lives. This belief was found
to recover, however, when adolescents began working, employment
bringing with it experiences of success and autonomy that increased the adolescent's conviction of his/her ability to personally control his/her future. Starting work also resulted in
a greater structuring of FO's occupational area, a finding
that adds further support to our contention that present experiences shape one's hopes, fears and expectations for the
future.

3.3. Influence of parental child-rearing

The concept "social role" is too global for studying the specific influences that social experience has on FO. We will
therefore base our discussion in what follows on different
types of social learning directly tied to specific experiences.
One implication of the theory of social learning (cf. Rotter,
Chance & Phares, 1972; Mischel, 1973) is that receiving positive reinforcement can induce a general expectancy of positive
outcomes, trust, and optimism. Parents who support their children by giving them warmth and love should thus, in contrast to
parents who give little support, foster an active and positive
attitude toward the future. As compared with children who receive little parental support, highly supported children should
believe more strongly in the success of their endeavors and
show a greater tendency to perceive their success as being the
result of their own effort and performance. They should also
show greater willingness to invest personal efforts in order
to achieve future goals. These hypotheses are in line with the

theoretical notions of Stapf, Herrmann, Stapf and Stäcker
(1972) on children's perceptions of parental child-rearing.

Results. The study reported by Burger (1975), Füchsle (1975)
and Trommsdorff et al. (1978) also included a measure of perceived parental support. In general, the results supported the
above hypotheses (cf. summary in Trommsdorff et al., 1978,
p. 123 ff.). It was found that children who felt they received little parental support were less hopeful and less optimistic about their future than were those who perceived high
support. They were also less convinced of their ability to
influence personal events and showed less differentiation and
extension with regard to the economic and occupational future.

Discussion. The findings of this study are consistent with the
hypothesis that children who perceive a greater degree of parental support show greater confidence and optimism regarding
the future and have a more highly developed FO. Children who
feel they receive little encouragement and recognition from
their parents do not learn to trust their own abilities and,
when reinforcements are withheld, have greater difficulty en-
visaging the kind of action that would lead to eventual success. They thus regard their future with greater pessimism
and uncertainty. As can be seen with this study, situational
variables can strongly influence the FO of the child. In the
following study, the influence on FO of another situational
variable - "institutionalization" - is demonstrated.

3.4. Influence of institutionalization

If the individual has, over a period of time, been subject to
social influences that greatly limit his/her freedom of choice
and action - as occurs, for example, in prison or (with certain
differences) in the army - then his/her FO should be particularly marked by anticipations of the time of release or dis-
charge (cf. Landau, 1975). Whether or not the FO is so completely dominated by this event that it remains otherwise un-

structured, and whether it changes with the approaching release to increasingly include subsequent possibilities, are all
questions that underline the importance of situational influences on FO. These and similar questions have been posed regarding delinquents, for whom a less structured and less extended
FO has been frequently postulated and often confirmed (cf.
Barndt & Johnson, 1955; Black & Gregson, 1973).

A limited extension and structuring of FO due to institutionalization might be derived from the assumption that the nature
of a person's FO reflects his/her previous experience. On the
other hand, this assumption may be inappropriate in the present case because the limitations of experience due to institutionalization are temporary and are constantly perceived as
such, especially as the date of release approaches. What may
occur, however, is that the FO is entirely fixated on the moment of release in the early part of the term but becomes progressively more differentiated and/or extended as the point
of release approaches.

Methods and results. In studies by Hormuth, Michelitsch, Scheuermann and Vögele (1975), Hormuth, Lamm, Michelitsch, Scheuermann, Trommsdorff and Vögele (1977), Trommsdorff (1978a) and
Trommsdorff and Lamm (1980), the FO's of 90 imprisoned delinquents and 90 German Army draftees in their first, second and
final trimester of institutionalization (n = 30 for each trimester) were examined and campared to those of 30 delinquents
released on probation and 30 male workers. The subjects were
also given a motor test to measure their impulse control and
a personality test, the MMPI. The sample was homogeneous with
respect to education and social class.

The results show that the institutionalized subjects noted
relatively more fears pertaining to family life and personal
development and more hopes pertaining to occupation. Their
FO's were, however, less structured with respect to politics
and world events and less extended with respect to family
life. Institutionalized subjects close to the date of release

structured their fears concerning family matters in a more detailed manner than did those for whom release was less immin-
ent.

Discussion. These results provide further support for the assumption that situational variables can shape FO. Although
their eventual release is certainly salient in the institutionalized subjects' minds, their FO extends far beyond this
date to include hopes and fears concerning events that are expected to occur at a later point in time. The FO of institutionalized subjects contained more fears concerning personal
development than did that of the noninstitutionalized, a finding that is to be expected when the experience of being almost
entirely cut off from the social environment and the knowledge
that - in many respects - a new beginning must be made following release is taken into account. This does not necessarily
mean, however, that the institutionalized see the future more
pessimistically than the noninstitutionalized; as Landau
(1975) has hypothesized, they prepare themselves for release
by concerning themselves with the negative developments that
are possible afterwards. This argument is consistent with the
view that institutionalized persons - including delinquents -
adopt a rational, problem-oriented approach that is well-suited under the given social circumstances. In order to interpret these results as causal effects of institutionalization,
longitudinal studies are needed to analyse the changes in FO of
institutionalized as compared to noninstitutionalized persons.

3.5. Summary: Conditions for future orientation

It has been demonstrated that an individual's experiences play
an important role in determining his/her FO. This relation
between experience and FO is complicated, however, by the fact
that FO is multidimensional, consisting of numerous thematic
areas largely independent of one another and thus differen-
tially susceptible to influence by any given experience.

Experiential variables that have been found to influence FO
include class membership, social roles (age, sex, occupation),
parental child-rearing and institutionalization. Depending
upon such life experiences,the specific content areas of FO
are more densely structured (that is, more highly differentiated and extended), evaluated more positively and/or judged
more susceptible to internal control. The effects of some
variables on FO are, however, more durable than others, with
those of class membership and sex-roles being especially resistant to subsequent modification.

3.6. Correlates of future orientation: Delinquency

One strategy for determining the behavior patterns that correspond to specific characteristics of FO is to select social
groups with prescribed behavioral differences and draw comparisons between their respective FO's. Though several authors
assume that delinquent actions are the result of a short-
sighted FO (cf. Barndt & Johnson, 1955; Black & Gregson, 1973),
a causal relationship between FO and these extreme behavior
patterns has not yet been empirically demonstrated. The present
section is devoted to a discussion of our studies on this problem.

If it is true that delinquent behavior is correlated with a
tendency to give inadequate consideration to the consequences
of one's actions, and if such a tendency reflects, in turn,
a poorly structured FO, then the FO of delinquents should be
less structured than that of non-delinquents. In line with
this reasoning, it should also be the case that delinquents
are less able to control impulses and less willing to delay
gratification in order to receive greater rewards at a later
time. These hypotheses were tested for (a) male prisoners (cf.
Trommsdorff, 1978c; Trommsdorff & Lamm, 1980) and (b) female
prisoners (cf. Trommsdorff, Haag & List, 1979).

Method. For the details of study (a), see section 3.4. For
study (b), the sample was composed of 45 female delinquents
(15 subjects were on probation, 30 subjects were in prison)
and 30 female workers. The subjects were homogeneous in respect to socio-economic background. All subjects completed a
questionnaire containing possible future life-events that pre-
study delinquent subjects had noted as being especially relevant with respect to their hopes and fears. For each item,
subjects were to indicate the probability (expectation) and
desirability (evaluation) of the event's occurrence, when the
event would occur (extension), and what would be the cause of
its occurrence (attribution). In addition, several other instruments were to test delay of gratification (e.g. choice of
an immediately available reward or a larger one four weeks
later) and a series of hypothetical choices between saving
or spending money.

Results. a) The findings from the study involving the male delinquents indicate that the delinquents' FO was less extended
than the non-delinquents'. Delinquents were found to structure
their self-reported hopes and fears concerning personal matters
more precisely than the non-delinquents, but the opposite held
true for political and world affairs. Delinquents were more
pessimistic about the near future than were non-delinquents.
Impulse control was lower and aggressiveness higher for delinquents than for non-delinquents. b) The results of the second
study show that female delinquents do not differ from non-delinquents with respect to the extension of their hopes into the
future, but do show considerably less extension with regard to
fears. Female delinquents also judged the occurrence of feared
events as being more probable than did the non-delinquent females.

Discussion. In general, these results do *not* support the frequently made assumption that delinquents have a less complex
FO and are less willing to delay gratification. With respect
to personal matters, male delinquents structured their FO more
complexly than non-delinquents did, especially when it concern-

ed their fears. If there was a consistent difference between
the FO of delinquents and non-delinquents, it was with respect
to extension, female delinquents' fears being extended less
far into the future than the non-delinquents'.

Is it possible to predict delinquents' future behavior or, furthermore, is it possible to draw conclusions as to the causes
of delinquency? The present data suggest some possible explanations that should be examined in further studies. The dominance accorded the self in their FO indicates that, in comparison to non-delinquents, delinquents may give their social environment too little consideration and thus develop a relatively poor understanding of social expectations, norms, values
and institutions. In order to study the conditions under which
such characteristics of FO influence action, it is necessary
to more closely examine the effects of relevant situational
variables.

4.   Conditions for delay behavior

4.1. Theoretical questions

Delay of gratification and future orientation. In the standard
delay of gratification paradigm, the individual has to choose
between two alternatives: a smaller but immediate reward or a
larger reward to be received later. While considerations bearing on the FO are no doubt relevant here (cf. Mischel, 1974),
functional relationships between FO and delay behavior have
not yet been systematically studied. Most research on delay
of gratification has been done in the laboratory and is hardly representative of real life situations where long-term consequences of decisions have to be taken into account. Yet even
in the laboratory-decision situation, the individual is confronted with alternatives where consequences for the near future must be weighed.

Basic theoretical assumptions. The most recent work on self-imposed delay of gratification has been based on the theoretical assumptions of cognitive social learning theory (cf. Rotter et al., 1972; Mischel, 1973). According to this theory, willingness to delay gratification is a function of (a) developmental, learning and cognitive processes and (b) the value that the person attaches to the object of gratification. These assumptions have been experimentally examined and confirmed (cf. for example, Mahrer, 1956; Mischel & Grusec, 1967).

Factors in delay of gratification. The attractiveness of the delayed reward can be affected by conditions that determine its availability, such as the length of the waiting period or the requirement to successfully perform an intervening task (cf. Mischel, 1974; Mischel & Grusec, 1967). When the delayed reward is to be obtained through effort (work) and/or chance, the certainty of the goal-attainment is affected as well and can imply additional costs that inhibit willingness to delay. In such cases, individual differences in the causal attribution of success and failure should play an important role. Fontaine (1974), for example, demonstrated that the belief in internal control of successful outcomes leads to higher expectations of success (and hence, presumably, a greater willingness in delay) than the belief that future success depends on chance and luck.

A further determinant of the willingness to delay is how the goal object is subjectively represented, the degree to which it is perceived as being instrumentally relevant to the individual's needs determining the level of frustration that the delay arouses (cf. Mischel, 1974).

Of course, individuals will often vary among themselves in the meaning that they attach to a given delay situation, their varying interpretations determining the expectations and values that they attach to the choice alternatives. Personality characteristics such as locus of control (cf. Rotter, 1966;

Mischel, Zeiss & Zeiss, 1974) and achievement motivation (cf.
Mischel, 1966) should be especially influential in this regard.

This assumed interaction between situational and dispositional
characteristics in determining delay of gratification underlies the empirical studies reported in the following section.

4.2.   Empirical studies

4.2.1. Situational and personality variables in delay of gra-
     tification

Study (1). The aim of the first study was to examine the general hypothesis that willingness to delay gratification decreases as the uncertainty and effort associated with such a delay
increases. In addition, it was hypothesized that the willingness to delay would be greatest in those cases where achievement motivation was most pronounced (cf. Trommsdorff & Schmidt-
Rinke, 1979). Furthermore, attribution tendencies should have
an impact on delay of gratification.

114 female and 129 male upper level Gymnasium pupils participated as subjects. They first completed questionnaires measuring internal and external locus of control and achievement
motivation. Afterwards, they were given a series of choices
between small, immediate rewards and large, delayed ones (the
rewards included candies, money, books, playing cards, etc.,
there being 20 different choices to make, altogether). The
major independent variable was the nature of the activities
required of subjects during the delay interval, they having
either to (a) merely wait for the delayed, larger reward
(cost: delay); (b) wait and complete a boring but easy task
(cost: perseverance); (c) wait and succeed at a difficult task
(50% probability of success) (cost: uncertainty).

Delay was chosen more often in the waiting-only condition than
in either of the other two conditions, the latter not differing from each other in this respect. The anticipation of com-

pleting a task - regardless of whether it was boring or difficult - apparently involved additional cost sufficient to inhibit the willingness to delay. How subjects responded to the
difficult task with its uncertain outcome, depended, however,
on their locus of control; persons believing in internal locus
of control, who presumably judge a situation according to their
ability to be successful, preferred the immediate, certain reward to the delayed, uncertain one. Persons believing in external locus of control, on the other hand, who attribute personal success to fate and/or luck, seemed to attend primarily
to the chance component in this situation rather than to the
performance requirements and were, as a result, readier to
accept the delay than persons believing in internal control.

El-Gazzar, Saleh and Conrath (1976) report a similar finding.
According to these authors, people believing in internal locus
of control prefer to avoid uncontrollable situations and are
therefore less willing to embark on difficult tasks than are
people who believe in external control. This result underlines
the interaction of situational and dispositional factors in
determining delay of gratification.

Study (2). This second study examines how willingness to delay
is affected by expectations, reward values, the cost of waiting, locus of control, and achievement motivation.

Seventy-two elementary school students (36 male, 36 female,
of an average age of 11 years) were randomly assigned to four
experimental conditions. Waiting for the delayed reward was
varied as follows: (a) waiting only, (b) waiting as well as
throwing the correct number on dice, (c) waiting as well as
correctly completing a performance task, (d) waiting as well
as throwing the correct number on dice *or* correctly completing
a performance task (choice). Twenty different items (candies,
books, money, etc.) were used as reward objects. The following
personality variables were tested prior to choosing a reward:
internal versus external locus of control; achievement motivation; subjective expectancy of receiving the reward; subjec-

tive expectancy of success with respect to the task to be completed (conditions b, c, d); causal attribution of successful
task completion; reward value of the objects. In addition, subjects made 20 hypothetical decisions in which the length of
delay to attain a given financial reward was varied in an attempt to measure the subjective cost of the waiting period.

Results and discussion. As in the first experiment, subjects
in the "waiting-only" condition showed greater willingness to
delay gratification than did subjects in any of the other conditions. Although expectancies of success were the same for
the two tasks, subjects given a choice of which task to perform
during the waiting period showed a significant preference for
the performance task, a finding consistent with the previously
mentioned position of El-Gazzar et al., (1976) that people
prefer situations that allow them personal control over the
outcome. Despite this preference for the performance task, however, willingness to delay in the performance task condition
(c) was no greater than in the dice throwing condition (b).

Other findings were that **w**illingness to delay varied positively with achievement motivation, and that subjects with internal
locus of control as compared to persons with external locus of
control were less willing to delay in the chance condition.

These results clearly show that additional cost inhibits the
willingness to delay. People interpret delay situations differently according to their level of achievement motivation
and locus of control and hence arrive at different delay decisions.

4.2.2. Class-specific and parental child-rearing influences

The expectation of actually receiving a delayed reward influences the reward's value and, hence, the willingness to delay. If
one learns, whether from direct experience or imitation, that
delayed rewards are uncertain, the preference for an immediate
as opposed to a delayed reward should be reinforced.

Class-specific influences. It has been repeatedly assumed, but
only sporadically demonstrated, that lower class members are
less willing to delay gratification than are members of the
middle class (cf. discussion in Trommsdorff et al., 1978). According to social learning theory, such differences should be
the result of class-specific learning experiences in the family and school. In addition, however, the material and economic
future is less certain in the lower than in the middle class.
Blue-collar workers have less influence at their jobs than do
white-collar employees and receive their material rewards at
shorter intervals: the weekly pay check as opposed to the salary. Such experiences could influence the behavior of the
parents and hence have modelling effects on the child with respect to the development of confidence in the future, locus of
control, and preference for delayed rewards.

On the basis of such reasoning, we hypothesized that lower
class children are less willing to delay reward and attach a
lower value to the future than do middle class children (Füchsle & Trommsdorff, 1980). To test this, we had elementary
school students (male and female, n = 123) in the first and
second grades first indicate which of a series of reward objects (toys) they liked best and then whether they wanted to
wait for two weeks to get this object or whether they preferred
receiving a less desired object immediately. In addition, subjects were to indicate, using coins of different value, the
subjective value of the past, present and future.

The results showed that lower class children valued the present more highly than did the middle class children and chose
the immediate reward more frequently. It thus seems that delay
of gratification is more costly for lower than middle class
children, the value of the reward becoming too small for them
when the waiting requirement is added. Lower class children
presumably have not yet learned that delayed rewards "pay off"
in the future. For them the present is all important.

The influences of parental child-rearing. In order to specify the influence of parental child-rearing on decisions to delay gratification, we studied the relationship between perceived parental support and delay of gratification (Füchsle,
1975; Trommsdorff et al., 1978) (cf. section 3.3.).

It was assumed that high parental support induces a willingness to delay rewards by promoting positive expectations for
future success, trust and confidence. This hypothesis was
tested in (a) a waiting-only condition (small immediate or
large delayed reward) and (b) a waiting condition linked to
performance (small immediate or larger delayed reward following completion of an essay-writing task). The hypothesis was
confirmed only in the second condition, children who perceived
less parental support being less willing to wait for the
greater reward linked to the performance task.

The highly supported child presumably learns early in life
that his/her activities are likely to be rewarded and that
the magnitude of the reward is proportional to the effort ex-
pended. The child who receives less parental support is less
confident in this respect and may therefore be more likely to
center his/her attention on the cost of the efforts involved
in the waiting interval when making his/her decision of
whether or not to delay gratification.

5. Summary and outlook

The decision to delay depends on situational and cognitive-
motivational factors such as the expectation of success, the
evaluation of the outcome, generalized beliefs in external or
internal control, and need for achievement. The future orientation of the person is part of such cognitive-motivational
schemata that serve to interpret the decision-making situation. As we have shown in the course of our discussions, FO
a) consists of both cognitive and motivational components and

b) though affected by situation-specific learning, can remain relatively stable over time. These characteristics of FO should be taken into account when studying the relationships between FO and individual action.

In future studies, the function of FO for delay decisions or other kinds of action should be explained in a way that makes clear the situational conditions under which various aspects of FO are or are not relevant. For example, when someone decides whether or not to embark on a long course of study (rather than pursue more immediate rewards), the aspects of FO involving achievement and career become especially relevant and are probably better predictors of the eventual decision than a global construct of FO would be.

Since the anticipation and evaluation of the future are integral parts of decision making and individual action, future research should focus on the specific structure of such anticipations and evaluations and their functional relationship to individual action.

Chapter 7   A Study of Social Information Processing: Some Experiments on Imitation

K. J. Groffmann, E. Kroh-Püschel and I. Wender

1. Introduction

Ever since the 1900s imitation has been regarded as an important means for transmitting cultural values, morals and customs.
With few exceptions (e.g. Guernsey, 1928), however, the beginning of experimental psychology around the turn of the century
marked a drop in the interest shown for research on imitation,
a trend that was to continue until Miller and Dollard's (1941)
learning-based studies many years later. During the '60s there
was a flood of imitation research initiated mainly by Bandura
and his associates, this work re-establishing imitation's importance both as a form of social learning and as a means of
socialization.

This last wave of research began by studying how the imitative
learning of simple responses is influenced by a wide variety
of factors such as the characteristics of the model and the observer and the pattern of reinforcement. Soon, however, the investigations spread to more complex behaviors as well as to the
transmission and modification of rules, norms, problems of con-
science, creativity and cognitive styles. This expansion in
scope was aided by Bandura's inclusion of cognitive activities
in his theory of social learning (see Bandura, 1977) as well as
by Kohlberg's (1968) and Langer, Kuhn and Turiel's (1972) cri-
tiques of the shortcomings of previous imitation research.

These relatively recent developments form the basis of our own
research program. In its first phase, our research was concerned primarily with following up hypotheses and results in the
social learning literature in order to form a basis for further

work. This part of our research centered on determining the influence that various characteristics of the observer, model and the behavior (especially its observable consequences for the model) have on social learning processes.

Our later experiments lay greater weight on cognitive issues raised in developmental psychology. Can behavior that has been shown to follow a certain developmental course (for example, delay of gratification on the distribution of rewards) be channelled in a different developmental direction through observational learning? Other experiments took the model performance itself as their object, trying to separate the model's informative and social functions in order to better grasp their separate and combined influence on the transmission of social information. An effort was also made to compare imitative learning with other forms of information transfer. This emphasis on cognitive factors was continued in studies in which we investigated the role that causal attribution plays in information transfer and behavioral persistence.

The practical applications of social learning research were addressed in a final set of experiments that attempted to use imitative learning to improve the quality of classromm performance of anxious grade school children and influence the information-seeking behavior of students and children in decision-making situations. These last studies form the link to another project in which it was attempted to improve young people's seeking and processing of information in actual career decisions (see Jeromin & Kroh-Püschel, 1979).

2. Theoretical perspective

Next to classical and instrumental conditioning, we consider learning through modeling to be the third main form of human learning, its distinguishing feature being the speed of transmission of information between social partners, the behavior

of one (the model) providing the other (the observer) with specific information that can influence the observer's behavior
in a characteristic way. "Especially important in this context
are imitation and identification, learning processes that are
considered by some authors equivalent, while others distinguish
between them. They can, however, be combined under the general
concept of learning from models or, from the point of view of
the learner, observational learning" (Groffmann, 1968, p. 90).
Learning processes that can occur through the observation of
social models include the acquisition of new, global behaviors
or single responses, an integration of already learned responses into new behavior patterns, the inhibition of already learned behaviors or their disinhibition, and a change in the frequency with which a particular behavior or response is manifested.

In the following,we prefer the concepts "learning from models"
and "modeling" to "identification" or "imitation", "identification" having too broad, and "imitation" too narrow, a connotation in the previous research literature. Learning from models, accordingly, will denote social learning, a process characterized by the transmittal of information either by the
model's demonstrating a particular behavior in a particular
situation or by informing the observer of the behavior's result. This learning process is distinguished from other forms
of learning in that the behavior is not overtly rehearsed. It
is acquired or learned before it is performed.

The theoretical basis of our own research centers around Bandura's (1977) social learning theory. Though he originally developed it in terms of traditional learning concepts, Bandura
has more recently extended his theory to take into account the
operation of cognitive processes, he being of the opinion that
it is overly restrictive to limit social learning to those
cases when the learning occurs through direct, as opposed to
vicarious, experience. In Bandura's view, cognitive symbolic
processes play an important role in social learning settings,

allowing the individual to reflect upon his/her environment and to make his/her own decisions on future behavior. The operation of self-regulatory processes is also assumed, these allowing the individual to control the consequences of his/her own actions. Thus, behavior is no longer treated only as a dependent variable determined by various situational and dispositional factors but rather as one element in the complex interaction that takes place between the person and environment.

On this problem of reciprocal influence Bandura writes, "It is true that behavior is regulated by its contingencies, but the contingencies are partly of a person's own making. By their actions, people play an active role in producing the reinforcing contingencies that impinge upon them. This behavior partly creates the environment, and the environment influences the behavior in a reciprocal fashion"(Bandura, 1974, p. 866).

Where he once spoke of a direct stimulus-response link, Bandura now thinks of the model as serving an informative function, whatever new information he/she transmits being actively organized by the observer in some sort of central, symbolic representational system. "... Modeling influences operate principally through their informative function, and ... observers acquire mainly symbolic representations of modeled events rather than specific stimulus-response associations" (Bandura, 1972, p. 40).

Stimulus contiguity during behavior acquisition is considered to be a necessary but in no way a sufficient condition for modeling to occur. Before, however, the socially transmitted behavior can be reproduced, the learner must codify, organize and integrate the information concerning it. The importance of symbolic processes like speech and imagination in directing behavior is substantiated by people's ability to describe with surprising exactness previously unfamiliar, model-demonstrated behavior patterns even before having the opportunity of performing the behavior themselves.

A cognitive transmission system is postulated between the perception of a model's behavior and its reproduction; though the
acquisition of response patterns is governed mainly by stimulus
contiguity, its eventual performance is influenced primarily
by reinforcement contingencies. New response patterns can thus
be learned without their actually having been performed (and
rewarded). As it seems likely that expectations of future utility determine individual attentional processes, social learning cannot, however, be considered without taking into account
motivational processes as well (Mischel, 1973).

Modeling, according to Bandura, is divided into four interlock-
ing systems, each of which is controlled by specific variables:

(1) Attentional processes
    The observer exercises a certain selectivity in his/her
    perception of the model's behavior and the relevant aspects
    of the stimulus situation. Mainly model and observer charac-
    teristics are the variables that exert the most important
    influence on this perceptual selectivity.
(2) Retention processes
    The observer stores the information in pictorial and/or
    verbal form and rehearses it in order to better recall it
    later on. The model's behavior is not, however, organized
    into new memory structures but rather is assimilated into
    pre-existing ones, thus often giving rise to inaccuracies
    in how it is represented.
(3) Motor reproduction processes
    The observer, of course, must be physically able to perform
    the behavior, his/her performance being guided by the cog-
    nitive representation that he/she had previously formed on
    the basis of having watched the model.
(4) Motivational processes
    The progression from merely having learned a behavior pat-
    tern to actually performing it is influenced by various
    reinforcement contingencies, the reinforcement here being
    either external, vicarious, or originating in the self.

Reinforcement not only stabilizes the behavior but also functions as an informative and motivating factor. For example, an action's consequences can be cognitively stored and provide information guiding the observer's behavior later on, this holding regardless of whether the consequences stem from one of his/her own acts or from a behavior observed in someone else.

Authors of the Skinner school - for example, Gewirtz (1971) - consider stimuli stemming from vicarious reinforcement to be discriminating stimuli (S^D) and posit that these stimuli are responsible for the effect of vicarious reinforcement in imitative learning. Bandura (1971a), however, sees several possible explanations:

(a) Vicarious reinforcement possesses informative value for the observer, enabling him/her to discuss which behaviors result in positive or negative consequences.

(b) Vicarious reinforcement serves the discrimination between environmental stimuli, the observer thus learning to discriminate between different situations.

(c) Vicarious reinforcement motivates the observer to imitate.

(d) Vicarious reinforcement leads to the vicarious conditioning or extinction of emotional arousal. The model's behavior, at first neutral, becomes associated with the ensuing positive or negative reinforcements and thus becomes a conditioned stimulus for the observer, the imitative response leading the observer to experience the same emotions as the model did.

(e) Vicarious reinforcement changes the status of a model. Punishment of a model can lead to a diminution of his authority and therefore to less imitation. Rewarding the model can contribute to an increase in his status and hence increase imitation.

(f) Vicarious reinforcement provides the observer with an opportunity for comparison and a standard for evaluating just or unjust punishments and rewards.

On the behavioral level, Bandura differentiates between three
important effects of modeling:

(1) Acquisition of new behavior that was not formerly present
     in the behavioral repertoire (observational learning effect).
(2) Modification of behavior already present in the repertoire.
     According to the behavioral consequences observed, such
     learning can result in an inhibitory or a disinhibitory
     effect.
(3) Facilitation of the performance of already learned beha-
     vior. Inhibitory or disinhibitory processes do not play a
     part here. The model's response serves as a discriminating
     stimulus and facilitates the observer's performance of the
     same behavior (response facilitation effect).

In summary, for modeling to occur, the model's behavior must
be observed, registered in memory and later retrieved under
appropriate stimulus conditions. Absence of a modeling effect,
on the other hand, implies a blockage at either the perceptual,
encoding or retrieval stages or an absence of appropriate stimulus and/or reinforcement contingencies. Each of social learning component processes can be affected by different sets of
variables. In the following section, we will take a close look
at some of these variables and consider their importance within the theoretical framework just presented.

3.   Independent variables affecting social learning processes

3.1. Model characteristics

Characteristics of the model serve as discriminating stimuli
influencing the degree to which observers follow the model in
their behavior. By "model characteristics" we refer to all properties of the model that do not form an integral part of the
key behavior. Hypotheses concerning these model variables can
often be deduced from commonplace observation. A girl, for

example, will usually expect and experience more positive responses from her environment for the imitation of female models
than she would for imitating male models, though the experimental findings concerning same - and different - sex models are
not, to be sure, uniform (Bandura, Ross & Ross, 1961; Bandura,
Ross & Ross, 1963; Hicks, 1965; Fryrear & Thelen, 1969). Along
with sex this section will cover the effects of age, nurturance,
power, status and similarity with the observer.

Considering these results, however, it seems senseless to investigate whether an isolated characteristic does or does not
influence modeling. The kind of behavior to be learned must be
taken into account, as well as the characteristics of the learner and the particular situational contingencies. It still has
not been explained, for example, when positive interaction
(such as nurturance) between model and observer leads to a modeling effect and when it does not (Yarrow & Scott, 1972).
Grusec and Skubiski (1970) hypothesized that nurturance had no
influence when task-relevant behavior was to be learned, while
Parton and Siebold (1975) claim that the dependence between
nurturance and imitation is mediated by the model's attractiveness. In our opinion, this problem can only be properly investigated when observer characteristics (e.g. achievement motivation) are also taken into account (see experiment 3).

The findings are a little more definite with respect to the
model's power and competence. Grusec (1971) proposed, for example, that the power of a model becomes important when subjects'
task is to learn a behavior unpleasant for them - as is often
necessary during socialization. Yet while power seems a central
ingredient in parent-child interactions, it seems somewhat over-
shadowed by the influence of model similarity when socialization occurs among peers. According to Hartup and Lougee (1975)
the kind of behavior in question is an important determinant of
whether peer or parental models are the most effective, peer
models being especially effective when the modeling involves
disinhibition. Since this difference in the effectiveness of

peer and parental models is extremely important for the practical application of modeling techniques, we thought it wise
to more exactly determine the varying effectiveness of different aged models over a range of different social conditions
(experiments 4 and 5).

Another model characteristic that has received attention is the
extent to which the model's behavior shows "coping" versus
"mastery", especially with respect to anxiety (cf. Meichenbaum,
1971; Sarason, 1975; Groffmann, Zschintzsch, Köster & Messer,
1979). In the case of avoidance behavior, research has shown
that a coping model - one who first shows avoidance behavior
but then overcomes his/her anxiety and masters the situation -
can be particularly effective. It is here necessary, however,
to take observer factors (e.g. achievement anxiety) into account before any general conclusions concerning coping and
mastery can be drawn (see experiment 10).

3.2. Multiple modeling

Though it is often the case that social learning situations
involve several models, each with different characteristics,
the effects that multiple models have on social learning has
so far been subject to little systematic research. We were particularly interested in examining possible sequence effects in
multiple model situations, choosing age as an independent variable. Assuming that an older model will have greater influence on the observer due to the status, competence and authority
usually attributed to age, will the magnitude of this age effect vary depending upon the older model's ordinal position in
a sequence of other models? Since the literature on this question involves conflicting results we sought to clarify the
situation in our own research (experiment 4). In experiment 12
we used the positive effect of multiple modeling and the adult/
peer variable to demonstrate the imitation of an adult model
by a peer observer.

3.3. Modality effects

Modeling can occur either directly, as when the model performs
the behavior in the presence of the observer, or indirectly,
the observer receiving the relevant information in symbolic
form through films and/or tape recordings. Both forms of modeling have been shown in experiments to be successful. It has
not yet been clarified, however, whether a visual transmission
(for example film) is superior to a purely auditory one (for
example tape recording), and whether the two combined are superior to either visual or auditory transmissions alone (experiment 6).

We also investigated effects of demonstrations in which the
model was neither directly nor symbolically present to the observer but could only be inferred from what happened during
the demonstration itself (experiment 8).

3.4. Informative and social function of the model

The typical demonstration provides the observer with information concerning the behavior in question and also social information pertaining to the model him-/herself. The former class
of information alludes to the particular response possibilities
in the given situation and fulfills what Parton (1971) has referred to as the model's informative function. The latter type
of information fulfills the model's social function, which,
Parton argues, provides observers with cues concerning his/her
suitability as a social partner. Our own analysis is similar
to Parton's except that we take the model's social function
as being one of indicating whether the demonstrated behavior
in a given situation is appropriate, socially acceptable or
even desirable. Holzkamp (1972) argues in a similar manner.

In order to determine whether the effect of a behavioral demonstration is due only to action components or also to model

components, the influence of various social components was tested (experiment 7). In an additional experiment (experiment 11)
pure action components - shown as a cartoon - were compared
to model action. Whether mere indication of model action can
influence the informative behavior of an observer was investigated in the study mentioned above (experiment 8).

Aronfreed (1968) claimed that a model can be replaced not only
by direct verbal instruction but also by nonsocial stimuli,
while Grusec and Skubiski (1970) similarly argue that the model's behavior serves as an implicit behavioral instruction.
Accordingly, in two of the experiments just mentioned (6 and
11), conditions were included to test the relative effectiveness of actually observing a model's performance with merely
receiving instructions concerning the behavior to be learned.

3.5. Observer characteristics

Bandura's theory of social learning attributes observes an active role in the learning process. The less precise, the less
structured and the more ambiguous the learning situation, the
more important these observer factors become, especially those
pertaining to learning and reinforcement history (Mischel,
1973). Experiments have shown that the effects of previous
learning appear immediately and persist over extended periods
of time (Akamatsu & Thelen, 1974; Zumkley-Münkel, 1976).

Occasionally social class has been discussed as an important
factor underlying certain learning differences. Reasoning that
such differences may be due to divergent child-rearing practices between different social classes (cf. Caesar, 1972), we
ran a series of experiments testing the effects of social class
and reinforcement contingency on learning from models over a
range of different behaviors (experiment 1 and 2). In another
experiment we extended our investigation to the possible interaction of the observer's achievement motivation (a factor closely tied to class differences) and various model characteri-

stics (experiment 3), while a final pair of experiments (experiments 10 and 11) examined the influence of observer achievement anxiety on the performance of model-relevant and irrelevant behaviors.

3.6. Reinforcement contingencies

A review of the literature on social learning shows that directly rewarding the observer for modeling increases the frequency of its occurrence, while direct punishment decreases modeling frequency (Flanders, 1968; Zumkley-Münkel, 1976). These results held across different age groups and for primary as well as secondary reinforcement.

Despite a great deal of controversy (cf. Kohlberg, 1969; Gewirtz, 1971; Groffmann & Schmidtke, 1977; Rice, 1976) social learning theorists attach particular importance to vicarious reinforcement. From the observer's perspective, vicariously experienced reinforcement contingencies have a functional value, determining the selective perception and retention of model stimuli and, of course, later serving as the basis for response selection when the observer him-/herself performs the behavior. In short, knowledge of behavioral consequences serves as a discrminating stimulus (Bandura & Barab, 1971).

The research literature on vicarious reinforcement does not, however, allow any firm conclusions to be drawn, vicarious positive reinforcement being effective in about half the studies (Thelen & Rennie, 1972) and vicarious punishment depending for its effectiveness on the model's emotional reaction (Montada & Setter to Bulte, 1974). In predicting the effects of vicarious reinforcement, furthermore, it appears necessary to take cognitive as well as motivational factors into consideration. Hamilton (1970) demonstrated that the observer must be, firstly, conscious of the contingency between the model's behavior and the reinforcement and, secondly, must be generally motivated to imitate the model's behavior. Liebert and Fernandez (1970)

argue that the learning effects of vicarious consequences only
become evident when the behavior in question is relatively
complex or uninteresting. According to Thelen and Rennie (1972),
highly structured tasks and the observer's expectation of having to solve the same problem as the model, both serve to facilitate the effect of vicarious reinforcement.

Kohlberg (1969) argues that the discrepancy in behavioral competence between the model and observer is the major determinant
of children's readiness to imitate (this varying negatively
with age), and several studies have shown vicarious reinforcement to have only secondary importance in such instances
(Preis, 1978; Waller & Preis, 1975, 1977). Our own research
further investigates this issue, trying to use vicarious reinforcement to encourage imitation while paying special attention to possible differences between social, material or informational reinforcement (cf. Spence, 1971) (experiments 3,
10, 11), and to the role played by children's previous learning histories (cf. Gewirtz & Baer, 1958a, 1958b; Zigler &
Balla, 1972) (experiments 1, 2 and 3).

3.7.   Type of model behavior

3.7.1. General aspects

In speaking of the "generality of modeling influences" Bandura
(1969, p. 252) claims that an extremely diverse range of responses and behavioral patterns can be acquired or modified by the
observation of a model. While research has verified that not
only simple motor, verbal and emotional responses but complex
behaviors as well can be learned through modeling, one finding
of particular interest is the importance of whether the model
performs desirable or undesirable behavior. Although models
performing undesirable behavior usually cause a distinct increase in the undesirable behavior manifested by the observer
models that behave socially desirable have only a limited and
temporary inhibiting effect on undesirable behavior (cf. Stein,

1967). In order to show modeling effects we used in our studies many different types of behavior - simple motoric tasks as well as complex cognitive tasks.

3.7.2.   Special topics

3.7.2.1. Modeling-up and modeling-down

Whether observational learning can instigate developmental progress or regression has been the subject of much controversy. The instigation of developmental progress is termed "modeling-up" (or "prodevelopmental change") and that of regression "modeling-down" (or "retrogressive change"). Cognitive developmental psychologists are of the opinion that, if alterable at all, a child's developmental progress can be changed most easily in the direction of natural development (Kuhn, 1973). Social learning theory, on the other hand, implies that, when appropriate models and reinforcement contingencies are presented, modeling-up as well as modeling-down are equally possible.

This controversy has centered around empirical studies on different areas of behavior, especially moral judgment and performance in Piaget's conservation problems. The results of this work show that modeling-up is more easily achieved than modeling-down (Dorr & Fey, 1974), though direct statistical comparisons between the two types of modeling have been lacking.

In our own research (experiment 5) we directly compared the effects of modeling-up and modeling-down by calculating an imitation score that reflected the degree to which our child subjects followed the behavior shown by an equitable (modeling-up) or egoistical (modeling-down) model in an allocation paradigm.

3.7.2.2. Abstract modeling

Theories of social learning originally assumed that imitation was limited to those aspects of the model's behavior that were

directly observable, and early research on social learning
tended to center on the imitation of concrete behaviors. More
recently, however, there have been quite a number of experiments on abstract modeling, the emphasis being placed particularly on concept learning, information seeking, strategies for
self-reward and self-punishment, moral judgments and cognitive
styles.

According to Bandura, the observers in abstract modeling experiments "extract the common attributes exmplified in diverse
modeled responses and formulate rules for generating behavior
with similar structural characteristics (Bandura, 1977, p. 42)."
Rosenthal and Zimmermann (1978) have concerned themselves in
detail with abstract modeling, concentrating especially on the
manner in which the to-be-learned rule is presented. Since
rules are abstractions, they must be operationalized on a behavioral level in order to be observable, this often with the
support of verbal means. Instructions can be given that point
out a rule's most important aspects, the rule itself can be
linguistically formulated, and the observer can be trained to
distinguish between relevant and irrelevant occurrences. Zimmermann and Rosenthal (1974, p. 40) summarize their studies as
follows: "Thus modeling, especially when combined with such
other operations as instructions, feedback, or rule provision,
is a powerful means to instate novel and relatively stable abstract performance."

Our studies on delay and allocation of reward (experiment 4
and 5) can be regarded as dealing with abstract modeling. The
new rule to be learned was in one case to accept a longer delay in order to gain a greater gratification and, in the other,
the equity norm. In another experiment (experiment 12), we
compared the relative impact on observers' behavior of a model
verbalizing a rule versus actually performing behaviors according to it.

3.8. Stability of modeling influences

Now and then objections to modeling experiments (especially
the modeling of socially desirable or undesirable behavior)
have been made on the grounds that the effects produced are
only observable for a limited period of time (Cowan, Langer,
Heavenrich & Nathanson, 1969; Turiel 1966). Some recent modeling
experiments have explicitly investigated this problem of stability; besides measuring observers' behavior immediately after
the observation phase, these studies each involved a second
measurement up to several months after the first session in order to establish the degree to which model-induced behavioral
changes had been retained. Some studies found the behavior
changes to be stable (e.g. Dorr & Fey, 1974), others did not
(e.g. Debus, 1970; Hicks, 1965).

One factor that seems to affect the stability of modeling effects is whether the modeling is "up" or "down", the model-induced behavior being consistently stable only in the former
case. Two of our experiments (experiments 4 and 5) were intended to further investigate the nature of the interaction between
the direction of modeling and its temporal stability.

3.9. Generalization of modeling effects

Generalization occurs when a response learned in connection to
a particular stimulus is also performed in connection to other
stimuli. While modeling can be thought of as involving such a
process when the observer performs a response that he/she has
seen performed before in another, similar situation, concern
with generalization began only with research on abstract modeling. Drever and Fröhlich (1972) describe the process of cognitive generalization as follows: Generalizing "designates a process of thinking, in which an opinion about a whole class of
objects or events is formed on the basis of a few cases ....
Generalization occurs, so to speak, with the perception and

recognition itself." Thus, in abstract modeling, the observer
does not simply learn to perform a particular, fixed response
to a given range of situational stimuli, but rather learns a
complex pattern of stimulus response relations; that is, a rule.
The acquisition of a rule can, in the last analysis, only be
tested on material other than that which the model had originally applied to it.

Research on abstract modeling has differed as to whether rule
acquisition was immediately tested on material different from
the models (cf. Bandura & McDonald, 1963; Bandura & Mischel,
1965), or whether such tests of generalization came only after
the observer had been tested on the same material that the model had performed with, the interval separating these two tests
ranging from several seconds to several weeks (cf. Zimmermann
& Rosenthal, 1972, 1974). In either case, generalization was
found in nearly all experiments testing for it, the learned behavioral patterns being as pronounced for the generalized as
they were for the original stimuli (A compilation of these
works was made by Gatting-Stiller, Stiller & Voss, 1978).

Generalization was studied in experiments 4 (delay of reward),
5 (allocation behavior), 10 and 11 (solving of anagrams). In
experiment 12, scores for direct imitation and generalization
were seperately calculated. All other studies used the same
material as the model when testing the performance.

4.   Experimental program

4.1.   Influence of model characteristics, observer attributes
       and types of reinforcement upon imitative behavior in
       children

4.1.1. Reciprocal influence of type of model reinforcement and
       observer characteristics

The two experiments discussed in this section each examine the
effects that observers' social class and the type of reinforcement that the model receives have on imitative learning.

Experiment 1:

It was hypothesized that: a) children who observe a materially
or socially reinforced model learn more than children who observe a model who is not reinforced; b) children from lower
socio-economic groups imitate the model's behavior to a greater
extent than middle-class children do; and c) materially or socially reinforcing a model increases his/her impact on lower-class
children but has little effect on middle-class children. These
hypotheses were tested in a 2 (subject social class: child of
an unskilled worker versus child of a professional) X 3 (type
of positive reinforcement: social/praise versus material/chew-
ing gum versus non) X 2 (subject sex) between subjects factorial
design. Sixty boys and sixty girls aged six to seven years
were tested. The model and the experimenter were female students.

The experimental task was a picture completion exercise, the
dependent variable being the number of times that each subject
chose pieces that had already been chosen by the model. The
maximum possible score was 8. (For a detailed description of the
task, which had not yet been used in a modeling experiment, and
a trial pretest see Wender, Neu-Weissenfels & Groffmann, 1974).

The results confirmed hypotheses a ($F = 6.59$; $df = 1/108$; $p<.05$)
and b ($F = 3.51$; $df = 2/108$; $p<.05$): When the model received a

social or material reinforcement, subjects in each social class showed a greater tendency to complete the picture with the same pieces as the model chose, this reinforcement effect being greater with the lower class children than it was for the middle class ones. Though the corresponding F did not attain standard significance level, the results were in the direction predicted by hypothesis c, type of model reinforcement having no effect on middle class childrens' tendency to imitate, but social reinforcement eliciting greater imitation than material reinforcement for the lower class children.

With respect to this last finding, the greater readiness of middle class children to produce their own solutions does not necessarily imply that middle class children are in general less prone to imitate model behavior than are children of the lower class. Since the picture completion task may have been better suited to the educational styles and aims of the middle class, more representative sampling of experimental tasks would have to be made before any general conclusion on this issue could be drawn.

Experiment 2:

To establish whether the working-class children's greater readiness to imitate is determined by the kind of problem posed, the experiment was repeated with the same factors but with a different experimental task and a "no-model" control group (Gassner, 1973). The task in question was intended to be monotonous and involved sorting marbles according to color. Since the model performed this task at a rate of 60 marbles per minute as opposed to 18 per minute for the children in the control group, "greater rapidity in sorting" was the behavior to be learned.

In the main experiment the subjects were 272 children between the ages of 6 and 8 years, divided into workers' and professionals' children by the criteria mentioned above. As in the first experiment, the adult model was female, whereas the experimenter this time was male.

The results indicated that there was no difference between the workers' and professionals' children as to the number of marbles sorted. There was, however, a significant difference between the conditions in which the model was reinforced and the condition in which she was not, children in the former condition sorting more marbles than those in latter (F = 62.78; df = 3/256; p<.01).

The results also show a reinforcement model x social class interaction similar to that found in experiment 1. The working class children responded more to social reinforcement of the model (praise), whereas the professionals' children, when they responded to reinforcement at all, were more influenced by material reinforcements (chewing gum) (p<.10). This difference is most likely due to different rearing practices in the two social classes. Taken together, the results of these first two experiments show that, in the course of their socialization, children learn key situational stimuli which help them to discern when it is appropriate to conform a model and when it is not.

4.1.2. Influence of model reinforcement, observer achievement motivation, observer model interaction and the relevance of model behavior

Experiment 3:

The results of the experiments described above led us to substitute a more psychologically defined observer dimension for the sociological dimension "social class." We chose achievement motivation as measured by Heckhausen (1963; cf. Schifferer-Kornfeld & Wender, 1974), recognizing that this variable is closely tied to subjects' social class and socialization history. The model in this experiment performed two kinds of behavior; besides performing the task (a grammar task found to be equally difficult for all of the children - cf. Taffel, 1955) that the subjects themselves would have to perform later

on, the model performed a variety of irrelevant behaviors; for
example, sticking a pencil behind his ear. For half the subjects, the experimenter reinforced each of the model's relevant
behaviors with "correct", while for the other half he did not.

Another question investigated in this experiment was the effect that positive attention (i.e. nurturance) by the model
would have on observer's imitative behavior. Previous experiments reported in the literature had shown conflicting results
with respect to nurturance. We suspected that consideration
not only of the kind of behavior to be imitated but also of
observer characteristics related to nurturance would allow
better prediction of nurturance's effects on imitative behavior.
Accordingly, the high- and low-achievement motivated children
were exposed to two different conditions: Before performing the
task, the model either interacted with them in a friendly way
and offered them juice and cookies or the model ignored them
entirely and withdrew into a corner to read.

The dependent variables were the frequency with which subjects
used a certain pronoun that the model had used particularly
often during the grammatical task, and spontaneous reproduction
of the task-irrelevant behaviors. These two dependent variables
were analyzed separately in a 2 (achievment motivation of the
observer) X 2 (model nurturance) X 2 (model reinforcement) between subjects analysis of variance. Subjects were 48 high-
and 48 low-achievement motivated boys with an average of 10,2
years. The model was a male student, the experimenter a female
student.

The results indicated that subjects hardly ever spontaneously
reproduced the model's irrelevant gestures, though they were
able to remember them when stimulated. With regard to task relevant behavior, however, significant main effects were obtained for each independent variable. The subjects with low achievement motivation increased their use of the pronoun after observing the model to a greater extent than did those with high-
achievement motivation ($F = 5.46$; $df = 1/88$; $p<.05$). Subjects

who had observed a nurturance model used the pronoun more often
than did subjects who had observed a neutral model (F = 10.46;
df = 1/88; p<.01) and the vicarious reinforcement of the model's
task-relevant behavior led to greater use of the pronoun among
the observers as compared to when no reinforcement was administered (F = 5.77; df = 1/88; p<.05). Furthermore, there was a
significant interaction between achievement motivation and nurturance such that high-achievement motivated subjects were not
influenced by this model characteristic, whereas the low-achievement motivated subjects responded by increasing their rate of
pronoun use (F = 5.17; df = 1/88; p<.05).

The results suggest that people with high achievement motivation
and similar characteristics prefer to find their own solutions
and problem solving strategies and thus are less likely to follow the model's performance or react to social stimuli (e.g.
nurturance of the model or social reinforcer). The findings for
this variable parallel those for social class in experiments 1
and 2. The strong effect of the different forms of model reinforcement points to the importance of vicarious reinforcement
in learning through modeling. Furthermore, in order to predict
modeling effects it seems necessary to take the type of imitated behavior into account.

4.2. Modeling of developmentally determined behavior patterns

In the following experiments modeling was extended to comply
developmentally determined behavior patterns, allocation and
delay of gratification. Of special interest to us in this part
of our research program was the role of social learning in
developmental processes and the function of adult models.

4.2.1. Modification in delay of gratification as a function of the age and sequence of appearance of two models

Experiment 4:
In this experiment, delay of gratification was to be modified,

a behavioral pattern that becomes increasingly dominant as children approach early adolescence. For example, a pre-test run in our own research program (Kroh-Püschel & Wender, 1979) revealed that boys who averaged 8;6 years of age were significantly less likely to select a delayed but more valuable reward than was another, older group of boys averaging 9;9 years of age (t = 4.11; p<.01).

The subjects in the present experiment were 184 boys with an average age of 8;0 years. Two models were presented to each group. Whether the models were children or adults, and the order in which they appeared, were systematically varied, each subject observing either an adult-adult, child-child, adult-child, or child-adult modeling sequence. Our selection of model age as an independent variable was determined by the fact that it is positively correlated with status, power, authority, competence, etc., each of which are model characteristics previously found to have important effects on observational learning.

In order to test the temporal stability of the learning effects, subjects were tested for delay of gratification either immediately after observing the two models or after an interval of four weeks.

It was hypothesized that: a) An adult model would be more effective at inducing delay of gratification than would the model who was the same age as the subjects themselves. This superiority of the adult model should hold regardless of the order in which the child and models appear; b) The model who is observed first has a stronger influence than the one who is observed second; and c) Modeling effects are durable, so that subjects tested four weeks after having observed the models should show greater delay of gratification than should a control group who saw no model.

The hypotheses were tested with a 2 (age of first model) X 2 (age of second model) X 2 (time of test) between subjects analysis of variance. Models' demonstrations were presented on film. The dependent variable was a delay of gratification index calculated from subjects' responses to a questionnaire. For a description of the experimental material and a discussion of the questionnaire see Kroh-Püschel and Wender (1979).

The results show that while the age of the first and second models both had significant, positive main effects on subjects' subsequent performance ($F_{1st\ model}$ = 27.65; df = 1/88; p<.001; $F_{2nd\ model}$ = 6.15; df = 1/88; p<.05), the time of testing made little or no difference.

A comparison of the variance attributed to each of these variables as well as multiple comparisons of the means show that the age of first model had a much larger influence than did the age of the second model. A comparison with the children who had not seen any model showed that all model contingencies, at least as far as adult models are concerned, caused a significant increase in delay of reward behavior (p<0.05). The boys who had seen two peer models, on the other hand, showed the same behavior as children of the control group.

The results can be interpreted in line with the concept of discrimination developed by Bandura and Barab (1971): When learning involves complex behavioral patterns that run against the observer's habits and needs, imitation occurs most readily when the behavior is demonstrated by adult (i.e., powerful) models, the imitation of whom brings with it an intrinsic reward. The greater influence of the first observed model was also found by Baron (1971) for the modeling of aggressivity but runs counter to the "recency effect" reported by McMains and Liebert (1968).

4.2.2. Modification of reward allocation by modeling-up and modeling-down

Experiment 5:

This experiment compares modeling-up and modeling-down as means of changing complex social behavior. As in experiment 4, the age of the model was varied as an independent variable, it being hypothesized that an adult model is more effective than a peer model regardless of the direction - up or down - of the modeling. The timing of the dependent variable was also manipulated, imitative behavior being measured either directly after the observation phase or following a delay of 9.5 weeks.

Numerous studies have shown the "norm of equity" (Adams, 1965) to be a decisive factor in negotiation and reward allocation, though a competing preference for equal distribution (without regard for inputs) has also been shown to be operant (cf. Lane & Coon, 1972). Several authors have attempted to interpret such behavioral differences as progressive steps in the course of development, making reference to Piaget's (1954) theoretical work on the development of moral judgment (see Crott, Möntmann & Wender, 1978).

In a study of children's reward allocation behavior, Mikula (1972) found that pre-school children allocate mainly egoistically, the principal of equality appearing in kindergarten and early grade school only to be superceded by the equity norm during the later grades. Crott, Wender, Oldigs and Reihl (1975) only partly replicated these findings for German children.

In the present experiment, each subject was faced with a situation in which his contributions to the joint achievement of the dyad was the lesser one, since it is only under this condition that it is possible to distinguish between egoistically and equitable behavior. 213 boys in the third grade were chosen with the purpose of provoking through modeling (film portrayal) an alternation in their allocation behavior either in the direction of prodevelopmental change (equity, modeling-up) or regression (egoism, modeling-down). A pre-study had shown, as the studies by Mikula and Crott et al. had found earlier, that the predominant tendency in this subject population was one towards equality.

The basic design was thus a 2 (model age) X 2 (direction of
modeling) X 2 (time of measurement) between subject factorial
with "no model" control groups being added at the time of both
the immediate and delayed measures. The dependent variable was
the number of coins which each subject claimed for himself.
The experimenter and all models were male.

The following hypotheses were tested: a) In comparison to the
control group, all of the experimental groups should show reward allocation behavior more closely resembling that of the
model; b) There should be a model age X direction interaction
such that influence of an adult model is greater than that of
a peer model in transmitting equity behavior, but inferior in
transmitting egoistical behavior; c) Even after an elapse of
9.5 weeks between observation and reproduction, differences in
behavior in accordance with hypotheses a) and b) should be evident. The delayed differences, however, should be less than
those measured immediately after the observation.

The results showed modeling-up was more successful than modeling-
down (F = 77.3, df = 1/68, p <.001); i.e. the children more
readily changed their allocation behavior in the direction of
a distribution proportionate to performance, performance in the
modeling-down condition failing to differ significantly from
that in the no model control group: $t_{up\ vs.\ control} = 5.68$; p <.01;
$t_{down\ vs.\ control} = 0.10$; n.s. Adult model: $t_{up\ vs.\ control} = 5.28$;
p <.01; $t_{down\ vs.\ control} = -2.33$; n.s.). Interestingly, it was
found that an egoistic allocation by an adult model tended to
have a reversed effect on the subject's imitative behavior,
prompting it to change in the direction of greater equity.

The results did not support hypotheses b) and c). Peer models'
influence was only slightly superior to that of the adults,
this effect due, in part, to the reversal for egoistical adult
models discussed above. For neither age model was the influence
persistent, the modeling effects having completely vanished by
the time 9.5 weeks had elapsed. It thus appears that observation of a single model is insufficient for inducing durable

change in developmentally significant behavior patterns. In
this context, it should be pointed out that the delayed changes
found in experiment 4 were the results of multiple modeling
and were measured after an interval of only four weeks. The modeling effect of the adult model (as found in experiment 4) was
not replicated. This may be due to task differences and differences in the experimental settings.

With regard to greater facility of modeling-up than modeling-
down, Lerner (1974) has argued that selfish motives play only
a small role in children's reward allocations, these allocations being instead determined by whatever concept of justice
happens to play the dominant role in shaping their perceptions
of the situation. Being part of a team and having a personal
relationship to one's partner should lead to the expectancy
that fairness in the sense of equality will underlie the relationship (Lerner, Miller & Holmes, 1976). Indeed, the children
in our pre-experiment seemed to follow such an equality principle in their distribution of the coins. In the main experiment, the pressure to imitate or to change their behavior in
the presence of an adult experimenter led subjects to decide
in favor of that behavior which, in their opinion, was appropriate and fair; i.e. an allocation proportionate to performance. It thus seems that observers play an active role in modeling situations, selecting and evaluating the incoming information before they react.

Both this experiment and experiment 4 thus show that complex,
developmentally dependent behavior can be modified through modeling, though modeling-up is apparently easier to achieve than
modeling-down is. In order to obtain a certain amount of learning stability, additional factors appear to be necessary; for
example, positive vicarious self-reinforcement, multiple modeling etc. The provocation of converse imitation in modeling-
down is something to be verified in further experiments.

4.3. Analysis of the model's function

In this section, we will discuss studies that attempt to analyze the form and content of effective modeling performances. Modeling is understood here to be a process by which information about the to-be-learned behavior and the model is socially transmitted, primarily through auditory and visual channels. Our strategy was to isolate each of these different aspects of modeling information transmission in order to better understand its contribution to overall modeling effects.

4.3.1. Information transmission via visual and/or auditory presentation as well as through given instruction

Experiment 6:

This experiment sought to determine whether modeling occurs when only auditory or visual information is received from the model and whether either type of information yields effects comparable to the two combined. This question has significance because modeling research has until now been indiscriminate in its use of various media like radio, tapes, films and television.

We were also interested in comparing the influence of auditory verbal instruction with that of the combined visual-auditory modeling. An earlier study by Allen and Liebert (1969) found that a model's informative value increases as a positive function of the number of reinforcing stimuli that it transmits concerning the behavior in question. The greater the model's informative value, the greater the influence he/she should have on the observer's subsequent behavior.

The following hypotheses were investigated: a) Isolated visual and auditory model information both yield learning though their combined effect is greater than that of either alone; b) Though auditory verbal instructions can change behavior, their impact is less than that of combined visual-auditory modeling.

The subjects were 80 five year old girls, the experimental design being a 2 (Sound vs. No Sound) X 2 (Visual vs. No Visual) between subjects factorial design with a control group of 50 girls of the same age who received verbal instruction without a model. The experimenter and model were female students, and the behavior to be learned was a fast-paced game of marbles (Rennert & Wender, 1975; Groffmann & Wender, 1975). The dependent variable was the number of marbles the subject threw in one minute.

The results indicated that auditory and visual model information had strong, positive impact on subjects' imitative behavior (F_{sound} = 34.11; df = 1/76; p<.001. $F_{vis.}$ = 34.66; df = 1/76; p<.001), both factors accounting for comparable shares of the overall variance. In addition, subjects who observed a combined model performance were significantly faster than those who received information in only one modality.

Though the instruction also produced a significant learning effect, the learning resulting from the combined model demonstration was significantly greater (t = 4.13; df = 70; p<.001), the learning from instruction being comparable to that which occurred in the single modality conditions ($\bar{x}_{1. minute}$: $\bar{x}_{instr.}$ = 26.07; $\bar{x}_{vis.}$ = 24.45; $\bar{x}_{sound}$ = 24.30). The social component in imitative learning apparently plays an unimportant role in such simple task settings. As the task becomes more complex, instructions should become more difficult to understand and the superiority of modeling thus emerges.

4.3.2. Modeling and reduction of model components

Experiment 7:

The advantage of the 'complete' model over the verbal instructions found in the above study imply that the model conveys more than the essential, 'task-relevant' information. The present experiment was intended to more closely analyze the nature of a model's impact when a complex behavior, delay of gratification, was to be learned.

It was hypothesized that the less visibly evident a model's
behavior was during the demonstration, the less impact the
model would have on observers' subsequent performance. To
test this, observers witnessed one of the following demonstrations:

(1) A model fills out a questionnaire,
(2) A hand fills out a questionnaire,
(3) A questionnaire is shown before and after it has been
    filled out,
(4) No model demonstration,

the questionnaire in each case dealing with delay of gratification (for details, cf. Kroh-Püschel, Rennert & Wender, 1976).
The dependent variable was the number of observer responses
the same questionnaire.

Subjects were 72 boys with an average age of 8,4 years. Experimenter and model were male university students.

The various demonstrations had the predicted effect, their
impact increasing as a positive function of their completeness
($F = 5.15$; $df = 3/68$; $p<.01$). A trend analysis showed a significant linear trend component ($p<.01$).

To summarize the experiments presented in this section, exclusively visual or auditory model demonstration have comparable impact, at least when it comes to learning simple responses, optimal learning occurring only when the two modalities are combined. This is consistent with the results from
research of abstract modeling (e.g. Zimmermann & Rosenthal,
1974).

Aronfreeds' (1969) assertion that verbal instructions can re-
place demonstrations by a model may be true for simple behaviors
(such as the sequence of movements in an isolated response) or
purely cognitive tasks (anagram-solving) but, as the above experiment on socially relevant modes of behavior show, does not
extend to cases in which complex or socially relevant behaviors
are to be learned. The above findings suggest that the model

conveys more than just the essential task relevant information
and that this added "social" information plays an increasingly
greater role in mediating the model's impact the more socially
relevant the behavior in question is (see also the study by
Parton & Geshuri, 1971, concerned with the modeling of aggression). In conclusion, we can formulate the following thesis:
The greater social relevance a behavior has, the more important
becomes the model's social, as opposed to its purely informational function.

4.4. Modeling and information-seeking

The experiments discussed in this section are concerned with
the information-seeking that precedes making a decision and its
susceptibility to activation through social influence.

4.4.1. The model's informative function and its influence on observer behavior

Experiment 8:

In this study, we examined how information concerning a model's
decision effects observers' pre-decisional information-seeking.

It was hypothesized that: a) The more he/she already knows, the
less likely the observer is to demand further information before making a decision; b) Observers will be more likely to
seek out further information when the model's decision conflicts
with what they already know than when it is consistent.

The subjects were ninety-six male and female students with an
average age of 21;9 years. The experimenter was a male student
of approximately the same age. The decision-making task involved estimating the distribution of various colored balls in an
urn, a task described in detail by Rühle (1975). The design was
a 2 (amount of initial information: much vs. little) x 3 (model decision: consisting vs. conflicting vs. none) mixed factorial, model decision being manipulated within subjects. The

data, however, were analyzed as a between subjects design, observers' first, second and third responses being analyzed separately.

An overall analysis of variance with repeated measurements
would have been preferable for a greater test strength, but is
here inapproporiate because of the risk of 'carry-over' effects
(Hays, 1963). The dependent variable was the amount of additional
information which the subject requested before making each of
his/her decisions.

Our first hypothesis was confirmed by all three measurements:
Subjects who received little initial information demanded more
additional information than did those subjects who had received a larger amount of initial information (F = 6.89; df = 1/78;
p<.05). Support for our second hypothesis was less strong, it
being upheld only with respect to subjects' third decision:
The conforming model decision led to fewer requests for additional information than did the conflicting one (F = 7.03;
df = 2/78; p<.01). The results for subjects' third decisions
also showed that those with little initial information were
more assured (i.e. desired less additional information) by a
corroborating model and less shaken by a conflicting model than
were subjects with more initial information. Assessing the
results of this study we must remember that the model was only
introduced by his behavior results, the social information was
minimal.

4.4.2. The influence of modeling and information cost on the demand for information

Experiment 9:

This experiment was intended to determine whether a model can
influence teenagers' pre-decisional information-seeking. Because numerous studies have shown that desire for information
may depend on its cost per bit, we introduced "information
cost" as a further independent variable.

The subjects were to decide which of three radios was the best
in terms of a set of criteria provided in a catalogue distributed by the experimenter. Information concerning the radios'
relative standings on the various criteria was available for
purchase. The model, disguised as an ordinary subject, gave
his performance at one of three different points in time: 1)
immediately after the distribution of the catalogue; i.e., at
a time in which the subjects had not yet read through the catalogue themselves; 2) after several minutes had passed during
which the subjects could have already decided on desirable information themselves; and 3) after the subjects had made their
own information requests.

The predictions were: a) The amount of cost of information influences the amount of information requested such that less
information is demanded at high cost than at low cost; b) Subjects who, before making their own decision about what information to buy, observe a model who demands a lot of information
will request more information than do subjects who see no model
before making their decision; c) If a subject learns of the
model's information request before he/she knows what information will be supplied by the experimenter, he/she will request
more information than if he/she had already known what information was to be supplied.

The hypotheses were tested with a 2 X 3 between subjects factorial design analyzed by a series of a priori multiple comparisons. The independent variables were "information cost" (high
or low), and "time of observation" (observation with knowledge
of information supply, observation without this knowledge, or
observation after own informational decision). The dependent
variable was the amount of information requested (cf. Kroh-
Püschel, Rennert & Silberer, 1978). The subjects were 90 male
and female students with an average age of 16 years. The model
and the experimenter were female university students.

Both independent variables yielded significant main effects in
the predicted direction, thus supporting the first two predic-

tions given above. The information costs clearly determined the demand; subjects who had to pay little for each unit of information requested more information than did subjects who had to pay more (F = 17.80; df = 1/84; p<.05).

The observation of a model before making an information decision led to an increase in the amount of information demanded (F = 8.03; df = 2/84; p<.05). A comparison of means, however, showed that this was only the case when the information costs were high. The subjects in the "high cost" condition who did not observe a model before making a decision on their own information needs demanded less information than did the subjects in all the other conditions (p<0.01). It appears therefore, that subjects in these other conditions had a certain conception of the amount of information necessary for a decision and were relatively uninfluenced by the models' request.

4.5. Achievement anxiety and modeling

Achievement anxiety has become a considerable problem for many individuals under present school conditions. In this study we attempted to use modeling as a means for showing achievement anxious children how to overcome their anxiety and increase their classroom performance.

4.5.1. The influence of vicarious coping on achievement and imitative behavior in anxious and non-anxious children

Experiment 10:

The following study investigates the effect of the observer's achievement anxiety and the model's behavior on the quality of the observer's own performance. We also wanted to investigate whether there is a connection between achievement anxiety and inclination to imitate, especially in behavior irrelevant to the problem at hand. The model behavior was varied to show different graduations of overt anxiety (Faust, Helmke & Wender, 1979).

The following hypotheses were formulated: a) School children
with high anxiety demonstrate a higher rate of performance after observing a model who overcomes initial anxiety (coping
model) than when they observed a model who appears sure of himself from the outset (mastery model); b) Highly anxious children
show a greater tendency to imitate behavior irrelevant to problem solving than do less anxious children. The quality of performance was measured by the number of anagrams solved and the
behavior irrelevant to problem-solving by the frequency with
which a pyramid was formed out of the anagram squares. Imitation of the model's relevant behavior was measured by the number of anagrams solved by rules that the model himself used.
Independent variables were the observer's achievement anxiety
(high/low) and whether the model exhibited coping or mastery.
Forty high- and 40 low-anxiety school children of about 9 years
of age took part in the experiment. The "Anxiety Questionnaire" from Wieczerkowski, Nickel, Janowski, Fittkau and Rauer
(1974) was used as the instrument of selection.

The evaluation of the quality of performance revealed a significant interaction between the observers' achievement anxiety
and the nature of the model; when the model was from the outset self-assured, the highly anxious children were inferior to
those children with low anxiety, but for the coping model, the
performance of the two groups were roughly equal ($F = 6.61$;
$df = 1/35$; $p<.05$). Though, as predicted, highly anxious observers showed a greater tendency to imitate the model's irrelevant behavior ($F = 6.24$; $df = 1/36$; $p<.05$), there was no difference found between observer groups with regard to the imitation of relevant behavior.

Unlike subjects in experiment 3, subjects in the present study
did not distinguish between relevant and irrelevant behavior
in their imitating. One reason for this difference may have
been that both relevant and irrelevant behaviors were, in the
present case, closely tied to the experimental task, thus making the dinstinction between them more difficult. When they

are shown very similar behaviors which refer to a given task, anxious children apparently imitate that behavior which attracts the most attention and which is the easiest to imitate.

4.5.2. The effect of chronic achievement anxiety and instructional set on imitative behavior and achievement

Experiment 11:

This experiment examines the influence of "stress" or "game" instructions on achievement anxious or non-anxious children and also seeks to determine whether the effects of these instructions are comparable to those of the coping or mastery model. We were interested not only in childrens' achievement behavior but in their imitative behavior as well (Helmke & Wender, 1979). It was predicted that the anxious children would, particularly under stress instructions, tend to imitate behavior irrelevant to problem solving and that their task performance would be highest under the game set. Low-anxiety children were predicted to be less prone to imitation than their high-anxiety counterparts regardless of whether the behavior in question was task-relevant or not.

Independent variables were achievement anxiety in the observer (high/low), task instructions (game/stress), and demonstration type (with/without model).

As in experiment 10, the dependent variables were:
- number of anagrams solved (performance level)
- frequency of arranging anagram pieces in a pyramid (imitation irrelevant to problem solving)
- proportion of anagrams solved according to the demonstrated rule (relevant imitation).

Forty children with high anxiety and forty with low anxiety in the third and fourth grades took part as subjects. (Selection instrument was, again, a modified form of the "Anxiety Questionnaire for Grade School Children" from Wieczerkowski et al., 1974). The results indicated that, as predicted, children

with high achievement anxiety imitated the model more than did
those with low achievement anxiety, this effect holding for
both problem-relevant (χ^2 = 9.92; df = 2; p<.01) and irrelevant
model behavior (F = 4.87; df = 1/36; p<.05). Though the result
differs from that reported for experiment 10 (in which we found
a difference only for the imitation of irrelevant behavior),
the discrepancy may only be an artefact stemming from the difficulty of measuring the two behavior types. Further studies
are necessary to clarify this point.

With regard to imitation effect, it was found that the performance of the highly anxious children was inferior to that of
the low-anxiety children after having received the stress instructions, whereas with the game instructions, both groups
showed a similarly high quality of performance (F = 8.96; df =
1/71; p<.01). The instructions thus had an effect on performance quality similar to that of the coping-mastery manipulation in experiment 10, the game instruction being comparable
to a model who overcomes anxiety, and the stress instruction
similar to a model which demonstrates self-confidence. The demonstration type of the modeling process had no effect, which
may be due, as argued earlier, to the fact that the imitated
behavior has little social value.

4.6. Modeling of causal attribution and the persistence of behavior in failure motivated children

Experiment 12:

Causal attribution is accorded a central role in most cognitive
theories of motivation (Heckhausen, 1977). Attempts to modify
the achievement motive and achievement-orientated behavior have
tended to proceed through influencing attribution tendencies
(Dweck, 1975) so that, for example, subjects' attributions
would change in the direction of self-determination and reflect
confidence in the subjects' own ability or effort. In this
study, we examine the effectiveness of learning through model-

ing as a means of modifying attribution tendencies and behavioral presistence.The question to be investigated was formulated as follows: Does a model's behavioral persistence and
manner of verbalizing causal relationships increase behavioral
persistence and affect attributions among failure-motivated
children?

One aspect of recent work on abstract modeling has been an interest in modifying observers' cognitive processes through varying models' verbalizations in support of their behavior. Thus,
in the present experiment, one way to reverse failure-motivated childrens' tendency to attribute failure to a deficiency in
their ability rather than to a lack of effort would be to ex-
pose them to models who account for their own failure in terms
of insufficient effort alone, while, according to Weiner (1976),
such a strategy might also result in an increase in observers'
behavioral persistence and the effect would be even stronger if
the models themselves showed persistence at their task efforts.

Accordingly, the two major independent variables manipulated
in the present experiment were the model's attribution tendency (effort vs. none) and the model's behavioral persistence
(high vs. none). The subjects were eighty failure-motivated
boys and girls in the fifth and sixth grades chosen by means
of the GITTER-Test (Schmalt, 1974) out of a larger random sample (n = 318). The procedure involved observing two video tapes
that showed how a female model behaved in the face of failure
in an easy task and a second female peer model, who imitated
the first adult model.

Immediately after the observation of the tapes, observers'
causal attribution and behavioral persistence were measured,
once in a situation similar to the one that they observed in
the video tapes and once in a different situation in order to
measure the generalizability of the modeling effects.

The principal findings were main effects for model attributional tendency (F = 8.72; df = 1/64; p<.01) and behavioral per-

sistence (F = 33.65; df = 1/64; p<.01), such that observers
tended to imitate the model both in the way they accounted for
their failure and their persistence at the experimental task.
While both effects showed some tendency to generalize to situations other than those observed on the video tapes, this generalization was statistically significant only with respect to
behavioral persistence (F = 13.00; df = 1/54; p<.01). Finally
there was no evidence that the two independent variables summat-
ed in their effects on either observer attributions or observer behavioral persistence. Perhaps a summation effect would
have occurred if some kind of connection between effort and
persistence had been shown in the modeling film (cf. Gatting-
Stiller, Gerlin, Stiller, Voss & Wender, 1979).

5. Conclusions

It seems justified to grant modeling, as a technique that can
produce relatively rapid modifications in behavior and cognition, an important place among other behavior modification
techniques. The extent to which modeling can be replaced by
the much discussed "learning by teaching" technique (Zajonc,
1979) remains to be established by comparative investigations.
Nevertheless, the experiments should be carried out in more
natural settings to overcome some criticism. Most studies on
imitative learning, including our own, employ a general experimental paradigm: The subjects are shown a model's behavior
in a certain situation and it is then determined whether the
subjects themselves behave similarly when placed in a situation
resembling or identical to that of the model. Criticisms of
this paradigm have centered on two different points. First, it
seems clear from the existing literature that the behavior of
the subjects in imitation experiments can often be attributed
to factors other than the experimental variables (cf. Rennert,
1975). Secondly, as discussed above, the stability of imitative
learning that occurs in this paradigm is open to question

(cf. Hartup & Coates, 1970). Both these points, along with imitation's close dependency on observer age (cf. Piaget, 1951; Lerner et al., 1976), suggest that some caution should be exercised in advancing imitative learning as a behavioral principle of wide applicability.

Chapter 8 Subjective Hypotheses in Diagnosis Problems

H. J. Grabitz and J. Haisch

1.   Introduction

1.1. Overview

This report concerns the role that subjective hypotheses play
in solving diagnosis problems. In what follows, we will first
make clear what we mean by "diagnosis problems" and "subjective
hypotheses" and then go on to survey some experimental findings
that bear upon subjective hypotheses' nature and function.
Finally, we will describe some theoretical accounts of the origin and the effects of subjective hypotheses and discuss specific conditions that determine the hypotheses' occurrence and
efficiency.

1.2. Diagnosis problems

Normally the term "diagnosis" is bound up with medical research.
The doctor makes the diagnosis - that is, determines the nature
of the illness - from observation of the symptoms. The symptoms
thus serve as the basis for determining the disease.

Generalizing beyond the medical context, "diagnosis" refers to
the process of using available or anticipated information to
decide which of several possible states of affairs in fact obtains. This description agrees with the characteristics of
diagnosis problems suggested by Kozielecki (1972):

1) There is a set of hypotheses concerning different possible
   states of nature. This complete set may be presented to
   (closed situation) or generated by the problem solver (open
   situation) (Kozielecki, 1969).

2) Each hypothesis indicates a certain subjective probability, this probability corresponding to the extent to which the hypothesis is supposed to be correct.
3) Sources of information exist that provide the set of data that might be used to modify the initial probabilities of hypotheses.

This formal description applies to more than just medical situations; in everyday life, we are often required to find out the actual state of nature by indicators, hints, circumstantial evidence and so on. In addition to medicine, there are other spheres of activity in which diagnosis problems frequently appear; e.g. the administration of justice, economics, politics, the army and psychology. But in addition to these, many everyday problems show the above mentioned attributes. In this connection, we will characterize all situations corresponding to the above description as "diagnosis situations" and the accompanying problems as "diagnosis problems".

1.3. Subjective hypotheses

Just as we did "diagnosis problem", we can describe the term "subjective hypothesis" quite generally: "Subjective hypothesis" refers to a person's supposition as to the actual state of one aspect of reality.

The person's confidence in his supposition varies from "uncertain" to "completely certain". The hypotheses can be based directly upon the person's experience, his/her inferences from that experience, or the experiences or thoughts of others. Later on, in section 2.1., we will consider the question of what are the necessary pre-conditions for the development of subjective hypotheses.

2. The role of subjective hypotheses in diagnosis-situations

The solution of diagnosis problems is often complicated by the incomplete reliability of available information, either as a result of measurement error, doubtfulness of information, etc.. Another difficulty arises from the fact that the information will not always discriminate sufficiently between the possible alternative states; that is, on the basis of the available information, not just one but all of the possible states may be favored with some probability. Thus, the selection of one state may often not be made with certainty (categorical diagnosis) but only with some probability of correctness (probabilistic diagnosis) (Kozielecki, 1971).

The factors mentioned above make it difficult to arrive at correct diagnoses. Nevertheless, correct diagnoses are often possible provided that the available data are carefully assessed and that the procedure is continued long enough for one of the possible states to be designated as correct with a sufficient reliability. Several studies concerning the solution of diagnosis problems show, however, that the actual processes employed often differ in typical ways from the ideal. Subjective hypotheses constructed before or during the diagnosis process may be regarded as one of the most essential causes for these deviations. The development, the period of maintenance and the effects of these hypotheses will be dealt with in the following sections as we discuss some empirical findings.

2.1.   Development of subjective hypotheses

2.1.1. Minimal requirements

First we will deal with the question of the minimal requirements necessary for the development of subjective hypotheses in diagnosis problems. Hints at the answer to this question are provided by studies by Pruitt (1961) and Brody (1965). In the

Pruitt study, subjects had to discover whether two lamps, a red and a green one, would light up in a ratio of .60 to .40 or .40 to .60. By pressing a button each time a sign was given. They could get information concerning the correct ratio by seeing which of the two lamps was illuminated.

The following two experimental conditions were set up: a "pre-decision" condition in which it was possible to decide in favor of one alternative any time during the informational series but, once the decision was made, impossible to alter it; and a "post-decision" condition in which subjects were allowed to make a decision prior to the presentation of any information, the informational series being arranged so that subjects' first guesses were invariably wrong. The dependent variable was the total amount of information required for the subjects to reach a decision for a given stimulus series. Pruitt found that con-siderably more information was required to modify the prelimin-ary guesses than for subjects in the pre-decision condition to reach a decision.

Brody's (1965) experimental arrangement was quite similar to Pruitt's (1961). Subjects were given two words and had to de-cide which would be presented 18 times and which 12 during one presentation sequence. In two of the three experimental groups subjects had to come to a decision before they received any information (i.e. they had to guess), this first decision being falsified by the following information for one group and sup-ported in the other. The third group did not have to make a preliminary decision. Brody discovered that:
1) A preliminary decision intensifies subjects' confidence in the correctness of the chosen alternative.
2) A preliminary decision that afterwards proves wrong lowers the level of confidence in the final decision but has no in-fluence on when that decision is made.

Both studies show that simply guessing has an effect on the diagnosis process. Pruitt found that considerably more infor-mation is required in dropping a once-guessed alternative than to arrive at the same conclusion when no preliminary guess had been made. These results are analogous to Brody's, where guessing prior to receiving any information increased subjects' confidence in the correctness of the chosen alternative.

It would have been thought that the procedures followed in these two studies would have discouraged the development of subjective hypotheses since, in the case of the preliminary decisions, subjects had no reason for preferring one alternative to the other. Yet subjective hypotheses were nevertheless developed, even though their foundations were either entirely lacking or irrelevant.

2.1.2. Automatic stabilization

The Pruitt (1961) and Brody (1965) studies demonstrate that subjective hypotheses are in some cases developed in the absence of any relevant supporting information. One possible explanation for these findings is that people form subjective hypotheses whenever they are urged to reach a decision favoring one alternative over the other(s) regardless of whether or not they have sufficient information available. It may thus be that when people are not placed under such decision pressure and expect to receive further decision-relevant information in the near future, they will refrain from developing hypotheses.

A study by Dailey (1952) is interesting in this regard. Dailey examined the conditions that influence the ability of clinicians to form a correct impression of an individual's character. He presented each of his clinician-subjects with an abbreviated version of a person's autobiography that was to serve as a basis for an individual characterization. The clinicians first read the autobiography and then responded to a personality inventory as if they themselves were the stimulus person. The actual answers of the stimulus person in question served as a criterion for the veracity of the clinician's prediction.

Some of Dailey's results are: 1) Clinicians who, after

having read one part of the autobiography, were asked for some
initial predictions concerning the stimulus person's responses,
were later - after having read the whole text - less able to
give correct predictions than were other clinicians who, though
having paused after reading the first part, made no prognoses
during the break. 2) Clinicians who read the autobiography without a break gave better predictions concerning the answers of
the stimulus persons than others who read the text in two parts
separated by a two-minute break (without any judgments requested).

The second of Dailey's results is especially interesting and
can be accounted for in two possible ways. It might be, for
example, that some of the initially presented information had
been forgotten during the break. Another study by Dailey (1952),
however, suggests that subjects arrive at conclusions and construct subjective hypotheses during the two minute interval
that influence their evaluation and processing of the subsequently presented information. Dailey found, for example, that
the accuracy of subjects' predictions especially suffers when
the first portion of the text contains unimportant information.

The knowledge that further information will follow evidently
does not keep people from constructing subjective hypotheses.
Once the volume of information exceeds a certain limit, a person may feel compelled to reduce the processing load by making
summary inferences or forming hypotheses. The differences between Dailey's conditions may have been due to subjects in the
no-break condition not having the opportunity to perform this
simplifying cognitive work. This explanation, however, does not
clear up why precocious conclusions influence further information gathering. Dailey (1952) assumes that precocious inferences are mistakenly regarded as facts during the final evaluation of information.

If, as Dailey's results seem to suggest, subjects given the
opportunity will develop precocious hypotheses whenever the
volume of information exceeds a certain level, one way to

prevent such activity should be to present the information in
a continuous sequence without break. It is questionable, however, whether this latter procedure will always turn out to be
successful, as two experiments by Peterson and Du Charme (1967)
demonstrate. In both experiments, subjects had to revise the
subjective probability of two possible alternatives on the
basis of a set of sequentially given data. Informational sequences were arranged in such a way to support one of the possible alternatives at first and the other later on, the objective Bayesian probabilities for the correct alternative being
at first below .50 and then rising towards 1.0. Peterson and Du
Charme found that subjects delayed in changing from the initially favored alternative, with half of the subjects not favoring
the correct alternative even when its probability climbed to
nearly 1.0. Peterson and Du Charme interpreted these results as
a "primacy" effect, referring to Asch's (1946) earlier work on
"primacy" effects in impression formation.

Peterson and Du Charme's study shows that even when stimuli are
presented sequentially and without a break, subjects have a
pronounced tendency to develop precocious hypotheses on the
basis of incomplete and/or erroneous data that later interfere
with their arriving at the correct alternative. It should be
considered, however, that in experiments concerning the revision of subjective probabilities, the person usually has to estimate the probabilities of alternatives after each given piece
of information. Such a procedure may involve an effect similar
to pressing people to make precocious decisions between the
alternatives. This objection, however, may not be raised with
regard to a study by Bruner and Potter (1964).

Bruner and Potter (1964) had subjects identify the contents of
color slides, these being at first projected out of focus and
then, over successive presentations, gradually sharpened towards
clarity. Initial clarity (relatively complete, intermediate and
low) and the duration of presentation (122, 35 and 13 sec) were
the independent variables. All pictures were shown for an equal

duration at the end of the presentation sequence but were still
so obscure that their correct identification was difficult. The
results showed that the slides were more often correctly identified the longer they had been presented, and that the initial
screening had a strong effect, so that the lower the slides
initial clarity, the less likely they were to be correctly
identified at the end.

Bruner and Potter argue that these results are due to "interference" from hypotheses that subjects tend to construct concerning the contents of out of focus pictures. Further, they
claim that the time necessary for disproving incorrect hypotheses is greater than the time required for constructing initial
ones. (This idea has also been mentioned by Pruitt, 1961).
Since incorrect hypotheses are more probable with increasing
obscurity, it follows that the probability of a correct final
interpretation will vary positively with the slides initial
clarity.

The studies summarized in this section suggest that people in
diagnosis situations show a strong tendency to spontaneously
generate subjective hypotheses. The following section will be
devoted to a discussion of these hypotheses' persistence.

2.2. Persistence of subjective hypotheses

As to the persistence of subjective hypotheses, it is of special interest to consider situations in which the data upon
which they are based becomes progressively more disconfirming.
The above mentioned studies by Peterson and Du Charme (1967)
and Bruner and Potter (1964) are of this type. In the Peterson
and Du Charme study, half the subjects kept to their original
erroneous hypotheses even when the Bayesian probabilities favoring the other were near 1.0, while Bruner and Potter found that
subjects maintained their wrong interpretations even after the
projection had improved to the point that correct interpretations were possible. Ross (1977) makes a similar point, doubt-

ing the common preconception that tentative decisions are changeable in the face of disproving evidence. Referring to results from research on "impression formation", Ross states, "These biased strategies and procedures produce initial impressions about oneself or other people that typically are premature and often erroneous. As long as they remain private and free of behavioral commitment, such first impressions may seem inconsequential, tentative in nature and free to adjust to new input. A gradually increasing body of theory and research, however, can now be marshaled to suggest the contrary." (pp. 204-205).

Valins (1974) impressively demonstrates this persistence of hypotheses in the face of disconfirming evidence. Valins presented his male subjects with pinups, at the same time leading them to believe that heart rate and GSR measures were being made. The subjects were given bogus auditory feedback of their heart rates, whose frequency varied with pinup. While increasing the bogus heart rate was previously found to increase subjects' liking for the corresponding pinup (Valins, 1966), Valins hypothesized that this would not occur if subjects were informed of the feedback's bogus nature before making their liking ratings. This hypothesis was not, however, confirmed. Pictures that had co-occurred with an accelerated heart rate were classified as being more attractive despite the debriefing.

Valin's results show that, once an inference has been drawn, its effects cannot be completely undone even when its whole basis is undermined. On the basis of post-experimental interviews, Valins argues that subjects do not passively relate the false heart beat feedback to the pinups' attractiveness but rather actively try to account for apparent variations in heart beat by searching for objective features in the corresponding pinups. Once these features are found, the picture's attractiveness becomes independent of autonomic feedback and is thus unaffected by the discovery that the feedback is false.

2.2.1. Perseverance

Ross, Lepper and Hubbard (1975) gave their subjects incorrect
feedback as to their performance on a discrimination task, varying whether subjects were told that they had succeeded (receiving repeated feedback of success) or that they had failed (receiving rare feedback of success). As dependent variables subjects were asked, among other things, to estimate,
a) their number of correct answers,
b) the average number of correct answers made by other subjects,
c) their probability of success in a second trial,
d) the extent of their abilities in this,
e) and other problems.

Before making these estimations, subjects received one of three
different information sets concerning the experiment, namely 1)
no information at all, 2) information that the success/failure
feedback was incorrect, and therefore useless as a basis for
any inferences, 3) in addition to information concerning the
incorrectness of the feedback, information that the present experiment dealt with the effects of debriefing (so-called "process" information). Besides the subjects, observers were present who recorded the subjects' performance on the discrimination task, received the same information set, and finally estimated the subjects' ability and performance. It was found
that:
1) The success-failure manipulation significantly affected observers' responses on all dependent variables and subjects'
   on all variables except the estimation of their abilities in
   other problems.
2) Debriefing had virtually no effect: though the absolute
   levels show a decrease across information conditions, all
   differences between success and failure groups that were
   significant in the "no information" condition were significant as well in the two others for both subjects and observers.

3) The 'process" information had the largest effect, though not
   on every dependent variable. As for the ability estimation,
   successful subjects are assessed as being much better than
   unsuccessful subjects, especially by the observers. The
   latter also showed significant differences in their judgments of successful and unsuccessful subjects' actual performance.

These results indicate that both subjects and observers maintained subjective hypotheses concerning subjects' ability and
performance on the discrimination task, even when the information that they later received showed that the hypotheses were
foundationless.

This ineffectiveness of debriefing in self-perception and
social perception situations had been termed by Ross (Ross et
al., 1975; Ross, 1977), "perseverance ."[1] Ross et al. argue that
perseverance in impression formation results from a weakness in
the social inference process and depends on two mechanisms:
distortion and autonomy. Distortion is the influence that initially formed impressions have on the interpretation of any
information that follows, with information that is consistent
with the initial impression being attributed to corresponding
dispositions of the actor, and information that is inconsistent
being attributed to external forces or to chance. By this, no
information evaluated after a first impression is formed can
serve as disconfirmatory evidence. This mechanism of distortion
exactly corresponds to what Kozielecki (1966) terms the "mechanism of self-confirmation of hypotheses" (see paragraph 2.3.3.).

Concerning "autonomy" Ross et al. follow Regan, Straus and
Fazio (1974) in arguing that any data that proves relevant for
an impression will not be reinterpreted if, at a later point in

_____

[1] The term "perseverance" is used by Lautmann (1972) with a similar content. By this he means a heuristic in decision making
by which a "tentatively accepted alternative will be fixed and
finally realized." (p. 158, translated by the authors).

time, the basis of its original coding has been discredited. Ross et al. (see also Ross, 1977) propose that "once coded, the evidence becomes autonomous from the coding scheme, and its impact ceases to depend upon the validity of that scheme" (p. 889).

As the studies reviewed here show, subjective hypotheses seem to become irreversible under certain conditions. Later on we will discuss the probable nature of these conditions. First, however, we will enter into the particulars of how subjective hypotheses and their persistance affect the processing of further data in the diagnosis process.

2.3.   Effects of subjective hypotheses

2.3.1. Cognition and behavior

Kelley (1950) manipulated subjects' expectations concerning a course instructor by describing the instructor as being either "warm hearted" or "cold". The subjects' task - after having watched the instructor lead a class discussion for 20 minutes - was to give free description of the instructor, as well as rate him on a set of scales. The results show that subjects who received a "warm-hearted" description of the instructor not only rated him as being more altruistic, informative, social, humorous, human, etc. but also conversed more frequently with him. The subjects' initial, subjective hypothesis not only affected their subsequent cognitive reactions to the instructor but their behavioral reactions as well. The initial hypotheses thus served in this case as "self-fulfilling prophecies" (Merton, 1957) in that they influenced the situation in such a way that it evolved in a manner that was consistent with the hypotheses themselves. "Self-fulfilling prophecy" may certainly be regarded as one of the results and, at the same time, as an efficacious mechanism for the maintenance and confirmation of subjective hypotheses (cf. Jones, 1977). The scope of this paper, however, does not permit us to deal with the particulars of this problem.

2.3.2. Incorrect solutions

One of the findings of the Peterson and Du Charme (1967) and
Bruner and Potter (1964) studies discussed above was the persistence of incorrect, subjective hypotheses in the face of subsequently received, inconsistent information, a persistence
that resulted in incorrect solutions to the experimental tasks.

Another experiment investigating the relation between incorrect
initial hypotheses and the percentage of incorrect final solutions was conducted by Grabitz (1969). In this study the subjects' task was to find out which of five cities (A,B,C,D or E)
a stimulus person was in. Each of the five cities was characterized by the relative proportion of its red, yellow, black and
white inhabitants, the subjects being, in addition, informed of
the color of each of the citizens that the stimulus person encountered on the street. In one of the experimental conditions,
subjects were told that the person decided to directly ask the
inhabitants for information on the name of the city, but that
the inhabitants would never mention the name of their city
directly, giving instead only hints - that were sometimes con-
fusing or even wrong - by comparing it with the neighbouring
cities. Though these hints all implied city C, the further information received concerning the inhabitants' color suggested
city D. The subjects receiving the inhabitants' hints thus
began the main experimental task with an incorrect initial
hypothesis. The results indicated that these subjects ended
with incorrect solutions 57% of the time, as opposed to 19% for
the subjects who had received no erroneous hints at the outset.

Given this three-fold difference in subjects' performance, we
might expect that the processes for evaluating information in
the two conditions were conceptually quite different. A study
of Kozielecki (1966) deals with the mechanism underlying this
difference.

2.3.3. Self-confirmation of hypotheses

Kozielecki (1966) had subjects choose either one, or a combination of two or three, of seven available fertilizers as being the best growth-promoter for plants. Subjects had at their disposal 24 specimens, each consisting of four fertilizers, along with messages presenting evidence concerning their positive or negative effectiveness. The subjects were told, however, that only 18 of the 24 messages were actually true, without specifying which ones.

The major findings were as follows:
1) Subjects tended to settle rather quickly on one of the available solutions as a subjective hypothesis.
2) More than 95% of the messages were evaluated as "true" if they supported the favored hypothesis. Of the messages disproving the favored hypothesis, on the other hand, only 22% were evaluated as "true". 78% were evaluated as "false".
3) 58% of confirming messages that had been regarded as true yielded increments in corresponding hypothesis' subjective probability. On the other hand, 72% of disproving messages that had been regarded as wrong had no decremental effect on the hypothesis' subjective probability.

Kozielecki argues that a person will settle upon the first hypothesis among the set of available alternatives that exceeds a certain "hypothesis threshold"; that is, when its probable truth reaches a certain minimal level. The subsequent evaluation as true or false of the confirmatory and disconfirmatory information, as well as the changes in the hypothesis' subjective probability, is termed by Kozielecki the "mechanism of self-confirmation of hypotheses".

The non-specific ratio of false messages in Kozielecki's study guarantees the "verification" of nearly any hypothesis. In the first phase of the self-confirmation process, subjects try to adapt the data to their hypotheses by classifying it as either true or false. In the second phase, this interpreted data acts

on the hypotheses' subjective probability. The question arises
whether there is a mechanism accounting for the maintenance of
subjective hypotheses when the reliability of information is
not threatened by a false-ratio. The evaluation tendency found
by Pitz, Downing and Reinhold (1967) may be regarded as a possible answer to this problem.

2.3.4. Inertia effect

Pitz et al. (1967) conducted an experiment on the way in which
confirmatory and disproving information is evaluated. One of
their findings was the confirmatory facts resulted in greater
modifications of hypotheses' subjective probabilities than disconfirmatory ones did. To account for this "Inertia Effect"
Pitz et al. offer two possibilities.
1) The effect may result from subjects' expectations of disconfirmatory instances, and their subsequent tendency to
   process these instances as exceptions (expectancy hypothesis).
2) Subjects may be unwilling to admit to a lowering of a previously stated subjective probability level (commitment hypothesis).

An empirical test of these explanations by Geller and Pitz
(1968) could not definitely decide between them, though another
study by Pitz (1969) supported the commitment hypothesis.

Grabitz and Haisch (1972) raised the question of whether distortion occurs only in the case of data that violate subjects'
hypotheses or whether it occurs as well in confirming instances.
They had their subjects modify, by examining a new set of relevant data, the probabilities associated with two, mutually exclusive and exhaustive hypotheses. The data consisted of visual
patterns, a part of which subjects had already seen during previous exposure. The modification of the subjective probabilities by employing the patterns as information was bound to one
condition: subjects were restricted to only make use of those
patterns that they had already seen during the preceding

presentation.

In the experimental treatment subjects performed this task
being fully aware of the confirming or disproving character of
the patterns received, while control subjects performed their
task without this awareness. The major finding was that subjects hardly ever decide upon "seen" in case of disproving data
but,in the case of confirming information, decide upon "seen"
more frequently than do control subjects. In other words, the
distortion tendency in information evaluation is not limited to
disproving data but affects confirming information as well.

2.3.5.   Subjective hypotheses and attribution

2.3.5.1. "Self-serving bias"

Pretending to study decision making, Snyder, Stephan and
Rosenfield (1976) asked subjects to play against one another in
a competitive number matrix game. The feedback as to the subjects' winning or losing was manipulated so that they could be
randomly assigned to the win or the lose condition. The subjects were afterwards asked about the role of skill, effort,
task difficulty and luck in determining their own and their
opponent's outcome. Snyder et al. found the following: 1) Losers
show a greater tendency than winners to attribute their losing
to bad luck. 2) Winners show a greater tendency to attribute
their winning to their own skill than the losers do. 3) Losers
show less of a tendency than do winners to attribute their
losing to lack of effort. 4) Winners show a greater tendency
than losers to attribute their winning to their effort.

The authors discuss their results in terms of "Egotism", this
term referring to the person's tendency to attribute win or
loss in a way that puts him/herself in the most favorable light.
In terms of our present discussion, Snyder et al.'s subjects
started with the subjective hypothesis that they, as persons,
could only be evaluated positively, this hypothesis being

either confirmed (winner) or disproved (loser) by the subsequently received data. The impact of this information on the
subject hypotheses was "managed" by means of the attribution of
causality, confirming instances being attributed to personal
factors (e.g. skill) and disconfirming instances being attributed to chance or external influences (e.g. bad luck). Such a
process is analogous to the "self-confirmation of hypotheses"
or the Intertia Effect discussed above.

Stephan, Presser, Kennedy and Aronson (1978) tested a supposition of Miller and Ross (1975) that subjects would be more
likely to make these "self-serving" attributions under conditions of cooperation or competition than when they perform independently. Specifically Stephan et al. tested the following
hypotheses: 1) During competition or cooperation, subjects are
more likely to attribute their own success to dispositional
factors and failure to situational factors than when performing
independently. 2) During competition or cooperation, subjects
are more likely to attribute their partner's success to situational factors and his/her failure to dispositional factors
than when they perform independently.

From a set of oil-paintings, presented two by two, subjects had
to discriminate the respectively 'prize winning' picture. In
order to increase their motivation, subjects were told that
they would be permitted to skip a further experiment and still
receive full credit if they performed successfully. In the cooperation condition the subject and his partner (a confederate)
worked together to reach this goal, while in the competition
condition, the one of them with the best performance would be
the only one excused from the future experiment. In the independent condition, their outcomes were determined solely by
their performance as individuals.

Subjects were randomly assigned to the success and failure condition and were afterwards asked to rate the degree to which
luck, skill, effort and task difficulty influenced their own
and their partner's outcome. Stephan et al. found no support

for either hypotheses, though there was a main effect such that
in all experimental conditions subjects attributed their own
success to dispositional factors and their failure to situational factors. Subjects in the cooperation and independence condition attributed their partner's outcome to dispositional
factors, while those in the competition condition centered on
situational factors. In summary, subjects' attributions concerning their own and their partner's outcome turned out to be
"self-serving" in each type of interaction studied.

Results similar to these had already been reported in several
earlier studies (e.g. Johnson, Feigenbaum & Weiby, 1964;
Feather, 1969; Fitch, 1970; Beckman, 1970; Frieze & Weiner,
1971; Davis & Davis, 1972; Wolosin, Sherman & Till, 1973). In
an attempt to systematize these findings, several authors have
proposed that the motive of "ego-defence" underlies the attribution effects. In a critical review of the research in this
area, however, Miller and Ross (1975) conclude that there is
little empirical support for a motivational explanation, as
individuals engage in self-enhancing attributions only under
conditions of success; under conditions of failure, the tendency towards self-serving attributions can barely be ascertained. Miller and Ross propose a cognitive explanation, arguing
that individuals discern a closer correspondence between behavior and outcomes in case of success than in case of failure.

Studies by Regan, Straus and Fazio (1974) provide further
evidence in support of the insufficiency of explanations having
to do with "self-servingness". Observers were asked to attribute an actor's success or failure in a game playing task to
personal or situational factors. Liking for the actor was manipulated beforehand by having subjects regard the actor's behavior during a videotaped interview. The major findings were as
follows: 1) Success of a liked actor and failure of a disliked
actor were attributed internally (i.e. to dispositional factors);
2) Success of the disliked actor and failure of the liked actor
were attributed to external (situational) factors, more often

to task difficulty.

Another experiment by Regan et al. in which observers made
attributions concerning the prosocial behavior of liked or disliked acquaintances yielded similar results; prosocial behavior
of a friend was attributed internally, whereas the very same
behavior performed by someone disliked was attributed to situational factors. Regan et al. suggest that the obtained patterns
of attribution serve as a means for subjects to preserve pre-
existing patterns of liking and disliking. Following Heider
(1958), they reason that the observers expect good people to
perform good acts and bad people to perform bad acts, any
deviations from this expectation being attributed to situational factors. Making use of external attributions in this case
has the advantage that the expected contingency between liking
and goodness remains undoubted and obviates any modifications
in observers' dispositional attributions. The notion of "self-
servingness" clearly does not apply in such instances.

2.3.5.2. "Discounting"

Two experiments by Thibaut and Riecken (1955) (the so-called
"North-Carolina" and "Harvard" experiments) had subjects work
with two other persons (both actually the experimenter's confederates), one of higher status than the subject, and the
other of lower status. The subject's task was to induce the two
confederates to help him (e.g. to lend him a dictionary). Eventually, both confederates agreed to do so.

One of the dependent variables of interest was the subject's
causal explanation for the other persons' compliance. Specifically, subjects were asked whether they thought each person complied because he wanted to (internal cause) or because he had
been forced to (external cause). The results for the "North-
Carolina" experiment indicate that a majority (18 of 19) of the
subjects attributed the high-status person's compliance to
internal causes and the low-status person's to external causes.

Kelley (1971) uses the principle of "discounting" in discussing these results, maintaining that "the role of a given cause in producing a given effect is discounted if other plausible causes are also present" (p. 8). According to Kelley, discounting is a rational response on the part of the naive attributor and is quite similar to behavior shown by scientists.

The "Harvard" experiment differed from the "North Carolina" one in that internal and external attributions were measured separately. The results show that, of 21 subjects, 12 attributed internal causes of the high status confederate and external causes to the low status one, 4 subjects showed the reverse attribution pattern, and 2 and 3 made exclusively internal and external attributions respectively. It may be supposed by these distributions that the possible cause "internal motivation" in case of a low-status confederate will not only be discounted but nearly neglected considering the available external cause. The confirmation of this suggestion would give rise to doubts of any rational basis of the actual behavior.

A study by Kruglanski, Schwartz, Maides and Hamel (1978) yielded findings that complement those of Thibaut and Riecken. Kruglanski et al. found that attributions to a "focal" explanation were not significantly weakened when subjects had equally variable alternative explanations available. Kruglanski et al. conclude that attributors take less account of evidence concerning alternative explanations than they do that concerning the focal explanation. More generally, once people construct a subjective hypothesis concerning the causal explanation of an effect, non-confirmations of this hypothesis (e.g. evidence in favor of alternative explanations) are discounted while confirmations of the hypothesis are accentuated.

3. Theoretical explanations

The preceding sections have been concerned with the development,

persistence, and consequences of subjective hypotheses in
diagnosis situations. The available evidence shows that subjective hypotheses arise nearly automatically and, once established,
are nearly immune to revision or disproof by subsequently received information or direct challenges to the hypotheses' base.
It was also found that this persistence is in large part due to
the effect that hypotheses have on the evaluation of subsequently received data. The following sections describe various theoretical accounts of diagnostic processes as well as review
empirical studies done to test these theories' implications.

3.1. Information evaluation and cognitive dissonance

One possible approach to diagnosis phenomena is provided by the
theory of cognitive dissonance (Festinger, 1957), especially as
reformulated by Irle (1975). We will confine our discussion to
those aspects of dissonance theory that seem especially relevant to diagnosis problems. The theory can be directly applied
to the problem of information evaluation by regarding the
latter as a series of cognitive decisions concerning a set of
alternatives that can lead ultimately to further, irreversible
decisions concerning behaviors. As we have seen, information
evaluation in diagnosis settings involves making decisions concerning the actual state of nature. Any information that is
inconsistent with the subjective hypothesis that the person
holds at a given moment will arouse dissonance. In order to
reduce this dissonance, such information will usually be discounted. "Any hypothesis (or theory, views etc.) will first be
processed from the environment into the Self, then will be reproduced as a cognition with the understanding that the subjective probability that this hypothesis proves correct or may
account for some empirical findings exceeds a certain minimum
threshold"(Irle, 1975, p. 313, translated by the authors).

In diagnosis problems, the cognitive decision refers to the
actual state of nature. Any information supporting an alterna-

tive state of nature is dissonance arousing. Such events normally will be discounted in order to reduce dissonance.

The theory thus seems able to account for the influence of sub-jective hypotheses in diagnosis problems, the predictions concerning the information evaluation falling in line with the empirical findings discussed above.

3.1.1. Diagnosis-process and strength of dissonance

An experiment by Grabitz (1971) tested dissonance theory's (1957) commitment hypothesis against an expectancy hypothesis, both hypotheses having been developed to account for the in-ertia effect described above. According to dissonance theory, once a person has decided on a particular alternative, any in-formation that disproves it will be dissonance arousing and is therefore likely to be discounted (Festinger, 1957, 1964). The magnitude of dissonance aroused in such instances should be a positive function of the ratio between the number and intensity of dissonant elements on the one hand, and the number and inten-sity of consonant elements on the other. Thus, the tendency to discount the disproving information should be more pronounced the sooner this information appears after the subjective hypoth-esis has been adopted (holding, of course, the amount of con-sonant information constant).

According to the expectancy-hypothesis, there should be a strong tendency to discount disproving information whenever such information is expected. Since the expectancy for disprov-ing data has been found to increase with the number of preced-ing supporting data (cf. Geller & Pitz, 1968), the tendency to discount disproving information should increase the longer the delay with which such information is received after the hypoth-esis has been adopted.

Grabitz had subjects decide upon two mutually exclusive alter-native hypotheses on the basis of a body of serially presented facts. The major independent variable was the point in the

information sequence that subjects first received information
disproving their hypothesis. The results indicate that the disproving information was discounted more the earlier it was presented, thus providing support for dissonance theory[2].

A further experiment pitting dissonance against expectancy
hypotheses was conducted by Grabitz and Grabitz-Gniech (1972a).
The authors argued: 1) That any event, E, disproves the favored
alternative, A, if the conditional probability, $P(E/A)$ is lower
than the conditional probability, $P(E/B)$, where "B" represents
a second alternative. 2) The degree to which the favored alternative is disproved depends on $P(E/A)$ just as much as on $P(E/B)$.
3) In case of constant $P(E/B)$ A's disproval by event E increases with decreasing amounts of $P(E/A)$. Thus, according to
dissonance theory, the tendency to discount disproving events
should vary inversely with the magnitude of $P(E/A)$.

According to the expectancy hypothesis, as we have already seen,
a disproving event is discounted the more it is expected. Since
such expectancies should vary positively with $P(E/A)$, disproving facts should be discounted more the greater the magnitude
of $P(E/A)$.

The results again favor dissonance theory, subjects' probability revisions concerning their favored hypotheses being smallest
for those events that disproved the hypotheses the most. Also,
subjects' tendency to classify a disproving event as "false"
increases when the diagnostic value of an information received
was high.

---

[2] It should be pointed out that the prediction of the reformulated version of the theory of cognitive dissonance would have
been in accordance with the expectancy hypothesis. Referring
to Irle (1975), the intensity of cognitive dissonance is regarded as "a function of a person's (P) subjective probability
as to the veracity of any hypothesis of the Self. This subjective probability is a) a positive function of the number of confirmations and b) a negative function of the number of non-
confirmations of the hypothesis ...." (p. 314, translated by
the authors).

3.2. Meaning theory

In a study by Judson and Cofer (1956), subjects were confronted
with "Four Word Problems." These problems consisted of four
words, three of them being related and the one remaining not.
The subjects' task was to select the one word not related to
the others. Actually, the members of each four word set could
be grouped in two, uncorrelated ways (e.g. add-subtract-multi-
ply-increase).

One of the variables that Judson and Cofer manipulated was the
serial position of the critical item; two possible orders of
the above mentioned example were as follows: 1) add-subtract-
multiply-increase, and 2) add-increase-multiply-subtract. The
experiment was conducted on the basis of the hypothesis that
problem solving is a function of the priority of the subjects'
response systems. In fact, as expected, the order of presentation had strong effects. For word order 1), for example, 26.5%
of subjects excluded "subtract", while 70.4% excluded "increase".
Similarly, for word order 2), "subtract" was excluded by 62% of
the subjects, whereas 30.7% excluded the word "increase".

Bransford and Johnson (1972) played the following tape recording to their subjects:

"The procedure is actually quite simple. First you arrange
things into different groups depending on their make-up. Of
course, one pile may be sufficient depending on how much there
is to do. If you have to go somewhere else due to lack of facilities that is the next step, otherwise you are pretty well set.
It is important not to overdo any particular endeavor. That is,
it is better to do too few things at once than too many. In the
short run this may not seem important, but complications from
doing too many can easily arise. A mistake can be expensive as
well. The manipulation of the appropriate mechanisms should be
self-explanatory and we need not dwell on it here. At first the
whole procedure will seem complicated. Soon, however, it will
become just another facet of life. It is difficult to foresee
any end to the necessity for this task in the immediate future,
but then one can never tell." (from Bransford & Johnson, 1972,
p. 722).

After having heard this passage, subjects had to make a scale rating as to its intelligibility and then recall as much of its content as possible. The major findings were that subjects knowing the passage's title, "Washing Clothes", before listening to the tape recording rated it as more intelligible and recalled its contents better than subjects who were not acquainted with the title.

In this case, the title obviously helps the subjects to classify the text with reference to past experience. Subjects construct what Bransford and Johnson call "semantic products", these being a joint function of the incoming information and the past experience.

Mayer (1977) has referred to this sort of analysis, as well as the earlier ideas of Bartlett (1932) and Gestalt psychology upon which it is based as "meaning" theory. According to meaning theory, a main problem for the subject in processing new information is to figure out which set of past experiences the new data should be related to in order to become comprehensible. Bartlett (1932), in referring to this process states, "... it is legitimate to say that all the cognitive processes which have been considered, from perceiving to thinking, are ways in which some fundamental 'effort after meaning' seeks expression" (p. 227).

Meaning theorists distinguish between two types of knowledge gotten from experience: "meaningful" and "rote" knowledge (Ausubel, 1968) or, alternatively, "propositional" and "algorithmic" knowledge (Greeno, 1973). Newly received information can be assimilated to cognitive structures of either of these two types. The Bransford and Johnson (1972) experiment demonstrates this point, the group knowing the title beforehand being able to meaningfully integrate the text into their cognitive system by addressing the appropriate categories found from past experience, while the second group was limited to using the less edifying, rote structures. It is interesting to know that a third group learning the title *after* having heard the story showed recall and clearness data no better than those of the group that did not receive the title at all. To be effective, cognitive structures probably have to be activated during the actual processing of the information and not after the information has already been incorporated into a different structure (see also Mayer, 1975; Bransford & McCarrell, 1974).

Early experiments by Dailey (1952, discussed above) and Kastenbaum (1951) touch upon this issue as well. Dailey investigated whether precocious inferences decrease subjects' understanding of subsequently received information by operating on specific aspects or by operating quite generally. The findings show that the precocious inferences made on the basis of the stimulus person's autobiography had a biasing influence on the way all other information was subsequently assimilated.

Kastenbaum's (1951) subjects listened to three tape recordings of telephone conversations, the voices being varied so as to sound either warm, cold or neutral. In one condition the subjects were told that the conversations involved three different persons and that their task was to note their impression of each. They were later told, however, that the conversations actually all involved the same person, and they were asked to give a detailed description of this person. This new description turned out to be rather difficult to render. Another experimental group, being told from the outset that the different tape recordings all involved the same person, were able to give the description without problem. Stotland and Canon (1972) interpret Kastenbaum's findings as follows: "Somehow the three schemata formed by the first group had independent coherences, a kind of life of their own that could not be simply abolished by fiat. The schemata were almost reifications, with respondents reacting as if they were real objects or entities" (p. 101). It becomes evident that this interpretation is quite similar to the mechanism of autonomy postulated by Ross, Lepper and Hubbard (1975) in order to explain the perseverance of hypotheses. As these studies show, the "after the fact" provision of appropriate contexts (or "meaning") has virtually no effect on how information gets registered in the cognitive system. Complementing this, the studies by Valins (1974) and Ross, Lepper and Hubbard (1975) show that the posterior withdrawal of "meaning" is equally impactless. Thus, it may be supposed that these findings reveal two sides of the same coin. In both cases, subjects make use of subjective hypotheses, or, in other words, the initially presented information gets assimilated to pre-existent cognitive structures (either rote or meaningful). These hypotheses create interpretive frameworks that are extremely resistant to subsequent modification.

3.2.1. Mechanism of consistency

Some different suggestions as to the integration of new information to already existent cognitive structures are presented by Singer (1968). Referring to experiments on information processing schemata (e.g. De Soto & Kuethe, 1959; De Soto, 1960; Zajonc, 1960; Zajonc & Burnstein, 1965), Singer maintains that besides a consistency mechanism that reduces tension within the person's cognitive system, there is a second, similar mechanism independent of the first that structures incoming data so that the person's cognitive system remains consistent. Since the limitations in a person's information processing capacity requires the continual simplification of incoming information, Singer regards this mechanism as being indispensible and feels that it operates in all cases so long as the discrepancy between the mechanism's basic rules of processing and the actual state of nature turns out to be not too large.

Grabitz and Grabitz-Gniech (1972b) hypothesized that simplifications in information evaluation using the above mentioned mechanism are reinforcing and, as a consequence, should become more and more frequent as the information processing progresses. The experiment was arranged so that subjects had to repeatedly revise - during three experimental phases - the probability of mutually exclusive, alternative hypotheses in response to

sequentially given information and finally decide upon one
alternative. Subjects did not receive any feedback as to the
correct solution. The prediction was that Inertia Effects due
to simplification would increase during the experiment's
successive stages. It was found, as predicted, that the inertia
effect increased significantly during the experimental stages
and that this increment was due to a progressively growing
underestimation of inconsistent information. The evaluation of
supporting information on the other hand, remained nearly constant. A follow-up study by Grabitz and Klump (1973) examined
whether the increment in the Inertia Effect occurs when feedback concerning objective decision criteria are available. The
subjects' were to perform six, sequentially given decision
tasks, the first and last task consisting of the very same
structure. There were two experimental conditions differing as
to whether subjects were or were not provided with feedback
concerning the objective probabilities after each probability
revision. The findings indicate that, as was expected, the
opportunity to examine and correct the subjective information
evaluation by means of an objective criterion can prevent the
increasing use of the consistency mechanism.

3.3.   Diagnosis Problems and "personal causation"

3.3.1. Personal causation

In discussing the concept of "motivation", De Charms (1968)
points to the inadequacy of simple analyses of human behavior
in terms of specific motives, corresponding goals and the subsequent satisfaction upon goal attainment. The author firmly
believes that the ways and means that people have of working
towards goals are more important for the understanding of human
motivation than is the nature of the goal themselves. De Charms
assumes that the individual's effort towards "personal causation" is the primary motivational element in the process of
reaching one's goal. This entails a general tendency on the part

of the individual to be the source of his actions, to be a
causal agent, to be effective in causing any modifications of
his environment, to be the real source of his/her own behavior,
etc. As a part of personal knowledge (Polanyi, 1958), "personal
causation" is a learned tendency for the person to appear - to
himself at least - as a causally effective individual (De
Charms & Shea, 1967; Mischel, 1969; Moore, 1970).

"Personal causation" cannot itself be considered as a motive
but rather interacts with motives to determine how a person
goes about realizing his/her goals in any particular situation.
Thus, the striving for own actions and personal causation can
manifest itself within all motivational contexts. According to
De Charms, the individual's striving for "personal causation"
results in his continuous struggle with constraints and restrictions posed by external forces. According to his success or
failure in the struggle, the individuals feel either like an
"Origin" or a "Pawn". An "Origin" is a person who believes his/
her behavior is caused by his/her own intentions. A "Pawn" on
the other hand, is a person, who believes his/her behavior is
caused by external forces outside of his/her control. In this
connection, Alderman (1976) found that the modification of
situations (freedom vs. constraint) has more impact on the feeling of "Origin/Pawn" than subject's disposition.

Sherrod, Hage, Halpern and Moore (1977) varied the degree to
which their subjects had control over the starting or stopping
of a disturbing background noise. Sherrod et al. found that
increasing control resulted in decreasing error rates in a
proof reading task and, afterwards, in increased tolerance of
frustration in dealing with an insoluble puzzle.

Assuming with De Charms that the individual's behavioral tendencies are dominated by a striving for "personal causation",
the question arises as to what influence personal causation has
in diagnosis situations. This question may be subdivided as
follows: a) what are the behavioral expectations in diagnosis
situations? b) in what way does the individual realize his

behavioral tendencies in these situations? c) what other variables affect behavior in these situations? (Grabitz & Haisch,
1976).

3.3.2. Behavioral expectations in diagnosis situation

The normative expectations for behavior in diagnostic situations are dominated by the demand for a correct diagnosis. The
individual's task is to classify and/or to evaluate the incoming data with the aim of ultimately arriving at one of the
alternative solutions, this procedure being carried out "objectively", making use of whatever criterion or previous experiences seem applicable. The person is expected to behave as a
passive and faithful recorder, any modifications of his cognitive set (e.g. any modifications of suppositions concerning
the veracity of probable diagnoses) being solely a function of
the incoming data. Not only the result - i.e. the diagnosis -
but also the ways and means of arriving at this outcome are
supposed due to factors external to the individual.

3.3.3. The realizations of behavioral tendencies

In dealing with the demands inherent in diagnostic situations,
the person should, in De Charms terms, feel himself a "Pawn".
On the other hand, the person should deviate from the situational demands in so far as they interfere with his or her
striving for "personal causation." If the person's behavior
primarily consists, as we suggested above, of establishing ways
and means for arriving at a definite diagnosis, then a specific
problem arises due to the fact that the goal pursued in diagnosis situations is an abstract one; namely, to determine the
actual state of nature by passively responding to the situational demands. Faced with this problem, the person establishes
his/her own goal by selecting one of the possible alternative
states of reality as an hypothesis. It is interesting in this
connection to consider an explanation that Pruitt (1961) gives,

on the basis of his subjects' comments, concerning the fact
that modifying a decision requires more information than making
a decision. Pruitt says, "... we might conclude that people
will require more information before changing a decision than
before making one because of an impatience in the latter case
to begin working toward goals" p. 439).

The adoption of probable solutions as hypotheses has been proposed by earlier theoretical approaches; for example, in the
Non-Continuity Theory of concept-learning (Tolman & Krechevsky,
1932; Kendler & D'Amato, 1955; Kendler & Kendler, 1962, 1975;
Levine, 1966), the problem solver being characterized - contrary to purely associational explanations - as an active information processor who plays the part of an hypothesis tester. In
seeking a solution, the problem solver will adopt different
hypotheses, test their implications, and reject whichever ones
lead to false inferences or classifications. This suggestion
probably originates with the feedback procedure normally used
in concept learning experiments that allows subjects to definitely falsify any erroneous hypotheses. In case of partial or
complete lack of feedback, however, other kinds of behavior
become evident (Levine, 1966; Kozielecki, 1961, 1964).

In testing hypotheses against subsequently received data, the
person is once again in a passive role, though in relation to
an actively chosen alternative. Indeed, the striving towards
personal causation in such instances seems limited to the
selecting of hypotheses to test; whether the hypotheses are
maintained or not depends, however, upon factors outside the
person's control.

It thus seems likely that people will not be so much drawn to
the role of "hypothesis tester" as they are to the one of "data
tester"; rather than testing the veracity of their hypotheses
against the incoming data, they should prefer testing the
data's compatibility with their favored hypotheses, rejecting
whenever possible those data that prove incompatible.

3.3.4. Behavioral tendencies and external factors

It has already been mentioned that the evaluation of information in light of a selected hypothesis is a characteristic behavioral feature in diagnosis problems. This selectivity in evaluation, however, is not the only factor operant, since people often do encounter evidence that violates their favored hypotheses and result in their rejection. The individual can thus be seen as being in a continual struggle against the environment (cf. De Charms, 1968), his/her actual behavior being a joint product of his/her own behavioral tendencies and external factors.

In a series of experiments, Katz, Cole and Lowery (1969) investigated the factors that contribute to the low levels of agreement in clinicians' diagnoses. They were interested in whether this lack of agreement is due to differences in the manner of physically perceiving patients or whether it is due to different ways of classifying patients for whom there was, otherwise, agreement concerning symptoms and behavior. Katz et al. presented their clinician-subjects with standardized video-taped interviews and found that they often diagnosed completely different symptom patterns.

In another experiment, Katz et al. presented a patient's interview to skilled psychiatrists whom they asked to indicate the symptomology, the psychiatrists being divided into two groups according to whether they diagnosed the patient as "schizophrenic" or "psychoneurotic". Afterwards, the symptoms observed by each group were contrasted. The authors found that the set of symptoms discovered by the two groups of psychiatrists were quite similar. Referring to these and other findings, Jones (1977) inclines to the view that clinicians obviously discover different symptoms in the medical examination of one and the same patient and, furthermore, diagnose quite different states even when regarding one and the same set of symptoms.

3.3.4.1. Reliability of information

If different clinicians, or a single clinician at different
times, discover different symptoms watching a patient's behavior on video tape, there can be little that is objective and/or
reliable in the way that these symptoms are perceived or measured. This deficiency in objectivity and reliability can occur in
different ways; e.g. the video tape may be too short and the
behaviors or statements recorded may be unrepresentative or invalid, thus making it difficult to identify the relevant cues.
Such low reliability can affect both the ascribing of symptoms
and judgments concerning their strength.

Applying this reasoning to the view that actual behavior in
diagnosis situations is a joint function of the individuals'
own behavioral tendencies and the external conditions, and keeping in mind that incoming information is one part of the external conditions, it may be concluded that the influence of
the person's behavioral tendencies will increase with decreasing reliability of the available data.

In cases of low reliability, the actual state underlying any
received piece of information is, by definition, not definitely
ascertainable. Depending upon the information's correlation
with the actual state of reality, this unascertainability may
have different consequences. Considering two possible states of
reality, A and B, a single aspect of reality, M, and two of its
possible manifestations, x and y, we can distinguish two cases:
1) A possible confusion of x and y due to a low reliability
concerning M has no effect on the indication of A and B; i.e.
irrespective of whether x or y is taken as the actual state of
M, A (or B) will be diagnosed. 2) A confusion of x and y
affects the indication of A and B, so that direction of the
diagnostic step depends on whether x or y is taken as the
actual state of M. In this second case, the low reliability of
information concerning M affects the subjective probabilities
assigned to A or B. This case will be termed *"interpretability*

of alternatives" or "interpretability".

3.3.4.2. Validity of information

Several different causes could lead a group of clinicians to give different diagnoses for the same set of symptoms. For example, the symptoms may be common to two illnesses, A and B, and thus provide no valid basis for distinguishing between them. Another possibility is that the two states themselves may not be exactly defined, so that certain symptoms are only occasionally connected with the state in question. This would result in a reduction of the symptom's validity (Tversky & Kahneman, 1977).

As already mentioned above, people in diagnosis situations intending to maintain personal causation have to adopt one of the potentially correct states as a hypothesis. This procedure, however, turns out to be impracticable when the possible alternative states are indefinitely defined. With decreasing definiteness, the basis of the diagnosis problem as well as the person's basis for striving for "personal causation" in the actual situation diminishes. In other words, the impact of the person's behavioral tendencies on his/her actual behavior in diagnosis situations diminishes the data's decreasing validity.

3.3.4.3. Measuring the effects of deficient reliability and validity

Though reliability and validity both seem rather closely connected to available information, they do not have the same implications for the individual's striving for "personal causation." If the states of reality to be decided upon defy any definition (i.e. if the symptoms that they generate are of low validity), the decision situation provides no basis for the individual's striving to exert influence. If the symptoms are valid, however, the influence of the person's striving toward

personal causation will be limited to the extent that the data
that he/she receive are reliable.

Nevertheless, the effects of both variables can be measured by
the same instrument since it is of little importance in diagnosis situations whether the behavior results from an absence
of motivational factors or simply the presence of situational
features that block the motivational factors from having their
effects.

3.3.5.   Experimental studies

3.3.5.1. Reliability, validity and interpretability of
alternatives

In an experiment conducted by Haisch and Grabitz (1979), the
solution process in diagnosis problems was examined as a function of the reliability of information and the clearness with
which the alternative states were characterized. The ideas
discussed above provided the basis for the following predictions: 1) The person's behavioral tendencies will become more
manifest with decreasing reliability of information; the information evaluation in support of the person's favorite hypothesis (Hypothesis Effect) should increase with decreasing informational reliability, as the person, for example, assigns lower
weights to disproving information (Inertia Effect) or reinter-
prets disproving information in a way that makes it appear neutral or even supportive; and 2) The basis for forming behavio-
al tendencies will decline as the alternative solutions become
less clearly delineated; the Hypothesis Effect, the Inertia
Effect and the tendency to reinterpret should thus decrease
with the declining clearness of alternative solutions.

As in the above mentioned studies of Pitz, Downing and Reinhold
(1967), Geller and Pitz (1969), Grabitz (1971) and Grabitz and
Haisch (1972), the present experiments were run using paradigm
in which subjects had to revise subjective probabilities.

Similar to the Grabitz and Haisch study (1972), the construction of diagnosis problems was affected by a combined "bookbag-
and-pokerchip" - and "recognition-test" - paradigm. In the
former, two (or more) possible states are created by, for example, having two different contents of an urn, the subjects'
task being to decide step by step which content he has before
him by taking (and returning) single elements, giving his revised diagnosis after each such sampling.

Haisch and Grabitz linked this paradigm to a "recognition-test"
paradigm by using stimulus patterns as "urn elements", these
patterns being square scanning-patterns in standardized sheets
of paper, each divided into 12 cells with either three or four
black points scattered about the cells irregularly. In addition
to being differentiable by number of points, the patterns also
differed in having either been presented during a preceding
presentation phase or being new. Subjects had before them a
chart indicating the four categories that resulted from combining the symptoms "three points/four points" and "old/new", as
well as the probability distribution for the four categories
under the two possible solutions A, B. In all experimental conditions, the probability distributions were such that, depending on the subjects' recognition judgment, either solution A or
B was favored. In addition, the distributions were balanced
over "three points/four points" in order to equalize any response tendencies in the recognition judgments.

In the beginning of the experimental session, subjects were
acquainted with the sequential revision of subjective probabilities in favor of one or another possible solution by detailed
instructions. In the following presentation phase, subjects had
to learn 20 (or 40 in the case of reduced reliability) different patterns (50% three-point-patterns/50% four-point). The
sequences of patterns was arranged so that no more than two
events in a row supported the same alternative, though those
events in the.first and the last part of the test sequence did
favor a single solution. Subjects' first task in information

evaluation during the exposure sequence was to identify, for
each pattern, whether or not they had seen it before, this task,
of course, also requiring that they discriminate for themselves
whether the pattern was of three or four dots. Based on the
relative frequency of events occurring in each category under
solution A or B, subjects had to revise the subjective probabilities concerning solutions A or B. Subjects were instructed
to process no less than 10 pieces of information and to not
decide upon a final judgment until having assessed the subjective probability of one alternative to be .90. As already mentioned, the reliability of information was manipulated by varying the number of patterns included in the presentation sequences (20 or 40). The clarity of the alternative solutions was
manipulated by varying whether there was a definite and fixed
linkage between the information categories and the probability
distributions representing A and B (high clarity) or whether
this linkage was changed by the experimenter prior to each
event's occurrence (low clarity).

In order to examine the predictions concerning the Hypothesis
Effect, the logarithmic subjective Likelihood Ratio (SLLR) was
computed with the subjective probabilities from the beginning
and end of a problems' test sequence. This index indicates the
diagnostic weight ascribed to any information in the sequence
and reflects not only the subject's tendency to assign different weights to supporting and disproving information but also
the tendency to reinterpret the information in light of the
favored hypothesis. For measuring Conservatism and the Inertia
Effect, the SLLR-values were compared to the log of the objective diagnostic value (OLLR) calculated according to Bayes
theorem, thus giving the ratio, SLLR/OLLR. Known as "Accuracy
Ratio" (AR) (Peterson, Schneider & Miller, 1965), this value
was converted to a logarithmic form (log AR) in order to guarantee symmetry with respect to over or underestimations. Finally,
reinterpretations were measured by comparing the percentage of
supporting information that was recognized correctly and the

percentage of disproving information not correctly recognized, (i.e. processed as supporting information).

The results partially supported prediction 1; The Hypothesis Effect turned out to become stronger with decreasing information reliability. In addition, the percentage of reinterpretations in case of disproving information was also found to increase with decreasing reliability. The Inertia Effect however, did not show any variations with reliability.

Prediction 2, on the other hand, was not confirmed by the present results. The Hypothesis Effect as well as the percentage of correct identification for supporting information turned out to be more considerable when the alternative solutions were specified with low clarity than when they were specified with high clarity. Another study by Grabitz and Haisch (1979) examined the effects of information reliability and the interpretability of alternatives on the information evaluation. The prediction concerning reliability was analogous to the one mentioned above, the Inertia Effect and the probability of reinterpretations increasing with decreasing reliability. The interpretability of alternatives was thought to promote reinterpretations, thus serving as a suitable basis for an effective data testing. In the "interpretability" condition, reinterpretations are therefore predicted to appear more frequently than in the "no interpretability" control group. The Inertia Effect, on the other hand, was predicted to be stronger under the "no interpretability" condition.

The experimental paradigm was essentially the same as above. "Interpretability" was manipulated by linking the information categories to probability distributions representing A and B. In case of "interpretability", the subject's judgment as to "seen" or "not yet seen" decided whether the information in question supported solution A or B. Under "no interpretability", the subject's judgment implied nothing about the information's supporting or disproving character. Table 1 (see page 273) supplies a schedule for the "interpretability/ no interpreta-

Information Categories	Interpretability				No Interpretability			
Number of dots	4	3	3	4	4	4	3	3
Subject's judgment	seen	not seen	seen	not seen	seen	not seen	seen	not seen
Available Solutions A	.35	.30	.25	.20	.35	.30	.25	.20
B	.20	.25	.30	.35	.20	.25	.30	.35
Information supports solution	A	A	B	B	A	A	B	B

Table 1. Schedule of Interpretability vs. No Interpretability

bility" conditions within the experimental paradigm.

The results indicate that the Inertia Effect did not increase with decreasing informational reliability while the tendency to reinterpret disproving information did. These results basically correspond to those of the study just mentioned. The results were more supportive, however, of the predictions concerning interpretability. With regard to the Inertia Effect, more weight was assigned to supporting information in the "no inter-pretability" condition than in the "interpretability" one, whereas there were no differences between these conditions in the weights assigned to disproving information. As for reinter-pretation, the probability of correct recognition of supporting information as well as an incorrect recognition of disproving information was higher in the "interpretability" condition. Interpretability thus results in subjects encountering fewer disproving instances and thereby enables them to verify their favored hypotheses without having to rely on the Inertia Effect.

This effect of interpretability had already been found in a study by Grabitz, Haisch and Kozielecki (1974). This study also manipulated the clarity with which the alternative solutions were characterized and yielded results different from those re-ported above, the Inertia Effect decreasing under "low clarity", this decrease being stronger in the "no interpretability" con-dition than in the "interpretability" one.

A study conducted by Bruner, Postman and Rodrigues (1951) can also be regarded as a test of the effects of informational re-liability. Bruner et al. tested the hypothesis that the proba-bility of confirming an initially established supposition in-creases as the amount of suitable information decreases. Bruner et al.'s subjects were to match the color of a stimulus-patch using a variable color-mixer. Two classes of stimuli were pre-sented, one consisting of ovaloid shapes corresponding to such familiar objects as a tomato, tangerine, lemon or neutral oval, the other consisting of familiar, elongated-ellipsoid objects such as a lobster claw, carrot, banana and neutral elongated

ellipse. These objects were cut from neutral grey paper, placed
on a blue-green background and covered by finely ground glass.
Thus, the colors that subjects had to match were actually of an
indefinite brownish-orange hue.

Subjects were assigned to four experimental conditions: The
"un-informed" group learned the name of each object before
selecting its color on the color-mixer; the "informed" group
was instructed as to the 'illusory quality' of the colors before them; the "stable color" group received appropriately
colored stimulus forms rather than ones that were colored
neutrally; the "optimal matching" condition used real colors
for the stimulus-patches and allowed subjects to make simultaneous (instead of successive) comparisons in arriving at their
color matches.

The results show first of all, that subjects' initial hypotheses affected their color judgments, so that an object identified
as a tomato was matched redder than other, same color objects
identified as lemons. Secondly, a subject's initial hypothesis
had the more influence the lower the input of adequate information, the colors matched to the different forms differing most
in the "uninformed" group and least in the "optimal matching"
group.

Quite similar results were yielded by a study of Haisch,
Grabitz and Prester (1979). Haisch et al. manipulated interpretability and allowed subjects to mention and reject hypotheses
concerning the correct solution at any time during the information evaluation. It was found that hypotheses developed under
high interpretability conditions were maintained more often
than under low interpretability, although this difference did
not prove significant for all the diagnoses problems used.
Altogether, in case of interpretability, subjects developed
hypotheses more frequently than under "no interpretability". In
addition, the Hypothesis Effect turned out to be stronger in
case of "interpretability" than in case of "no interpretability",
and reinterpretations also were found to be more frequent under

"interpretability", especially when an hypothesis had been adopted.

3.3.5.2. Preference for situations

The person's striving for "personal causation" may not be equally realized in all situations. Subjects who are continually confronted with situations that do not allow any personal influence end up feeling as "Pawns" to use De Charms' (1968) term. Striving for "personal causation" must therefore entail the attempt to avoid any situation that frustrates the person in this respect.

Haisch, Grabitz and Trommsdorff (1975) examined this question by having subjects decide between two information processing problems, one with interpretability of alternatives and the other without. The authors hypothesis that subjects would prefer interpretable problems was not, however, confirmed.

3.3.5.3. Reliability and "multiple cue learning"

An experiment by Ebert, Grabitz and Haisch (1977) used a multiple cue learning paradigm to study how informational reliability affects subjects' tendency to confirm their subjective hypotheses. Subject's task was to assess a person's qualification for a certain activity by means of some "experts' evaluations". In a preliminary learning phase, subjects were acquainted with the correlation between the cues (experts' evaluations) and the criterion variable (qualification vs. missing qualification) by being given correct feedback after each estimation. The reliability of the cues was signalled by their green-blue color, the hues associated with the low reliability cues being less distinct. The results show that low cue reliability promotes reinterpretations, the color of the low reliability cues often being erroneously identified so as to confirm the subject's initial diagnosis.

3.3.5.4. Supervision by an observer

As we have seen, actual behavior in diagnosis situations is a
joint function of the individual's behavioral tendencies and
external factors, the latter increasing in their importance
to the degree that the incoming information proves reliable.
Other factors, however, may also account for limitations in the
relative influence of the individual's behavioral tendencies. A
study of Grabitz, Haisch and Wolfshörndl (1979) was devoted to
the controlling influence of a competent observer. It was
hypothesized that the external control provided by an observer
would reduce - by exerting social pressure - the person's influence on the solution process. Using the "bookbag and poker-
chip" paradigm described above, the experiment manipulated the
clarity with which the alternatives were specified as well as
whether an observer was present or not. The specific predictions were that: 1) Deviations from an objective evaluation of
information would diminish with decreasing clarity of alternatives and 2) the presence of a competent observer would give
rise to objective information evaluations, especially in the
case of clearly specified alternatives.

Prediction (1) was not confirmed by the present results, the
Inertia Effect being more distinct in the case of low clarity.
As for reinterpretations, prediction (1) was only confirmed
with respect to objectively disproving information, this being
less prone to reinterpretation in the low clarity condition.
The presence of an observer did result, as predicted (2), in
the decrease of the Inertia Effect when the alternatives were
clearly specified, while it did not have an effect under low
clarity conditions. The percentage of reinterpretations was not
affected by the presence or absence of an observer.

4. Final remarks

The preceding statements as to the development, maintenance and
effects of subjective hypotheses in diagnosis problems give
reason to conclude that the individual does not proceed rationally in problem solving situations. Referring to the discussed
theoretical explanations for this behavior, especially to the
ideas developed on the basis of conceptions by De Charms (1968),
the individual does not seem to be striving for correct results
in the problem solving process, this despite the fact that
people seem to do an adequate job solving the problems that
they encounter in their everyday lives. On the basis of our
preceding discussion, we might offer the following reasons for
Man's inadequacy as a problem solver.

1) In some complex problems, the actual veracity of any diagnosed solution may not be examined. This may be due to the fact
that a) the available information is of low reliability and
therefore open to interpretations, b) lack of clarity in the
specification of alternatives leads to a reduction in the validity of information, c) the incorrect solutions do not have
immediate negative consequences, d) the negative consequences
that do occur can be attributed to factors other than the incorrect decision, or e) the effects of alternative solutions
are not at the person's disposal. Each of these possibilities
decrease the likelihood of the person's favored solution being
falsified by the facts.

2) Many everyday problems represent routine diagnoses in which
individual's subjective hypotheses will prove right with some
probability on account of the problem solvers previous experiences with the effects resulting from incorrect solutions.

3) In case of data consistently supporting one solution, the
problem solver is quite likely to set up the correct hypothesis.
In such instances, a person deciding on *any* hypothesis and
arriving at a solution on the basis of only few data will be
regarded (by both himself and others) as energetic and success-

ful, irregardless of the outcome.

4) Situations providing reliable and relatively consistent bodies of data do not comply with the individual's striving for "personal causation". Instead of this, they make possible a larger number of correct solutions that may then be ascribed (by both the problem solvers and others) to problem solver's competence, a factor regarded by some authors (e.g. White, 1959; Deci, 1975) as a central motive of human behavior.

Considering all these factors, the comparatively favorable impression that one has of the problem solver in diagnosis situations seem due more to his/her actual or supposed success than to the methods he/she uses for reaching this goal.

Chapter 9 Cognitive Dissonance: Experiments and Theory

D. Frey, M. Irle, V. Möntmann, M. Kumpf,
R. Ochsmann and C. Sauer

1. General introduction

The theory of cognitive dissonance is one of the most controversial theories in social psychology. One of the reasons for
this may be that many of the theory's predictions contradict
common sense. In any case, no social psychological theory has
initiated more empirical research than dissonance theory has
during the last 20 years. Möntmann and E. Irle (1978) document
that there have so far been more than 800 publications dealing
with dissonance theory, the bulk of these coming in the 60's
and the early 70's.

Dissonance research has touched on an extremely wide range of
different behaviors: reactions after rewards and punishments,
changes in attractiveness of alternatives after decisions, pre-
and post-decisional information-seeking and avoidance, the consequences of idle efforts, reactions to expectancy-discrepant
events, the impact of low credibility communicators on attitudes, helping behavior, and all kinds of group processes.

The aim of this project was to test some selected aspects of
dissonance theory, our more important findings being presented
below. We begin with a discussion of forced compliance (2.1.)
and then go on to cover a) the effects of receiving attitude-
or belief-discrepant information (2.2.), b) postdecisional
attitude change (2.3.1.) and c) postdecisional information
seeking (2.3.2.). In closing, we briefly outline a revised
version of dissonance theory that derives from our research
findings (3. and 4.).

2. Empirical evidence concerning dissonance theory

In what follows we do not discuss the basic assumptions of
dissonance theory, these being more than amply covered in a
number of recent German and American publications (cf. Frey,
1978a, 1978b, 1979a, 1981a; Irle & Möntmann, 1978; Wicklund &
Brehm, 1976; etc.). It should only be remembered that dissonance exists when two cognitions are incompatible with each
other, and that dissonance is a negative drive state that
prompts behaviors aimed at dissonance reduction. The stronger
cognitive dissonance, the stronger the pressure to reduce the
the dissonance; the way dissonance is reduced depends, however,
on the resistance to change of the cognitions involved.

Festinger (1957) indicates four basic paradigms for testing
dissonance theory: "forced-compliance", "confrontation with
discrepant information","postdecisional dissonance" and "selective exposure to information after decisions." During the
period 1968 - 1978, we carried out research in each of these
fields, the results of which are separately reported in the
following four sections.

2.1.Forced compliance

Forced compliance is the topic that has stimulated the greatest number of dissonance studies. Dissonance theory predicts
an inverse relation between the amount of reward and attitude
change following counter-attitudinal behavior. According to
dissonance theory, persons who are induced to behave contrary
to the way they think or feel will be more favorable towards
their actions the *less* they are rewarded for performing them.
This paradoxical prediction can be explained as follows: persons have less justification for behaving as they did following a small reward than following a large one and, therefore,
experience a greater degree of dissonance. Persons can, however, reduce this dissonance by changing their attitudes to

fall more in line with their behavior; that is, by becoming more favorable towards the counter-attitudinal act. Other theories - for example incentive theory (Elms, 1967) or affective-cognitive consistency theory (Rosenberg, 1965) - make predictions contrary to those of dissonance theory, maintaining that there is a positive relationship between reward and attitude change. Our own research in this paradigm was intended to check whether, and under what specific conditions, the predictions of dissonance theory are born out.

2.1.1. Reward level, freedom of decision, commitment, actual vs. anticipated behavior

The variables most frequently tested in the forced compliance paradigm have been level of reward, freedom of decision, and commitment, these variables playing a key role in attempts at determining the conditions under which dissonance predictions concerning the negative incentive effect do - and do not - hold. For example, Frey and Irle (1972) did an experiment in which subjects were asked to write a counter-attitudinal essay arguing that the voting age should not be reduced from 21 to 18. For this they were promised either 1 or 8 DM. Since the essay was supposedly going to be used by experts preparing a government report, subjects should have anticipated some potential negative consequences for their behavior, a necessary pre-condition for dissonance to occur (cf. Collins & Hoyt, 1972). The counter-attitudinal behavior was performed under either high or low choice, and the essay-writing was either public (subjects had to write their names in the essay) or anonymous (subjects did not have to sign their names).

Frey and Irle found that the dissonance prediction held only in high dissonance conditions; the low reward elicited greater attitude change only when subjects perceived that they were free to choose whether or not to perform the counter-attitudinal behavior and performed the behavior non-anonymously. When perceived freedom was low and the counter-attitudinal behavior

performed under conditions of anonymity, incentive theory
yielded the most accurate predictions.

In a later study, Frey (1975 a) found that, under high dissonance conditions, subjects need not actually perform the
counter-attitudinal behavior for the dissonance effect to occur. Rather, all that is necessary is that they make a "commitment" to behave counter-attitudinally. In this experiment, female subjects were asked to write counter-attitudinal essays
advocating a mandatory year of social service for females
equivalent to the draft for men. As in Frey and Irle (1972),
the anticipation of potential negative consequences was induced by telling subjects that the essays were to be used for
a government panel. Half of the subjects actually wrote the
essay, the other half only expected to write it. All subjects
were given high freedom of choice. Half of the subjects were
promised a high, the other half a low reward. It was found
that regardless of whether subjects actually wrote the essay
or were merely committed to writing it, the attitude toward
mandatory social service was more favorable under low than
under high reward. It is interesting to note, finally, that in
both the Frey and Irle and Frey experiments, the "quantity"
and "quality" of subjects' counter-attitudinal behavior (number of written words and the apparent conviction of the essay
writers) varied positively with reinforcement level. That changes in attitudes followed the reverse pattern suggests that,
contrary to both incentive and affective-cognitive consistency-
theories, the processes that mediate attitude change in forced
compliance settings are independent of what occurs during the
performing of the counter-attitudinal behavior itself.

2.1.2. Reward level and attitude discrepant vs. attitude-
    convergent behavior

One problem inherent in much of the forced compliance research
is that reward is often varied over just two levels, thus mak-

ing it impossible to test hypotheses concerning a curvilinear relation between reward level and attitude change (cf. Gerard, 1967). To remedy this, Frey, Irle, Kumpf, Ochsmann and Sauer (1979) performed an experiment in which reward was varied over five different levels (0, 3, 5, 8, 12 DM). While these authors did find dissonance effects for the low reward conditions (there was greater attitude change in the 0 than in the 3 DM condition), there were no dissonance effects found for the high rewards, the findings in the latter case conforming to what would be expected on the basis of incentive theory, there being more attitude change as the rewards increased. Frey et al. also investigated what influence the variations in reward level had on subjects' attitudes after *attitude-convergent* behavior and found that attitudes polarized (i.e. changed in the direction of the behavior) in a manner inversely correlated to reward level. While dissonance theory itself does not yield predictions for such situations, this last finding can be explained by Bem's (1965, 1966) attributional approach to dissonance phenomeny together with the assumption that the high rewards were "over-sufficient" and elicited uneasiness on the subjects' part (see also Frey 1979b, Schwarz, Frey & Kumpf 1979).

Besides attitude change, Frey et al. also measured changes in the perceived attractiveness of the experimental task and found that while the attractiveness of the attitude convergent task increased with reward level, that of the discrepant task followed a curvilinear (positive, non-monotonic) pattern, the task being judged most attractive in the intermediate reward conditions.

2.1.3. Financial gratification and deprivation, and time of information

According to dissonance theory, an important factor influencing the amount of dissonance is the timing of dissonance-arousing information, the resulting dissonance being greater when such information is received prior to the decision than when it is received afterwards.

Frey, Irle and Hochgürtel (1979) conducted another forced compliance study in which subjects performed a boring task and then received rewards that were either more than, less than, or equal to the amount they expected. The critical independent variable, however, was whether subjects were informed of the reward before or after having had performed the task. When payment information was given after task performance, task attractiveness increased with the amount of payment received. It seems reasonable to suppose that little dissonance was aroused in these latter conditions and that reinforcement effects predominated, greater rewards producing greater attraction to the task. When payment information was given prior to. the task, however, subjects judged the task most attractive when they were to be paid either more or less than they had expected; that is, there was a negative curvilinear relationship between payment and task attractiveness. In the decreased pay condition, task attractiveness was higher for pre-informed subjects than for subjects informed after the task, consistent with dissonance theory predictions. Frey et al. also asked their subjects to indicate how much money they thought was adequate as a reward for performing the task. It was found that the amount of payment believed to be adequate was greater under increased pay conditions than it was under either the same pay or decreased pay conditions. In the "before" condition, the amount of pay believed adequate increased directly with the level of pay actually received, whereas in the after-condition it was much greater when payment was either greater or less than that expected.

2.1.4. Attitude-discrepant behavior evoked by situational factors

In the "forced-compliance" paradigm it is generally the experimenter who uses his influence to induce the subject to behave counter-attitudinally. Kumpf (1978), however, performed
a study in which subjects were induced to behave passively in
the face of an emergency simply by the characteristics of the
experimental situation itself; i.e., without any direct verbal
influence from the experimenter. Kumpf found that, as predicted, subjects were later more likely to justify their passivity
when intervention on their part would have been possible than
when it was impossible. Kumpf also predicted that those subjects who, before the experiment, were the most convinced that
they would intervene would be the ones who later showed the
most justification of their passive behavior. This prediction
was not, however, borne out clearly in the results.

The effects of such dissonance in emergency settings can also
generalize to affect intervention behavior in subsequent emer-
gencies. Kumpf was able to show that subjects who remained
passive during a theft intervened in a later emergency significantly less often than did those subjects who had not been
previously faced with deciding whether or not to intervene in
an emergency situation.

The inducement of counter-attitudinal behavior by "non-per-
sonal" influences makes it easier to eliminate possible confounding factors like "demand compliance" (Wyer, 1974) or
"evaluation apprehension" (Rosenberg, 1965) from tests of
dissonance hypotheses. Such procedures should, therefore, be
taken into account whenever experiments on the effects of
counter-attitudinal behavior are being planned.

2.1.5. Conclusion

As already mentioned in the introduction, counter-attitudinal behavior is the area in dissonance theory which has stimulated the most research. Also most of the theoretical alternatives to dissonance theory - for example, self-perception theory, Nuttin's (1975) response-contagion theory or the impression management theory of Tedeschi et al. (1971) - focus more or less on the field of counter-attitudinal behavior. In general, our research in the field of forced compliance confirms the dissonance hypotheses. Our experiments show, however, that the negative linear relationship between amount of money and attitude change predicted by the original version of dissonance theory must be modified when excessive amounts of money are involved, attitude change increasing again in the latter conditions.

2.2. The response to dissonance-arousing information received from an external source

According to Festinger (1957), one can assume that dissonance exists whenever a person receives information that is inconsistent with his expectancy or self-esteem, the level of dissonance being higher the greater the discrepancy. Classical experiments on this issue have been performed by Deutsch and Solomon (1959), Johnson (1966) and Hamilton (1969) among others. Our own experiments on this topic all deal with cognitive reactions that occur when a subject receives unexpected or "belief-inconsistent" information from an external source.

2.2.1. Different amounts of positive and negative discrepant information

A typical paradigm was to have subjects work through an intelligence test and then give them fictitious results that deviated positively or negatively from their own self-evaluations. Irle and Krolage (1973) used this paradigm to demonstrate that the evaluation of a source of information (in this case, the intelligence test) varies positively with the favorability of the information received from it. Subjects who received scores lower than they expected devalued the validity of the test and rationalized their "poor performance" by reporting that they put low amounts of effort into their test responses, all the while maintaining their self-estimates of their intelligence. Studies by Frey and Kumpf (1973) and Fries, Frey and Pongratz (1977) replicated these findings, the latter demonstrating also that subjects receiving scores that are positively discrepant from their self-estimates a) report greater amounts of effort in completing the test, b) change their self-estimates to correspond more closely to the received results and c) evaluate the test more positively than do subjects who receive a negatively discrepant result. The three studies thus seem to show that subjects reduce the dissonance resulting from the positively or negatively discrepant test results by ascribing their cause to either externally (e.g., validity of the test) or internally variable factors (e.g., amount of effort) in the test situation.

2.2.2. Discrepant information and public vs. private results and reactions

In the experiments mentioned so far, subjects completed the dependent variables under conditions of complete anonymity. Frey (1975b), however, investigated subjects' responses to dissonance when their reactions are made in public. Frey's subjects again received fictitious, strongly or moderately negative test results concerning their intelligence, the results being in all cases received in the presence of the experimenter and the fellow subjects. The subjects were then asked to evaluate the intelligence test, the evaluations being made either publicly or anonymously. The design was thus a 2 x 2 factorial consisting of two independent variables - result discrepancy (strong vs. moderate) and evaluation setting (public vs. private).

The results show that the tendency to increasingly derogate
the intelligence test the more negatively discrepant the scores
occurs only when the test evaluations were made anonymously.
It thus seems that subjects who score poorly and who think
that others know about their poor scores do not apply dissonance-reduction methods that they assume are negatively sanctioned
by the audience.

Frey (1978a) continued this line of investigation by performing a similar experiment in which he varied the degree to
which subjects' test scores as well as their test evaluations
were accessible to other subjects. Frey found the greatest
amount of dissonance reduction - that is, the least favorable
test evaluations - when the test scores were public but the
test evaluations made anonymously. The least dissonance reduction (i.e., the most favorable test evaluation), on the other
hand, occurred when both the test scores and the test evaluations were "public".

Götz-Marchand, Götz and Irle (1974) used the same paradigm to
demonstrate that the extent of dissonance reduction depends
on the availability of the various dissonance-reduction mechanisms. The authors varied the ordering of the two main
dependent variables (subjects' evaluations of the test and
estimations of their own intelligence) in the post-test
sequence and found that items at the beginning of the questionnaire generally showed stronger dissonance effects than
those at the end. Subjects thus appear to have reduced all the
dissonance they experienced at the first opportunity that presented itself. One prerequisite for this effect, however, was
that the subjects had no prior knowledge of the questionnaire
contents; when subjects were completely informed of the questions they had to answer, these sequence effects disappeared.

2.2.3. Discrepant information, self-esteem and anxiety

A study by Kumpf and Götz-Marchand (1973) established that sub-

jects with high self-esteem reduce cognitive dissonance differently from those with low self-esteem. Kumpf and Götz-
Marchand's subjects were engaged couples who were given 'test
results' indicating that their chances to have a happy marriage
were somewhat middling and considerably lower than the subjects
themselves had expected: as predicted, derogation of the test
and positive distortion of the test result increased sharply
with increasing discrepancy, whereas attitudes towards the
test and evaluations of "the importance of being happily
married" were affected less. The authors also found, however,
that low self-esteem subjects devaluated the importance of
being happily married and derogated the test more than high
self-esteem subjects did.

2.2.4. Anticipation of discrepant information

Dissonant information need not actually be received in order
to affect cognitive change, the mere anticipation of a dissonant event being sufficient to trigger dissonance reduction.
In a field experiment by Sauer, Frey, Kumpf, Ochsmann and Irle
(1977) on the occasion of the provincial diet elections in
Northrhine-Westphalia and Lower Saxony, students were asked
which party they would vote for and which party or party-con-
stellation would win the election. The authors reasoned that
those persons who expected an opposition victory would be in
a dissonant frame of mind and, in order to reduce this dissonance, would tend to dismiss the elections' prognostic value
for national elections. The results supported this reasoning,
as did those from a similar study done by Frey, Götz and
Marchand (1972) before the provincial elections in Baden-
Württemberg.

2.2.5. Conclusions

This last set of experiments shows that many factors must be
considered when predicting reactions to discrepant information.

It was found, for example, that the "publicness" of the discrepant information and the subjects' reactions to it, the
order of presentation of dependent variables, and individual
differences all play a role in determining how subjects respond
in such cases.

2.3.   Postdecisional dissonance

2.3.1. "Postdecisional dissonance" and changes in attractive-
ness[1]

According to Festinger (1957), dissonance exists whenever a
person makes a decision, the positive aspect of the non-chosen
alternative and the negative aspect of the chosen alternative
being dissonance arousing. Dissonance theory predicts that in
such situations cognitive activity directed at reducing dissonance should result in the chosen alternative increasing in
attractiveness while the unchosen one decreases. There are
several experiments in the literature in which this effect is
tested (cf., for example, the classical experiment by Brehm,
1956).

An experiment by Irle, Grabitz-Gniech, Frey and Kumpf (1980)
introduced the variable of whether the decision alternative
was eliminated by the subjects themselves (by free choice) or
by another person (the experimenter). In addition, half the
subjects were told that the elimination was reversible, while
the others were told that it was final. Subjects' reactions
were measured at four different points in time after the alternative was eliminated.

As we have already seen, dissonance theory predicts that the
freely chosen alternative will increase in attractiveness
while the rejected alternative will decrease. The difference

---

[1] Ochsmann and Frey (1978) reviewed the most important studies
in this area from the German and American literature.

in attractiveness between chosen and non-chosen alternative
should, furthermore, increase with time following the decision
- at least in the case of irreversible decisions. For decisions that are reversible, the initial difference between
chosen and non-chosen alternatives should diminish with time.
The results of Irle, Grabitz-Gniech, Frey and Kumpf supported
these hypotheses.

With respect to the elimination of a choice alternative by a
third person, the reactance theory implies that the attractiveness of the eliminated alternative should increase - this
all the more so the greater the time lapse after elimination.
The data show that this effect only appears when the elimination is reversible; in the case of final elimination, the
attractiveness of both the eliminated and the available alternative decreases with increasing time. Interestingly, during
the past years there have not been many experiments further
testing this point.

2.3.2. "Postdecisional dissonance" and selective reception of information

Dissonance theory postulates that people experiencing dissonance as a result of a decision seek information that supports their decision and avoid information that contradicts it.
Freedman and Sears (1965) cast doubt on the validity of this
reasoning after having discerned a preference for dissonant
as opposed to consonant information in their experiments. Frey
(1981a) performed a series of experiments in an attempt to
specify the conditions under which selective information-seeking takes place. Frey's paradigm was to have subjects choose
one from among several decision alternatives and then choose
from information that supported or contradicted the chosen
alternative. The following independent variables were examined:
subjects' familiarity with supporting and contradicting items
of information, the information's refutability, degree of

decision freedom, the information's cost for the subjects, decision reversibility and the amount of cognitive dissonance. Frey's findings, grouped by dependent and independent variable, are the following (for an overview see Frey, 1980 a, 1981).

2.3.2.1. Results for information seeking

2.3.2.1.1. Familiarity with supporting and contradictory information

Two experiments (Frey, 1981, Exp. 6 and 7) were done to investigate this variable, both of which yielded the same result: subjects prefer the type of information with which they are least familiar. When subjects were equally familiar with both sorts of information, they showed a uniform preference for consonant information. A cognitive system that is stable can risk exposure to dissonant information in order to refute it, whereas one that is already weakened by dissonant information must seek out consonant information in order to bolster the decision. This accumulation of consonant items of information will only continue, of course, as long as the original decision or hypotheses is adhered to.

2.3.2.1.2. Degree of refutability of the arguments

Three experiments (Frey, 1980 a, Frey, 1981 a, Exp. 8-10) were carried out to test this variable. In all three, degree of refutability was operationalized, as in Lowin (1969), by varying the competence of the source of (both dissonant and consonant) information. When the competence of the source was low, the preference of consonant over dissonant information was lower than when the source's competence was high (difficult refutability). This effect can be explained as follows: dissonant information which is easily refutable is welcome since refuting is an effective strategy (far more effective

than simple avoidance) for reducing dissonance. In the case of
the highly competent source, on the other hand, the difficult-
to-refute dissonant information is threatening to the self
while gathering the corresponding consonant information represents an effective strategy towards dissonance reduction.

2.3.2.1.3. Degree of freedom of decision

Frey and Wicklund (1978) manipulated freedom of decision by
varying the extent to which subjects were free to choose
whether or not to perform a counter-attitudinal behavior. It
was found that subjects' tendency to seek out decision-consonant information varied positively with the extent to which
they had been free to make their own decision. Presumably, the
decision to behave counter-attitudinally aroused more dissonance in the complete freedom condition than in any of the
lower freedom conditions, thus driving the "complete freedom"
subjects to look more earnestly for decision-consonant information. This was the first experiment in which a link between
attitude discrepant behavior and selective search for information was established.

2.3.2.1.4. Costs of information

An experiment (Frey, 1980b) featuring this variable shows
that attaching a price lowers the amount of information seeking and raises subjects' relative preference for decision-
consonant information. The effect of cost on the absolute
level of information seeking was already demonstrated by Frey,
Kumpf, Raffée, Sauter and Silberer (1976) and is consistent
with the theoretical approach of Lanzetta (1963).

The effect concerning the preference for consonant information
bears an interesting parallel to those findings from the field
of sequential information processing that indicate that the
inertia-effect (i.e. the overevaluation of the diagnostic

value of the preferred alternative, and the underestimation of
that of the rejected alternative) is more pronounced when the
search for information is combined with costs than when the
information is free.

2.3.2.1.5. Decision reversibility

Two experiments (Frey, 1981a Exp. 9 and 16) were performed to
investigate this variable, each showing that there is a greater preference for consonant information following irreversible
decisions than there is following reversible ones. In both
types of decision situations, however, subjects were found to
prefer consonant to dissonant information. These findings are
consistent with both the original and the reformulated versions
of dissonance theory (see section 3 below); since, by definition, irréversible decisions cannot be changed, subjects will
experience greater dissonance and attempt to reduce it by ac-
cumulating information that supports their decision. In the
case of reversible decisions, on the other hand, subjects will
first of all experience less dissonance and, secondly, might
prefer to reduce this dissonance by changing rather than bol-
stering their original decision.

2.3.2.1.6. The magnitude of cognitive dissonance

Dissonance theory implies that the preference for consonant
information should increase as subjects experience greater
magnitudes of cognitive dissonance. If, however, the dissonance
is so high that it exceeds the resistance to change of the
cognitions concerned, the search for consonant information is
then reduced and, in the extreme case, subjects begin to look
for dissonant information. The curvilinear relationship comes
about because, beyond a certain dissonance level, it appears
more effective to the subject to revise his decision than to
continue the search for consonant information in order to bol-

ster the chosen alternative. The theory thus postulates an
inverted u-shaped relationship between the magnitude of cognitive dissonance and the selective search for consonant information.

In an extended replication of Festinger's classical experiment
(1957), Frey (1981a Exp. 17) found a curvilinear relationship
between the magnitude of dissonance (operationalized by the
amounts of gains and losses) and the intensity of selective
information seeking.

One precondition for this curvilinear relationship is that the
subjects feel that their original decision is reversible; that
is, cognitions concerning the decision must not have too high
a resistance to change. If decisions are irreversible, the
search for consonant information ought to increase with increasing dissonance (Irle, 1975). Frey (1981a Exp. 16) found
support for this derivation in another experiment. He had subjects rank-order fourteen books according to attractiveness
and then, according to experimental conditions, had them
either choose between the second and third, second and seventh
or the second and thirteenth alternative, it being assumed
that the amount of dissonance aroused by the choice would increase with the similarity in attractiveness of the two alternatives. Half the subjects were told that the decision was
reversible, while the rest were told that it was irreversible.
It was found that, as predicted, the tendency to selectively
search for consonant information either increased or decreased
with the similarity of decision alternatives (i.e. the magnitude of dissonance), depending on whether the decision was
irreversible or reversible, respectively. In the reversible
decision condition, however, the preference for dissonant information exceeded that for consonant information only when
dissonance was maximal, though Frey speculated that a similar
difference might have been obtained at the other end of the
spectrum if conditions with still lower dissonance had been
run.

2.3.2.2. Results concerning information avoidance

Dissonance theory postulates that, in addition to selectively searching for consonant information, people who experience dissonance try to avoid receiving further dissonant information. Our own research provides clear support for this prediction; in some experiments where subjects were asked which pieces of information they did *not* want to see, there was a significantly greater tendency to indicate dissonant as opposed to consonant information. Unlike selective information seeking, however, the magnitude of their avoidance did not vary as a function of any of the variables discussed above.[2] We explain these results as follows: though cognitive dissonance can indeed be reduced by the search for consonant information, the avoidance of dissonant information merely hinders a further increase in the already existing dissonance. Furthermore, the avoidance of *all* dissonant information would not be effective for the cognitive system because the subject can never exclude the possibility that some items of dissonant information might be useful for future decisions. That is, while subjects can actively reduce dissonance by buttressing "weak" cognitions with additional consonant information, the avoidance of further dissonant information serves only as a strategy for maintaining the status quo. Selective avoidance should therefore show less variation with dissonance level than selective searching does.

2.3.2.3. Results for perceived reliability of consonant and dissonant information

In some of the experiments (Frey, 1981a, Exp. 1, 3 and 6)

---

[2] In only one of the experiments was there a significant difference: subjects under the high dissonance conditions avoided dissonant information more than subjects under the low dissonance condition.

subjects' judgments as to the reliability of the consonant
and dissonant information was measured. The results indicate
that no matter how pronounced the subjects' tendency to selectively seek consonant information, such information was always
judged to be more reliable than dissonant information. This
finding again parallels findings from research on sequential
information evaluation (cf. the summary by Grabitz & Grabitz-
Gniech, 1973; Irle, 1971; 1975) though, while the latter experiments generally make these measurements *before* a decision,
our own experiments measured subjects' judgments *after* the
decision had been made.

2.3.3. Conclusion concerning selective information seeking

The results of the experiments concerned with selective information seeking show that Festinger's original assumptions
that people seek consonant and avoid dissonant information
have to be modified, there being certain conditions under
which they do not apply. These conditions are the following:
a) when subjects are already familiar with the consonant information, b) when subjects expect the dissonant information
to be easily refutable, c) when subjects judge the dissonant
information to be more useful, d) when subjects experience
extremely high dissonance and have the opportunity to revise
their decision. Expressed more abstractly, subjects will seek
dissonant information whenever:
1) the cognitive system is so stable that dissonant information can easily be integrated (e.g. by means of refutation
   or differentiation) and a further stabilisation of the cognitive system thereby achieved; or
2) the cognitive system is so weakened that the accumulation
   of consonant information, in the long term, offers a less
   effective and more unstable reduction of dissonance than
   does the changing of the cognitive system itself.

The curvilinear relationship implied by dissonance theory between the level of cognitive dissonance and the selective
search for consonant information also cannot be taken as un-
restrictedly valid. Rather, a necessary precondition is that
subjects perceive that their original decisions are reversible.
When decisions are perceived as irreversible, the tendency to
search for consonant information increases linearly with increasing dissonance. That the intensity of the avoidance of
dissonant information is dependent on the degree of cognitive
dissonance could not be confirmed by the present investigations.

In spite of these restrictions, our findings indicate that the
position advanced by Freedman and Sears (1965) with respect
to selective information seeking and avoidance is untenable.
Besides the obvious methodological flaws in the experiments
(their own and others) that they draw on, their analysis is
weakened by their failure to consider the resistance to change
of the involved cognitions. By taking resistance to change
into account, it becomes evident that the search for supporting information is the favored form of dissonance reduction
only under certain initial conditions. When these conditions
are not fulfilled, the failure to find evidence for selective
information seeking does not, in itself, contradict dissonance
theory.

3. The revised theory of cognitive dissonance

One essential result of the empirical work inspired by
Festinger's (1958) original version of dissonance theory was
Irle's (1975) revision, the most important modifications being
as follows:

1) In specifying the conditions necessary for dissonance to
   occur, the original theory only provided examples of
   instances when one cognition did or did not follow from

another but offered no generic characterization of the
"follows from" relation. The revised version of dissonance
theory corrects this deficiency by introducing the notion of
"hypotheses", drawing a parallel between the naive subject
and the deductively reasoning scientist. According to Irle,
whenever a person expects one event to follow from another,
he/she can be said to have an implicit hypothesis concerning their inter-relation. This hypothesis constitutes a
"third cognition", and its violation is the necessary and
sufficient condition for dissonance to occur. By defining
dissonance in terms of subjective hypotheses, Irle not only
provides experimenters with an objective criterion for determining whether a given experimental treatment aroused
dissonance, but also established a conceptual bridge between dissonance research and work on cognitive theories of
learning and concept formation.

2) The original theory defines the "magnitude of cognitive
dissonance" and "a cognition's relative resistance to
change" as being dependent on one another, the former increasing as result of increases in the latter. The revised
theory separates the two definitions, defining the magnitude of cognitive dissonance as a function of the subjective probability associated with the violated hypothesis,
thus allowing greater precision in specifying dissonance's
antecedent conditions.

3) The original theory analyzes a cognition's resistance to
change in terms of the degree to which the cognition is
removed from objective reality, with zero-order cognitions
(i.e., cognitions based directly on sensory input) being
the most resistant. Applied to the revised version, this
analysis implies that hypotheses, as cognitions representing abstract (descriptive and/or prescriptive) facts,
should be of relatively low resistance. The reformulated
version, however, rejects this conclusion both as a result
of several non-supportive empirical findings and in recog-

nition of the fact that a cognitive change, although re-storing consonance in the particular relationship being studied, might create dissonance in other relations that the changed cognition enters into. In light of this, resistance to change was re-analyzed in terms of the degree of dissonance over the entire cognitive system, a particular cognition being more resistant, the greater the number of relations that it enters into (see Götz-Marchand, Götz & Irle,1974).

4) The revised version further developed Festinger's original dissonance theory in order to explore the commonalties between dissonance phenomena and those dealt with by attribution theory, the theory of social comparison, the hypothesis theory of perception and the theory of curiosity and exploratory behavior.

4. Empirical evidence concerning the revised theory of cognitive dissonance

4.1. Dissonance reduction by hypothesis change

An experiment by Frey, Irle and Kumpf (1974; see Irle, 1975, pp. 343-346) derives directly from the revised theory. Using a visual detection task, the experimenters induced subjects to form a specific hypothesis concerning the optically presented events and then violated this hypothesis in the critical, test trial. The dependent variable was the subjects' probability estimates concerning whether or not the violating event had actually occurred and the validity of their hypotheses.

The central hypotheses were the following:

1) If an event takes place that contradicts a subjective hypothesis, the resulting dissonance will be reduced by lowering the subjective probability with which the hypothesis is held.

2) The higher the subjective probability concerning a hypothesis' truthfulness, the greater the cognitive dissonance
aroused by a disconfirmatory event.

3) Events predicted on the basis of a subjective hypothesis
are likely to be reported even in cases when they did not
actually occur.

The results provided unequivocal support for hypotheses 1 and
3, and were in the predicted direction (though of only border-
line significance) for hypothesis 2. The findings thus support
the revised theory's claim that cognitive relations involve
three cognitions; the two cognitions X and Y, and the subjective hypothesis (H) concerning their relationship.

Thus cognitive dissonance can be reduced not only by altering
one of the cognitions X or Y but also by modifying the hypothesis cognition H. According to Irle, there are at least two
ways of reducing cognitive dissonance by changing a hypothesis
cognition: a) by lowering the subjective certainty with respect to the truthfulness of the subjective hypothesis and b)
by modifying the hypothesis in such a way that it is confirmed
by an originally contradicting event. The latter reduction
mode results in an immunisation of the hypothesis. If a subjective hypothesis can explain all conceivable events - that
is, if the hypothesis is totally immunized - it can not longer
be refuted, and thus no dissonance can arise.

4.2. Subjective hypotheses and cognitive dissonance

According to the revised theory, dissonance occurs only when
internalized hypotheses are refuted. The refutation of hypotheses held by other people but not held by the person him- or
herself is not dissonance arousing. An empirical test of this
point was carried out by Möntmann, Katz and Irle (1979).

Subjects were presented with two event-pairs that they had
never before, in all probability, thought about. For one of

the event-pairs, they were asked to indicate one reason why,
in their opinion, event Y (e.g., an increase in forest land)
might follow as a consequence from event X (e.g., a reduction
in the production of artificial cellulose), a task intended
to prompt subjects to form a subjective hypothesis concerning
the relation between the two events. The subjects then received two printed communications, each dealing with one of
the event-pairs and arguing against the possibility of there
being any relation between the component events. Each subject
thus received two refutational arguments, one dealing with an
internalized hypothesis, the other dealing with a non-inter-
nalized one.

The dependent variable was again the subjective probability
assigned to the relation between the components of each event-
pair. As already known from the investigation conducted by
Götz-Marchand, Götz and Irle (1974), the sequence in which
dissonance-relevant, dependent variables are presented plays
a very important role as to which cognitions are changed; if
the sequence is unknown to them, subjects tend to take the
first possibility offered for reducing cognitive dissonance.
Thus, one way to establish that reactions to the refutations
were due to dissonance reduction was to vary when the subjective probability measure was presented in a battery of other
dissonance-relevant measures (evaluation of X, evaluation of
Y), the predictions being that a) probability change should
be greatest following the refutation of the internalized hypothesis, and b) probability change should be greater the earlier
the probability measure appears in the test battery.

The results were as predicted. The refutational communications
had greater impact when the hypothesis that they attached was
internalized than when it was not, and changes of the hypotheses' probability were greater the earlier the probability
measures occurred in the series of dependent variables, the
latter effect, too, being most pronounced for the internalized
hypothesis.

A study by Ochsmann (1979) also demonstrates dissonance reduction by hypothesis change, using a decision making paradigm
and monitoring post-decisional changes in the evaluations of
the chosen and rejected alternatives and the subjective probabilities associated with decision correctness and competence.
The results showed that subjects who were initially certain in
the correctness of their decision reduced dissonance not by
changing their evaluations of the alternatives but by changing
the subjective probabilities (i.e., hypotheses) associated
with decision correctness and their competence as decision
makers. Subjects, on the other hand, who were not certain in
the correctness of their decision, reduced dissonance primarily by re-evaluating the chosen and rejected alternatives.

4.3. Preference for differently resistant cognitions for the reduction of cognitive dissonance

Besides a more precise specification of dissonance's antecedents, the revised version of dissonance theory also aims at
greater precision in dealing with the consequences of dissonance arousal. As already mentioned above, a cognition's resistance to change is re-analyzed in terms of its relatedness to
other cognitions. More precisely, resistance to change is defined as number of third cognitions with which a given cognition (X) stands in a consonant relation and as "a negative
function of the number of third cognitions with which X stands
in a dissonant relation (Irle, 1975, p. 316)."

An experiment by Haefele (1978) tested several hypotheses
derived from this definition of resistance to change. Subjects were again presented with two event-pairs that they had
probably never before thought about and whose component events
were, therefore, not likely to be firmly anchored to other
units in their cognitive systems. For each pair, subjects were
asked to generate a reason why one event (X) would result in
the other (Y), a task designed to internalize an hypothesis

between X and Y. The same task was then used to establish cognitive relations between the X- and Y-cognitions and other related cognitions, Z_x and Z_y, respectively. The two major independent variables - the resistance to change of the X- and Y-cognitions - were separately manipulated by varying whether the X- and Y-cognitions were anchored to no, two or five Z cognitions.

As in the study discussed above, each subject received printed communications that refuted the hypotheses that he/she had formed between the X and Y cognitions of each event-pair. Dependent variables were the subjective probabilities attached to the occurrence of event X, the occurrence of event Y, and the causal connection between X and Y, for each event-pair.

The hypothesis was that the dissonance aroused by the refutational communications would be reduced by changing the least resistant cognition, so that, for example, the greater the number of Z cognitions that X had been anchored to, the more likely it would be that the dissonance reduction would take place at the cognition on the X-Y hypothesis, and vice versa. The results, however, were not supportive of this reasoning.

Though the predicted inverse relation between degree of anchoring and amount of change was found with respect to the Y-cognition, increasing Y's resistance to change did not result in a greater change at X or the X-Y hypothesis. No anchoring effect at all was found with respect to the X-cognition.

4.4. Conclusion

Taken as a whole, the results discussed above provided solid support for the revised theory of cognitive dissonance. It was shown, for instance, that dissonant relations involve at least three cognitions (the X- and Y-cognitions and the subjective hypothesis (H) relating them) and that all three cognitions must be specified in order to make clear predictions about

dissonance reduction. Changing hypothesis strength was found
to present an especially attractive avenue for reducing dissonance, and subjects were in some cases found to change hypotheses' content as well as to render them "immune" to refutation.

The results also support the revised theory's contention that
a hypothesis must be internalized in order for a refutation of
it to create dissonance, the dissonance aroused in such cases
being a positive function of the subjective probability with
which the hypothesis is held to be true. Though the revised
theory makes specific predictions concerning the locus of
dissonance reduction, it so far has met with less empirical
success in this respect. Though some evidence was found to
support the hypothesis that anchoring a cognition to other,
consonant cognitive units increases its resistance to change,
that such resistance leads to greater changes at other points
in the dissonant relation remains to be demonstrated.

Appendix

The Revised Theory of Cognitive Dissonance

1. Definitions

1.1 A *cognition* is defined as a part of psychological reality.
    A cognition is responsive to other, non-psychic realities,
    that can be defined in terms of physics, biology, sociology,
    etc. A cognition is a *psychological representation* of other
    realities, but not necessarily a veridical one. *Perceptions*
    can become cognitions via memory storage.

1.2 A person has a set of cognitions (at a specific place in
    space and time). Each two cognitions out of a set may or
    may not have a cognitive relation. A set (or 'cognitive
    map', 'life space') becomes a *cognitive field* to the ex-
    tent that the number of cognitive relations rises within

the set. A cognition can also be called a *cognitive element* if it cannot be broken into components by the cognizing person.

1.3 A cognitive relation is called *irrelevant* if it arises on- ly from the fact that two cognitions happen at the same place in space and time. A cognitive relation is called *consonant* if the cognizing person believes in a hypothesis (H) explaining that cognitions X and Y happen at the same place in space and time (space and time are here used as psychological terms, according to Lewin): 'X implies Y', or 'Y follows from X'. A *hypothesis* is a cognition that re- presents a part of an abstract reality (of theories, etc.). The expectation that Y will happen when X is given is the most simple form of hypothesis; i.e., H = X causes Y. A cog- nitive relation is called *dissonant* if X and a NON-Y happen at the same point in space and time in contradiction to H.

1.4 A person may recognize two parts of a cognitive set; one consisting of those cognitions presenting the self, and another consisting of cognitions presenting the environment. X and Y may both be located in the self, one in the self and one in the environment, or both in the environment. A cognition may be part of the self (or the environment) at one point in space and time but not at another. A person may cognize an hypothesis H as part of the environment only, as part of the environment and of the self, or as part of the self only. An hypothesis H is part of the self and/or of the self and the environment, whenever a person believes in its truth or empirical validity. Hypotheses of the self (or of the self and environment) are denoted as H_s.

2.   Propositions

2.1 Cognitive dissonance is accompanied by tension. The stronger cognitive dissonance is, the stronger this tension will be, and therefore the stronger the force in direction of reduc- ing cognitive dissonance.

2.2 The strength of cognitive dissonance is a function of the combined subjective certainty in the truth of the involved cognitions (H_s, X, NON-Y), with at least $p > 0.5$.

The strength of cognitive dissonance is a function of the subjective certainty in the truth of H_s.

The strength of cognitive dissonance is a function of the subjective certainties in the truth of the cognitions of concrete, singular facts (X, NON-Y).

2.3 The subjective certainty in the truth of H_s is a function of:

   a) the proportion of empirical verifications to falsification, the person P has experienced before in applying this hypothesis;

   b) The social support P experiences from reference persons/ groups in applying the same hypothesis;

   c) the level of aspiration of P in applying his/her hypothesis H_s, according to successes/failures in applying other hypotheses;

   d) the unambiguousness of H_s. (H_s is maximally ambiguous if it allows as much that X happens with NON-Y, as with Y.)

2.4 Cognitive dissonance will be reduced by cognitive change.

The magnitude of cognitive change is a function of the magnitude of cognitive dissonance.

The ease of reducing cognitive dissonance is a function of the availability of cognitions to add and/or subtract; that is, the ease of substituting some cognitions for others.

2.5 The resistance to change of each cognition is a function of the proportion of consonant to dissonant relations which this cognition has to other, third cognitions (Z).

Cognitive change follows the principle of optimizing cognitive consonance by least effort. The cognition with relatively least resistance to change will be changed first.

The more third cognitive relations exist in case of cognitive dissonance of H_S (X with NON-Y), the less cognitive change is apt to lead to maximal cognitive consonance within the cognitive field.

The above statements (2.5) are valid for H_S, too. The more H_S has relations to other hypotheses ('hypothetical system', theory) of P, the stronger will be the resistance to change of H_S.

Chapter 10   The Theory of Psychological Reactance
D. Dickenberger and G. Gniech

1. Reactions to social influence attempts: Conformity and Opposition

Attempts at forcing a person to do or not to do something are not always successful. When such attempts serve what are consensually accepted as legitimate aims, there is generally no problem. More complicated, however, are those cases in which the person conforms with the influence attempt even though he/she rejects the aim towards which it is directed, a state that Allen (1965) refers to as "public conformity with private disagreement." The psychological processes occurring in this latter, ambivalent state should differ fundamentally from those in which the overt behavior and underlying attitude are consistent with one another.

There are, of course, other possible reactions to social influence besides these two different types of conformity. The person may, for example, completely ignore the influence attempt, his/her behavior being instigated by personal aims that may or may not coincide with those towards which the influence attempt is directed. The person may also, however, react against the attempted influence, purposefully behaving in a way that resists or counters it. The present chapter is primarily concerned with these cases of "anti-conformity", the theoretical background being provided by the theory of psychological reactance (Brehm, 1966, 1972). According to reactance theory, people have a basic motivational drive to resist social influence and preserve personal freedom.

2. The theory

The theory of psychological reactance, formulated by Jack
Brehm in 1966, deals with how individuals respond when their
behavioral freedom is threatened. According to this theory,
threatening an individual's freedom to choose between several
possible behavioral alternatives results in motivational arousal directed towards restoring the threatened possibilities
and avoiding future restrictions. Brehm (1966) refers to the
motivation aroused in such instances as "reactance", and
states: "Given that a person has a set of free behaviors, he
will experience reactance whenever any of these behaviors is
eliminated or threatened with elimination (p. 4)." Summaries
of recent research on reactance theory can be found in Wicklund (1974) and Gniech and Grabitz (1978).

2.1. Conditions for the arousal of reactance

According to Jones and Brehm (1970), the necessary pre-conditions for the arousal of reactance are that a) the person feels
free to choose between a set of given alternatives, b) this
freedom of choice is important to the person, and c) the
person perceives that the freedom is threatened. Though Wicklund (1974) lists the prior existence of freedom as being the
only necessary pre-condition, those just given also appear in
formulations by Wortman and Brehm (1975) and Dickenberger
(1979).

2.2. Strength of reactance

According to Brehm (1966), the strength of reactance is a positive function of:

1) the *absolute* importance of the threatened freedom for the
   individual; i.e., its instrumental value for the satisfaction of potentially important needs,

2) the *relative* importance of this freedom compared to other
   freedoms at the time the threat is made,

3) the proportion of freedoms eliminated,

4) the implication the threat carries for future threats,

5) the strength of the threat.

Wicklund (1974) and Wortman and Brehm (1975) both give four
determinants of reactance strength, the former not distinguishing between absolute and relative freedom importance and
the latter listing expectation of freedom, strength of the
threat, importance of freedom and implication for other
freedoms.

In discussing determinants of reactance strength, Dickenberger
(1979) draws a distinction between what she refers to as the
"importance of freedom to" and the "importance of freedom from".
The former of these has to do with the freedom's instrumenta-
lity with respect to certain needs and, as such, is similar
to Brehm's (1966) "absolute freedom". The latter is defined
as the product:

$$P_F \cdot (1 - P_F)$$

where P_F is the person's expectation of having freedom, defined in terms of subjective probability. It follows that as
the person's expectations of freedom decrease, the "importance
of freedom from" will first increase and then decrease. Thus,
contrary to Wortman and Brehm (1975) who propose a positive
linear relation between expectancy and reactance strength,
Dickenberger posits an inverted U-shaped relation, with reactance being at minimal strength when freedom is either completely or not at all expected.

Aside from the above determinants, some authors postulate the
presence of individual differences in reactance potential.
Schwartz (1974), for example, raises the possibility that there
are people with lowered reactance thresholds, while S.S. Brehm
(1976) argues that a heightened vulnerability to reactance can

explain the frequent occurrence of violent anger and hostility
found among certain clinical groups. Dickenberger (1979) accounts for the heightened reactivity of certain individuals
by pointing out that a general reduction in a person's expectation of freedom may actually result in an increase in both
the expectation and valuation of freedom in those few areas
of the person's life that the reduction had not affected.

2.3. Effects of reactance

As mentioned above, the reactance motive is aroused whenever
a person's behavioral freedom is threatened or actually eliminated and is directed towards the re-establishment of the
freedom and the prevention of further freedom loss. If, for
example, a person's freedom to choose between drink A and B is
threatened by someone telling him/her not to take drink B, the
person can re-assert his/her freedom by choosing drink B. If
drink B is no longer available, he/she will manifest some
other sort of behavior aimed at freedom restoration. Alternative responses to reactance that have received previous empirical attention include changing the attractiveness of the
available and eliminated or threatened alternatives, engaging
in behavior that is in some way equivalent to the behavior that
is threatened, getting a peer to engage in the threatened behavior, and aggressing towards the source of the threat (Brehm,
1966, Wicklund, 1974).[1]

Brehm (1972) separates the possible responses to reactance into
two groups. He (p.3) refers to the first group of responses
as "perceptual or judgmental effects consistent with the motivational change of reactance", these consisting primarily
of subjective reactions that result in a cognitive restructur-

---

[1]There is agreement in the publications about number and kinds
of reactance effects; only Guydosh 1974 names over-compliance
as a further manifestation of reactance.

ing of the reactance-arousing situation. The second group, on
the other hand, consists of overt behavioral responses such as
attacks against the threat's source or withdrawal from the situation. Though Brehm does not specify the conditions under
which responses from either group will occur, it seems likely
that the "subjective" responses would be the more frequent
since they are less susceptible to control by the person's
peer group and also less anti-social than the overt behavioral
responses. Heilman and Toffler (1976), however, argue that the
reactance motive will be reduced only in those cases where the
person's response succeeds in re-establishing the status quo
in his/her relationship to the threat's source thus implying
that the subjective responses will be less effective than behavioral responses as means for reactance reduction.

3. Empirical studies

We will now turn our attention to empirical studies of reactance, dividing our discussion between the following categories: individual differences in responses to reactance, the
effects of the relationships to the source of threat, variations in the amount and importance of freedom, variations in
the strength and nature of threats, and, finally, measurement
problems in reactance research.

3.1. Individual differences

People can differ both in the amount of reactance that they
experience in any given situation and in whether they choose
to reduce this reactance by subjective or overt, behavioral
responses.

Grabitz-Gniech (1971) investigated the influence of "feelings
of inadequacy" on the amount of reactance experienced. Since
Wicklund and Brehm (1968) had previously shown that a person's

competence with respect to an object determines the strength of the reactance that he/she experiences when his/her access to the object is threatened, Grabitz-Gniech tested the hypothesis that high "feelings of inadequacy" will lower reactance by increasing the person's tendency to conform with the freedom limitation. The results provided indirect support for the hypotheses, with those subjects who showed reactance after an influence attempt reporting less "feelings of inadequacy" than those who had complied.

Grabitz-Gniech and Niketta (1971) investigated whether increasing ego-involvement in the threatened freedom leads to heightened reactance, but their results offered no support for this hypothesis.

Crowne and Marlowe (1964) argue that an increasing need for social approval should lead a person to show more culturally sanctioned, acceptable behavior, thus implying that persons with a high need for social approval should have a low need for independence. In support of this, Dickenberger and Grabitz-Gniech (1972) found that subjects with a low need for social approval showed stronger (though non-significantly so) reactance effects than subjects with high need for social approval.[2]

As far as age and sex differences are concerned, Dickenberger and Bender (1980) studied variations in the learning of reactance behavior in kindergarten pupils ranging from three to six years of age and found that, as hypothesized, the percentage of children showing reactance behavior increased with increasing age. Though Dickenberger and Bender found no differences

---

[2] The authors presume the Marlowe-Crowne Social Desirability Scale to be the reason for the unexpected nonsignificant result. Dickenberger, Höltz and Gniech (1978) demonstrated that a) the M-C scale postulates norms that are no longer accpeted in many groups of adolescents, and that b) the questionnaire cannot distinguish between answers given because of a high need for approval and answers due to internalized norms.

in the reactance shown by males and females, a study by S.S.
Brehm and Weinraub (1977) using a similar age sample does report such differences, with males showing significantly more
reactance than females.

Grabitz-Gniech and Benad (1972) also found differences in reactance responses between male and female subjects. Their subjects were asked to help sort computer cards by a stooge with
whom they had played a prisoner's dilemma game and who either
had (High Moral Pressure) or had not (Low Moral Pressure)
given up a part of his winnings for the subject. Female subjects showed more reactance - that is, helped less - under
high moral pressure, while male subjects helped less when the
moral pressure was low.

Dickenberger and Link (1980) had subjects state how they would
react if their partner threatened their freedom with respect
to two specific behaviors. The subjects were to do this by
giving the probability that they would 1) be privately angry
about the threat ("Thinking without behavioral consequences")
and 2) show annoyance and insist that in the future they participate in the decision ("Doing"). The results indicate that
women favored "doing" and men favored "thinking". There also
was a significant difference between first and later borns,
with firstborns showing a greater tendency for "thinking"
than the later borns.

3.2. Relation between individual and source of threat

An important aspect of a relation between two individuals or
between an individual and a group is the desirability that
this relation has for the two parties; in influence situations,
for example, increasing attractiveness of the source of influence reduces subsequent resistance to the influence attempt
(Cartwright & Zander, 1968). Accordingly, reactance to social
influence should vary inversely with the desirability of the
person's relation to the influence source.

Dickenberger and Grabitz-Gniech (1972) manipulated the attractiveness of a relation by telling their subjects that they
either would or would not get along harmoniously with another
person who was, in fact, a confederate. As hypothesized, subjects in the high attractiveness condition complied with a
subsequent influence attempt made by the confederate, while
subjects in the low attractiveness condition showed reactance
effects.

Dickenberger and Papastefanou (1980) manipulated the attractiveness that a class had for a group of its students by informing them - in accordance with Cartwright (1968) - that
their class was either very homogeneous and that the students
would harmonize or that it was not homogeneous and that the
students would not harmonize too well. Half of the subjects
in each condition received, in addition, a bogus "mean class
attitude" with respect to a certain attitude object along
with a demand to adopt their own attitude to this position.
The remaining subjects simply received the bogus mean attitudes with no accompanying demand. Contrary to the hypotheses,
the subjects in the low attractiveness condition who received
the demand to conform ended up more similar to the class position than did those who did not receive the demand, while
in the high attractiveness condition, the opposite effect
was obtained.

Brehm and Mann (1975) argue and provide empirical evidence
that the importance of the threatened freedom determines what
impact the attractiveness variable has on the amount of reactance; when the threatened freedom is relatively unimportant,
reactance decreases with rising attractiveness, but when the
threatened freedom is very important, reactance will increase
with attractiveness. If we categorize the experiments discussed above according to the importance of the freedom
threatened, the Dickenberger and Grabitz-Gniech (1972) experiment would fall in the low importance category (subjects
could choose which 14 out of 21 relatively uninteresting

questions to answer), while the Dickenberger and Papastefanou
(1980) study will be considered among the high importance
group (subjects were to form opinions about how to go about
buying jeans and tape-recorders). Categorizing these two studies in this way, the opposing patterns of results fall in
line with Brehm and Mann's predictions.

Borrowing from the earlier work of French and Raven (1959),
Grabitz-Gniech and Niketta (1971) examined the influence of
"power by legitimacy" (teacher of music) and "power by identification" (Popstar) on a high-school student population when
students were told by either teacher or popstar which one out
of several records to prefer. As predicted, the subjects
showed greater conformity with the influence attempt when it
came from the source with power by identification, though with
neither source was the anticipated derogation of the attractiveness of pop records obtained.

Gniech, Schmidt and Dickenberger (1976) investigated the influence that status has on anticipated reactance. The subjects
read a story in which someone (an official) threatened either
a higher (a director) or lower (an apprentice) status person
than he. The subjects were to anticipate the apprentice's or
director's resulting thoughts and actions. It was predicted
that the apprentice would be ascribed greater subjective
reactance than the director on account of his dependent position, but the director would be ascribed greater overt, behavioral reactance. Though the results did not support this
prediction, they did indicate that status interacted with the
strength of threat, so that the director was ascribed considerably more reactance than the apprentice when the threat was
weak than when the threat was strong.

3.3. Freedom

For freedom restriction to result in reactance, it is of course
necessary that the freedom be at first perceived and be of some

consequence for the person. Should a perceived freedom be totally unimportant for an individual, threatening or eliminating it will not arouse reactance.

In this section we will review experiments dealing with the
effects that varying the amount and/or importance of the freedoms threatened has on subsequent reactance responses as well
as consider what happens with respect to reactance when these
freedoms are later restored.

According to Brehm (1966), the *amount of reactance* aroused as
a result of threatening or restricting freedom should increase
with the proportion of freedoms affected. Though Brehm,
McQuown and Shaban (reported in Brehm, 1966) and Wicklund,
Slattum and Solomon (1970) found support for this hypothesis,
their procedure was critizised by Grabitz-Gniech and Grabitz
(1973a) because it confounded the proportions of freedoms
threatened with the "size of the freedom space." To remedy
this, Grabitz-Gniech, Auslitz and Grabitz (1975) varied the
proportion of restriction over two levels (33%, 66%) for
"freedom spaces" of either six or twelve alternatives. They
found that the size of the freedom space determines the amount
of reactance effect; for 12 alternatives, there was no reactance no matter how many alternatives were eliminated from
choice, while for 6 alternatives, the attractiveness of the
eliminated alternatives showed greater increase when 66%
(i.e., 4 alternatives) were eliminated than when 33% (i.e.,
2 alternatives) were eliminated. The authors explain this
finding by saying that individuals with too large a freedom
space would be overcharged with respect to their capacity for
assessing decision alternatives and would therefore not experience freedom loss when the number of alternatives was
reduced. One could also, however, advance the simpler explanation that subjects with the large initial freedom space still
had appreciable freedom available after even 66% of the decision alternatives were eliminated, while those with a small
initial space were left a restricted choice repertoire.

As discussed above, reactance theory posits that reactance should increase with the *importance* of the freedoms threatened or eliminated. Experiments by Burton (reported in Brehm, 1966) and Brehm and Cole (1966) operationalized freedom importance by telling subjects that the experiment was either a pretest conducted by a student (low importance) or that it was a test of personality designed by a psychology professor (high importance), an operationalization in line with the definition of importance as "instrumental value for the satisfaction of relevant needs". Worchel (1972) advances another conception of "importance", arguing that "seeing a behavior in a film increases importance of this behavior." As long, however, as the film character's behavior does not appear to satisfy special needs, this kind of operationalization would seen more relevant to Dickenberger's (1979) notion of 'freedom from' than to the more absolute types of freedom dealt with by Burton and Brehm and Cole, since watching someone perform a behavior on a film could affect the viewer's expectation of freedom to perform this behavior his- or herself.

With respect to "freedom from", Dickenberger (1979) found in a study on children between ten and twelve years of age that increasing the number of restrictions on their freedom of activity in various areas of every day life first resulted in an increase and then, as the number of these restrictions increased even further, a decrease in the importance with which these areas were held. This positive, non-monotonicity of freedom importance (and hence also of reactance) as a function of freedom expectancy contradicts Wortman and Brehm (1975), who propose that, "The amount of reactance that an individual experiences is a direct function of ... the expectation that he possesses freedom ..." (p. 283)

Reactance following freedom restriction is directed towards *re-establishment of the freedom*. If, however, the freedom is in some way re-established before the person can respond, reactance should decline and no reactance effects appear.

Worchel and Brehm (1971) had subjects work together with two confederates; after one confederate threatened the free choice of topic for a following discussion, the other confederate immediately re-established this freedom by insisting on a joint decision. Worchel and Brehm found that the second confederate's intervention led to a statistically significant reversal in the reactance-inspired tendency to derogate the topic that the first confederate had insisted upon.

Grabitz-Gniech and Grabitz (1973b) had subjects rate 4 pictures, one of which the subjects were told they could take home after the next session of the experiment. During the second session, however, the subjects were told that certain pictures had not arrived and thus could not be chosen to be taken home. In the "re-establishment condition", another experimenter brought the missing pictures before the subjects made the second ratings so that the freedom to choose between all 4 pictures was restored. The hypothesized reactance-reducing effect of freedom re-establishment was not found, reactance effects appearing in both the "re-establishment" and "continued restriction" conditions. In discussing these results, Grabitz-Gniech and Grabitz argue that the re-establishment of freedom was outside their subjects' control and that it therefore may have been in itself insufficient in reducing reactance: "One can imagine a two component model for reactance reduction: psychological reactance will only be reduced if, first of all, the freedom space is re-established, and, secondly, if there is control over the threatening agent." (p. 365)

Starting from a different theoretical position, Heilman and Toffler (1976) reach a somewhat similar conclusion concerning the nature of the reactance motive. They assume that the reactance motive is not directed towards re-establishment of threatened freedoms per se, but rather that threatening a freedom changes the relative status of the involved persons and motivates the threatened person to demonstrate his/her independ-

ence in order to re-establish the former status relationship.
Heilman and Toffler (1976) demonstrated that a partner's giving subjects the possibility of free choice resulted in
greater conformity than in a "no choice" condition, while
there was no difference between choice and no choice when the
possibility of choosing appeared randomly.

Schwarz (1980) critizises the experiments on freedom restoration by pointing out that the restoration appears directly
after freedom restriction, and that the results could thus be
interpreted as being due to a reduction or cancellation of the
threat. In that case, the existing studies would not be evidence for the reactance reducing effect of freedom restoration,
but rather for different amounts of reactance after varying
levels of threat.

3.4. Freedom restriction

Wicklund (1974) discriminates between 3 kinds of freedom restriction; social influence, barriers and self-imposed restrictions. Wicklund defines barriers as incidents that keep
a person from reaching a goal, while social influence refers
to those situations in which people are compelled to comply
to the demands of others. A self-imposed threat develops in
the processes of bargaining or decision making as a result
of the successive elimination of alternatives. In each case,
as the freedom space gets continuously smaller, the eliminated
alternatives gain in attractiveness. S.S. Brehm (1976) developed an alternative scheme for classifying freedom restrictions according to whether they are personal, impersonal or
self-imposed.

The freedom to choose between several alternatives can be
restricted either by explicitly eliminating some of the alternatives or by pressing the decision maker to make a particular
choice. Both processes are implicitly existent in any freedom
restriction: If, out of three alternatives, one is eliminated,

the remaining two are imposed upon the person, whereas alternatively, if one alternative is insisted upon, the other two
are, in effect, eliminated.

In the above mentioned study by Grabitz-Gniech and Grabitz
(1973b), both kinds of freedom restriction led to reactance:
Out of 4 pictures, the one that subjects had initially rated
as third was either explicitly eliminated or implicitly eliminated by telling subjects they could choose only one picture
to take home. Reactance appeared in both conditions, the eliminated picture increasing in its rated attractiveness during
the final measurement.

With respect to implicit freedom elimination, it will be recalled that one of the five determinants for the amount of
reactance postulated by Brehm (1966) is the implication that
one threat has for further threats. Sensenig and Brehm (1968)
demonstrated that subjects who were told they would be working
together with their partner in three further experiments
showed more reactance when their freedom was threatened than
subjects who knew they would only be with their partners once.
Pallak and Heller (1971) used a similar paradigm but instructed their subjects explicitly that the forthcoming sessions
would be completely independent. Contrary to Sensenig and
Brehm, they found that the expectation of future interaction
resulted in greater conformity, reactance occurring only in
the single interaction condition. Pallak and Heller argue in
line with Kiesler and Corbin (1965) that future interaction
with a partner would lead to reflections upon the social
climate (one does not like to work together with an "enemy")
and thus bring subjects to comply in order to avoid conflict.

Dickenberger (1979) attempts to integrate Pallak and Heller's
theorizing with reactance theory. Dickenberger argues that by
conforming in the "implication" condition, the subjects lower
their expectation of freedom. Accordingly the "importance of
freedom from" in this condition increases, thus increasing
as well the amount of reactance that subjects should experience

in response to any further threat. If a further threat is indeed received, the reactance motive should outweigh the social motive and result in considerable reactance being manifest. Dickenberger's findings support this reasoning: Subjects expecting further interaction with the source of the threat showed reactance only after receiving the third threat, this reactance being considerably stronger than the reactance effects found in the single interaction condition.

3.5. Reactions to threats of freedom

The most effective way to re-establish a threatened freedom and reduce reactance is to choose the alternative that was threatened with elimination. This response, however, is the easiest to socially control and, accordingly, has a low probability of appearance. The responses least easily controlled are cognitive changes; e.g., increasing the perceived attractiveness of a threatened alternative. These latter responses are the most frequently used as dependent variables in reactance experiments.

There are serious problems in measuring these cognitive reactance effects. Grabitz-Gniech (1971) and Schmidt, Dickenberger and Grabitz-Gniech (1978) point out the possibility of regression effects when the same stimuli are repeatedly rated. Upshaw (1975) argues that the changes in attraction may be simply scale effects resulting from changes in the parameters of a hypothetical "personal reference scale." Gniech, Gumbel and Dickenberger (1980) followed Upshaw's suggestion and measured changes in attractiveness with both interval rating scales and by paired comparisons, the latter - according to Upshaw - eliminating the effect of the personal reference scale. Reactance was found with both measuring methods, thus rendering it unlikely that all reactance effects found with scale ratings have been due exclusively to measurement artefacts.

The study by Dickenberger and Grabitz-Gniech (1972) demonstrates how people will directly re-establish a threatened
freedom by exercising it when social control is not possible.
The experiment had 3 phases. The first was to establish the
freedom of choice for the subjects by allowing them to decide
which 12 out of 21 questions to answer. In the second phase,
subjects had to again select a subset of questions to respond
to, but this time their partner (a confederate) had told them
not to answer certain questions. In the third phase the confederate was absent and had no way to find out which questions
the subjects selected. The set of questions in the 3 phases
were very similar. The results indicate that the subjects
complied to the confederate's request when the latter was in
a position to monitor their choice (phase 2) but showed reactance in the third phase, answering a greater number of the
"forbidden questions."[3] A further, unexpected result was that
subjects who showed a greater tendency towards reactance in
the third phase rated their partner as being less attractive
than did those subjects who tended more towards conformity.

Dickenberger and van Kaick (1980) used the same paradigm but
measured both the changes in subjects' choice patterns and
their aggressiveness toward the confederate-partner, the
source of threat. The aggressiveness against the partner found
serendipitously by Dickenberger and Grabitz-Gniech was found
again, the effect being stronger when aggression was measured
before the other dependent variables than when it was measured
afterwards. This order effect points to reactance's motivational nature, as it implies that reactance conforms to a
hydraulic model when release through one response channel
reduces the likelihood and/or level of release through another.

---

[3] A similar delayed-reactance effect was found by Brehm and
Mann (1975) who referred to it as a "sleeper-effect".

4. A conflict model of opposing behavior tendencies in freedom restricting social influence attempts

4.1. Opposing forces

Reactance is simply defined as the motivation to restore a lost or threatened freedom, its behavioral manifestation being any kind of opposition against the freedom-eliminating pressure (cf. Brehm, 1966, 1972). In practice, however, reactance is often difficult to isolate, since the situations in which reactance occurs often elicit other, competing motivations as well. For example, besides eliciting reactance, freedom-limiting social influences also involve pressures for compliance, these pressures often masking whatever effects reactance might have.

Though numerous authors have pointed to the presence of competing motives in reactance settings (cf. Brehm, 1966, p. 14; Brehm & Cole, 1966, p. 420; Brehm & Sensenig, 1966, pp. 703-704; Brehm, 1968, p. 285; Sensenig & Brehm, 1968, pp. 324 and 327; Schwartz, 1970, p. 292; Brehm & Rosen, 1971, pp. 263 and 265-266; Doob & Zabrack, 1971, p. 408; Grabitz-Gniech, 1971, pp. 189 and 195; Worchel & Brehm, 1971, pp. 300 and 303; Brehm, 1972, p. 4; Dickenberger & Grabitz-Gniech, 1972, p. 179; Dickenberger, 1979), no one has as yet devised a model like Lewin's (1938) homological model or Miller's (1944) model of approach and avoidance gradients that would yield precise behavioral predictions in the case of such conflict.

In discussing situations in which reactance is opposed by pressures towards conformity, Worchel and Brehm (1971, p. 300) state that the result of such conflict is the summation of the opposing forces and that, in cases where the conformity pressure is stronger than the reactance, the latter may be expressed not as an overt opposing of the social influence but simply as a reduction in the tendency to conform. In general, however, there seems to be three different ways in which the

two opposing forces could interact: 1) they could be mutually
exclusive, so that either one or the other has full behavioral
expression; 2) they can complement each other, so that as
reactance increases, the tendency to conform decreases, and
vice versa; or 3) the two forces are entirely independent of
one another, it being possible that both gain full behavioral
expression in one and the same situation.

4.2. The conflict model

The latter possibility is consistent with Miller's (1944)
above mentioned conflict model. According to this model, the
tendencies to approach and avoid a particular goal both increase with increasing goal proximity. The conflict, according
to Miller, occurs between the tendencies to behave, the relative dominance of either tendency being ascertainable by the
overt behavior (i.e., approach or avoidance) shown at each
distance from the goal.

Applying this model to reactance settings, goal proximity
might be linked to "pressure towards compliance", this latter
construct being operationalizable as a decrease in the time
allotted for making a decision (cf. Linder & Crane, 1970;
Linder, Wortman & Brehm, 1971), increasing physical proximity
to the source of influence or decision objects (cf. Dabbs,
1971; Hammock & Brehm, see Brehm, 1966, p. 78), etc.. One can
assume that this pressure towards compliance increases as a
positive function of the strength of the social influence,
but when the influence reaches a point where it jeopardizes
the individual's freedom, the competing reactance motive is
also aroused. Reactance in this case corresponds to Miller's
avoidance tendency, its strength increasing at a rate more
rapid than that of the motive for compliance. This difference
in slope between compliance and reactance gradients might be
explained by the fact that as influence increases, more and
more freedoms become threatened by implication.

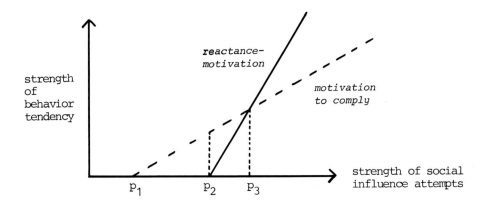

Figure 1. A conflict model of the opposing behavior
tendencies concerning psychological
reactance

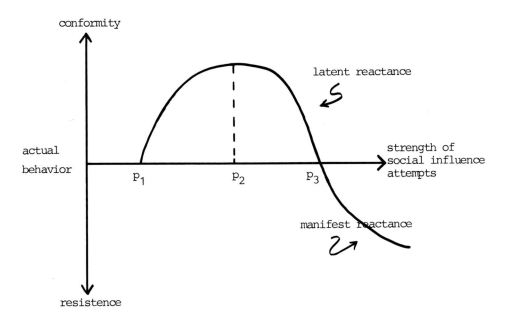

Figure 2. Behavioral effects of combination
of the two forces

In Figure 1, the reactance effect can be gotten by substracting the dotted line from the solid one. This gives us the pattern presented in Figure 2. Thus, as social influence increases, one would first expect an increasing tendency to comply (from p_1 to p_2), this being followed by a gradual decrease in conformity (p_2 to p_3) and finally an overt opposition to the influence attempt (p_3).

4.3. Empirical evidence

The distinction between latent and manifest reactance can be illustrated with respect to the findings of several different experiments. In one of these studies (Brehm, 1966, p. 82; Weiner-Regan & Brehm, 1977), shoppers' freedom was threatened either by asking them to purchase a specific brand of bread or by offering them a monetary incentive to buy the bread. As the amount of money offered was greater than the cost of the bread, this second influence technique was considered the stronger of the two and should therefore have elicited the greater reactance. The results show that the rate at which the bread was purchased was higher than normal in each condition, thus indicating that the two influence techniques both elicited compliance. As reactance theory would predict, however, compliance was lower in response to the monetary incentive than it was for the verbal request, the stronger influence attempt creating reactance that partially counteracted the tendency to comply. According to Brehm, this study lends some support to reactance theory in that it shows that monetary inducement, and probably verbal inducements, too, can result in less compliance as their strength increases (1966, pp. 89-90).

This experiment was replicated by McGillis and Brehm (1973), who added an additional condition in which a model implicitly restored the shoppers' threatened freedom by refusing to comply with the verbal or monetary influence. As in the ori-

ginal study, compliance was found to decrease with strength
of influence attempt, this effect being due to what we have
called "latent reactance" being elicited by the stronger,
monetary influence. In those conditions, however, where the
model publicly refused to follow the recommendations, the
latent reactance was substantially reduced, the degree of compliance shown to the two influence attempts being approximately
equal.

Doob and Zabrack (1971) used a similar paradigm in the context
of an opinion survey and found that, while monetary reward
increased the return-rate of their questionnaires, rewards
that were excessively larged tended to elicit reactance,
prompting the people to either return the money or to send
the questionnaire back without filling it out.

A further example of "latent reactance" can be found in a study by Schwartz (1970). In a Red Cross center, blood donors
were asked to donate bone marrow, one of the independent
variables being the reported likelihood of actually being
selected as a bone marrow donor after having had volunteered,
and another being how salient the possible negative consequences of giving bone marrow were made. The results show that,
when subjects thought that the probabilities of being accepted
as a donor were high, the rate of volunteering increased when
the possible negative consequences were made moderately salient
but decreased when these consequences were made highly salient.
Schwartz argues that the decrease in the legitimacy of the
request in the high salience condition permits the reactance
aroused by the request to be more freely expressed. As in the
other studies discussed in this section, however, the reactance
effects took the form of a reduction in the level of compliance
and did not involve active opposition to the request itself.

5. Applications of the theory

The theory of psychological reactance makes behavioral predictions for situations in which restrictions are experienced.
According to reactance theory, behavior in such cases will be
directed towards a restoration of the restricted (or threatened) behavioral freedom. In the research to date, the
theory's applicability to certain applied areas has been stressed. Among these are the so-called "boomerang-effects" in attitude change research, negativistic behavior by subjects in
psychological experiments, various aspects of consumer- and
political behavior, territorial behavior, the refusal to help
others, and a special case of interpersonal attraction: "romantic love".

5.1. Boomerang effects in attitude change

Several experiments have used reactance theory as a basis for
explaining negative attitude change (cf. Brehm, 1968; Frey,
1971; Grabitz-Gniech & Grabitz, 1973a; Kiesler & Munson, 1975).
Censorship, for example, seems often to give rise to reactance
effects, the censored information growing more attractive to
a public whose freedom of access to that information has been
limited. In such cases, negative attitude change (i.e., change
in favor of the censored viewpoint) is likely (Worchel &
Arnold, 1973; Arnold & Baker, 1975). A similar process can
occur when people find themselves committed to a certain position or behavior; the behavior or position, though perhaps
desirable at the outset, becomes less so as people feel themselves restricted in their freedom to change their stand
(Raven & Kruglanski, 1970; Heller, Pallak & Picek, 1973;
Gniech, 1977). A special case of this occurs when people are
given predictions concerning their own behavior; the more
authoritative the predictions, the greater the tendency to
behave otherweise (Bermant & Starr, 1972; Hannah, Hannah &
Wattie, 1975; Frey & Gniech, 1976).

5.2. The negativistic subject

It is never possible to achieve complete control over experimental settings, and a large part of the unavoidable variability arises from the subject and his/her motives and perceptions (Grabitz-Gniech, 1972a,b; Grabitz-Gniech & Schmidt,
1973). Though subjects are often motivated to behave in ways
that they perceive as being "helpful" to the experimenter
(i.e., they support what they believe to be the experimenter's
hypotheses), subjects who feel that the experimenter places
undue limitations on their behavioral freedom can respond in
the opposite manner, seeking to restore their freedom by behaving in a way contrary to what they perceive as being the
experimenters intentions (Bermant & Starr, 1972; Lange, 1972;
Mertens, 1975; Gniech, 1976).

Such reactance-inspired, negative behavior can be elicited by
a) forcing subjects to participate in experiments (Grabitz-
Gniech & Dickenberger, 1975; Rosenthal & Rosnow, 1975), b)
suspicion of deception (Grabitz-Gniech & Schmidt, 1973;
Grabitz-Gniech & Dickenberger, 1975), c) forced commitment to
a certain position or behavior, either through aggressive instructions (Grabitz-Gniech & Zeisel, 1974) or behavioral prognosis (Bermant & Starr, 1972; Frey & Gniech, 1976), and d)
giving subjects the feeling of being merely an object of
measurement (Gniech, 1977).

5.3. Territoriality

Territorial behavior in man relates to people's tendency, more
or less pronounced depending upon the situation, to retain
control over the physical space that they inhabit or in which
they behave. Usually, this sense of possessing a territory
becomes conscious only when the territory is threatened, the
result in such instances being behavior directed towards
territorial defense. The dynamics that underly human terri-

toriality are thus formally similar to those that underly behavior in all reactance-arousing situations (Edney, 1975).

There is copious evidence that people feel invasions of their
personal space as being freedom restricting and, therefore,
unpleasant. For example, if people are brought together for a
discussion in a very small room, the mere fact of bodily proximity arouses hostile feelings and leads to attempts at esca-
ping the uncomfortable situation (Dabbs, 1971). In his work on
crowding, Stokols (1972) uses reactance theory to explain the
unpleasant feeling aroused in situations where personal space
is excessively limited. Manderscheid (1975) integrated Stokol's
ideas in a more general theory of spatial effects.

5.4. Buying behavior

The classic purchasing study in the reactance field was done
by Weiner, Regan and Brehm (1977; cf. also Brehm, 1966, pp.
82-90) and was already discussed above in chapter 4.3.: Strong
attempts at influencing consumer's purchasing decisions resulted in reactance, which in this case took the form of a lower
rate of compliance with the influence attempt. This study was
replicated under modified conditions by McGillis and Brehm
(1973). A more recent application of reactance theory to purchasing and consumer behavior can be found in Wiswede (1979).

5.5. Consumer and political behavior

Kroeber-Riehl (1973, 1975) was one of the first authors who
stressed the importance of reactance-theoretical findings on
consumer reactions and marketing behavior. He was especially
interested in its bearing on resistance against influence
attempts. Heilman (1976) conducted an experiment in which
people at a supermarket were asked to sign a petition advocating price controls on meat and vegetables. The subjects were

asked to read one of the following two texts before they decided to sign or not to sign the petition:

"Raymond T. Finster ... has spoken out against this resolution
and claims that it would endanger the economy." (low pressure)

In the high pressure condition the words "He had said, that
people absolutely should not be allowed to distribute or sign
such petitions" were added to the above statement.

As predicted, the second, stronger text elicited a considerable
boomerang effect, leading a significantly larger number of
people to sign the petition.

Other field studies have shown how people react to attempts at
prohibiting their use of certain products or resources. West
(1975) for example, found that the attitudes concerning the
food in a certain campus cafeteria became more favorable when
students learned that the cafeteria would be closed for several
weeks and that they would have to eat elsewhere. Mazis and
his colleagues (Mazis, Settle & Leslie, 1973; Mazis, 1975)
studies housewives' reactions to local restrictions against the
use of phosphate detergents and found that such restrictions
led the housewives to become more favorable to phosphate detergents and more opposed to the local government's ecological
policies.

With respect to political behavior, Kornberg, Linder and
Cooper (1970) used data from a national pre-election study to
test whether people are more interested by elections when they
think that their preferred candidate is in danger of losing
than they are when they are sure that he/she will win. In
support of their hypotheses, supporters of Goldwater who most
feared a Johnson victory (or Johnson supporters fearing a
victory by Goldwater) reported the greatest interest in the
pre-election polls.

5.6. Interpersonal attraction and romantic love

Another, more recent application of reactance theory has been
to the relations within romantic couples. Two different cases
seem susceptible to reactance explanations: a) when affection
between partners is so strong as to pose a threat to either
on both's behavioral freedom, and b) when the possibility of
the relation being terminated or the couple being temporarily
separated threatens the partners' freedom of access to one
another. Only the latter case, however, has so far been dealt
with in the reactance literature.

Also relevant here is the phenomenon of "playing hard to get"
(Walster, Walster, Piliavin & Schmidt, 1973). Wicklund and
Ogden (1974) report an experiment in which female subjects
read questionnaires that ostensibly had been filled out by
five different males, the apparent purpose of the experiment
being to determine what male characteristics females find
most pleasing. The subjects were told that they would have a
chance to meet one of the five males later on, it being varied
whether or not the subjects could choose which male they would
meet. At the end of the session, after having had completed
attraction ratings for the five males, the subjects were told
that one of the males would not be available for meeting with
the subjects and that another would be late. A second set of
attraction ratings showed that for subjects who had a choice
in the matter, the relative attractiveness of the absent and
delayed males had increased.

A similar phenomenon has been designated by Driscoll, Davis
and Lipetz (1972) as the "Romeo and Juliet effect" and refers
to cases in which parental interferences in a love-relation
intensifies the young couple's feeling for each other. The
authors conducted a survey of people whose parents had objected
to their choice of romantic partner (mostly on the basis of
social, racial, religious, socio-economic, or moral grounds)
and found empirical evidence that the phenomenon does indeed

occur. As in the case of playing hard to get, reactance arousing threats to lovers' freedom of access to one another results
in an increase in the lovers' mutual attraction.

6. Connection to other theories

There exist several theories of smaller scope that are, in
essence, extensions of reactance theory to specific problem
areas. Some of these are discussed below.

6.1. Refusal to help (deficient altruism)

The refusal to help has been a topic of discussion and research
ever since the case of Kitty Genovese (cf. Rosenthal, 1964),
where a young New York woman was assaulted and killed in front
of 38 witnesses, none of whom were willing to intervene.
Reactance theory has been especially useful in analyzing the
refusal to help when the person feels his freedom of choice
limited by the moral weight carried by the request for aid
(cf. Berkowitz, 1970). As Schwartz (1974) has pointed out (cf.
4.3. above), such requests often imply future obligations for
helping as well and thus are perceived as being illegitimate
by the person to whom they are addressed (cf. also Guydosh,
1974). Indeed, studies by Jones (1969, 1970) have shown that
people, when given a choice, are less likely to help others
whom they perceive as being dependent on them.

A special threat to the potential helper's freedom arises when
the person requesting help has previously done him/her several
favors (Drews, 1970). To the extent that the potential helper
regards these favors as bribes intended to influence his/her
decision of whether or not to help, he/she is likely to experience reactance and re-assert his/her freedom by refusing
to help (Kahn & Tice, 1973; Organ, 1974; Gergen, Elsworth,
Maslach & Seipel, 1975).

If one wants to relate reactance theory to altruism, one has
to keep in mind that prosocial behavior is generally ruled by
a reciprocity-norm. For this reason, Harris and Meyer (1973)
reach the conclusion that hypotheses derived from reactance
theory cannot be applied to questions of altruism. A further
factor that has to be kept in mind is whether the person can
refuse to help or whether he/she is bound to help by situational factors. Even in cases where helping is mandatory, however, reactance can be manifested in the person's private
reactions. In a study by Regan (1971), for example, stronger
normative pressures led to almost universal helping, but there
was nonetheless evidence of a discrepancy between subjects'
overt actions and private attitudes. Guydosh (1974) argues
that even over-compliance can be a sign of reactance in those
cases where non-conformity is impossible.

6.2. Learned helplessness

One of freedom's essential aspects is the power to control
one's own activities and those features of the surrounding
environment upon which the activities depend. Wortman and
Brehm (1975) have related reactance to Seligman's (1975) notion of "learned helplessness", arguing that the link between
them lies in the control of an individual over his/her environment. While reactance theory holds that a person motivated by
the loss of control (i.e. loss of freedom) strives to regain
it, the theory of learned helplessness states that organisms
in uncontrollable environments become passive.

The two theories thus seem in apparent contradiction. Yet
reactance is assumed to occur only in those cases where freedom or control over one's own actions is expected and held to
be important. If, on the other hand, the person expects neither freedom nor control and attaches little importance to
them, he/she will react in accordance with learned helplessness theory, showing passivity and, in extreme cases, depression.

6.3. Brock's Commodity Theory

Brock's commodity theory (1968) relates objects' attractiveness to their scarcity: the more unattainable an object is, the more attractive it will seem. Reactance theory, of course, can provide a framework for analyzing the psychological processes that mediate such fluctuations in attractiveness with supply and demand, the assumption being that the more scarce an object is, the greater the threat to the person's freedom to attain it. An example of an experiment done in the commodity theory framework is provided by Worchel, Lee and Adewole (1975). These authors had subjects rate a variety of biscuits according to preference, the independent variables being a) the supply of biscuits available (large or small), b) the stability of the supply (stable or fluctuating) and c) the demand for these biscuits by the other subjects (high or low). The results show that scarcity, decrease in the available supply, and a high demand all lead to an increase in the commodity's value.

6.4. Regret

Both reactance theory and the theory of cognitive dissonance (Festinger, 1957) make predictions concerning the attraction changes of alternatives in decision situations. Reactance theory applies primarily to pre-decisional processes: a person threatened with having to forego one or several decision alternatives by deciding for another will, as a result of the reactance aroused, see these alternative(s) as being more attractive than before. Dissonance theory refers primarily to the post-decisional phase: once the decision is made, the person will attempt to reduce the resulting dissonance by emphasizing non-chosen alternatives' undesirable features and the desirable features of the chosen alternative.

Another way of stating the reactance prediction is to say that prior to a decision, the attractiveness of the various decision alternatives should converge. Linder and Crane (1970) as well as Linder, Wortman and Brehm (1971) were able to demonstrate that this convergence increases the nearer the decisionpoint draws. Though dissonance theory predicts as divergence of chosen from non-chosen alternatives following the decision, some research (Festinger, 1964; Walster, 1964) has found that for a very short period of time immediately after the decision has been made, the chosen alternative decreases in attractiveness while the attractiveness of the non-chosen alternatives increase. This phenomenon is referred to in the literature as post-decisional regret.

While dissonance theorists (e.g. Festinger, 1964) tried to explain this post-decisional regret in terms of a fluctuation in the salience of dissonant and consonant cognitions, reactance theory offers a more straightforward account. According to the latter, the decision maker's commitment to the chosen alternative limits his/her freedom with respect to the other non-chosen ones. Reactance is thus aroused and results in a convergence of the attractiveness of chosen and non-chosen alternatives for the same reasons as apply to pre-decisional reactance processes.

Research testing the relative merits of the dissonance and reactance theory accounts for post-decisional regret has not allowed any consistent conclusions to be drawn. Rather than review the conflicting experimental results in detail, we should simply state that both accounts seem at least partially correct by apply to different circumstances (cf. Rodrigues, 1970).

Miller (1968) concludes that post-decisional regret arises from the fact that decisions often have to be made under time pressure, the decision maker having to state a choice before he/she is actually ready to do so. Furthermore, whatever dis-

satisfaction or insecurity the decision maker feels with his/
her decision is no doubt often compounded with anxieties arising from evaluation apprehension. Miller hypothesizes that one
way to circumvent post-decisional regret is to make sure that
decision makers have adequate time to weigh the decision alternatives.

Chapter 11 Deviancy: An Attributional Analysis
C. Sauer, R. Ochsmann, M. Kumpf and D. Frey

1. Introduction

The term "deviant" covers such different and complex states of
affairs as homosexuality, prostitution, drug addiction, delinquency, vandalism and religious or political extremism.
People who are stigmatised by their outward appearance or abnormal behavior - for example, the physically deformed or the
mentally retarded - are also referred to as "deviant". Finally,
people can be labelled as "deviant" simply by belonging to a
minority ethnic or racial group.

In the following, we reserve the term "deviant" for behaviors
that represent real - not imputed - norm violations. Though
there has been nearly as many attempts at explaining deviant
behavior as there are forms of deviant behavior itself (cf.
Springer, 1973; Taylor, Walton & Young, 1973),there has yet
been no comprehensive theory of deviancy developed. Such a
theory would have to integrate the preceding theoretical
assessments, drawing a connection between the deviant action on
the one hand and the social structural conditions on the other;
between the deviant's own cognitive and motivational processes;
and between these latter processes and the direct and indirect
reactions of people in the deviant's social environment.

A social psychological approach to deviance could contribute to
the development of such a comprehensive theory by clarifying
the nature of the relation between the social, structural conditions and the various interpersonal processes that result in
deviant action. A basic assumption here is that such social

structural conditions operate only through cognitive mediation, and that the characteristics of these cognitive processes themselves are as important as the external social conditions in determining whether deviant behavior occurs and the form it takes.

2. Theory

2.1. Cognitive explanation for deviant behavior

The proposed cognitive explanation for deviant behavior is based on four assumptions:

Assumption 1: Discrepancies that a person experiences between his expectations and reality arouse psychological tensions.

People have expectations concerning the occurrence of events both within themselves and in their environment, these expectations varying according to the degree to which the person perceives the events as being, in fact, predictable. Discrepancies occur whenever an unexpected event takes place. The greater the perceived discrepancy between the unexpected event and the expectation, the greater the resulting psychological tensions. Discrepancies can become manifest in areas of varying importance for the person: The more important the area is, the greater the number of expectations contradicted and, hence, the greater the resulting psychological tension. Finally, unexpected negative events (i.e. events having unpleasant consequences) bring in their wake greater psychological tensions than unexpected positive events.

Assumption 2: Persons seek causal explanations for the discrepancies experienced between their expectations and reality.

Heider (1958) sees the function of social perception as being the discovery of relations between events: A world in which

events occur unconnectedly is not easily brought under control
and is therefore threatening. According to the attribution
theories of Jones and Davis (1965) and Kelley (1967, 1971,
1972), people strive whenever possible to apply simple and reliable causal explanations to events that they witness and, if
no such explanation is available, seek to develop one from
whatever information they have at hand. Correct causal explanations increase the probability of bringing events under some
sort of control.

Irle (1975, p. 312) has used the term "hypothesis" to refer to
units in the cognitive field that enable people to generate relations between individual cognitions. These hypotheses are
not independent of one another but form a "hypothesis mesh",
this latter being describable as a naive theory that the person entertains for the explanation of events. Such naive
theories are functional in that they subject events to "a
limited number of invariant categories" (Laucken, 1974).

Assumption 3: The person can perceive the causes of the discrepancies between expectation and reality as being either
dependent on himself (internal) or on the environment (external). In addition, these causes can be considered more or less
variable or invariable.

The individual pattern of attribution for the causal explanation of events is formed by two orthogonal and theoretically
independent dimensions: Internal versus external and variable
versus invariable causal attribution. These dimensions give
rise to the following four possibilities:

Internal - invariable attributions: The person sees himself as
the invariable cause of the discrepancies between his expectations and the actual events.

Internal - variable attributions: The person sees himself as
the cause of such discrepancies but feels also that this
causal responsibility can shift with time.

External - invariable attributions: The person sees his environment as being the invariable cause of discrepancies
experienced.

External - variable attributions: The person sees his environment as the cause of the discrepancies, but feels that at a
later point in time the causal responsibility could shift to
himself.

The greater the frequency with which empirical reality is in
accordance with the person's "hypothesis mesh", the more resistant the latter will be to change, with sporadically occurring disconfirmatory events resulting only in small amounts
of psychological tension. Chronic tensions arise only at the
permanent failure of these subjective explanatory systems.
We assume that one function of deviant behavior is to reduce
the tension that arises in such instances.

The extent to which persons consider the cause(s) of certain
discrepancies between expectation and reality to be variable
or invariable, and internal or external, depends among other
things on previous experience, on the availability of various
explanations applicable to the present situation, on the
explanation's social desirability, etc.. In any case, we
assume that people strive towards stable attributions, generating similar explanations for similar events.

Assumption 4: People try to reduce psychological tension, the
reduction strategy employed being determined by the person's
attributional style.

The psychic tension evoked by discrepancies between expectations and reality is unpleasant and sets off mechanisms
aimed towards its reduction. The pressure towards reduction
increases with the magnitude of the discrepancy, the mechanisms each operating by removing the discrepancy's perceived
causes.

The particular mechanism employed will depend, however, upon

the person's attributional style. People who attribute discrepancies to external, variable factors, for example, tend to
direct their efforts towards altering the conditions in the
environment, whereas an attribution to internal, variable
factors results in attempts to reduce the tension by changing
one's own person. A person who attributes discrepancies to
internal, invariable factors can so change or distort his or
her own state that he/she no longer perceives the discrepancies, while with attributions to external, stable factors, the
person's efforts are directed towards the distortion of the
external reality itself.

These four different attributional styles each imply a different sort of behavioral orientation in the face of expectancy-
reality discrepancies. The perception of variable causes for
experienced discrepancies implies primarily active reduction
strategies, while the perception of stable causes implies
passive ones. The specific forms of each of these tendencies
cannot, however, be predicted since, for example, collective
attempts at altering reality will vary with the circumstances,
and the various means of distorting reality (drugs, alcohol)
differ from situation to situation as to their availability
and/or the degree to which they are normatively sanctioned.

In order to test the theory, specific forms therefore have to
be assigned on an a priori basis to each attributional pattern.
We assume, for example, that alcoholism and drug-addiction are
characteristic of people with internal-invariable attribution
tendencies, while people who suffer from delusions of madness
and depressions should typically show attribution patterns
that are external-invariable. To complete this picture, delinquents should primarily show external-variable attribution
tendencies, whereas making individual attempts at altering
reality should be especially characteristic of people with
internal-variable attribution patterns.

Our strategy for testing the theory will be to select groups of subjects showing each of the various deviant behavior patterns mentioned in the preceding paragraph and then conducting tests to ascertain a) whether, in comparison with non-deviant controls, the deviant groups show a greater discrepancy between expectations and reality with respect to a variety of content areas, and b) whether the different deviant groups vary among themselves in the causes that they attribute to the discrepancies. With respect to the first of these comparisons, if the "deviant groups" do not differ from the "normal group", the entire theory can be considered falsified. No differences with respect to the second would, on the other hand, constitute only a partial disconfirmation.

2.2. Hypotheses

The following hypotheses, derived from the theory outlined above, were tested on three different deviant populations: Juvenile alcoholics, drug addicts and delinquents.

Hypothesis 1: Deviants should perceive greater discrepancies between their past expectations and reality than a control group of non-deviant people.

Hypothesis 2: Alcoholics and drug addicts should manifest greater tendencies towards internal attribution than do delinquents.

Hypothesis 3: Alcoholics and drug addicts should manifest greater tendencies towards invariable attribution than do delinquents.

3. Method

Selection of the populations: The three deviant populations
(juvenile alcoholics, drug addicts and delinquents) were
chosen for study on the basis of their social-political importance and availability. Juvenile alcoholics were questioned in the sanatorium at Kirchheimbolanden (Pfalz) and juvenile
delinquents in the juvenile penal institution at Adelsheim
(Baden-Württemberg)[1]. Drug addicts were recruited by placing
posters in bars known to be frequented by addicts, the poster
mentioning that participation in the study would be financial-
ly renumerated. The possibility that normal healthy people
would present themselves as drug addicts in order to receive
this cash payment (DM 35.00) was controlled for by means of
several screening questions set by our experienced interviewer.

The Interviewees: Combining the three deviant groups, the
initial subject sample consisted of 210 people. It was felt
necessary, however, to eliminate 37 of these subjects because
they either showed a) combined forms of all three deviant behavior patterns and could therefore not be used in testing
our hypotheses concerning attribution differences, or b)
evidence of overstraining and lack of concentration at the
end of the interview (average duration: 2 hours) that led
to the interview itself being broken off or a considerable
amount of faulty data being gathered. The final sample therefore consisted of 46 alcoholics, 66 delinquents (different
crimes, mainly criminal acts against property) and 57 drug
addicts. In all cases, the subjects were male juveniles between 16 and 28 years of age.

The control group: The control group consisted of 60 males who

---

[1] We would like to thank the direction and staff of both these
institutions for their cooperative support.

showed no deviant behavior patterns with respect to alcoholism, drug addiction and delinquency. The control subjects parallel-ed the deviant groups with respect to age, education and occupation.

Interview material: In addition to collecting data concerning subjects' expectation-discrepancies and attributional styles, a wide range of further information was gathered concerning things like demographic, biographical and socioeconomic variables, attitudes towards members of other marginal groups and personality ratings on instruments such as the "self-image" (Bills, Vance & McLean, 1951) and "purpose-in-life" (Crumbaugh, 1968) scales.

Procedure: The interviews were the same for each sub-sample, the subjects being interviewed singly by trained interviewers who recorded in pre-coded categories the subjects' responses to the prepared questions. The interviews lasted on the average 75-90 minutes, after which subjects were given a set of personality scales to complete. The total duration of each session was approximately two hours, a detailed description of the procedure being given in Sauer et al. (1976). Only the drug addicts and control subjects were paid for their part-icipation (35 and 15 DM, respectively), though comparable donations were made to the alcoholic's sanatorium and the juvenile penal institution.

4. Results

One of our central hypotheses was that deviant persons per-ceive greater discrepancies between their expectations and reality than do non-deviants. The magnitude of "expectation-discrepancy" was measured by means of the question, "How often have your expectations been fulfilled?", the subjects' responses being coded on a five-point scale (1= never; 5= always). The results are presented in Table 1.

Table 1. Magnitude of previously experienced discrepancies; Means and standard deviations.

	Alcoholics	Drug Addicts	Delinquents	Control Group
$\bar{x}$	2.78	3.12	2.89	3.32
s	0.89	0.88	0.88	0.71
n	46	61	66	57

A series of Duncan's a-posteriori-contrasts revealed that, as predicted, the control group had significantly smaller expectation-discrepancies than either the alcoholics ($p<.01$) and the delinquents ($p<.03$). The difference between the control subjects and the drug addicts, though in the predicted direction, did not attain statistical significance. It should be noted that no significant differences were found among the deviant groups themselves.

Our second hypothesis was that alcoholics and drug addicts would manifest stronger tendencies toward internal attribution than delinquents would.

The internality/externality of attribution was measured by means of an abbreviated version of Rotter's (1966) IEC-measure containing ten items (0 = extremely internal, 10 = extremely external attribution tendency). Table 2 presents the results (see page 352).

A simple inspection of the means reveals that neither of our predictions were confirmed; though the alcoholics show a tendency towards greater internality than the delinquents, the large difference between drug addicts and delinquents is in the opposite direction than was predicted. A Duncan a-posteriori-contrast revealed that this latter difference was significant at the .05 level. Also in contradiction to our

Table 2. Internal or external pattern of attribution;
         Means and standard deviations.

Alcoholics	Drug Addicts	Delinquents	Control Group
$\bar{x}$ 5.13	6.31	5.25	4.44
s 1.88	2.33	2.03	2.05
n 46	39^2	63	52^3

theory was the significant difference (by Duncan test) between
alcoholics and drug addicts, though the program of therapy
that the alcoholics were undergoing at the time of the study
may have induced unusually strong tendencies toward internal
attribution.

The data from previously reported comparisons of attribution
styles between deviants and non-deviants have been extremely
inconsistent (cf. Sauer et al., 1976). In the present study,
however, the deviant groups showed a consistent tendency to be
more external in their attributions than were the non-deviants.
The corresponding significance levels (determined by Duncan
tests) for each of these differences were as follows: Drug
addicts ($p<.01$), delinquents ($p<.09$), and alcoholics ($p<.10$).

In addition to Rotter's notion of generalized attribution
tendency, we tried to gather information concerning situationally-specific attribution tendencies by asking subjects to
indicate the extent to which they held themselves, others or
chance responsible for what they had so far achieved in life.

_____

[2] In the case of the drug addicts, it proved to be extremely
difficult to complete the final parts of the interview because many of these subjects found it too long and were not
willing to continue any further.

[3] Due to mistakes on the part of one interviewer the data from
eight subjects could not be used.

Table 3. Situationally-specific attribution tendency.
        (Responsibility for what has so far been achieved
        in life)
        Means and standard deviations.[a]

	Alcoholics			Drug Addicts			Delinquents		
	self	oth.	chance	self	oth.	chance	self	oth.	chance
$\bar{x}$	59	26	15	44	39	17	52	32	16
s	25	22	12	19	24	18	17	21	17
n		46			61			66	

	Control Group		
	self	others	chance
$\bar{x}$	65	24	11
s	17	15	1o
n		60	

[a]
  Cell entries represent distributions of perceived attribution sources
  averaged over subjects; each subject indicated the contribution of each
  source in percentages which had to add up to 1oo%.

Once again, drug addicts show less tendency for internal attribution than either the delinquents ($p < .08$) or the alcoholics
($p < .01$). While neither of these differences are consistent with
predictions derived from our theory, the former, as we have seen
above, is in the opposite direction from what was predicted.
As already mentioned, the latter difference may have been
caused by the type of therapy then in use in the alcoholic's
sanatorium.

The non-deviants were again found to show the strongest tendency of all groups to attribute their past achievements to
themselves as opposed to the environment. With the exception
of the comparison with alcoholics, all differences involving
the non-deviants were significant at or beyond the .05 level.

Turning now to hypothesis 3, our theory implies that the

various subject groups should differ among themselves according to the stability-instability of their attribution styles.
Stability was measured by three items relating to the perception of variability in events and states.

Table 4. Stable or variable pattern of attribution
         Means and standard deviations (over three items)
         Answer scale: 1 = very stable
                       5 = very variable

	Alcoholics	Drug Addicts	Delinquents	Control Group
$\bar{x}$	3.34	3.13	3.14	3.40
s	1.18	1.25	1.23	0.84
n	46	61	66	67

Though there were some differences with respect to single
items, their pattern was not systematic and, when an overall
score was calculated, no difference between groups obtained
(see Table 4). Thus, hypothesis 3 must be, for the time being,
rejected. It should be noted, however, that, in the absence of
more standardized alternatives, the ad-hoc operationalisation
of attributional variability is a point of methodological
weakness that stands in the way of further progress on this
question.

4.2. Additional analyses

Before discussing and interpreting the results reported so far,
we should present some further findings that are relevant to
other explanations of deviant behavior that have been proposed
in the literature. Non-deviant persons, for example, experienced a *family atmosphere*[4] as children that was significantly

---

[4] Measured with the question: "How pleasant was the prevailing
atmosphere in your family?" (5-point-scale from 'not' to
'very').

more pleasant than that experienced by any of the deviant
groups. The worst family atmosphere, on the other hand, was
reported by the drug addicts and alcoholics.

There were also some differences found with respect to *style
of upbringing*[5]. Drug addicts, for example, perceived having
had significantly less paternal support than did the non-
deviant controls (p<.01). Interestingly, the different group's
perceptions of their mothers' behavior were largely similar,
there being no significant differences with respect to either
"perceived support" or "perceived strictness".

When directly questioned on how lonely they felt, all deviant
groups reported significantly more frequent feelings of loneliness than the control group did. Those suffering the greatest loneliness were the drug addicts and alcoholics, though it
is unclear whether this was the cause or an effect of their
particular deviancies.

As would be expected, a large number of deviants had either no
occupation (22%) or were without a permanent place of work
(21%)[6]. All the people in the control group, by comparison,
had had occupational training, and only two were unemployed
at the time of the interview. Here also, however, it is impossible to distinguish causes from effects.

5. Summary and discussion

The hypothesis that deviants experience greater discrepancies
between expectations and reality than non-deviants was, on the

---

[5] Measured with the Styles-of-Upbringing-Questionnaire (reduced
to eight items) by Stapf, Herrmann, Stapf & Stäcker (1972).

[6] In the case of the delinquents, this was the situation before
the moment of imprisonment.

whole, confirmed with the present sample of juvenile alcoholics, drug addicts and delinquents. The central assumption of
our cognitive explanation for deviant behavior was thus corroborated: Deviant behavior results from the deviant's attempt
to reduce the heightened (relative to the non-deviants) levels
of tension they feel as a result of experiencing discrepancies
between their expectations and reality. Though such a causal
interpretation should not be attempted here (a longitudinal
study would have to be performed before causal inferences
could be made), one can at least agree on the basis of our
findings that there is a positive correlation between the degree of expectation-discrepancy experienced and deviant behavior. Though subjects in the present study were not asked to
specify the types of events that resulted in the discrepancies
they experienced, this variable should be investigated in the
future since what information we have available suggests that
the specific form that deviant behavior takes (e.g. criminal
acts against property) is determined by the specific area in
which the greatest and/or most important discrepancies were
experienced (e.g. financial area).

The second and third hypotheses dealt with the relation between specific forms of deviance and attributional style, the
argument being that how a person attributes the causes of the
discrepancies he/she experiences (i.e. whether he/she attributes them internally or externally, variably or invariably)
is a major determinant - along with normative inferences,
social models, etc. - of the sorts of deviant behavior that he/
she will perform.

Hypothesis 2 proposed that drug addicts tend more towards making internal attributions than do delinquents and was not confirmed, the results conforming to a pattern that was the
opposite from what was predicted. In addition, though our
theory led us to expect that alcoholics and drug addicts would
manifest similar attributional styles, the two groups were
found to differ significantly, the alcoholics showing a degree

of internality comparable to that found for the delinquents. It thus seems that, contrary to what we had claimed, alcoholism and drug addiction are not comparable forms of deviance with respect to their underlying attributional dynamics.

The therapy that alcoholics were undergoing at the time of the interview clearly had the effect of producing an unusually pronounced tendency toward internal attributions, thus rendering comparisons with this group with respect to attributional style of limited interest. It should be also noted, however, that social factors like the availability and the normative sanctioning of drug use and drinking are so important in shaping deviance patterns that it may be impossible to find homogeneous and consistent attributional tendencies within any given deviant group. This was supported by the way that members of these two deviant groups perceived members of the other in a significantly more negative light than members of their own: Concerning the question: "On what terms are you with alcoholics/drug addicts?", the alcoholics' mean response was +0.22 for themselves and -0.30 for the drug addicts, while the drug addicts' was +0.51 for themselves and -0.28 for the alcoholics[7].

It should finally be noted that, on both the "generalized" and "specific" attribution measures, the non-deviant control group showed a greater tendency towards internal attribution than the deviants did. This result might mean that deviants perceive the fact that they are deviant but can accept it neither in terms of the salient norms nor their self-image. Whatever dissonance they experience as a result of this might be reduced by ascribing the responsibility for their present status to external circumstances.

The third hypothesis led us to predict more attributions to invariable factors for the drug addicts than for delinquents,

---

[7]On a 5-point-scale from -2 to +2.

but the results indicated no differences between groups with respect to this attributional pattern. This failure to confirm ought not, however, to be blamed directly upon the theory, since the dependent variable used was operationalized in an ad-hoc-manner and may have therefore been faulty.

In summary, one can say that the central assumption of the outlined cognitive theory of deviant behavior was supported: Deviants report a greater experienced discrepancy between their expectations and reality than non-deviants. The further claim that people showing similar patterns of deviance attribute the causes of these discrepancies in similar ways was not confirmed.

Chapter 12   Justice Norms and Other Determinants of Allocation and Negotiation Behavior

H. Lamm, E. Kayser and T. Schwinger

1. Introduction: Allocation of material resources in experimental situations

Interpersonal conflict can result whenever material resources
are to be distributed among two or more persons. For example,
if the shares demanded by each person add to a sum greater
than the fund of resources available, then at least one of
them has to renounce part of what he/she aspires to. Who is to
renounce how much? Distribution conflicts of this kind can be
solved at least in two ways: a) through negotiating an agreement, usually by a process of mutual concession-making, or b)
through the application of norms and/or contracts (cf. Lamm,
1975, pp. 11-19; Thibaut & Kelley, 1959; Pruitt, 1972).

Negotiation can be time- and energy-consuming and can involve
processes that are detrimental to the "social climate" (e.g.
lies, threats, and false promises). In long-term groups with
recurring distribution problems, group-specific *norms* may be
developed to enable a quick solution without negotiation. But
even when there are no group-specific norms available, there
are *general* norms - in particular, societal principles of justice - that can guide, and thus facilitate, conflict resolution
(cf. Pruitt's [1972] distinction between group-specific and
general norms).

For both group-specific and general norms, however, further

---
[1] The authors are grateful to G. Mikula and G. F. Müller for
critical readings of earlier drafts.

conflict can arise over their applicability and the mode of application; this latter type of conflict may be resolved through negotiation.

A strict separation between negotiation and norm application is justifiable only as a first step in analysing conflict resolution. While early research on negotiation (Siegel & Fouraker, 1960) was largely limited to an analysis of the concession-making process, with individual profit maximization being the main motivational orientation, more recent work (e.g. Crott, 1972; Messick & McClintock, 1968) points to "social orientation" as an additional motive. This social orientation is, in the main, directed toward a solution consistent with participants' normative conceptions (in particular, their justice-related beliefs).

This dichotomization of conflict-resolution modes into negotiation versus norm application is, however, clearly reflected in experimental paradigms. Research on negotiation, for example, usually involves ad-hoc groups having no group-specific norms. Moreover, these groups are assigned the problem of distributing among themselves a commodity (usually money) supplied by the experimenter rather than something that they themselves produced through joint work. In what follows, we will refer to the situation created by the standard negotiating paradigm as having an "externally given resource" or "external reward", holding this in contrast to the "self-produced resource" typically allocated in justice research.

All theories of justice prescribe equal allocation as being the just way of distributing an external reward, this following from the fact, that, by definition, each negotiator's contributions to the attainment of the reward is equal - namely zero. Indeed, such a solution is found when the situation is maximally "transparent"; that is, when each party knows exactly what the other receives (as net value) in any given agreement alternative (cf. Crott, Kutschker & Lamm, 1977; Crott, Möntmann & Wender, 1978; Lamm, 1975, pp. 55-59).

Most negotiation games, however, are characterized by a lack of transparency, this lack having two consequences (among others): 1) There is a "search problem" in that, a) participants have to determine which solutions are most preferred with respect to joint profit (i.e. the Pareto-optimal solutions) and b) to the extent that participants are interested in arriving at a just solution, they have to find out what such a solution would be, and 2) each party may try to represent as "just" a solution that maximizes his/her own gains.

The first set of experiments (Part 2) described here deals with negotiations concerning external rewards, while a second (Part 3) deals with the allocation of rewards stemming from the recipients' own work. In the latter set, the primary question is how do participants allocate rewards when each has made qualitatively or quantitatively different contributions.

2. Negotiation over the distribution of external rewards

2.1. Theoretical introduction

The experimental investigation of negotiation processes can serve two purposes. First, it can clarify the processes and outcomes of everyday negotiations with a view to recommending "optimal" methods for the solution of distribution conflicts. Depending on the goals of the practitioner (or counsellor), this "optimization" may be based on considerations such as individual profit maximization or avoidance of egoistical and competitive behavior. Second, negotiation research can provide analyses of behaviors important for conflict resolution; for example, the development of trust (Deutsch, 1958), the application and consequences of threats (Crott, Lumpp & Wildermuth, 1976; Deutsch & Krauss, 1960), and the effects of communication restrictions and role obligations (Holmes & Lamm, 1979; Lamm, 1975; our own research program, see below).

One crucial aspect of negotiation situations is that the parties must come to an agreement over the distribution of the external reward in order to obtain any of that reward. This means that in the case of incompatible initial demands, at least one of the parties must make a concession. The more concession-making by a party, the smaller its share of the reward, while the greater its resistance, the greater the risk of negotiation failure. Thus, each party to the negotiation finds itself in an approach-avoidance conflict.

Negotiators can behave in any of three general motivational orientations. An *individualistically* motivated negotiator tries to handle the situation in such a way that the resulting material gain (i.e. share of the reward) is maximal for his party. A *competitively* oriented negotiator, on the other hand, is often prepared to renounce his profit in order to prevent his opponent from getting an equal or better share himself. The negotiator can also, however, be *socially* oriented, being ready to renounce potential profit in order to attain a "just" distribution or to help the opposing party (though this latter altruistic motivation had rarely been evident in experimental negotiations).

Of course it is the third category - the social orientation - that is of particular interest here. Given the usefulness of social norms for rapid, enduring and cost-saving conflict resolution (cf. Pruitt, 1972; Thibaut & Kelley, 1959), these "social" behaviors are less "irrational" than might appear from a decision-theoretical perspective, the latter with its assumption that individual profit maximization is the one and only goal in conflict settings.

Negotiation behavior is determined by a multitude of factors that can be classified as either *structural* (e.g. the payoff matrix, or the number of agreement alternatives), *situational* (e.g. social) or *personal*, though these three categories (and especially the first two) are not entirely independent (cf. Vinacke, 1969; Crott, Kutschker & Lamm, 1977).

A central aim in our own research has been to identify the
situational factors that determine the relative dominance of
egoistic and social motivations in negotiations (see also the
theoretical considerations in Apfelbaum, 1974). Specifically,
we were interested in finding the social variables responsible
for determining whether a negotiator responds with toughness
or works with his counterpart(s) to arrive at a "just" solution.[2]

We focused on two sources of social influence, the counterpart's behavior and the negotiator's constituency or reference
group, investigating their effects under various conditions.
By varying the experimental procedure, it is possible to independently vary the importance of either influence source in a
given negotiation. At one extreme, both sources of influence
can be eliminated by procedures such as a) limiting the possibility for interaction between negotiators to the exchange of
written notes (cf. the concept of the "minimal social situation" - Kelley, Thibaut, Radloff & Mundy, 1962) and b) isolat-
ing the negotiator from his constituency for the period immediately preceding, during and after the negotiations. At the
other extreme, however, the negotiators could be provided with
multiple channels over which to interact and be allowed to
guard close contact with his/her constituency at all phases
of the negotiation.

These two factors - the counterpart's behavior and the negotiator's constituency - are represented in Figure 1.

2.2. Situational influences on negotiation: The negotiators' interaction possibilities

The breadth of interactional possibilities between a negotiat-

---

[2] Indices for toughness are: a high initial demand; small and
infrequent concessions; lies (under-representation of own payoff possibilities); threats; and breakoff.

Figure 1

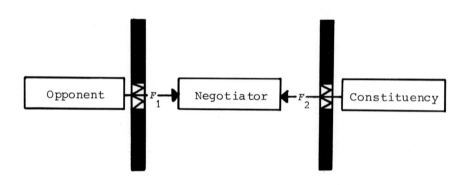

F_1 and F_2 ("F" standing for "factor" or "force"; cf. McGrath, 1966) indicate social influences emanating from the opponent and from (the negotiator's) constituency, respectively. The vertical bars indicate the "barriers" that may shield the negotiator from these influences.

---

or (A) and his opponent (B) can vary widely between situations. With respect to the operation of norms of justice, it is important to note that better interaction possibilities can lead to more information; i.e. to more transparency concerning the structural basis of conflict. It is only by having complete information on each other's payoff possibilities (i.e. the net value of each agreement alternative) that they can identify "just" and "egoistic" solutions. Egoistic demands can, under certain conditions, lead to sanctions, deviations from justice

norms being punished through verbal disapproval, threat, or
breakoff. A broader spectrum of interaction possibilities
implies enhanced opportunities for mutual influence and exchange of information, especially with regard of payoff possibilities. Thus a) the just solution is more recognizable and
b) deviations from it are more easily sanctioned.

In addition to having an effect on the interpersonal level, an
increase in the range of interaction possibilities can also
have an "intra-personal" effect: The *resultant increase in
transparency* will make it harder for a negotiator to shirk the
"force" of the social-normative solution. Since justice norms
are internalized, recognizable deviations from the just solution will lead to intrapersonal sanctions. Note that this
means that increasing the range of interaction possibilities
reduces the occurrence of counter-normative or "unfair" behavior. The greater the barriers against free interaction,
therefore, the less inhibited will a negotiator be in behaving
counter-normatively.

2.2.1. Hypotheses concerning situational influences

In light of the above considerations, the possibilities for
social contact between the negotiators were experimentally
varied in order to study the influence that the content, form
and breadth of the communication has in the negotiation process. More specifically, we wanted to know the conditions under
which information concerning payoff contingencies is or is not
distorted, or not exchanged at all, and the influence that
these conditions have on the process and outcome of the conflict resolution.[3]   The following paragraphs provide an

---

[3] When in the following we use the term *"information"* - as in
"information exchange" - it is meant to apply specifically to
information concerning one's *payoff contingencies*. The latter
term refers to the value (or net profit) accruing to a negotiator from the various agreement alternatives (or

overview of the independent variables investigated.

Exchange of information. The early stages of negotiations are frequently characterized by *non-transparency,* neither negotiator knowing the payoffs that his opponent would receive from the various agreement alternatives.

This opens up possibilities for distorted presentation of one's own payoffs (e.g. bluffing, understatement). In what follows (Section 2.2.1.1.), *"transparency"* will refer to situations in which a negotiator knows the payoff contingencies of his opponent. In our experiments, we varied whether information exchange was obligatory, voluntary or prohibited, as well as whether or not it was possible for the negotiators to bluff one another.[4]

Verbal communication. We investigated (Section 2.2.1.2.) the effects of varying whether or not negotiators were allowed to converse with one another, or restricting their communication to standardized cards. When conversation was allowed, we also tested the effect of giving either negotiator the power to block the communication channel.

Visual contact. In these studies (Section 2.2.1.3.) it was varied whether or not negotiators had a barrier between them that blocked visual contact and therefore eliminated all gestural and mimic components of non-verbal communication be-

---

[3] "solutions"). These payoff contingencies are provided by the experimenter, usually in the form of a payoff table (or schedule) given to the negotiator. The term *"communication possibilities"* refers to the number and type of available communication channels (e.g. verbal-oral, verbal-written, visual).

[4] Two other experiments were conducted to investigate the effects of providing information asymetrically. The role of "agreement pressure" (cost of bidding) was also investigated in these experiments, which are reported in Lamm (1976a,b). This research will not, however, be described further in the present chapter.

tween them.

Anticipation of future interaction with the opponent. In our
experiments, the negotiators usually did *not* anticipate having
any further contact with their opponents following the negotiations. In one experiment, however, one group of negotiators
were told at the start of negotiations that they would be
brought together to talk with one another following the session.
(Section 2.2.1.4.).

2.2.1.1. Exchange of information

Information on the opponent's payoff contingencies is a prerequisite for the identification of a "just" solution. Such
information is also necessary, therefore, for negotiators to
take sanctions against one another, since sanctions are generally triggered by the perception that the opponent has acted
egoistically rather than justly. All social psychological
theories of justice (see Part 3) predict that, in the usual
paradigm, the just solution will be perceived as an equal
allocation of the available resources, this following from the
fact that the inputs of the two negotiators are generally equal
(as we have seen above, in the usual case of "external rewards", neither negotiator makes any input to the resource
pool, the latter being provisioned entirely by the experimenter).

In virtually all research using *asymmetrical* payoff matrices,
the advantageous payoff contingencies are assigned through
random assignment and not "earned." In Siegel and Fouraker's
(1960) pioneering work on the "bilateral monopoly", maximal
transparency led to more equal allocations even in the case of
asymmetrical payoff schedules (cf. also, Morgan & Sawyer, 1967).
In the case of non-transparency, negotiators appeared to assume
that the payoff contingencies were equally distributed (cf.
Kelley, Beckman & Fischer, 1967); that is, they assumed that
over all possible alternatives, the payoff opportunities were

the same for both.

As an example of an asymmetrical payoff matrix, take the situation where two partners have to distribute a profit but have
differential costs to deduct before arriving at their net payoffs. The just solution would be an equal distribution of the
net profits, because these different costs do not represent
contribution differences but are externally caused (by the
experimenter). This means that the equal division of the sum
allotted to the parties would, in fact, be an unequal and
therefore unjust distribution of the net profits.

Consider now the role of transparency - that is, the presence
versus absence of information concerning the other's payoff
contingencies - in the asymmetric situation. The clearer it
becomes that the equal distribution of resources is not the
just solution, the weaker will be the position of the advantaged negotiator (i.e. negotiator with lower costs), as social
norms (as well as the sanctions that support them) require that
a person with unjustified advantage refrain from making unjustified demands (as would be the case, in the above example,
if the person with lower costs demanded an equal share). By
refusing to exchange information or by bluffing, the advantaged
party can, however, attempt to prevent the other from suspect-
ing the payoff asymmetry. Our own hypotheses are that the
possibility of bluffing and withholding information results in
less equal outcome allocations, and that the negotiators
favored by the payoff matrix will be more likely to withhold
information and/or bluff than ones who are not. In addition, we
expected that negotiators having the possibility to bluff would
be "tougher" (e.g. would make higher opening demands), Fischer
(1969) having previously argued that possibilities for bluffing
generally have a destructive effect on the negotiation process.
For asymmetrical payoff matrices, we expected the largest payoff differences to occur in a condition where information exchange was not allowed.

Experiment 1. In a study by Lamm and Rosch (1972), a modified
version of the "Game of Nines" (Kelley et al., 1967) was used.
In this type of game, nine points are to be distributed in each
of several negotiation trials. At the beginning of a trial,
each player receives a "cost" card indicating the amount he
has to subtract from his share of the nine units in order to
arrive at his net payoff. The instructions state that this cost
card must not be shown to the opponent. The negotiations were
done without visual contact, and verbal communication was
possible only via cards with prepared statements (e.g. "make
a concession - I made one last time").[5] The subjects (72 **male**
university students) were paid five German marks (DM) per
hour; in addition, each payoff point was worth 0.10 DM. The
following experimental conditions were created with respect to
the exchange of information concerning payoff contingencies:
no information exchange; obligatory, honest information exchange; and obligatory information exchange with possibilities
for bluffing.

Results: Negotiators in the "no information exchange" condition
behaved similarly to those who could bluff. Their opening demands (corrected for costs) were significantly higher, and the
intradyadic payoff differences larger, than in the "obligatory,
honest information" condition. Negotiators in the latter condition communicated less with one another than those in the
other two, a finding that seems to indicate that verbal communication is not very important for arriving at agreement in
high transparency conditions.

Indeed, in the "Game of Nines" a single piece of truthful
information concerning one's cost makes known to the opponent
one's entire payoff schedule (i.e. the value of all agreement
alternatives) on the given trial, since a fixed number of

---

[5] In our later presentation of the negotiation experiments in
this section (Part 2), only those procedural details will be
mentioned which deviate from the procedures described here.

points are to be distributed. This peculiarity of the negotiation situation may explain why information exchange, with
bluff permitted, results in no more cooperation among negotiators than occurs in the "no-information exchange" condition:
Even a single instance of perceived bluffing (i.e. a statement
of information that the recipient does not believe) results in
continuing non-transparency.

Experiment 2. A second study (Kayser, 1974; Crott, Kàyser &
Lamm, 1980) examined the influence of information exchange
using another kind of negotiation game. In this game, the
transmittal of one piece of information does not (as in the
"Game of Nines") make known the whole payoff schedule; only
clues are provided. Subjects in this experiment (156 male
university students) participated in only one negotiation trial.

The subjects' task was to agree on one of 45 alternatives. On
the average, the payoffs of player *A* were higher than those of
player *B* by a ratio of 1.6 : 1.0. This fact was not known to
the participants, but they could theoretically infer it through
appropriate information exchange - see below. *A* could win a
maximum of 30 DM, *B* only 18 DM, each alternative yielding a
different payoff. A Pareto-optimal, *equal* allocation (11.25:
11.25) was possible as well as a Pareto-optimal, unequal allocation based on each player's maximal possible payoff (15.00:
9.00).

At the beginning of the game, each player knew only his own
payoff schedule; that is, for each alternative he knew only
what he himself would get if that alternative were agreed upon.
At any given information exchange subjects could transmit information about a single alternative only. Thus, each piece of
information, if it was true and accepted as true by its recipient, rendered transparent only a single point of the sender's
payoff matrix - not the entire matrix as in the "Game of Nines."

Results: The greatest disparity in payoffs between dyad members
came in the condition where no information exchange was

possible. When bluffing was possible, it too led to a disparity in payoffs. Those negotiators favored by the payoff
asymmetry bluffed more frequently than did the disadvantaged
players; they also communicated less and reduced their information requests over time, whereas the disadvantaged players
requested information constantly. In contrast to what we had
expected, the advantaged player seldom refused to answer the
other's request for information.

This last finding becomes plausible if one remembers that the
attempt, on the advantaged player's part, to maintain non-
transparency is a means to "dodge" the normatively prescribed,
equal payoff solution. Now, explicit refusal to provide requested information concerning the payoff associated to a
given alternative is likely to make the opponent suspicious
that one is trying to "hide" one's advantage. More preferable
are less direct tactics such as bluffing and not requesting
information from the other. Refusal to give information is
more apt to be interpreted by the disadvantaged opponent as
uncooperative behavior and may thus lead to reactions of toughness.

The fact that, in this experiment - in contrast to the above-
mentioned investigation (experiment 1) - the exchange of information in conditions with a bluff permitted led to more
equal payoffs than negotiators without any information exchange
shows that Fischer's (1969) assumption on the destructive influence of bluffing possibilities must be modified. Our results
in experiment 1 and 2 show that the availability of bluffing
possibilities may have different consequences, depending on
the structure of the negotiation task.

2.2.1.2. Possibilities for verbal communication

Verbal communication between two or more parties can facilitate
the coordination of their behavior. The extent to which verbal
communication actually fulfills this function is, however,

dependent upon the parties' dominant negotiation goals. In
competitive situations that are "enriched" by possibilities
for threat and punishment (cf. Deutsch & Krauss, 1962; Nardin,
1968; Smith & Anderson, 1975), verbal communication appears to
work against such coordination by serving the dominant competitive goals.   In more cooperative game situations, on the
other hand, verbal communications has been observed to facilitate the finding of mutually satisfactory solutions, not only
by permitting direct appeals for cooperation, but also by opening the way for the sanctioning of non-normative or unethical
behavior on the part of the adversary. Studies by Wichman
(1970) with 2x2 matrix games imply, furthermore, that, under
conditions of adequate transparency, communication can itself
promote such cooperative motives on the part of negotiations.
From this we hypothesized that, given high transparency, unrestricted possibilities for communication would facilitate
conflict resolution.[6]

Experiment 3. In this experiment (Lamm & Kayser, 1976) we used
a modified version of the "Game of Nines" (see experiment 1) in
which negotiations had to partition 18 units in each trial.
There were three different experimental conditions: free oral
communication; restricted written communication via pre-
prepared cards; and a condition in which no communication was
permitted other than the written exchange of bids. The subjects
were 72 female university students.

Results: Negotiations were broken off most frequently in the
no communication condition, thus providing evidence that communication possibilities facilitate the "coordination" problem
posed by a negotiation task. In the Game of Nines, where a
fixed amount is to be distributed, a smaller number of

---

[6] "Unrestricted" means that participants can talk freely,
without any restriction on the contents of their utterances;
that is, they can even say things that are not related to the
negotiations.

breakoffs implies a higher number of Pareto-optimal solutions, since breakoff means choice of the one-and-only Pareto-non-optimal solution (i.e. no agreement and, therefore, no attainment of the reward). However, initial demands - discrepancies among which can be considered to be an index of initial manifest conflict - and payoff discrepancies within the dyads were not affected by communication conditions. Thus, communication possibilities do not necessarily lower initial conflict or lead to equal net gains.

As regards initial demands, a special procedural feature of this experiment should be mentioned. Before being informed about the communication condition, subjects were asked to indicate, for each of the oncoming negotiations, the initial demand they intended to make. In later analyzing this data, we calculated a "relative initial demand" by taking the difference between these intended demands and the initial demands that the subjects actually made. In terms of this index, possibilities for communicating were found to have an effect, with subjects in the free communication condition showing the greatest drop from their intended to their actual initial demand.

A final result of this experiment was that, in the post-negotiation ratings, subjects in the free communication condition judged their opponent's behavior to have been more cooperative, more reasonable and less hostile than did subjects in either of the other two conditions.

On the whole, the experiment seems to indicate that the availability of free communication had positive rather than negative effects. The decrease of communication-restriction resulted - in other tasks than that used by Deutsch & Krauss (1962) - in refraining from bluffing. Moreover, possibilities for free communication were conducive to mutual trust and honesty and resulted in positive evaluations of the negotiation situation and opponent.

2.2.1.3. Possibility for visual contact

Our hypothesis, as stated above, was that visual contact impedes deviation from normative, social behavior. Unless the situational context is such as to evoke competition, the sight of the partner should operate as a "conditional signal" for more cooperative, less egoistical behavior. Furthermore, an egoistical negotiator visually observable to his opponent is in greater danger of being recognized as egoistical and retaliated against through unyieldingness, verbal aggression, etc. Wichman (1970) shows that free visual contact, together with free communication possibilites, facilitates cooperation, while Jellison and Ickes (1974) analyze the relation between competitive interaction and avoidance of visual contact.

Experiment 3 (continued). In the experiment described above, visual contact was manipulated by varying whether or not an opaque screen separated the negotiators.

Results: Subjects in the visibility condition made lower initial demands and, as would be expected if there was less initial conflict between opponents, reached a final agreement in shorter time than did subjects in the no visibility condition.

2.2.1.4. Anticipation of future interaction with opponent

In line with our general assumption - that justice-oriented behaviors facilitate conflict solutions as well as create a "good" social climate for future interaction -, we hypothesized that behavior during negotiation will be less egoistical when future interaction with the same opponent is expected.

Experiment 4 (Lamm & Kayser, in preparation). The 18-point version of the "Game of Nines" was used. Subjects were male and female high school students. In the "anticipation" condition,

the two negotiators were told at the beginning that they would
get together with each other after the negotiation for a fif-
teen-minute free communication period. In the "no-anticipation"
condition, subjects were told that they would not get together
after the negotiation. Negotiations were conducted with visual
contact and free oral communication.

Results: In comparing the anticipation with the no anticipation
condition, it was found that in the former: a) initial demands
were lower (and thus there was less initial conflict), b) the
average concession was higher, c) there were fewer threats of
breakoff, d) the final demands were lower, and e) the opponent's behavior was judged on a final questionnaire to have
been more cooperative. Thus, our predictions were generally
confirmed.

2.3. Influences of the constituency: Negotiation by represent-
   atives

Consider again Figure 1. The questions examined so far have
concerned the effects of the "height" of the barrier existing
between the negotiator and his opponent. The experimental results were on the whole supportive of our proposition that the
dominance of individualistic behavior tendencies is positively
related to the height of that barrier. Lowering the barrier by
increasing the possibility for communication, visual contact
or transparency of the payoff matrix facilitates not only the
coordination of behavior aimed at attaining higher joint payoffs (e.g. Pareto-optimal solutions) but also the attaining
of balanced, "just" solutions.

The negotiator, however, may not only have to deal with his
opponent but may also be subject to influences from persons or
groups *external* to the negotiation relationship; that is, from
a reference group and/or constituency (F_2 in Figure 1) (we will
use the latter term to refer to both kinds of groups). Such
group influences may operate in several ways, depending on the

specifics of the group-negotiator relationship. First, the
negotiator may derive his/her normative beliefs about just allocations from his/her group (cf. Walster, Berscheid & Walster,
1973). In our paradigm, based as it is on external rewards,
such beliefs usually imply equal allocation.

Secondly, the negotiator may feel that his/her group share
some of the responsibility for his/her action and may, as a
result, feel less inhibited from acting counter-normatively.
We will focus on two aspects of such responsibility sharing:
a) If the group members deliberate before the negotiation takes
place, they then may become polarized towards a more egoistical
stance and hence encourage the negotiator to pursue a tougher
(and possibly more risky) negotiation strategy; b) The group
may provide the negotiator with an explicit mandate that, besides specifying the goals towards which he/she is to strive,
may override his/her normative obligations vis-à-vis his opposing counterpart. The group is in more of a position to justify
egoistic tendencies since it is not directly exposed to the
presence and influence attempts of the opposing negotiator
(cf. F_1 in Figure 1).

Now, the greater the "barrier" between the negotiator and his/
her opponent, the more easily can he/she serve his/her group's
egoistic interests. Also, the more egoistic the stance of the
group and the more directly the negotiator is subject to its
influence (F_2) (i.e. the lesser the barrier vis-à-vis the
group), the more "immune" will he/she be to the opponent's
influence (F_1). These are the basic propositions guiding the
experiments discussed below.

The consideration of group influences on individual negotiation
behavior is a step toward greater "realism" in experimental
negotiation research and thus also a step toward a greater
understanding of everyday negotiation behavior. At the same
time, it permits the investigation of important social-psychological processes that are not specific to negotiation situations (for example, group-induced polarization; role behavior).

A review of the existing research concerning social or group influences on negotiation behavior can be found in Crott, Kutschker, and Lamm (1977, pp. 89-173).

2.3.1. Group influences upon a person negotiating for himself

A person facing a negotiation will often consult with members of a group to whom he/she belongs (e.g. friends, family, colleagues), being especially prone to turn to those people who either face or have had previous experience in similar situations. Such group discussions may lead to a modification of an individual's proclivities. As has been shown by previous research on the group-induced choice shift, group discussion frequently leads to *polarization*; that is, an extremization of participants' positions in the initially dominant direction (cf. Lamm & Myers, 1978, for a review and discussion of recent research). In one of our experiments, we applied the group-polarization hypotheses to a negotiation context, predicting that discussion among individuals espousing the same side of an issue would lead to a toughening of their position.

Experiment 5. This experiment (Lamm & Sauer, 1974) used a modified version of the "Game of Nines", the participants being assigned to one of two bargaining positions and asked to note down their prospective initial demands for nine negotiation trials. In the *discussion condition*, subjects were then to discuss, in triads of which all members were assigned the same position, the question of the initial demand. No consensual group decision was required. Subjects in the *control* condition were asked to go through their notes again, individually.

Results: The preparatory group discussion led to higher initial demands, whereas going through notes individually had no influence on demand level.

It should be noted that Lamm and Sauer's subjects were *not* representatives of the groups within which the discussion took place. A smilar polarization effect may, however, occur when

the preparatory discussion takes place among a set of individuals, one of whom is to represent the others in an upcoming
negotiation.

2.3.2. Group influences upon representatives

Following McGrath (1966), group influence in a negotiation representative may be seen as a force operating on him/her, the
influence of the opponent and that of the social environment
(e.g. a mediator, an audience) being two other such forces.
Yet while the two latter forces act usually in the direction
of an agreement (and hence concession-making), influence from
the negotiator's own group usually acts in the direction of
resistance to concession-making and hence entails the risk of
non-agreement and the subsequent failure of the negotiation
process.

In making concessions, the negotiator risks that his group will
disapprove of his performance, which in turn may lead to a
withdrawal of the negotiator's representative status, material
punishment, expulsion from the group, and so on. Adams (1969,
1976) sees the representative as being in a "boundary-role
position", as he is a member both of his own group as well as
of the negotiation unit (for more detailed analysis, cf.
Holmes & Lamm, 1979). This may result in his loyalty being
doubted by his group and his concession-making being interpreted as disloyal behavior. Hence the representative must reckon
with the possibility that the group may try to exert even
greater control over his/her negotiating behavior. These considerations add up to the general hypothesis that negotiators
representing a group behave with greater toughness than do
those negotiating for themselves. Indeed, this hypothesis has
been supported by several experiments (e.g. Benton, 1972;
Benton & Druckman, 1973, 1974; Druckman, Solomon & Zechmeister,
1972; Vidmar, 1971).

2.3.2.1. Elected and non-elected representatives

If the representative is the elected spokesman of his group
and subject to recall, he presumably experiences a particularly
high level of group pressure and should, as a result, identify
especially strongly with his group and its goals (cf. Lamm &
Kogan, 1970). A non-elected representative, who, for example,
was appointed by an external agency, would feel less obligated
by his representative role and hence show less group identification (cf. Lamm, 1978b).

Experiment 5 (continued). Before the negotiations, two separate
three-men groups were formed from which, after some preparatory
discussion of issues, a representative was either elected or
selected on a chance basis: The negotiating behavior of these
elected and selected representatives was then compared to that
of a third group of negotiators who, though they took part in a
preliminary group discussion, were instructed to negotiate for
themselves. The design also included a fourth group of negotiators who negotiated without having gone through a preliminary group discussion.

Results: Elected representatives broke negotiations off more
frequently (thus demonstrating greater toughness) and consequently attained lower payoffs than non-representatives.
Elected and selected representatives showed a greater tendency than non-representatives to underestimate their opponent's
costs. There were no significant differences found between
elected and selected representatives.

This last result may be due to the fact that the group election
was secret and without discussion. In Lamm and Kogan (1970),
election was through open discussion and representatives were
found to be tougher than non-representatives. Also, Clark and
Sechrest (1976) demonstrated that group representatives elected
by a clear majority show greater risk taking than representatives elected by a less decisive margin. Lamm (1978a) discusses other possible reasons why no differences were found

between elected and selected representatives, some of which
may provide hypotheses for future research.

2.3.2.2. Risks involved in the representatives' tough negotia-
tion behavior

In most experiments dealing with negotiation behavior by representatives as opposed to non-representatives, the negotiations did not involve any material payoffs (e.g. Kogan, Lamm
& Trommsdorff, 1972; Lamm, 1973). Since cooperation is generally lower when negotiation is for imaginary than real money
(Gallo, 1963; Müller, 1976; Müller & Crott, 1978a,b), an experiment was designed to investigate the effects of the nature
of the payoffs in negotiations between both representatives
and non-representatives. If non-agreement means not receiving
real money, a representative may hesitate more before risking
- through toughness - a breakoff and subsequent loss for his
constituency than he would if only imaginary money were at
stake.

Another risk of toughness lies in the time span which is given
for reaching an agreement: If time is short, toughness means
greater risk of breakoff. Therefore we expected representatives to be tougher in negotiations than non-representatives if
payoffs are imaginary and/or time is long. If payoffs are real
and time is short, no difference in toughness is to be expected.

Experiment 6 (Lamm & Schwinger, in preparation[a]*)*. Subjects
(120 male university students) played four trials of the
above-mentioned version of the "Game of Nines", each trial
involving the partitioning of 18 points. The nature of the payoff was varied, it being either real money (.30 DM per point)
or just the points themselves. A second independent variable
was the time given to the subjects to reach an agreement, this
being either 2.5 or 17 minutes.

In each session, two subjects were placed together and asked
to choose a representative to negotiate with an alleged representative from another dyad. The latter, however, was in fact
negotiating for himself and thought his opponent was doing
the same.

Results: There were no significant differences found between
representatives and non-representatives. Since the represen-
tative-toughness effect has previously been found for constituencies of one (Benton, 1972; Druckman et al., 1972), the
reason for the similarity of representatives and non-representatives in the present experiment may have been due to the
fact that the constituents had, unlike those in the previous
experiments, no power of material sanction.

2.3.2.3. Reactions of a non-representative to a representative

Research comparing representatives and non-representatives has
been confined to situations in which both negotiators are in
the same role. The opposite situation, however, occurs quite
frequently in everyday life, one party being a representative
(e.g. salesman or civil servant) and the other acting in his/
her own self-interest (a client or citizen). The "asymmetric"
situation also allows the examination of some theoretically
relevant questions that can, for convenience, be divided into
two categories:

1) What kind of negotiation behavior does a non-representative
(i.e. a person acting on his own behalf) expect of a representative? We start with the assumption that the non-representative anticipates relatively tough behavior from an opponent who
is a representative, since he/she has an idea of the latter's
difficult situation vis-à-vis the group. Furthermore, we hypothesize that the non-representative's reaction will be a joint
function of these *expectancies* and the opponent's *actual behavior*. As Jones and Davis (1965) have shown, observers interpret behaviors that are discrepant with their expectations as

being indicative of intentionality or personal disposition.
Also, such role-discrepant behavior tends to be judged more
extremely (positively or negatively) than role-conforming
behavior (Holmes, 1976). Thus, if a person expects a representative to show toughness on the basis of the latter's role
obligation, he will attribute the representative's unyieldingness less to internal (person-specific) causes than he would
the same behavior from a non-representative. Such "external"
attribution should be especially likely when the representative is perceived as being under strong group pressure.

When the opponent is compromising, however, his behavior should
be seen as role discrepant and, by the same logic as above,
result in his being positively evaluated - unless he is perceived to be acting under directions from his group, in which
case an external attribution will ensue.

2) The second hypothesis to be examined is that a) a person
acting on his own behalf will be less likely to attribute an
opponent's tough or soft negotiation behavior internally if
the opponent is believed to be a representative, and that b)
the person will be less confident in predicting the opponent's
behavior in future situations when the latter acts only for
himself. Following the reasoning of Jones and Davis (1965)
given above, people will be unlikely to attribute a representative's behavior to features of his personality when they
perceive that he acts according to instructions received from
his constituency. This reluctance to attribute behavior to
internal characteristics will also make people less certain
of how the opponent will act in future situations when he is
not bound by instructions from his group.

Experiment 7 (Lamm & Schwinger, in preparation [b]). This experiment again used the 18-points version of the modified
"Game of Nines", the subjects (36 male and 36 female high
school students) each playing five trials against an opponent
who was an experimental confederate. Half of the subjects negotiated against a tough opponent who made a relatively high

initial demand, few concessions and frequent threats of breaking off, while the other half negotiated against a soft opponent. For both, the tough and the soft opponent, subjects were
told either that he was acting individually (i.e. as a non-
representative), acting on instructions from a group whom he
consulted before each trial, or acting in representation of a
group without consultation. After the five trials, the subject
was asked to complete a questionnaire concerning the causal
attribution of the opponent's negotiation behavior and was then
told that there would be five other negotiations against the
same opponent but that the latter would now negotiate for himself. The subject was then asked to complete a questionnaire
asking about the opponent's likely behavior in the oncoming
negotiations.

Results: Before the negotiation, the subjects did *not* perceive
the representatives and non-representatives as differing in
their negotiation goals. They did, however, show some differences in their attributions concerning the opponents' behavior, making greater use of external attributions when an instructed opponent was tough than when he was yielding, which
suggests that yielding behavior was perceived as being counter-
normative in this instance. There were no differences found in
either of the other two opponent-role conditions with respect
to the internality-externality of attributions. As to the subjects' predictions concerning the opponent's future behavior,
however, our hypothesis was confirmed: The behavior of non-
representatives was predicted with greater certainty than that
of representatives.

2.4. Summary

The first part of our report has been concerned with the "classical" experimental negotiation situation in which rewards are
distributed among negotiators as a result of the agreement process. We investigated the effects of two types of influence;

that stemming from the opponent, and that originating within one's own group. In the latter case, we also asked how a negotiator's perceptions and expectations are affected by his knowledge that the opponent is subject to direct influence by a constituency.

Our results show, first of all, that as possibilities for social interaction increase, so does the influence of social norms for fairness. An exception must be made here, however, for bluffing: Allowing subjects to bluff increases the mistrust between them and encourages negotiation strategies aimed at profit maximization, though allowing free verbal communication between the subjects (as opposed to limiting them to the use of standardized messages as did Krauss and Deutsch [1966]) can prevent this degradation of the negotiation process.

Secondly, we saw that negotiating as a group representative can lead to an increase in toughness (experiment 5), though such an effect is unlikely when the constituency has no means of material sanction (see experiment 6). Subjects were found to attribute toughness in their opponents to the effects of role pressures exerted by the opponents' constituencies, while "soft" or accomodating behavior was perceived as being role discrepant and attributed to dispositional factors (experiment 7).

3. The roles of justice norms in the allocation of team-produced outcomes

3.1. Theoretical introduction

Unlike most of the negotiation games used in laboratory research, *real* negotiation situations often involve the distribution of outcomes that were *produced* or earned through production either by the negotiators themselves or by the group that they represent. In such cases, the "just" solution is

usually agreed on as representing the amount of each party's
contribution to the outcome to be distributed. Problems arise,
however, in agreeing to the size of these contributions and,
hence, to the size of the share to which each party is entitled.
The respective claims may be divergent if the two parties contributed in different ways toward the outcome or if a precedent
favors a particular way of dividing the outcome that, though
formerly just, works now to one party's disadvantage. The
communication in such allocation settings will thus deal not
only with how the outcome is distributed but will also be concerned with assessing each party's relative contribution.

There are a number of theoretical approaches to interpersonal
justice that describe and explain the concepts of just distributions persons may have in these types of situation. We will
here, however, center our discussion on two basic theoretical
stances.

3.1.1. Equity theory

Walster and her colleagues have attempted to develop Adams'
(1963, 1965) equity theory into a general social-psychological
theory (Walster et al., 1973, 1977, 1978; Walster & Walster,
1975). They assume that, in social interaction, a condition
will be experienced as equitable - and will be aspired to - if
the "relative gains" of the interaction participants are equal.
As in Adams (1965), relative gains are conceived as a ratio
between outcomes and inputs.[7] When a person feels that inequity
- an inequality of relative gains - exists, he will experience
distress, and will try to re-establish equity through some

---

[7]While Adams (1965) proposed the ratio O/I, more complex versions of the outcome-input relationship and the equity formula are presented and discussed in the writings of the
Walsters (referred to above) and in Harris (1976), Walster
(1975, 1976) and Samuel (1976a,b).

form of cognitive and/or behavioral reactions (e.g. changing the inputs and/or outcomes). Equity theorists have analyzed numerous types of social interaction with respect to reactions to inequity (e.g. victim/exploiter; recipient/philanthropist; employee/employer; friendship and intimate relationships), assuming in each case that the interaction is directed towards achieving justice as equity theory prescribes. Equity exists, however, only in the eyes of whoever happens to be judging the interaction, and this makes agreement among several persons with respect to what is equitable unlikely (cf. Adams & Freedman, 1976, p. 45; Walster et al., 1978, p. 10). Equity theory has been criticized by Deutsch (1975), Lerner (1977), Mikula and Schwinger (1978), Müller and Crott (1978a) and Sampson (1975), among others.

3.1.2. Classification approaches

Other approaches to justice postulate several principles that are applied according to the situational conditions present at the time of outcome distribution (Deutsch, 1975; Leventhal, 1976a,b; Lerner, 1977; Lerner, Miller & Holmes, 1976; Mikula, 1980; Mikula & Schwinger, 1978; Sampson, 1975; Schwinger, 1980). They all agree, however, on three essential justice principles: the *equality principle* (to each an equal amount), the *contribution principle* (to each according to his contributions[8]) and the *need principle* (to each according to his needs). Each approach, furthermore, develops a classification system that groups situations according to the probabilities that each of these principles will be applied. Leventhal (1976b) postulates a compromise model in which the shares,

---

[8]An exact definition of contribution is not given. In addition to causally relevant contributions toward outcome production, Leventhal (1976a,b) lists other characteristics, such as social origin - as perceived by the participant/observer - as potential contributions. Lerner (1977) too fails to provide a precise definition of the term.

calculated independently for each principle, are combined
according to each principle's situational weighting. Lerner
(1977) and Mikula and Schwinger (1978) assume, on the other
hand, that, in any given situation, only one justice principle
will be taken into account. All of these authors agree, however,
that the social relationship between the allocator and recip-
ient(s) is an important situational determinant of a principle's dominance; the higher the interpersonal attraction,
the less consideration will be given to the contribution
principle as compared to the equality or need principles.

3.1.3. Problems of applying equity theory

1) The theory is vague as to the inputs considered relevant
in deciding on a just allocation. Though the theory directs
attention to the group(s) in which the allocator is a member,
it specifies neither which of the group characteristics are
relevant nor what concepts a person brings with him into the
allocation situation. Some a priori assumptions as to the list
of inputs would be extremely useful.

2) Research results indicate that the type of social relationship between the participants co-determines allocation behavior (Lerner, 1974; Mikula & Schwinger, 1978), a finding more
in line with the classification approach than with equity
theory.

3) The breadth of the exchange concept assumed in equity
theory is also problematical since the terms "input" and "outcome" are virtually unlimited in what they can encompass. This
permits little clarity concerning the prediction of the influence of justice concepts on allocation behavior. Due to
the wide range of possible inputs and outcomes, *every* allocation could be seen, post hoc, as being "equitable", equal
allocations of money given unequal performance being explainable by invoking additional, relevant inputs or outcomes (e.g.
Mikula & Uray, 1973, p. 137).

The various classification approaches, on the other hand, assume that a person's justice concepts contain specific allocation rules. According to these approaches, which particular rule is seen as appropriate, and which ones are seen as inappropriate, depends largely on the type of situation in question. Due to the greater ease of deriving predictions from these approaches, we will use the classification perspective in this paper.

3.1.4. Which allocation of team-produced outcomes is just?

In the negotiation paradigms discussed in part one, an equal allocation satisfied both the equality and contribution principles. When recipient produced outcomes are to be distributed, however, the allocator must, in the event that there are qualitative differences in the negotiators' contributions, determine a) whether contributions are to be considered at all, and if so, b) which of their characteristics are to be taken into account (cf. Mikula, 1977). This gives rise to two questions for the justice theorist. First, are the specified variables and their hypothesized effects on justice considerations adequate for predicting allocation decisions made by "socially" oriented people in fully transparent settings, transparency here referring not only to full knowledge of outcome possibilities but of the individual contributions to outcome production as well? Secondly, are people's justice concepts uniform enough to permit prediction from random samples?

3.1.5. Experimental control of the various decision determinants

Figure 2 presents the assumed determinants of negotiation decisions along with several paradigms in which the number of these determinants is reduced. (Figure adapted from Lamm & Kayser, 1978.)

We limit ourselves here to distribution situations in which
the interaction comes to an end with the distribution decision;
if the distribution decision took place in a group in which interactions were possible following allocation, the other determinants could become active, depending upon the particular
group type. For example, a distribution decision for a long-
term work group could be influenced by the goal of spurring
the group members to high performance and could, therefore,
deviate from what would be predicted from justice norms (cf.
Leventhal & Whiteside, 1973; Leventhal, 1976a,b).

FIGURE 2

Determinants	Orientation: "just" distribution	Orientation: personal gain maximization	Orientation: politeness and modesty	Negotiation tactics
Paradigms				
1) Individual allocation deci-sion for others (Section 3.2.)	X			
2) Individual allocation deci-sion for self and others (Section 3.3.)	X	X	X	
3) Collective allocation deci-sion in the group (Section 3.4.)	X	X	X	X

In negotiations on the allocation of jointly produced outcomes
(paradigm 3, Figure 2), other determinants probably play a
role in addition to the motives for gain-maximization (or loss
minimization) and "just" distribution. It may be, for example,
that rules of politeness and modesty prescribe choosing an
allocation type that gives the partner a larger share (cf.

Mikula & Schwinger, 1978; Schwinger, 1980; Section 3.4.). Tactical considerations (e.g. intimidation of the opponent through
use of a high opening demand, or distorted presentation of the
importance of own contributions) bound to the negotiation
situation could also play a role. These tactical considerations
play no role in paradigm 2, the allocator in the latter case
making his decision without interacting with the recipients.
In paradigm 1, the allocator is not a recipient - nor does he
participate in the outcome production -; he only makes the allocation decision for the producers. In this case, the justice
motive should, all else being equal, be more influential than
in paradigms 2 and 3. Once the decisions in this simplified
paradigm are understood, it will then be possible to investigate, in more complex situations, the extent to which behavior
is dependent on a just-solution orientation.

3.2. Making allocation decisions for others

With respect to paradigm 1, we have researched the following
questions: a) What are considered as relevant contributions in
allocation settings and how can these contributions be systematically characterized? b) How effective are allocators in
evaluating contributions on more than one dimension? c) To
what extent do the different needs of the recipients receive
consideration in allocation decisions? Is it possible to combine such consideration with a concern for "just" allocation,
and what characteristics influence the role that needs play in
determining the final solution?

Our experiments were conducted using questionnaires in which
subjects were given a story involving two persons, A and B.
The story said that A and B had worked together to write and
publish a paper on problems of education, and that the sale of
this paper resulted in a financial gain (or loss - depending
on the version of the story). In this way, precise information
concerning the recipients could be given while at the same

time ensuring that the entire sample of decision-makers received exactly the same information.

Our first problem was to see whether unequal distribution
appears at all in questionnaire paradigms, in the case of differing contributions or needs. While it is known that team
members who have to distribute a joint profit among each other
often prefer equal allocations (cf. for example, Lerner, 1974),
the extent to which the social relationships among recipients
influence the allocation behavior of a third party has not
been empirically investigated. According to Lerner (1975, 1977),
such relationships should be important, as justice principles
are social norms whose range of applicability are determined
in part by the type of social relationship under consideration.

3.2.1. Consideration of contributions or equal allocation? Specifying the characteristics relevant for allocation

As we have already pointed out, equity theorists have largely
neglected the question of what gets considered as a relevant
input. The classification approaches do, however, specify the
conditions under which specific inputs become relevant in determining the final allocation, distinguishing between cases in
which a) the recipients' contributions, b) their specific needs
or c) no distinguishing characteristics are taken into account.
"Contributions" here refers to those characteristics that are
perceived as causally important for the production of the outcomes to be allocated.

3.2.1.1. Perceived volitional control over contributions and their consideration by the allocator

Experiments by Leventhal and Michaels (1971), Cohen (1974) and
Uray (1976) indicate that externally caused differences in
individual contributions will not receive consideration in a
final allocation. In addition to this internal/external

dimension, however, a second important dimension underlying
naive causal explanations (cf. Heider, 1958; Weiner, 1975)
concerns stability/variability, with variability being one condition for attributing intentionality or "volitional control."
One assumption in our own work is that the perception of volitional control is crucial in determining whether an input is
seen as relevant or not. We hypothesize that contributions
perceived as being variable and due to internal, dispositional
factors should be rewarded more fully than those perceived as
internal but stable.

Experiment 8 (Kayser & Lamm, 1980). It was hypothesized that,
if two recipients make differential contributions on a dimension that the allocator perceives as relevant to outcome production, the final allocation will be more proportional to the
recipients' inputs when the latter are perceived as variable
than when they are perceived as stable. In the present experiment, we manipulated the recipients' contributions such that
differences appeared either in effort or in ability.[9]

Subjects were 14 male and 10 female upper level "Gymnasium"
(high school) students who were to allocate a sum of 300 DM
"jointly produced" by the two stimulus persons. In one experimental condition, *A* was said to have made twice the effort
of *B*; in a second condition *A* possessed twice as much ability
as *B*.

Results: Allocations were more frequently proportional to contributions when differences were present in effort rather than
in ability.

In order to verify the processes that we assumed mediate these
findings, subjects were asked to indicate the extent to which
effort, ability, task difficulty and chance had determined the

---

[9]In the present investigation, as in the following ones, information was given to the subjects concerning only the stimulus
persons' effort and/or ability; no information, however, was
given concerning the stimulus persons' performances. Exceptions to this method will be noted.

recipients' outcome,as well as the extent to which they perceived effort and ability as being under the recipients' volitional control. The data show that ability and effort were
judged as being almost equally important for outcome production,
but that effort was thought to be more under the recipients'
volitional control than ability was. Similar results appeared
in Lamm, Kayser, and Schanz (1978).

The experiment thus demonstrates that 1) unequal allocations do
appear in this paradigm and 2) that perceived control is a useful factor for predicting the allocation behavior of people who
are not themselves recipients.

3.2.1.2. The effects on allocations of the perceived causal relationship among contribution dimensions and outcome

If a specific contribution dimension X is perceived as having a
more tenuous relationship to the jointly produced outcome than
another contribution dimension Y, will X receive less consideration in the allocation decision? Attribution theories have
hypothesized that personal failure is more likely to be externally attributed than personal success is, the explanation for
this being that doing so answers the need to protect one's
self-image (cf. Heider, 1944; Heckhausen, 1972; see also Miller
& Ross, 1975). Shaver (1975) argues that the same pattern
occurs when attributing the causes of third person's success or
failure, provided the person is *similar* to the observer. The
goal of the present experiment was to ascertain whether, in the
case of failure and the allocation of negative outcomes, less
consideration is given to contributions than when positive outcomes are to be allocated.

Experiment 8 (continued). In an additional condition of experiment 8, ten male and ten female subjects were presented with a
version of the stimulus story in which the stimulus persons
were presented (as in experiment 8) as being similar to the

allocator in age, education and sex. The stimulus persons'
joint work was said to have resulted in a *loss* of 300 DM.
The stimulus persons were said to have made different amounts
of effort.

Results: It was found that the losses were allocated equally
despite the differing contributions. Thus, the allocation of
loss differs from that of profit, in which recipients' contributions were taken into account. Indeed, this seems to
follow from the additional finding that external factors were
perceived as being significantly more important in causing loss
than they were with profits; differences in contributions are
more likely to be considered the greater their perceived causal
relationship to outcome production. This is presented in Figure 3.

FIGURE 3

Perception of the (internal) contribution dimension as having high causal relevance for the outcome production	Perception of the (internal) contribution dimension as being variable and under vol- itional control	Extent of considera- tion given the contribution dimension (dependent variable)
yes	yes	very large
yes	no	medium
no	yes	very small (zero)
no	no	very small (zero)

3.2.1.3. Changing relevance assessments of contributions

If we define the "relevance" of a contribution dimension as the
average extent to which differences on this dimension are considered in allocation decisions, we can then state the relevance
indices for ability and effort from the results of experiment
8. In the condition with information on *effort differences,*

stimulus person *A* was said to have made 33% more effort than *B*
and was allocated, on the average, 27% more outcome than *B* was:
thus, the difference in effort received a little bit less than
100% consideration (83% exactly). In the condition with *ability
differences*, *A* was said tó have 33% more ability than *B* but was
allocated an average of 5.61% *less* than *B* was. In this case
lack of ability seemed to be a positive input. If *lack* of ability had been given its full weight (100% consideration), *B*
should have received 33% more of the outcome than *A* did. In
fact, however, differences in (lack of) ability received only
17% consideration.

In order to use these relevance indices as algebraic weights,
they were transformed so that they added to 1.00. "Effort" has
an index value of .83 and "lack of ability" has a value of .17.
We now turn to the question of whether these relevance values
are constant or whether they vary (and if so, how?) when information is given on *both* dimensions (ability and effort)
simultaneously.

The assumption (e.g. Parsons, 1970) that the creation of
equality through distribution processes is buttressed by special legitimacy pressure in modern societies leads one to sus-
pect that allocators prefer the equality principle above all
others, deviating only when recipients differ in a way that is
both relevant to outcome production and under volitional control. In such cases as the latter, the allocator has the choice,
however, of breaking either the equality or the contribution
principles, though he can avoid making the choice (and thus
avert concomitant distress) by finding an allocation mode that
satisfies *both* principles (cf. Kayser, 1979). In that the
equality principle is "inflexible", reinterpreting the contributions so that an equal allocation is consistent with the
contribution principle is, in our opinion, the only way out.
This can be done by neglecting those contributions on which
recipients differ and emphasizing those on which they do not ,

so that congruence between the two principles obtains.[10]

If this re-interpretation assumption is valid, any information indicating that the participants made equal contributions on one or more dimension should "facilitate" an equal allocation by rendering it consistent with the contribution principle. Thus, for example, information on equal ability should gain in "relevance" when presented together with information indicating unequal effort in comparison to a condition where information is given only on unequal ability.

This re-interpretation process can be investigated quantitatively by transforming the results of experiment 8 into weights for the effort and ability dimensions. Farkas and Anderson (1974) have offered an algebraic model (the "equity summation rule") for prediction of allocations based on multi-dimensional contributions in situations where the aspects of the contributions are independent of one another.[11] According to this model, the allocator first determines equitable shares for both recipients according to each contribution dimension and then builds a weighted average of the resulting proportions. The weights are determined according to the estimated"relevance" of the dimensions. Using this model, our calculated weights (see above) yield the following parameters for the allocation of 300 DM: For the condition in which the stimulus persons made unequal effort and were equally able, the parameters are

---

[10] Equity theory, rooted as it is in dissonance theory, also contains these kinds of re-interpretation processes ("psychological restoration of equity" - cf. Walster et al., 1973, 1978). In our analysis, these re-interpretation processes apply to incongruencies among allocations resulting from different justice principles, whereas equity theorists do not differentiate among justice principles.

[11] "Independence" in this case refers to the presence of different contribution dimensions; "dependent" would refer to the case of several performance indices regarding the same kind of contribution.

192.33 : 107.67 (German marks); while for the conditions in which the stimulus persons had unequal ability and made equal effort, they are 141.33 : 158.67.[12] Of course, one cannot expect the allocation to have exactly these values, but they should be more or less normally distributed around this parameter. In contrast, if our re-interpretation hypothesis is true, the empirically determined allocations should deviate clearly from this parameter in the direction of an equal allocation.

Experiment 9 (Lamm, Kayser & Schanz, 1978). The subjects (12 male and 12 female German Gymnasium students) were assigned in equal numbers to one of the two conditions.

Results: In the "unequal ability/equal effort" condition, all allocations were equal. In the "unequal effort/equal ability" condition, a 75% majority of the allocations were equal.

---

[12] These parameters resulted from the following formula:

$$\text{Outcome}_A = w_P \left(\frac{P_A}{P_A + P_B} \right) T + w_E \left(\frac{E_A}{E_A + E_B} \right) T$$

w_P and w_E are constant weights of two input dimensions "P" and "E". P_A, P_B, E_A, and E_B are the inputs for persons A and B. (Farkas & Anderson, 1974). T is the sum to be allocated. The parameters for the first-mentioned condition were calculated in the following manner: Dimension P is "effort" and dimension E is "lack of ability". The weight of "effort" is $w_{EFF} = 0.83$ and the weight of "lack of ability" $w_{L-ABIL} = 0.17$ (see above). If "team effort" ($EFF_A + EFF_B$) is given as 1.00, then A's effort (EFF_A) is equal to 0.67; if "team ability" ($L-ABIL_A + L-ABIL_B$) is given as 1.00, then A's lack of ability ($L-ABIL_A$) is equal to 0.50. The team gain (T) = 300.

$$\text{For outcome}_A = w_{EFF} \left(\frac{EFF_A}{EFF_A + EFF_B} \right) T + \left(\frac{L-ABIL_B}{L-ABIL_A + L-ABIL_B} \right) T$$

the result is 0.83 x (0.67/1.00) x 300 + 0.17 x (0.50/1.00) x 300 = 192.33 (German marks).

Kayser and Lamm (1980) interpret these findings as indicating that, in the last-mentioned condition, the ability dimension is given greater importance than the effort dimension, while the contribution principle is handled "flexibly" due to the subjects' preference for equal allocations.[13]

Experiment 10 (Lamm & Kayser, 1978a). In another experiment the contributions of the stimulus persons were constructed as follows: Person *A* was said to be twice as able as *B* but to have made only half as much effort. If the resulting "relevancies" of experiment 8 are transferable, allocations should favor person *B* for having made the greater effort. In contrast, the re-interpretation hypothesis implies that the application of the equal-allocation principle to cases in which two people differ on two contribution dimensions is facilitated when the ratios of these differences a) are equally large and b) favor one person in the first case and the other in the second. In fact, the majority (83.3%) of our subjects (12 male and 12 female upper level Gymnasium students) made equal allocations, thus supporting the re-interpretation hypothesis.

In contrast to experiment 8, there was no sign of a sanctioning of the "lazy" team member in this last study: He did not receive a smaller share than his partner. We were interested in the further question of whether subjects would persist in making equal allocations when the stimulus persons were presented as friends. According to the classification approaches to justice, the equality principle should be preferred in close social relationships, though these approaches do not distinguish between different contribution types and the different claims for reward that can be derived from them. From the general observation that friends are expected to support one another as much as possible (cf. Rubin, 1970), it seems plausible that friends' lack of effort on each other's behalf would

---

[13]Loss allocation situations were investigated using the same method and a new sample of the same population: In this case, only equal allocations occurred.

be evaluated negatively by an outsider. This should be especially the case if the team had suffered a loss that was, at least partially, explainable by this neglect. We thus replicated experiment 10 with stimulus persons described as friends.

Experiment 11 (Lamm & Kayser, 1978a). Subjects were 12 male and 12 female upper level Gymnasium students. In the case of gain, there was a marginally significant deviation from equal allocation, with the person making lesser effort receiving a smaller share. In the case of loss, however, this deviation was more pronounced, the person making the lesser effort being more severely penalized. This result demonstrates the importance of differentiation among different contribution types. When the type of contribution so clearly shows that one of the team members has broken a norm of mutual support, an equal allocation is seen as being less appropriate.

3.2.1.4. Causal explanation of performance differences in allocation situations

As mentioned earlier, there is evidence that performance differences presented as being externally caused receive less consideration from allocators than those presented as internally caused. This is true for allocators who allocate between themselves and another person (e.g. Uray, 1976) as well as for those who make allocations between two or more other hypothetical persons (Leventhal & Michaels, 1971). In connection with this, we wanted to test the effect that the perceived variability/stability of the cause of performance has on allocations (cf. Weiner, 1972).

Experiment 12 (Kayser & Lamm, 1979). We hypothesized that performance differences explainable by stable, ability factors will receive less consideration in the allocation of jointly produced outcomes than will performance differences explainable by the more variable, effort factor, as only the latter will be perceived as being under the stimulus persons' volitional

control. In this experiment, stimulus person A was said to have
produced 60% of the team performance and person B, 40%. In the
"effort" condition, person A was said to have made 67% (B 33%)
of the team effort while possessing, however, only 33% (B 67%)
of the total ability. In the "ability" condition, the situation
with respect to effort and ability was reversed (effort: A 33%,
B 67%; ability: A 67%, B 33%). The subjects were 12 male and
12 female upper level Gymnasium students.

Results: The data supported the hypothesis, the allocations in
the "ability" condition being nearer to equal than those in the
"effort" condition.

3.2.2. Consideration of need by the allocator

Though the "need principle" is considered in each of the various classification approaches to allocation justice, it has
been the subject of little empirical investigation. Our own
research addressed four questions concerning it.

a) *Is there a need principle of distributive justice?* It is not
clear whether allocations that take recipients' needs into
account are motivated by a desire for justice or whether they
are simply the product of a norm for social responsibility (cf.
Berkowitz, 1969). Leventhal (1976b) assumes that this norm is
encompassed by the need principle. In other words, are need-
considering allocations seen as just? In order to answer this
question, subjects were informed of two hypothetical recipients' differing needs and asked to make a *just* allocation
between them. If responding to the recipients' needs runs
contrary to subjects' conceptions of justice (because, for
example, it violates claims derived from the equality or contribution principles), then needs should, in this case, receive
less consideration than in an otherwise similar condition in
which no request to make a *just* allocation is made *(hypothesis
1)*.

b) *Under what situational circumstances will the need principle be applied?* Lerner (1977) and Mikula and Schwinger (1978) postulate that in situations characterized by high interpersonal attraction and participant interdependence (e.g. families, close friendships etc.),goods are distributed almost exclusively according to the need principle. If this is so, then allocators who have to distribute an outcome between two recipients should give greater consideration to the latter's individual needs if the recipients are friends with each other than if they are non-friends *(hypothesis 2).*

c) *What weight will differences in neediness receive relative to differences in contributions?* The research literature contains discrepant answers to this question. Lerner (1977) and Mikula and Schwinger (1978) assume that in close social relationships only the need principle is used, whereas Leventhal (1976b) postulates a compromise model. According to the latter, a recipient with greater needs but who made smaller contributions than his co-recipient should receive less than a similarly needy recipient who matched the co-recipient's efforts. Our third hypothesis concerns this point.

d) *What needs are considered?* We hypothesized that internally caused need states would receive less consideration than externally caused need states *(hypothesis 4).* This hypothesis derives from Leventhal's (1976b) analysis, he having observed that findings from helping research (e.g. Berkowitz, 1969; Schopler & Matthews, 1965) suggest that help is more likely to be given when "legitimate" needs are involved. We recognize, however, that internal/external causation and lesser/greater legitimacy are not identical concepts and that the relationship between them remains to be elaborated.

Experiment 13 (Lamm & Schwinger, 1980). In a first experiment subjects (64 male and 64 female upper level Gymnasium students) read a stimulus story similar to the one used in the previously described questionnaire experiments in which persons' *A* and *B* were said to have made equal performance contributions but to have different needs. While both needed to purchase books for examinations, *A* needed 200 DM and *B* only 50. The subjects had 300 DM to allocate. Independent variables were *interpersonal attraction* (*A* and *B* presented as close friends or as superficial acquaintances) and the *internality/externality of need* (having forgotten to check the books out of the library versus needing books not found in the library).

Results: The data supported the second hypothesis concerning attraction, the subjects considering need to a greater extent in allocations between friends than among non-friends. However, even in the latter condition a significant deviation from equal allocation (which in this case is identical with the allocation prescribed by the contribution principle) in favor of need consideration was found. The allocation behavior of male and female subjects differed in that women showed a greater tendency to make equal allocations than men. No support was found, however, for hypothesis 4: The perceived cause of neediness did not affect allocations.

Experiment 14 (Lamm & Schwinger, 1979). This study used the same procedure as in experiment 13. Subjects were 72 upper level Gymnasium students. Independent variables were interpersonal attraction (see above) and the allocation situation: In a performance difference condition, *A* (the needier person) was said to have provided only 33% of the recipients' total performance and *B* 67%; in a control condition, *A* and *B* were each said to have contributed 50%; in a third condition, the latter story was combined with the request to make a just allocation.

Results: Where there was no performance difference, high attraction between recipients lead to need-based allocations, while low attraction resulted in equal allocations. Explicitly demanding a "just" allocation did not reduce the needier recipient's share, thus failing to support hypothesis 1. It seems, therefore, that a significant portion of subjects regarded need consideration as being *compatible* with justice principles. Hypothesis 3 received only partial support: In the

case of performance differences, low performance resulted in
share reductions when the two recipients were friends but had
no effect in the low attraction condition.

Discussion of experiments 13 and 14. a) The finding that the
needier recipient was favored even in those cases where allocators were especially requested to make just allocations
supports the contention that there is a *specific need principle
for allocational justice.*[14]

b) As far as the *situational conditions* for the application of
the need principle are concerned, we can conclude that the need
principle is, in part at least, relationship-specific from the
findings that need consideration allocations were more often
made when the recipients were friends than when they were not.
The application of the need principle is not, however, completely limited to close social relationships. Need-consideration
allocations appear with more than chance probability when the
recipients are not friends whenever such an allocation is seen
as being compatible with justice.

c) The question as to the *relative degree* to which needs and
contributions receive consideration can only be partially
answered with the present data.

One can derive some idea of the weights of the need and contribution principles from the allocations made when there were
both need and performance differences. According to Leventhal
(1976b), a needy person who contributes less than his co-
recipient should receive less than if he matched the co-recipient's performance. Our data show, however, that this holds
true only when the recipients are friends. One can thus conclude that the weights of the two justice principles in

---

[14] It is unlikely that these need-consideration allocations were
used to demonstrate a special moral posture as there was *no*
correlation between need consideration and need for special
approval as measured by a German version of the Crown-Marlowe
Scale (cf. Grabitz-Gniech, 1971).

question depend on the recipients' social relationship, a determinant not included in Leventhal's model.

d) Concerning the influence of causal locus on the relative weighting of needs (and contributions) in allocation decisions, we found that there was no difference in share size whether needs were perceived as caused by the recipient himself or by external, situational factors. Apparently, causal locus plays a smaller role in allocation situations than in helping situations, a finding that suggests caution in generalizing from one research area to the other.

3.3. Individual allocation decisions to self and others

In the experiments discussed above, we were concerned with the allocations made by "third person" or "neutral" allocators. This paradigm permits observation of decisions for which the primary motive is the desire to be just. The question remains, however, as to what role this motive plays in situations in which the allocator is himself a co-recipient, having earned the right to a share through joint work with another person. Figure 2 shows three classes of determinants that are, in our opinion, important for this situation. In addition to the motive toward a just allocation, a desire to maximize gain, a tendency toward polite and/or modest behavior (cf. Mikula & Schwinger, 1978) and/or a desire toward "neutral" self presentation (cf. Leventhal, 1976b) could influence the decision. The fact that allocators apparently see several allocation rules as appropriate (see above) suggests that justice rules are unclear, leaving a certain freedom of movement with which motives other than the desire to be just can be influential. Our own research examines 1) the extent to which allocation behavior is limited by justice rules, and 2) the relative influence of egoism and modesty or politeness in determining allocations.

We used an experimental situation in which two subjects worked towards the same goal in separate rooms, their work resulting

in either a positive or a negative joint outcome. Before the
allocation of this outcome, the recipients received information
on their relative contributions. If the subsequent allocations
are primarily governed by justice considerations, the following hypotheses (already mentioned above) should hold:

Those making more effort should receive a more positive outcome
(win more, lose less) than those making less effort, and ability differences should play a smaller role in the allocation
decision.

Experiment 15 (Kayser & Lamm, 1978b). The two team members -
who could not see one another during the entire course of the
experiment - were first given a test of verbal ability. Following its completion, each could then decide whether he wanted to
participate in a task in which he could work with another person and win or lose a maximum of 10 DM. Subjects who agreed
to participate worked 45 minutes on the experimental task which
involved 90 verbal problems with differing degrees of difficulty. They were then given a fictitious result, with half the
dyads winning and the rest losing 8.80 DM.

In the "no performance infomation" condition, subjects were then
to make a first allocation decision without contribution information, while in the "performance information" condition, subjects
were first told that A had correctly solved 60% of the items and
B, 40%. After making the allocation, subjects were then given
false ability and effort feedback indicating that A had surpass-
ed B in ability (the "ability" condition) or effort (the "effort" condition). Note that in the"performance information"condition, the ability/effort differences can be interpreted by
subjects as explaining the performance differences. In all conditions, a second (final) allocation decision was made after
receipt of the ability/effort information. In sum, the design
of this experiment involved three factors, which were varied
orthogonally: a) presence versus absence of performance information; b) differences in effort versus differences in ability,

c) gain versus loss. The subjects were 94 male university students.

Results: Unlike our findings for neutral allocation decisions in experiment 9, subjects who received no performance information did not weight ability less heavily than effort in making their allocations and, in fact, made a large number of equal allocations. Whereas no subject in experiment 9 took ability differences into account, eight of 24 allocators did so in the present case. When "performance information" was provided, 44% of the first allocations were unequal allocations that favored the high performance partner, this differing significantly from the number of unequal allocations made in the "no performance information" condition. When, as a result of further information, these performance differences became explainable by differences in ability, as opposed to differences in effort, the allocators rescinded their initial consideration of performance to a significant extent, allocating in a far more egalitarian fashion.

The hypotheses that in the case of a team failure (loss), more equal allocation would occur than in the case of success (gain) (see 3.2.1.2.), was not confirmed. Allocations were, on the whole, less egoistical in the gain than in the loss condition. Politeness and modesty also appear to have been more influential in gain situations than in loss situations. Causal attribution may be of importance here: Whereas in the case of success, an allocation favoring the other still results in personal gain, in the case of loss it might imply acknowledgement of greater responsibility for the failure, something which the subjects seem to avoid. Clear differences in the allocation behavior of better contributors and poorer contributors were not found. The less able recognized the greater ability of their partner about as often as the latter requested that his greater ability be recognized. In contrast to the decisions of neutral allocators, it was apparent here that ability in a large number of cases constitutes a relevant input (i.e. provides a sense of entitlement).

3.4. Negotiations on allocation of jointly produced outcomes

Experiment 15 (continued) (cf. *Lamm & Kayser, 1978b*). Following the second allocation, the subjects were asked to negotiate an agreement on a final allocation of the (positive or negative) outcome using verbal communication (oral and written). They still had no visual contact. The negotiations were recorded and coded as to whether a negotiator demanded consideration of effort or ability differences. As illustrated in Figure 2, *tactical* considerations may become important in a negotiation situation. The question of the form which these tactical considerations take in connection with arguments concerning entitlement has not received attention in previous research. The present investigation was exploratory in nature and not designed to test hypotheses derived from justice theories. Our hypothesis was that negotiators use effort information more often than ability information to justify their allocation proposals. In addition, we expected the conflicts of interest typical of the beginning of normal negotiation situations to be the exception here because, through the joint work situation and contribution information, the situation is normatively prestructured and leaves little room for gain maximization.

Results: It was found that the initial demands of fewer than 10% of the 94 subjects lay outside of the area between an equal allocation and a 60 : 40 allocation in favor of the negotiator who had contributed the most (60% versus 40%). Thus, in most cases, the conflict was clearly limited from the beginning. Only in 17 of 47 dyads did the opening demands generate a conflict situation in which the two parties' demands were incompatible. In fact, in the vast majority of cases, both dyad members presented identical suggestions at the start which obviated the need for negotiations. In those cases in which an initial conflict appeared (i.e. *incompatible* opening demands),

egoistical demands were justified more frequently with arguments based on effort than on ability: Those having made *more*
effort argued *for* consideration of this contribution type,
whereas those having made *less* effort argued *against* its consideration.

Some additional interpretative remarks seem appropriate. The
question - that negotiators may ask themselves - of whether
the opponent's arguments are sincere in their appeal to justice
or based on egoistical gain considerations is reminiscent of
our investigations on bluffing in negotiations. It is useful
to compare the negotiation in experiment 14 with Schwinger's
(1975) experiment in which interaction was unrestricted (eye
contact and oral communication) and modest behavior dominant.
We should also reconsider the allocation patterns found in
experiment 14's gain and loss conditions. From all this, it
could be concluded that "egoistical" interpretations are a
negative function of the range of interaction possibilities and
a positive function of the extent of personal involvement, the
latter being particularly high when losses are to be allocated.

3.5. Summary

Decision behavior was investigated in experiments 8 through 14
reported in Part Two under conditions in which the allocation
had no consequences for the allocator and had only fictitious
consequences for the hypothetical participants. It was necessary to construct this situation in order to crystallize the
justice aspect and narrow (i.e. make more precise) the concept
of "social orientation" (cf. Figure 2). Using this paradigm,
the application of justice-oriented theoretical approaches
proved useful for the explanation and prediction of allocation
decisions. At the same time, the necessity and possibility of
increasing the precision of such approaches became clear. Our
attribution theory approach to the weighting of contributions
was found to be fruitful. The perceived relationship among

types of contributions (experiment 12), between contributions
and the outcome to be allocated (experiment 8), and the perception of the contribution as being volitionally controlled
by the contributor (experiments 8-12) all help answer the
question of the extent to which contribution differences enter
into the determination of allocations that deviate from equality. If was found, too, that the type of social relationship
between the potential recipients influences the extent to
which contributions are taken into consideration (compare experiment 10 with experiment 11).

Though this last factor is dealt with by the classification
approaches to justice theory, none of these approaches could
predict the results obtained in our experiments, where friendship interacted with effort differences in strongly affecting
allocation patterns. Our research on "allocations to self and
others" shows, however, that the weights of individual contribution dimensions can vary from one type of allocation situation to the other.

The results of the experiments on need consideration (experiments 12 and 13) supported the classification approach assumption that needs would be taken more into account in positive
social relationships. The above-mentioned investigations show
that allocators apparently assume that recipients who are
friends do their best in joint work and support one another in
emergency situations. It follows that contribution differences
receive consideration only when they are a) the result of lack
of effort toward the joint goal and b) result in failure and
loss for both recipients; otherwise an equal allocation is
made. *Need* differences receive less consideration when the prerequisite of maximal effort is broken. In the case of recipients who are not friends, allocators do not begin with such
prerequisites: Contribution differences have generally greater
importance and need differences, less. Only under this limitation is the assumption that the equality or need principle
applies to friends and the contribution principle to non-

friends valid.

In sum, the theoretical approaches outlined above were seen to
be capable of predicting allocation behavior in closely controlled laboratory situations. Much research remains to be done,
however, in order to refine these approaches so that the allocation behavior can be predicted in the real world.

Chapter 13   Interpersonal Conflicts and Bargaining
G. F. Müller[1]

1. Introduction

Interpersonal conflicts often occur when scarce resources have
to be distributed among individuals and groups whose demands
cannot be satisfied simultaneously. It is, for example, the
job of lobbyists in economy, society and politics to pursue
their constituents' interests in the face of competing interests of other groups, organizations or federations. Conflicts,
however, can also arise in "normal" social interaction; for
instance, between spouses, friends or colleagues. Undoubtedly,
these conflicts are seldom related to struggles over such spec-
tacular resources as market-control in economy, influence in
society, or power in politics. Rather, in most cases, interpersonal relations come in conflict over everyday resources
like the household budget, leisure time to be spent in common,
or opportunities for job advancement. The patterns of behavior
that can be observed in these simple conflict situations do not,
however, differ greatly from the conflict reactions that occur
within competitive markets, international debates or fiscal
policy. In each case, the greater disagreement over an acceptable device of distributing, allocating or commonly using
scarce resources, and the more emphatically individuals insist
upon unilateral advantage, the more likely it is that threats
and aggression will appear in the course of interaction.

---

[1]The author extends his appreciation to H. W. Crott, L. Katz,
E. Kayser, M. Kutschker and Th. Schwinger, all of whom offered helpful comments on earlier version of this chapter.

The behavioral analysis of interpersonal conflict has many different theoretical and empirical aspects. Analyzing conflicts between nations or organizations, for example, requires that one makes use of case studies, since these conflicts are highly complex, occur with relatively small frequency and offer limited possibilities for participating as a neutral observer (cf. Crott, Kutschker & Lamm, 1977b). Conflicts between group representatives or between individuals acting on their own are, on the other hand, less complex and are therefore easier to simulate in experimental settings (cf. Crott, Kutschker & Lamm, 1977a). While case studies are valuable for their detailed descriptions of conflict situations and resolution processes, experiments enable one to control and manipulate relevant situational and dispositional variables and hence to make critical comparisons between the various theoretical approaches developed to apply to conflict situations.

With regard to conflicts between individuals acting on their own, researchers have made use of social psychological constructs such as social motivation, social learning or social perception to guide their thinking (cf. McClintock, 1972; Crott & Müller, 1978; Apfelbaum, 1974; Kelley & Stahelski, 1970). For conflicts between group representatives, constructs borrowed from sociology have proven to be of greater heuristic value, special emphasis being placed upon the importance of social roles and group obligations in these situations (Adams, 1976; Holmes & Lamm, 1978). For reasons already mentioned, conflicts between nations or organizations are less readily subject to theoretical analysis, though the laboratory simulations of labor conflicts conducted by Tietz (1976) and Morley and Stephenson (1977) represent exceptions to this rule.

Frameworks for systemizing behavioral analyses of interpersonal conflicts have been provided by game theory (Luce & Raiffa, 1957), behavioral decision theory (Lee, 1971), and theory of interdependence (Thibaut & Kelley, 1959; Kelley & Thibaut, 1978). Each of these theories defines interpersonal conflicts as decision making situations; people are seen as entering conflict situations with certain goals in mind and having to choose strategies from a fixed number of available alternatives for goal attainment. Though people might be independent with respect to particular goals that they aspire to, their respective strategy decisions lead to joint outcomes. This requires that each person takes the potential strategies of his/her opponent into consideration when deciding his/her own strategy.

Differences in outcome or "payoff" structure[2] enable one to distinguish between pure conflict, co-ordination and mixed-motive situations. In pure conflict situations, a positive outcome for one person means a negative outcome for the other, the conflict here being defined as a pure conflict of goals. In co-ordination situations, there are no conflicts concerning goals, as both parties work together towards a mutually attained outcome, though problems of coordinating bilateral actions may sometimes emerge and thus give rise to strategy conflicts. Mixed-motive situations are characterized by a partial conflict of goals; though people can obtain positive outcomes by coordinating their strategies, these outcomes are less favorable than those obtainable by acting egocentrically. So, while cooperation assures one of a moderate positive outcome, attempts of maximizing one's own outcome will result in conflict. As the tension between cooperation and conflict can be looked at as an essential and basic attribute of social interaction, research on interpersonal conflict has focused primarily on these mixed-motive situations (cf. Lee, 1971; Schelling, 1960; Thibaut & Kelley, 1959; Rubin & Brown, 1975).

Decisions in mixed-motive situations are mediated by two cognitive processes. The first is *interpersonal* in nature and involves people perceiving that their goals diverge. At the

---

[2] Throughout this chapter, the discussion will focus upon conflicts between two persons.

beginning of interaction each person is unfamiliar with his/her opponent's strategy and must therefore make his/her own strategy decision under conditions of uncertainty, either trusting or distrusting the opponent's goal intentions. During the course of interaction, mixed-motive situations potentially can evolve towards either cooperative coordination or pure conflict, depending on whether the strategies adopted by the two parties create an atmosphere of mutual trust or distrust. The conditions under which mixed-motive situations become cooperative or competitive is thus a question that must be analyzed in the context of joint decision making (Kelley & Thibaut, 1978).

The second process that mediates strategy decisions in mixed-motive situations is *intrapersonal* in nature and refers to cognitions of goal attractiveness. It is an inherent characteristic of mixed-motive situations that people involved experience difficulty in deciding between several, equally attractive goals. For example, when distributing scarce resources, it will often be difficult to decide between trying to maximize one's own gain and agreeing on a fair allocation of payoffs. During the course of interaction, however, people usually learn which goal can be asserted most effectively from seeing how effective their strategies are in influencing their opponent's behavior.

In **section** 2 of this chapter, we present a theoretical framework for analyzing the motivational basis of cognition in mixed-motive situations. We then go on to summarize the results of a research program on interpersonal conflicts and bargaining and close by discussing both the framework and the results in the more general context of exchange theory.

2. Motivational orientations in conflicts of interest

This paragraph describes a theoretical approach to interpersonal conflict inspired by motivational models of social choice
(cf. McClintock, 1972), bargaining behavior (cf. Raiffa, 1953),
gaming (cf. Deutsch & Krauss, 1960) and justice (cf. Walster,
Berscheid & Walster, 1973; Lerner, 1977). We do not explicitly
deal with the process by which this approach developed, and so
the description of its present state will only sketch some
basic ideas of its origins in the motivational models just mentioned. A more detailed account of the theory's development can
be drawn from the publications by Crott (1972b, 1974), Crott,
Kutschker and Lamm (1977a), Crott and Müller (1978), Müller and
Crott (1978a) and Müller (1980a).

2.1. A structural analysis of interpersonal conflicts

One of the strengths of formal *game theory and behavioral decision theory* is that they are based on the analysis of the
logical structure of interpersonal conflict situations (cf.
Lee, 1971). We will demonstrate what we mean by "structural
analysis" by applying it to a situation where conflict can be
resolved by bargaining. We focus on negotiable conflicts because the overwhelming majority of the experiments described in
the following paragraph use a bargaining paradigm.

According to game theory and behavioral decision theory, all
bargaining situations can be reduced to a structural degree
that allows the investigation of basic psychological processes
underlying bargaining decisions. From this point of view, bargaining situations have two minimal characteristics: there are
at least two "pareto-optimal" bargaining alternatives, these
being joint outcomes that represent the *maximum* payoffs both
bargaining participants can have; and there are two "security
levels", one for each bargaining participant, these being related to a joint "status-quo" outcome that represents the *lowest*
payoffs both participants would accept.

The pareto-optimal alternatives have the property of "dyadic optimality"; that is, no other solution, compared with a specific pareto-optimal solution, gives a higher outcome to *both* bargaining participants (though other solutions can give equally high payoffs at least to one of them). If the participants have information about all possible bargaining solutions, and if they discuss no additional ("integrative") solutions, the set of pareto-optimal solutions can be illustrated by a payoff diagram (see Figure 1). In Figure 1, pareto-optimal solutions are localized on the fat line that encloses the set of possible joint payoffs on the diagram's upper right side ("pareto-optimal set").

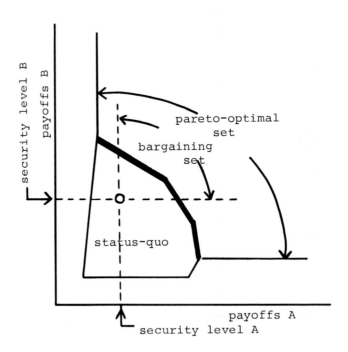

Figure 1. Payoff diagram of bargaining participants A and B

Not all pareto-optimal alternatives, however, are potential
bargaining solutions, because in order to be a solution an
outcome must fall above the security levels of both participants. This set of potential solutions (the "bargaining set")
must, of course, be non-null for bargaining to occur at all.
To obtain the solution corresponding to the intersection of
two security levels a person does not need to bargain; he/she
can "secure" this outcome anyway.

2.2. Individualistic motivation

It is the implicit or explicit assumption of numerous psychological theories that people are motivated to seek reward and
avoid punishment. This simple reinforcement model has also
been used to explain and predict behavior during interpersonal
conflict. Both game theory and behavioral decision theory make
implicit use of a reinforcement model with regard to the concepts "homo oeconomicus" and "rationality", when tacitly assuming that individuals make decisions so as to maximize expected gains and/or minimize expected losses.

Luce and Raiffa (1957) show that bargainers will manifest
"individualistic" gain maximization or loss minimization whenever they a) reduce the possible solutions to the pareto-optimal set of payoff alternatives and b) settle on one of the
pareto-optimal payoff alternatives lying above security levels.
At the same time, however, Luce and Raiffa give reasons why
it is impossible to define a *specific* solution within the bargaining set without weakening the assumption of pure gain maximization. As soon as the number of solutions within the bargaining set exceeds one - and this is typically the case in
bargaining situations - each participant would be strongly
motivated to enforce the solution that guarantees him/her the
maximum payoff and would be unwilling to make any concessions
to his/her opponent. As a result of mutual intransigence,
both bargainers will finish with smaller payoffs than two,
more yielding bargainers would.

To avoid this "dilemma of rationality", game theory and behavioral decision theory define criteria for arbitration. According to a criterion postulated by Raiffa (1953), for instance
two rational bargainers should agree on the pareto-optimal
solution that provides shares proportional to their maximal
payoffs in the given situation. It is implicitly assumed here,
however, that *both* bargaining participants consider this criterion as relevant to the arbitration - an eventuality unlikely, as indicated above, when both bargainers adhere to pure
gain maximization.

Characterizations of individualistic motivation in bargaining
situations tend to emphasize gain maximization and loss minimization, the assumption being that individualistically motivated bargaining behavior should be oriented towards winning
much and losing little. The relevant empirical evidence indicates, however, that a linear increase of monetary incentive
does not automatically intensify bargaining toughness. Apparently, a more important factor in individualistic motivation
is the bargainer's *aspiration level,* this reflecting both his/
her personal values and the specific situational demands operant at any given moment. According to Siegel (1957), aspiration level can be defined in terms of subjective utilities.
It refers to the upper point of that section in the utility
function showing the steepest slope. In bargaining research,
aspiration level can serve as a dependent variable (measured
by questions such as, "Which bargaining payoff would be more
satisfying than dissatisfying to you?") or an independent
variable (manipulated, for example, by the instruction: "In
our experiments good bargainers usually get at least an outcome of X"or "if you at least obtain a settlement X, your payoff will be doubled"). Aspiration level and monetary incentive are both "individualistic" in nature since they are not
directly related to the opponent's outcome. In this context,
even the cooperative search for pareto-optimal solutions can
be seen as an individualistic phenomenon insofar as it en-

ables both bargainers to maximize their own gains. Although concessions in such instances should conform to the bargainers' aspiration levels, a problem still remains in determining - especially when the aspiration levels are disparate - which final solution the bargainers will agree upon. In order to define this "rational arbitration", it becomes necessary to supplement individualistic motives with "social" motives, these latter inducing bargainers to identify adequate criteria of arbitration and mutually satisfying solutions.

2.3. Distributional justice

If people sought only to maximize individual need satisfaction and strove for their own advantage regardless of possible consequences to the social environment, a constructive resolution of interpersonal conflicts would be difficult to achieve. That such constructive resolutions do occur implies that people accept and follow certain norms of "fairness" in treating one another in conflict situations. The general process of socialization provides a person with knowledge of the norms that apply to social interaction and the behavior expected from people acting in accordance with these norms.

The norms governing the resolution of social conflict can be placed under the generic category "norms for reward allocation" (cf. Crott & Müller, 1978). The problem of specifying which norm will be applied in which given conflict situation has been dealt with by the social psychological theory of justice (Lerner, 1977; Mikula, 1978; cf. Müller & Crott, 1978b). Justice theory distinguishes three principles of reward allocation - the equity-principle, the need-principle and the equality-principle - and states that which of these principles is actually applied depends upon the nature of the specific social relationship under consideration. If the relation is primarily objective or "economical" in nature, the equity principle should apply, whereas if the relation is characterized by solidarity and friendship, rewards should be allocated to the equality principle. The principle of need, on the other hand, is thought to apply primarily to intimate relationships.

Our present concern will be with objective, economic interactions. Here, conflicts often arise because persons have divergent opinions on how to weigh their individual contributions, judgments of fairness being directly related to the perceived degree of proportionality between bargaining inputs and outcomes (cf. Adams, 1965). Relevant inputs in such cases include pre-bargaining performance, knowledge, experience, and bargaining status or power. If - as a result of explicit discussion or implicit reflection - bargainers arrive at a consensus on how to relate specific inputs to specific shares, applying the equity principle will result in what is judged a just and fair settlement (cf. Müller & Crott, 1978c).

It should be noted that justice theory differs from game theory and behavior decision theory in the way arbitrational criteria are defined. While the latter two define arbitrational criteria objectively in terms of outcomes and payoff alternatives, justice theory treats these criteria subjectively in terms of the bargainers' perceptions and their evaluations of bargaining inputs. This aspect has important consequences for the prediction of interpersonal conflict behavior. As we have already seen, Raiffa (1953) argues that bargainers should settle on a solution that provides a share proportional to the maximum individual payoffs possibly attainable. If, however, the bargainers judge that differences in maximum payoffs are not justified by different pre-bargaining contributions, such a solution will be impeded, the disadvantaged bargainer striving for a share more commensurate with his/her actual inputs (Walster, Berscheid & Walster, 1973). Despite this potential source of conflict, however, the equity principle has a strong appeal in arbitrating diverging demands of reward allocation. It usually forces a bilateral accommodation towards a pareto-

optimal solution satisfying the attempts of *both* bargainers.
If the mutual contributions are perceived to be equal, the
equity principle leads to the same solution as the equality
principle.

We assume here that the justice motive is unaffected by variations in monetary incentive or level of aspiration. The motivation to behave equitably should exist even when, for instance, small profits are at stake. If the two contributions of
the two bargainers are perceived to be equal, a distribution
of $ 5 : $ 5 should be judged as just as one of $ 10 : $ 10,
while a distribution of $ 3 : $ 7 should be judged as unjust
as one of $ 6 : $ 14. Commonly observed preferences for higher
outcomes can be explained, of course, referring to individualistic motives like gain maximization.

2.4. Competition

Bargainers who are individualistically motivated and/or motivated to establish a fair and equitable outcome usually consider conflicts of interest as problems to be solved "rationally". That is, they try to "depersonalize" the conflict and
act toward constructive solutions that are "task-adequate"
for the given payoff situation. It is obvious from everyday
experience, however, that conflicts are sometimes difficult
to completely depersonalize and that conflict resolution is
often accompanied by *ad hominem,* opponent-centered behavior.
Especially when there is reason for distrusting the opponent,
bargainers are often not able to act rationally towards cooperation and justice, showing more interest in outcomes that
demonstrate superiority and strategies for competition.

It is possible to relate individual competition to the need
for social comparison (McClintock & Avermaet, 1975). In conflict situations, abilities such as bargaining efficiency or
dominance can become material for comparison processes, the
bargainers being motivated to determine how good they perform

relative to their opponent. These processes are most likely to appear when people face opponents similar in ability, status or power (cf. Festinger, 1954). Hence in situations of conflict, competition should become more predominant as bargaining abilities and bargaining abilities and bargaining positions become increasingly equal. Bargaining abilities here refer to variables such as eloquence or interactive competence, while bargaining positions refer to variables such as threat capacities or social support.

As competition is directed towards superiority and better performing, it evokes a struggle for advances in interpersonal influence. Whereas for justice-motivated bargainers, the actual opponent might be seen of subordinate significance insofar as the optimal settlement is concerned, bargainers who are competitively motivated use their opponent for establishing the standard for bargaining success. The latter tend to approach the bargaining situation more as a *medium* for demonstrating superiority and dominance than as an *end in itself* which, rationally handled, brings a profit to both participants. As competition permits only one to be the winner, it implicitly bears the risk of destructive consequences for conflict resolution and bargaining (Deutsch, 1973).

2.5. Alternative motivational approaches

Evidence concerning the three basic conflict motives described above can be drawn from both theoretical and empirical studies. While other motives such as aggression, altruism or pure cooperation may also play a role in interpersonal conflicts, their contribution to bargaining behavior seems less convincing. With regard to cooperation, for example, Crott and Möntmann (1973) show that bargainers seldom arrive at solutions that maximize the sum of their individual payoffs but rather agree on solutions that minimize the difference. Cooperation thus appears to result from individualistic motivation and the motive for distributional justice.

The various motivational approaches that have appeared in the
literature differ in the number of basic motives that they
postulate. The McClintock model of social choice (McClintock,
1972; McClintock, Messick, Kuhlmann & Campos, 1973) features
individualistic motivation (maximizing own outcome), a motive
for competition (maximizing relative outcome), a motive for
cooperation (maximizing joint outcome), and one for altruism
as well (maximizing other's outcome). Walster, Berscheid and
Walster (1973, 1976) propose two basic motives - an outcome
maximization motive and a motive for outcome fairness - and
do not take competition into consideration. MacGrimmon and
Messick's (1976) social choice model contains six motives:
altruism, individualism, aggression (i.e. minimizing the opponent's outcomes), self-sacrifice (i.e. minimizing own outcome), cooperation and competition, the latter two being defined in the same way as in the McClintock model. MacGrimmon
and Messick extended the notion of cooperation, however, by
distinguishing between "basic" and "proportional" cooperation,
the former referring to the sum, and the latter to the ratio
of joint outcomes. While McClintock and Walster, Berscheid and
Walster proposed theories of *actual* behavior, MacGrimmon and
Messick's model is a logical analysis of outcome-interdependent
situations that has no direct grounding in empirical evidence.

Although there is a body of experimental studies on the McClintock model and justice theory, this research is seldom explicitly related to "interpersonal conflict", "conflict resolution" or "bargaining." In the above approaches, "conflict"
is seen as a possible byproduct of specific motives like competition or gain maximization. Consequently, only limited conclusions can be drawn from these frameworks concerning the
effects that specific structural and situational variables
have on interpersonal conflict resolution and bargaining.

3. Experimental studies

Before starting our research, we had to select an appropriate
conflict paradigm. Since "standard" conflict paradigms like the
Prisoner's Dilemma Game or the Trucking Game had been criticized as being operationally ambiguous (Nemeth, 1972; McClintock,
1972; Smith & Anderson, 1975), we thought it preferable to work
with the "explicit" bargaining game. This paradigm will be
described in the following section. The results from our research will be presented in two separate sections, the first
concerning the effects of situational characteristics (exogenous variables), and the second the effects of interaction
characteristics (endogenous variables) on conflict resolution
processes.

3.1. The experimental paradigm

In social reality, complex motivational, perceptual and cognitive processes typically mediate interpersonal conflict behavior, the persons involved responding to a multitude of situational, personal and interaction variables. For this reason,
it did not seem advisable to begin testing our theoretical
framework with studies done in field settings. Rather, our aim
to explore the conditions that elicit specific motivations and,
as a consequence, evoke specific forms of conflict behavior
made it necessary to start with less complex situations, since
reducing real-life conflicts to a small number of clearly defined behavior alternatives enables better control of relevant
variables.

To accomplish this reduction, we decided to use a bilateral
monopoly bargaining game. As already outlined in section 2,
bargaining games are operationalizations of distribution conflicts, the players having divergent conceptions of how to di-
vide certain resources. The conflict resolution process starts
with offers and counter-offers and, ideally, ends with a mutually satisfying payoff distribution. One essential feature,

therefore, is that the bargaining game presents a number of payoff-alternatives or solutions with varying attractiveness to the bargainers. By carefully selecting these alternatives, the experimenter can create a tension between cooperation and conflict that is typical for mixed-motive situations (cf. Crott, 1972a).

In most of our experiments, the set of solutions was specified on a bargaining schedule that contained various possible prices of an imaginary product and the corresponding payoffs for the buyer and seller. The status-quo-outcome usually was a zero-payoff; i.e. no profit could be drawn from interaction without settlement. Many experiments were conducted using *incomplete* bargaining situations, the bargaining alternatives being restricted to pareto-optimal solutions. Figure 2 shows a typical bargaining schedule consisting of identical payoffs for both anticipants ("symmetrical" situation). Other bargaining-schedules had an asymmetrical payoff structure. In some experiments, subjects also could apply threats and punishments.

In most experiments, the bargaining intraction took place without verbal communication or face-to-face-contact, the subjects being assigned to separate cubicles and communicating via note or electronic display systems. By restricting the channels of communication in this way, we were able to minimize the influence of verbal abilities and related personal dispositions on our findings and, by this, to increase our context control (cf. Druckman, 1971).

Subjects for all the experiments were male economics students at the University of Mannheim. The homogeneity of the population assured that the results from the different experiments would be comparable. All subjects participated on a volunteer basis. The standard experimental setting was as follows: Without having opportunity to see one another, subjects were placed into cubicles where they found the experimental instruction (either buyer's or seller's instruction, these roles being randomly assigned by the experimenter) and the price-

price[+]	payoff A	payoff B		price	payoff A	payoff B
70	20.00	0.00		49	9.50	10.50
69	19.50	0.50		48	9.00	11.00
68	19.00	1.00		47	8.50	11.50
67	18.50	1.50		46	8.00	12.00
66	18.00	2.00		45	7.50	12.50
65	17.50	2.50		44	7.00	13.00
64	17.00	3.00		43	6.50	13.50
63	16.50	3.50		42	6.00	14.00
62	16.00	4.00		41	5.50	14.50
61	15.50	4.50		40	5.00	15.00
60	15.00	5.00		39	4.50	15.50
59	14.50	5.50		38	4.00	16.00
58	14.00	6.00		37	3.50	16.50
57	13.50	6.50		36	3.00	17.00
56	13.00	7.00		35	2.50	17.50
55	12.50	7.50		34	2.00	18.00
54	12.00	8.00		33	1.50	18.50
53	11.50	8.50		32	1.00	19.00
52	11.00	9.00		31	0.50	19.50
51	10.50	9.50		30	0.00	20.00
50	10.00	10.00				

[+]in units of DM

Figure 2. Schedule of bargaining participants
A (seller) and B (buyer)

payoff table on the base of which bargaining took place. After
being informed of technical details of the bargaining task,
the subjects exchanged offers via luminous dial projectors
in front of the cubicles. Controlled by an elctronical apparatus, the offers were not visible until both participants had
switched a certain price alternative (simultaneous bidding).
Threats, bluffs or punishments were also communicated via non-
verbal media (display, information sheets). The bargaining

range usually consists of 30 to 50 possible price alternatives.
Bargaining time was fixed, the subjects having to reach an
agreement within a period of 30 to 60 minutes. Payoffs connected with the settlement price were cashed, in addition to
which the subjects received 7.50 DM for participating in the
90 minute session (instruction, bargaining interaction, post-
experimental questionnaire). Each experiment was run with a
subject sample sufficiently large to allow robust F-Tests of
the hypothesized treatment effects.

3.2.   The influence of exogenous variables

3.2.1. Payoff structure and information

The research program began with an investigation of the expectations that bargainers have with respect to settlement
alternatives. As described in paragraph 2, game theory provides objective definitions of arbitration criteria. To find
out what sort of criteria are prominent in settlement expectations, Crott (1971b) varied payoff structures with regard to
status-quo-outcomes, security levels and relations of maximum
payoffs. As the subjects were allowed to make only *one* settlement offer ("one-shot"-bargaining), Crott was able to determine which payoff characteristic had the highest "normative"
prominence for settlement. The results showed that, within the
most of the presented payoff structures, the favored offers
could be predicted by the arbitration device postulated by
Raiffa (1953). The subjects preferred settlements that divided
outcomes in accordance with maximum individual payoffs.

In order to test the generality of this result, two further
experiments were conducted in which *extensive* bargaining (i.e.
a free and unlimited exchange of offers) was possible (Crott,
1971a; Crott & Möntmann, 1973). In addition to asymmetry of
payoff structure,these two experiments also varied the degree
of information about the opponent's profits: Under the condi-

tion of "complete" information, subjects knew how much the opponent could actually win, while under the condition of "incomplete" information, subjects knew only their own payoffs. These findings indicated that the bargainers agreed on alternatives around the Raiffa-solution only when they did not know the opponent's payoffs. Under conditions of complete information, variations in the payoff structure did not differrently effect the bargaining settlements. The participants in all cases agreed on solutions that approximated equal split of payoffs.

Despite these information effects, the obtained results do not contradict the findings obtained in the "one-shot" experiment, since settlement *expectations* did not vary over the different information conditions: The participants in all cases expected settlements closely aorund the Raiffa-solution. The observation, however, that having complete information ultimately led to more equalized payoff divisions is relevant to the derivations from justice theory. The subjects perceived "other" contributions as being more important as determinants of the final solution than were the different maximum payoffs assigned by the experimenter.

These findings led us to formulate the following proposition. *Proposition 1:* The more information the bargainers have about joint payoffs and bargaining positions, the greater the influence is that pre-bargaining justice motivation will take on the final settlement.

Additional evidence for this proposition can be derived from experiments in which information effects were analyzed together with those of other situational bargaining variables. Here too, it was found that, on the average, completely informed bargainers divided the payoffs more equally than did bargainers who were incompletely informed (Morgan & Sawyer, 1967; Lamm & Rosch, 1972), and that - under complete information - unequal divisions had to be justified by different pre-bargaining contributions (Messé, 1971).

3.2.2. Aspiration level and bargaining experience

Crott and his colleagues (Crott, Simon & Yelin, 1974; Crott & Müller, 1976; Crott, Müller & Hamel, 1978) performed a series of three experiments to examine the relative influence of individualism and justice motivation on bargaining behavior, manipulating the former by varying the bargainers' aspiration levels and the latter by varying the completeness of the payoff information. In accordance with earlier research by Siegel and Fouraker (1960), aspiration level was manipulated by promising double payoffs if the participants could manage a certain minimum price settlement, low versus high corresponding to whether the buyer or seller was assigned the inferior or superior payoff position. The Crott and Müller, and Crott, Müller and Hamel studies, also manipulated the degree of bargaining experience by having some of the subjects participate several times in the same experiment.

The first study by Crott, Simon and Yelin (1974) was intended to investigate pure gain maximization effects of aspiration level, the bargaining interactions taking place under conditions of incomplete payoff information. As expected, bargaining participants with high aspiration levels were found to have higher settlement-expectancies and to agree on better prices than were bargaining participants with low aspiration levels. The study by Crott and Müller (1976) examined whether aspiration levels have similar effects when there is complete payoff information; that is, when bargainers are torn between fairness and gain-maximization. The results show that even with complete payoff information, bargainers having high aspiration levels achieved better outcomes than those with low aspiration levels, these outcomes at the same time being higher than an equal division of the payoffs. It should be noted, however, that high aspiration settlements in the complete information condition did not deviate as greatly from the equal division solution as did those achieved in the incomplete information

condition. This difference implies that the justice motive had
at least *some* influence in the complete payoff condition when
aspiration levels were high. In the experiment by Crott, Müller and Hamel (1978) aspiration level and payoff information
were manipulated simultaneously and an identical pattern of
results was obtained.

The findings from Crott and Müller,and Crott, Müller and Hamel
studies also showed significant effects for bargaining experience such that increasing bargaining experience led to more
favorable price settlements and higher payoffs.In the Crott
and Müller study, subjects in the high experience conditions
participated four times, while Crott, Müller and Hamel had
their high experience subjects participate three times, the
opponents in both studies always being inexperienced, not having previously taken part in a bargaining experiment. The results of both studies show that subjects used their experience
to their own advantage, thus favoring individualistic attempts
as opposed to justice considerations.

Similar conclusions can be drawn from the results of an experiment conducted by Crott, Scholz and Michels (1978) in which
pareto-optimal and non-pareto-optimal bargaining alternatives
were presented. Within this payoff-structure, it was found
that higher outcomes of experienced bargainers also were related to more agreements on pareto-optimal price alternatives.
This study, in conjunction with the three others described
above, led us to our second proposition:

Proposition 2: The higher a person's aspiration level is and
the more bargaining experience a person has, the greater the
influence is that individualistic motivation will play in
governing his/her behavior during conflict resolution.

Additional support for this proposition is provided by the
studies of Yukl (1974) and Hamner and Harnett (1975), both showing effects of aspiration level on bargaining expectations and
bargaining outcomes that are entirely consistent with those

discussed above. With respect to bargaining experience, additional evidence in support of proposition 2 is available from
research on the Prisoner's Dilemma Game. Conrath (1970), for
example, found that experienced subjects were more cooperative
and thus got higher payoffs than inexperienced subjects. Similarly, Horai and Tedeschi (1975) showed that experienced bargainers employed more threats and punished more often than inexperienced bargainers did as long as they could increase outcomes by doing so.

3.2.3. Strategy of the opponent

Another series of experiments (Crott, Lumpp & Wildermuth, 1976;
Crott, Müller & Maus, 1978; Crott & Müller, 1980) investigated
behavior effects of justice motivation, when subjects are confronted with exploitative opponents. Using pre-programmed confederates, Crott, Lumpp & Wildermuth, and Crott, Müller and
Maus varied the opponent's strategy with regard to equal versus
unequal joint outcome, while Crott and Müller exclusively
observed reactions to exploitative intents. Within each of
these experiments the subject could punish the opponent by
taking cost-raising actions.

The Crott, Lumpp and Wildermuth study examined the differences
in bargainers' punishing behavior towards an opponent whose
strategy either led to a settlement with equal payoffs or to
a payoff higher than what could be expected by a fair outcome
distribution. The results show that subjects made use of punishments whenever the opponent insisted upon a unilateral advantage. This behavior was remarkable in that the punishments reduced the subjects' own payoffs and, hypothetically, exposed
them to the possibility of retaliatory acts from the opponent.
The findings thus indicate that bargainers will punish whenever
they perceive the opponent following unfair bargaining strategies, and that this concern with justice or equity restoration
can take precedence over mere gain maximization or cost mini-

mization considerations. The Crott, Müller and Maus experiment showed,however, that punishment is the last strategy that subjects adopt when faced with a potentially exploitative opponent. The findings from this study indicate that punishments are primarily used when the opponent does not respond to other means of influence such as tough bargaining or threats. As long as the opponent showed signs of conceding - no matter how grudgingly - to equalized payoffs, the bargainers rarely punished.

Crott and Müller (1980) investigated two instrumental aspects of justice motivation first discussed by Walster, Berscheid and Walster (1976), these latter authors distinguishing between "compensation" and "retaliation" as possible ways for victims of exploitation to restore equity. Crott and Müller devised a matrix-game that allowed subjects four alternative response strategies: exploitation, cooperation, compensation and retaliation. The game was played over 14 trials, each trial beginning with an initial choice between exploitation and cooperation. A preprogrammed opponent always chose the exploitation alternative and thus attained the lion's share whenever subjects chose to initially cooperate. As in the Prisoner's Dilemma, bilateral exploitation led to the worst possible outcome; in the present case, zero-payoffs. Subjects were, however, given the possibility of withdrawing from the trial by choosing either compensation or retaliation, the former restoring equal payoffs to both players and the latter giving zero payoffs to the opponent and a compensation payoff to the subject. One problem with these strategies, though, was that they were costly for subjects to employ, as the payoffs attainable by compensation or retaliation were below those that were possible by choosing either exploitation or cooperation. The findings of Crott and Müller indicate that, despite its cost, the retaliation alternative was the one most frequently chosen. This led us to our third proposition.

Proposition 3: The more unyielding and exploitative the opponent, the more likely it is that a person will use destructive

modes of justice restoration during conflict resolution and
bargaining.

Benton, Kelley and Liebling (1972) found that inflexibly exploitative opponents can even force persons to break off bargaining. Müller (1980b) reports that his subjects used superior
coercive power to break off bargaining, and thereby punished
the opponent with monetary losses, if they could not at least
attain an equal division of payoffs.

3.2.4. Monetary incentive and conflict orientation

Following up results of the Crott, Lumpp and Wildermuth study,
Müller and Crott (1978a, 1979) performed two experiments to
investigate the nature of competition motivation. Crott, Lumpp
and Wildermuth had found that punishment was mediated by monetary incentive and symmetry of the bargaining positions, being
most frequent when payoffs were small and outcome-possibilities
identical. This finding led Crott et al. to assume that punishment plays a role not only with respect to justice motivation,
but with respect to competition as well.

To examine this conclusion in a more sophisticated manner,
Müller and Crott (1978a, 1979) observed "real" groups in bargaining situations that were symmetrical in both payoff structure and punishment power. As expected, punishments are used
more often when monetary incentives were low than when they were
high. There was, however, another, even clearer effect; punishment behavior was also influenced by the degree of bargaining
experience subjects had. The experience variable had been introduced to analyze whether aggressive acts in bargaining typify "naive" conflict behavior or whether - and if so, under
which conditions even experienced bargainers behave destructi-
vely. The results indicate that, while experienced bargainers
punished less and perceived the bargaining interaction as being
less competitive than did the inexperienced bargainers, pitting
experienced bargainers against inexperienced opponents often

led to an intensive exchange of aggressions. Generally, it was
the inexperienced bargainers who started the employment of
punishment, the experienced subjects answering with similar
actions that, in turn, led to counteractions, etc.. Consequently, both bargainers rated the interaction as being highly
competitive in nature.

This shift to competition among experienced bargainers appeared to be connected with discrepancies of conflict orientation
between them and the inexperienced bargainers, the former
being more gain-orientated and thus more susceptible to frustration by the behavior of their inexperienced opponents.
This conclusion was also suggested by an analysis of cooperation ratings made during the course of the conflict resolution
(see below). These findings led us to advance a fourth proposition:

Proposition 4: Within punishment-equalized groups, the level of
competition in conflict resolution increases as a negative
function of monetary incentive and the initial gain orientation of the bargainers.

Further evidence for the role of incentive is available in
Gallo (1966) and Kelley, Deutsch, Lanzetta, Nuttin, Shure,
Faucheux, Moscovici, Rabbie and Thibaut (1970) as well as in
the Crott and Müller (1980) experiment discussed above in
which subjects either played for pfennigs or DM. Low incentive stimulated competitive bargaining led to increased attempts at outdoing the opponent. Harrison and McClintock (1965)
and Braver and Rohrer (1978) report additional evidence concerning different conflict orientations of experienced and inexperienced subjects, both studies finding greater competition
in Prisoner's Dilemma settings when subjects were completely
naive than when they had either direct or vicarious experience
with the experimental situation.

3.2.5. Bargaining goals

Müller (1979) conducted a questionnaire study designed to further test the validity of propositions 1 and 4. Müller confronted his subjects with three bargaining situations and, for each,
had the subjects rate, from a buyer's viewpoint, several alternative goals with respect to desirability. The three situations
differed according to the extent of information about mutual
profits (payoff transparancy) and in terms of incentive value,
the object of transaction either being a used car (high incentive) or an exotic souvenir (low incentive). The results showed
that gain maximization is accentuated in a situation low in
payoff transparency and high in incentive level, while fairness is accentuated in the highly transparent, high payoff
situation. Among various competitive goals, the purpose "to
consider bargaining as a personal challenge and to dominate the
opponent" was rated highest in the situation conceptualized
as low in incentive, a finding consistent with those concerning
competition and incentive level reported above.

3.3.   Interaction effects

3.3.1. Mutual accommodation

As a large part of a bargainer's behavior depends upon the ability to influence the opponent's willingness to concede, a
final settlement of any bargaining process will be as much a
consequence of interaction-inherent variables of the conflict
as it is of exogenous variables like payoff-transparency, incentive level, etc.. Crott, Simon & Yelin (1974), Crott & Müller (1976) and Crott, Müller & Hamel (1978) analyzed the concession behavior within bargaining dyads to get evidence about
mutual influence processes during conflict resolution. They
tested the predictive accuracy of two controversial concession-
models: Siegel and Fouraker's (1960) aspiration-level adaption-

model and Osgood's (1962) reciprocity-model. According to
Siegel and Fouraker, yieldingness of one opponent should elicit toughness of the other opponent, or vice versa, while Osgood contends that one opponent's "tempered" yielding should
stimulate yielding by the other opponent, thus leading to a
process of increasing mutual concessions.

The results of these analyses indicate that both models are
correct in assuming that bargainers modify their behavior in
response to the behavior of their opponents and do not act
according to "autistic" behavior schedules. Apart from this,
however, the predictive accuracy of the models varied from
situation to situation depending upon conditions of payoff
information and bargaining experience. Inexperienced subjects
with incomplete payoff information, for example, reacted in
accordance with the aspiration-level-adaption-model, conceding
when the opponent was unyielding, but slowing down their concessions when the opponent himself yielded. On the other hand,
subjects with complete payoff information (whether they were
experienced or inexperienced) acted in accordance with the
Osgood model, conceding when the opponent made concessions
but not when the opponent was unyielding. Even with complete
payoff information, however, the subjects' behavior was not
entirely reciprocal, the more experienced subjects especially
following a strategy of always making concessions smaller than
the ones they received from their opponent. A fifth proposition derives from these findings.

Proposition 5: The more yielding the opponent is during the
course of a bargaining interaction, the more prevailing the
influence of individualistic motivation on the bargainer's
concession behavior.

Evidence for proposition 5 can also be drawn from Komorita and
Brenner (1968), Komorita and Esser (1975) and Esser and Komorita (1975), these studies all showing that subjects tend to
take advantage of unconditionally conceding bargaining participants.

3.3.2. Orientation shifts

To analyse the dynamics of conflict motivation more deeply, Müller and Crott (1978a, 1979) had subjects respond to short questionnaires after a fixed number of bargaining trials, the items on the questionnaires relating to the basic conflict motivations like gain maximization, cooperation and competition. This measurement was made of five points during the bargaining interaction thus permitting trend-tests that gave insights into changes of behavior orientations and conflict motivations. The overall-results of these studies reveal that response trends in bargaining dyads with comparable conflict experience markedly differ from the response trends of those whose experience - and, therefore, motives - diverge. Thus, though inexperienced participants on the average rated the bargaining process as being more competitive than experienced participants did, all subjects tended to perceive bargaining increasingly cooperative in nature the longer the process continued, as long as they were dealing with opponents of the same level of experience as themselves (Müller & Crott, 1978a). Since experienced subjects in the study of Müller and Crott (1979) showed a reverse trend, a combined analysis of both studies was performed to directly compare the response data (see Müller, 1980a). Results of this re-analysis revealed that the changing judgment pattern found for experienced subjects apparently was due to their sensitivity in perceiving their opponent's intentions. While the responses of inexperienced subjects did not differ significantly, experienced bargainers rated their opponents as being more cooperative and less competitive if they were also experienced, and as being less cooperative and more competitive if they were inexperienced. It thus seems plausible to conclude that the experienced subjects in the second study became frustrated in their gain-oriented efforts and had to face the problem how to react, replying with aggressive acts and thus increasingly assimilating their opponent's competitive stance. From these results we derived proposition 6:

Proposition 6: The greater the extent to which aggressive acts
by an opponent frustrate a bargainer's own orientation, the
more prevailing competition will become in motivating the bargainer's behavior as the interaction proceeds.

Proposition 6 can be related to findings of Kelley and Stahelski (1970) and Teger (1970), which indicate that subjects with
cooperative intentions (for example to make some profit in the
game playing situation) were highly sensitive to abuse of
trust and neglection of their own constructive efforts. Conflicts between cooperative and competitive subjects often esca-
lated (even if the initial competitor disclosed himself as
"reformed sinner") and came to a point where resolution was no
longer possible (see also Harford & Solomon, 1967)[3].

4. Social interaction and bargaining behavior

Social interaction can be dealt with theoretically from a
variety of perspectives (cf. Graumann, 1972). One very general
perspective is provided by "social exchange theory", in which
interpersonal relations are seen as a transaction of material
and/or immaterial rewards (Homans, 1958; Thibaut & Kelley,
1959; Jones & Gerard, 1967). Depending on the anticipated or
actual outcomes of interaction, their subjective evaluation
relative to previously experienced outcomes and the presently
available outcome-alternatives, conditions for the start, con-
tinuance and termination of interpersonal relations can be

---

[3] It should be apparent, proposition 6 is based on conclusions
that exceed a purely motivational approach to interpersonal
conflict behavior. However, as the results of the Müller &
Crott studies show, attributional processes have to be assumed,
especially for explaining shifts of orientation during the
course of bargaining. This issue is further discussed in Müller
(1980a), where an attempt is also made to specify some "critical" conditions under which the predictions of a motivational
approach do not match those from an attributional conflict
approach.

specified. Bargaining processes often contribute to each of
these stages. An initiation of contact and communication between the representatives of competing organizations, for example, in most cases is motivated by the egoistic expectations
that joint actions will be more profitable than separate actions or cooperation elsewhere. Outcome-expectations for joint
actions are located above a "comparison level for alternatives"
(i.e. CL alt.) (cf. Thibaut & Kelley, 1959). This CL (alt.)
corresponds directly to the concept of "security level" discussed in section 2. Compromising divergent interests becomes
attractive whenever solutions exist that, at worst, exceed
the security levels of both parties.

Continuing with the same example, there is another important
reference point in the making of corporate decisions: This
point represents the decision makers' actual expectations and
is referred to as the "comparison level" (CL). The CL is based
on the decision makers' previous experiences with similar situations and interactions and, in bargaining, it can be compared with aspiration level. Solutions that exceed the aspiration levels of both parties are usually highly satisfying. The
more the bargainers' CL's diverge, however, the more difficult
it generally is to bring interaction to a mutually satisfying result. Thus, if persons can anticipate a certain degree
of divergency in interest even before having started interacting
(for example, because of resource scarcity), it might be
rational for them to adjust their expectations so as to fall
within a specific range of satisfying and/or at least acceptable outcomes; that is, outcomes that exceed the CL_{alt} regardless of whether or not they exceed the CL as well. In exchange
theory, especially in the approach of Thibaut and Kelley (1959),
bargaining processes are looked at as activities of high relevance for interaction. The reason lies in the nature of bargaining agreements. They constitute *binding* contracts and are
obligatory behavior devices for the persons involved. As persons can trust in what they agreed upon, further interactions

are facilitated. Persons save lengthy, cost- and time-inten-
sive discussions and are able to concentrate on other activities inside and outside the respective social relation.

The motivational model outlined in paragraph 2 of this chapter
extends social exchange theory with respect to conflict interactions in that its assumptions and propositions define the
conditions under which specific conflict motivations operate
and specify the kinds of behavior that result. The model also
specifies the circumstances that lead to competitive behavior
being more rewarding than outcome maximization or distributional justice and hence complements those "advanced" social exchange theories (e.g. Walster, Berscheid & Walster, 1973, 1976)
that do not specify a competition motive.

From a more applied point of view, experimental studies on conflict resolution and bargaining are often considered as simulations of real-life conflicts and exchange situations (Tietz,
1976; Druckman, 1968; Pruitt & Lewis, 1975; Morley & Stephenson,
1969; Sawyer & Guetzkow, 1965). If regarded in this way, these
studies indicate that even within a complex situational context,
the process and outcome of bargaining activities can be explained and predicted by postulating a relatively limited number of
basic behavior determinants. For example, a formal behavior
model of labor negotiations developed by Tietz (1976) works on
the basis of only six discrete levels of wage expectation. So,
the motivational approach proposed here might potentially be
usefully applied for achieving better solutions of real-life
distribution problems, suggesting more efficient bargaining
strategies or formulating more adequate arbitration criteria.
The extent, however, to which the presented approach is, in
fact, applicable to such problems is an issue that has to be
elaborated by further experiments in more complex settings or
simulation studies.

The prediction of behavior in more realistic situations will
surely necessitate attending to multiple effects of personal,
structural, situational and social variables. However, as Crott

and Müller (1978) pointed out, the research done so far allows
one to concentrate on specific "central" conflict variables
like level of experience and aspiration, degree of payoff information, amount of coercive power or extent of prospective
costs in the case of deadlocks. From a "conflict diagnosis"
with respect to these central variables, it should be possible
to derive testable hypotheses about behavioral effects even
within more complex situations than have been realized so far.
Preliminary results from ongoing research suggest that the
proposed model does indeed have predictive value for conflict
resolution behavior in complex buyer-seller-simulations
(Scholz & Fleischer, 1980) and field settings (Müller, 1981).

Chapter 14   Marketing and Buying Decisions in Industrial Markets

W. Kirsch and M. Kutschker

1. Introduction

The present project focused from the beginning on collective
decision processes. As our theoretical and empirical frame of
reference, we adopted what we call the "multiorganizational
interaction approach", an orientation that differs fundamentally from traditional approaches to research on industrial
marketing. Currently, however, such interaction approaches have
become more and more frequent and seem to be becoming the predominant trend in marketing research, thus displacing the earlier concern with the organizational buyer behavior.

Following an outline of what we perceive as being the central
problems in industrial marketing, we will turn to a discussion
of the interaction approach that forms the basis of our work.

2. Origins and development of industrial marketing

An overview of the marketing literature indicates that research
on marketing has tended to become increasingly consolidated and
that, at the present time, two main research trends can be discerned. These two trends differ on the level at which their
analyses are carried out, one proceeding on the level of the
individual, the other on the level of the organization. Nevertheless, the problems addressed within these two trends are
roughly analogous (see Table 1).

Table 1. Main Trends in Research on Industrial Marketing

Inidividualistic	*Organizational*
- Approaches to explain and improve salesman effectiveness	- Approaches to improve the marketing decisions of the producers of industrial goods
- Approaches to explain buyer behavior	- Approaches to explain intra-organizational interactions
- Approaches to explain the inter-personal relations in the industrial buyer-seller-dyad	- Inter- and multiorganizational interaction approaches

In the following we will separately consider each of these research problems, comparing for each the individualistic and organizational formulations.

Management approaches to industrial marketing

The first general work in this area was Alexander, Cross and Hill's (1956) *Industrial Marketing*, a monograph that stimulated a great deal of research in industrial marketing and that was followed (up to the present) by a series of similar manuals, each of which is characterized by the same mixture of instrumental - and management approaches borrowed from consumer-marketing[1].

In the German marketing literature, such monographs are rare[2]. Here, as in the Anglo-American literature, research progress results primarily in a large number of individual articles

---

[1] cf. Baker (1975); Coram and Hill (1970); Corey (1962); Denning (1969); Dodge (1970), Fisher (1969); Haas (1976); Hill (1973); Lonsdale (1966); Wilson (1968).

[2] cf. Pfeiffer (1965); Scheuch (1975); Six (1968)

dealing with particular marketing instruments and/or special
aspects of the industrial market, such as:

- marketing organization[3],
- marketing planning[4],
- price policy[5],
- service[6],
- advertizing[7],
- market research[8],

---

[3] cf. Klemm (1957); Batzer & Laumer (1961); Sherman (1965);
Weber (1967); Marettek (1967); Altefelder (1970); Rasche
(1974); Scheuch (1974); Backhaus (1974).

[4] cf. Tacy (1961); Fromm (1962); Pressel (1965); Kneschaurek
(1966); Stern (1968); Lohse (1969); Hoffman (1970); Ames
(1972); Lehmann (1973).

[5] cf. Beckarath (1965); Farley, Howard & Hulbert (1971); Sultan
(1971a, 1971b).

[6] cf. Löbel (1965); Kroos (1966); McGuire (1970); Hillman (1973);
Schlupp (1974); Cunningham & Roberts (1974); Perreault & Russ
(1976).

[7] cf. Blasberg (1955); Kassner (1959); Berekoven (1961); John
(1961); Sonnek (1962); Kropff (1962); Blasberg (1962); Messner
(1963); Smith (1963); Todtmann (1964); Bruder (1964); Wenzel
(1964); Münster (1964); Kohlmann (1964); Strothmann (1965);
Linder (1966); Goehrmann (1967); VDMA (1967); Strothmann
(1968b); Hessenmüller (1969); Uherek (1970); Blickenstorfer
(1970); Walter & Lorenz (1970); Antonoff (1970); Webster
(1971); Meffert (1972b); Schäfer (1973); Lehmann & Cardozo
(1973); Bunkenburg (1974); Bossert (1975).

[8] cf. Peres (1952); Fratz (1957); Müller-Eckert (1960); Geisser
(1961); Killias (1961); Grünwald (1962); Nahrmann (1962);
Serke (1963); Ringel (1963); Bulach (1964); Wilhelm (1965);
Knüvener (1967); Fiedler (1968); Zinßer (1963); Traub (1968);
Fratz (1968); Eichholz (1968); Meyer & Fischer (1969); Gerth
(1969); Danckwerts & Eggert (1969); Fischer & Meyer (1970);
Gerth (1970); Meyer & Fischer (1971); Jacob (1972); Enquin
(1972); Kesten (1973); Meyer & Wolf (1973); Chisnall (1973);
Franzen (1974); Andritzky (1974); Meffert (1974).

- arrangment of payment terms[9],
- sales promotion[10],
- international industrial (export) marketing[11].

The contributions to personal selling deserve special consideration because they emphasize the aspect in which industrial marketing differs most clearly from consumer marketing. Besides the voluminous normative literature on selection, training and "optimal" strategies for salesmen[12], it is the empirical (descriptive) research on the coherence of salesmen's motivational structures[13], their environment[14] and the determinants of their contentedness and success which gives a relatively comprehensive and realistic picture of the industrial salesman.

This work makes it clear that it is useless to attempt to develop normative strategies for salesmen since the optimal sales approach varies widely from one situation to another. One important determinant of sales effectiveness is, of course, the salesman's partner in the transaction, and buyer-seller interactions were an important early topic in individualistic

---

[9] cf. Tesmar (1964).

[10] cf. Banting and Blenkhorn (1974); Blom (1960); Cunningham & White (1974); Haeberle (1970); Lorenz (1964); Plesse (1965); Schulz (1974); Ullrich (1972).

[11] cf. Cogdale (1973); Klemm (1957); Linder (1966); Walde & Berlinghoff (1967).

[12] Summaries are to be found in Evans (1968); Downing (1969); Boyd & Davis (1970).

[13] cf. Belasco (1966); Pruden (1969); Sales (1969); Hise (1970); Pruden & Reese (1972); Walker, Churchill & Ford (1972); Greene & Organ (1973); Mattheis, Durand, Muczuk & Gable (1974); Walker, Churchill & Ford (1975); Donelly & Invancevich (1975); Pruden & Peterson (1971); Greene (1972); Pruden, Cunningham & English (1972); Darmon (1974a, 1974b); Winer & Schiffman (1974).

[14] cf. Johnson (1971, 1974); Johnson & Cannon (1972).

approaches to research on industrial marketing. Before, however,
the same problem could be formulated on the organizational
level, further research progress had to be made on the nature
of the processes involved in collective purchasing decisions.
Though at first intended only to provide theoretical support
for marketing management decisions, this work eventually developed into a separate area of industrial marketing research.

Individual and organizational buying behavior

When changing from a marketing to a buying approach, one does
not encounter an abrupt transition, since the former is always
based on at least rudimentary assumptions about the target of
the marketing effort: the industrial buyer or the buying organization.

Contrary to consumer behavior research, first approaches assume
industrial buyer's behavior to be rational. The controversy
about the rationalistic or emotional motivational base of industrial buying decisions ended in a still ongoing process of
theoretical and empirical research. On one side, the role of the
individual buyer in a collective organizational decision process is looked down upon, the multi-personality and structure
of the decision process forming the focal point of the analysis.
On the other side, however, it is the industrial buyer's embedd-
edness in organizational structure that is neglected. Models of
buyer behavior concentrate on the cognitive structure of the individual, the best known among these being Howard and Sheth's
(1969) model of the purchasing behavior or private and industrial buyers. Frequently discussed empirical topics include information selection in industrial buying decisions, supplier selection and source loyalty, these being accounted for mostly in
terms of personality variables among which readiness for risk
taking and previously experienced uncertainty play a dominant
role. According to Sheth (1973, 1975), the individual buying process changes to a joint one if the experienced risk becomes too

great and if the interests of others are concerned.

Although it seems that the interaction approaches to industrial marketing (outlined in the next paragraph) are becoming increas-. ingly important, the models and research on organizational buy- ing processes still enjoy a great popularity and theoretical influence. One reason for this continuing importance may be the great degree of similarity between the various approaches to buying processes. Regardless whether one chooses the Buy-Grid- Model by Robinson, Fajris and Wind (1967), the "Nielsen-Box" (1975), Robinson and Stidson's (1967) Compact Model (also Stidson, 1967), or the frame of reference by Webster and Wind (1972a,b; also Webster, 1965), one finds a joint buying pro- cess divided into phases and decision type and influenced by a great number of variables. Most approaches differentiate be- tween the individual group, organizational and environmental system levels, and center empirical attention on those deter- minants that operate most directly on the individual and/or buying group: i.e. on the so-called "buying center." Numerous empirical studies have been done to weigh the relative merits of these various approaches (cf. review by Kirsch, Kutschker & Lutschewitz, 1980). As we agree with Nicosia and Wind (1978) that the modelling of industrial marketing should follow an interaction approach, our **own** work enters into direct competi- tion with the Webster and Wind model.

Personal and organizational interaction approaches

The explication of the term "marketing" has already shown that the paradigm of interaction and exchange is traditional with the marketing theory. One of the first persons who introduced the exchange-concept into marketing theory was Anderson, whose law of exchange holds that an exchange takes place only when it is of mutual interest for the parties concerned (Anderson, 1965; Anderson & Martin, 1965). Similarly, Kotler (1972a) states that a transaction between two or more parties depends on the fact that each possesses a product that is scarce for each of the other(s) and is able to transact and communicate. We thus include under the heading "interaction approaches" all theoretical frames of reference centering on processes of mutual influence and communication linked to the transaction of industrial goods. Personal interaction approaches posit only a thematic link between dyadic interaction of individuals, while organizational interaction approaches see transactions as joint decision processes between organizations.

The experiment by Evans (1963a,b) is regarded as being an important early study in the personal interaction approach, even though insurance policies hardly fit the classical definition of industrial goods. The study shows that the probability of a sales agreement becomes higher the more demographic, individual and cognitive traits the interaction partners have in common. Subjectively perceived similarity among transaction partners is a better predictor of final agreement than objective similarity is. Other studies show that the relation between buyers and sellers is influenced by their values, consensus concerning role expectancies, expertise, credibility and social power. In the German research literature, Schoch has been principally responsible for developing the personal interaction approach, regarding social interaction as the result of closely interrelated verbal and non-verbal behaviors of two or more individuals in immediate physical proximity (Schoch, 1969).

The chief merit of such interaction approaches is no doubt the empirical proof they provide that there is no ideal "salesman personality", sales success is dependent instead on the social distance separating seller and buyer. The concentration of personal interaction approaches on the microcosm of the dyadic interaction and the detailed empirical and theoretical specification of individual and social influences has yielded a body of empirical factors influencing dyadic interaction that could be a starting point for empirical research on more complex, joint decision processes on the

organizational level. Though we welcome the replacement of the
salesman approach by a personal interaction approach, the sim-
plicity of decision situations and types of goods to which
they apply render them unsuitable as a basis for developing an
approach to multi-organizational interaction.

The move from personal to organizational interaction approaches
not only involves a jump to the next higher system-level but
necessitates the adoption of an interdisciplinary orientation.
It is for this reason that these approaches are characterized
by a strong reliance on organization theory itself being interdisciplinary in its scope.

Hakansson and co-workers (Hakansson & Östberg, 1975; Hakansson
& Wootz, 1975a,b) place less emphasis on the transaction's
component processes than on its determinants, their work making
use of three different research areas. First, they use previous
work on risk-management, also applied to marketing theory by
Bauer (1960) and Cox (1967), to account for the effects that
the uncertainty resulting from the transaction has on participants' adaption behavior. The research also leans heavily on
the contingency approach of organization theory and the theory
of inter-organization relations. From the first comes their
claim that the transaction's progress and structure will reflect the constellation of influences stemming from the relevant product technology, the characteristics of the involved
organizations and the dynamics of the environment.

From the latter, which is still in its early stages, comes the
heuristic claim that the interaction is both the cause and the
result of power and dependency relations (cf. Litwak & Hilton,
1962; Levine & White, 1965; Emerson, 1962; Heskett, Stern &
Beier, 1970; Warren, 1967).

The close entwinement between organization theory and modern
management theory may be the reason that the differences between the work of Hakansson et al. and our own interaction
approach are less pronounced than are those between our

approach and other well-known frame of references for the study
of industrial marketing. The basic differences between the two
approaches should not, however, be ignored. While Hakansson et
al. have analysed ongoing business relations, our prime consideration has been for complex decision processes. In spite
of basic differences in detail, the two approaches' common background makes collaborative research possible, and such a project was started in 1977 simultaneously at the Universities of
Bath, Lyon, Manchester, Munich and Uppsala and at ISVOR-Fiat
Turin[15].

3. The interaction approach to the industrial marketing

In calling our approach the multiorganizational interaction
approach, we want to emphasize that the interaction processes
involved in industrial market transaction take place in a socio-
economic field that extends over many different organizations.

The concept of the socio-economic field pervades our following
discussion. The socio-economic field of an industrial market
transaction is the sum of all social factors (taking into
account their isolated effects and their interactions with one
another) that we must refer to when trying to explain why an
interesting industrial market transaction has been realized
under certain conditions. In the following, we shall progressively refine this definition and illustrate how it can be operationally specified in specific research settings. First, we
characterize the industrial marketing transaction and the complex decision problems that have to be coped with. We then
propose a definition of the transaction episode and show that

---

[15] Apart from the empirical testing of the status quo regarding
interaction approaches, their further development was a substantial aim of this project. The extended conception of the
interaction approach that we present here has been the dowry
to this project, resulting from our work in the SFB.

many classical marketing activities (price-, product-planning,
conditions, etc.) are analyzable as joint decision processes
(negotiations) involving representatives of several organizations within the specific transaction-episode. Moreover, there
are a variety of marketing activities by producers, users and
other participants (parties) aimed at establishing and developing potentials that we will discuss in detail in the third
section. Finally, all this happens, as we said before, in a
socio-economic field, whose features and limits will be considered in detail in the final chapter.

3.1. Industrial marketing and complex problems

It is often the practice to talk of "complex" industrial goods
and to see in this complexity a main cause for a series of
phenomena typical of industrial transactions. When talking of
"complex" industrial goods, we refer not so much to the characteristic and configuration of such goods as to the problems
that have to be coped within transactions concerning them. In
the following, we want to briefly outline the problems of industrial goods transactions.

The problems of industrial marketing transactions

Capital goods are often presented as configurations of industrial investments comprising of a variety of interdependent technical and structural sub-systems and elements. Even single
aggregates, therefore, sometimes show high complicated configurations that make great demands upon the producers' technical
know-how. Suppliers are often compelled to supplement the "hard-
ware" of the configuration itself with some "applied software",
the latter often being restricted to the "systems and procedures" necessary for the operation and control of complex pro-
duction- or communication systems. In addition, users on
industrial markets expect additional service that extends
partly to maintenance but also to the training of personnel.

Apart from technological problems, the development and transaction of capital goods is often connected with considerable
organizational problems for the suppliers as well as for the
buyers. These problems are especially great when such transactions involve more or less radical changes in the organization's structure and/or procedure. This is why procedural rules
have to be established and institutional preventive measures
have to be taken that facilitate a smooth transaction of investment projects. Besides a technological software which
primarily enters into the design of the capital goods, there
must also be an organizational software covering all methods,
procedures and institutional preventive measures that can be
applied to optimally introduce the necessary technical know-
how even with the most complicated problems. This organizational software thus requires a diversified knowledge base as well
as methodological tools (developed with respect to both organizational praxis and theory) that are applicable to the design,
production and sale of capital goods.

The decision situation just outlined is surely not typical for
all transactions on industrial investment markets. There are,
indeed, a series of investment goods for which transactions
create far less complex problems. In addition, one and the same
capital good can create decision situations of different complexity depending upon the situational factors that are apparent at any given moment.

The complexity of the problems for suppliers and buyers of investment goods will increase with the relative value of an investment object, the novelty of the problem to be coped with,
the complexity of the organizational change required for the
development and production or introduction and use of the investment object. Before looking closely into these central
determinants of problem-complexity, however, it is necessary to
describe more precisely what we mean by complexity itself.

The definition of complex problems

A basic assumption in current work on problem solving is that
the definition of a problem and the generating and testing of
solutions take place in a context established by a problem
space and that one and the same task may be defined in different contexts as different problems. When stuck on a problem's
solution, people often gain new impetus by recasting the problem in a completely different context.

There are many tasks that by their very nature span several
contexts, and transactions concerning investment goods normally
belong to this category. Such cases call for the know-how of a
range of specialists and experts and are likely to confound
those interested parties concerned with determining problem
type and strategy. These specialists and/or interested parties
will often have a variety of different contexts at their disposal in which they alternatively cast the problem at hand. We
refer to such multi-context-problems as being complex problems.

Problem complexity is a positive function of
1) The number of the different, relevant contexts, and the
   number of specialists or interested parties concerned;
2) the difference between these contexts and
3) the difficulty of transferring statements from one context
   to the next (i.e. the degree to which the contexts correspond).

We propose that the problems arising with capital goods transactions are generally complex, and that these transactions can
be differentiated from each other and labeled according to complexity level. Normally such transactions affect many specialists and/or interested parties who, on account of their widely
varying background, perceive the problem differently and experience considerable difficulties in communicating with one
another.

We presume that the complexity of a decision situation

increases with the relative value that the investment object
has for the suppliers and buyers organization (judged by the
turnover or investment volume), the newer the tasks linked
with the transaction are for suppliers and buyers and the greater the organizational change required for the producers and
users after the transaction has been successfully closed.
Relative value, novelty and organizational change are the key
factors upon which, in our opinion, the complexity of decision
situation depends.

In the following, we are mainly interested in those transactions characterized by a high problem complexity. In order to
analyze such transactions, we shall first, however, introduce
the concept "transaction episode", the second important element
of our interaction approach.

3.2. Transaction episodes

In a socio-economic field relevant to a specific capital goods
transaction, there is a continuous stream of activities and
interactions. The transaction episode comprises all activities
and interactions connected with the preparation, arrangement
and realization of the transaction in question. Not all transaction episodes, however, end with a transaction. The quota of
interrupted episodes is - especially within the capital goods
market - relatively high.

Normally, there are a considerable number of organizations
(or their representatives) involved in transaction episodes
for capital goods. The wide range of parties concerned in such
transactions takes on significance when we consider transaction
episodes' main features.

Main characteristics of episodes in capital goods transactions

The episode for a highly complex capital goods transaction includes more than just the actual transaction itself. Typically,

it includes also the various activities relating to the development and set-up of facilities as well as the actual production, assembly and even maintenance. Thus, the range of parties involved extends well beyond the producers and users to include a wide spectrum of third parties (e.g. advisory engineers).

With complicated investment goods configurations there are often numerous organisations who supply different aggregates and who team up with associations and syndicates in order to control the development, production and installation. Moreover, it is not at all unusual that there are several organizations engaged on the user-side who mutually use these facilities and who therefore (possibly during the period of transaction) establish a joint subsidiary. During a complex transaction episode, there is an inter-woven chain of single transactions; development-, delivery- and maintenance-contracts are drawn up as well as secondary transactions concerning insurance, financing contracts with banks, shipment contracts with forwarding agents and advisory contracts with advisory-engineers. These secondary transactions stand, of course, in very close relation with the primary transaction.

The operation of complex industrial facilities involves a great deal of legal groundwork. Thus, public authorities (e.g. unions, liaison offices) will also play an important role in the transaction episode, not only in granting permits or delivering sanctions but also in serving as sources of official contact.

The methodological status of the episode-concept

The socio-economic field, relevant for the explanation of capital goods transaction is usually a complex structure, consisting of numerous actors and the network of their social interactions. The analysis of such complex structure calls for a relatively high level, macroscopic analysis. As opposed to decision theory analysis, which accounts for events in terms of the volition of individual decision makers, the macroscopic analysis of organizations proceeds on the collectivistic level, generating explanations without recourse to the decisions made by individual actors.

We believe that a theory of industrial goods marketing based on an interaction approach should provide a bridge between microscopic and macroscopic analyses in order to take advantage of both. The episode concept, in our opinion, enables such a synthesis to be made. Our approach will be to analyze the given episode itself microscopically, giving primary concern to the voluntaristic and individualistic elements, while at the same time treating the context (i.e. all system activities not belonging to the episode in question) macroscopically. In as much as the mutual influences of the episode and context are taken into account, the micro- and macroscopical views are combined in a single theoretical framework.

The operational definition and demarcation of an episode is chiefly an heuristic matter. Generally, those occurrences, activities and interactions are relegated to the episode's context that, in the opinion of the researcher, are not worth while analyzing microscopically. This does not exclude the possibility that, when analyzing a specific episode, further episodes can be identified and analyzed with instruments specially adapted to their particular characteristics. Ultimately, defining episodes is a strategic decision to be done in such a way that enables the researcher to concentrate more strongly on individual parts of the socio-economic field without neglecting the influence of (or their influence on) the context.

The decision characteristics of transaction episodes

Complex transactions cannot be coped with by treating them as single collective decisions or problem solving processes. Rather, it is generally more effective to handle such complex events as a sequence of partially parallel, loosely connected decision processes, each of a collective nature and each referring to different aspects of the transaction episode.

The activities and interactions occurring within transaction episodes can be divided into 5 classes.

1) Transactions and transformations of physical objects
2) The generation and distribution of evidence (perception, explanation, intelligence)
3) The building, exercise and securing of power
4) Development of consensus
5) Securing of commitments

These classes are not, of course, mutually exclusive; one and the same activity can simultaneously represent, for example, the transformation of physical objects and securing of power.

The collective decision processes can be thought of as (sub-) episodes of interrelated activities and interactions of all five classes, though not every such activity or interaction constitutes a decision episode. A great deal of what occurs within and between organizations lies beyond a strictly decision-oriented voluntaristic point of view. This becomes especially significant with respect to what political scientists have called "nondecision" phenomena; that is, organizational processes concerning power and/or consensus whose (possibly latent) function is to avoid the initiating of definite decision episodes.

Decisions can be characterized as "joint-decision-processes" when there are several inter-acting decision makers, each having his/her own task in mind, who actively influence each other in order to motivate them to arrive at decisions favorable for their own tasks. Thus, when two representatives of different organizations cooperate in their respective organizational tasks, they can only in a very rudimentary sense be said to be working at a common task requiring a collective problem-solving effort.

This does not exclude, however, the possibility that representatives will arrive at such common tasks during the course of

their interaction. The likelihood of this occurring is greater
the more integrative these decision processes are; that is, the
greater the willingness of those concerned to cooperate.

Cooperation will often reflect a general willingness to accept,
in conflict situations, substantive and procedural restrictions
in favor of one's counterparts. If this readiness is small, the
decision process will be of a distributive nature, integration
being greatest when all concerned look upon the decision as a
process of collective problem-solving where impartial assessment and consensus without coercion prevail.

To the extent that collective decision processes include participants' mutual exertions of power, they take on the character
of negotiations. One can see the texture of collective decision
processes as consisting of the alternation of inter- and intra-
organizational negotiations, the latter serving as an occasion
to develop the negotiating strategies of the organizational representatives as well as to confront members of the mother
organizations with whatever results the inter-organizational
negotiations have so far achieved.

3.3. Potentials for capital goods transactions

The discussion above makes clear that a lot of what is determined in a transaction episode is analyzed in marketing research
in the context of general decisions about the marketing-mix
(price, product promotion, conditions, etc.). In this, our own
frame of reference differs substantially from the theoretical
conceptions developed in industrial marketing. We too, however,
can formulate the general hypothesis that with the increasing
complexity of the decision situation, decisions about the relevant marketing parameter will be made within the transaction
episode and that, additionally, they will be subject to negotiations.

Within the industrial goods market there are, of course, marketing activities and decisions that take place outside of the

individual transaction episodes and that are of a general
character. According to our own point of view based on the episode concept, these general marketing activities serve to develop and promote potentials that can later be activated within
transaction episodes.

Development and activation of potentials

The meaning of "potential" in our interaction approach is
schematically illustrated in the following flow-chart:

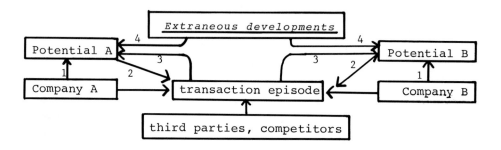

The flow-chart represents the marketing activities of the suppliers and buyer organizations within a single transaction
episode. Besides general activities aimed at developing and
promoting potentials (arrows 1), many things happening within
the transaction episode are the result of activating the potentials either directly (arrows 2) or by their indirect repercussions (arrows 3). An interrupted transaction or a non-recur-
ring price-concession may weaken the potential of the organization and thus the chances for future episodes. The potentials are thus also a function of non-intentional side-effects or
of extraneous developments not under the control of the organizations concerned (arrows 4).

The promotion and development of such potentials is initially
subject to standard marketing activities like advertisement,
sales promotion, marketing research, the development of new
products, etc. They also reflect, however, organizational

regulations, procedures and structures (project-management) insofar as these facilitate the individual transaction episodes.

Consequently, our interaction approach is not restricted to the interaction within transaction episodes but also tries to take into account, through the concept of "potential", the import- ance of general marketing decisions for the opening, arrange- ment and outcome of industrial goods transactions.

Socio-economic field and markets

Judging from text-books on industrial marketing, the socio- economic field in which transactions of investment goods of interest take place is the capital goods market. This market is often called a social system, the attempt being to bring into play certain concepts from micro-economic price-theory and the theory of social systems (Philipps, 1960; Cyert & March, 1963; Williamson, 1963). This attempt depends heavily on the modern theory of management- and marketing channels, the latter often being treated as very specific sorts of social systems (Breyer, 1964; Bowersox, 1969; Stein, 1969a,b; Steffenhagen, 1975). An example of such treatment is the frame of reference developed by Evan (1965) who, following a closer analogy with social psychological role concepts, sets out from what he calls an "organization set". This reduction to social-psychological terms in theorizing about macro-systems has initiated a rather broad program of empirical work that, for example, analyses conflicts in marketing channels as being primarily conflicts with regard to role-expectancies and requirements.

Inquiring as to which types of social systems best characteriz- es a market leads to difficulties, since there is no apparent a priori criterion for deciding on one rather than another and it is not clear whether markets in fact represent still another type of social system, like groups, coalitions, organizations or collectivities.

In recent empirical tests on industrial goods marketing, it has

been denied that the market constitutes a social system (cf.
Webster, 1969b, 1970, 1971). Social systems are considered as
being relatively isolated systems, the members of which are
connected by an especially close pattern of social interaction
(a communication net). The competitors' concealing of information from one another, the geographical separation of market
participants and the necessity of avoiding problems with anti-
trust laws are all factors that act against the market satisfying the basic conditions for being a social system. These plausible arguments are, on the other hand, confronted by results,
supporting the assumptions of the industrial market, being a
social system (Czepiel 1973, 1974; Martilla, 1971). Our own
approach is to avoid any a priori classification. In our term-
inology, a market is first of all an abstract summary of two
social categories ("suppliers" and "demanders") within the relevant socio-economic field. The interaction connecting the members of these different social categories need not be especially intense; the communication pattern linking the "suppliers"
and "demanders" is not a fixed criterion for distinguishing
markets from non-markets but rather an aspect that can vary
from one market to another. The closer the link between
"suppliers" and "demanders", the greater the market's transparency. Usually, only those parties are considered as being
part of a given market who have at least a minimal chance of
contacting one another and of being acquainted. Since this implies, however, the presence of communication nets in the socio-
economic field, this requirement ties the "market" concept to
the pattern of relations in the socio-economic field and the
nature of its component social categories. Based on the morphology of the social systems in the socio-economic field, there
may well exist a great number of suppliers and demanders integrated into independent communication nets. It is these subsets
of suppliers and demanders, then, that constitute the individual markets of interest.

3.4. Concluding remarks

The interaction approach that we propose centres on the idea of
"the transaction episode", highlighting a complex variety of
interactions that can occur among representatives of different
organizations (as well as other social systems). These interactions are closely tied to collective decision or negotiation
processes that are, in turn, conditioned by a multitude of situational factors specific to transactions (e.g. prices, product
design, terms, etc.). Procedure and results of these transaction episodes also depend on incidents and structural traits of
the socio-economic field, the concept of "potential" serving as
a link between structural traits and processes.

Admittedly, our theoretical frame of reference is quite abstract. This abstractness is due in part, however, to the material with which we deal. Although the investment projects that
concern us involve transactions of great complexity, our choice
of these projects was motivated by the desire to make a contribution to the development of a general marketing theory, especially for the marketing of industrial goods. At the beginning of our investigations in 1970/71, we felt that the then
current approaches to marketing theory were too concentrated
on relatively simple consumer and industrial products. By
choosing investment goods transactions, we hoped to remedy this
shortcoming.

4. Empirical tests of the interaction approach

The recent literature in marketing research shows an increasing trend towards empirically testing predictions generated by
interaction approaches to industrial marketing. These empirical
tests are primarily carried out with respect to interpersonal
interaction models (Tosi, 1966; Willet & Pennington 1966; Evans,
1968; Schoch, 1969). The only empirical tests of an organizational model that we know of were those performed by the

International Marketing Group in Uppsala mentioned above (cf. Hakansson & Östberg, 1975).

4.1. Method

The theoretical frame of reference discussed above was not the starting point of our research program but rather the result of a series of studies employing unstructured interviews, negotiation games and questionnaires submitted to manufacturers, purchasing firms and "third parties" (e.g. consulting engineers) (Huppertsberg, 1972, 1975; Kirsch & Huppertsberg, 1972; Kirsch, Huppertsberg & Kutschker, 1977). The questionnaires dealt with both general problems (e.g. investment planning and application, investment policy, marketing-mix, diffusion strategy, organizational information and adoption behavior) and specific issues concerning the initiation and completion of a single transaction episode. In a first study this questionnaire was distributed, on the purchaser side, to a representative cross-section of all registered companies in West Germany having more than 900 employees while on the side of the manufacturers, the questionnaire was sent to a representative sample of industrial goods manufacturers having more than 50 employees and belonging to either the VDMA, ZVEI, building, shipping, aviation and space industries.

A second field study concentrated on manufacturers and purchasers of standard application software, the sample consisting of 71 manufacturers (among them were 9 computer manufacturers and 56 software companies) and 47 purchasers (cf. Kirsch, Börsig, Englert & Gabele, 1975 ; Kirsch, Englert, Börsig & Gabele, 1975; Englert, 1977 for detailed descriptions of random tests and test design).

Survey of empirical findings

The research program outlined above has generated several

research reports in which we conduct primarily exploratory
analyses of our data with the aim of testing and further developing our theoretical frame of reference. In addition to hypotheses on the characteristics and component processes of
transaction episodes, our research was directed mainly at testing hypotheses concerning the nature and effects of the environment within which transaction episodes occur. Furthermore,
a series of research reports were published containing purely
descriptive-statistical evaluations in order to provide the
companies participating in our research program with rapid
feedback (Huppertsberg, Roth & Schneider, 1974; Kirsch, Börsig,
Englert & Gabele, 1975; Kirsch, Englert, Börsig & Gabele, 1975;
Kutschker & Schneider, 1974; Roth, Huppertsberg & Schneider,
1975).

The following is a brief survey of the issues addressed by our
research program.

1) The literature on buyer behavior in industrial milieux contains frequent, controversial statements as to the rationality of individual or collective decision processes. It comes
as no surprise, therefore, that decision-makers in purchasing
organizations have certain ideas about what constitutes
"correct" rational behavior and that organizational regulations
exist dictating the use of "rational" profitability calculations. If one compares, however, these individual attitudes
and organizational regulations with actual behavior, one finds
that the parties in question make only limited use of profitability calculations. From this point of view, the behavior of
purchasing organizations seems only partly rational, even when
rationality is evaluated in terms of criteria established by
decision-makers and/or organizations themselves.

This discrepancy might be an indication of a "rationality veil"
that, in practice, deliberately or undeliberately gets spun
around investment decision. It is obviously difficult, however,
to be entirely "rational" during interactions with a negotiation partner.

2) Economic science places the question of rationality in close connection with information behavior and the use of systematic information processing methods (e.g. profitability or investment calculations). Two of our research reports (Kutschker & Roth, 1975; Roth, 1976), concern information behavior that occurs prior to purchasing decisions. In this connection the following questions were examined:

- What is the relation between a purchaser organization's traits (especially its degree of organization) and its information behavior?
- What importance do investment calculations have during the preparation of purchase decisions?
- What influence does information behavior have on the purchasing process?

If investment calculations and the general results of the information behavior are regarded as a "potential" of the organization in question, then empirically, examining information behavior should also provide insight into a significant aspect of the construction and use of potential in the field of capital goods marketing.

3) If we focus our attention on the decision processes that occur within transaction episodes, the question of decision criteria for the purchase of investment goods takes on a special significance. According to our empirical findings (Kutschker, 1975; Huppertsberg & Kirsch, 1977), the purchasers of investment goods act mainly according to criteria based on the following factors:
- technical problem solution
- commercial conditions
- producer reliability

An examination of the question to what extent producers realistically estimate purchasers' decision criteria indicates that the producers (1) underestimate the importance of the technical problem solution, (2) correctly estimate that of the commercial conditions and (3) overestimate the importance of producer reliability.

This led us to ask how far such errors influence the process of the transaction episodes, especially inter-organizational nego-tiations. Furthermore, the producers' efforts to create "acqui-sition potentials" by means of advertising are apt to be highly influenced by the degree of realism in estimating the purchas-ers' criteria.

4) The results concerning the decision criteria used by the purchasers of investment goods were confirmed by a parallel investigation of software marketing (Börsig, 1976; Englert, 1977). Here, too, we were able to demonstrate that the produc-ers estimate the purchasers' decision criteria incorrectly. We also found that, when launching public relations activities, producers do not act on the basis of what they believe to be the purchasers' decision criteria, their advertising corres-ponding to neither the actual nor the presumed decision cri-teria.

5) The complexity of the problems surrounding an investment good are particularly high when it is an innovative good presented on the market for the first time. Foremost among these are diffusion problems; the diffusion of the object it-self and of the innovative technological ideas behind it. In addition, besides diffusion problems within the whole multi-organizational complex, there are also problems concerning the diffusion of the new technological ideas within the purchasing organization that arise partly during actual transaction epi-sodes. Diffusion problems, therefore, give vent to questions concerning the development of a manufacturer's "potential" out-side and within transaction episodes. Research report by Lutschewitz and Kutschker (1977) deals with three out of a wide range of questions concerning diffusion problems:

- How are innovations within the investment goods industry received, how do they affect the managers' cognitive

structure regarding knowledge of and attitude towards innovation, and which influencing factors dominate this attitude?

- Which introductory strategies are selected for the diffusion
  of innovative investment goods and which factors determine
  the selection of these strategies?

- What are the characteristic traits of the adoption process
  for investment goods by the purchasing organization and how
  does this process differ from "normal" investment decisions?

Our empirical analysis was, of course, subject to certain practical limitations. One of these was a restriction in the range
of our data gathering to processes within the actual transaction episodes themselves, thus preventing us from exploring the
morphology of the socio-economical field, a topic that we consider basic for the discussion of diffusion processes.

6) Our interaction approach was focused from the start on problems of intra-organizational and inter-organizational negotiations. The empirical findings pertaining to these negotiations,
and therefore based on research design, are strongly influenced
by our differentiation between episode and environmental field.
Consequently, our research on negotiation behavior provides
the main source of empirical support for the central components in our frame of reference.

We intended to demonstrate the following:
- The complexity of the decision situation accounts for a portion of the variation in processes that occur within the
  transaction episode.
- The analysis of the negotiation processes within the transaction episodes is of particular significance for explaining
  the market behavior of both producers and purchasers.
- Structural traits of the socio-economic field influence the
  processes that occur within the transaction episode.

Test plan

The literature on the various sub-topics in negotiations shows
no shortage of paper aimed at integrating the different theoretical approaches and manifold empirical results within a unified
frame of reference. For the most part, however, such attempts
remain at the level of mere classificatory schema (cf. Crott,
Kutschker & Lamm, 1977a,b; Druckmann, 1977; Morley & Stephenson,
1977; Sawyer and Guetzkow, 1965). The variables in the following
studies, on the other hand, are related by means of the theoretical categories of the interaction approach presented in the
second chapter and were *jointly* submitted to an empirical test.

Figure 1 presents a rough diagram of the relations between
variables of the transaction episode and environmental field
that were tested. As can be seen, the individual variables
are united into variable groups and characterized by means
of a corresponding "summary" variable. Nearly all of the
variables listed, therefore, represent a vector of dependent
or independent variables.

As to dependent variables for the transaction episode, we followed the literature on inter-individual, organizational and
international negotiations in selecting those variables commonly accepted as being representative of negotiation behavior.
The environment, on the other hand, was operationalized in
terms of a series of structural and/or descriptive variables
concerning the organizations and their representatives of the
organizations involved that precede, succeed or accompany the
transaction. Many of the preceding activities are no longer
recognizable as such, but leave traces in the shape of more or
less consolidated structural traits in the systems under consideration. Characteristics such as company size, market position, sales development, etc. are relatively invariant consequences of earlier company activities and have been classified
together as "attributes of the organizations". We consider the
organizations' strategic behavior and transaction and negotia-

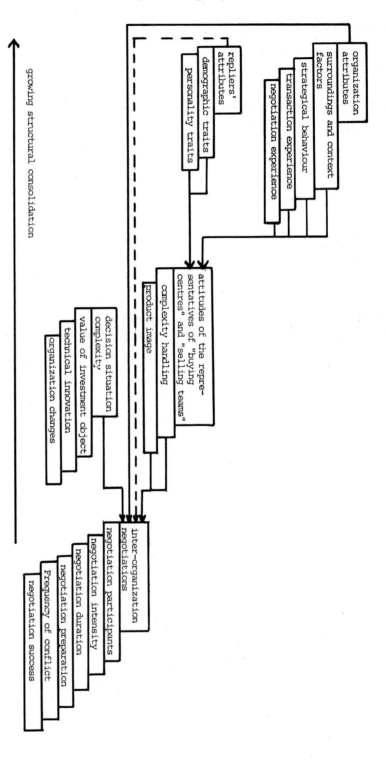

Figure 1. Test plan for the analysis of negotiations between suppliers and purchasers of investment goods

tion experience to be attributes of a more variable nature. Here, incidents such as the appearance of a new competitor, personnel changes in the purchasing department or increased sales promotion may accentuate, cancel or even reverse outcomes gained during the transaction episode itself.

A similar dichotomy exists with respect to our respondent sample; demographic data such as age, sex, length of professional experience appear less variable than personality traits such as readiness for innovation. These traits, however, are not expected to account for the negotiation behavior during transaction episodes but rather to provide a means for assessing the representativeness achieved by our having had individuals respond for organizations of which they were members. In the case of variables containing factual statements such as size and growth of the company, advertising budget, etc., the choice of competent persons as respondents should have, if not completely, at least considerably reduced problems of reliability and representativeness. The persons answering our questionnaires belonged mainly to the top management and were involved in the transactions being studied. It therefore seems likely that all equally informed members of the organization would have responded in a similar manner.

We also, however, collected data on a series of variables concerning values, customs, attitudes, etc. typical of the organization, buying center or selling team. We believed that such attitudes are strongly influenced by the organizational atmosphere; that, for instance, losses suffered in the past influence the readiness for compromise during subsequent negotiations. We feared, however, that the persons answering our questionnaires would not act as spokesmen of "prevailing" opinions, customs, etc., but that their judgments concerning such problem situations would be distorted by their own subjective feelings. In order to have some basis for estimating this bias, we included the respondents' attributes in all our evaluations as control variables.

The prevailing values and attitudes in an organization, classed
under the heading "Attitudes of representatives of the 'buying
centers' and 'selling teams'", act as intervening variables,
our position being that their attitudes are both influenced by
the attributes of the respective organization, and, in turn,
influence the representatives' own behavior during the transaction process. Another reason, however, for assigning these
variables an intervening position is that they seem far more
susceptible to change than, for example, the organizational
attributes are. This is clearly demonstrated in the case of
attitudes towards the product (product image), these - and this
is typical for capital goods marketing - being subject to
mutual manipulation attempts during the transaction episode. In
the course of the evaluation we shall also investigate whether
these attitudes are not explained by the negotiation behavior
taking place during the episode.

It is obvious that all possible independent - dependent variable relationships cannot be presented here. It is our aim
rather, to demonstrate the overall connection of the variable
groups relevant to determining the role that episode and
environmental field play in determining negotiating behavior.
To do so, we must omit describing the construction of the
global variables and the multi-variate connection within the
individual variable groups. As a representative of the other
independent variables, we present the construction of variable
"problem complexity" in some detail.

4.2. Complexity of the decision situation

Problems that arise in the marketing of investment goods tend
to be complex in that they usually involve multiple contexts.
It will be recalled that a problem becomes more complex the
greater the:
1) number of relevant contexts
2) dissimilarity of the contexts

3) lack of correspondence of the contexts
4) variability of these dimensions.

Three determining factors were selected as being especially
influential with respect to the above four dimensions: The relative value of the investment, the novelty (innovativeness) of
the relevant activities and the degree of organization changes
caused by the investment object. Our operationalization of
complexity is in line with these factors.

A problem's novelty to the purchasing organization depends on
whether it is a straight rebuy situation, a modified rebuy or
a new task. The producers, on the other hand, must differentiate between investment goods that result from mass production, modified mass production or production by special
order. To measure respondents' perceptions of problem novelty,
we had them rate their respective problems on five-point novelty scales. To aid them in their ratings and establish an objective basis for comparison, a number of examples were given for
each scale point. A similar five-point scale was used to measure respondents' estimates of the organizational change triggered by the product in question. Value was assigned by taking the
logarithm of each product's absolute price and then distributing these logarithms over a ten-point value scale.

Figure 2a and 2b on the following pages show the distribution
of marketing and purchasing decision-situations in the three-
dimensional "complexity" space. The n for the producer sample
was 168 and that for the purchaser sample was 116.

For easier empirical handling, the data can be reduced to a
single dimension by means of various methods of index formation,
regression or factor analysis. The latter is suited very well
to identify and test the hypothesis of a general factor "complexity" being hidden behind the three operational measures of
problem complexity: The goods value, its novelty and the amount
of organizational change, caused by the capital good's production and installation. According to our theoretical model, one

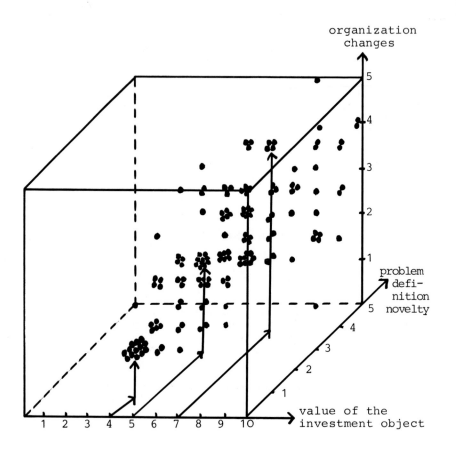

Figure 2a. Distribution of the test units according to the
          complexity of the decision situation (producer)

(N.B. In order to achieve a better three-dimensional impression,
the dots become smaller with growing distance from the reader.)

factor should be extractable when applying the usual criteria
and this factor should act as the starting point for further
calculation and classification of the 168 (or 116) cases on a
continuum. The factor analysis should, in this manner, serve as
a means of one-dimensional scale construction.

By means of factor analysis with iterative communality estimation, and by applying Kaiser's criterium (need reference), a

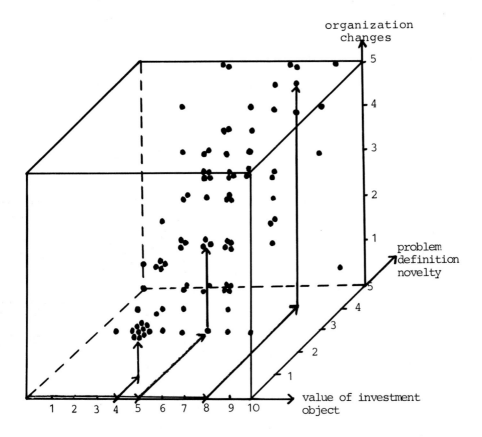

Figure 2b. Distribution of test units according to the com-
          plexity of the decision situation (purchaser)

single factor F_1 was extracted that we labelled "Complexity of
the decision situation". This factor explains roughly 53% (50%)
of the overall variance and 99.38% (98.25%) of the communality.
Through the multiplicative connection of the factor coefficient
matrix with the actual answers of respondents we will get a
value corresponding to its position in the threedimensional
space of all cases.

4.3. Testing the distinction between episode and surrounding field

The frame of reference schematized in Figure 2 can be transformed into a test plan with numerous evaluation steps. Five relatively independent "knowledge" elements result from such an evaluation process (for greater detail see Kutschker & Kirsch, 1978):

1) Knowledge of the internal connections between the elements of negotiation processes;
2) Knowledge of representatives' attitude structure;
3) Knowledge of the relationship between attitudes and behavior during negotiations;
4) Knowledge of the influence of organizational and individual attributes on these attitudes;
5) Knowledge of the direct influence that these attributes and the situational context has on the negotiation behavior observed during transaction episodes.

The position of these five elements in the overall patterning of events in capital goods transactions is shown in Figures 3a and 3b.

The central portion of both figures represent the hypothetical causal models linking the directly measured negotiation variables during a transaction episode. They correlate with representatives' attitudes being themselves influenced by the attributes of respondents and the respective organization. The left side of the illustration shows the direct influence of these attributes and the situational context on negotiation behavior. For clarity's sake, we no longer differentiate between the global variables "context", "strategy", "transaction" and "negotiation experience".

These two figures can be compared with the frame of reference presented in Figure 1. The stipulated connections between organizational attributes, situational factors and negotiating behavior (arrows No. 4 and 5), between organizational and

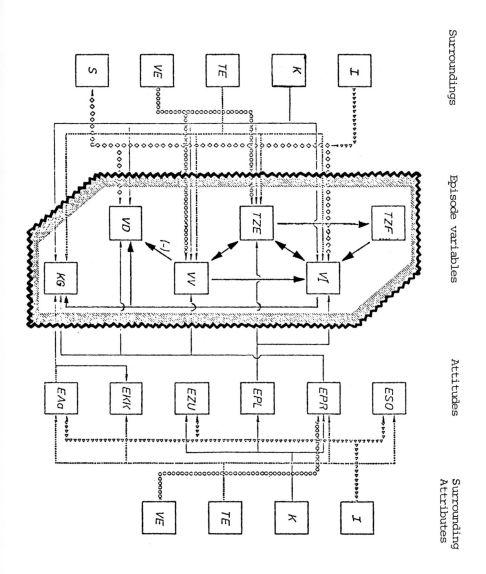

Figure 3a.   Empirical relations between
             model variables for producers

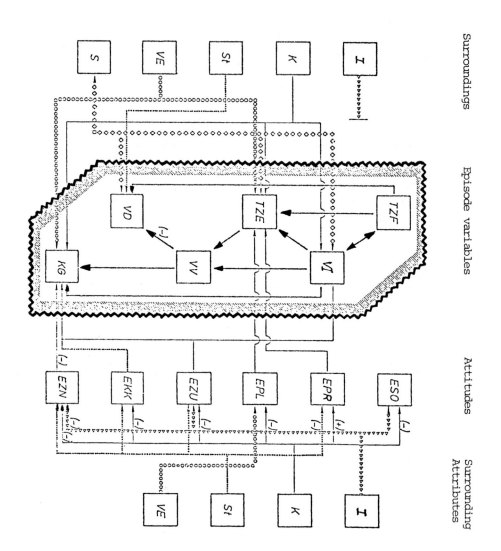

Figure 3b.   Empirical relations between
model variables for purchasers

Legend:

I   = Characteristic traits of the answering person-
           Age
           Attitude to innovation measured as a semantic differ-
           ential.

K   = Context factors describing the company and its
           market position.

TE   = Transaction experience = sum index of variables in-
           dicating success and failure components of a company
           during transactions in the past.

VE   = Negotiation experience = sum index of the respond-
           ent's knowledge regarding the other company and its
           representatives.

S   = Problem complexity.

St   = Strategic investment behavior.

ESO, EPR
EZU, EPL = Factor-analytically determined, decision-relevant
EAa, EKK   attitudes concerning the respondent's satisfaction
  EZN   with the article and the partner company.

TZF   = All representatives delegated by the other company.

TZE   = All representatives delegated by one's own company.

VI   = Negotiation intensity - sum of the number of prob-
           lems under negotiation.

VD   = Negotiation time = number of negotiation sessions
           multiplied by the average duration of one session.

VV   = Negotiation preparation = number of tactical re-
           flections made prior to the negotiation.

KG   = Degree of conflict = sum of disputed items during
           Negotiations.

---

individual attributes and attitudes (arrows 1 and 2) and between attitudes and behavior (arrow 3), reappear in each figure.
On the basis of the apparent identity between the postulated
frames of reference and summarized findings, Figures 3a and 3b
can be seen as presenting synthetic models of the investment

goods transaction that offer proof both for the validity of
the "episode" concept and interaction approach on the one hand,
and the dissimilarity of producer and purchaser models on the
other.

Unfortunately, however, such a claim would be invalid since it
is based simply on a summary of isolated findings without taking into account the varying importance of the statistical
methods employed. It seems clear that these methods do not
operate on the same level, and nor is the role of attitudes as
an intervening variable sufficiently considered. The ambiguous
status of attitudes as dependent *and* independent variables
(this also goes for the episode variables) prevents the transformation of the factors shown in Figure 2 into a system of
multiple regression equations. It is for these reasons that we
chose to apply path analysis instead of multiple regression
analyses or canonical correlations.

The causal model distinguishes between exogenous (i.e. not explained in the model) and endogenous (i.e. explained in the
model) variables[16], the former being labeled "x" and the latter
"y" in Figure 4. (The residuals for the endogenous variables
are labeled with small letters.) The arrows show the causal relations posited by the model. These were checked by calculating
the path coefficient for each; if a coefficient was below a
fixed value ($p_{yx} < .10$; cf. Land, 1969), it was taken to signify
falsification not only of the individual relationship but of
the causal model as a whole.

Several methods have been developed for the calculation of the
path coefficient. The varying applicability depends on the specification and recursiveness or non-recursiveness of the model
(cf. Opp & Schmidt, 1976, p. 301). Recursive causal models do
not contain any direct or indirect reactions of the endogenous

---

[16]For further information, see Blalock (1971) and Goldberger
& Duncan (1973), as well as Weede (1970a,b; 1972). Our work
is based especially on Opp & Schmidt (1976), Kießler & Scholl
(1976) and Weede (1970a).

variables, whereas non-recursive models do. In the scene, our
causal models of negotiation behavior are non-recursive. The
proposed calculation methods are variants of the regression
technique, their application - as in all calculation so far -
proceeded on the following assumptions concerning the characteristics of our data: Multivariate normal distribution, linearity
of relations and low multi-collinearity of the exogenous variables.

Causal model for purchaser negotiation behavior

A comparison of Figures 3 and 4 shows that our causal analyses
do not cover the entire model outlined above (cf. Kutschker &
Kirsch, 1978). In order to ease our calculations and simplify
such problems as the under-specification of equation systems,
we thought it advisable to limit the analyses to the manageable
set of what we considered were the most important relations
among variables.

Whereas the model in Figure 4 conserves the distinction between
the episode and environmental field central to our interaction
approach, we cannot here provide theoretical arguments in support of
choice of which dependent and independent variables to retain[17].
In order to empirically validate the episode/surround distinction, equal consideration should be given to variables in both
domains. The analysis is, however, further complicated by our
testing as exogenous variables that, in previous analyses, had
been found to be good predictors. In the case of such variables,
that common effects cause them to attract a variance which until now has been explained by the endogenous episode variables
on the basis of correlation. It should finally be noted that
the purchaser's satisfaction with the product (EZU) is assumed
to be a dependent variable linked to the negotiation process.

[17] A model for producer negotiation behavior should be developed
in an analagous manner. Space shortage prevents us from doing
this here. See Kutschker and Kirsch (1978, p. 293) for further details.

Calculation of path coefficient

In order to determine the path coefficients in Figure 4, the structural equations must be transformed into so-called r-equations (as a simplification, we have labeled the endogenous variables y_1 - y_4 and the exogenous as x_a - x_d).

Figure 4. Path-diagram for purchaser behavior in negotiation

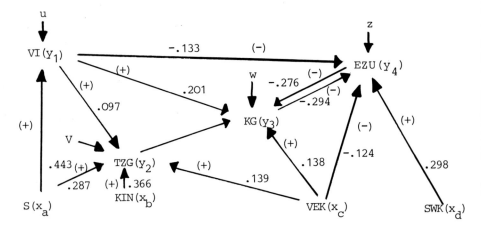

Legend: y_1 = VI = negotiation intensity; y_2 = total number of participants; y_3 = KG = degree of conflict; y_4 = EZU = satisfaction with product; x_y = S = complexity of decision situation; x_b = KIN = absolute investment volume; x_c = VEK = experience that negotiation will end in compromise; x_d = SWK = acceptance of profitability calculations.

According to Opp and Schmidt (1976, p. 254), causal diagrams such as the one in Figure 5 are over-specified equation systems because the number of pre-determined variables excluded from the equations is higher than the number of non-recursive endogenous variables on the equation's right hand side. For calcula-

Table 2. Correlation matrix (purchaser)

		1	2	3	4	A	B	C
Intensity	1							
Participants	2	.235						
Satisfaction	3	-.206	-.165					
Conflict	4	.316	.249	-.363				
Situation	A	.444	.386	-.157	.131			
Invest. volume	B	-.036	.394	-.067	.046	.080		
Compromise	C	.205	.227	-.166	.256	.209	.026	
Profitability Calculation	D	.131	.021	.266	-.027	.154	-.054	.186

tions based on Figure 5, we recommend recursive as well as non-recursive connections that vary according to the state of ident-ification. For over-specified and specified recursive model structures, we recommend the "classical" method of multiplica-tion by the pre-determined variables, also called "ordinary least square" (OLS) (cf. Opp & Schmidt 1976, p. 276ff) because it is easy to apply and gives the same results as the other methods (instrumental variables, indirect least square and two stage least square). In the case of over-specified non-recurs-ive model structures, the "2-stage lease square" system gives the most reliable results. Weede (1970, p. 545) uses OLS as a fair approximation when the r-equation is established by direct multiplication with the pre-determined variables. Because of our model's "mixed" structure, we apply the method already illustrated above for y_2 and arrive at the path coefficients shown in Figure 4.

Criticism of the causal model

All path coefficients are larger than or, as in the case of P_{21} (the effect of negotiation intensity on the number of partici-pants = .097), almost equal to .10, the standard cut-off point for the relevance of causality effects. Thus, our initial model was not falsified. Comparison of the assumed indicators, discussed in detail in the preceding chapters, with the determined indicators also confirms the initial model. The variances accounted for by the endogenous variables were: for y_1: 19.6%; for y_2 : 27.8%; y_3: 14.8%, and for y_4: 23%.

Dependent variable	Predictor variable	Total causal effect	Indirect effect	Direct effect	Other effects	Bivar.
y_1	x_a	.44	0	.44	0	.44
y_2	y_1	.10	0	.10	.141	.24
	x_a	.33	.04	.29	.05	.38
	x_b	.37	0	.37	.03	.40
y_3	y_1	-.19	-.06	-.13	-.02	-.21
	y_4	-.28	0	-.28	-.03	-.36
	x_a	-.10	-.10	0	-.06	-.16
	x_b	-.02	-.02	0	-.05	-.07
	x_c	-.17	-.04	-.12	0	-.17
	x_d	.30	0	.30	-.03	.27
y_4	y_1	.25	.05	.20	.06	.31
	y_2	.13	0	.13	.121	.25
	y_3	-.29	0	-.29	-.07	-.36
	x_a	.15	.15	0	-.02	.13
	x_b	.05	.05	0	0	.05
	x_c	.19	.05	.14	.06	.25

Table 3. Split-up effects of purchaser model

With the exception of two connections, the correlation coefficient split-up gives no indication of a possible model alteration. For the relation between number of participants (y_2) and degree of conflict (y_4) the path coefficient seems to have been elevated by "third variable" effects stemming from negotiation intensity (y_1) and compromise experience (x_c). At the same time, the connection between negotiation intensity (y_1) and number of participants (y_2) appears to have been non-causally influenced by the variable "decision situation" (x_a). Thus those connections bearing on the hypothesis that purchaser representatives respond reactively to increasing negotiation intensity are strongly threatened by elimination.

We are able to follow up these indications, checking our model's causal arrangement with test equations. By comparing the actual correlation coefficients with the theoretically implied correlations calculated from the calculated path coefficients, possible sources of error can be found. This consistency test can be carried out with all over-specified equation systems by multiplying the structural equations by the non-causal and/or the indirectly pre-determined variables. The equations for y are as follows:

$$y_2 = P_{2a} x_y + P_{2b} x_b + P_{21} y_1 + P_{2c} x_c / \cdot x_d$$
$$r_{d2} = P_{2a} r_{ad} + P_{2b} r_{bd} + P_{21} r_{d1} + P_{2c} r_{cd}$$
$$.02 \neq .09.$$

The results of all consisting tests are given in Table 4.

falsification equation for	empirical correlation	correlation implied by model	difference
2) $x_d : r_{d2}$	.02	.09	.07
3) $y_2 : r_{23}$	-.17	-.12	.05
3) $x_a : r_{a3}$	-.16	-.08	.08
3) $x_b : r_{b3}$	-.07	-.08	.01
4) $x_a : r_{a4}$	.13	.21	.08
4) $x_b : r_{b4}$	.05	.07	.02
4) $x_d : r_{d4}$	-.03	-.02	.01

Table 4. Test equation for purchaser model

By convention, deviations between empirical correlation and
model implication that do not exceed .10 are regarded as acci-
dental. Since none of the deviations exceeds this figure, the
causality arrangement of our model remains unfalsified. Our
fears regarding negotiation intensity effects were thus not
borne out, and our causal model is interpretable as it stands.

In view of the problem that we set out to analyze the results
of the causal analysis can be interpreted as follows:

The distinction between episode and environmental field central
to our interaction approach was sustained by the test results.
The model's endogenous episode variables exert mutual influence
in no way inferior to that of the exogenous variables. For instance, the degree of negotiation conflict cannot be explained
without taking recourse to negotiation intensity, number of
participants and the representatives' attitudes, nor without
consideration of the variables in the episode's environmental
field. Besides showing the direct influence of the exogenous
variable "compromise experience", the causal model also reveals
an indirect effect of the decision situation not found in the
simple regression models. In addition, a high degree of problem
complexity was found to entail a high degree of conflict.

Regarding the number of participants as well as conflict frequency, the purchaser organizations and their representatives
act according to situational influences arising from the episode variable "negotiation intensity" and the complexity of the
decision situation. This situational influence is also demonstrated by the fact that the overall effect of negotiation intensity on the other endogenous variables amount to .54, and
that of problem complexity to .58, half of these effects being
indirect.

We should point out that the multivariate causal analysis does
not provide definitive "proof" of our model, since the same
data could provide a basis for constructing other models that
would test out equally well. In view of the inconsistent

results of empirical negotiation research (cf. Crott, Kutschker & Lamm 1977a,b), we consider causal analysis, despite its un-solved methodological problems, together with other multivari-ate methods to be the only means of achieving an at least approximate picture of the correspondence between a complex reality *and* complex theoretical frames of reference constructed to account for it.

Other difficulties arise from our having only approximately operationalized the "potential" concept discussed above. "Potential", together with the idea of a transaction's "socio-economic field" (cf. Kirsch & Kutschker, 1978, Kutschker 1980), constitute extensions of our theoretical position carried out after we had performed the above-reported empirical work. The questionnaire used in our studies was largely based on inter-actions and factors that influence them and thus enabled us to demonstrate the influence of organization attributes resulting from context, previous experience in transaction and negotia-tion, and strategic behavior. These structural traits, however, can only be interpreted as "substitute" indicators for the theoretically more exciting "potential" concept. Simplifying somewhat, an organization's potential reflects the ensemble of attributes of all organizations taking part in the transaction and the representative's ability to use this constellation during transaction episodes. Empirically validating the "poten-tial" concept thus implies an examination of the attributes of all the organizations and their representatives, while such an examination can be limited to a given moment in time, it may in some cases be necessary to extend it to include the development-al history of the organizations' and/or representatives' potentials. Even though the exogenous variables used in our causal models might turn out to be rich indicators for measur-ing potential, the attributes "transaction-" and "negotiation experience" suggest that incorporating an organization's "history" and/or its interactions with other organizations into the empirical analysis of the potential concept would prove

fruitful. In any case, we hope that further development of the
"potential" concept and that of the socio-economic field with
respect to investment goods transactions will open the door for
a more general research program analysing inter-organizational
relations and decision processes.

Chapter 15 Consumer Information Requirements and Information Acquisition with Regard to Decision Making Processes in the Private Household

H. Raffée, K. Grabicke, M. Hefner, T. Schätzle and M. Schöler

1. Introduction

Although interest in consumer problems has increased greatly in recent years both in the social sciences and in commerce, there are still large gaps in what has been so far achieved. Commerce has only gradually become aware that the comparatively weak position of the consumer or private household can be improved by measures of consumer policy. While the social sciences have augmented their efforts in consumer research, knowledge in this area still remains deficient in many respects.

One of the central and, as yet, inadequately exploited areas of consumer research is the field of consumer information. Adequate information is a prerequisite for any high quality decision and is particularly critical for the consumer. Though the extreme complexity of his/her environment increases the importance of being well informed, the consumer has at his/her disposal only limited personal and material resources for acquiring, processing and using the necessary information.

The present studies center on the problems of consumer information requirements and information acquisition. Apart from two laboratory experiments on brand and product choice (done in collaboration with J. Jacoby, Purdue University), our efforts have been directed primarily towards field research. Here, we were first of all concerned with developing a criteria-oriented

measure of the learning that occurs during the course of purchasing decisions. This measure was employed in a time-sequence
study of the effects of utilizing the results of consumer-
commodity tests when making actual purchasing decisions. In
addition, field interviews to explore consumer information
acquisition and its determinants were carried out in urban
and rural settings. A further interview survey was carried out
to investigate how the relation between information requirements
and information acquisition vary over different product types
and consumer segments. A separate survey was aimed at foreign
workers in their role as consumers.

The variables that appear in each of our studies can be classified under the headings, "consumer segments", "information
types" and "decision items". Our project's aim was to investigate the influence of each variable type on consumer information processing and decision making, considering the variables
both independently and in interaction with one another. The
accompanying chart provides a schematic view of our research
program (see page 491).

2.   Theoretical background

2.1. Determinants of consumer information behavior

The quality of every decision is largely determined by the information upon which it is based. Due, however, to limitations
on time, money, cognitive capacity and other resources, decision makers are rarely able to base their decisions on all relevant information but rather must proceed on the basis of only
a subset of all potentially available facts. Selecting this
information in turn requires that decisions be made as to
the kind of information to be selected and the intensity of the
information search. The outcome of these decisions depends on
variables that pertain either to the decision maker's person-

	Consumer Segments	Information Sources and their use	Decision Items
Consumer Segments	1) Consumer behavior in foreign workers *field 1*	1) Information acquisition behavior and its determinants – comparative survey in Mannheim and in the district of Neckar-Odenwald *field 2*	1) Information requirements and information acquisition in relation to different product types and particular consumer segments *field 3*
Information Sources and their Use	cf. field 2 *field 4*	1) Development of a criteria-oriented test for measurement of learning achievements 2) Time-sequence study of effects of using results of consumer-commodity tests when making actual purchasing decisions 3) Information acquisition behavior when choosing brands *field 5*	 *field 6*
Decision Items	cf. field 3 *field 7*	 *field 8*	1) Decision behavior with differing decision items *field 9*

ality (internal system) or environment (external system) (cf.
Lewin, 1963). The personality characteristics of the consumer,
his/her motives and attitudes, and his/her perceptual, learning
and thinking processes are the main elements of the internal
system. The existing commodity-environment, membership in
social groups, codified and non-codified norms and other, similar factors are the main components in the external system.

Perceptual, learning and thought processes constitute the link
between stimuli operating on the consumer from the external
system and the variables of the internal system (cf. Howard
& Sheth, 1969). In addition to these basic cognitive processes,
however, cost-benefit considerations, risk perception and information overload also exert important influences on the consumer's decision making and constitute the essential elements
of the theoretical frame of reference which will be set out in
more detail in the following.

2.1.1. Cost-benefit considerations

Experienced and/or anticipated rewards and punishments constitute the main criteria in terms of which individuals evaluate
behavioral alternatives (cf. the theoretical principle of gratification, Schanz, 1977). The more often an action is rewarded,
the greater is the probability that it will be repeated, this
probability increasing at a rate proportioned to the value that
the individual attaches to the reward received (cf. the success
and value hypothesis in Homans, 1968).

To decide in favor of one activity often, however, entails the
loss of possible rewards for other activities, these foregone
rewards constituting the costs of the activity actually undertaken (Schanz, 1977). The probability that an activity will be
carried out is thus determined by its *net* gratification as determined on the basis of - at least approximate - cost-benefit
considerations.

When examining information behavior from the point of view of

the gratification concept, one can proceed on the assumption
that here, too, cost and benefit expectations are relevant,
though often in a manner that is not directly quantifiable. In
general, it can be said that information activities are always
undertaken if the expected benefit from these activities is
rated more highly than the expected costs (Raffée et al., 1975).

The costs of information activities include, in addition to the
expenditure of time and money, the consumption of mental and
physical energy in obtaining and processing the information
(Kuhlmann, 1970; Silberer, 1975; Irwin & Smith, 1975). These
costs will be compensated for to the extent that the information activities result in an increase of decision quality.

The cost-benefit concept, which can also be characterized as
subjective-formal rationality (cf. Raffée, 1969), is, of course,
in its basic form rather imprecise, and it is necessary to
specify some additional, peripheral conditions before being
able to operationalize it. Nevertheless, even in its basic form
the concept yields considerable powers of explanation and prediction.

2.1.2. Learning-theory aspects

The reference to rewards and punishments in connection with the
cost-benefit concept already touches upon the field of learning.
The established theories of learning, however, supply only
limited points of reference for explaining information behavior,
as they deal for the most part with narrowly defined learning
forms. Of all the learning theories, those of cognitive learning - especially Tolman's theory of 'purposive behavior' (Tolman, 1967) - afford, in our opinion, the most useful approach
to the explanation of consumer information behavior. According
to Tolman, an individual learns behavioral plans, or cognitive
maps, rather than individual behaviors themselves, having
acquired on the basis of repeated experiences certain anticipa-
tory attitudes concerning situations, possible behavior and

the resultant behavioral consequences.

Applying Tolman's theory to information behavior during purchasing decisions, we are led to conclude that the form of such
behavior will depend on the individual himself (his/her cognitive abilities, his/her socio-demographic characteristics, etc.)
as well as on the specific situation, including the nature
(e.g. complexity) of the article under consideration. Learning,
according to Tolman, is a process of hypothesis confirmation in
which the individual uses experience to test the validity of
hypotheses he/she has concerning some valued goal and means for
attaining or avoiding it (cf. Hilgard & Bower 1975, p. 237).
This too has its parallel in purchasing decisions if we assume
that a purchase that satisfied the individual constitutes a
strong positive influence on his/her future behavior in similar
situations.

2.1.3. Risk perception

A purchasing decision carries risk in so far as it has consequences that cannot be predicted with certainty (Bauer, 1967).
The extent to which this risk is subjectively experienced -
that is, the perceived purchase risk - is a function of a) the
perceived possible negative consequences of the purchasing
decision, and b) the decision maker's uncertainty concerning
these negative consequences (Cox, 1967; Cunningham, 1967; differently, Bettman, 1973). Typical negative consequences include
product insufficiency (the economic risk), social disapproval
(the social risk), frustration (the psychological risk) and
health impairment or injury (the physical risk) (cf. Panne,
1978). As a rule, consumers make only those choices that carry
limited perceived risk (Cox, 1967), decisions whose risk is too
high being either abstained from or altered by certain strategies for re-organizing information gathering (e.g. augmented or
selective information seeking, habituation, etc.).

In addition to the consumer's personality and class specific

features, the kind of product under consideration exerts an
important influence on the type and level of perceived risk and
on the choice of risk reduction strategy (cf. Roselius, 1969;
Schweiger, Mazanec & Wiegele, 1976).

2.1.4. Information overload

Assuming that every individual is limited in the capacity for
the assimilating, storing and processing of information (cf.
Chestnut & Jacoby, 1976), and taking into account the ever increasing abundance of information, it can be supposed that a
consumer engaged in making a purchasing decision may often
reach a point where he/she can no longer cognitively handle the
amount of information available (cf. Jacoby et al., 1973). This
"information overload" gives rise to a cognitive stress that
can lead to changes in the consumer's information behavior (cf.
Kirsch, 1970). Though these changes in behavior are functional
in so far as they enable the consumer to pursue his/her original goal (e.g. purchase of a certain article), the resulting
information behavior is usually far less comprehensive and not
as consistently organized. The consumer thus no longer makes
use of information normally necessary for an objectively correct decision, with the result that his/her decisions tend to
be impulsive and/or inconsistent (Jacoby et al., 1974).

The level of perceived "information overload" is determined by
a number of situational and dispositional factors. Environmental complexity is an example of a situational determinant; in
actual purchasing situations, this is determined by the number
of alternative goods and shops, the variety of different information available per alternative and the information's intelligibility. The time factor, which is part situational and part
dispositional, also has a decisive effect on perceived information overload in so far as the probability of information overload increases with increasing time pressure. The dispositional
determinants of perceived overloading center primarily on the

cognitive abilities of the consumer to assimilate, store and process information. The higher the consumer's cognitive complexity (cf. Streufert & Driver, 1965), for example, the longer it will take him/her to reach the stage at which he/she feels over-burdened by a surplus of information.

As mentioned above, the possibilities open to the consumer for reducing perceived information overload - or for avoiding it altogether - lie mainly in avoiding excessive cognitive and physical strain in the course of his/her information activities. Information behavior that has been referred to as "chunking" (cf. Miller, 1956) is one example of a response in line with this relief principle.

2.1.5. Socio-demographic aspects

Significant criteria for social class membership are profession, education, and income (cf. Berelson-Steiner, 1972). It is one of the characteristics of social classes that individuals that belong to the same class show almost identical forms of behavior. An early study by Katona and Mueller (1955) demonstrated the influence that socio-demographic factors have on consumers' behavior, with age, education and profession being the most important. Several later studies (e.g. Der Hamburger Verbraucher als Wirtschaftspartner, 1974) confirmed this result.

Members of well-educated social classes generally have higher incomes and are more mobile, flexible, and interested in procuring information than are consumers belonging to less educated classes (cf. Kuhlmann, 1970). Since acquiring information prior to purchase is an intellectual activity that requires that the consumer maintain a certain distance between himself and the product as well as sample a variety of sources, it seems reasonable to assume that consumers from better educated classes will be more efficient at information gathering than those with lesser educations.

Age also exerts a strong influence on the consumer's behavior.
Due to their limited buying experience, young consumers must
often carry out extensive information searches before being
able to arrive at a decision, while older consumers are able to
use their previously acquired experience as a basis for their
decision making. Besides the difference in past experience, however, young consumers' greater readiness to search for information may be due also to their greater open-mindedness, flexibility and their comparatively small budgets.

2.2.   Work related to theories and fundamentals

2.2.1. The usefulness of cognitive dissonance theory in explaining consumer information behavior

Prominent social scientists hold Festinger's theory of cognitive dissonance (Festinger, 1957) to be one of the few social
science theories whose informativeness compares favorably to
that of theories in the natural sciences. Examining this
theory's usefulness for the investigation of consumers' information behavior therefore seems warranted.

In a critical review of dissonance theory from a consumer psychology perspective, Raffée, Sauter and Silberer (1973) came to
the following conclusions:

1) Dissonance theory shares the same problems fundamental to
   all theorizing in the social sciences. The hope of having
   found in dissonance theory a nomological statement system
   comparable to theories of natural science remains unfulfill-
   ed. One problem rests in the fact that the universality of
   dissonance theory is lower than is often supposed. One can
   by no means assume, for example, that decision-induced dissonance (postdecisional regret) is something that arises
   following *every* decision. Moreover, the theory's precision
   is subject to considerable limitations both as to the antecedent conditions necessary for the theory to apply and to
   the behavioral consequences.

2) Despite these weaknesses, dissonance theory has considerable
   heuristic potential both for empirical decision research and
   for practical decision programming. Dissonance theory, for
   example, has been instrumental in bringing greater attention
   to postdecisional processes that were, until recently,
   largely ignored. In the field of practical programming, this
   enables commercial and non-commercial organizations to reduce any post-purchase dissonance that customers may experience by means of a calculated communications policy. From
   the point of view of consumer interests, on the other hand,
   it seems necessary to inform the consumer of such communication strategies since, in an economy based on competitive
   trade, it is essential that consumers react to inferior services either by protesting or withholding further business
   (cf. Hirschman's concept of voice and exit, 1970). Negative
   sanctions of this type will not occur if negative cognitions
   are harmonized and learning from negative experience, thereby, hindered (Raffée, Sauter & Silberer, 1973).

   Another way in which dissonance theory is relevant to consumer research is with respect to the "inference" that dissonance reduction can be present in the measurement of consumer
   satisfaction. Whenever the degree of satisfaction with a
   particular consumer article is measured, the possibility
   that satisfaction judgments are positively distorted as a
   means of reducing dissonance cannot be discounted.

3) The suggestions for practical programming derivable from
   dissonance theory can be criticized as being non-innovative,
   many of these (e.g. the necessity to avoid communicating
   negative information about a product already sold) having
   been known and practiced beforehand. It has been argued
   (e.g. Weber, 1978) that even the recent development of dissonance theory has not been able to rectify this deficiency in
   innovative potential.

4) With respect to research on consumer information behavior,
   dissonance theory seems unsuited as a comprehensive

theoretical foundation as it does not sufficiently allow for
the influence of personality variables, these being extremely important determinants of consumer response.

2.2.2.   The construct "information requirements"

2.2.2.1. Its aim

"Information requirements" is a construct that has proven useful in the analysis of consumer information behavior. In that
the demand for commodities is generally viewed as a variable
that aids in explaining commodity-oriented behavior, the same
perspective can be applied to the field of information; that is,
information can be seen as a special kind of commodity. Investigations of demand can provide starting points for consumer
policy measures. In the area of consumer information, for example, the problem arises of whether, and in what way, information requirements that are not adequately met through the resources of a private household should be satisfied by special
organizations (e.g. institutes which test consumer goods).

2.2.2.2. Subjective information requirements

A person's subjective information requirement can be defined as
all information that he/she considers as "necessary within the
scope of a (purchasing) decision" (Raffée & Silberer, 1975).
The determinants of subjective information requirements can be
classified as either motivational, cognitive or situational.
Some specific examples of determinants in each category being
given in the chart on the following page.

The listed determinants are taken, for the most part, from current theoretical approaches. The consistency motive, for example, is taken from dissonance theory, while "need for safety"
has its origins in risk theory (cf. Cox, 1967; Bauer, 1967;
Cunningham, 1967; Panne, 1978). Work on achievement motivation

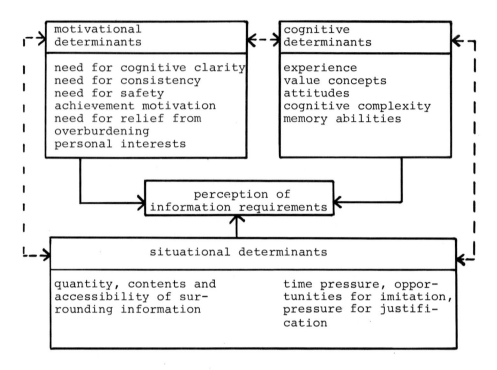

Determinants of subjective information requirements
(source: Silberer, 1975)
(---; interactive connections)

has also hypothesized that these variables affect information
behavior (McClelland, 1961; Atkinson, 1964). Cox (1967) stres-
ses the importance of the need for cognitive clarity, and Raffée (1969) discusses the role played by the need for relief
from overburdening.

As for the cognitive determinants, the influence of the decision maker's cognitive complexity has been investigated chiefly by Streufert (1970). It seems reasonable that discriminati-
ve and integrative ability, as components of cognitive complexity, are also important determinants of consumer information
behavior. The notion of "information overload" discussed above
alsc emerges directly from Streufert's work (cf. Streufert &
Driver, 1965).

Since they are easily distorted by external influences, subjective information requirements are extremely difficult to
measure. Asking consumers what information they want is no more
valid than observing their actual demand for information (cf.
Sauter & Raffée, 1973 and Raffée & Silberer, 1975). In the
first case, demand characteristics can falsify the results,
while in the second, external factors like information cost can
cause the apparent demand to diverge from its real level.

2.2.2.3. Objective and normative information requirements

Despite the importance of subjective information requirements,
their utility is limited by the fact that they are strongly
affected by the decision maker's general and product-specific
knowledge. Someone, for example, who has never heard anything
about possible health hazards or about environmental problems
caused by certain products is unlikely to consider information
requirements concerning them. It is in response to this problem
that attempts have been made to formulate objective and/or normative information requirements.

Objective information requirements specify, according to Sauter
(1974), the amount of information necessary for a rational solution of a decision problem. It can, however, be proven that
such a specification is possible only in a restricted decision
model. Since, for real purchasing decisions, open-ended models
are the more applicable, it is not as a rule possible to ascertain the objective information requirements. Only by providing normative guidelines (e.g. comparative tests of consumer
articles) can the shortcomings of consumers' information processing be rectified.

2.3. Summary

(1) A survey of the most important determinants of information
    behavior pointed to cost-benefit considerations, learning

phenomena, risk perception, information overload and, to a somewhat lesser extent, socio-demographic factors. Cost-benefit considerations play a role in determining whether or not a consumer undertakes information activities, while the consumer's capacity for learning allows him/her to make cognitive referral to past experience and to re-use decisional strategies that have proven successful. Though the influence of perceived risk centers more direct-ly on determining the actual purchasing decision itself, it too influences information behavior since it is by ga-thering information that the level of risk associated with the various decision alternatives can be reduced. The ex-tent of information gathering in such cases is milited by the individual's capacity for assimilating, storing and processing information. An overburdening of these capaci-ties owing to "information overload" brings with it the risk of confused and disfunctional behavior. Finally, mem-bership in different age, professional, educational and income groups exerts an important influence on purchasing and information behavior. Group membership can, for example, be one of the decisive factors with regard to the level of perceived purchasing risk, previous purchasing experience, preference for certain information sources and other, similar things.

(2) A critical analysis of dissonance theory led to the conclu-sion that the theory is unsuitable as a foundation for examining information behavior because of its lack of pre-cision and its almost total neglect of personality vari-ables. The discussion of subjective and objective infor-mation requirements emphasized the problems encountered in measuring these two concepts, it being suggested that normative parameters on consumer information behavior be used as a means of circumventing the measurement problems for the subjective information requirements. Due to these concepts' importance for consumer policy issues, the pre-

sence of such measurement problems should not stand in the
way of further research in this area.

3.   Field studies

3.1. The determinants of consumer information seeking - a comparative survey in an urban and in a rural region

This study of information acquisition is the first systematic
analysis of the following issues in a German speaking population:
a) Incidental information acquisition versus intentional information seeking before and after buying.
b) Having subjects rate their information deficits and needs
   for information as means for measuring information requirements.
c) The influence of "socio-demographic features", "cost-benefit
   considerations" and "information overload" on the consumers'
   information acquisition.
d) The influence that the infra-structural conditions in the
   consumer's residential area has on his/her information
   seeking.

3.1.1. Procedure and subjects

The present analysis makes a city-country comparison of consumers' need for information and their subsequent information
acquisition activities. Durable goods were the subject of the
investigation, the purchase of which generally entails complex
information seeking. Interviews were carried out with a fully-
structured and standardized questionnaire that, in order to
assure the interpretation of the data, consisted almost entirely of closed-format questions and Likert scales. Particular
care was taken in selecting the multidimensionally-structured
random sample. The sample consisted of 300 people, half from

Mannheim and half from Neckar Odenwald, a weakly-structured, rural region outside of Mannheim. The sample was stratified in terms of four age groups and sex.

3.1.2. Findings concerning information acquisition

a) The incidental acquisition of information before buying

21.9% and 29.7% of the city and rural respondants, respectively, who had bought a product had incidentally obtained information relevant to the purchase beforehand. These astonishingly high figures accentuate the importance of such information acquisition and call into question previous research on information seeking that has largely neglected this aspect.

The results indicate that information on costs was the least likely to be obtained incidentally for both the city and rural dwellers (13% and 24.2%, respectively). Whereas the city dwellers were most likely to have received incidental information concerning the products' comfort and practicality (60.8%), the rural dwellers most frequently learned of the products design and appearance (63.6%).

For both city and country dwellers, the most frequently listed source for such information was "family, relatives, and friends" (47.8% and 63.3%, respectively), a finding that points to the immense importance of private communication. Indeed, such private networks should serve as pools for a large variety of purchase-relevant information, the information gotten in this way being particularly influential due to the ease with which it is obtained and the high credibility of its sources (see, for example, Raffée, 1969).

b) Intentional search for information before buying

The intensity of activities directed at obtaining information prior to purchase can be derived from the number of brands considered, the number of shops visited, as well as

from the number of methods used and sources addressed. If one
first of all restricts the analysis to the number of brands
considered and shops visited, it becomes evident that the rural
population was less intense in its information seeking than the
urban population; only 18.3% of the rural respondents (as opposed to 28.2% of the urban) considered more than 3 brands, and
only 15.4% (as opposed to 38.4%) visited more than 3 shops.
This lower information seeking on the part of the rural population reflects, no doubt, one of the disadvantages of country
living, where the costs in gathering information may often exceed whatever benefits the information would bring.

While all previous research on intentional acquisition has
been restricted to analysing the information's source and content, we were interested in determining the extent to which
this information affects the purchase decision. The following
percentages of urban and rural respondents reported that their
decisions were influenced by information of each type: technical comfort 73.3%, 73%; efficiency and duration 66.7%, 68.5%;
prices 67,6%, 64.9%; services 59%, 67.6%; stores with large
selection of goods 52.4%, 34.2%; design and appearance 51.4%,
48.6%; and running costs 30.5%, 25.1%. Unlike the data for
information seeking, there is little difference between the
percentages for urban and rural populations, each reporting
comparable degrees of influence by the various information
types.

We were also interested in determining the effect that its
source has on information's eventual impact on consumer purchasing decisions. Among those urban and rural respondents who
visited only one shop, 47.6% and 65.8% reported that the information gained influenced their decisions. The corresponding
percentages for "family, relatives and friends" were 46.7% and
58.6%, while those for "store demonstration" were 51.4% and
50.5%. Again, there are only minor differences between urban
and rural populations.

The information behavior of the rural respondents is typi-
fied by their tendency to have visited only one shop and
the particular importance that they attached to private
communication. The relatively minor importance that both
groups attached to neutral, consumer-oriented sources such
as magazines (28,8%, 17.1%, respectively) and advice centers (7.6%, 7.2%) was as hypothesized. Advertising, whether
on the radio or television, or in magazines and newspapers,
was also reported as being relatively unimportant, a result that casts some doubt on advertising's efficiency as
a marketing instrument. It should be kept in mind, however,
that these conclusion are based on self-report data and
that caution should therefore be exercised in basing generalizations upon them.

32.4% of the urban respondents and 25.2% of the rural limited their information seeking to a certain brand, model,
and/or shop. Reasons given for this limitation were: the
model's special qualities (70.6% and 64.3%), quality of
service (50% and 39.2%), reference from friends and neigh-
bors (47% and 57.2%) and radio and TV advertising (5.8%
and 7%). Of special interest here is the small influence
attributed to advertising and the greater importance of
private communication channels for rural than urban dwellers. Of the respondents actually making a purchase, 50.4%
of the urban dwellers and 63% of the rural bought at a shop
with which they were already familiar. The figure for the
urban population is surprisingly high and is probably due
to limited information seeking. Previous experience must
also have played a part, however, as 83% of the urban and
71.4% of the rural respondents stated that they had previously purchased articles at the same shop that were rea-
sonably priced and of good quality. Learning from prior
success thus also seems to be of considerable importance
in influencing consumers' decisions.

c) Respondents' rating of informational deficits and desire
for information as indicators for information need

In order to get an idea of respondents' perceptions of the extent to which they were informed, we had them rate the magnitude of their information deficit. 20.9% of the urban and 15.3% of the rural dwellers had unanswered questions. For the urban dwellers, the greatest deficit was with information concerning the product's comfort and practicality (36.4%), while for the rural dwellers it was with information concerning the product's efficiency and durability (64.7%). It is surprising that these were the kinds of information regarded as most decisive when making the purchase. Thus, though they thought the information important, the respondents were dissatisfied with the results of their efforts to seek it out.

Consumer reports provide one means of meeting consumer information needs, being particularly effective in that their credibility, completeness, and topicality are taken for granted. That there is a general demand for information provided by test reports is shown by the finding that, of the urban und rural respondents, 98% and 98.7% wanted information from test reports concerning the practicality of larger electrical appliances, 96.7% and 88.3% about durability, 94.7% and 92.6% about technical characteristics, and 92.7% and 96.7% about prices. There was a similarly pronounced demand for the other types of information as well, only 9% and 7.3% of the two respondent populations regarding test reports as unnecessary. It is interesting to note the large discrepancy between the need for information and the actual consulting of test reports, a phenomenon due perhaps to the high effort required for obtaining and reading the test reports.

d) Incidental and intentional acquisition of information
   after buying

Incidental and intentional acquisition of information after buying were apparently of little importance; of the urban and rural respondents, 11.4% and 9.9% reported having acquired information incidentally, and 12.4% and 16.2% intentionally. Dissonance theory posits that post-decisional information seeking should be directed towards a gathering of decision-supportive information (cf., Raffée, Sauter & Silberer, 1973). Our present design, however, did not enable us to test this dissonance theory prediction.

3.1.3. Determinants of information acquisition

In order to compare the intensity of information seeking prior to purchase in the urban and rural samples, an intensity index was created on the basis of four items: The number of the shops considered, the number of brands/models considered, the number of different types of information needed, and the number of the sources of information used (different variants are specified by Newman and Staelin, 1972). Responses to each item were converted to percentages and an index score assigned to each respondent by taking his average response over all four items. Specifying an index score of 50 as the boundary between low and high intensity, the frequency distribution for the urban sample (n= 105) was 57 low and 48 high, while for the rural sample (n= 111) the frequencies were 77 and 34.

Suggestions as to the determinants of information seeking's intensity are available from previous research carried out in the U.S.A. (Katona & Mueller, 1955; Newman & Staelin, 1972) as well as being derivable from the assumptions guiding our present research.

a) Socio-demographic influences

Katona and Mueller (1955) assume that families with many children are subject to greater financial restrictions than families with few children and are therefore more sensitized to the financial advantages of information seeking. We, however, were not able to find this relation by means of cross-tabulation, nor were Newman and Staelin (1972). Our own result could be explained by the fact that households with several children belong mainly to the lower social

classes, a sub-population characterized by less intensive
searches for information (cf., Caplovitz, 1967). A cross-
tabulation of income (incomes higher and lower than DM 1.500)
and intensity of information seeking showed, for both the
urban and rural samples, that people with higher incomes
look less intensively for purchase-relevant information. A
lower financial risk in the case of bad bargains and a different ordering of time preferences due to different utility-
costs considerations might explain this lack of intensity
on the part of the high income respondents.

As for the influence of employment on the intensity of information seeking, urban respondents with medium-ranked jobs
(non-managerial civil servants, white-collar and skilled
workers) sought after information more intensely than did
those from lower or higher occupational categories, a finding that corresponds to findings from other analyses (e.g.
Newman & Staelin, 1972). This pattern was reversed, however,
in the rural sample, the number of this "middle" category
searching for information the least. This discrepancy may
be accountable for by the education differences between the
two samples with 74% of the rural respondents with "middle"
jobs not having studied past elementary school, whereas the
comparable figure in the urban population was 49%. This city-
country comparison is particularly important because only
the results for the urban sample conform to those of other
analyses (Katona & Mueller, 1955, Newman & Staelin, 1972).

b) Information overload

The importance of information overload as a determinant of
the consumers' behavior was dealt with in an earlier part of
this investigation (cf. 2.1.4.), it being hypothesized that
the intensity of information seeking is reduced by confusion
concerning the existing opportunities for informing one's
self. This hypothesis was confirmed only with respect to the
rural sample ($\chi^2 = 13.4$, df = 2), the greater impact of confusion in this case being due, perhaps, to the sample's low
level of education.

c) Cost-benefit considerations

It can be hypothesized that people not yet committed to a
given brand, model, or shop and who have not yet found a
suitable information source are more likely to value - and
therefore profit from - an opportunity for an intensive information search before purchasing. This hypothesis was confirmed for both the urban and rural populations both with
respect to respondents who had not yet decided on a brand
or model (χ^2 = 25.4 and 7.65, respectively; df = 1) and
those who hadn't decided on a store (χ^2 = 7.65 and 31.85;
df = 2).

It could also be hypothesized that the more readily available
and, hence, more easy to find, certain types of information are considered to be, the more intensely will people
look for them. This hypothesis was confirmed for the urban
sample (χ^2 = 4.20, df = 1) and appeared as a trend in the
data from the rural respondents.

The same pattern of results was obtained for the hypothesis
that people will look less for information the more they
are led to believe that their purchase will require little
in the way of time and effort (χ^2 for urban sample = 7.93,
df = 1). Finally, the hypothesis that test reports will be
used more frequently the more readily available they are
believed to be was confirmed for both urban and rural samples (χ^2's = 9.33, 5.26; df's = 1). This cost result is
particularly important from the point of view of consumer
politics as it shows that a more widespread diffusion can
lead to an increased application of test results.

3.1.4. Summary

A sample of 300 people, equally partitioned between urban
(drawn from Mannheim) and rural (drawn from the Neckar Odenwald) populations, was surveyed concerning information acquisition behavior when buying durable commodities like

appliances. For both respondent groups, the results point to the outstanding importance of relatives, friends, and acquaintances as a source of information. In comparison to this "private communication", public information channels like advertising and consumer interest publications proved to be of minor importance.

A considerable number of the people interviewed (15.3% of the rural respondents and 20.9% of the urban) said that they felt as if they had lacked sufficient information at the time they made their purchase decision. It is worht noting that this expressed information gap could have been filled by consulting the magazine issued by "Stiftung Warentest", but that the latter was used as an information source to only a very low degree.

To rate the intensity of pre-purchase information seeking, an index was constructed from 4 items: the number of brands and models considered, of shops visited, of types of information searched for, and of sources of information employed. Among urban respondents, those from the middle-ranked professions showed the highest intensity of information seeking, while among rural respondents, the information seeking shown by the middle-ranked professions was the lowest; a finding that, in our opinion, is due to the latter group's relatively inferior level of education. A comparison among the different age groups showed that, for both urban and rural samples, the middle-aged respondents looked for information most thoroughly.

Regarding the perceived obtainability of purchase-relevant information, there was a clear difference between urban and rural samples, the urban respondents perceiving such information to be far more easily obtainable than did the rural respondents and, as a result, seeking after it more intensely. On the other hand, the urban respondents seemed more susceptible to the desire to expend a minimum time and effort, an influence that tended to reduce the intensity of this information seeking.

3.2. Information need and acquisition as a function of product type and consumer segment

Previous studies of consumer information gathering indicate that the extent of information seeking and the kind of sources used depend on the type of goods in question and the personal characteristics of the consumer (cf., Katona & Mueller, 1955; Newman & Staelin, 1972; Davis, 1976; Kuhlmann, 1970, 1974; Bucklin, 1969; Grabicke & Hilger, 1980; Raffée et al., 1975 and 2.1. above).

The present field study aims at extending these previous findings by carrying out a more differentiated analysis, investigating information gathering's variation over the following product types and consumer segments:

Product Type
durable goods   prescription free medicines   food

Consumer Segment
LI   =   low income /social security claimants
YS   =   secondary school and university students
YE   =   young employed persons
MAE   =   middle aged employed persons
O   =   older people

The group "middle aged employed people" functioned as a control for the other consumer segments. In addition to measuring information need and the intensity of information gathering, we analyzed how these two variables were influenced by "cost-benefit considerations", "risks", "information overload", and the socio-demographic factors "age" and "income" (cf. 2.1.).

3.2.1. Procedure and subjects

Information need was measured with an open-ended question in order to minimize answers intended to please the interviewer. The wording of the question was as follows: "What do you think,

should one obtain product information before purchasing durable goods, for example? If so, what information should one
have?"

After having answered this question, the respondent was asked
to rate the types of information he/she desired on six point
scales (1 = not important, 6 = very important). In analyzing
the data, these separate ratings were added up to obtain an
overall index of information need.

Information acquisition was measured by a series of closed-
response questionnaire items concerning information dimensions
and information sources. Respondents in each segment were to
indicate on a six point scale (1 = not at all, 6 = extensively) the extent to which they had acquired information about
each of a list of 15 information dimensions specific to their
consumer segment and product type (e.g. side effects of medicines) and addressed 14 information sources common to all segments
(e.g. family, friends, newspapers ...). The 29 different responses were added to obtain an index of information acquisition
for each respondent.

With regard to the independent variables, "product type" was
nested within the three product categories given above, "Food"
encompassing "semi-prepared", "ready-cooked", and "deep-frozen
food", "Prescription-Free Medicines" encompassing "pain kil-
lers" and "influenza medicines", while "Durable Goods" included a series of products each over DM 100 in value. Further
independent variables were constitued by the above mentioned
consumer segments as well as additional segments created on
the basis of subjects' responses to items concerning cost-
benefit considerations, perceived risks, and information overload.

As for the consumer segments, the "middle-aged employed people"
were drawn from the pool of all registered voters in Mannheim
between the ages of 30 and 35. Three different middle-aged
samples were taken (n for each = 80), one each for questioning

with respect to durable goods, food and non-prescription medicine. Two separate samples of older people (n for each = 80) was drawn from the pool of Mannheim voters from 65 to 75 years old, one of these samples being questioned about "food", the other about non-prescription medicine. Consumers with low incomes (n = 80) were defined as social security claimants, while the segment "young employed people" (n = 80) consisted of apprentices and young workers from Mannheim between 16 and 21 years of age. The sample "secondary school and university students" (n = 80) was drawn from several Mannheim secondary schools and the different departments of Mannheim University. An important condition for membership in the "durable product" sample was, of course, that the respondent had, during the last year, bought a durable product worth more than DM 100.

3.2.2.   Hypothesis and results

3.2.2.1. The influence of product type and consumer segment on information need and acquisition

Concerning the influence of product type, it seems reasonable to expect that the need and acquisition of information are greatest for the purchase of durable goods. Because of their complexity, durable goods need to be explained to many consumers. It can also be expected that the accompanying functional, financial and - often - social risks stimulate information acquisition behavior.

Non-prescription medicines, on the other hand, probably give use to a medium level of information need and acquisition. Here, need and acquisition levels are the result of a balance between competing elements; low price, previous experience and consumer trust of pharmacists as information sources tending to minimize need and acquisition, and uncertainty concerning health risks and product reliability tending to augment them. (Jacoby & Kaplan, 1972; Jacoby et al., 1973; Fritz, 1977).

The lowest need for and acquisition of information should occur with respect to food purchases. Considering the wide range
of food products (e.g. canned food, deep-frozen chicken etc.),
one can expect relatively low prices, high purchase frequency,
and, accordingly, a large amount of prior experience. Furthermore, semi-prepared, ready-cooked, and deep-frozen food all
belong to the category "convenience foods" (Schleicher, 1978),
products that the consumer purchases habitually and without
much reflection. Regarding the effects of the different consumer segments, we hypothesize that older people, although
having enough time, show a minimum need for and acquisition of
information. Due to their product specific stock of information,
previous buying experience, and the complacency that often
comes with old age, it can be supposed that this population
has only a weak motivation to procure information, and that
they succeed in meeting whatever subjective information needs
they might have. (Schiffmann, 1971; Schleicher, 1978; Feldmann,
1966; Fritz, 1977).

The low income segment, also, should show a reduced subjective
need for and acquisition of information, this even though -
from an objective standpoint - increased information activities would seem necessary in order to achieve optimal returns
from their limited financial resources (Wiswede, 1972; Schör-
ner, 1977). Previous research indicates, however, that people
who are objectively most in need of information are the least
likely to obtain it, low income and low education conspiring
to make these people more reluctant to invest the efforts required for acquiring information and less aware of the benefits that such information would bring (Caplovitz, 1967). In
addition, these people's capacity for dealing with information is comparatively small, thus bringing them, for example,
to make less use of results from test reports (Silberer, 1977).
Finally, low income consumers seem especially sensitive to the
emotional hindrances to making use of certain kinds of information; for example, information provided in retail shops.

The middle-aged, employed consumers should should show a moderate need and acquisition of information (Katona & Mueller,
1955). Since they work and have only a limited amount of lea-
sure time, these consumers should tend not to have enough time
to meet their information needs. The needs themselves, however, may be psychologically discounted and held at a level
comparable to the actual possibilities for acquiring information, thereby avoiding the arousal of cognitive dissonance.

The greatest need for and acquisiton of information should be
found among young consumers. On the one hand, this consumer
segment usually lacks buying experience, while on the other,
the young consumers' limited financial means should increase
their motivation to procure information. In addition, these
young consumers are characterized by a relatively high degree
of cognitive complexity (cf. Katona & Mueller, 1955; Hilger,
1977).

3.2.2.2. Results and discussion

Level of information need and acquisition in the segments
analyzed

The accompanying tables present frequency distributions showing the level of information need and acquisition in each of
the consumer segments.

Table 1. Information Need as a Function of Product
Type and Consumer Segment

	Durable Goods				Food		Medicines	
Information Need[a]	LI	MAE	YS	YE	MAE	O	MAE	O
Low	47	35	17	22	48	56	71	69
Medium	31	43	43	46	28	22	9	11
High	2	2	20	12	4	2	0	0

[a]The three levels are determined from the index values:
Low = (0 - 18 points), medium = (19 - 37 points), and
high = (28 - 55 points).

The n for each group was 80.

Table 2. Information Acquisition as a Function of Product
Type and Consumer Segment

	Durable Goods				Food		Medicines	
Information Acquisition[a]	LI	MAE	YS	YE	MAE	O	MAE	O
Low	7	8	5	3	16	24	27	32
Medium	54	51	49	55	48	33	51	44
High	19	21	26	22	16	23	2	4

[a]The three levels are determined from the index values:
low = (30 - 70 points), medium = (71 - 111 points), and
high = (112 - 151 points).

The n for each group was 80.

The effect of product type on information need and Acquisition

As predicted, information need and acquisition were higher
with respect to durable goods ($\bar{x}$ = 22.04 and $\bar{x}$ = 97.48, respectively) than for any other product type, though only the
differences with the medicines was statistically significant

(F_{need} = 33.1, df = 2,237, p<.001; $F_{acquisition}$ = 20.8, df = 2,237, p<.001). Contrary to our hypothesis, however, was the finding that information need and acquisition were lower for medicines than they were for food products (see Table 3).

Table 3. Mean levels of information need and acquisition for food and medicine

	$\bar{x}$ information need	$\bar{x}$ information acquisition
Food	18.71	91.31
Medicines	11.53	77.10

Further analyses revealed that the chemist plays a central role as a high-competence information source, and that, relying on his expertise, consumers tend to reduce their information seeking elsewhere. As information concerning these medicines is relatively complex and not so readily accessible as information on foods, the perceived information need with regard to medicine is also lower.

Variations in information need and acquisition over Consumer segments

Separate analyses of variance comparing "old" and "middle-aged employed" consumers with respect to information need and information acquisition revealed that the two segments did not differ with respect to either criterion (see Table 4 for the corresponding means). Presumably, a "ceiling effect" was in operation here, middle-aged consumers already having gained so much experience in purchasing the products in question (medicines and foods) that they feel no further need to acquire additional information as they become older.

Table 4. Information need and acquisition among the old and
middle-aged for medicines and foods

| | Product Type | | | |
| | Need | | Acquisition | |
Segment	medicines	food	medicines	food
older people	11.13	16.34	76.72	91.70
employed middle-aged persons	11.52	18.71	77.10	90.31

Table 5. Information need and acquisition as a function of
consumer segment: food and non-prescription drugs

Segment	Need	Acquisition
persons with a low income	19.74	97.18
employed middle-aged persons	22.04	97.48
pupils, students	28.30	103.01
younger employed persons	27.30	101.15

Two other analyses of variance were done comparing low income,
students, young- and middle-aged- employed segments with respect to need and acquisition of information concerning durable goods. Though the various segments did not differ according to their acquisition of information ($F = 1.81$, $df = 3,319$,
$p<.14$), they did differ with respect to reported need
($F = 12.70$, $df = 3,319$, $p<.001$), the students and young-employ-
ed people reporting the greatest need and the low income people
the least. Practical difficulties in acquiring and comprehend-
ing information on durable goods may have prevented the effect
on acquisition from reaching significance. In any case, as can
be seen in Table 5, the ordering of means for both information
need and information acquisition conform to our predictions.

3.2.3. Summary

The results reported above concern how the need for and acquisition of information vary over consumer segments and product
types. The product types examined were durable commodities,
non-prescription medicines and foods. The consumer segments
were:

1) Persons with low incomes   n = 80
2) high school and university students   n = 80
3) young employed people   n = 80
4) middle-aged employed people   n = 240
5) elder people   n = 160

The "middle-aged employed" consumers showed significantly
greater need for and acquisition of information concerning
durable goods than they did for either non-prescription drugs
or food. Of all consumer segments, however, the "low income"
and "young employed" respondents reported the greatest need
for information concerning durable goods, the results for acquisition following a similar but less pronounced pattern.

3.3. An investigation of foreign workers' consumption behavior

As a part of our research on specific consumer segments, we
analyzed the consumption behavior of foreign workers. A comprehensive description of this complex analysis can be found
in "Der Gastarbeiter als Konsument - segment-spezifische Analyse des Konsumentenverhaltens ausländischer Arbeitnehmer in
einer westdeutschen Großstadt" (Hefner, 1978).

3.3.1. Theoretical aspects

A main reason for the problems that face foreign workers in
the Federal Republic of Germany is that they are a peripheral
minority (Mehrländer, 1974; Borris, 1973), diminutive both
in numbers and influence. The percentage of foreign workers

in West Germany at the end of 1972, as compared to the overall
number of poeple working in dependent jobs, was 10.8% (representative analysis, 1972). Their lack of influence is evident
in their difficulties in finding employment (cf. Geiselberger,
1972; representative analysis, 1972) and housing (cf. Zieris,
1972) as well as by their inferior legal status (cf. Kanein,
1966; Peters, 1972). Their inability to obtain an influential
position is even more distinct than for other socially inferior
groups. This is caused by the fact that besides the usual social deficits, differences in skin color, gestures, language,
manners, and religious customs come into play. As inter-group
relations frequently give rise to (or augment existing) social
tensions, conflicts, suspicion, prejudices and, eventually,
result in discrimination, the present analysis centered on the
following issues:
- the importance of social groups for the individual
- the forming of in-groups vs. out-groups in majority - minority relations
- the influence of such group relations on the opinions and
  behavior of the individual group members, especially with
  respect to the development of rules, viewpoints, stereotypes,
  prejudices, and discrimination (cf. Markefka, 1974; Kruse,
  1972; Brandt & Köhler, 1972; Irle, 1967).

The minority position of foreign workers seems especially to be
aggravated by their problems in communicating with the majority, "German population" (cf. results about linguistic competence of foreign workers in the representative analysis, 1972;
Bingemer, 1970). Therefore, in addition to level of education,
linguistic competence was chosen as an independent variable
to investigate with respect to minority - majority relations,
it being assumed that verbal communication influences the development of almost all other types of communication processes.

An additional reason, of course, for the foreign workers' socially peripheral situation is the common view that, in some
fields of life, they show deviations from the commonly accept-

ed behavior. Their own rules of conduct seem to be in conflict
with those of the majority and hence present the foreign workers with problems concerning their will and ability to adapt.
Moreover, the attitude of the German population towards foreign
workers is predominantly negative (cf. Neubeck-Fischer, 1972).
Particularly characteristic are economic prejudices (reinforced
by press reports - see Delgado, 1972) such as: "Foreign workers
are snatching 'our' jobs and are sending 'our' money back home",
and similar such statements.

In order to find the root of these problems, it was first of
all necessary to analyze the foreign worker's consumption behavior, to isolate its determinants, and to work out a possible
influence of these determinants on certain other areas of behavior.

We define consumption behavior broadly, meaning not only on
the actual purchasing of products but also the saving of money,
the acquisition of information and behavior during leisure
time. Furthermore, foreign workers were not regarded as an
amorphous mass, but segmented according to nationality, age,
and accomodation.

The most important hypotheses and results are summarized below.

3.3.2. Type of analysis sample

Each nationality (Turkish and Italian) was represented by 50
respondents, each of whom were living in private flats on their
own or together with their families. The questioning took the
form of individual interviews based on a structured, standardized questionnaire with primarily closed-format items and
translated into the workers' native tongue.

3.3.3. Hypotheses and results

a) The general information behavior of foreign workers

Hypothesis 1: The greater their linguistic difficulties, the
more likely it is that foreign workers address sources in their
own language when searching for information on their home
country or on life in the Federal Republic (χ^2 = 4.15; df = 4;
α = 0.3861).

Hypothesis 2: The higher their level of education, the more
likely it is that foreign workers make use of official, city
advice centers (χ^2 = 12.86; df = 5; α = 0.0247).

b) Money saving behavior

Hypothesis 3: Residents of dormitories state a higher monthly
savings rate than non-dormitory residents (χ^2 = 30.07; df = 8;
α = 0.0002).

Hypothesis 4: As workers stay longer in Germany, their stated
quotas for money saving become lower (χ^2 = 55.60; df = 48;
α = 0.2102).

c) Buying behavior for foreign workers

(1) The purchase related information behavior

Hypothesis 5: The greater the foreign workers' linguistic problems, the more likely it is that information sources requiring
little linguistic competence are used before buying larger
electrical appliances.

- family, friends. relatives
  χ^2 = 2.98; df = 2; α = 0.2256
- shop windows
  χ^2 = 2.94; df = 2; α = 0.2296

Hypothesis 6: The greater their linguistic competence, the less likely it is that foreign workers regard statements about product quality, as made by advertising, as being credible ($x^2 = 4.02$; df = 4; $\alpha = 0.4038$).

Hypothesis 7: The higher their education, the less likely it is that foreign workers regard the statements of advertising as credible ($x^2 = 17.69$; df = 2; $\alpha = 0.0604$).

(2) Purchasing decisions

Hypothesis 8: Foreign workers with great linguistic difficulties tend to prefer brand-name articles when buying larger electrical appliances to a greater extent than do those with few linguistic difficulties ($x^2 = 3.67$; df = 2; $\alpha = 0.1596$ [correlates negatively]).

Hypothesis 9: Foreign workers with great linguistic difficulties are more likely to passively accept German shop prices than those with few difficulties ($x^2 = 0.36$; df = 1; $\alpha = 0.5501$).

Hypothesis 10: The greater the linguistic difficulties of foreign workers are, the more often larger electrical appliances are bought in
- department stores
  $x^2 = 6.80$; df = 2; $\alpha = 0.0333$
- self service stores
  $x^2 = 6.43$; df = 2; $\alpha = 0.0401$

(3) Post-buying period

Hypothesis 11: After a "bad" buy, foreign workers with low linguistic competence are less likely than their more fluent counterparts to show
- activities of complaint
  $x^2 = 8.03$; df = 2; $\alpha = 0.0181$
- exchange activities
  $x^2 = 13.38$; df = 2; $\alpha = 0.0012$

The hypotheses were tested on a sample of 200 respondents, the sample consisting of 4 segments (of 50 respondents each) cor-

responding to the four cells created by factorially combining
the factors "Nationality - Turkish vs. Italian" and "Residence
(Dormitory vs. Non-Dormitory)". The Chi-square analyses were
performed by making median splits in the combined sample in
terms of independent variable (e.g. linguistic competence,
education level, etc.) mentioned in the particular hypothesis
being tested.

As these results show, the presumed influence of linguistic
competence on the type of information sources used - German
or native language - was not confirmed, all respondents markedly preferring sources in their own language. The foreign workers may regard vernacular sources of information as links to
the home country, thus making these sources helpful for over-
coming problems of non-integration.

Hypothesis 2, however, shows that their level of education
affects foreign workers' readiness to address public advice
centers. The psychological "costs" of acquiring information,
such as fear of being treated with impatience or hostility,
are evidently lower for better educated people. Another factor
may be that a higher level of education improves the understanding of the duties of the different administrative offices,
thus minimizing fears of possible controls, discrimination, or
refusal.

The supposition that dormitory residents have greater capacity
for saving money than non-dormitory residents was borne out by
the data. Dormitory residents normally have families to support
back home and therefore tend to spend less money on consumption in Germany (including rent), greater savings and greater
transfer of money to their home countries. It may be, moreover, that dormitory living, per se, encourages money saving
by restrictions that are imposed on dormitory resident's life
styles.

No significant results were obtained for the influence of
length of stay on monthly saving quotas. Foreign workers' willingness to save and their saving objectives seem resistant to

various influences towards increased spending possible with
the Germans' higher standard of living.

Regarding purchase-related information behavior, linguistic competence was not found to have an effect, all workers showing a
marked preference for linguistically non-demanding sources of
information: 53% family, friends, acquaintances and 42.5% shop
windows. As a lack of language knowledge cannot be decisive
for the popularity of these sources, other factors must be
responsible; trustworthiness, perhaps, in the case of family,
friends and acquaintances and anonymity in the case of shop
windows.

The influence of linguistic competence on the perceived credibility of advertizing claims concerning product quality was
also found to be negligible, with a substantial proportion
(59%) of the respondents regarding advertizing statements as
unreliable. This may be caused by a critical attitude towards
advertizing already acquired in the home country that, regardless of level of comprehension, is transferred to German advertizing. This critical attitude seems to become more pronounced with higher education, the relation tested in hypothesis 7 attaining a statistical significance of 0.06.

As for the influence of linguistic competence on the preference for brand-name articles, the data indicate a weak relation
($p < .15$) that is in a direction opposite that what we had hypothesized. As a whole, the respondents' appreciation of brand-
name articles was rather high, 81.5% of them saying that a
well known brand was important to them. This may be due to the
fact that quite a few German brands are known abroad and thus
already familiar to foreign workers. On the other hand, it is
likely that those foreign workers living in Germany for longer
periods have had positive experiences with German brand name
articles that they later relate to their compatriots.

Language knowledge, contrary to our hypothesis, was found to
have no influence on bargaining about the prices demanded by
German shop owners. 95% of the respondents, against the customs

they are familiar with, agree with the demanded prices. The
unfamiliar situation in Germany may place a strain on the
foreign worker and thus bring him/her to discard customs in
order to prevent conflicts.

Linguistic competence did have an effect, however, on the
choice of shop for buying large electrical appliances; with
growing language problems, the preference for department stores
and other self service shops increases. The corresponding frequency distribution shows that larger electrical appliances
were most often bought in department stores (60.5% of the
respondents) and self service shops - valid also for food and
clothes - can be seen as a reflection of foreign workers' self-
consciousness, especially their fear of being confronted with
prejudices and discrimination. Besides the possibility of buying goods directly without having to talk to a shop assistant,
another attraction of these stores is, no doubt, their more
reasonable prices and larger quantitative and qualitative se-
lections, particularly in department stores. With regard to
post-purchase activity, the data indicate that linguistic competence plays a significant role in determining the frequency
of complaints and exchanging goods, these activities increasing, of course, as language difficulties decrease.

The results confirming hypotheses 2, 7, 8, 10 and 11 suggest
that foreign workers show a tendency towards rational information and purchasing behavior. The rejected hypotheses -
mostly dealing with the influence of linguistic competence,
present us with new questions to investigate. The variations
in the frequency distribution of the individual samples suggest, for example, that the influence of nationality, accomodation, and age should be examined more thoroughly. It would
also be interesting, however, to determine the extent to which
the determinants chosen in this investigation hold valid for
the purchasing and information behavior of other peripheral
communities in the Federal Republic of Germany.

3.3.4. Summary

The buying and information behavior of foreign workers in Mannheim were thoroughly analyzed through standardized, closed-
response interviews. The repondent sample was drawn from two
nationalities (Italians and Turks) and represented two different life-styles (dormitory and non-dormitory living), these
two factors being combined factorially with fifty respondents
falling in each nationality - life-style condition.

Besides the theoretical concepts developed earlier (cf. section 2.1.), reference was made to social psychological concepts
such as in-group - out-group relations - minority - majority
relations and intra-group interaction processes in advancing
the hypotheses and interpreting the results. Also, from the
perspective of communication theory, the influence of linguistic barriers on respondent behavior seemd particularly important.

The results of this investigation show that deficient linguistic competence is responsible for foreign workers preferring
the anonymity of department and self service stores when making
their purchases. The assumption that a lack of linguistic competence presents a barrier in respect to activities of complaint
and of exchanging goods could be clearly proved. However, language knowledge did not affect the respondent's choice of pre-
purchase information source, nor did it influence their perception of advertizing credibility. Contrary to what we had
hypothesized, the foreign worker's willingness to save money
was not affected by the length of time they had been in Germany.
However, the dormitory residents interviewed reported significantly higher saving quotas than non-dormitory residents. It
was also observed that the respondents seemed reluctant to bargain about the prices wanted in German shops and were attracted
to German brand names. To sum up these results, it can be stated that the consumer behavior of the foreign workers interviewed - when a lack of language knowledge does not present an

insurmountable barrier - shows a tendency similar to that of
their German colleagues.

3.4.   The study of learning processes in purchase-oriented
         information behavior

3.4.1. Statement of problem

In the field of consumer research, considerable attention is
presently being given to a discussion of the pros and cons of
increasing the amount of purchase-relevant infromation available to the consumer. While, on the other hand, there is assumed to be a positive correlation between the quantity of
available information and the quality of purchasing decisions
(cf. French & Barksdale, 1974), this conflicts, on the other
hand, with empirical studies on the problem of information
overload (e.g. Jacoby et al., 1974, also Raffée et al., 1976).
The development of information programs to aid the consumer
does not, therefore, automatically imply an increase in product information but rather should first deal with the consumers ability for processing whatever information is already
available and the efficiency of the existing information programs.

In the present study, a selected information program (comparative tests of consumer articles) was subjected to such an examination with reference to real purchasing decisions. It is,
to the best of our knowledge, the only study outside the laboratory which is devoted to this, until now, completely neglected question of efficiency monitoring.

3.4.2. The development of a criteria-oriented test for the
         measurement of learning during the making of purchasing
         decisions

The registering of informedness changes during the course of

purchasing decisions required that we develop a new measurement instrument. Any previous attempts in this area have been
based on question and answer data gathered, as a rule, during
interviews. Apart from the known inadequacies of "standardized interview" techniques (cf. e.g. Kreutz, 1972), the shortcomings of this method of measuring informedness changes becomes evident when results obtained by it as compared to more
objective measures of changes in information level. We attempted to counteract these shortcomings by developing a criteria-
oriented test in which respondents' acquisition of information
during the making of actual purchasing decisions would be measured in terms of their level of performance on a standardized
task. By using this measure, we hoped to be able to monitor
respondents' informedness with respect to product-related and
purchase-related, legal information at various points in time
during the making of real purchasing decisions and thus be
able to compare the efficiency of various consumer articles
published in a "test" magazine published by the German consumer service.

The stimulus materials used in the study were articles drawn
from the magazine *Stiftung Warentest* dealing with either comparative tests of durable, technical products[1] or reports on
legal information relevant to purchasing. The former set of
articles dealt with 17 different product types, these being
selected from an initial pool of 45 on the basis of the comparability of the tests performed. These products were: all-
purpose slicers, laundry presses, electric sewing machines,
do-it-yourself tools, window ventilators, coffee machines,
storage heaters, refrigerator-freezer combinations, humidifiers,
lawn-mowers, electric shavers, spin-driers, tumble-driers,
vacuum cleaners, space-saving fully automatic washing machines,
fully automatic washing machines in the medium price range
and hedge cutters. Applying Bormuth's linguistic transforma-

---

[1] in order to encourage extensive problem-solving behavior in
connection with goods worth more than 100 DM.

tion procedure (Bormuth, 1970), 33 test items were constructed by remodelling the test and legal information reports.

The test sample consisted of 80 adults of either sex drawn at
random from the population of Mannheim. All subjects stated
that they were generally interested in consumer questions. They
were given an additional incentive through being able to choose
the product group that they would be tested on.

The learning measure was employed in a before-after design,
the subjects having an interval of one week between pre- and
post-tests to study the learning material. Cox and Vargas'
pre-test - post-test difference index procedure (Cox & Vargas,
1973) was used for selecting test items for the final analysis.
Although selection according to item difficulty is ordinarily
not done in criteria-oriented measurement, we felt it necessary in the present case in order to assure the comparability
of the results obtained from the 17 different product tests.

The validation was made by ascertaining the L - coefficient
according to Herbig (1975)[2]. The test reliability was examined by the test-retest method; the reliability coefficient was
r_{xy} = .46, a value sufficiently high for the field of criteria-
oriented measurement (cf. Brickekamp, 1975; a detailed account
of the test construction can be found in Grabicke et al., 1977).

3.4.3. Time sequence study of the effects of using consumer test results in actual purchasing decisions[3]

Although many consumers are aware of the existence of consumer

---

[2]This L-coefficient is an indicator of the experimental validity
of a criteria-oriented test. It results from an analysis of
variance of the pre- and post-test values and describes the
percentage of total variance (of the whole test or single
items) accounted for by the learning that occurs between the
two measurements.

[3]A detailed account of this study can be found in Grabicke et
al., 1980.

advisory bureaus, the degree to which these bureaus are utilized is comparatively low (cf. Raffée et al., 1975). This discrepancy is probably due to the fact that, for the consumer,
the utilization of a consumer advisory bureau often results in
an unfavorable cost-benefit relationship. The consumer will,
therefore, resort to other sources of information less exact,
complete and correct but more easily accessible. Communication
among friends and family members, for example, plays an important role in the acquisition of purchase-relevant information
(cf. Raffée et al., 1975), but usually cannot bring about the
level of informedness necessary for a "good" purchasing decision.

It might be assumed that consumers provided with consumer test
information are more comprehensively informed than consumers
who have tried in other ways to obtain a clear view of the
market and thus assess their personal situation from a different perspective. This perspective difference is likely, in turn,
to affect their degree of satisfaction with the product purchased, their conviction in the correctness of their decision
and their willingness to use a similar information strategy in
future purchasing decisions.

Against this background, the following individual hypotheses
emerge:

H1: Consumers to whom information material is made available
     before a purchasing decision (test group I) have a higher
     level of knowledge than consumers who have used other
     sources of information (test group II).

H2: Personal communication has less bearing on purchasing
     decisions for consumers who have test information avail-
     able than it does for those who do not.

H3: Consumers to whom test information has been made available
     are more likely to use such information when making future
     purchasing decisions than are those who received no test
     information.

H4:   Consumers given test information are, at the time of the purchase, more strongly convinced of the correctness of their decision than consumers not provided with this information.

H5:   Consumers provided with test information show more satisfaction with the purchasing decision than do consumers not provided with this information.

Concerning the organization and running of the test:

Subjects in this field experiment were either, consumers of both sexes who declared themselves willing to take active part in a long term research project (test group I), or consumers who happened to have made a purchasing decision concerning a product from the 17 product groups listed above and who were recruited after their purchase in cooperating stores in Mannheim (test group II). The N for each group was 81.

The subjects in test group I received a list of the 17 product groups, general instructions and 2 pre-stamped postcards, their first task being to indicate their intention to purchase one of the products listed by sending a postcard to the research team stating the name of the product and giving a time and date for a visit. A co-worker visited the subject at the appointed time and administered the criteria-oriented test as a measure of the subject's baseline informedness. The subject was then given an information folder containing a consumer test report on the relevant product and some other legal information of general relevance to purchasing decisions[4]. After the purchase had been made, the subjects were to send the second postcard to the research team, announcing the purchase and giving a new time and date for a visit during which the criteria-oriented test of informedness was to be given a second time. Subjects were informed neither of the theoretical background nor the procedure until the agreement was completed, being told only that the

---

[4] The subjects could keep this information material until their final purchase decision.

experiment dealt with consumer test information and would involve their being visited and interviewed several times.

At the second measurement, subjects in group I (i.e. those who
were given consumer test information) received in addition a
standardized questionnaire concerning their level of satisfaction with the purchase, the helpfulness of the test information
and other, similar points. Consumers in group II (i.e. those
who had not received the test information) were administered
the criteria-oriented test directly after their purchase and
the same standardized questionnaire without, however, the
questions dealing with the test information. The same questionnaires were re-administered to both groups six months after the
purchase, thus enabling us to determine whether consumer satisfaction varies over time. (A detailed account about panel studies can be found in Schätzle and Grabicke, 1979.)

Results and discussion

Hypothesis 1, which led us to predict a higher level of product relevant knowledge in test group I, was tested by comparing the two groups' performance on the criteria oriented test
using a t-test for independent random samples and unequal
variances. The results were in the predicted direction and
highly significant ($t = 6.98$, $df = 167$, $p<.001$)

Hypothesis 2 states that private communication will have less
influence on future purchasing decisions in test group I than
test group II. The findings show that, as predicted, group II
attached greater importance to private communication than group
I did, the associated t - value being highly significant ($t = 3.45$, $df = 143$, $p<0.01$).

Hypothesis 3 led us to predict a greater use of consumer test
results for guiding future decisions in group I than group II,
this prediction too being significantly confirmed by our findings ($t = 3.05$, $df = 143$, $p<0.01$).

The prediction, derived from hypothesis 4, that the consumers
supplied with test information (i.e. group I) would be more

convinced about the correctness of their purchase decision was
not confirmed, a comparison of the average values yielding
identical figures for the two groups. This failure to confirm
hypothesis 4 is probably due to a ceiling effect, the means
for both groups equalling 5.02 on a six point scale. As the respondents made their confidence ratings shortly after having
made their purchases, the high values may reflect a positive
emotional mood experienced directly after buying. On the other
hand, it is possible that the consumers in group I had no previous experience with consumer test information and were thus
not familiar with it's advantages. If this were so, the predicted difference in confidence would only arise after the
group I consumers had had positive experiences with such information.

Hypothesis 5, like hypothesis 4, led us to predict that consumers in group I would be more satisfied with their purchasing
decisions than would those in group II. While the data gathered
shortly after the purchase did not confirm this prediction,
those gathered six months afterwards did (t = 5.50, df = 83,
p<0.01).

3.4.4. Summary

The presented investigation aims at measuring the consumers'
informedness when making purchase decisions. A prerequisite for
this measurement was the development of an instrument for the
detection of increases in product- and general, purchase-relevant legal knowledge.

With the help of a linguistic transformation procedure, a
criteria-oriented knowledge test was constructed on the basis
of test reports from the Stiftung Warentest on 17 durable commodities and reports on purchase-relevant legal matters. This
test was validated on a preliminary sample of 80 respondents in
a "before and after" learning paradigm, thus allowing us to
eliminate all unnecessary or inaffective test items.

The test was employed in a field study on the influence that consumer test reports have on informedness, the quality of purchase decisions, and consumer satisfaction in the purchasing of durable goods. Two experimental groups were created, one being drawn from a panel study sample and consisting of people who said they planned a purchase of one of the 17 products featured in the knowledge test, the other of people contacted in shops after having bought one of the 17 different products. The first group was given consumer test report data and purchase-relevant, legal information before making their purchase. Both groups were tested shortly after their purchase and again, six months later.

The results show that the respondents who received the consumer test data were significantly better informed about the products purchased and - after six months of product use - were more satisfied with them than the respondents of the second sample. It was, moreover, found that this positive experience led to a change of attitude, the informed respondents reporting themselves to be more ready to refer to consumer test reports when making future purchases than were those who received no test information. This last result indicates that the regular use of test reports can be initiated by a single positive experience resulting from their usage.

4.   Laboratory experiments

4.1.   Information acquisition and brand choice

4.1.1. Overview

This experiment (Raffée et al., 1976) is a replication of a study carried out in 1973 by Jacoby, Szybillo and Busato-Schach at Purdue University and is intended to examine possible inter-cultural, behavioral differences between the German and

American subject populations. The subjects were 84 female
students at the University of Mannheim.

The design was a 3 (product information about 4 vs. 8 vs. 12
brands) x 2 (brand name and manufacturer provided vs. not provided) between subjects factorial. The test product was, in
this case, toothpaste.

Outline of procedure:

1) Subjects rate the importance of toothpaste.
2) Simulated purchase: subjects were to "purchase" one from a
set of 4, 8 or 12 brands of toothpaste, basing their decision
on information posted in a matrix with brand names (or numbers
representing brand names) heading each row and characteristic
type (e.g. price, consumer test result, etc.) heading each column and ordered alphabetically. Each information item in the
matrix was covered by removable paper strip. In order to make a
purchase decision, the respondent could, according to their
requirements, remove none, one, more, or all strips. The time
needed for decision process and the number of information items
used were recorded by the test supervisor.

4.1.2. Hypotheses and operationalizations

The experiment was aimed at critically examining the widespread
opinion underlying much of present-day consumer legislation
that consumers are better off the more product information
there is available. In this view, it is of no importance
whether the consumers make use of this information or not; it
should, in any case, be available in order to meet their moral,
ethical, and legal rights (Jacoby et al., 1974, p 1). It is, on
the other hand, possible to derive a competing viewpoint from
some recent experimental evidence that consumers are overstrain-
ed when they receive "too much" information and that, in such
cases, they base their purchase decisions on only a small subset of the information available. Brand name and price seem to
be especially important in this respect, each having a high

probability of being used in overload situations, the former
usually being "chunked" with the name of the manufacturer
(Jacoby et al., 1974, pp 3-4).

The following hypotheses were advanced:

H 1a: Consumers, when given a packet with a large amount
      of information, will tend to use only a part of it when
      making their purchasing decision.

H 1b: The information utilized will pertain to between 3 and 7
      different product characteristics.

H 2a: When selecting on-the-packet information, consumers are
      more likely to choose brand names than any other product
      characteristic, and will utilize it at an earlier stage
      in their information processing.

H 2b: Given a choice of on-the-packet information from which
      brand name is missing, consumers are most likely to
      choose price information, and to utilize it earlier in
      the decision making process, than any other information
      type.

4.1.3. Results and discussion

Results on Hypotheses 1 a/b:

Hypotheses 1a and 1b were confirmed in both the American and
German studies. It is true that consumers, when being allowed
to choose from a pool of information, do not use all the information for one decision, but only a part of it. While in the
United States an average of 5.05 items of information was used,
the average in our study was 6.01 (the mode was 6, and the
standard deviation = 2.068).

Results on Hypothesis 2a:

The results in America show that, as expected, the information
dimension "brand name" in the experimental situation "brand and

manufacturer's name available" is more often and earlier picked as all other information in the information gathering process. In contrast, the German results show that the information dimension "overall judgment of the Stiftung Warentest" is first in preference.

Results on Hypothesis 2b:

While this hypothesis was confirmed with the American sample, the German subjects tended to choose information as to price only after having already chosen information on "particularly efficient components" and "overall judgment given by the Stiftung Warentest", this pattern holding regardless of whether brand information was available or not. The importance attached to consumer test results suggests that the consumer testing program in Germany is more efficient in achieving its aims than its counterpart in the United States (cf. Raffée et al., 1976). Caution should be exercised, however, when generalizing the results of this experiment, especially with respect to the absolute figures obtained concerning the number of information items used.

4.1.4. Summary

This study replicates an earlier one carried out in the U.S.A. to determine whether it is better for consumers to receive as much product information as possible or whether the information supplied should be limited to a few "essentials" in order to avoid information overload. To answer this question, 84 subjects were brought into a laboratory situation designed to simulate the purchase of toothpaste, the subjects having a choice between 4, 8, or 12 different brands. Information concerning the different brands could be obtained from an information board, there being no prescriptions as to what and how much information to make use of, though only half the subjects were able, if they wanted, to obtain information concerning brand name and manufacturer.

The results show that consumers use only a fraction of the available product information when making a purchasing decision. It is particularly striking that certain bits of information are used particularly often, especially information concerning product price, brand name, manufacturer, and performance in comparative test reports. This information is apparently of high value to the consumer and invested with special significance.

4.2. Decision behavior concerning different objects

The question raised here is whether individuals always make decisions in the same manner, according to so-called "behavioral maps", or whether different objects evoke different forms of decision making behavior. The same question can be raised as to the effects of risk, experience, importance, etc.; are they invariable or do they change depending upon the nature of the decision making situation?

In order to assure between-condition comparability, our previous experiments each employed a single type of decision making situation that varied only slightly from one condition to the next. In order to address the above questions, however, the present experiment requires that subjects make simulated decisions about five very different kinds of things; the brand of stereo tuner and toothpaste to purchase, the bank in which one should take out credit, the particular member of the opposite sex whom one would like to date and, finally, a favorite branch of study.

4.2.1. Type of experiment sample

a) Methodological Improvements in Recording Information
   Acquisition Processes

The measures of information acquisition used in this study circumvent four main disadvantages inherent in the measures

previously employed and thus permit a more realistic simulation
of actual decision making situations (cf. Jacoby, 1975).

1) The previously discussed experiments were mostly based on
   hypothetical decision-alternatives and product information.
   For this study, the decision alternatives and corresponding
   charts and figures were real. Only in the case of "making a
   date" did we use hypothetical decision alternatives and
   information.

2) Subjects in the previous studies received fixed amounts of
   information which they were to employ in arriving at their
   decision. In the present study, subjects were free to decide
   how much or how little information to employ, a situation
   more characteristic of real decision making.

3) A third improvement has to do with a refinement in monitoring the cognitive processes that mediate the acquisition of
   information, the results from which are currently being
   evaluated.

4) Unlike the previous experiments, the data from the present
   study are not based on "verbal statements" but on "actual
   behavior". This advantage is quite important, because it has
   been empirically established that there is a difference
   between intended and actual behavior in information seeking.
   Jacoby, for instance, found in several analyses (e.g. Jacoby,
   1975) a correlation-coefficient of only +.4 between the two
   indices (cf. also Raffée et al., 1975).

The data were collected in December 1977. Each subject was
questioned individually, the order of the decisions being
counterbalanced between subjects to avoid order effects. For
each decision, the subjects had eight alternatives. These were
offered in the form of 8 blocks of information posted on an
information board and labeled by the letters A to H. Each block
consisted of a stack of information sheets, each one longer
than the one above it, the exposed part of each sheet containing a description (cost, content, etc.) of the kind of infor-

mation it contained. An example of the content of an information sheet (this concerning toothpaste) is given below:

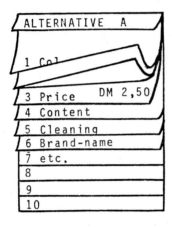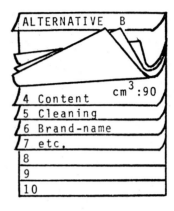

As mentioned above, subjects were able to procure all the
information they wanted for each decision trial and were not
restricted to any special sequence. Also, the same piece of
information could be referred to several times if need be.
After the subject had acquired all the information that he/she
felt necessary, he/she decided on one of the 8 alternatives.
The subjects were 55 male and 45 female students at the University of Mannheim.

4.2.2. Hypotheses and results

a) Similarity and differences in decision making processes

Various standpoints in learning theory, most notably Tolman's
theory of "sign-learning", posit that behavior is purpose-
oriented and that learning involves the learner discovering
signs that lead, as a map would, to his/her behavioral objectives. For decision making behavior, this translated into the
individual learning patterns of behavior, so-called "cognitive
maps", that lead to a reasonable decision. Such an analysis
would seem to imply that the individual's pre-decisioned behavior would remain constant irregardless of the particular

decision situation. In the present case, there should thus be no differences in the processes found to mediate each of the five different decision types.

Other theoretical analyses as well as the results of some empirical work argue against, however, the application of learning theory concepts to decision making. Risk theorists, for example, contend that as perceived risk increases, the level of information acquisition should increase too, thus reducing uncertainties about the decision and its possible consequences (Cunningham, 1967). As the level of perceived risk varies with different decision objects, the intensity of information acquisition should vary from one decision situation to the next (Kaplan et al., 1974; Jacoby & Kaplan, 1972).

Decision importance and cost-utility considerations should also play a role in shaping situation-specific decision behavior. Findings from previous research in this area (e.g. Katona & Mueller, 1955; Newman & Staelin, 1973) support this presumption, demonstrating that the processes that mediate decision making vary as a function of the decision object. For durable goods, for example, a more extensive planning and acquiring of information was found than was the case for, for instance, the purchase of sport-shirts (Katona & Mueller, 1955).

These last discussed results led us to propose the following hypothesis:

Hypothesis 1: For each of the five decision types studied in this experiment, a given decision maker will
- make use of different amounts of information,
- need varying amounts of time for reaching a decision.

Previous analyses have shown socio-demographic characteristics to be potent determinants of decision making behavior, especially sex, income, education and age (cf. Newman & Staelin, 1973; Katona & Mueller, 1955), thus suggesting that, in the present study:

Hypothesis 2: In working towards their final decisions, male
            subjects will differ from female subjects with
            respect to
            - the amount of information used,
            - the time needed for making the decision.

Results on hypothesis 1

The overall findings from a multi-variate analysis of variance
shows that the 5 decisions differ in a highly significant way
($F = 20.33$, df = 8/838, p<.001), and the corresponding univariate F's show that this difference becomes manifest both with
respect to the amount of the information employed ($F = 19.92$,
df = 4/420, p<0.001) and the amount of time needed for reaching
a final decision ($F = 16.39$, df = 4/420, p<0.001). These highly
significant results suggest that decision behavior - or, more
precisely, the information behavior before deciding - is strongly influenced by the decision object.

Table 6. Information use and decision time as a function of
         decision type

Decisions	Amount of information used			Time required in seconds		
	Min/Max	$\bar{x}$	Median	Min/Max	$\bar{x}$	Median
1. tuner	7/114	29.6	23.3	40/750	235.9	209.7
2. credit	11/87	35.0	29.8	90/950	327.3	275.0
3. date	3/109	35.2	30.5	70/832	307.3	276.5
4. toothpaste	6/94	26.7	23.5	25/660	185.3	156.0
5. branch of study	0/64	16.4	12.0	1/825	217.5	209.8

With respect to individually paired comparisons between the
five decisions, the only decisions not found to differ signifi-

cantly from one another were decisions 2 (credit) and 3 (date), these two differing neither with respect to the amount of information used nor the time needed to reach a final decision. Though the reasons for this lack of difference cannot be definitely determined, it should be pointed out (see Table 6) that these two decision types were the ones that required, on the average, the most information and the longest decision-time. Perhaps a psychological ceiling effect was operating here, subjects' limits for handling information preventing them from any further information acquisition.

Results on Hypothesis 2

Besides decision type, sex also produced significant differences in decision behavior, the multi-variate F with respect to sex being highly significant (F = 4.25, df = 2/419, p<.01). The separate univariate F's with respect to information use and decision time each showed significant effects for sex as well (F = 8.41 and 4.42, df = 1/420 and 1/420; p<.004 and .04 respectively). The corresponding means show that female subjects generally ask for less information than do male subjects ($\bar{x}_f$ = 26.09, $\bar{x}_m$ = 30.59) and require less time ($\bar{x}_f$ = 239.12, $\bar{x}_m$ = 267.3).

Situational determinants of decision making processes

Correlational analyses showed that the different situational factors monitored (risk, decision importance, desired decision quality, decision transparency) had variable, weak effects on the amount of information used and time needed for reaching a final decision. The results of the correlational analyses are summarized in Table 7. It cannot be determined from the present data whether the low correlations indicate that the variable in question has little effect on decision making or whether its influence lies in aspects other than amount of information used and decision time.

Table 7. The effects of situational determinants on decision
          processes

decision	situational determinant	amount of information used		time required	
		r	α	r	α
tuner	risk	0.176	0.04		
	importance	0.219	0.01	0.221	0.01
	difference in quality of the product	0.232	0.01		
	transparency of decisions			0.173	0.04
toothpaste	importance	0.316	0.00	0.218	0.15
	quality re-quired for the decision	0.298	0.00	0.185	0.03
	differences in quality of the product	0.226	0.01	0.207	0.02
branch of study	differences in quality of the object	−0.221	0.01		

4.2.3. Summary

The present study investigated whether decision making processes vary from one decision situation to the next. Subjects
(55 male, 45 female) were asked to make five different hypothetical decisions (purchasing of a tuner and of toothpaste,
choosing a bank to take out a credit, choosing a university
major and a person of the other sex one would like to meet).
For each decision, subjects had 8 alternatives to choose from.
For each alternative, there was an equally high amount of information. The respondents were free to decide which, how much,
and in what order they would use the information offered. The

experimenter recorded only the amount of information used and the time needed for reaching a final decision.

The results show that decision behavior varied greatly between the five different decision types, all except "credit" and "date" differing significantly from each other with respect to both information use and decision time. With respect to "credit" and "date" decisions, a ceiling effect may have been operant in that the level of information use found for these two decisions seemed likely to tax subjects' capacity for information processing.

Sex was also found to affect decision making processes, the female subjects requiring less information and less time for making decisions than male subjects did. Situational factors like "risk", "decision importance", "expectancies of decision quality", "decision experience", and "decision transparency" had only slight influence on the amount of information used and decision time.

The significance of this experiment is, above all, methodological, as the standardized interview was replaced by an experimental task that embodied the essential aspects of real-life decision situations. The results point to the importance of the decision-object as a determinant of decision processes. Furthermore, it is interesting that our hypotheses were only partly confirmed with respect to the influence of risk and decision importance. Further research concerning these factors is clearly needed [5].

---

[5] A detailed account of this study can be found in Raffée et al. (1979).

Chapter 16 Needs and Satisfaction with Respect to the Supply of Daily Goods: A Consumer-Oriented Approach

E. Dichtl, W. Beeskow, G. Finck and S. Müller

1. Summary

The supply of goods according to consumers' needs is a problem
of increasing social-political relevance in Western societies
due to the trend towards concentration in the food retail trade
and the disappearance of small stores. The quality of supply
in an economy based on the division of labour cannot be satisfactorily ascertained either through economic efficiency
criteria or by objective measures of supply conditions alone,
particularly as far as essential goods are concerned. The
empirical finding that there is a low correspondence between
standard of living and well-being thus calls for a qualitative
examination of the supply sphere.

The purpose of the analysis presented here is to provide politicians and planners with a methodology and a measure that
sheds light on problems of supply and that can serve as an aid
for political decisions. Such a measure will enable decision
makers to contrast consumers' interests with the interests of
other economic groups.

Public and scientific discussion has shown that the so-called
objective measures of retail density - such as villages without stores or distance from consumers' homes to the nearest
store - are inadequate indicators of supply quality. First of
all, such indicators describe nothing but inputs (e.g. the
number of stores) and, secondly, they ignore the complexity of

the problem at hand. For instance, objectively identical levels of supply conditions can have different effects depending upon situational factors in households. One way of improving these indicators would be to expand their focus and take into account the outputs of the supply process as well, for example, by considering consumers' own subjective evaluations of their supply situations.

This extension of the research objective towards consumers' subjective experience, together with our aim to provide detailed information with regard to problems of supply, requires the application of a recipient-orientated, multi-attribute research approach. The results of a pilot study indicated that the object of our analysis can be sufficiently represented by ten single attributes, and we assumed that consumers' satisfaction/dissatisfaction is a suitable measure of the quality of the supply situation. The consumers interviewed in several surveys, however, expressed their degree of satisfaction only with respect to those supply attributes that they considered being salient.

A further characteristic of our approach is the household perspective. Considering the high degree of consumer mobility and, what results from this, that consumers are not constrained to one particular shopping area, it appeared to be necessary to define the object under investigation in terms of the subjective supply area (i.e. the sum of the perceived shopping possibilities) and not in terms of a pre-specified geographical area. In order to be able to draw segment-specific conclusions, we subdivided our sample into discernible units of analysis according to supply needs and household characteristics pertaining to the supply process. Intra-individual and regional comparisons were made possible by an Index of Supply Satisfaction (ISS) developed on the basis on an additive attitude model.

With respect to regional factors our investigations showed that the quantity and structure of consumers' supply needs vary greatly between urban and rural populations: 71% of an urban sample and 67% of a rural sample expressed between 4 and 7 out of 10 possible supply needs. The rural population in particular pointed to wants related to the process of acquisitioning goods, while the urban population tended towards more subtle, qualitatively oriented supply needs. In both groups, however, a preference for good value was dominant.

Utilizing multidimensional scaling we identified linkages between supply needs. For the urban population we found a strong linkage between "low prices" and the "number of similar stores available" and attributed this fact to the perception of the existence of price competition. The rural population, however, linked the price variable first and foremost with the possibility of "purchasing all the desired goods at one single store", thus pointing to a distinct preference for large retail establishments among this segment. Nonmetric profile analyses indicated trade-offs between certain supply needs. Thus, town-dwellers consider qualitative (quality of goods, shopping atmosphere) and quantitative (distance, prices) aspects of supply to be more or less incompatible, whereas for the rural population, short shopping distances and good value shopping are mutually exclusive.

Number, strength and linkages between supply needs do not in themselves, however, allow any conclusions to be drawn on perceived supply problems: Supply deficits only become visible through weighted satisfaction/dissatisfaction ratings for the individually salient attributes. One problem not yet resolved is to determine whether the salience of attributes can be traced back to the perception of shortage or to the wish to maintain a somewhat positively evaluated situation.

In terms of our ten supply attributes and the applied satisfaction scales, the level of satisfaction expressed by the urban population was 74.5% of the maximum possible satisfaction level, while that expressed by the rural population amounted to 68.1%.

For the former, low prices, high quality and a wide range of goods could be identified as problem attributes (although there were 64 smaller stores for daily necessities in an area of 1 sq.km); for the latter, low prices, a wide range of goods, accessibility of stores and the possibility of one-stop shopping seemed to be the weak points.

Segmentation analyses show that the interpretation offered here is in line with the escalating consumer aspirations brought about by increases in mobility and, consequently, widening opportunities to draw comparisons. If, however, mobility is job-linked, the satisfaction deficit decreases proportionally with the extent commuters manage to combine travelling to work and shopping. It is interesting to note that the segment of immobile old people, which was always thought to be a problem group, expressed the highest level of satisfaction with their supply situation.

Analyses carried out on an individual level with the aid of our ISS demonstrated that 20.2% of the people living in the country and 13.6% of the town population felt themselves to be undersupplied to at least some extent. An attempt, however, to typify these consumers on the basis of socio-demographic criteria more or less failed. The only positive correlation which we observed was a small one between age and ISS-value.

We chose the respondents' overall satisfaction rating as the criterion for the concurrent validation of the ISS. The correlation coefficients (0.41 for the urban and 0.44 for the country population) remained within the boundaries typical for behavioral research.

The approach described here certainly needs further improvement. Nevertheless, it represents a relatively simple and manageable tool for tracing supply problems and yields results that are far more informative than those obtainable by merely counting the number of stores.

2. Introduction and exposition of the problem

The advent of new types of stores (e.g. discount houses, supermarkets) and increased consumer mobility has led to continuing
structural changes in the retail trade and in the service
sector. Particularly in the Federal Republic of Germany, this
development has resulted in a concentration of supply outlets
and in a weakening of the retail network, especially with regard to the grocery trade and food manufacturing (bakeries,
butchers etc.)[1]. In view of the fact that these two sectors
are supposed to meet basic needs, we assume that this selection
process not only raises problems for smaller retailers (Finck
& Müller, 1978) but also has an unwanted impact on the supply
of households unable to adapt themselves to the prevailing circumstances.

In market oriented economies, the evaluation of the supply
situation has been dominated by criteria of economic efficiency
(cf. Ihde, 1976). Thus, the nature and structure of supply
with commodities has until recently been looked at solely on
the basis of purchasing power. In an economy with division of
labour, however, the supply of the population cannot be regarded from a purely economic perspective on account of the fundamental function that it serves for society. As supply in general belongs to the basic subsistence functions (Partsch, 1970),
it cannot be evaluated by quantitative aspects alone. There is
a qualitative side of the matter, too. In our view the supply
situation constitutes a facet of the quality of life just as
housing, education, work or leisure. Most comprehensive studies
carried out in this area (e.g. Campbell, Converse & Rodgers,
1976; Andrews & Withey, 1976) failed to take notice of this
particular aspect.

The last decade has seen a gradual abandonment of the material-

---

[1]Within a time-span of one decade the number of grocers decreased from 187,000 to 99,000, while the retail area increased from 10.6 millions sqm to 15.1 millions (1968-1978).

istic values of earlier years (Inglehart, 1977) with their
tacit equalization of material prosperity and quantitative
growth, on the one hand, and quality of life on the other. This
reorientation will inevitably have an impact on domestic trade
policy. Nowadays, the presentation of more and more items on
an ever-increasing retail space in fewer and fewer stores can
no longer be quickly passed off as progress. Quantitative
growth indicators such as an increase in turnover, parking area
or variety of products have only little, if any, predictive
value for the quality of consumer life. Apart from the prevention of material shortcomings in supply that may occur as a
result of this concentration process (in the sense of insufficient accessibility of stores), recent inquiries reveal that
there is an additional need for a qualitative improvement in
the supply with shopping and convenience goods,and that merely
increasing the number and variety of goods does not necessarily
further the well-being of the people (cf. Prinz, 1977).

In the Federal Republic of Germany, there so far exist only
vague conjectures as to the connections between the potentially available supply and its perceived quality. These
conjectures have, however, already had consequences in the form
of drastic political interventions in the supply structure
organized on a market economy basis. These interventions rest
on the assumption that keeping up local competition in the
supply of food, semi-luxuries and other household goods period-
ically required guarantees, at the same time, a supply that
corresponds best to consumer needs (cf. Dichtl, Beeskow &
Finck, 1979a).

Though the Federal Republic of Germany does, in principle, adhere to freedom of trade, recent requests to open up large retail establishments have been subjected to controls similar to
those adopted in France and Italy. Thus,in section 11, 3 of the
1977 "Bau-Nutzungs-Verordnung",it is assumed that retail outlets with a retail area of $1,500m^2$ and over have a negative
impact on local supply. Such establishments are, therefore,

permitted only in areas that are mainly non-residential. An even tougher restriction of the planning autonomy is imposed on communities by several state requirements that make the admissibility of large retail establishments dependent on the type of centre laid down in plans for the development of a region.

In West Germany, Switzerland and Austria the attitude of legislators towards the supply structure has been influenced by various investigations (some government-commissioned) on the provisionment of daily necessities (cf. Dichtl, Bauer & Finck, 1978a). As a common feature they use objective measures like retail density (e.g. villages without any stores) or location of consumers in relation to grocery stores (e.g. 15 minutes walk) as indicators for the presence or absence of supply problems.

Such objective indicators do not appear to be a suitable basis for deciding whether and how to create or guarantee a supply situation that meets consumers' needs because they neglect differences between social groups and the fact that objectively identical supply situations exert different effects with regard to household factors (e.g. mobility, self-supply). For both describing the situation at hand and prescribing appropriate actions for improvement, the focus should not be exclusively on "reasonable" norms of supply developed by experts but should also take into account the subjective evaluations of the consumers concerned. So, ensuring a supply adequate to needs, for instance, not only depends on the number of stores to be found in a district but also on the fact whether, in the eyes of the consumers, the range and availability of the merchandise offered are adequate to their needs (cf. Dichtl, Bauer & Finck, 1978b).

In evaluating supply quality, however, it is not enough to rely on overall judgments, since these yield little information as to possible actions for improvement. Rather, it would appear to be necessary to have consumers rate all the relevant criteria of supply and to determine supply quality on the basis of these

ratings. To do this, a measure must be devised that
- yields reliable information about the supply situation of
  the population in general and of certain social groups in
  particular
- shows up weaknesses in supply and
- is easy to handle.

3. Theoretical framework for consumer-oriented research on supply

The central concern here is the development of decision aids
for institutions directly or indirectly involved in the supply
process. These aids could take the form, for example, of recommendations to politicians concerned with infra-structural
problems like the granting of permission for the establishment
of large supermarkets or shopping centers, or a subsidy for a
local store. One precondition, however, is to know what effects
such interventions have on the satisfaction of supply needs
(cf. Dichtl, 1979).

The lack of correspondence between objective criteria and judgments based upon them can be demonstrated in various spheres of
life (e.g. Atteslander, 1976; Irle, 1975; Glass & Singer, 1972).
So the amount of purchasing power linked to a number of stores
selling daily necessities (so-called retail centrality) cannot
be regarded as the only indicator of the quality of supply; the
consumer is imbedded in a supply structure - arising from the
temporal and spatial restrictions imposed upon him by his
choice of residence and place of work - which may not correspond to his supply needs. For these reasons, the quality of
supply cannot be derived from objective criteria or from the
purchasing behavior of consumers alone. What is needed is the
development of indicators on the basis of subjective judgments.

3.1. The supply situation as a multiattribute attitude construct

The consumers' supply situation as a complex system of conditions made up of supply and demand modalities is regarded as
an object of social judgment. In contrast to persons or products, it is of a somewhat singular nature, since a consumer
can, as a rule, only choose between individual stores but not
between different supply areas. It may be assumed, however,
that consumers are able to make a differentiated assessment of
their own supply situation because they are in a position to
identify their supply needs and draw comparisons based on incomplete (e.g. newspaper advertisements of suppliers outside
their reach) and/or "historical" (e.g. suppliers known from
previous places of residence) information.

Here attitude research can serve as a basis for explanation
and prediction (Triandis, 1975). A prediction of shopping behavior based on the relationships between cognitive, affective
and conative aspects (Fishbein, 1973; Ryan & Bonfield, 1975)
appears to be possible only under extreme conditions of supply,
however. Therefore, the present approach aims above all at
describing the supply situation perceived by the individual and
to elaborate the meaning of the term "supply adequate to needs".

Due to the diagnostic requirements to be fulfilled by the
measuring instrument and the relative singularity of the object
of assessment, a holistic measuring approach seems less suitable than a constructive, elementaristic one (cf. Schümer,
1971). This calls for an assessment of consumer attitudes concerning all relevant facets of supply. Thus, the identification
of the dimensions on which supply situations are perceived to
vary as well as the proper rule of combination that governs
consumers' satisfaction judgments are the first steps in our
approach. The resulting index should allow comparisons of the
assessments put forward by members of households in different
living spaces (cf. Anderson, 1974).

3.2. Consumer segmentation

A fundamental criticism put forward against the use of objective indicators of the quality of supply is that they consider
consumers to be a homogeneous group, a position that is clearly
untenable. The consumer-orientated approach, is geared at the
individual and his specific supply needs and the peculiarities
of his situation. Since, however, economic and political decisions cannot be based on individual peculiarities, the consumer
group whose supply situation is to be analysed must be split
up into sub-groups that are as homogeneous as possible. This
segmentation is usually carried out only on the basis of those
socio-demographic characteristics that are likely to be correlated with differences in perception of the supply situation. A
more promising approach to segmenting a population of consumers
would be to identify clusters on the basis of similar evaluations of the supply situation *and* an analysis of dominant socio-
demographic characteristics of the clusters.

3.3. Supply and household characteristics

Due to the relatively high proportion (61.8%) of households in
the Federal Republic of Germany who have at least one car at
their disposal, improved possibilities for storing perishables
(e.g. the availability of freezers), and the increase in discretionary income available for consumption purposes, shopping
habits of most consumers have changed. In particular, higher
mobility of a large proportion of the population expedites a
kind of shopping behavior which overcomes traditional geographical boundaries. When analysing the supply situation of the
population in a geographically defined entity (e.g. a village),
it would, therefore, not make sense to simply take local shopping facilities as the object of judgment. What is needed is an
assessment of the supply area realised by the household, since
it may be assumed that the stores patronized represent - apart
from possible situational and household related restraints -

the relatively best combination. In order to classify consumer evaluations, therefore, a detailed knowledge of shopping behavior with regard to the type of outlets favored is essential.

4.   Design and results of a pilot study

4.1. Operationalizing the supply construct

In our research, we considered the supply situation as an analogue to product image. Our first aim was to identify the attributes necessary for its description with respect to daily commodities. Fifteen housewives were asked in unstructured interviews what they considered to be important when shopping for groceries and other household items. From the records of these interviews we derived the following supply attributes (abbreviations in brackets):
- price level of daily commodities (price)
- quality and freshness of the goods available (quality)
- distance to the store (accessibility)
- possibilities of comparisons and competition between stores (number of stores)
- variety of store types available (variety of stores)
- image and atmosphere of stores (atmosphere)
- agglomeration of stores or the possibility to purchase everything under one roof (one-stop shopping)
- choice from a wide line of products (assortment)
- availability of goods in desired quantities or units (quantity).

Very much to our surprise, not even housewives with a full time job mentioned store opening hours as a relevant supply characteristic. This may be due to the fact that a very restrictive law on closing times has been in force since 1956 and people seem to have become accustomed to its regulations[2]. However, proceeding on a "good reasons approach", we included this variable in our list of attributes. We assume that this list represents the cognitive elements of consumers with regard to the supply situation.

In order to assess the intensities of the attributes, a 5-point scale was used. With regard to a total of five attributes, it was possible to construct the scales directly according to their content (e.g. "very long" to "very short" distance to stores); for the remaining five only an evaluative scale was used (e.g. "very negative" to "very positive" impressions when shopping). The weighting of the 10 attributes was also accomplished by means of a 5-point scale ranging from "very relevant" to "not relevant at all". This type of scale proved to be superior to an "importance scale" in several pretests (in so far as it revealed more discriminatory power). In addition, respondents were asked to pass an overall judgment of their supply situation on a 5-point scale ranging from "very good" to "very bad". The questionnaires were distributed to 10% of households randomly selected in each of five districts of Nuremberg, which were quite different according to age and proximity to the city centre. 403 out of 522 questionnaires (77%) distributed could be analysed.

4.2. A test of multiattribute attitude models

Identifying the integration rules for attitude formation is

---

[2] In West Germany there exists a law that prohibits shop owners from opening their shops between 6.30 p.m. and 7 a.m. on workdays and from 2 p.m. on Saturday (6 p.m. once a month) to 7 a.m. on Monday. Exceptions are made for pharmacies and stores which carry travelling necessities, journals, souvenirs etc. Originally this law was to protect employees in the retail trade from exploitation. Nowadays the law is regarded as a means to maintain equal chances in competition between large and tiny retailers.

necessary to establish a subjective index of the quality of supply and to identify those facets which are most typical of an adequate supply situation. Since we may assume that these rules vary both between and within individuals according to situation and judgment object, that model should be selected that yields the best average for all consumers or for particular consumer segments (least squares property).

Since there is no suitable external criterion at hand (e.g. the supply area actually realised by the consumers), which could serve for validation purposes, we took the degree to which the overall judgment and the scores calculated on the basis of different attitude models concurred as the criterion of model quality. Various linear compensatory and non-linear non-compensatory models (cf. Beeskow & Finck, 1979) drawn mostly from the literature on attitude research were subjected to that type of validation. The best validation result was obtained with the multiple linear regression model neglecting explicit weightings of the variables ($R^2=.52$). Second in line was a multiple regression model using the logarithms of the judgment scores (conjunctive model; $R^2=.51$). This was followed by a multiple linear regression model in which the independent variables consisted of the weighted discrepancies between the perceived value and the maximum value of an attribute ($R^2=.50$). These maximum values served as an indicator for the ideal state of affairs. By means of the simple additive model which neglects weightings of relevance, we still managed to obtain a correlation coefficient of .69 (see Table 4.1, page 562).

We would be overhasty in concluding from the present results that consumers implicitly weight the variables in their attribute judgments and that we would thus forego the weighting procedure (cf. Mikes & Hulin, 1968). We would be equally rash in favoring the ideal value concept proposed by Beckwith and Lehmann (1973). Apart from possible distortions due to the violation of the assumptions that the scales are interval scales and that the scale values are comparable over all

Rank	Type	Model	R	R^2
1	LC	$R^2 \rightarrow (V_i)$		.52
2	NC	$R^2 \rightarrow (\log(V_i))$		.51
3	IV(LC)	$R^2 \rightarrow (W_i|V_i - I_i|)$		.50
4	LC	ΣV_i	.69	
5	IV	$R^2 \rightarrow |(V_i - I_i)^2|^{1/2}$		.45
6	IV(LC)	$\Sigma(W_i|V_i - I_i|)$	-.67	
	NC	$\Sigma \log(V_i)$	.67	
8	IV	$\Sigma(W_i|V_i - I_i|^2)$	-.65	
	IV	$(\Sigma|V_i - I_i|^2)^{1/2}$	-.65	
	NC	$R^2 \rightarrow (-W_i \log(K - V_i))$		.42

Table 4.1: Eleven model algebrae, which produced the highest degree of correspondence with the overall judgment.

Legend:

LC = linear-compensatory

IV = ideal value

NC = non-linear, non-compensatory

V = judgment value

W = weighting

I = max. positive judgment value

i = attribute (i=1,2,....,10)

variables, model-specific effects should bear on the results.
It can easily been shown that the interval scale degenerates in
all models as soon as the components are multiplied or divided
by each other. The same effect appears when a component is
raised to a higher power. The size of this effect depends on
whether the calculations are based on unipolar or bipolar scale
values and on how many scale points are used. For example, a
unipolar scale ranging from 1 to 5 for judgments as well as
relevance weightings yields a span of 1 to 25 after multiplication, within which 11 numbers do not appear. If the overall
attitude is recorded on a 5-point scale too, its poor variability leads to a decrease in the measure of association. If,
instead, we use scales ranging from -2 to +2, the range of
variation of the products and the number of unoccupied values
decrease. However, the nature of the statement also changes:
an attribute which is assessed positively (+2) although being
irrelevant (-2), results in a decrease of the attitude value
(-4).

Empirical tests of the multiplicative attitude model yielded a
correlation coefficient of R=.45 for the unipolar variant and
an R^2 of .29 for the disaggregated analysis, while the corresponding values for the bipolar variants were .55 and .36,
respectively.

The comparatively good fit of the "ideal value model" can be
explained by the structure of the raw data. With the exception
of the "price level" variable, the distributions of the ratings over the supply attributes display negative skewness. Thus,
the weighted differences between scale maxima and original ratings vary only scarcely with the result that a larger proportion of the criterion variable's variance can be explained.

The non-linear, non-compensatory models suggested by some
authors (e.g. Einhorn, 1970) as an approximation of the disjunctive and conjunctive decision rules constitute an interesting group. The models for disjunctive and conjunctive decisions
rest, however, on different basic assumptions with regard to

judgment formation. The former type of model is dominated
by positive judgments, while the latter is dominated by
negative judgments. However, concurrent validation does not
allow any clear conclusions to be drawn as to which of the two
models works better in approximating the cognitive structure of
a sample. When eliminating the relevance weightings the value
of R^2 for the conjunctive model in a multiple regression
analysis rose from .31 to .51. The corresponding values for the
disjunctive model amounted to .41 and .42, respectively.

The comparatively poor validation results for linear-compensatory models incorporating explicit relevance weights could be
due to the violation of either or all of three of the model's
essential premises:
1) The judgments on supply attributes are correlated (multi-
   collinearity).
2) The weightings for the supply attributes are correlated.
3) Correlations exist between the judgment and the weighting
   dimensions.

With respect to the first premise, if judgments concerning supply attributes are inter-correlated, the evaluation score calculated by means of linear-compensatory algebrae will be excessively influenced by overlapping characteristics. For 7 out of
a total of 45 correlations, highly significant coefficients
with values greater than .30 were found.

Concerning the second point, 22 correlation coefficients between importance weights were >.30, while the variances of the
weights did not exceed 1.0. In connection with the extreme
negative skewness of the attribute weighting distributions, a
multiple degeneration effect was found for the multiplicative
models that led to frequent violations of the proportionality
premise.

With respect to the third point, violations of the proportionality premise should occur more frequently insofar as attitude
judgment and weighting are interdependent, since in this case

single supply attributes exert a biasing influence on the
model's score. Only in one out of 10 possible cases, a correlation coefficient of >.20 was found.

A principle component analysis (cf. Harman, 1960) of the attribute judgments, weightings and the overall judgments yielded a
structure of factor loadings that had to be expected in view
of the above considerations (see Figure 4.1, page 566).

Hence, judgments on the attributes and their weightings belong
to different principle components. We conclude from this observation that weightings of attributes possess an information
value of their own which, however, is not adequately taken into
account by the algebraic models investigated. The high loading
of the overall judgment on the judgment dimension indicates
that it is strongly related to the attribute judgments.

4.3. The pattern of associations between overall judgment and attribute judgments

Due to the complexity of the mental processes that mediate the
formation of impressions, algebraic models can only be taken
as approximations, even if the problem of scaling may be regarded as solved. Thus, if one wishes to restrict oneself to
ordinal data, the pattern of association between the supply
attributes and the overall judgment can be ascertained with the
aid of nonmetric multidimensional scaling (Shepard et al., 1972;
Kruskal, 1964a,b). Using the gamma coefficient (Goodman &
Kruskal, 1954) as a measure of association between the judgments regarding the supply attributes, the MINISSA program
(Lingoes & Roskam, 1973) yielded a very close fit (stress value
of 0.04) of the Euclidean distances between the supply attributes and the rank orders of the association coefficients in
three dimensions (see Figure 4.2, page 567).

Although this approach cannot account for individual differences in judgment (Feger, 1974), the solution provides hints

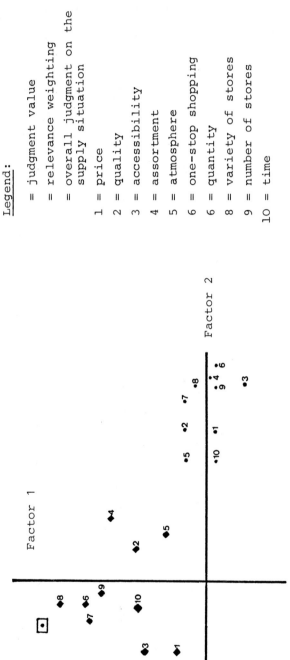

Legend:

■ = judgment value

◆ = relevance weighting

□ = overall judgment on the
    supply situation

1 = price

2 = quality

3 = accessibility

4 = assortment

5 = atmosphere

6 = one-stop shopping

6 = quantity

8 = variety of stores

9 = number of stores

10 = time

Figure 4.1. Graph of the factor structure of the judgment values and relevance weightings

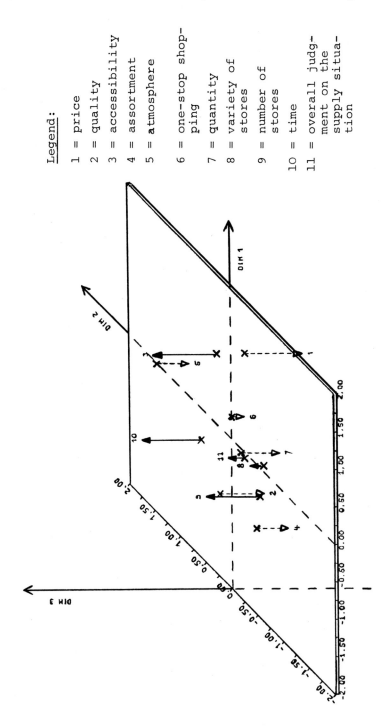

Legend:

1 = price

2 = quality

3 = accessibility

4 = assortment

5 = atmosphere

6 = one-stop shop-
    ping

7 = quantity

8 = variety of
    stores

9 = number of
    stores

10 = time

11 = overall judg-
     ment on the
     supply situa-
     tion

Figure 4.2. Three-dimensional MINISSA-representation of the pattern of association between
the overall judgment and the judgments on attributes of the supply situation.

about which of the ten supply attributes have a special impact
on the perception of the supply situation. Since, even in a
three-dimensional solution, clusters are hard to be identified
visually, we subjected the configuration of the solution to an
additional hierarchical cluster analysis (Bock, 1974). Figure
4.3 (see page 569) displays the dendrogram of the fusion process according to Ward's method (1963).

This dendrogram illustrates the fact that the attributes concerning the possibility of choosing between different types of
stores, obtaining the required quantity of a product and one-
stop shopping have the greatest influence on the overall judgment. On the other hand, we see that price level, shopping
atmosphere and the objectively definable attributes "distance",
"number of stores" and "opening hours" represent more self-
contained clusters.

4.4. Discussion

With the help of algebraic models we attempted to establish
the best approximation of attitude organisation. At first
glance, the results of the concurrent validation seemed quite
encouraging. However, the empirical results are affected by
some interference that throws doubt on the validity of the
operationalization chosen.

4.4.1. Suitability of quality judgments

Although, from a teleological point of view, quality can be
defined as a bundle of satisfying elements (Kupsch, Hufschmied,
Mathes & Schöler, 1978), the question remains whether the scaling method selected for the cognitive attitude component sheds
any light on the extent to which needs are satisfied. For this,
knowledge of the optimum quality aspired to would be necessary.
This optimum would have to represent an ideal situation based
on functional connections between the supply attributes. It is

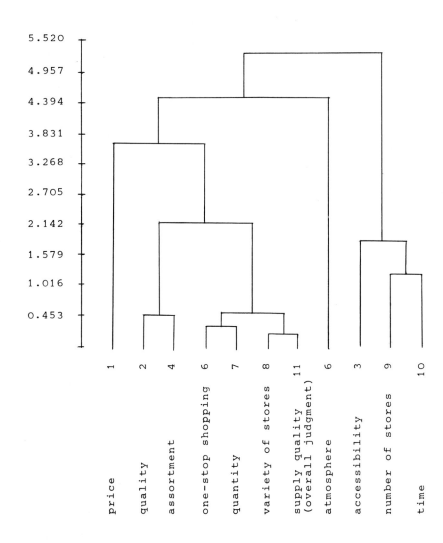

Figure 4.3. Dendrogram of the hierarchical cluster analysis

not possible, for example, to offer good-quality products at extremely low prices. Maximum targets on each dimension cannot, therefore, be taken as indicators of a supply situation which best meets existing needs.

Furthermore, we should not blindly assume that maximum points are aspired for all attributes. For instance, a very wide and deep assortment could reduce the clarity of the range of goods and consequently lower a store's attractiveness. As this example shows, the verbal expression of ideal concepts is extremely difficult. Thus, depending on the terms of comparison used, a medium range of products could comprise several hundred or even several thousand items.

4.4.2. Weighting the characteristics

The very low variances of the attribute weightings and their negatively skewed distribution could, on the one hand, be due to the possibility that each attribute was *in fact* important to all respondents or, on the other hand (and more probably), that the subjects' isolated weighting of each attribute led to a tendency of maximize aspirations. When ascertaining evaluation scores with the aid of algebraic models incorporating weighted judgments, invariant maximum weightings merely serve as constants.

The question of the degree to which the given set of attributes is relevant for all respondents is closely connected with the weighting problem. Though subjects could "choose" among attributes by giving those they found irrelevant a zero-weighting, the pilot study showed that subjects allocated this zero weight to only one attribute, "opening hours", and this by only 6.2% of the sample.

4.4.3. Independence of attributes

Probably the most stringent requirement of additive attitude models is that the attributes must be independent (e.g. Wilkie & Pessemier, 1973). Because of the above-mentioned functional connections between aspects of supply (e.g. price level and product quality), this requirement cannot be upheld in the present case even if this results in double countings and a subsequent bias of impression values.

A more important argument against the elimination of highly correlated variables is that the stress laid on the statistical aspect does not necessarily lead to a higher degree of iso-morphy in algebraic models since the synthetic, average struc-ture determined by correlation is not comparable with the indi-vidual judgment structures (Kupsch et al., 1978). One aspect related to the problem of duplicate countings concerns the loss of information. If, for instance, the coefficient of determina-tion for two variables amounts to .25, this measure does not only indicate a remarkable association between the two varia-bles but also that 75% of this total variance is not accounted for by the covariance. This argument supports, in our view, the inclusion of attributes with moderately high intercorrelations in attitude models.

5. Satisfaction as a measure of supply quality

Lack of knowledge of consumers' ideals and the problem of com-parability of attributes when using scales specific to attri-butes nourished doubts as to whether the quality judgment, in the sense of an evaluated subject-object relationship (Kawlath, 1969), serves as a suitable indicator of perceived quality of supply. Contrary to quality judgment, satisfaction judgments permit comparable statements to be made about the degree of fulfillment of individual aspirations without having to pry in-to the nature of these claims.

5.1. The construct of supply satisfaction

Viewing consumers' supply with daily commodities as one of many facets of the quality of life, as we do here, suggests looking for parallels in other spheres of life. In particular, research on job satisfaction can look back on a long tradition without having yet arrived at a comprehensive and consistent theory to support it (Bunz, Jansen & Schacht, 1974). This is partly due to the fact that the concept of satisfaction is borrowed from everyday speech and is applied to differing subject matters according to the particular theory employed at any one time.

In motivational approaches, job satisfaction is taken as a construct called upon to explain working behavior. There are, however, considerable differences between definitions of satisfaction. Neuberger (1974a), for example, distinguishes between homeostatic, hedonistic, cognitive and humanistic concepts of satisfaction. The basic assumption underlying homeostatic conceptions is that the satisfaction of a need cancels out a perceived shortcoming. Satisfaction is regarded, however, as a relatively short-lived state of satiation. The various versions of this approach differ as to the proposed nature of the processes underlying satisfaction, with some authors regarding satisfaction as the fulfilling of instinctive needs and others (e.g. Vroom, 1964) merely as knowledge gained from experience with respect to possible ways to realize desires.

While the homeostatic approach emphasises the inner, almost physiological equilibrium of an individual, hedonistic theories accentuate the incentive concept. Striving towards pleasure and avoiding pain interact with environmental conditions which thus take on an instrumental character. Satisfaction is achieved when the balance of pleasure and pain is at its maximum (cf. the expectancy theory; Porter & Lawler, 1968).

Cognitive conceptions of satisfaction emphasize successful orientation in the environment, those objects or states of affairs being satisfying that either are instrumental in attaining a highly valued objective or that appear equitable when compared to those of the person's reference group. (cf. Adams, 1965; Homans, 1961).

Finally, the satisfaction theories developed by Maslow (1954) and Herzberg (1966) focus attention on the specifically human problems of coming to terms with existence and achieving life fulfillment (humanistic conceptions). Both assume two basic sets of needs: Maslow distinguishes between basic and higher order needs and Herzberg between hygienic needs and motivators. Maslow's hierarchy of needs seems, however, to be much too general and extensive for having any direct bearing on supply satisfaction since it covers the entire, complex pattern of human existence. Herzberg's two-factor theory, on the other hand, cannot be denied any analogy to the supply question be- cause it rests on "critical incidents". It will be discussed below, however, in connection with the individual's ability to influence the facet of life under investigation.

A typical aspect of research on satisfaction based on motiva- tional theories is that the individual himself can take action to bring about the state of satisfaction. Hence, the considered fields of research must be characterised by a high propensity to be influenced by the individual. In the case of market pro- cesses, we can observe that the individual consumer has virtual- ly no possibility to influence the supply situation. His pur- chase behavior is effective solely in conjunction with that of other consumers (except for extremely highly priced products with high profit margins). Thus, the only chance available for the individual consumer is to adapt to the supply offer. Keep- ing within his financial, temporal and physical limits, he can then - for example, by using a car to get to his shopping place - influence his supply situation to a small extent. Finally, he can come to terms with supply problems by means of cognitive adaptation (e.g. reduction of cognitive dissonance).

In general, however, supply satisfaction is something that is experienced passively and determined by the conditions of

supply as well as situational household factors. At first
glance, two factors appear to determine how consumers overcome
supply problems: conditions of supply (analogous to Herzberg's
hygienic needs) and acquisition efforts (analogous to Herzberg's
motivators). Both physical and psychical shopping efforts, however, depend on the supply conditions, so that as a result the
more consumers value the conditions with respect to a narrowly
bounded geographic supply area, the lower the probability that
acquisition efforts are taken to overstep these boundaries.
Contrary to Herzberg, we therefore assume a unilateral dependence of the two supply "factors". Moreover, it does not seem
appropriate to draw a parallel between shopping activities and
Maslow's self-actualisation philosophy which, in the last
analysis, is at the root of Herzberg's motivators.

Shopping for daily necessities is a continuously recurring process for the consumer. Because of this continuity, supply satisfaction cannot be equated with the settlement of needs on the
basis of a homeostatic instinct concept. It is of no interest
which "degree of saturation" consumers reached on a particular
day or whether they were perhaps annoyed by a sales assistant.
Rather, it is the perceived possibility to supply oneself
according to one's needs that is the gist of supply satisfaction.

Apart from irradiations of satisfaction with life in general,
supply satisfaction is influenced primarily by environmental
conditions; i.e., the existing structure of supply and the consumers spatial location in this structure. Incentive-based conceptions concentrate not on the satisfaction with needs but on
satisfaction with an environmental condition (Neuberger, 1974a,
p. 159). In line with the cognitive concepts, we regard social
comparisons to be essential for supply satisfaction; an individual compares his subjective cost-benefit relation with that
of reference persons (Lawler, 1973). This subjectively estimated cost-benefit relation of others represents the level of
aspiration of the individual. If the individual attains this

level a feeling of equity arises and non-attainment leads to
dissatisfaction. In contrast to equity theory (Adams, 1965), we
postulate that exceeding this level does not provoke feelings
of guilt but rather a switch to other reference persons or
groups.

Thus, the consumer's supply satisfaction is determined by the
possibility to find one's way in the supply environment which
corresponds to his particular aspirations. The aspiration level
is determined by processes of social comparison, which in turn
are responsible for changing expectations with respect to the
environment. We regard a longing for supply not as an elementary human motive, but merely as a condition for the freeing of
physical and mental energies in other spheres of life. To some
extent, supply satisfaction can be equated with the satisfaction of maintenance needs as defined by Maslow. It should be
emphasized that we intend to use the hypothetical construct of
supply satisfaction not primarily to explain shopping behavior,
but to describe consumers' "Einstellung" towards the supply
situation.

5.2. The validity of satisfaction judgments

Using expressions of satisfaction to describe the supply situation is not without problems, since such expressions are
susceptible to falsifying response sets (Pfaff, 1977) and, in
addition, depend on the prevailing situation (Smith, Kendall &
Hulin, 1969). Furthermore, satisfaction is influenced by the
particular cultural sphere and the degree of socialization.
The dynamics of the aspiration level, moreover, lead to expressions of satisfaction that have come about as a result of differing cognitive processes (cf. Bruggemann, Groskurth &
Ulich, 1975, p. 134f). If, for instance, a comparison between
the actual and the target state of affairs turns out to be
negative, resignation can lead to a lowering of the aspiration level or to a distortion of the perception of the current

state (with aspiration level being constant) to bring them into closer accord. Von Rosenstiel (1977) points out that satisfaction judgments do not speak for themselves but rather must be interpreted and evaluated in the context of the particular conditions under which they were obtained.

Even if one assumes perfect consistency between peoples' mental states and their responses to survey items, it does not follow that different ratings of supply satisfaction reflect either objectively different levels of quality or bad faith on the part of the respondents. Rather, satisfaction ratings reflect the degree of the subject's mastering of the environment as a result of habit and learning. What might appear to be a "poor" supply situation at first glance can thus be experienced as quite satisfactory if a person has become accustomed to it over the years for lack of an alternative.

By these considerations we are not trying to evade the challenging question as to whether the present trend towards mass distribution by large shopping establishments leaves the consumer more satisfied than the small shops of the past used to do. The question to be resolved is not, however, whether the supply of goods was formerly perceived more positively than it is today, but in what respects the present supply system falls short of meeting consumers' needs.

5.3. Claims for a method of measuring supply satisfaction

As we have already mentioned, supply of daily necessities, as it is perceived by consumers, represents a multi-attribute construct influenced by the consumers' perception of the supply situation itself and by certain situational household factors. Satisfaction ratings, therefore, have to be ascertained on the supply attributes which are relevant to the individual. This is why it is particularly important to determine the individual range of needs.

When using batteries of standardized items, there is always a danger that the respondents are faced with attributes that are totally irrelevant to their satisfaction and are likely to lead to an ad hoc elaboration. An elimination of variables on the basis of correlation coefficients at a later time does not do justice to attribute sets varying between individuals. The problem of obtaining an adequate representation can be resolved by giving each respondent the opportunity to generate his own set of needs by selecting attributes out of a list of conceivable items.

A similar problem arises with respect to relevance weighting. Although in a number of surveys (for a summary, cf. Neuberger, 1974a, p. 149) as well as in our own pilot study the relevance weighting of variables did not bring about any increase in concurrence between the model indices and the overall judgments, we nevertheless still consider the weighting of variables to be necessary since the equal relevance of individual supply need may not be assumed a priori. Our pilot study showed, however, that having subjects weight attributes one at a time (so-called absolute weighting) leads to nearly every attribute being rated as particularly relevant. One way to avoid this is to limit the total number of weighting points that subjects have at their disposal. Due to this usage of a constant scale sum and the possibility to select and rate only relevant attributes (relational weighting),

- only those supply attributes will be assessed and weighted that form the individual's evoked set,
- the interdependences of the attributes are made clear to the respondents,
- judgments of persons who generally consider everything to be important will become comparable with those made by persons capable of making subtle distinctions,
- each respondent will have the same resource to assert his aspirations, and
- it will be possible to rank order the supply attributes

according to respondent's preference.

The relevance vectors obtained by this method have an ipsative character (Cattell, 1944). This implies that the relational weighting reveals which supply attribute is the most important one for the individual, although it does not indicate what position it occupies on a normative scale. Moreover, the relative weightings of the supply attributes depend on the number of attributes perceived as salient, with higher average weightings being allotted in smaller sets of needs than in larger ones. This corresponds with our notion that an increase in the number of supply needs is likely to bring about a weakening of their relevance and, hence, that consumers with extensive sets of needs should not be granted a greater influence on decision-making in the supply sphere than consumers with few supply needs.

Interpersonal comparability of the relative weightings is given when one assumes that quality of supply has the same degree of significance for every consumer. The relative weightings can be totalled for consumer aggregates since all that is aimed for is a statement on the relevance of single attributes to the over-all concept of supply. In the case of the obtained satisfaction ratings, we also assume inter-attributive comparability, since the satisfaction scale employed is valid for all variables. We postulate here that differing degrees of satisfaction and dis-satisfaction can be represented on a common (bipolar) scale.

5.4. An index of supply satisfaction

Apart from the analysis of weaknesses specific to particular attributes, it would be of particular interest to determine how many and which households are dissatisfied with their general supply situation. This is not only necessary in order to render the individually perceived object of supply comparable, but it would also serve as an indicator of the extent to which actual supply situations fall short of consumers' comparison levels.

The aggregation problems arising here have already been sketch-
ed out in part 3.2. Similar to multiattribute utility theory,
we argue that the overall judgment should not be used here because the decomposition principle enables the analyst to consider more specific attitudes. Therefore, combining these by
means of a suitable mathematical model is superior to an overall judgment.

When aggregating weighted judgments, we assume that the supply
needs perceived as relevant have a compensatory relationship
to each other. It should be possible, for example, for every
consumer, even in poorly supplied areas, to do his/her shopping
at relatively low prices simply by covering longer distances.
In such a case, the consumer would be highly satisfied with the
prices asked for in shops a long way from home, but at the same
time highly dissatisfied with the distance to be covered.
Should the consumer attach more importance to distance than to
price, his/her overall judgment would be negative. On the other
hand, if he/she were very price-conscious, his/her overall judgment would be positive.

The formal structure of the ISS, based on relationally weighted attributes, is

$$ISS_i = \sum_{j \in J_i} w_{ij}\, s_{ij}$$

$$\text{with} \sum_{j \in J_i} w_{ij} = const.$$

Here: i = subject, J = object space
 j = element of the object space (attribute)
 w = relative weight of an attribute
 s = satisfaction rating

Due to the constant sum of weights, the index possesses a
definable range. If 20 weighting points and a satisfaction
scale ranging from -3 to +3 are used, the resulting index
range is 120 points. When weighted satisfaction and dissatisfaction balance, the resulting index value is zero, a point
that we define as the threshold of perceived undersupply (comp.
Figure 5.1). Fully satisfied consumers are indicated by index
values of >40. Scores between zero and forty indicate that
some desires are not being met. Consumers whose index value
indicates the existence of dissatisfaction can be subdivided
in a similar fashion.

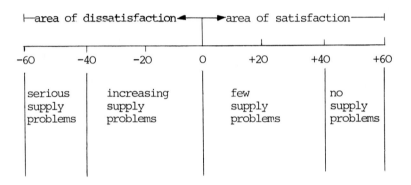

Figure 5.1. Range of the Index of Supply Satisfaction

6. Some empirical results

The judgment model presented in part 5.3 was used as a basis
for two field studies. A rural and an urban population were
selected to analyze supply satisfaction taking into account
the structure of respondents' needs and to test the sensitivity of the model described.

6.1. Design of the survey

Various differences between living conditions in urban and
rural areas led us to expect significant differences in the
purchasing behavior of the people concerned, primarily because
of the traditional difference in the structure of the retail
trade in the respective areas. In both surveys, we proceeded
from the hypothesis that differences, due to environmental
circumstances, are reflected in the extent and structure of
supply needs and in the level of supply satisfaction.

In the first survey a stratified sample of 162 subjects from
households in a district of Mannheim[3] that comprised of no less
than 64 smaller stores in an area of not more than 1 sq.km was
drawn at random. Although this district is very close to the
downtown area, access to the centre and to neighbouring districts is impeded by natural and artificial barriers (railroad
tracks, highway, river). The second sample of 188 subject represents four communities near Heidelberg, two of which with a
grocery store, one without any source of local supply and one
with two tiny stores.

While the urban population and 50 subjects of the rural sample
were interviewed personally, the bulk of the rural sample (n=
138) had to fill out a questionnaire. Nevertheless, conditions
were such that the comparability of the two samples was maintained, thus enabling us to analyse the respective data sets
together as well as apart from each other.

In order to acquaint respondents with the subject matter, they
first had to answer several questions concerning their shopping
for daily commodities. The next crucial step was the selection of individually relevant supply attributes. This was
facilitated either by having subjects select these from a deck
of cards upon which supply attributes were printed (urban

---

[3] Mannheim is an industrial city in southwestern Germany (20
km from Heidelberg) with slightly more than 300,000 inhabitants.

sample) or simply by checking the relevant attributes on a master list (rural sample). Subjects were then given 20 points to allocate to the relevant attributes according to their importance. Finally, subjects were asked to indicate their degree of satisfaction with each of the attributes which they had indicated as being relevant.

6.2. Selection of supply needs

The selection of individually relevant supply needs made by the subjects in step 1 of the procedure already enables us to draw some conclusions on the nature of supply needs. Of particular interest here are the number of supply needs selected, the frequency of selection of specific needs with respect to the two samples concerned (both overall and depending on the size of the individual set of needs), and the combination of supply needs when forming sets.

6.2.1. Size of need sets

The amount of supply needs selected displays an approximately normal distribution for both samples (see Figure 6.1., page 583).

71 % of the urban sample and 67 % of the rural sample selected between 4 and 7 supply needs, with a mode of 6 for each of the two distributions. This finding supports our initial postulate that the use of standardized attribute list discourages respondents to voice differentiated opinions and desires with regard to complex subject matters. Rather, the number of individually relevant object attributes varies greatly between subjects. Apparently, the human capacity of information processing - depending on the respondent's cognitive complexity and/or the complexity of the object of assessment - is limited to between 4 and 7 attributes (cf. Jacoby et al., 1977).

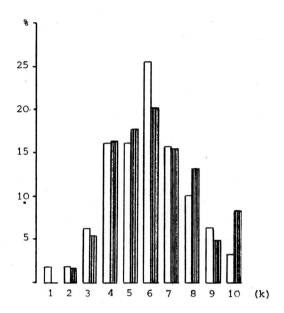

Figure 6.1. Frequency distribution of the number (k)
of supply needs picked in the urban (☐)
and the rural (▥) sample

6.2.2. The relative frequency of selection of supply needs

The frequencies with which individual supply needs were selected (see Figure 6.2. on page 584) reveal several remarkable
differences between the urban and the rural population.

The latter is more interested in utility dimensions that are
tangible and easy to operationalize, while urban residents
articulate, as it were, more subtle wants pertaining to facets
of their shopping. This comes to light with special clarity

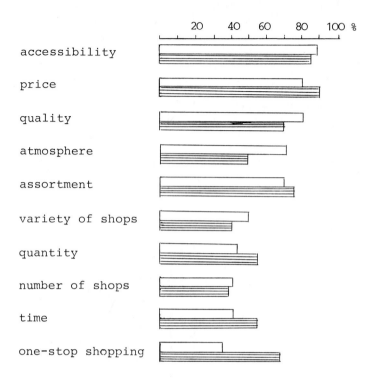

Figure 6.2. Relative frequency of selection of the supply
            needs for the urban (☐) and for the rural
            (▨) population

in the rural population's desire "to buy all daily commodities
in one store", whereas town people far more frequently expressed a desire to shop in a pleasant atmosphere.

6.2.3. The relative frequency of selection of supply needs
         within need sets of various sizes

The analysis of the relative frequencies of selection does not
take into account variations in sizes of need sets. Figure 6.3.
(see page 585) presents the observed selection frequencies f_j
of the attributes as a function of the size k of the need sets.

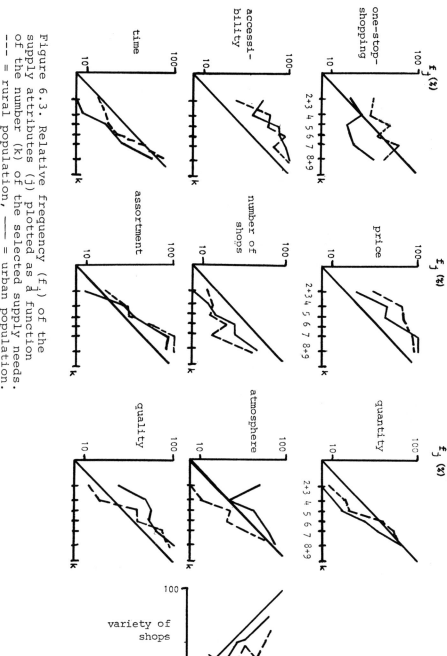

Figure 6.3. Relative frequency (f_j) of the
supply attributes (j) plotted as a function
of the number (k) of the selected supply needs.
--- = rural population, ——— = urban population.

Only two supply needs - good accessibility of stores and the
possibility to shop at low prices - appear to an extent which
is above average with both groups of the population. For the
townspeople, the same applies to shopping atmosphere and the possibility to buy good-quality goods, whereas country people
attach a great amount of importance to being able to purchase
all daily necessities in *one* store.

It would seem to be logical to speak of *basic needs* when referring to these supply needs which appear with a frequency higher
than average in small sets of needs ($k \leq 4$). Correspondingly,
those attributes which only appear with higher than average
frequency in larger sets of needs ($k \geq 4$) will be labelled as
supplementary needs. Table 6.1 summarizes the basic and supplementary needs for both samples.

Basic needs		Supplementary needs	
urban population	rural pop.	urban population	rural pop.
price quality accessibility atmosphere	price one-stop shopping accessibility assortment	assortment	quality

Table 6.1. Basic and supplementary needs for the rural and
           urban population

6.2.4. The linkage of supply needs

While the frequency with which they are selected indicates the
relevance of supply attributes, the frequency with which attribute dyads appear can serve as an indicator for their psycho-

logical nearness.

If one assumes that our respondents selected sets of attributes that typify their habitual ways of thinking, it is plausible to assume a complementary relationship for attributes that are frequently selected together.

In principle, there are numerous coefficients of association for binary variables suited to quantify the intensity of linkage of two supply attributes (cf. Böcker, 1978; Bock, 1974, p. 48ff.). We developed an invariant coefficient (L), in which the joint frequency of selection of two supply attributes j and l is normalized with respect to the frequency of selection of one of these attributes taken alone. The coefficient L can be written as follows:

$$L_{jl} = \frac{f_{jl}}{\lambda}$$

with $\lambda = \min \{f_j, f_l\}$

and $f_j, f_l > 0; \; j, l = 1, 2, \ldots, 10, \; j \neq l$

where:

f_{jl} = joint selection frequency of the supply needs j and l

f_j, f_l = absolute frequency of selection of the supply needs j and l.

This coefficient appears to be particularly suitable for our purposes because it is - due to the minimum normalization (instead of the usual normalization on the basis of the expected value) - not subject to a bias which would arise from the inclusion of all of the cases in which neither of the two supply needs was selected.

Having been quantified with the aid of the coefficient and having been assembled in a matrix, the intensities of linkage can now be investigated as to whether they possess a specific structure for both samples. For this purpose, the geometric model of non metric multidimensional scaling (Kruskal, 1964a,b)

is applicable, as it enables items (here supply attributes) to
be arranged in a spatial configuration, in which any pair of
objects (here linked supply needs) can best be represented in a
way that is directly interpretable (cf. Beals et al., 1968).
If a structure can be identified and if it can be adequately
depicted within a low-dimensional space, then the degree of
psychological nearness of the supply needs can also be visually
distinguished.

The analysis of the linkage matrices for both samples using
the MINISSA program developed by Roskam and Lingoes (1970)
yielded, with stress values of .11 (urban) and .05 (rural population), adequate fits (cf. Wagenaar & Padmos, 1971; Young,
1970) of the Euclidian distances to the ranking of the coefficients in three dimensions. Figure 6.4 (see page 589)
shows the empirical structure for the urban and the rural population.

The shorter the distance between two attributes of supply, the
stronger is the linkage between them. However, as we already
stated, there are limits to the direct visual identification
of attribute clusters in the three-dimensional space. Hierarchical cluster analysis can come to our aid here (see, also,
section 4.3.).

The dendrograms of the fusion process (see Figure 6.5, page 590)
support our assumption of the existence of inter-population
differences in patterns of linkage of needs. We consider the
linkage of the needs "low price shopping" and "shopping in
several similar stores", displayed by the urban sample, to be
particularly informative. Clearly townspeople expect competition between stores to have a positive impact on the price
level of goods. Furthermore, the desire for having a variety
of stores at their disposal and the opportunity to buy high-
quality goods are also closely linked in this group.

For the rural population, on the other hand, the need to choose
from a number of stores is not closely linked with any of the

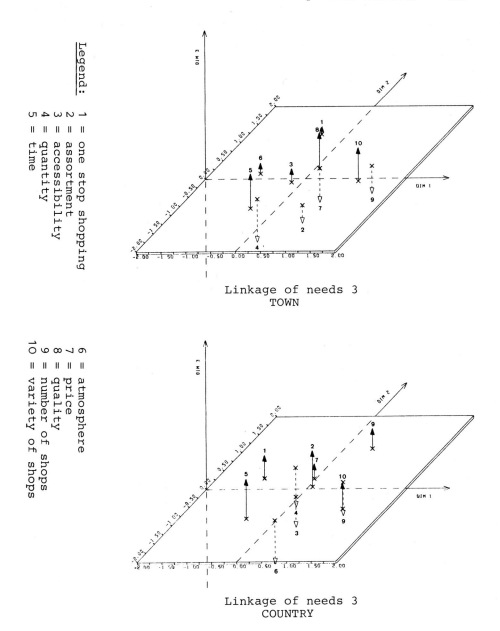

Legend:

1 = one stop shopping
2 = assortment
3 = accessibility
4 = quantity
5 = time
6 = atmosphere
7 = price
8 = quality
9 = number of shops
10 = variety of shops

Linkage of needs 3
TOWN

Linkage of needs 3
COUNTRY

Figure 6.4. Three-dimensional MINISSA representation
of the linkage of needs by the town and
country population

Legend:
—————

1 = one stop shopping
2 = assortment
3 = accessibility
4 = quantity
5 = time
6 = shopping atmosphere
7 = price
8 = quality
9 = number of stores
10 = variety of stores

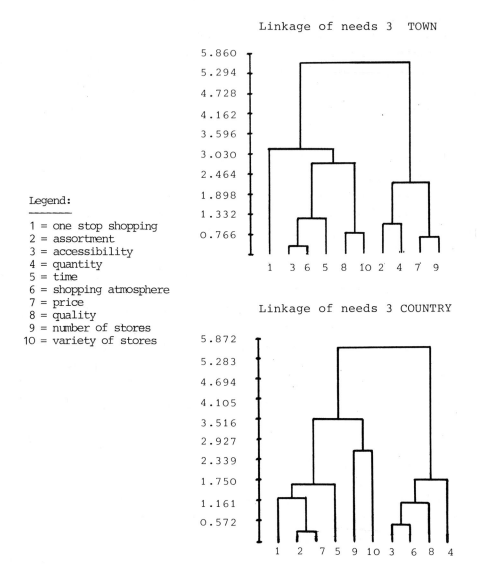

Figure 6.5. Dendrogram of the hierarchical cluster
analysis for town and country population

other supply attributes. Rather, the linkage between one-stop
shopping, a wide range of goods and low prices serves as evidence for the rural population's preference for large shopping
establishments. Common to both population groups is the linkage of pleasant shopping atmosphere and easy accessibility of
stores. In the case of the town population this is complemented
by a desire for store opening hours fitted to their particular
needs.

This finding suggests that when subjects express the need for
a pleasant shopping atmosphere, they are not only thinking in
terms of store climate (e.g. friendliness of the sales personnel, hygiene, presentation of goods, etc.) but are also thinking of their monetary efficiency of shopping with respect to
the expenditure of effort (e.g. costs for the coverage of the
distance to the store, for the parking space etc.). It also
must be questioned whether the concept of quality means the
same thing to both population groups. For instance, one could
imagine that the rural population fancies more traditional
items whereas the urban population longs for slightly unusual
goods usually to be found in specialised stores. In order to
back up this assumption it will, however, be necessary to establish a content oriented definition of the quality aspect in
a follow-up study.

6.3.1. Intensity of supply needs

As a measure of intensity (I) we used the proportion of weighting points allotted to a given attribute (j) relative to the
total number of points allotted in each sample.

$$I_j = \frac{\sum\limits_{i} w_{ij}}{\sum\limits_{j} \sum\limits_{i} w_{ij}} \; 100 \; [\%]$$

j = 1,2,...,10 (attributes).

i = 1,2,...,n (persons)

w = weighting

Figure 6.6 (see page 593) illustrates the intensity of the
various supply attributes for the urban and the rural population.

If the attributes attaining a proportion of at least 10% in
both samples are arranged according to the actual percentages
observed, the result shown in Table 6.2 is obtained.

urban population		rural population	
need	intensity (in %)	need	intensity (in %)
price	17.8	price	20.6
quality	16.6	accessibility	15.8
accessibility	15.4	one-stop shopping	12.7
assortment	11.3	assortment	12.3
atmosphere	11.0	quality	10.5
	72.1		71.9

Table 6.2. Lists of priorities with respect to supply for
the urban and the rural population

Comparison of both priority lists, in which 72% of the weighting points were allotted in each case to the five needs listed
in Table 6.1, supports the finding mentioned above (see 6.2.2.).
For the rural population, the rational component of the acquisition of goods plays a more important role than for the urban
population.

While the rural respondents view one-stop shopping more important than product quality, the urban population attributes to
this item an intensity of only 5.6%, well below the 10% barrier.
In contrast, the rural population appears to place far less
value on a "pleasant shopping atmosphere" (5.4%) than the urban
population (11%). Surprisingly, there is only little desire for

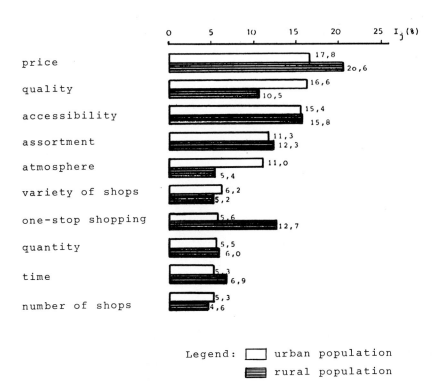

price   17,8
                20,6

quality   16,6
                10,5

accessibility   15,4
                15,8

assortment   11,3
                12,3

atmosphere   11,0
                5,4

variety of shops   6,2
                   5,2

one-stop shopping 5,6
                   12,7

quantity   5,5
                6,0

time   5,3
                6,9

number of shops 5,3
                4,6

Legend: ☐ urban population
         ▤ rural population

Figure 6.6. Proportions I_j of the supply needs j
relative to the total number of
weighting points

the availability of a variety of stores and for easy accessibility of stores in the sense of longer opening hours in both
groups.

6.3.2. The intensity of the supply needs in different sized
need sets

Due to the procedure employed here, weightings of elements in
small attribute sets have a greater impact on the measure of
intensity I_j than weightings of elements in large attribute
sets. The question arises, therefore, as to whether attributes
vary in intensity depending on the size, k, of the attribute
set. In order to answer this question, we divided each sample
into three groups according to the size of the attribute set
(small: $2 \leq k \leq 4$; medium: $5 \leq k \leq 7$; large: $8 \leq k \leq 10$). Table 6.3 (see
page 595) shows the intensities found for each group.

It can be seen that easy accessibility of stores and the need
for stores with extremely low prices are, by and large, independent both of set size and sample. On the other hand, the
possibility for buying daily commodities of high quality, which
is always fairly important to the urban population, comes to
the fore in the case of the country people only with increasing
size of the set of needs (see also section 6.2.2.).

The low weights assigned to the so-called weak supply attributes were not affected by set size or type of population.
With an increasing number of needs voiced, availability of
goods in any quantity desired (e.g. package sizes suited to
consumers' needs) and store opening hours gain slightly in
importance.

A method of metric preference analysis was used to analyze
(according to set size) the differences in needs between the
rural and urban populations. The method represents subjects
(the 5 segments shown in Table 6.4) and stimuli (the supply
attributes) in a joint space.

supply needs	Segment 1: 2 ≤ k ≤ 4		Segment 2: 5 ≤ k ≤ 7		Segment 3: 8 ≤ k ≤ 10	
	S_1 (n=39)	L_1 (n=43)	S_2 (n=89)	L_2 (n=95)	S_3 (n=31)	L_3 (n=48)
One-stop shopping	⑥ 5,5	③ 16,2	⑨ 5,0	③ 13,1	⑩ 4,8	⑤ 8,6
assortment	⑤ 8,6	④ 11,4	④ 13,0	④ 12,7	④ 10,6	④ 12,2
accessibility	② 19,0	② 18,7	③ 15,1	② 15,7	③ 13,2	② 13,4
quantity	⑧ 4,6	⑨ 3,4	⑩ 4,9	⑥ 6,4	⑦ 8,5	⑧ 7,4
time	⑩ 1,4	⑥ 6,4	⑦ 5,7	⑦ 6,3	⑥ 9,3	⑥ 8,4
atmosphere	④ 14,5	⑩ 1,7	⑤ 10,3	⑧ 5,8	⑤ 9,7	⑦ 7,8
price	③ 18,7	① 23,7	① 17,9	① 21,0	① 15,0	① 17,1
quality	① 19,5	⑧ 5,9	② 15,6	⑤ 11,6	② 14,0	③ 12,4
number of shops	⑨ 3,2	⑦ 4,2	⑧ 5,4	⑨ 3,7	⑧ 8,1	⑨ 6,7
variety of shops	⑦ 5,0	⑤ 7,8	⑥ 6,7	⑩ 3,6	⑨ 7,1	⑩ 6,0
Sum	100,0	99,4	99,6	99,9	100,3	100,0

Table 6.3. Intensity I of the supply needs j depending on the size k of the need set

(S = urban population, L = rural population;
O = rank of intensity of the supply need)

The MDPREF program developed by Carroll and Chang (1969) con-
verts an intensity matrix as given in Figure 6.7 (see page 597)
into a metric point vector representation, with individual supply attributes being displayed as points and the subject groups
as vectors in a common space. The projections of the facets of
supply onto the respective segment vectors serve as the best
possible representation of the intensity of needs of each segment. The numerical values given in brackets after the segment
vectors indicate the range of size of the attribute sets. The
variance accounted for by the two-component solution is approximately 95%.

The three vectors representing the urban segments are all situa-
ted in the fourth quadrant and, moreover, are less dispersed
than the rural segments located in the first quadrant. The most
substantial differences in intensity appear between the rural
segment with only modest supply requirements (2-4 needs) and
the town segment with the widest range of requirements (8-10
needs). Thus, the first-mentioned group rates the feasibility
of one-stop shopping as the attribute which is number 3 in line,
whereas this attribute is rather unimportant to the latter. The
latter group, however, rates high quality of goods and a pleasant shopping atmosphere as far more important than the former
is inclined to do.

6.3.3. Classification of consumers according to their judgments of relevance

The intensity measure of the ten supply attributes suggests
that need priorities are on the whole almost identical for the
two respondent populations (see Table 6.2). It is impossible,
however, to deduce from this measure whether the attribute
weightings were consistent over the entire population of respondents or whether the respondents varied among themselves,
some evaluating a given attribute as being highly relevant
while others evaluating the same attribute as being irrelevant.

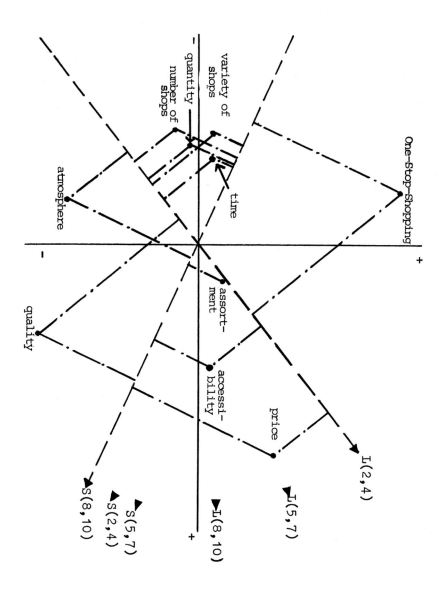

Figure 6.7. MDPREF representation of supply attributes
            and consumer segments with need sets of
            different sizes

            (L = rural sample, S = urban sample)

In addition, it seems reasonable to assume that various attributes compensate each other to a certain extent, a high weight for one leading to a low weight for the other one. This would be the case, for example, if respondents were found to attribute either "easy accessibility of stores" or "low prices" (but not both) a high relevance. This kind of dependence between attributes no doubt has a levelling effect on the intensity measure and thus bears upon its utilization.

We shall address the following two questions with respect to the judgments of relevance:
1) How similar are the relevance profiles of the individual attributes of supply when considered over all subjects, and can trade-offs between them be established?
2) Is it possible to distinguish between consumer segments by means of relevance profiles and can these segments then be identified by means of socio-demographic data?

6.3.3.1. Relevance profiles of the supply needs

Subjects' relevance weightings for the selected attributes can be thought of as constituting the attributes' "relevance profiles". The latter, in turn, can be compared with one another with respect to profile similarity (cf. Beeskow, 1979).

We assume here that:
- profiles can be represented in a reduced space as points,
- points which lie close to each other represent similar profiles, and
- changing values of the coordinates in this space lead to a continuous change of the corresponding profiles.

The program PARAMAP (Shepard & Carroll, 1966), which meets these assumptions, was used to parametrically represent the relevance profiles[4]. This method may be described as a non-

_____

[4] For a detailed discussion of the procedure see Carroll (1972).

metric factor analysis. It enables the analyst to reduce the
size of the data set far more radically than it would be possible by means of a linear factor analysis procedure, especially when there are strong linear or non-monotonic relations between variables. In addition, PARAMAP is, in principle (cf. Ca-
roll, 1972), able to uncover at least the topological properties
of the structure underlying subjects' relevance ratings about
as well as a multidimensional scaling of similarity judgments[5].

The results presented in Figure 6.8 (see page 600) yielded
"badness-of-fit" values of 1.045 and 1.025, respectively, for
the urban and the rural populations. With a theoretical minimum of 1.00, these figures can be regarded as very good.

The interpretation of configurations will be restricted to the
five supply needs which are evaluated as especially relevant
as regards their overall intensity (comp. part 6.3). The distances between these attributes portrayed in a two-dimensional
space reveal that urban people tend to attach importance either
to easy accessibility of shops and low prices or to shopping
atmosphere and good-quality products. The fairly central position occupied by the attribute "assortment" in the PARAMAP
solutions for both samples indicates that this need is fairly
balanced with regard to the other needs under consideration.

Differences in the weightings of both population groups occur
insofar as the rural population does not link the desire for
low prices with easy accessibility of shops, the country people
evidently being aware that it would be unrealistic in their
environmental circumstances to demand easy accessibility and
low prices at the same time. Their judgments reveal, instead,

_____

[5] It will be recalled that subjects were allowed to select those
supply attributes that they found relevant for themselves and
that the resulting attribute sets varied in size. In order to
apply PARAMAP (which is based on the comparison of squared non-
euklidean-distances) to this data, we assigned a zero weighting to any attributes not selected. Though this would result
in inflated correlation coefficients in linear factor analysis
procedures, PARAMAP remains unaffected.

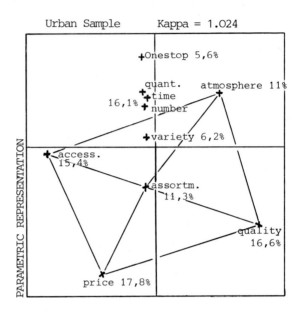

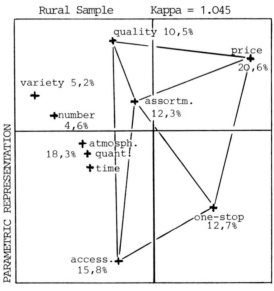

Figure 6.8. PARAMAP-representation of supply needs
and of their intensity at a urban and
a rural sample

an association of low price level and one-stop shopping, a
combination which materialises in the shopping centre out "in
the middle of nowhere." The ideal for the country population
seems to be the possibility to buy any daily commodities in a
single store that is easy to reach and that offers goods at
reasonable prices (see also section 6.2.4).

6.3.3.2. Classification of consumers on the basis of similar relevance vectors

After analysing the relevance profiles of the ten supply attributes (R-analysis), we next investigated (in the sense of a Q-
analysis) the relevance vectors of the urban and rural respondents. Our aim was to group consumers, who could be characterised by their relevance vectors, into homogeneous and clear-cut
classes on the basis of a suitable distance measure, and by
means of hierarchical cluster analysis.

Since an a priori standardization is afforded by the fixed sum
of weights, the individual relevance vectors were directly comparable. As a measure of dissimilarity of relevance vectors, we
chose the Euclidean distance. Accordingly, the following holds
for two consumers A and B with the relevance vectors being X_A
and X_B:

$$d_{AB} = \left[\sum_{j=1}^{10} (x_{jA} - x_{jB})^2 \right]^{1/2}$$

The classification of the consumers was carried out according
to Ward's (1963) method, which uses the within-group variance
as the criterion for fusing two classes. Figure 6.9 (see page
602) shows the dendrogram resulting from this fusion process
for the town population.

The increasing within-group-variance with mounting aggregation
level calls for a limitation of the interpretation to the six
and five group solutions for the urban and rural samples, respectively. In Tables 6.4 and 6.5 (see pages 603 and 604) the
average relevance vectors of the ten supply needs in the six

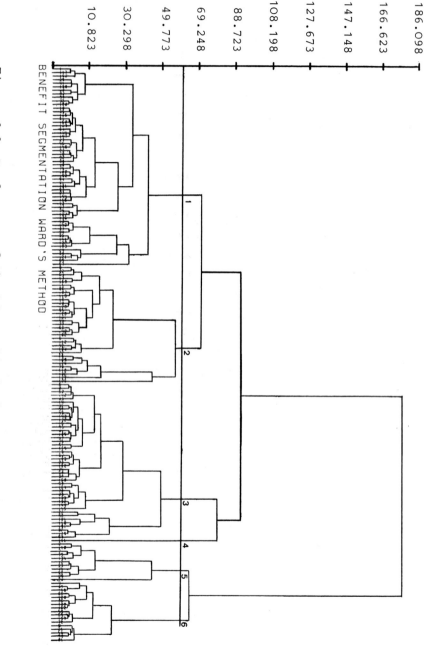

Figure 6.9. Dendrogram of the hierarchical cluster analysis
of the urban population

No.	supply need	Mean of the relevance weightings segment						
		I (n=56)	II (n=33)	III (n=44)	IV (n=1)	V (n=1)	VI (n=17)	total
1	one stop shopping	1.37	0.48	1.06	20.00	0.00	1.35	1.12
2	assortment	2.94	2.87	1.20		4.70	0.00	2.25
3	accessibility	3.30	2.36	3.29		1.70	4.23	3.08
4	quantity	0.69	1.72	1.52		1.09	0.11	1.09
5	time	0.65	0.51	2.36		1.09	0.11	1.05
6	atmosphere	1.57	0.72	2.96		1.70	5.58	2.20
7	price	5.12	4.96	2.68		0.12	0.41	3.56
8	quality	3.50	1.30	2.58		7.00	6.35	3.31
9	number of shops	0.33	2.39	1.34		0.93	0.23	1.05
10	variety of shops	0.51	2.63	1.00		1.54	1.48	1.24

Table 6.4. Average relevance weightings of the supply needs for various segments of the town population formed according to similar weighting vestors.

		Mean of the relevance weightings					
		segment					
No.	supply need	I (n=39)	II (n=67)	III (n=17)	IV (n=45)	V (n=20)	total
1	one stop shopping	0.82	2.04	1.00	5.82	1.15	2.50
2	assortment	2.58	2.44	4.29	2.06	1.30	2.43
3	accessibility	2.20	3.22	1.70	3.06	6.00	3.13
4	quantity	1.12	1.01	1.35	1.26	1.50	1.18
5	time	1.38	0.85	0.64	1.42	3.50	1.36
6	atmosphere	1.30	1.47	0.35	0.48	1.15	1.06
7	price	2.25	4.70	7.64	4.46	1.65	4.07
8	quality	2.23	3.23	0.94	0.66	2.00	2.07
9	number of shops	1.92	0.58	1.64	0.48	0.35	0.90
10	variety of shops	3.12	0.44	0.41	0.20	1.25	1.02

Table 6.5.   Average relevance weightings of the supply needs for various segments of the country population formed according to similar weighting vectors

town and five country segments are presented.

Ignoring cluster VI for the urban sample (which consists of only one respondent), we are in a position to identify nicely separated consumer segments in spite of the high level of aggregation in both population groups. Their weighting behavior indicates once again the existence of trade-offs between individual attributes of supply (as discussed above in section 6.3.3.1.).

For both populations our interpretation will be restricted to three segments and the five most heavily weighted attributes. The average relevance vectors together with the relevance vector of the whole sample are presented in Figure 6.10 (see page 606).

Comparison of the vectors for the urban segments II, V and VI confirms the finding that the importance attached to the qualitative aspects "pleasant shopping atmosphere" and "high quality of goods" varies inversely with that attached to "low price level." Contrary to our findings above (section 6.3.3.), however, there is no correlation to be observed at this level of aggregation between "easy accessibility of stores" and "low price level", with accessibility being allocated about the same weights by each urban segment. Comparison of the segments V and VI, on the other hand, confirms the largely independent nature of the need for a wide range of goods. For the rural sample, and particularly for the comparison between segments III and V, the expected trade-off between low prices and easy accessibility of stores is rather evident. Whereas segment III links its strong need for low prices most closely to that for a wide range of goods (which it would like to see realised in a number of similar stores), segment VI, which also puts an above average stress on the price aspect, would prefer to purchase all of its daily commodities under one roof.

Attempts to describe cluster segments by means of demographic data are not often successful (cf. Böhler, 1977). As for us,

Urban population

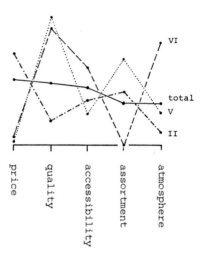

Rural population

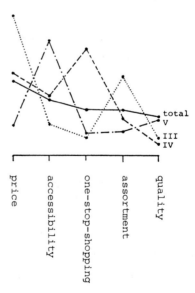

Figure 6.10. Weighting profiles of selected segments and the average profile for the urban and rural populations.

we could not establish any remarkable difference between clusters with respect to variables such as sex, education, occupation, and shopping activity. Segments V and VI of the
urban sample, both of which place greatest emphasis on the
quality aspect, had the highest average age and the highest (V)
and lowest (VI) income, respectively. In contrast, the members
of the price-oriented segment II were of low average age. In
the rural sample, too, the consumers with a remarkable price-
orientation (III) were among the youngest. The rural segment V
resembled urban segment VI in the following respect: Though its
members were the oldest and had the lowest income, they were
not at all price-oriented; instead, they believed that the
greatest benefit could be gained by easy accessibility of
stores and greater flexibility with regard to store opening
hours.

6.4. Satisfaction with supply

The structuring of consumer supply needs cannot by itself provide a basis for drawing conclusions concerning the extent to
which these needs are satisfied, since subjects' responses to
our questions might have been motivated in various ways. The
relevance weights, for example, could have been allotted either
on the basis of a striving towards security or on the basis of
a perception of deficiency (cf. Beeskow & Finck, 1979). In order
to get an idea as to how the respondents are satisfied with
their respective supply situations, we need to consider the
information contained in the satisfaction judgments with respect to individual attributes.

The ratings given by the rural population illustrate that satisfaction judgments only make sense for attributes which enter
into an individual's cognitive representation of the object
under investigation. One part of the 138 subjects who answered
questionnaires gave judgments on satisfaction on all supply
attributes irrespective of the fact whether these were of any

relevance to them or not. For six out of ten attributes, those
subjects to whom an attribute was irrelevant used the scale
point marking indifference (neither satisfied nor dissatisfied)
far more frequently than those to whom the attribute was relevant (chi square; $\alpha=.05$). The same trend is also reflected by
the mean values of the judgments on satisfaction; whereas the
figure for the relevant attributes was 5.11, a mean of 3.66
applied to the irrelevant attributes which is not far from the
value of indifference which is 4.00.

6.4.1. Deficiencies in supply

By breaking down supply satisfaction into its determining factors, it was possible to ascertain in detail the weak points in
respondents' supply situation. An analysis of the mere satisfaction ratings for the urban and the rural sample yielded
significant differences for 6 out of 10 supply attributes ($\alpha=$
.05; see Figure 6.11, page 609.

It can be seen that the rural population is less satisfied than
its urban counterpart with respect to almost all supply needs.
In particular, their less favorable response to the accessibility of stores indicates that the objectively larger distances
covered by the rural population when shopping (Finck &
Niedetzky, 1979) find their expression in the satisfaction ratings. The difference existing between the urban and the rural
population is, however, less than one would expect on the basis
of studies on supply which use only objective indicators (cf.
Dichtl et al., 1978a).

Looking at the means of the satisfaction ratings does not suffice to detect the type and the possible extent of perceived
supply deficits. It is necessary, rather, to take into account
the particular relevance of each variable as it is reflected in
its relevance weighting. Thus, small satisfaction deficits with
deficits with attributes that constitute an essential part of
the supply situation must be weighted against higher satisfac-

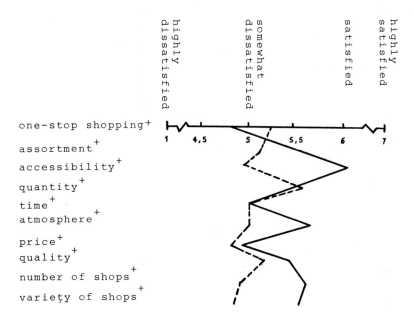

one-stop shopping[+]

assortment[+]

accessibility[+]

quantity[+]

time[+]

atmosphere[+]

price[+]

quality[+]

number of shops[+]

variety of shops[+]

Legend:

————— urban

- - - - - rural

[+]: significant
   mean differences
   (p< .05)

Figure 6.11. Comparison of the satisfaction profiles of the
            urban and rural populations with supply of daily
            commodities

tion deficits for attributes that are relevant only for a
minority. The following indicator was developed for analyzing
the satisfaction deficits (SD) of sub-samples or segment(s)
with a view to being able to identify the supply attributes for
these.

With respect to an ideal state of complete satisfaction with a
deficit of zero, this deficit amounts to 31.9% and 25.5% for

the rural and the urban population, respectively. The extent
to which single attributes are responsible for these (deficit)
states can be taken from Table 6.6 (see page 611).

Deficit Formula

$$SD_s = \frac{\sum\limits_{j=1}^{m} (s_{max} - \bar{s}_j) \cdot \bar{w}_j{'}}{s_{max} \sum\limits_{j=1}^{m} w_j} \cdot 100\%$$

Where:

s_{max} = maximum satisfaction value on a transformed satisfaction scale ranging from 0 to 6

$\bar{s}_j$ = average satisfaction value for attribute j over all respondents if j is selected

$\bar{w}_j{'}$ = average weighting of the attribute j over all respondents in segment s

$\sum\limits_{j=1}^{m} w_j$ = constant (20)

j = attribute (j=1,2,...,10)

The type of aggregated analysis carried out here yields a pattern of findings that may be taken as the ordinal analogue to
the simple frequency counts presented in Figure 6.2 above.
Though shortcomings with respect to "good value" shopping makes
the largest contribution to the satisfaction deficits for both
populations, the urban population considers this to be less
serious by 16.3% than does the rural population. For the former,
on the other hand, the deficit regarding the availability of
high quality goods is, in absolute terms, 33% larger than for
the consumers living out in the country.

The urban households investigated are in a position to choose
between a number of different types of local stores, an option
not open to the rural population. Since, in 63.3% of the rural

| Supply attribute | contribution to supply deficit | |
	rural population (in % of total deficit)	urban population (in % of total deficit)
price	22.7 (1)	23.7 (1)
accessibility	16.8 (2)	9.1 (4)
assortment	11.8 (3)	10.7 (3)
one-stop shopping	11.4 (4)	8.3 (6)
quality	10.0 (5)	16.7 (2)
time	7.1 (6)	6.8 (7)
variety of stores	5.7 (7)	5.7 (8)
atmosphere	5.2 (8)	8.8 (5)
number of stores	4.9 (9)	4.9 (10)
quantity	4.4 (10)	5.3 (9)
total deficit	31.9	25.5

Table 6.6. Relative proportions of the supply attributes
           to the perceived supply deficit (including
           ranking of the problem variables)

households, at least one member of the family works outside the
village, we might reason that members of these commuter households are more satisfied with their supply situation than members of households with stronger ties to their village,
especially as 83.2% of the commuters happened to do regularly
at least part of their shopping outside the village. The data
show, however, that the satisfaction deficit is considerably
higher (34.1%) with the commuter households than with the non-
commuter households (27.7%). Further segmentation of the commuter households according to the frequency with which shopping
is done on the way to or from work, and of the non-commuter
households according to whether or not a car is available for

shopping purposes, yield results as shown in Table 6.7 (see page 613).

This analysis can be put into perspective by considering the following hypothesis: greater mobility - whether job-linked or not - goes in hand with an increase in personal experience and, thus, causes a rise in the level of aspiration. This, in turn, increases the satisfaction deficit. Conversely, the more people manage to overcome spatial and temporal restrictions so as to enable them to patronize more attractive shopping outlets outside the village, the smaller will be the satisfaction deficit.

How far age per se causes a lowering of the level of aspiration cannot be causally inferred from the data. It may be assumed, however, that old age is connected with lesser mobility and that this fact, in turn, limits exposure to new experiences that could push up the level of aspiration. A comparison of the size of the satisfaction deficit and the age of motorised urban respondents (SD = 22.9%, average age = 42.7 years, n = 93) and non-motorised urban respondents (SD = 20.0%, average age = 58.8 years, n = 69) supports this assumption to a fairly large extent. From the results shown in Table 6.8 (see page 614) we can see that the joint effects of low mobility and old age lead to an increase in respondents' supply satisfaction.

According to these results, households of pensioners with no car at their disposal display the lowest satisfaction deficit. Since the number of pensioners with cars in our sample was small, we cannot be sure whether the deficit in these households, as Table 6.8 suggests, is at a level comparable to that of non-pensioner households. If this last finding is reliable, it seems due to problems regarding the availability of high quality goods which is considered to be more important than the price aspect, otherwise dominant.

segment	n	⌀ age (in years)	supply deficit (in %)	problem variables (proportion > 10% of supply deficit in %)
commuter households				
– no linking of shopping and journey to work	20	43.1	37.5	1.price (19.4) 2.accessibility (18.6) 3.assortment (13.5) 4.time (12.3)
– infrequent linkage	47	42.0	33.9	1.price (24.5) 2.accessibility (18.6) 3.assortment (12.0) 4.one-stop shop. (11.5) 5.quality (10.4)
– frequent linkage	40	38.8	31.3	1.price (25.8) 2.accessibility (14.7) 3.assortment (13.2) 4.quality (11.7) 5.one-stop shop. (10.1)
non commuter households				
– with car	26	58.8	33.7	1.price (24.2) 2.accessibility (15.2) 3.one-stop shop. (13.3) 4.quality (12.1)
– without car	43	70.0	22.9	1.accessibility (21.8) 2.price (17.7) 3.one-stop shop. (12.0)

Table 6.7. Supply deficits and problem variables for five segments of the rural population

segment	n	⌀ age (in years)	supply deficit (in %)	problem variables (proportion > 10% of supply deficit in %)	
non pensioner households (total)	119	42.8	23.7	1.price 2.quality 3.assortment	(24.7) (15.5) (10.2)
– with car	84	39.9	23.4	1.price 2.quality 3.assortment	(26.1) (25.7) (10.4)
– without car	35	49.6	24.7	1.price 2.quality 3.atmosphere 4.one-stop shop.	(21.4) (15.0) (12.5) (10.1)
pensioner households (total)	43	68.1	16.5	1.price 2.quality 3.assortment	(21.4) (19.5) (12.4)
– with car	9	67.4	24.3	1.quality 2.assortment 3.variety of shops 4.price	(28.4) (19.6) (16.4) (11.4)
– without car	34	68.3	15.4	1.price 2.quality 3.atmosphere 4.assortment	(23.0) (18.9) (10.9) (10.7)

Table 6.8. Supply deficits and problem variables for four
segments of the urban population

6.4.2. Pinpointing differences by means of the supply
satisfaction index

The a priori segmentation of the sample of respondents by means
of socio-demographic data permits only comparatively general
statements on variation of supply satisfaction to be made. The
index discussed in section 5.4 tells us something, however, on
how many households conceive themselves as being undersupplied.
The distribution of individual satisfaction indices given in
Figure 6.12 (see page 616) indicates, first of all, that the
proportion of consumers who claim to have no supply problems
at all (see, for comparison, Figure 5.1) is much larger with
the urban population (43.2%) than with the rural one (33.0%).
More serious supply problems (ISS $\leq$ 0) seem to exist for 20.2%
of the rural population and for 13.6% of the urban population
according to the respective indices.

Because of the fact that the index is of a compensatory nature
and one-dimensional, it is not possible to infer the existence
of particular supply problems from the index values. The size
of the contribution of the variables to the supply deficit,
which is given separately for each sample (cf. Table 6.6), can
have an impact of considerable variance on low or high ISS
values. The main point of interest is to determine which supply
attributes are primarily responsible for low index values and
whether there are household or personality variables which are
closely related to high or low index values.

6.4.2.1. Variables responsible for more serious supply
problems

In order to identify those variables primarily responsible for
low ISS values, each sample was split into two groups of respondents, one with ISS scores less than or equal to zero and
the other one with scores larger than or equal to forty. The
satisfaction deficits for the groups with negative ISS values

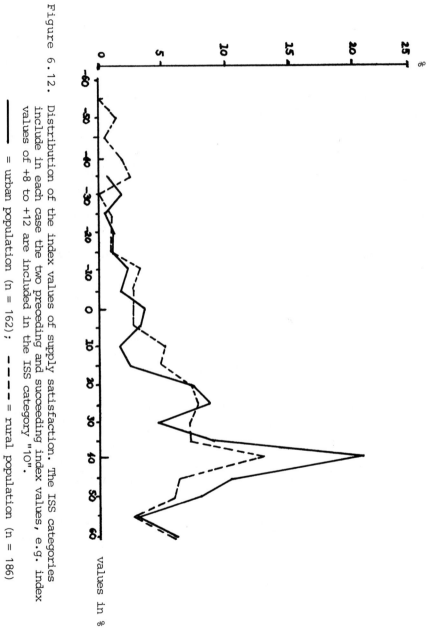

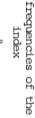

Figure 6.12. Distribution of the index values of supply satisfaction. The ISS categories
include in each case the two preceding and succeeding index values, e.g. index
values of +8 to +12 are included in the ISS category "10".

———— = urban population (n = 162); ― ― ― ― = rural population (n = 186)

were 3.2 (urban population) and 4.5 (rural population) times
those of the groups with high ISS scores in the urban and the
rural population, respectively. A comparison of the satisfaction deficits specific to particular attributes for the two
contrasting urban groups revealed that one-stop shopping, store
opening hours and the range of goods carried have a disproportionate effect on the latter group's dissatisfaction. For rural
households, dissatisfaction was found to centre around distance,
prices and the range of good available. For the low ISS groups
in the urban and rural populations these "problem" variables
accounted for 37.7% and 48.8% of the total satisfaction deficit,
respectively.

The average ISS values for the inhabitants of the four villages
express clearly that the ISS score not only reflects the
existence of subjective supply problems but also corresponds to
conditions of supply measured in an objective manner: While the
mean ISS values for the three villages with shopping facilities
at their disposal spread between 21.2 and 24.3, that for the
village without a shop amounts to only 9.8.

6.4.2.2. Identifying subjectively undersupplied consumers

Just as we pinpointed the variables essentially responsible for
the existence of dissatisfaction with supply conditions, we can
also establish whether dissatisfaction is influenced by certain
household factors. If so, readily observable characteristics
could serve as indicators of supply satisfaction, and social
policies suited to maximize such satisfaction could be developed. Using Chi square tests, we examined whether there are socio-
demographic characteristics which are significantly connected
with membership of one of the two contrasting ISS groups. We
were unable, however, to establish such connections for either
of the two populations.

Postulating that the extent of supply satisfaction is not only
a result of the supply conditions but also determined by what

people are accustomed to, we looked into possible connections
between the length of time the respondents had lived at their
present place and the value of the ISS. For the urban population the ISS values of the "inhabitants of long standing"
(those residing there since 1960 and earlier) and "new arrivals"
(those living in the town since 1975) showed an appreciable difference (α=.05), whereas the difference for the rural population just failed to reach the 5% level of significance. We were
thus led to conclude that supply satisfaction increases inas-
much as people accommodate to the environment, part of which
being shopping conditions. We also noticed, however, that
length of residency was confounded with age of the respondent
and, therefore, repeated the analysis holding the latter constant. Partial correlation analysis correcting for age resulted
in an r-score relating residency and satisfaction with supply
of 0.04. This suggested that our original hypotheses had to be
rejected. The key co-variate is not the extent to which people
are accustomed to existing conditions of supply, but rather
their age.

Positive correlations between ISS and age were found for both
population groups (r_{town} = .32; $r_{country}$ = .19; α = .001).
Obviously the level of aspiration with respect to the availability of daily commodities either decreases with age or is
adjusted in accordance with previous experience. The widely
held contention that elderly people regard themselves as being
underprivileged in modern consumer society cannot be supported
by these results, at least not in this simplified form. Thus,
the comparatively low scores (see also the benefit segments in
section 6.3.3.2.) indicate once more that the elderly should
not be regarded as a homogeneous group of the population. In
order to get more precise results, this segment should be
further subdivided according to the particular angle of investigation.

6.4.3. The adequacy of the index of supply satisfaction

It will be recalled that respondents' overall judgments on
satisfaction (OS) measured on a 12-point scale ranging from
"strongly dissatisfied" to "strongly satisfied" served as
criterion for assessing the validity of the ISS. With $r_{OS/ISS}$ =
.41 for the urban and $r_{OS/ISS}$ = .44 for the rural sample, the
correlation coefficients for the present study reach levels
attained in the pilot study, even though in the latter we pursued a different measurement approach. In contrast to the pilot
study, however, neglecting relational weights when aggregating
the individual judgments does not yield an increase in the correlation coefficients. We assume that the factors having the
greatest influence on the ISS's goodness of fit are the number
of individual attributes selected and weighted and the order in
which the overall attribute judgments are made. Using the data
of the urban respondents we checked upon the influence exerted
by the number of attributes weighted and found evidence for a
U-shaped relationship (see Figure 6.13).

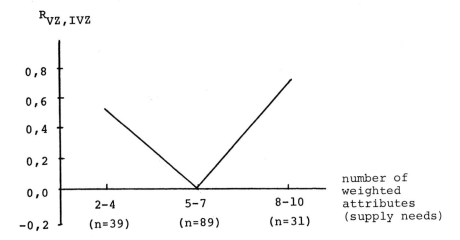

Figure 6.13. Correlation coefficients between overall satisfaction (OS) and the Index of Supply Satisfaction
(ISS) as a function of the number of weighted supply needs (urban sample)

While it seems reasonable to expect that the fewer attributes
there are, the more easily they can be integrated to form an
overall judgment (cf. Miller, 1956; Jacoby, 1977), the fact
that correlations again increase when attribute sets are larger
is, at first glance, puzzling, since consumers with large attribute sets have the most (i.e., 8-10 attributes) information to
process. In our view, the reason for this second rise in the
size of the correlation coefficient lies in our having limited
the number of weighting points available to a fixed sum of 20.
As the attribute sets increase in size, the relevance weightings act more and more like constants, thus reducing the amount
of information which subjects actually have to process. It remains to be seen, however, whether this pattern still holds
when the degree of freedom increases by raising the sum of
points to be allotted.

In order to control a conceivable effect resulting from the
sequence of the questions when measuring attribute and overall
satisfaction, three types of questionnaires were administered to
different subgroups of the urban sample:

type 1: The overall judgment had to be made *directly before* the
        judgments on attributes.

type 2: The overall judgments had to be made *directly after* the
        judgments on attributes.

type 3: The overall judgment had to be made *some time after* (20
        minutes later) the judgments on attributes.

Figure 6.14 (see page 621) shows how the sequence of questions
affected the degree of correspondence between the overall judgment and the index calculated from the judgments on specific
attributes. The higher concurrence in sequences 2 and 3 (in
which the overall judgment follows the judgments on attributes)
is most likely due to the fact that respondents become increasingly aware of the number of facets to be considered in their
judgment as a result of the breaking down of the supply construct into single attributes, while the slight decrease in
sequence 3 may result from forgetting the given judgments on

attributes during the 20-minute interval.

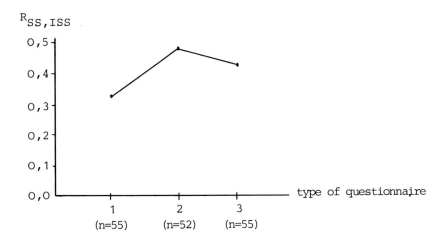

Figure 6.14. Correlation coefficients between overall satisfac-
            tion (OS) and the Index of Supply Satisfaction
            (ISS) as a function of the three types of question-
            naire (urban sample).

The size of the correlation coefficients does not shed any
light on the extent and direction of the difference between
overall judgment and ISS values aggregated from judgments on
attributes. We, therefore, re-coded the scale points used in
measuring overall satisfaction into corresponding intervals of
ISS values (see Table 6.9 on page 622).

For the 45.8% of the urban and the rural respondents together,
the overall judgment and ISS value fall into corresponding categories. In 29.1% of the cases the category for the ISS value is
lower than the one for the overall judgment, and for the 25.1%
it is higher. In only 6.1% of the cases was there a discrepancy
of two categories, and in no case was there a discrepancy of
more than two categories.

Scale points of the overall judgment	ISS intervals	Category
1,2	[-60,-40]	serious supply problems
3,4,5,6	[-39, 0]	less serious supply problems
7,8,9,10	[1, 39]	slight supply problems
11,12	[40, 60]	no supply problems

Table 6.9. Scale points of the overall judgment and corresponding intervals of ISS values

6.5. Evaluation of the research carried out and future prospects

In closing, we would like to comment on our findings both from a methodological point of view and with regard to the contents. A certain amount of overlap is inevitable here since, in the final analysis, all the results of any empirical work done are determined in large part by the methods employed.

6.5.1. Progress in research methods

Our approach to have each subject pass judgment only on those supply attributes which are relevant to him/her seems to have proven worthwhile; our data reveal that subjects' need sets vary widely with regard to the underlying structure (see section 6.2.2.) and subjects who had to respond to all of the ten attributes more frequently gave indifferent or evasive answers (neither satisfied nor dissatisfied). Any statements concerning the strength of supply needs made in absolute terms should be tempered, however, by referring to the ipsative nature of the weighting process and the different sizes of the sets of needs which vary from one person to another.

Even in view of these constraints the technique of using relative weights served the purpose of preventing an inflation of
weights, as found in our pilot study. A replication study about
to be completed should shed some light on whether the conflict
of objectives in absolute vs. relative weighting can be reduced
by increasing the sum of weights (20 vs. 40 vs. 60) available
to the respondents.

Taking the overall judgment on satisfaction as criterion of
validity of the multi-dimensional ISS model corresponds to the
usual practice but nevertheless is open to criticism on the
grounds that the validity of the overall judgment itself is
questionable. An infinite regress is likely to occur. Our findings concerning the relative timing of attribute and overall
judgments (see section 6.4.3.) underline this problem. Obviously, overall attitudes towards complex objects are too diffuse
or unstable to resist influence exerted by context factors, and
these too must be taken into account (e.g., other dimensions
of the quality of life).

The extent to which "supply with daily commodities" is described adequately by the catalogue of attributes employed here can
only be concluded indirectly from the respondents' reactions:
none of the 350 subjects, whether interviewed personally or
asked to fill out a questionnaire complained that the catalogue
of attributes was incomplete, that some facet had been neglected, etc. No doubt this is poor evidence but, on the other hand,
it is certainly no less hazardous to regard the fit between
overall satisfaction and aggregated judgments on attributes as
a criterion suitable for assessing the adequacy of the set of
attributes used. Completeness of the set of attributes, reliability of the attitude measures, as well as validity of the
attitude model also determine the size of the coefficient of
correlation.

In our view, one should not set one's aims too high. Our task
of developing a manageable instrument to measure supply satisfaction calls for cuts to be made where the marginal utility of

further methodological precision becomes negligible and the
gap between theoretical investigation and applicable research
becomes too wide.

We would like to draw to attention the following points which,
in our view, require further research:
- detection of existing relations between consumers' manifest
  shopping behavior and their satisfaction with supply,
- development and testing of measurement instruments (cf.
  Atkinson, 1977; Maddox, 1976) which are suited to describe
  consumer satisfaction/dissatisfaction in a more differentiated manner than the type of pseudo-semantic differential scale
  usually employed (cf. Dawes, 1977; pp. 201-209),
- deduction of normative weights from ipsative measures.

It also remains to be established what impact changing environmental conditions have on supply satisfaction and the ensuing
process of psychological adaptation (cf. Kuhl & Blankenship,
1969). In addition, in order to better understand consumer responses further study of the construct "satisfaction/disatis-
faction with supply" should be carried out using suitable
social-psychological approaches (cf. Anderson, 1973).

6.5.2. Material findings

A lack of transparency of the market and continuing appeals
from consumer advocates are largely responsible for what has
been referred to as consumers' price-fixation. In the present
study, this fixation was reflected in the consumer's judgment:
the most important satisfaction deficit centered around the
need for low prices; in fact, however, meeting, or rather not
meeting this need, as it turned out, hardly made any difference
to the degree of satisfaction with supply.

Looking at our data, it would seem that the discrepancy between
the situation of the urban population and that of its rural
counterpart with respect to supply problems is much smaller
than expected. While the dissatisfaction of the urban population

tends to focus on quality of goods, that of the rural population centres around the process of obtaining goods.

Contrary to expectations, based on common-sense considerations,
mobile consumer groups displayed the least degree of satisfaction with supply. The group of "immobile old people" which from
a socio-political point of view had been seen as being especially problematic, turned out to be the one which was most satisfied. These two cases illustrate the crucial consequences which
differing standards of comparison may have when assessing the
supply situation. This once again focusses attention on the
need to better integrate the aspiration level (cf. Cantril,
1965) in future applications of our approach to assess consumer
satisfaction.

According to our results the degree of supply satisfaction does
not depend on household characteristics directly observable. We
therefore assume that, alongside the ability to adapt, instill-
ed moral and religious norms determine the extent of life satisfaction and its effect on the supply sphere. In this case,
expressed supply satisfaction should be corrected by this "non-
object-linked" satisfaction.

If research on supply following a subjective approach is intended to reveal relevant facts for decisions concerning the organisation and structure of the distribution of goods, it should
go further than merely describe the state of the art. The
message of our findings is that more consideration should be
given to the interests and needs of the consumers affected by
marketing decisions. Questions that should be taken seriously
into account when making such desision include the following:

1) What needs do consumers have and to what extent can these
   be forecast?
2) What particular benefits as well as drawbacks do consumers
   attribute to the various types of retail outlets (cf.
   Andritzky & Finck, 1978)?
3) Where and to what extent does technical progress in the

retail trade have a bearing on consumer interests (cf. Moll, 1978)?

4) What should be the future shape of the structure of the distributive trades so as to meet consumers' needs?

5) What impact is a higher level of information concerning the problems of retail distribution likely to have on supply satisfaction (cf. Dichtl, Beeskow & Finck, 1979b)?

6) What mechanisms of incorporating the public in a market economy can be developed in order to be able to avoid any misallocations of resources in the retail trade right from the start?

Chapter 17 Aiding Decision Making and Information Processing

K. Borcherding and R. E. Schaefer

1. Introduction

Life is a sequence of decisions. Though many of these decisions are more or less trivial and do not require extensive deliberations, some decisions are important. In this paper we will be concerned with such inportant decisions, whether they be made on an individual or societal basis. Since these decisions are important, we will assume that the Decision Maker (DM) wants to make a 'good' decision, that is in accordance with his preferences, that effectively uses all available information, that considers all relevant options, etc. Life is complicated and so are decisions: Often many options exist with an abundance of data that may or may not be informative, credible and/or reliable.

In what follows procedures and approaches will be described that aid the DM in such complex decision situations. The need for decision aids results primarily from man's limited capacities for information processing, but it is also a consequence of his tendency to use heuristic, ineffective and often incorrect rules when making intuitive judgments.

Three examples may illustrate some of the problems that arise during information processing and decision making:

a) *Medical prognosis*. A patient with continuous heart trouble learns about an operative treatment that, though difficult and risky, may result in a substantial improvement of his condition. The patient must now decide whether or not to have an operation. To make this decision, he has to determine whether the advantages that would follow from a successful operation justify taking the risk of dying. Only the patient himself can make this decision, the crucial factor being the operation's probability of success. The patient hopes to get this information from his physician.

The physician faces the problem of processing all the data available to him: Among other things, he must consider the patient's age and state of health as well as his own previous experiences from similar operations. The question thus arises as to how to aggregate these different pieces of information to best predict success probability of the operation.

b) *Selection of nuclear waste disposal site*. An industrial society that has decided to use nuclear power for energy production faces the problem of nuclear waste disposal. Potential waste disposal sites must be discovered, and their suitability must be examined. If, after this first examination, several sites seem suitable, the problem of selecting the 'best' site still remains. The final selection will depend on criteria such as the following:

> Minimizing the costs and risks associated with transportation of nuclear wast from reactor(s) to the disposal site;
>
> Minimization of construction costs;
>
> Maximization of geological safety;
>
> Minimization of the expected protests from the population;
>
> Minimization of the probability of ground movements;
>
> Maximization of the distance to densely populated areas; etc.

If one potential site is preferred to others by all the criteria, this site will be selected. Since this is rarely the case the necessity of a "trade-off" between criteria arises. For example, to what extent is the decision maker (in this case the government or its representative organization) willing to give up advantages on one criterion for an improvement on another?

c) *Product decision*. A company wants to decide whether it
should continue to export a product to a certain country or
whether it should shift its production to that country. There
are arguments pro and con (e.g. labor might be cheaper in the
country under consideration, transport costs and import taxes
would be circumvented, difficulties with workers due to cultural differences, etc.) and a variety of decision alternatives
(e.g. construction of the plant abroad vs. no construction,
initial construction of a small plant vs. immediate, full-scale
production, etc.). In making its decision, however, the company seeks to maximize its outcomes in terms of the following
set of criteria:

> Assurance that its market share will be maintained at
> its present level, if not increased;

> Guarantee of sufficient labor;

> Maximization of profit;

> Independence of company policies from regulations of
> the foreign government; etc.

Although a single alternative has to be chosen, it is difficult
to tell beforehand which is the most promising; that is, which
alternative best fulfills all of the above mentioned criteria.
Furthermore, though a given plan's success can be determined
in part by the company itself (by selecting a good pricing
policy, taking the appropriate public relations measures,
choosing an appropriate site, etc.) there are also events outside of the company's control (e.g. political uncertainties
and strikes, sabotage, dispossession, prohibition of gain
transfer) that are likely to be important determinants as well.
The global decision of whether or not to build the plant will
thus depend on the outcome of a large number of more specific
decisions. The latter decisions are not independent of one
another, and their success cannot be predicted with certainty.
Therefore benefits as well as uncertainties are important and
have to be considered.

These three examples demonstrate that decision-making is often
very difficult and that the method for arriving at the best

decision is closely dependent upon the situation in which the
decision is made. It is in recognition of these difficulties
that the question arises of whether or not it is possible to
provide help for decision makers with respect to information
processing and decision making.

2. Aiding decision making and information processing

Before going into procedural details, we will first give a
general characterization of the processes involved in making
decisions. Two main steps will be distinguished which we will
call *diagnosis* and *selection*, respectively.

"Diagnosis" refers to the selection and processing of information with the aim of determining which one of a set of states
is the 'true state of nature'. The physician in example 1 *a*
above is faced with such a problem. By definition, the DM cannot influence or determine what state of nature will occur.
He can only select and process information to arrive at a probabilistic estimate of the true state. Although several models
can be used to formally describe this procedure, we will concentrate here on probabilistic Bayesian information processing.

"Selection" is the process of choosing one alternative from a
set of alternatives, as was the case in the nuclear disposal
example give in 1 *b* above. Often the alternatives are complex
and vary on several different value relevant attributes. Though
it might be easy to order the alternatives with respect to
each single attribute, the final decision will require that
all attributes be considered simultaneously, each weighted by
its importance to the DM. A set of models that is helpful in
such instances is called "multi-attribute utility theory",
which provides a means of aggregating preferences with regard
to single attributes into a global preference measure if certain conditions are met.

Sometimes, both diagnosis *and* selection have to be considered;
as for example, when the attractiveness of alternative courses
of action depend upon the particular event or state. In such
cases it becomes important to have a precise diagnosis (i.e.
a diagnosis that concentrates as much probability density as
possible on only one state) before selecting among alternatives.
The product decision example given in 1 *c* is a case in which
both diagnosis and selection are involved.

2.1. Steps of decision process

A decision situation is characterized by five assumptions:
1) There exists a set of hypotheses, situations, states of
   nature: $\mathcal{H}$
2) There exists a set of actions: $\mathcal{A}$
3) There exists a set of consequences or outcomes: $\mathcal{X}$
4) There exists an outcome function: $\mathcal{H} \times \mathcal{A} \to \mathcal{X}$. A specific
   situation and a specific action will lead to consequences
   or outcomes that occur with certain probabilities.
5) The consequences can be measured with respect to their
   utilities.

The following diagram illustrates the various steps that could
be taken in a decision situation. There are three basic areas
of interest: The diagnosis concerning $\mathcal{H}$, the evaluation concerning $\mathcal{A}$ given a specific situation H_i, and the selection of
one action $A^* \in \mathcal{A}$.

Diagnosis: $\mathcal{H}$ is the set of possible states of nature upon which
the decision maker has no influence and whose specific realization he usually cannot observe directly. In medical diagnosis,
for example, $\mathcal{H}$ represents the set of illnesses that a patient
might have. Since one mostly assumes mutually exclusive and
exhaustive states, the patient has exactly one illness, H^*.
The doctor does not know which illness the patient actually
suffers from, but he has some idea about their probabilities
which we call prior probabilities $p_o(H_i)$.

Diagram 1. Steps of the decision process

D I A G N O S I S

1. Assumed are possible states or hypothesis..... H_i; i=1,n
   with prior probabilities..................... $p_o(H_i)$; i=1,n
2. Considered are relevant data variables........ $\mathcal{D}_j$; j=1,m
   with observations............................ $D_j \in \mathcal{D}_j$
   and likelihoods.............................. $P(D_j/H_i)$; i=1,n; j=1,m
3. One object is to be classified
   according to observations.................... D_1, D_2,...
4. Prior probabilities and
   likelihoods of observations are aggregated
   to posterior probabilities................... $p_m(H_i)$; i=1,n

E V A L U A T I O N   O F   A C T I O N

1. Assumed are different possible actions........ A_k; k=1,K
2. Considered are relevant variables for the
   evaluation of actions........................ x_ℓ; ℓ=1,L
   with specific consequences................... $x_\ell \in X_\ell$
   and utilities associated with consequences.... $u(x_\ell)$
3. Depending on the hypothesized state and
   the specific action, there are
   probabilities of consequences................ $p(x_1|A_k,H_i)$
4. Probabilities and utilities of consequences
   are aggregated to the utility of an action.... $U(A_k|H_i)$

A C T I O N   S E L E C T I O N

1. The information given by 'diagnosis' $p_m(H_i)$; i=1,n
   and the 'evaluation of actions' $U(A_k|H_i)$; i=1,n; k=1,K
   are aggregated to form....................... $U(A_k)$; k=1,K
2. The best action A* is to select according to.. $A^*=MAX_k[U(A_k)]$

R E E V A L U A T I O N

The true state may turn out to be............. H^*
The best action would have been (1)........... $MAX_k[U(A_k|H^*)]$
The utility of the selected action is (2)..... $U(A^*|H^*)$
The loss is................................... (2) – (1)

The set $\mathcal{D}$ is the set of variables whose values provide information about $\mathcal{X}$. These are sources of information that lead to
a revision of prior to posterior probabilities. Remaining within the example of medical diagnosis, instances of such variables would be blood pressure, appetite, special aches etc. The
values of the variables are obtained from the patient through
medical tests or interviews.

One such result of the variable blood pressure may be the event
'extremely low blood pressure'. The occurrence of this event
allows probabilistic conclusions about the illnesses, since
some events are symptomatic for certain illnesses and rarely
occur with others. The probabilistic connection of symptoms
(data) with hypotheses is formally given by what is called a
likelihood matrix. The vector of m symptoms transforms by use
of the likelihood matrix the prior probabilities $p_o(H_i)$ into the
posterior probabilities $p_m(H_i)$. Given the true state, H^*, the
posterior probability, $p_m(H^*)$, is expected to be much greater
than the prior probability, $p_o(H^*)$. The process of proceeding
from a relatively diffuse prior probability distribution to an
informative posterior probability distribution is the essence
of diagnosis, or diagnostic information processing.

Evaluations of actions: The set $\mathcal{A}$ is the set of possible courses
of action from which the decision maker can select one. In medical diagnosis, the set would consist of various therapies.
Even under the assumption that the doctor would know which
illness, H^*, a patient has, the selection of an appropriate
therapy would be a difficult task. In the case of drug treatment, for example, a variety of different drugs may exist which
have roughly the same therapeutical effect but with different
side-effects.

$\mathcal{X}$ is the set of attributes on which the courses of action vary
and that are important for evaluation. Since an overall evaluation of an action's consequences might be too difficult a task
for intuitive judgment, it might be necessary to separately
analyze all its single attributes (e.g. probability and degree

of remedy of some discomforts, probability and degree of occurrence of various side-effects) together with the attribute
weights. In the next step, the outcomes of these separate analyses are combined to form an overall evaluation of the action,
$U(A_k/H_i)$. Here we are dealing with the problem of multi-attribute utility measurement. The consequences of one action have
to be established for each illness.

Selection. If we except the SEU Model as the selection criterion, the final evaluation of a course of action is equal to
its expected utility, where the probabilities come from the
diagnosis, the utilities from the evaluation of actions:

$$U(A_k) = \sum_{i=1}^{n} P_m(H_i) \cdot U(A_k/H_i)$$

Each action is now described by one value, and the selection
rule dictating the choice of that action having the maximal
expected utility, $MAX_k [U(A_k)]$.

2.2. Aids for diagnosis

A diagnostic problem is a problem of classification. It is
generally assumed that the classes form a partition; i.e.
are mutually exclusive and exhaustive. Then an individual or
object belongs to just one class. In practice, an unequivocal
assignment of an object to one and only one class is often
not possible; in these cases, all one can merely make is a
probability statement concerning the objects' membership in
a certain class of the partition.

The basic strategy underlying probabilistic classification or
diagnosis begins with the notion of a prior probability distribution. On the basis of previous experience it may turn
out that some classes are more likely than others. Thus, if
one knew nothing about an object that had to be classified,
one would classify it probabilistically in terms of this prior
distribution. As data became available concerning the object,

one would revise the prior probabilities accordingly, thus
yielding what is called posterior probabilities; i.e. probabilities posterior to observing data. The central question that
we ask here is: "How can one assist the decision maker in revising his prior probabilities into posterior probabilities?"
The situation is schematically represented in the following
diagram:

Diagram 2. A Model of Information Processing

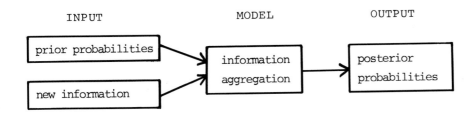

The approach pursued here is based on Bayes' theorem as a model
of probabilistic information processing and hence, as an aid
for diagnosis.

Bayes' theorem is a simple fact of probability theory. As such,
it is completely uncontroversial. For two events D and H, the
multiplication theorem of probability theory yields

$$P(D,H) \;=\; P(D) \cdot P(H/D)$$
$$\;=\; P(H) \cdot P(D/H)$$

That is, the probability of the joint realization of two events
equals the product of the probability of one event times the
probability of the second given the first had already occurred.

Equating the two right sides of the above formula yields Bayes'
theorem in its simplest form:

$$P(H/D) \;=\; P(H) \cdot \frac{P(D/H)}{P(D)}$$

In its simple form, the theorem applies to a single informa-
tion source, $\mathcal{D}$, with a current information $D \in \mathcal{D}$. The theorem
can be extended, however, to apply to a whole series of infor-
mation sources $\mathcal{D}_1, \ldots \mathcal{D}_j, \ldots \mathcal{D}_m$ each having a current information
$D_j \in \mathcal{D}_j$. In this extended form, the theorem is as follows:

$$P(H/D_1, \ldots, D_m) = P(H) \cdot \frac{P(D_1, \ldots, D_m/H)}{P(D_1, \ldots, D_m)} \tag{1}$$

Equation (1) can be written, without any additional
assumption as:

$$P(H/D_1, \ldots, D_m) = P(H) \frac{P(D_1/H) \ P(D_2/H, D_1) \ldots P(D_m/H, D_1, D_2, \ldots, D_{m-1})}{P(D_1, D_2, \ldots, D_m)} \tag{2}$$

If conditional independence holds true this can be simplified:

$$P(H/D_1, \ldots, D_m) = P(H) \frac{P(D_1/H) \ P(D_2/H) \ldots P(D_j/H) \ldots P(D_m/H)}{P(D_1, D_2, \ldots, D_m)}$$

$$= P(H) \frac{\Pi_j \ P(D_j/H)}{P(D_1, \ldots, D_m)} \cdot \tag{3}$$

The conditional independence assumption states that the data
classes are independent for each H, although they may be dependent across different H's. We will get to the importance of
this statement later.

If one wants to interpret Bayes' theorem in the form of Eq. (2)
as a system for decision aid, then $P(H)$ is the prior probability of state H; prior to the observation of $D_1 \ldots D_m$. $P(H/D_1,$
$\ldots, D_m)$ is the probability of state H after observation of m
data sources; i.e. the posterior probability. The determination of this probability can be very difficult. For example,
even if there exist only two data classes for each variable,
observing m variables yields 2^m different possible observations,
each of which must be taken into account when calculating the
posterior probabilities.

This high degree of complexity renders it unlikely that the form of Bayes' theorem given in equation 2 could serve as an aid for information processing. The form given in Eq. (3), on the other hand, contains only simple statements like $P(D_j/H)$ and seems well-suited for this purpose. If the conditional independence assumption is valid, only very simple associations of data and hypotheses need to be calculated and the posterior probabilities can be easily determined. The following steps would then be involved:

(1) The statements $P(D_j/H)$ have to be calculated, or estimated, for all data classes of $\mathfrak{D}_j$ and all $\mathfrak{D}_j$ $(j=1,\ldots,m,)$, and all H in the form of the likelihood matrix,

(2) the prior probabilities must either be estimated or assumed to be diffuse;

(3) for each object that has to be classified, the true state of each datum, i.e. of each variable, has to be determined. Given this information, the posterior probabilities can be computed.
Steps (1) and (2) have to be done only once at the beginning. Then, for as many objects as necessary, classification can be carried out using the results of step (3).

In order to apply Bayes' theorem according to Eq. (3) as a decision aid, the following conditions must be fulfilled:

(1) The set of hypotheses must form a partition. This condition is necessary so that the prior as well as the posterior probabilities sum to 1. The condition of a mutually exclusive and exhaustive classification of states presents no great difficulty because the states that are not classified can be lumped together in a residual class. The practical difficulties that may result from this must, however, be kept in mind.

(2) The data must be conditionally independent from each other, as it is only under this condition that Eq. (2) can be reduced to Eq. (3). In practice, an approximation to conditional inde-

pendence is all that is required since the conditional independence is rarely, if ever, fulfilled.[1]

(3) The data classes must be observed and reliably reported,
i.e., without any mistake. If, however, perfect data reliability
does not obtain, the Bayesian algorithm can be modified to take
this into account; see, for example, Gettys and Willke (1969),
and Schum and DuCharme (1971). Although these two approaches
may seem completely different, Schaefer and Borcherding (1973b)
were able to show the consistency between them. The solution
to incorporate unreliable data consists in a two-step induction:
On the basis of a single observation one can draw conclusions
as to the data class to which the observed event actually belongs and, from that, to the validity of hypotheses. See e.g.,
Schaefer (1975) for a formal account of this.

(4) The final condition is "stationarity". This requires that
the probabilities $P(H)$ and $P(D_j/H)$ do not change over time.
Only under this condition can the prior probabilities and likelihoods be used repeatedly for calculating the posterior probabilities. If conditions change, it may still be possible to
continuously modify these values with the use of updating, or
learning programs, and to adjust them to the prevailing conditions. Such a procedure, however, would at most allow for the
adequate consideration of gradual changes. In Schaefer (1975)
Bayes' theorem is considered as a special case of probabilistic induction; it then becomes clear at which point the condition of stationarity enters into the model.

---

[1] It is obviously problematic to state, on the one hand, that a
condition is necessary and, on the other hand, that it is never actually fulfilled. The question thus arises as to how
sensitive the technique is with regard to violations of the
assumptions; i.e. how much do the posterior probabilities according to Eqs. (2) and (3) differ for a set of conditionally
non-independent data. Moreover, one has to ask how the errors
made in intuitive diagnosis compare to those made by using
Bayes' theorem when the conditional independence is neglected.
A detailed discussion of conditional non-independence can be
found in Schaefer (1976a), where different forms of non-independence are distinguished.

The use of Bayes' theorem as a decision aid has been called PIP (Edwards, 1965), an acronym for probabilistic information processing. PIP denotes the process of deriving posterior probabilities from estimates of likelihoods and prior probabilities via the use of Bayes' theorem.

This technique contrasts with POP (posterior probability), the intuitive and wholistic processing of information as it usually occurs in diagnosis. With regard to the inputs used, Edwards (1965, p. 147) states: "Specifically, the hypothesis underlying PIP is that men can serve as transducer for P(D/H) that is, they can be taught to estimate such probabilities.....with accuracy sufficient to serve as a base for decision making even when the probabilities cannot be calculated by any other procedure."

The simplest way of comparing PIP and POP is by examining the degree of convergence between the posterior probabilities obtained by both methods. In those cases, however, where the actual state can eventually be learned, it is more satisfactory to directly evaluate the two approaches by checking which approach had assigned the higher probability to the true state, H*. This might be done, for example, in medical applications when the true state becomes known during or after an operation or after the death of a patient. A review and evaluation of Bayes' theorem as an aid in medical diagnosis can be found in Kistner and Schaefer (1977), Schaefer (1978a), and Kistner (1980).

Schaefer (1976b) experimentally compared several kinds of posterior probabilities. His subjects' task was to estimate the proportion of students having different characteristics (e.g. the proportion of males and females wearing spectacles, voting for a certain party, etc.). The terms to be evaluated were chosen in such a way that some could be used as prior probabilities, others as likelihoods and posterior probabilities. For example, from estimates like P(H): the probability of a female psychology student, $P(D_1/H)$: the probability that a female

psychology student has her own car, and $P(D_2/H)$: the probability that a female psychology student wears spectacles, you can
derive (calculate) via Bayes theorem the posterior probability
$P(H/D_1, D_2)$: the probability that a psychology student wearing
spectacles and possessing a car is female, which can be compared with the directly estimated posterior probability. The actual proportions were known because a survey among all psychology students had been conducted at the same time. These proportions were taken as "true probabilities". It was therefore
possible to compare the posterior probabilities via PIP as
well as subjects' direct intuitive estimates of the posterior
probabilities (POP) with the "true" ones. The results are summarized in Table 1.

Table 1. Mean deviation of the various posterior probabilities
from the true probabilities

	BT_{II}	BT_I	PIP_I	PIP_{II}	POP
Mean relative deviation	0	0.00	−0.04	−0.06	−0.10
Mean absolute deviation	0	0.03	0.08	0.09	0.12

Notes: Negative values denote conservative estimates.
The various posterior probabilities were derived as follows:
BT: true percentages for priors and likelihoods via Bayes'
    theorem
PIB: subjects' estimates for priors and likelihoods via Bayes'
    theorem
POB: subjects' direct posterior probability estimates
Index I: assuming conditional independence
Index II: taking conditional dependencies into account

Of course, calculation of the true percentages via Bayes'
theorem was always better than calculations on the basis of
estimates, as shown by the comparison of BT and PIP in Table 1.
A comparison between PIP and POP, however, clearly shows that
PIP led to better estimates of posterior probabilities.

In general one would expect a model that reflects conditional dependencies (index II) to be better whenever conditional dependencies occur. This holds for the comparison of BT_I and BT_{II}. As for PIP_{II}, more complex likelihoods served as inputs. The advantage to give estimates that reflect conditional dependencies was more than compensated by the fact that the estimation task was more difficult and, as a consequence, performance was less good.

Aufsattler and Schaefer (1978) systematically examined how the accuracy of posterior probabilities depends on the complexity of the decision task. Using a disguised urn paradigm, special hypotheses (urns) were described to subjects. After observing data they had to associate posterior probabilities with these hypotheses according to the likelihood that the data were generated by one of them. The complexity was varied by manipulating a) the number of hypotheses that could have generated the data b) the number of different data (information, different colors in an urn) and c) the amount of information (number of observations) to be processed. Generally speaking, the goodness of the posterior probabilities decreased with increasing task complexity.

Our own and others' research has confirmed the value of Bayes' theorem as an aid to probabilistic diagnosis. The theorem seems especially useful in those cases when diagnoses must be made on the basis of large amounts of data of relatively low diagnosticity. The possibility for sequential information processing and the ability to use discrete as well as continuous data are attractive features of this algorithm. The problem of how to handle conditional non-independence merits, however, further theoretical and empirical work.

2.3. Decision aids for selection

To "select" means, in this case, to choose the best from a certain number of available alternatives. Such decisions are

simple if the alternatives vary only on one dimension or attribute, or if only one attribute is relevant to the decision.
The choice rapidly becomes much more difficult, however, if the
alternatives are complex; i.e., if the alternatives vary on
many dimensions that are all more or less important. The selection of a nuclear waste disposal site, discussed at the beginning of this paper, is an example of a selection problem.

The goal of selection is to choose the alternative that corresponds most closely to the preferences of the DM. The more
complex the problem, the more difficult it is to establish
and express these preferences. In such complex cases, decision
aids are called for. Systematic questioning can help the DM
to structure the situation and to establish his preferences
concerning the alternatives. Methods of multi-attribute utility theory serve this purpose. As a first step toward their
application, the complex decision task must be decomposed into
less complex attributes relevant to the establishment of preferences. The set of attributes to be chosen is not fixed,
but some desirable properties can be defined. For example:

(1) Completeness. Taken as a whole, the set of attributes
should describe the alternatives. Only then can one expect
the attribute set to be sufficient for the evaluation of the
alternatives.

(2) Non-Redundancy. The attributes should cover different,
non-overlapping aspects of the alternatives.

(3) Operationalizability. One should choose attributes that
are easily operationalized and, as a consequence, alternatives
are measurable on these attributes.

(4) Decomposability. One should be able to decompose the total
utility function into partial utilities on these attributes,
so that the total utility can be put together from the partial utilities.

(5) Minimal set. This criterion, one might assume, results
from a joint consideration of criteria (1) and (2), as a com-

plete and non-redundant set would seem to be minimal. But it
must not be forgotten that the partition of the total utility
of alternatives into partial utilities can be continued by
further decomposing the attributes; that is, decomposing them
into sub-attributes and thereby generating a hierarchical attribute structure. Taking a hierarchical attribute structure,
a minimal set of attributes is one where the level is as high
as possible and still fulfilling requirements one to four.

If a satisfactory set of attributes has been established, the
utility of each decision alternative on every single attribute can be determined with or without taking uncertainty into
account. As the problem of uncertainty will be discussed later
(see part 4.), a simple riskless case will be considered here.
Such a decision alternative, A_i, has known consequences that
occur with certainty. A consequence is a label or value on an
attribute. For m attributes, a decision alternative i is characterized by the m-tuple:

$$A_i: (x_{1i}, x_{2i}, \ldots, x_{ji}, \ldots, x_{mi}),$$

where A_i denotes the decision alternative showing outcome
x_{ji} on attribute x_j. Utilities can be assigned to the attribute values; the utility assigned to x_{ji} being denoted as u_{ji}.
Thus, $u_{ji} = f_j(x_{ji})$ and, given simple independence, the overall
utility of the alternative i is

$$U(T_i) = g(u_{1i}, \ldots, u_{ji}, \ldots, u_{mi})$$

The utilities in parentheses correspond to one column of the
outcome matrix shown in Diagram 1, where the outcomes are
preferentially ordered. Under certain conditions, the utility
of a decision alternative is just a weighted sum of the
partial utilities on the m attributes:

$$U(T_i) = \sum_j w_j u_{ji},$$

where w_j is the relative weight of the attribute A_j, the importance of this attribute for the overall utility. The additive representation is the simplest approach to determine the total utility from the partial utilities.

Dawes and Corrigan (1974) have shown that the simple additive model can be used to effectively approximate more complex functions. Under conditions of no risk, the total utility of the alternatives can be determined by the following procedure:

(1) For each attribute, utilities have to be assigned to the different outcomes on this attribute. This assignment can be done in accordance with utility theory, where $u_{ji} > u_{jk}$ iff outcome a_{ji} of alternative i is preferred to a_{jk} of alternative k on attribute j, and $|u_{ji} - u_{jk}| > |u_{jl} - u_{jm}|$ iff utilities of outcomes i and k differ more than those of outcomes l and m.

(2) Each attribute must be assigned a relative weight that reflects the degree to which the attribute determines the total utility of an alternative. In determining the weights, trade-off procedures have to be used. These procedures allow the direct comparison of outcomes on two different attributes and answer questions like "how much of a gain on one attribute is necessary to compensate for a specified loss on another attribute?"

(3) Finally, given the vector of outcomes for a single course of action the total utility can be calculated. This must be done for each alternative course of action under consideration.

Steps (1) and (2) have to be done before the total utility can be determined according to (3) for as many decision alternatives as wanted. The selection rule is, of course, to choose the alternative which maximizes total utility.

The empirical validation of a decomposition approach to determine the overall utility of alternatives can be done in several different ways. Whenever possible, the validity of the model should be decided in terms of an outside criterion; e.g., comparing the amount of money gained using a decomposition model

in an investment decision against the gain achieved by deciding intuitively. Though it is rarely possible to make such a
comparison in real life situations, an external criterion can
also be framed in terms of actual behavior. This is the case,
for example, with consumer decisions, where preferences established by a model were used to predict actual consumer behavior.

Another validation technique is to directly compare intuitive
preferences with those established with the aid of a model.
Since such a comparison can only reveal convergence of the two
preference orders, this technique is less satisfactory than
the one described above. If the task is not very complex (i.e.
if only few attributes have to be taken into consideration when
establishing preferences) a much higher agreement is expected
between the model-generated and the intuitive preference order
than would be the case with a decision among complex alternatives. As the decision becomes more complex, the correlation
between the modelled and intuitive judgments will become smaller. But this cannot be taken as evidence against the model's
validity, because it is exactly in such cases that aiding the
DM to express his preferences is necessary. Thus, a model developed to improve intuitive decision making can be validated
against holistically determined preferences only if considerable caution is exercised.

In what follows, two experimental applications of the additive model of multi-attribute utility theory are described. For
more detailed information the reader is referred to the original research.

2.3.1. Multi-attribute evaluation of automobiles

The investigation conducted by Schaefer, Borcherding, Grabicke,
Raffée and Schöler (1975) was designed to test the usefulness
of multi-attribute utility determination for aiding consumer
product choices. The alternatives were automobiles selected
from the lower price ranges (and thus thought to be of parti-

Brand	Unit	Auto-bianchi A 112	VW 1200	Renault 4 L	Fiat 128	Citroen 2 CV 6	Mini 1000	Peugeot 100	Citroen Dyane 6	Daf 44 de Luxe	Simca 1000 LS	Renault 6 L	Simca 1100 LS
Power	hp	44	34	34	55	28	36	45	32	34	40	48	60
Acceleration 0 - 100 km	sec	16	30	29	17	31	28	20	32	35	21	21	17
Maximal speed	km/h	143	118	120	144	111	123	139	116	119	134	133	145
Consumption per 100 km	liter	7-8	9-10	7-9	9-10	6-8	9-11	8-10	7-9	9-10	8-10	9-11	9-12
Security rating	points	10	4	8	9	5	10	8	5	4	4	5	8
Comfort rating	points	6	7	8	7	7	3	10	7	8	5	10	9
Hold	liter	144	188	200	288	160	92	208	196	248	156	199	204
Frequency of damage	in %	98	54	90	98	107	109	100	100	62	114	65	89
Resale price after two years	in %	51	54	53	51	51	53	59	51	47	50	50	51
Total costs per km with depreciation and interest for 15.000 km per year	DM	.38	.36	.35	.43	.33	.37	.40	.33	.37	.38	.42	.47

Table 2. Product information about cars

cular interest to students). The 29 subjects had to rank order
the automobiles according to preference three times, each time
using a different set of information. The information available
for the three rankings was (see Table 2):

  (A) 10 different technical facts about
       the products;

  (B) Exact brand information;

  (C) Both technical and brand information.

Two additional rank orders were developed with the help of an
additive multi-attribute utility model. To do this, (1) the
utilities on the attributes and (2) the relative importance
have to be known. A linear relationship between attribute outcomes and their utilities was assumed. The relative importance
of the attributes was measured in two ways: by a graphical rating approach and a trade-off approach for indifference construction, yielding preference orders D and E:

  (D) Preferences derived by multi-attribute utility model,
       attribute weighting by graphical rating;

  (E) Preferences derived by multi-attribute utility model,
       attribute weighting by a trade-off approach.

Some intercorrelations are given in Table 3.

The upper left quadrant summarizes the intercorrelations among
the intuitively determined rank orders. As can be readily seen,
the correlation between individual rankings established on the
basis of product information and those on the basis of brand
information is very low, $\bar{r}$ = .22. Thus subjects' preferences
among the cars depended very much upon the kind of information
given. Both rankings are more highly correlated with ranking C
(product *and* brand information) than they were with each other,
which may result from A and C as well as B and C having partly
identical information. The exact brand information of a car,
B, has implicit all information, out of which the presumably
relevant information without the brand name is explicitly used

in A. One explanation of the low correspondence between A and B could be that A does *not* contain the relevant information that subjects base their preferences on, though this is contradicted by the modest correlation between A and C. So the only explanation could be, that subjects were not expert enough to see the similarities of both descriptions and show consistent preferences.

Table 3. Average rank correlations among the various preference orders

	A	B	D
B	.22 (-.12; .67)[a]	-	-
C	.52 (.03; .85)	.47 (.15; .82)	-
D	.24 (-.36; .79)	-	-
E	.33 (-.36; .82)	-	.68 (.34; .94)

[a]The range of the correlation coefficients is given in brackets

The lower right-hand quadrant gives the relationship between the two rank-orders developed from the decomposition model. As can be readily seen, the different methods of attribute weighting had a rather strong influence on the resulting preference orders, the correlation between them being only .68. Here a correlation of .68 is rather low because the rank order of automobiles on attributes is the same for D and E - no randomness -, and multi-attribute utility is not sensitive to small fluctuations of weights in linear weighting procedures.

As product information was used as a basis for the decomposition approaches, it seemed to be useful to compare them to the
intuitive preference order based on product information. The
correlations presented in the lower left-hand quadrant, are
very low in comparison to those mentioned in the literature.
Fischer (1972, 1976), who also conducted an experiment on the
evaluation of cars, reported correlations around and above .90
between intuitive preference orders and preference orders generated by an additive multi-attribute model. The difference
between Fischer's findings and ours may be due to differences
in the stimuli used since Fischer's cars were less homogeneous
with regard to price. A higher price will more likely lead to
better outcomes on all attributes, so that attributes are pairwise positively related. Preference judgments then are easier
because they are less complex. If price is not one of the attributes, we felt having a narrow price range to be important.

2.3.2. Multi-attribute evaluation of research projects

The decision whether research projects should be supported is
an extremely difficult evaluation task due to the many criteria that have to be taken into account. Schaefer (1973) suggested methods of multi-attribute utility theory as decision
aids in such situations. Aschenbrenner, Borcherding, Kasubek,
Schaefer, Schümer and Schümer (1975) experimentally examined
one of these approaches.

As a first step, those attributes relevant for project evaluation had to be defined. The following list of criteria was
derived from questions posed by the German National Science
Foundation ('Deutsche Forschungsgemeinschaft') to experts
nominated to evaluate research programs:

1) How do you estimate the quality of the proposals put forward by the various projects?

   - Theoretical explanation of the research question
   - Concreteness of the research question

- Is the procedure proposed appropriate to the research question?
- How do you estimate the practicality of the project?
- Can new findings be expected?

2) How much does each project contribute to the program of the institute as a whole?

- ... with regard to content?
- ... with regard to theoretical considerations?
- ... with regard to 'selling' the institute to the DFG and its directors?

3) To what degree does the project cooperate with the other projects in the institute?

4) How much does the project contribute to integrating the research endeavors of the institute as a whole?

5) How do you evaluate the final outcome of the project?

- ... with regard to the amount of output (research reports, publications, etc.)?
- ... with regard to the quality of the output?

6) What is the project's cost-effectiveness?

The options to be evaluated were the projects existing at the SFB 24 of the University of Mannheim at that time. The evaluaters were 29 colleagues, members of the SFB 24. We assumed that they could properly use all criteria and would know the projects and their work quite well. The subjects were required to:

1) Establish an intuitive rank order of overall projects concerning their supportability;

2) Rate the projects on the attributes;

3) Assign weights to the first- and second-order attributes;

4) Answer questions about non-professional relations to colleagues.

The data obtained from each subject permitted the construction of several different preference orders based on the following procedures:

MAUT I: Additive utility model described above using the six first-order attributes

MAUT II: This differed from MAUT I in that the first-order
             attributes 1, 2, and 5 were substituted by their
             sub-attributes, making a total of 13 attributes to
             be taken into consideration.

REG I: Regression on the basis of the six first-order at-
             tributes; weights were determined so as to maximize
             the correlation with the intuitive total rank order.

REG II: As in REG I except that the first-order attributes
             were substituted by their sub-attributes.

REG III: Regression on the basis of ratings of the eight
             additional questions.

Table 4 summarizes some of the results.

Table 4. Correlations between the intuitive rank order and
         the ones resulting from the application of various
         models.

Model	Number of Predictors	Correlations Median	Range
MAUT I	6	.85	(.42 - .98)
MAUT II	13	.85	(.52 - .98)
REG I	6	.91	(.63 - .99)
REG II	13	.98	(.91 - .99)
REG III	8	.96	(.78 - .99)

For the three regression models (REG I, II and III), it can be
readily seen that the size of the correlation coefficients in
Table 4 vary positively with the number of predictors that the
various models are based on. The extremely high correlation in
the case of REG III is not surprising when it is considered
that 13 predictors were used for matching the intuitive rank

ordering of 17 projects. It should also be noted that the correlations for the rank orders generated by MAUT are also quite
high. In all cases, however, the reservations concerning the
use of intuitive rank orders as a validation criterion apply.
It remains to be seen which order best reflects the subjects'
true preferences; i.e. which rank ordering subjects would
choose as best representing their preferences if all six of
the above rank orders were presented to them.

Further data analysis showed that all variables, attribute
ratings as well as responses to the additional questions, were
highly intercorrelated. A project with a high score on, for
example, 'qualification of the proposal' was likely to be evaluated as a project that cooperates, has a high output, ...,
people working there are friendly and helpful, one has private
contact with, and so on. This means that any variable could
have been used to predict the intuitive rank order quite well.
A factor analysis generated one main factor that explained
73% of the total variance, the next two factors explaining
only 13% and 7%, respectively. It seems, therefore, that the
data can be almost completely described in terms of a single
dimension.

This strong linear relationship between the variables is of
primary interest among the results of the study and seems
accountable for by several different explanations:

1) It is, in principle, possible that all evaluative attributes
refer to the same underlying dimension. If this were so, the
attributes used in the present study would have been redundant
and thus not well chosen. An examination of the attributes
employed, however, reveals that they seem to cover very different aspects of quality of research projects.

2) Another possibility is that the dimensions are themselves
independent but that the options (i.e., research projects)
induce high intercorrelations. This would be the case, for
example, if researchers applying for grants have learned to
more or less satisfactorily fulfill all relevant requirements.

3) Finally, the possibility has to be considered that the subjects might not have had enough information about the projects,
their judgments being more or less determined by the 'image'
of the project or project leader.

It seems unlikely that the last explanation would be relevant
to the case of outside experts. It is, however, only by further studying the actual evaluation of projects by a number
of experts using decision aids such as those proposed above -
or similar ones - that issues concerning the relationship among
attributes can be clarified.

2.4. Conclusions

The structuring of decision situations discussed in this chapter is by no means the only one possible, but it does make it
feasible to investigate with considerable detail the mutual
importance and dependency of diagnosis and selection in decision making. Experimental results were reported that bear upon
these two processes, the data requisite for testing the various models being readily obtainable. As the quality of a decision via a model is dependent upon the degree to which the
necessary conditions are fulfilled as well as upon the quality
of the input information, this latter aspect will be discussed in the following.

3. Assessment and evaluation of probability judgments

Decisions often depend on variables and parameters that are
unknown and have to be estimated. This is especially characteristic of diagnoses, where the probabilities (the likelihoods)
have to be obtained before any technique for aiding information processing can be applied. The quality of the output of
a model aided diagnosis will very much depend upon the quality of the input information. In this sense, the assessment and

evaluation of probability judgments is a sub-problem relevant
to all decision situations using subjective estimates.

3.1. Assessment of probabilities

There are different ways to obtain uncertain quantities. The
true value of an uncertain quantity can be assessed as a point
estimate, one number being assigned to the uncertain quantity
in question; e.g., the probability of someone wearing glasses
is p = .3. Such an estimate contains enough information for
many applications and is generally sufficient as an input to
decision aid methodologies.

In evaluating the goodness of a probability estimate, a point
estimation is insufficient, because there is no information on
how sure an assessor is about his or her estimate. In the
above example one cannot know whether the asessor believes
that the percentage of people wearing glasses is exactly .30,
or whether he or she also considers any other values of the
uncertain quantity as being possible candidates for the 'true
value'. An assessor has given his complete information only
when he also states a confidence with his point estimation,
which will give probabilistic information about 'true value's'
range. This information is available only when the complete
subjective probability distribution has been assessed.

There are a number of approaches available for the assessment
of subjective probability distributions. For uncertain quantities that are discrete or discretized, the simplest way is to
assign probabilities to the n classes of the uncertain quantity. Such a probability indicates how probable the assessor
thinks it is that the true value of the uncertain quantity
will fall into the respective class. Schaefer (1976a,b), Schaefer, Borcherding and Laemmerhold (1977) and Borcherding (1977,
1978) used this approach, its principle advantage being that
it is easily understandable, a consideration that seems especially important for people without any statistical background.

For uncertain quantities that are continuous, more complicated assessment methods are available; see, for example, Winkler (1967). In such cases, either the density function or the distribution function can be obtained through skillfully graduated questioning. If, however, previously obtained expert information can be described in terms of an analytical statistical distribution function, then it is only necessary to assess the parameters of this distribution. This latter approach is referred to as indirect assessment technique because the subjective probability distribution is inferred from the estimates of the parameters. Schaefer and Borcherding (1973a) and Bülles and Borcherding (1980) used both direct and indirect methods for the assessment of probability distributions, a detailed description of assessment techniques can be found in Schaefer (1976a).

3.2. Evaluation of probability judgments

When speaking of the quality of probability judgments, various aspects of "quality" can be distinguished. These can be grouped into the following categories:

1) *Normative aspects*. These comprise all quality criteria that refer to consistency in the sense of an absence of logical contradictions in a set of statements. Such criteria are developed from the axioms of probability theory.

2) *Substantive aspects*. Substantive criteria of goodness always refer to the share of valid information contained in the estimates. As such, they depend upon the amount of knowledge that the assessor can be thought to possess about the uncertain quantities. Substantive goodness can be assigned to an assessor only with regard to a specific domain of knowledge.

3) *Aspects of empirical validity*. This involves the degree of correspondence between the probabilistic estimates on the one hand, and the actual occurrence of events, on the other. Depending on the context, the terms "realism" or "calibration" are used to refer to this aspect of goodness.

4) *An overall measure of goodness.* This is a score calculated according to a proper scoring rule (PSR). Such a rule takes into account all three classes of aspects mentioned above. Four different proper scoring rules have been formulated, each having its own advantages and disadvantages. For a detailed discussion of these four rules, see Schaefer (1969).

If only point estimates are available, the capabilities for evaluating the quality of the estimates is limited to substantive aspects; once the actual value of an uncertain quantity becomes known, the distance between the point estimate and the actual value can be used as a measure of the estimate's substantive quality and, hence, of the assessor's expertise.

If complete probability distributionsare available, a variety of evaluations are possible. Normative aspects would ask for probabilities of complementary events, and identity between probabilistic statements derived from different assessment procedures, or the fulfillment of axioms in the case of a measurement-theoretic approach to subjective probability. Substantive aspects would ask for a high probability or density assigned to the event that actually occurs, a small distance between the mean of the subjective probability distribution and the actual value of the uncertain quantity, and partly as consequence, a tight subjective distribution. Empirical validation of estimates is only possible if many estimates are available, preferably from the same assessor. In such cases, the probability assigned to an event is compared with the relative frequency with which the event occurs.

If estimates for uncertain quantities have to be obtained one will always try to get substantive experts to make them. A major problem is to determine whether experts can adequately express their knowledge in terms of probability distributions, and whether they can get trained to do a better job.

3.3. Empirical studies of the evaluation of probability
     estimates

A number of studies have been carried out to investigate the
realism of probability judgments, most finding that assessors
overestimate the extent to which they are informed about uncertain future events, their resulting probability estimates
being far too concentrated around too few events. In other
words, the ranges of the subjective probability distributions
that subjects have generated in these experiments have generally been too narrow.

In two experiments, we attempted to lead subjects to make more
realistic assessments when generating subjective probability
estimates. Schaefer and Borcherding (1973a), for example, asked subjects during four sessions to estimate subjective probability distributions for uncertain quantities according to two
different assessment methods. Schaefer (1976b) conducted five
sessions, using still another method. Realism in both studies
was defined in terms of both the interquartile score and the
surprise score. The interquartile score is the percentage of
true values of the uncertain quantities falling in the interquartile range of the subjective probability distributions.The
surprise score is the percentage falling outside the 1st and
99th percentile. If a subject estimates realistically, one
would expect 50% of the true values to be located within the
interquartile range and 2% outside the 1st and 99th percentile,
respectively. As shown in Table 5, the interquartile scores
were far below the ideal of 50%, and the surprise scores far
above 2%, for both experiments. This strongly suggests that
people tend to exaggerate the definitiveness of what they
know and therefore generate subjective probability distributions whose ranges are too narrow. As can be seen in Table 5,
there was some improvement over the training sessions, but the
scores were generally still far from being perfect.

Table 5. Percentage of the true value in the interquartile
and surprise range

Range	Method	Session				
		1	2	3	4	5
Inter-quartile	indirect continuous*	15.7	38.1	37.4	48.2	-
	direct continuous*	22.5	30.3	36.9	37.9	-
	direct discrete**	27.1	7.9	32.8	35.7	34.0
Surprise	indirect continuous*	49.8	21.5	15.5	5.6	-
	direct continuous*	38.8	14.9	16.0	11.9	-
	direct discrete**	25.0	27.6	21.0	18.0	14.7

*   Schaefer and Borcherding (1973a)

**   Schaefer (1976b)

In the case of genuine discrete events, realism can be examined
in terms of the probabilities assigned to the different classes. Ideally the probability assigned to one class should correspond to the relative frequency with which the true value
of the uncertain quantity falls into that class. In Schaefer,
Borcherding and Laemmerhold (1977), subjects had to predict
results of soccer games during the 1974 World Championship
played in Germany. Probabilities were assigned to the three
possible outcomes of one game; first team wins, tie, second
team wins. These probabilities should sum to one. Since there
were 3 outcomes for each game, 12 games to predict for each
group, and 25 subjects, 3 x 12 x 25 = 900 probabilistic predictions were done for one group. Out of 3600 predictions for
groups 1-4, there were 844 outcomes subjects thought very unlikely to occur and consequently gave a probability of occurrence below .05, out of which actually 17% occurred, which has

to be compared with an expectation by empirical evaluation of about 2,5%. It can be seen from the table that for low subjective probabilities, the actual relative frequencies are too high while for the high subjective probabilities, the actual frequencies were too low, a pattern of findings that would be expected if subjects were over-reliant on whatever information

Table 6. Realism of probability estimates as a comparison between the subjective probabilities for events and the relative frequency of occurrence of these events

Subjective Probability Range	Relative Frequency of True Value in Range		Number of Estimates	
	Group		Group	
	1-4	5+6	1-4	5+6
.00 - <.05	.17	.11	844	243
.05 - <.15	.21	.18	408	174
.15 - <.25	.29	.19	476	315
.25 - <.35	.33	.25	528	370
.35 - <.45	.29	.36	290	223
>.45 - .55	.38	.49	237	143
>.55 - .65	.38	.55	176	124
>.65 - .75	.40	.71	120	68
>.75 - .85	.62	.70	156	64
>.85 - .95	.66	.78	105	12
>.95 - 1.00	.79	.84	260	64

they had available. Only in the range (.25 - < .35), where the actual frequency was 33%, were the estimates reasonable, but it has to be kept in mind that this is the range indicating absence of any information concerning the three outcome classes (win, loose, draw); correspondence between objective percentages and subjective probabilities will, in such a case, necessarily occur.

A further study by Borcherding (1978) critically examined the concept of realism, considering it in conjunction with subjective certainty (see also Schaefer & Borcherding, 1978a,b; Lichtenstein, Fischoff & Phillips, 1977). A tendency to over-rely on information may have two consequences: 1. Subjects overestimate the impact of the information, leading to overly tight distributions that are too much concentrated around some mean value, 2. Subjects overestimate the representativeness of their information, leading to misplaced subjective distributions centered around already biased values.

Although realism is always interpreted according to the first argument, both effects will influence the realism of assessments and should therefore be distinguished. From the result of a pilot study, 30 items out of 78 were classified into three classes according to the degree they induce a bias in the localization of the probability distribution. Each class contained 10 items. In the main study a second group of subjects had to give probability judgments regarding these 30 items. The results of this investigation all point in the same direction: with an increase of bias in localization, the quality of the probability estimates, defined as probability assigned to the true class or as the score of a proper scoring rule, decreases. As can be seen in Figure 1, the form of the realism curves were also very much dependent upon the degree of mis-information. For perfectly realistic estimates, one would expect a 1:1 correspondence between the responses r_i and the percentage of true statements c_i, as reflected by the diagonal. A bias in location could be used in such a way that it either facilitated the correct choice (left column) or made the choice more difficult (right column). If the bias in localization is strong and if it systematically leads the assessor to the choice of the wrong alternative, then the following holds true: The higher the assessed probability for one event, the lower the probability of such an event occurring (upper right quadrant). In the case of two alternatives, of which one is correct, one would talk about a bias when it systematically

induces the choice of the wrong alternative (and obstructs the
identification of the correct one), then this is the condition
under which the bias in localization has its strongest influence. In this narrower sense of the term the quadrant I to VI
contain increasing degrees of biases.

This result calls into question the simplest interpretation of
low realism as an over- or under-estimate of the degree of subjective certainty. The Borcherding study demonstrates that
there are other relevant factors, like bias in localization,
that have a strong influence upon the realism of estimates but
that cannot be subsumed under the notion of subjective certainty.

Schaefer (1976b) critically analyzes how useful realism data
is as feedback in the training of probability assessors. It was
found that subjects who were given feedback concerning the realism of the distributions assessed became more realistic in
their probability estimates. Since the estimated terms could
be used as likelihoods in Bayes' theorem to compute posterior
probabilities, the substantive goodness of the posterior probabilities could be tested. Realism improved over training
sessions. Completely contrary to this was the finding that the
goodness of posterior probabilities calculated with the help
of the model deteriorated over the sessions. Schaefer mentions
several factors that could have led to this surprising result.
Nevertheless, the findings seem to imply training has to be
provided in the context of the quality of probabilistic estimates relevant to the decision model. If the estimates are
processed by the Bayesian approach, then their most important
property is that they accurately reflect the likelihood ratios.
Realism in itself is hardly of any importance then. Somewhat
similar results were obtained by Borcherding (1977), who
showed that training has no effect on differential predicta-
bility, the single most relevant criterion in that study.

Figure 1.   Realism curves

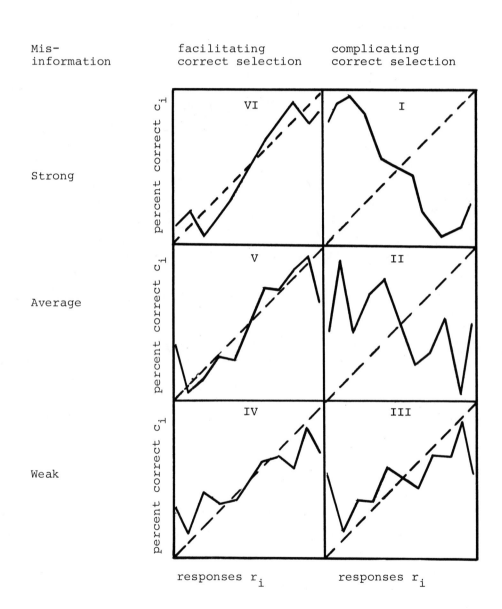

It seems very important to gain experience with assessment and
evaluation of inputs for decision aid techniques and with
training of experts, where only those criteria relevant to the
decision situation are used as criteria of goodness. There is
a dearth of systematic investigations in this area.

4. Portfolio theory as a decision aid

Portfolio theory is concerned with 'mixing' courses of action
and involves a selection process. In the typical case, there
exists a set of courses of action out of which one course can
be chosen, but also any combination is possible. For example,
certain crops are available to a farmer for the cultivation of
his land, and he can grow just one, but, moreover, he can choose any possible combination of the various alternatives, like
50% for growing wheat, 20% for corn, 22% for sugar beets, etc.
Besides the 'pure' course of action, each combination also represents a course of action in itself.

Here, combining courses of action especially makes sense if
risk is involved. If, as is the case in no risk situations,
the alternatives' utilities can be determined beforehand, then
the alternative with the highest utility can be pre-determined
and should be chosen all the time. If risk is involved, however, utilities cannot be known beforehand, and mixtures of
'pure' courses of action shall be preferred.

4.1. Problem

The problem of portfolio theory is a selection problem that can
be described as a problem of maximizing future utility. As before, utility can be influenced by many factors (attributes).
The personal utility of some state of affairs at a future point
in time might depend very much upon how problems regarding
family, housing, or profession are by then resolved. For a

commercial enterprise, an alternative's utility might depend
mostly upon the future state of the economy. Although, in ac-
tuality, all factors that determine utility should be included
in these considerations, portfolio theory generally reduces
the utility concept to financial terms. Since one can assume
that utility on attributes can be expressed in monetary values,
we will also reduce the utility concept to monetary utility.
With this convention, the problem of portfolio theory can be
described more specifically as a problem of maximizing the
utility linked to future capital. It is a normative theory for
decision making in the case when the different possible outcomes of pure courses of action are uncertain and intercorrelated.

The paradigmatic decision problem for portfolio theory is the
investment decision. The investor has a certain capital at his
disposition that he wants to distribute on i = 1, 2, ..., n
investment possibilities (courses of action) in such a way to
insure a high and certain gain. Though, in practice, the investment possibilities can differ very much among themselves,
they will have to be identified as shares. Obviously, the investor faces a very complex problem: Should he spend all his
capital on the purchase of shares of one single corporation
(pure course of action) or should he buy shares of different
firms? If he chooses the latter option, how many different
shares of each firm should he buy?

When making a portfolio decision, three steps can be distinguished that are more or less consciously executed when deciding intuitively:

1. *Analysis of shares*. Evaluating the quality (i.e. profitability) of single shares requires knowledge about the firms
involved, about the market situation, the inter-dependencies
of the various firms due to the market trends, etc. If a decision aid technique is to be applied, all this knowledge has
to be combined and expressed in numerical values.

2. *Portfolio analysis.* The set of all possible portfolios is considered and their respective qualities established. If this is to be done with a decision aid technique, it has to be possible to establish the quality of every single portfolio from characteristic indices of its components.

3. *Portfolio selection.* The problem of portfolio selection consists in selecting, from all possible portfolios, the one that most closely corresponds to the investor's preferences. The investor's utility considerations enter in here; once these are known the portfolio with the highest (subjective) utility can be determined.

4.2. The Mean-Variance approach of the portfolio theory[2]

The four main assumptions of the Mean-Variance (MV) approach are:

(1) The utility of an investment depends upon the expected return (gain). The higher the expected return, the greater the utility.

(2) The utility of an investment depends upon the variability (variance) of returns, i.e., the risk. The smaller the risk, the greater the utility.

(3) The utility of an investment depends only upon the expected return and the risk.

(4) The two variables are compensatory: Greater risk can be compensated by a higher expected return, and a lower expected return by less risk.

---

[2] Markowitz (1952) developed the Mean-Variance approach, completing it in Markowitz (1959); Sharpe (1963) considerably simplified it; see Borcherding (1978) for a detsiled description and references.

The expected return of a portfolio P is given as:

$$E(R_p) = \Sigma_i \, w_i \, E(R_i) \, .$$

(4)

The corresponding risk is:

$$\sigma_p = \sqrt{\Sigma_i \, \Sigma_j \, w_i \, w_j \, \sigma_i \, \sigma_j \, \rho_{ij}} \; \le \Sigma_i \, w_i \, \sigma_i$$

(5)

where:

w_i	part of the capital invested in investment i, with $\Sigma_i \, w_i = 1$
$E(R_i)$	expected return of investment i
$E(R_p)$	expected return of portfolio P
σ_i	risk associated with investment i
ρ_{ij}	correlation between returns of investment i and j.

The expected return of a portfolio is linearly related to the expected returns of the investments, which is not true for risk. The equality in Eq. (5) holds, if all intercorrelations $\sigma_{ij} = 1$, $i \ne j$. Most likely, for $i \ne j$, $\rho_{ij} < 1$, and $\sigma_i \ne \sigma_j$ for at least some i and j, the unequality holds: The risk of a portfolio is smaller than the corresponding linear combination. Under certain conditions, the risk of a portfolio is even smaller than the risk of the investment with the smallest risk.

In determining efficient portfolios according to the mean-variance approach, the expected return and the risk of the components (investments) have to be known as well as the intercorrelation matrix of the returns. Portfolio selection then reduces to finding the weights w_i that maximize $k \cdot E(R_p) - \sigma_p$; k reflects the numerical value of the trade-off between expected return and risk.

4.3. The use of the portfolio theory as a decision aid

If the mean-variance approach to portfolio selection is to be used as a decision aid, it is necessary to quantify the model inputs. There are two ways to do this. One can use historical

data to obtain predictions about future returns and risks and
to construct the intercorrelation matrix. This can be done
in terms of frequency or time-series analysis. The second
possibility is to ask experts to give these inputs as subjective estimates; this second possibility was empirically
investigated.

Four groups of subjects participated in this experiment. Seven
psychology students (laymen), seven students of business administration, five professors from the business administration
faculty and five professors in statistics. The latter two
groups served as experts in the subjective and normative sense,
respectively. The subjects were asked to give predictions for
future share-quotations in form of subjective probability distributions. The predictions had to be made for ten German
shares for intervals of 1 month, 2 months, ..., up to 6 months.
After each month, subjects received feedback concerning their
estimates and then had to make predictions again for the next
one to six months period. The experimental design is given in
Table 7.

The quality of the share-quotation predictions was evaluated
according to several criteria: i.e., the score of a proper
scoring rule, the probability for the class containing the true
value and the distance between the true value and the 'best
guess' estimation among others. In addition, a 'theoretical
subject' gave predictions corresponding to the relative frequencies derived from documentation of the two years before the
experiment. The results showed that the experts' predictions
were better than the non-experts, that quality of predictions
declined the longer the period that they covered, and that
predictions improved over sessions relative to the theoretical
subject.

All the criteria mentioned above can be used for evaluating
individual probability assessments. In connection with portfolio theory as a decision aid technique, it is necessary that
the estimates resemble the eventual, actual state of affairs.

Table 7. Time sequence of share-quotation predictions

Dates of Predictions

Dates of Estimates	1974								1975		
	t_1	t_2	t_3	t_4	t_5	t_6	t_7	t_8	t_9	t_{10}	t_{11}
	June 10-14	July 8-12	Aug 5-9	Sep 2-6	Oct 30-4	Nov 28-1	Nov 25-29	Dec 23-27	Jan 20-24	Feb 17-21	March 17-21
t_0: 05/20-22/74	+	+	+	+	+	+					
t_1: 06/17-19/74		+	+	+	+	+	+				
t_2: 07/15-17/74			+	+	+	+	+	+			
t_3: 08/12-14/74				+	+	+	+	+	+		
t_4: 09/9-11/74					+	+	+	+	+	+	
t_5: 10/7-9/74						+	+	+	+	+	+

Did a share for which a higher return was predicted actually
yield higher returns? For this purpose, a rank correlation
coefficient was calculated between the medians of the assessed
probability distributions from the various shares and the rank
orders stemming from the true values.

As can be seen from Table 8, the correlations are extremely
low and sometimes even negative. Negative correlations mean
that the subjects expected relatively high gains from such
shares which finally yielded relatively low ones. Two explanations are possible to account for these findings:

(1) Subjects had no knowledge which they could have used for
valid differential predictions. Positive and negative correlations must then have occurred randomly.

(2) It might have been possible that single shares showed especially untypical and unexpected fluctuations. This would then
have led to a greater number of negative correlations.

To check if at least some of the subjects had valid differential information, the number of negative correlations per subject was tabulated. The result is shown in Table 9. The substantive experts had slightly fewer negative correlations, but
this difference is not significant. The only significant finding was that subjects showed a greater number of positive than
negative correlations.

The small amount of differential quality contained in the estimates, as is shown by the frequency of negative correlations
and by the low values of the correlation coefficients, obviously, makes them unsuitable for use as input for portfolio evaluation according to the mean-variance approach.

Perhaps this task was too artificial and subjects were not used
to it? Subjects had the possibility to put together a portfolio of their own at each assessment session. Subjective experts are familiar with this kind of a task. The highest gain
obtained during the total time period was 9,4% and the greatest loss 15,1%. A subject investing an equal amount of money

Table 8. Average correlation between class predicted (point estimate of subjective probability distribution) and the class actually realized (true class)

Dates of Estimates

Dates of Estimates	Dates of Predictions										
	1	2	3	4	5	6	7	8	9	10	11
1	-.07	.17	.07	.04	.12	.15					
2		.15	.15	.05	.12	.17	.15				
3			.03	-.03	.11	.17	.12	.04			
4				-.03	.02	.09	-.04	-.09	-.04		
5					.02	.07	.22	.15	-.01	.04	
6						.17	.06	-.09	-.02	-.02	-.02

Prediction Intervals in Months: 1   2   3   4   5   6

Table 9.   Frequency of negative correlations out of a total of
           36 correlations for each subject

Subject Group	Frequency	Mean Probability
Psych.Stud.	9;12;18;15;16;10;19	.39
Bus.Adm.Stud.	15; 7;21; 9;18;14;14	.39
Normative Experts	16;11;15;19;10;	.39
Substantive Experts	12;13; 8;11;18;	.34

in each share would have had a loss of 7.4%. Only six out of
24 subjects had higher losses.

Table 10 shows the ranks of the gains obtained by the various
subjects, where rank 1 denotes the highest gain. It can be seen
that the substantive experts seem to have established better
portfolios than other subjects, but differences between experimental groups failed to reach standard significance levels.

As before, it can be seen that subjects possessed some task-
relevant information; most got higher gains on the average
than the theoretical subject, and substantive experts showed a
tendency to do best.

5. Summary and conclusions

The research summarized here reported some empirical findings
on the assessment and evaluation of probabilities and utilities. The central issue was how such judgments could be incorporated into decomposition models for aiding diagnosis and
selection. The quality of assessments was considered from two

Table 10. Ranks of gains obtained with the portfolio

Subject Group	Rank
Psych.Stud.	8; 19; 17; 11; 12; 5; 14;
Bus.Adm.Stud.	21; 16; 20; 7; 10; 22; 23;
Normative Experts	9; 1; 18; 15; 24;
Substantive Experts	3; 4; 2; 6; 13;

points of view: their goodness as individual assessments, and their usefulness for decision aid models. Wholistic intuitive judgments were often compared with model-generated judgments, it being our a priori expectation that the latter would be superior. This was found to be most certainly true for probabilistic diagnosis and held true for many selection problems as well.

The experiments reported above dealt with decisions made by individuals. But if an organization is the decision maker, and if many people participate in the decision-making process, then questions concerning consensus arise. Should consensus be reached with regard to the evaluation of single components, or is consensus only necessary with regard to the final decision? We have recently begun research on this and other closely re-lated problems; see, e.g., Borcherding & Schaefer (1976), Schaefer (1977), Seaver (1977, 1978).

Whenever a consensus is required, there are two different ways of obtaining it; either as an agreement of the group via nego-tions and discussions, or as a solution obtained by using some kind of a model to aggregate individual opinions. When indivi-dual members have to justify a group's decision, it becomes

especially important that they feel that their opinion was
taken into account when the consensus was reached, thus rendering the former behavioral approach very important. A variety
of studies on choice shifts indicate that the group situation
can induce certain judgmental trends like polarization. Such
group-induced shifts may have to be taken into account with
respect to the quality of estimates reached by a consensus. A
review of the literature and a translation of some choice shift
problems into the language of decision theory can be found in
Schaefer (1978b).

Methodologies for aiding information processing and decision
making have by now been developed to an extent that they can
be used with good success on a large-scale basis, especially
for important, information-loaded, time-constrained, or otherwise complex problems. Further research is still needed, however, to resolve the practical and methodological problems
that remain.

Chapter 18 Theory and Application of Utility and Decision Analysis

*K. M. Aschenbrenner, M. Zaus, N. Mai and
M. I. Ksiensik*

1. Introduction

In real decision situations, a decision maker must carefully
weigh the consequences of an impending decision in order to fix
priorities for his behavior. That these consequences are usually
quite complex is the result of two different factors: not only
may the consequences vary simultaneously on more than one important dimension, but there may also be some uncertainty as to
which consequences will in fact occur, since this often depends
on further events over which the decision maker has no control.

If decision alternatives or their consequences vary on several
dimensions simultaneously, we speak of multiattribute decisions.
Daily needs, for instance, vary frequently on attributes such
as price and quality. Living accomodations vary on attributes
such as size, location, rent, quietness, etc.. In most cases,
none of the alternatives offers optimal values for all evaluation criteria; rather, maintaining positive values on some attributes often requires accepting negative values on others.
Thus, a person who wants a lodging close to work and with easy
access to shops and cultural events may, for example, have to
put up with more noise, air pollution and a higher rent. The
decision maker must consider the advantages and disadvantages
of the various alternatives in order to make the best possible
personal choice.

When the consequences of a decision do not occur with certainty,
we speak of decisions under uncertainty. The consequences of a
medical treatment, for instance, depend on the patient's disease which, in turn, must be accurately diagnosed. Often,

however, a given set of symptoms can characterize any one of
several different diseases. Thus, in order to assess the success of a treatment, it is necessary to calculate the probabilities of the possible diseases on the basis of the symptoms.

Thus, the choice of complex decision alternatives requires a
simultaneous consideration of multiple information. Since, however, a person's capacity for processing information is limited
to about seven items at a time, most decision situations will
overcharge the decision maker's ability for processing all relevant information. As a result, decision makers often apply
simplifying strategies and heuristics to reduce the complexity.
With regard to the decision maker's intentions, this can often
lead to suboptimal or even wrong decisions (cf. Aschenbrenner,
1977b, 1978a; Slovic, Fischhoff & Lichtenstein, 1977, Tversky
& Kahneman, 1974).

The deficiencies and weaknesses of decision and judgment processes point at the necessity of decision-aiding procedures
that allow appropriate information processing and an optimal
selection of alternatives. Our own research has shown that prescriptive decision analysis can adequately serve such a function. Up to the early seventies, decision theorists distinguished between descriptive and normative decision theory
(Coombs, Dawes & Tversky, 1970, Luce & Suppes, 1965). *Descriptive* decision theory tries to establish rules and models to determine how a naive, unguided decision maker considers the different aspects of a decision problem in arriving at a decision.
Normative decision theory, on the other hand, develops models
to be applied in certain situations when a given objective
criterion - for instance profit - is to be maximized.

In contrast, *prescriptive* decision theory aims for optimization
according to subjective criteria. In this way, it is a synthesis of the two other approaches, since the decision maker's objectives are often not accessible to objective measurement, or
the decision maker wants to accomplish several competing objectives simultaneously. Prescriptive decision analysis proceeds

by structuring a decision problem in such a way that a mathematical model can be applied to integrate the evaluations of the
problem's various aspects. The selection of an adequate model
depends on the decision maker's preference structure, which
can be assessed by some simple questions.

The basic principle of decision analysis is decomposition: the
decision problem is decomposed into its individual aspects.
The global evaluation of a complex problem is thus replaced by
many, more simple evaluations. A mathematical model is then
used to integrate these partial evaluations. For value judgments, this aggregation is achieved by multiattribute utility
theory (MAUT). Probability judgments are processed correspondingly with the help of probabilistic information processing
systems (PIP).

An important aspect of our research is the testing and application of these procedures as decision aids in complex decision situations. In section 2, we describe MAUT and its application to the evaluation of cortisone drugs, research projects,
urban parks, and student lodgings, as well as another procedure, partially oriented towards MAUT, that was used to help
pupils in their occupational choices. Section 3 illustrates
the application of probabilistic information processing systems
to indicate brain-angiography and to classify comatose states.
It contains also a review of research on the elicitation of
subjective probability judgments. Section 4 describes our research on unguided decision behavior. It analyses the question
of how decision makers perceive risk and how they incorporate
it into their decisions. Section 5 discusses the contribution
of measurement theory to the foundations of subjective probability and utility analysis and compares alternative ways of
handling measurement error.

2. Multiattribute Utility Theory (MAUT)

The design of our studies on decision analysis is based primarily on multiattribute utility theory (MAUT; Keeney & Raiffa, 1976). In line to this theory, the decision alternatives are first decomposed into individual attributes so that the decision maker can determine each alternative's standing with respect to each attribute and, additionally, each attribute's importance for the overall evaluation can be assessed.

MAUT proceeds by the following steps:

(1) *Determination of a set of attributes* that
(a) includes all aspects that allow the decision maker to distinguish between the decision alternatives,
(b) can be operationalized in such a way that a clear evaluation of the levels can be determined for each attribute,
(c) can be processed by a mathematical aggregation model.
This set allows to define each decision alternative A_i as a vector of attribute levels $A_i = (X_{i1} \ldots, X_{in})$. In the context of risk, decision alternatives are defined as vectors of probability distributions over the attributes. The attributes will be elicited and defined principally by a goal system analysis. We will discuss this in more detail when describing applications of MAUT.

(2) *Determination of an evaluation model.*
Before the decision maker's preferences can be quantified on the basis of a real-valued utility function, at least two independence-conditions must be tested to arrive at a suitable evaluation model. First, preference independence must be tested to make sure that the trade-offs between two attributes X_1 and X_2 do not depend on the other attributes $X_3 \ldots X_n$. The utility independence test, on the other hand, examines whether each attribute X_j ($j = 1, \ldots, n$) can be evaluated independently of the other attributes. This analysis of the decision maker's preference structure informs us on the question of whether the overall utility of an alternative is representable (a) as the sum of its partial utilities (b) as the sum of its interacting partial utilities or (c) as the product of its partial utilities.

(3) *Determination of utility-functions.* After the independence
conditions have been verified, an utility function is assessed for each attribute. The choice of the scaling method (Fishburn, 1967; Keeney & Raiffa, 1976) depends on the operationalization of an attribute. There are by now about 30 alternative
scaling methods for MAUT (Fishburn, 1967; Keeney & Raiffa, 1976;
Zaus, 1975) so that, from a practical point of view, there
should be no difficulties encountered with respéct to scaling.

(4) *Determination of attribute weights.* By comparing the attributes with one another, the decision maker may find that some
attributes are substantially more relevant than others. In
this case, the attributes should contribute with different
weights to the global evaluation. Similar scaling procedures
can be used for the determination of weights as for the determination of utility functions. In addition, there are scaling
procedures that allow the simultaneous assessment of utility
values and attribute weights (Aschenbrenner & Kasubek, 1978a;
Keeney & Raiffa, 1976; Raiffa, 1969; Toda, 1974).

(5) *Calculation of the overall utility for each alternative*
on the basis of the model determined in step (2).

(6) *Sensitivity analysis.* Sensitivity analysis is a method designed to measure the sensitivity of the final evaluation
against variations of the chosen attribute weights and possible
inaccuracies in the scaled utility functions.

2.1. Applications of Multiattribute Utility Theory

MAUT has been applied in various fields in order to demonstrate
its usefulness as a decision aid and to solve more specific
problems; for instance, comparisons between different scaling
procedures. We applied MAUT to evaluate research projects,
urban parks and green spaces, student lodgings, and cortisone
drugs. Here the fundamental question arises of how to assess
the success of a decision aid. What standard can we use to
establish MAUT-judgments' superiority over the intuitive, un-

guided judgment? Since the main reason for developing subjective evaluation procedures is the absence of a single, objective criterion for evaluating the alternatives, simply comparing the MAUT-judgment with such a criterion is not possible.

Of course, a specific model's appropriateness can be inferred
from its fulfilling the necessary conditions of independence.
Referring to these or to similar arguments, Shepard (1964) and
Edwards (1971) argue that MAUT procedures should be accepted
as valid when they appear appropriate in a given situation.
Even if the model is appropriate, however, the question remains
as to whether the elicitation procedures can actually achieve
what we expect from them. Do the utility scaling procedures
really reproduce the differences in value which the decision
maker perceives between different attribute levels? Does a
weighting procedure reflect true differences in the importance
of individual attributes? The verification of internal consistency and convergent validity can contribute to answering
these questions.

Internal consistency allows to check whether a decision maker
applies a procedure adequately. If, for instance, the decision
maker judges an attribute A to be three times as important as
attribute B, and attribute B again to be twice important as
attribute C, then he should also evaluate attribute A being
six times as important as attribute C. If not, then he either
has not understood the procedure, or he lacks insight into
the subject matter.

Miller, Kaplan and Edwards (1967, p. 367) introduced the basic
idea of convergent validity into decision research: "The basic
idea of construct validity is that a test should make sense
and the data obtained by means of it should make sense. One
form of making sense is that different procedures purporting
to measure the same abstract quantity should covary". In MAUT,
the most commonly used form of convergent validity is to compare MAUT-judgments with intuitive overall evaluations of the
alternatives (Fischer, 1975). One objection to this is that

validating a judgment aid by comparing it to what it was supposed to improve involves some circularity. On the other hand,
when considering only a few attributes, intuitive evaluations
are relatively good (Yntema & Torgerson, 1961). We can therefore argue that if there is a good agreement between MAUT-judgments and intuitive ones with few attributes, the corresponding elicitation procedure should also yield valid results when
more attributes are involved.

Checking convergence between judges or methods appears to be a
more valid procedure, even if it requires more effort. An evaluation method will therefore be considered valid if (Aschenbrenner & Kasubek, 1978a):
- two or more judges with similar objectives and similar information arrive at similar judgments
- the same judge reaches similar judgments by different elicitation methods
- an elicitation procedure yields coinciding parameters (e.g.
  weights) between judges
- a judge generates coinciding parameters with different elicitation methods.

2.1.1. Evaluating the dangerousness of cortisone drugs

By applying these convergent validation criteria to the evaluation of cortisone therapies, we were able to demonstrate
MAUT's effectiveness in improving medical therapy decisions
(Aschenbrenner & Kasubek, 1978a, Kasubek & Aschenbrenner, 1977,
1978). The specific decision problem consisted in selecting
one from a variety of alternative chemical derivatives of cortisone. Certain diseases (e.g. bronchiale asthma or arthritis)
call for a prolonged therapy with cortisone as the last possibility of relief for the patient. The selection is problematic
because alternative derivatives of cortisone cause possible
side effects that vary in their nature and extent (table 1).
Since the desired effect is similar for all drugs, equally ef-

Table 1

Relative Frequencies of Six Undesired Side Effects of Cortisone Drugs[a]

Drug	Efficiency equivalent dose in mg	Increased weight	Increased blood pressure	Cushing face[b]	Ulcus, hyperacidity	Hypertrichosis hirsutism[c]	Myopathy[d]
Cortisone	50	58%	49%	78%	30%	65%	4%
Dexamethasone	1.5	64%	2%	70%	9%	8%	6%
Hydrocortisone	40	24%	18%	76%	10%	58%	4%
Prednisolone	8 - 10	20%	11%	86%	36%	68%	1%
Prednisone	10	20%	11%	86%	36%	68%	20%
Triamcinolone	8	40%	2%	70%	12%	19%	62%
6-α-methyl-prednisolone	8	30%	5%	78%	5%	47%	1%

[a] Data for side effects 1 to 5 are from Zicha (1961), 100 randomly selected patients per drug. Data for myopathy are from Braun et al. (1965) and Grabner (1972).
[b] Obese face.
[c] Abnormal growth of hair.
[d] Weakening of the muscles.

ficacious doses of each could be evaluated on the basis of a multiattribute index of dangerousness. For this purpose, the side effects in table 1 were used as attributes and their relative frequencies of occurrence as objective measures of the alternatives' attribute levels.

Five internists took part in the evaluation task. First, they were presented with the information in table 1 and asked to rank the seven drugs intuitively according to their dangerousness. Two different elicitation procedures were applied for MAUT evaluations; an indifference curve procedure (Thurstone, 1931) and a conditional weighting procedure initially developed by Aschenbrenner (1977a, cf. 2.1.4.).

Indifference curves (cf. Fig. 1) connect points of equal dangerousness on a coordinate plane defined by two attributes. Accordingly, each physician was first instructed to imagine a hypothetical cortisone that would cause, for example, myopathy in 10% of the cases and an ulcer in 50% of the cases. He was then asked what myopathy frequency would render another alternative equally dangerous if it caused an ulcer in only 30% of the cases. The points identified in this way are all of equal dangerousness and, when connected, form an indifference curve. Using an adequate pairing of attributes, this procedure allowed to estimate "dangerousness functions" and importance weights for all attributes using an algorithm of Toda (1974).

At the same time we were able to check the preference independence of attribute pairs required by the additive model. When determining the points of equal dangerousness, the physicians were to imagine that the uninvolved attributes remained fixed at some constant level. Preference independence requires that changing this constant level should not influence the tradeoffs between the two attributes involved in the comparison. This was found to be the case with respect to the comparisons made by the five physicians involved in our study.

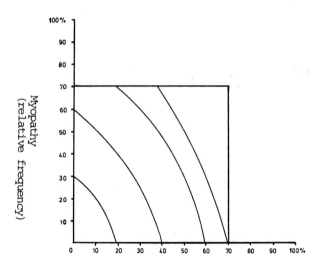

Ulcus, hyperacidity
(relative frequency)

Figure 1. Sample indifference map from
           Physician 3,
           myopathy vs. ulcus, hyperacidity

The conditional importance weighting procedure (Fig. 2) allows
a direct evaluation of the weights on the basis of the actual
variability of the attributes. In this procedure, cards were
presented to the judge indicating for each attribute the extreme
positive and negative poles that occurred in the alternatives.
The judge was then asked to imagine a hypothetical alternative
with the most negative standing on each attribute and to decide
for which of the attributes he would most like to exchange its
worst for its best level. We assume that the attribute chosen
shows the greatest subjective value difference between its positive and negative extreme and should thus be the most important. Likewise, the order in which the remaining attributes are
selected should reflect their respective rank order of impor-

tance. In performing this task, the judge becomes aware of the
meaning of the weighting and subsequently has little problems
in numerically evaluating the importance of the individual
attributes relative to the one chosen last.

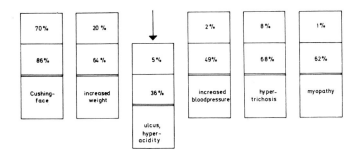

Figure 2. Conditional importance
rating

Dangerousness values of the individual drugs were first assessed on the basis of the dangerousness functions and weights determined by the indifference curve procedure. The weights were
also replaced by the conditionally evaluated ones and the dangerousness values recalculated. Two factor (physician x drug)
analyses of variance were done for each judgment method (i.e.
intuitive, indifference curve and conditional weighting) in order to assess convergent validity. Of interest here were the
portions of judgmental variance accounted for by drugs and by
physician x drugs interaction[1], the latter reflecting the degree of disagreement and error in a procedure. The MAUT-judgments were found to be fairly consistent between physicians
with only 13 % (indifference curve method), and 5 % (condi-

---

[1]The portion of variance accounted for by physicians is meaning-
less, since the origin of the scales of dangerousness is
arbitrary.

tional importance weighting) of the judgmental variance being accounted for by interaction. In contrast, agreement between intuitive judgments was low showing 57% of the variance being accounted for by interaction. Furthermore, whereas the MAUT-judgments determined by the two different procedures agreed well with one another,both differed considerably from the intuitive judgments.

Good agreement was also found with respect to the weights, these showing considerable convergence both over physicians and procedures. Once again, however, the conditional weighting procedure yielded a higher between-physician agreement than the indifference curve procedure did. An internal consistency analyses showed that this was due to the fact that two of the five physicians evaluated inconsistent indifference curves, whereas the three others gave comparable judgments in both procedures. That the conditional weighting procedure led to good results for all physicians suggests that this method is superior to the one based on indifference curves.

These results illustrate the usefulness of MAUT as a judgment aid. Whereas the physicians agreed in how to evaluate the components and how to aggregate the partial evaluations, their intuitive overall judgments showed considerable divergence. In this study, the decision problem was very precisely defined and the attributes were objectively measurable. The following study however will deal with a problem in which the goals are far more abstract and difficult to measure.

2.1.2. Evaluation of research projects

Together with the project X.10 (Aschenbrenner, Borcherding, Kasubek, Schaefer, Schümer & Schümer-Kohrs, 1975), we attempted to evaluate the quality of the different research projects in the SFB itself - a complicated task that external experts invited by the DFG have actually to deal with at regular intervals. Here quality refers to the degree to which a project is

worth being funded.. Besides being informative to our colleagues within the SFB, the study served as a comparison between
MAUT and the so-called "Bootstrapping" approach (Bowman, 1963).
The latter, based on Brunswik's (1956) lens model, assumes that
though a human judge bases his/her judgments on all essential
aspects of the judgment object, these judgments can be subject
to random errors arising from internal and external influences.
By applying statistical procedures (multiple regression or analysis of variance) to a series of different judgments, one attempts to extract a model of the judgment process in form of
the individual attributes' weights (cf. Aschenbrenner, 1977b,
Dawes & Corrigan, 1974, Slovic & Lichtenstein, 1971).

Seventeen different research projects were judged anonymously
by 29 collaborators in the SFB. Comparison with the intuitive
global judgment served as convergent validity criterion. For
this reason, each judge was first asked to rank order the projects holistically according to the degree that they deserved
being funded. MAUT evaluations followed the two-step hierarchy
of attributes for evaluating projects' worth displayed in table
2 (see next page) which was based on the guide-lines proposed
by the DFG (DFG notes, Feb. 1972, p. 29) for the evaluation of
SFB's. Graphical rating scales ranging from 0 to 100 were used
to evaluate the projects' standings on each attribute. In order
to provide anchors and to increase discrimination, the judges
first had to indicate the two projects that they considered
being the best and the worst on each respective attribute,
these projects being assigned the values 100 and 0. This procedure was used both for the super-attributes in the upper part
of the hierarchy and for the subattributes in the lower part.

The MAUT and Bootstrapping approaches differed only in the
way the weights were calculated. MAUT weights were directly
estimated by the judges. For each super-attribute the judges
had 100 points to distribute over the subattributes according
to the extent to which the latter contributed to the superattribute's fulfillment. For weighting the super-attributes,

Table 2. Attributes for determining quality of individual research projects in a SFB

Supergoals	Subgoals
1. Quality of the proposal	1.1. Theoretical foundation of the research problem
	1.2. Concreteness of problem formulation
	1.3. Is the proposed investigation adequate to the problem?
	1.4. Workability of the project
	1.5. To which extent can one expect new results?
2. Project's contribution to the completion of the SFB's program	2.1. with regard to content
	2.2. with respect to theoretical advancement
	2.3. as to "selling" the SFB to the DFG and its judges
3. How close is the cooperation between this project and others?	
4. How well does the project fit into the SFB's overall research plan?	
5. The project's yield	5.1. with regard to output quantitiy (reports, publications, etc.)
	5.2. with regard to output quality
6. Relation of scientific output to the project's cost	

these were first rank ordered according to importance. Then a
numerical estimate was made about how much more important each
superattribute was as compared to the last ranked superattribute.
The additive model was first used to calculate the MAUT ratings
directly from the superattributes and secondly with the respective superattributes being replaced by their subattributes, the
latters' weights being calculated as the product of their
point-allottment and the weight of the superattribute. Bootstrapping weights were evaluated by multiple regression with the
overall evaluation as criterion and the evaluations of the projects on the individual attributes as predictors. Once again,
two regressions were done, one using only the superattributes
as predictors and the other using the subattributes (both analyses, however, included the simple attributes 3, 4 and 6).
This form of regression is called a hybrid model (Huber,
Danshgar & Ford, 1971); it facilitates future evaluation tasks
as far as the judge will only have to evaluate the alternatives
on the individual attributes. Aggregation of the partial evaluations is then done by the model using the weights estimated from the judge's previous judgments.

For analysis, each judge's model judgments were compared to his/
her intuitive overall judgments. These comparisons showed relatively high correlations between model and intuitive judgments for all four models and for nearly all judges: the median
correlation for both MAUT-procedures was .85, while those for
the regression models based on super- and subattributes were
.91 and .98, respectively. The fact that the regression models
yield higher correlations than the MAUT-procedures results from
the fact that no cross validation took place. At first glance,
these results seem to indicate that all the procedures used
were appropriate for evaluating the quality of the research
projects.

This conclusion was called into question, however, by a subsequent factor analysis showing that ratings on all attributes
were highly inter-correlated so that the first factor could

account for 73 per cent of the overall variance of all the attributes' evaluations. It thus seems that the latter were not
independent evaluations of individual aspects but simply repeated measurements so that the good fit of all models would be
a trivial result. Aschenbrenner et al. (1975) discuss various
ways of explaining this. It is, of course, theoretically possible that the attributes are really redundant or that the individual researcher, as a result of his/her socialisation, has
come to satisfy all criteria to similar degree. Neither explanation appears likely, however, if one looks at the formulation of the attributes. Rather, it is more probable that the
majority of the SFB-members had previously formed overall
judgments concerning the individual projects and that these
judgments dominated their rating of the individual attributes.

Although external judges would be less subject to such a halo
effect, we can conclude from this work that a decomposing evaluation procedure must not only decompose the goals (attributes)
but must also decompose the alternatives as well. One cannot,
for example, simply ask judges directly how concretely a given
project has formulated its research problem; rather, this concreteness has to be operationalized and measured for all projects, and the various degrees of concreteness have to be evaluated independently of the respective projects. Such a procedure would have revealed the reasons underlying the unidimen-
sionality of the multiattribute judgments in the present case
and would prove insight as to whether it could be avoided.
The attributes used in this study may not, however, be appropriate for this procedure. Research should be undertaken
to determine the kind of scales - maybe only qualitative ones -
that should be used to measure the projects' attribute levels.
Only then could utility functions be elicited for these scales independently of the projects. The next study presents the
formulation of such objective measure by means of a hierarchical goal structure and clarifies the effect of the attributes'

concreteness on the convergence of two importance weighting
procedures.

2.1.3. Evaluation of urban green and recreational areas

This study attempted to construct a hierarchical goal structure for the development of green and recreational areas. City
planners were asked to weigh the subgoals according to their
importance (Zaus, 1977; Zaus & Wendt, 1977, 1980).

For new recreational areas in Hamburg, a criteria system had
to be worked out according to which the areas could be compared. The chief problem in urban park planning consists in recognizing the need for attractive installations and equipment
and, after having checked these needs against the existing
possibilities, introducing a goal-oriented management. The sum
of all material, institutional and personal installations that
characterize a recreational park is here defined as the *recrea-*
tional infrastructure. The supergoal in this case consists in
the optimal management of the infrastructure.

In view of resolving the problem of how to adequately represent this totality as a system of supergoals and subgoals, a
hierarchical decomposition technique must be selected that
enables one to decompose the recreational infrastructure into
a functionally and substantially ordered set of sufficiently
precise elements. In sight of various decomposition criteria
(Zaus & Wendt, 1977), two goal structures were developed in
collaboration with 10 professional city planners.

Figure 3 (see page **692**) shows a goal structure that can serve
as basis for the development of regional recreational parks
and that can be operationalized with respect to alternative
regions; that is, the attributes 1 to 100 are to be transcribed
into measurable dimensions so that the regions in question
can be evaluated and compared unequivocally by applying MAUT.

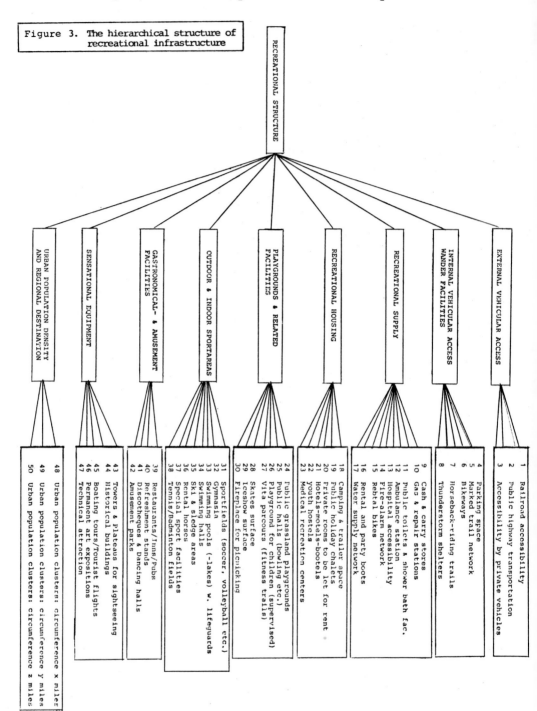

Figure 3. The hierarchical structure of recreational infrastructure

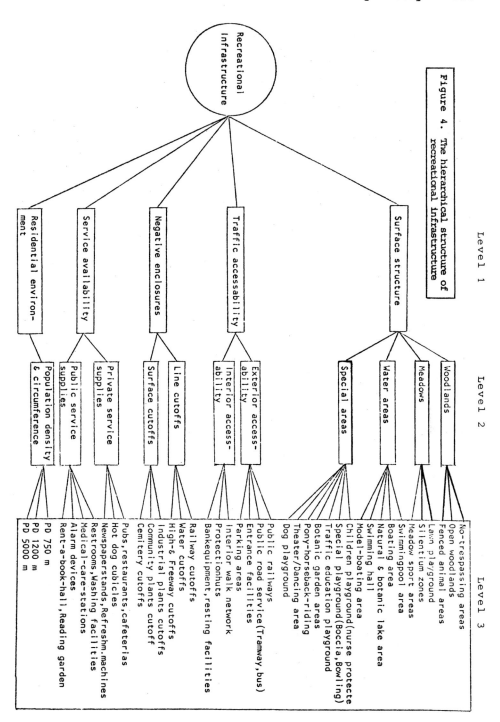

Figure 4. The hierarchical structure of recreational infrastructure

Along with this rather complex goal structure, a simple goal
structure was worked out for the recreational areas in Hamburg
mentioned above. It orders, on two levels, relatively abstract
subgoals (attributes) and indicates, on a third level, the
quantitative attributes that can be considered for comparing
the recreational areas. This goal structure is presented in
Figure 4 (see page 693). It was used to compare two weighting
methods.

To measure the relative importance of the subgoals for the
supergoals, the former were evaluated on each level by both
a hierarchical and a sequential weighting method. In the hierarchical method, a fixed number of points (1,000) was distributed
among each supergoal's subgoals, while in the sequential method
each level of the hierarchy was evaluated independently by
using a rating scale. As a measure of the degree of convergence among the experts, we used the portion of total variance
in the weights that was accounted for by the attributes in the
respective method and hierarchy level. For the hierarchical
method, the convergence among experts amounted to 0.702 on
level 1 (five subgoals), 0.857 on level 2 and 0.914 on level 3,
while the corresponding convergence levels for the sequential
method were 0.795, 0.209 and 0.860, respectively. These findings indicate that the hierarchical method was in all respects
superior to the sequential weighting procedure. In both methods
convergence was best for the most concrete level of abstraction.

2.1.4. Evaluation of student lodgings

Multiattribute evaluation of student lodgings provided an opportunity to determine the extent to which MAUT evaluations
depend on the specific formulation of the attributes (Aschenbrenner, 1977a; Aschenbrenner & Kasubek, 1975). The more the
alternatives of a decision become complex and the more abstract
and intangible the decision maker's objectives are, the more
difficult it becomes to specify a unique attribute set to eva-

luate the alternatives, this becoming increasingly dependent
on the intuition of the people involved. The same problem can
be broken down into attributes in various ways which, in turn,
can be variably operationalized. Bauer, Gebert and Meise (1973)
or Wendt and Zaus (1975) provide some examples of the diversity
of possible attribute sets for a basically similar evaluation
problem.

The question we are concerned with here is how MAUT evaluations
depend on the specific attribute formulation. Are they sensitive to such variations or, as we assumed, does any attribute
structuring, although possibly equivocal, still lead to a better evaluation than no structuring at all? If the latter supposition holds, the convergence of MAUT-judgments based on divergent attribute sets should still be greater than the convergence among intuitive overall evaluations of the same alternatives.

In order to get a realistic divergence in attribute sets, two
groups of five students each independently developed an attribute set for evaluating the suitability of offered lodging.
Several attributes turned out to be strictly identical in the
two sets (table 3). Larger subsets of the two attribute sets
(including the strictly identical ones) were weakly identical
in the sense that the attributes in these subsets in general
referred to the same aspects of quality of housing, but were
differently formulated and structured. Finally, each group generated some attributes not mentioned by the other.

Fifteen descriptions of actual student lodgings were then prepared that gave information about the lodgings' standings on
all attributes generated by the two groups. The descriptions,
each on a separate sheet of paper, were independently evaluated by the groups in group-work. First, each group ranked the
lodgings holistically according to suitability. For multiattribute evaluation each group used its own attribute set. First,
all lodgings' standings on an attribute were written on a blackboard, e.g., with respect to kitchen equipment. These standings

Attributes of group A	weighting method rating	BRLT	Attributes of group K	weighting method rating	BRLT
costs-					
A1 Monthly costs	.136	.112	K1 Monthly costs	.150	.154
A2 Investment costs (security renovation, etc.)	.255	.008	K2 Investment costs (security, renovation, etc.)	.065	.278
strictly identical attributes					
A3 Distance to university	.085	.075	K3 Distance to university	.120	.074
A4 Ecological influences of surrounding	.123	.119	K4 Disturbance by noise, smell, and vermin	.125	.086
A5 Duties and restrictions	.017	.067	K5 Restrictions by the owner	.005	.012
			K6 Duties of tenant	.025	.049
weakly identical attributes					
A6 Size and ground plan of the living room	.027	.090	K7 Structure of the lodging	.100	.099
A7 Further usable rooms	.059	.112	K8 Kitchen equipment	.035	.006
A8 Outfit (furniture, lamps, heating, etc.)	.042	.149	K9 Quality of sanitary facilities	.090	.086
A9 Structure and state of the house	.136	.149	K10 Outfit of the living room	.015	.012
A10 Access to the lodging (separate or not, stairs)	.021	.037	K11 Type of heating	.070	.006
			K12 Separate entrance	.110	.068
A11 Distance to shopping and service facilities	.030	.052	K13 Tenancy agreement	.040	.037
A12 Disturbance through vs. readiness to help of neighbors	.034	.008	K14 Communication facilities in the neighborhood	.050	.031
A13 Social intrastructure of neighborhood	.034	.022			
A14 Type and family status	.001	0			
A15 Duration of owner's presence			Group A decided to drop these two attributes		
A16 Tolerance of owner			in the evaluation phase		

Table 3.   Attributes that contribute to quality of lodgings for student housing and their importance weights, estimated by two MAU methods.

were then rank-ordered independently of the alternatives, and evaluated consecutively. For this, a simple riskless rating procedure similar to the one used for evaluating the research projects and the risky BRLT procedure (Raiffa, 1969) were employed (we will discuss the latter in more detail in 2.3.). Importance weighting under risk also followed the BRLT procedure, whereas the conditional weighting procedure (cf. 2.1.1.) was used for the riskless weighting.

The additive model was used to calculate the two groups' MAUT evaluations and the convergence among these was compared with

the convergence among the groups' overall judgments. Although
the correlation of the overall judgments between the groups
was unexpectedly high (0.84), the correlation between the riskless MAUT judgment slightly exceeded it (0.86). If restricted
to the use of weakly identical attribute sets, the riskless
MAUT evaluations showed even greater convergence (0.91). The
convergence shown by the risky MAUT procedures was somewhat
lower, attaining the convergence of the overall judgments only
for weakly identical sets. The reason for the lower convergence
of the risky MAUT evaluations was found in the BRLT-importance
weights rather than in the attribute sets' divergence. In contrast to the riskless weights, the groups' BRLT-weights for identical attributes differed considerably. Obviously, the BRLT
procedure puts too much strain on the judges (Aschenbrenner &
Kasubek, 1978b, cf. 2.3.).

These results lead to the conclusion that MAUT procedures are
relatively robust against the discussed differences in attribute formulation, at least as long as the judges are able to
make adequate use of the other scaling procedures. In contrast,
intuitive judgments can be extremley dependent on the attribute
formulation (Aschenbrenner, 1978c, cf. 4.).

2.2. A decision aid for Hauptschul-pupils choosing an apprenticeship[2]

The importance of structuring by decomposing is even better
illustrated by our efforts to construct a decision aid for
Hauptschul-pupils. We (Gerdts, Aschenbrenner, Jeromin, Kroh-

---

[2] The Hauptschule is the lowest of the three levels of schooling
in the traditional German school system. After leaving this
school at about the age of 15 the pupil usually starts learning a trade by apprenticeship. This is a three year practical
education in a firm backed up by some theoretical education
in a vocational school. After passing a final exam, the
apprentice is qualified for working autonomously in his field.

Püschel & Zaus, 1979a,b) were able to show that simply structuring a decision problem in form of a goal hierarchy can
lead to a substantial improvement in choice behavior. Our initial observation was that the Hauptschul-pupils' performance
in seeking and processing information leaves much to be desired. The pupils seem to have only a very limited idea of their
educational goals and rely on what they hear by chance. Our
conclusion was that the pupils at first need a better idea of
their objectives. Only, if the pupils know what they want can
they effectively search for the appropriate information.

With the goal system analysis, decision analysis provides an
ideal instrument for this purpose. Of course, its application by
people who are not highly educated requires some modifications.
Therefore, we developed a six step procedure by which the pupils
could learn to generate hierarchical goal systems of their own.
In order to get a preliminary idea of the problems involved,
we started not with the choice of a profession itself but with
the choice of an apprenticeship in an already chosen field.

Sixteen pupils were individually guided in their hierarchy
construction. As a first step, the pupil was asked to name all
aspects coming to his/her mind that might be relevant to the
choice of an apprenticeship. In the second phase, he/she was
asked to sort the aspects into specific and general ones. The
third step was a first hierarchization, the pupil being asked
to group the more specific aspects under the more general ones,
considering whether the former contribute to the attainment of
the latter. In the fourth step, these goal aspects were written
on magnetic plastic chips that the pupil could arrange and re-
arrange on a metal blackboard and, as shown in Fig. 5 (see next
page), connect by lines. At this stage, the pupil was asked to
complete his/her goal system by considering all that is relevant to attaining each of his/her higher level objectives and
by seeing whether his/her goals were complete within the levels of the hierarchy. In step 5, the pupil was then given an
unsorted pile of plastic chips containing objectives from a

Figure 5. Expert goal hierarchy for evaluating and
choosing apprenticeship offers
(see also page 764)

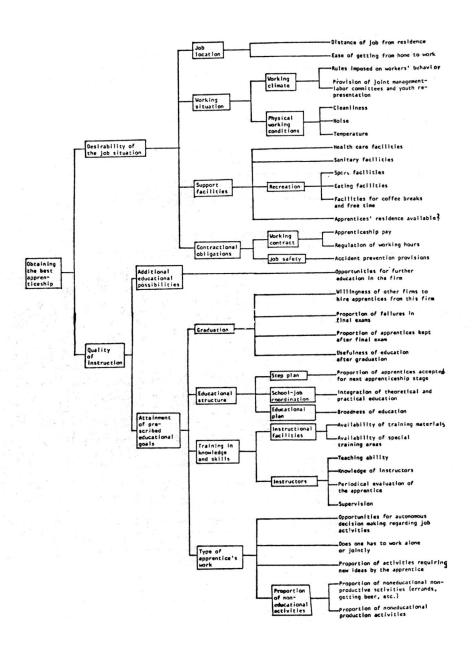

goal hierarchy (Fig. 5) constructed by a panel of experts but in which the bottom level was deleted. The pupil could integrate as many additional goals as he/she liked into his/her own hierarchy. Finally, the pupil was presented the attributes from the bottom level of the expert hierarchy and was allowed to integrate any of them into his/her hierarchy. Our purpose in presenting the expert hierarchy's objectives was first of all to make sure that no essential aspects of the apprenticeship situation were overlooked as a result of time limitations. Secondly, the apprenticeship offers used in the subsequent control task were constructed on the basis of the expert hierarchy's attributes.

The goal trees of the 16 pupils were surprisingly diverse. Nine developed a hierarchy with four levels of abstactation and seven with as many as five levels. The goal trees included a mean of 46 aspects; two thirds were generated by the pupils themselves, the remaining third having been adopted from the expert hierarchy.

Sixteen control pupils read and discussed a text most of which was taken from information brochures issued by the state employment office and which dealt thoroughly with the aspects contained in the expert hierarchy. The control and experimental groups were thus similarly informed, but only the latter carried out their own structuring operation, whereas the treatment of the control group did not go beyond the usual preparation received in school.

A process tracing technique (Aschenbrenner, 1977b) was used to determine the success of the decision aid. Such techniques permit the observation of the sequence in which pieces of information are sought out and thus allows one to draw conclusions about the course of information processing and the decision rules being applied. The technique centered on an information display board (cf. Aschenbrenner, 1979, for a complete description of these methods), an attribute x alternatives matrix whose cells are actually drawers containing information on the particular alternative's standing on the par-

ticular attribute. If, for instance, the pupil wants to know
how noise disturbance is like in apprenticeship 2, he has simply
to draw a card out of the drawer in the second column of the
noise row, read the information on the reverse side and lay it
down. The board described three or five hypothetical alternatives on the 35 lowest level attributes from the expert hierarchy. The alternatives were constructed in such a way that none
clearly exceeded the others.

The information display board was explained to the pupils and
they were asked to select their most preferred apprenticeship.
For this, they were allowed to draw as much information as
they wanted, proceed in any sequence, and refer to the same
piece of information several times.

Four criteria were used to evaluate subjects' information processing: .the number of observed attributes; the average number
of alternatives considered per observed attribute; the "goal-
orientedness" of the information search, measured by the rank
correlation between the sequence in which the attributes were
considered for the first time and their previously elicited
importance rank order; and the unstructuredness of the searching process. The latter criterion was defined in terms of the
so-called transitions from one kind of information to another,
the extent of "unstructuredness" increasing with the number of
jumps in which attribute and alternative are changed simultaneously (Aschenbrenner, 1979).

A multivariate analysis of variance showed that the experimental group used better information processing strategies. Though
experimental pupils took only a few more attributes into consideration than control pupils did (19 vs. 17), they considered a far greater number of alternatives per attribute observed
(66 v. 40 per cent). In addition, their information search was
significantly more goal-oriented ($\overline{\text{Tau}}$: 0.44. v. 0.00) and
structured (35% v. 60% jumps) than was that of the control
group. The latter's proportion of jumps (60%) corresponds approximately to the expected value of a random search, whereas

the proportion in the experimental group comes close to a strategy based on systematic attributewise comparison of the alternatives.

The construction of a personal goal hierarchy leads to a substantial improvement in information processing that is greater
than that achievable by merely discussing the relevant decision
criteria. The explanation for this is that hierarchical structuring enables decision makers to deal more intensively with
partial aspects without losing sight of the whole problem.

Recently, Aschenbrenner, Jaus and Villani (1980) put the goal
structuring procedure to two field tests. In the first test, the
pupils' subsequent verbal behavior in a consultation at the
employment office was analyzed. The second experiment tested
the same pupils' occupational knowledge and preferences three
months later. Here we found that experimental pupils required
twice as much and more specific and concrete information and
that they were better equipped to process this increased amount
of information.

2.3. Determination of utility functions in risky context

The elicitation of risky utility functions always requires
that the judge states indifference judgments between bets and
certain outcomes, or that he varies individual parameters of
such stimuli until he feels indifferent (cf. Fishburn, 1967).
One such procedure is Raiffa's (1968) basic reference lottery
ticket method (BRLT). The judge is presented a bet in which
he/she can receive either a good (X^*) ot a bad ($X*$) outcome;
these outcomes being the upper and lower bounds of the range
of the attribute whose utility function is to be assessed. The
judge is then asked to indicate the probability (p_i) of winning
X^* that he/she would have to be assured in order to be indifferent between the bet (X^*, p_i, $X*$) and the option of receiving,
without risk, an intermediate outcome (X_i). If we assign 1 and
0 to the utilities of X^* and $X*$, respectively, the chosen p_i
indicates the utility of X_i.

This method has the theoretical advantage of enabling one to
determine the utility of any attribute level, X_i, relative to
X^* and X_*. It requires, however, a very complex and unusual
judgment from the decision maker. For this reason, Aschenbrenner
and Kasubek (1978b) were interested in determining how consistent such judgments are and whether they can be improved by
training and group discussion.

A criterion of internal consistency served to answer these
questions. If we have evaluated the BRLT-utility, u, for three
increasingly preferable outcomes X_i, X_j, X_k, we can then predict indifference judgments for further combinations. For instance, the indifference probability p_{ijk}, where the judge
should be indifferent between the bet (X_k, p_{ijk}, X_i) and the
certain outcome of receiving X_j, is predicted as:

$$[u(X_j) - u(X_i)] / [u(X_k) - u(X_i)] = (p_j - p_i) / (p_k - p_i).$$

Aschenbrenner and Kasubek compared seven such predicted indifference judgments with actually observed ones for outcomes ranging from 0 to 10 DM. A bidding procedure was developed to motivate subjects to give honest answers. Similar bidding procedures had been applied by Becker, de Groot and Marschak (1964)
for utility evaluations according to another method and by
Aschenbrenner and Wendt (1978) for probability evaluations. The
procedure is based on a principle of sharing cake: One splits,
the other chooses. Once the judge has stated his/her indifference probability (p_{ijk}), another probability (q) is drawn at
random from a uniform distribution over the interval [0,1]. If
q exceeds p_{ijk} or is equal to it, the judge is allowed to play
the bet (X_k, q, X_i). Otherwise, if q is inferior to p_{ijk}, he/
she receives X_j immediately. Aschenbrenner and Kasubek proved
that, in this procedure, the judge does him-/herself wrong by
not stating his/her indifference probability (p_{ijk}).

This procedure was repeated on 60 subjects in three individual
sessions in order first, to evaluate a utility function over
the interval from 0 to 10 DM and then to check the consistency

of the seven judgments. In addition, each subject participated
in a final group session with four others in which group members had to arrive at consensus indifference probabilities. To
increase their motivation, the subjects' payment was determined after each session by the actual playing of the bidding
procedure for a bet/certain outcome combination randomly selected from the one used in the session.

The results showed a large discrepancy between the observed
indifference probabilities and the ones predicted from the
judges' utility functions. The average absolute difference was
0.4 in the first session and 0.28 in the third. Thus, though
training brought an increase in internal consistency, the judgments do not appear compatible with utility theory.

Consensus judgments turned out to be substantially more consistent. With a mean discrepancy of 0.17, however, they still
do not appear compatible with utility theory. The group judgments' consistency was found equal to the consistency of the
respective group members' average individual judgments in session 3.

The inconsistency with EU-theory was explained in terms of the
judges' use of an anchoring and adjustment heuristic (cf. Tversky
& Kahnemann, 1974). The indifference judgments at different
bet/certain outcome combinations signified that the judges
oriented their probability judgments above all on the certain
outcome. Since the stakes ranged from 0 to 10 DM, a transformation into probabilities was easily feasible; for example, with
a certain outcome of 2.70 DM the subject used 0.27 as a starting probability. This probability was then adjusted to the
bet's outcomes as follows. If the optimal outcome is only
7.50 DM instead of 10, then the estimate would be somewhat
increased; for example, up to 0.30. As has also been found in
other studies (cf. Slovic, Fishhoff & Lichtenstein, 1977), the
adjustment is usually too small and thus results in inadequate
judgments.

Judges are obviously overtaxed by the kind of judgment required by utility theory and must, as a consequence, have recourse
to simplifying strategies such as anchoring and adjusting heuristics. We can infer from this that the complicated procedures
required by theory are hardly applicable in practice. Indeed,
they appear to lead to larger errors than the use of simple
evaluation techniques such as rating scales, even though the
latter are themselves inadequate as measures of judges' attitudes towards risk.

Interestingly, the consensus evaluations did not show the pattern typical of the anchoring and adjustment heuristic. The
groups must therefore have applied a more complex judgment strategy than their individual members that resulted in greater
consistency. It thus seem that group discussions offer not only
a quantitative but also a qualitative improvement of judgment
behavior. In eliciting utility functions, however, this possibility is questionable when individual differences in the utility functions are expected.

An alternative explanation for these inconsistencies with EU-
theory finds fault not with the complexity of the required
judgment but with the nature of the bidding procedure. The
principle "one splits, the other chooses" implies that if one
wants to maximize one's own outcome, one must make the split
in such a way that both parts are equally large or, in the
present case, that the preferences for the bet and sure outcome are truly identical. Aschenbrenner (1976a), however, calculated the loss in expected utility as a function of the difference between the judge's "true" indifference probability
and a false indication and found that the expected loss varies
as a flat quadratic function of this difference increasing
only very slowly around the apex. Thus, large differences lead
to comparatively small losses.

A difference of 20% between true and stated indifference probability, for instance, will lead at most to a loss in expected
utility of 2% of the utility difference between X^* and X_*.

The mean expected honorarium loss resulting from the subjects' inconsistent judgments was, in fact, only 0.03 DM. Comparable results could be derived for the Marschak bidding procedure.

As a consequence, the EU bidding procedures may possibly achieve exactly the opposite of what they were intended to. If the judge actually behaves according to utility theory, then the bidding procedure teaches him not to spend much effort in making his/her judgment because the gain stemming from a better evaluation is, in most cases, minimal.

3. Probabilistic information processing systems

In cases where the consequences of alternative actions do not occur with certainty, but only with certain probabilities, the question of how to determine these probabilities has so far remained open. In real-world situations, it is often not possible to base such probability estimates on simple frequency counts. Rather, reference must be made to many single pieces of information. In cases, for example, where medical diagnoses cannot be made with certainty, the probabilities of each alternative diagnosis must be determined. Knowledge of the incidence rates (prior probabilities - $P(H_i)$) of the observed disease H_i helps only slightly in judging an individual case. The physician must instead collect relevant data (D_j) about the patient in order to further differentiate between diagnoses (hypotheses).

Such data collection is thus aimed at reducing as much of the uncertainty as possible. In medicine it is generally postulated that no single or composite piece of information can be taken as definite proof in favor of a diagnosis. Rather, the individual data are only probabilistically linked to the various diseases, this connection being representable in terms of conditional probabilities of the form $p(D_j/H_i)$. Once all the relevant data have been collected, however, the probabilities

associated with the hypotheses are of interest. These latter
probabilities are called posterior probabilities and are of
the form $p(H_i/D_1, \ldots D_m)$.

It is evident that a direct evaluation of posterior probabilities requires very complex judgments. Ways to simplify these
complex judgments can be derived from the formal connection of
the probabilities involved. If the prior probabilities $p(H_i)$
and the conditional probabilities $p(D_j/H_i)$ can be determined,
Bayes theorem will then, under various restrictive conditions,
indicate an optimal connection of the information to the posterior probabilities $p(H_i/D_1, \ldots D_m)$ we are interested in. The
following version of Bayes theorem is the one most frequently
applied:

$$P(H_i/D_1, \ldots, D_m) = \frac{\prod\limits_{j=1}^{m} P(D_j/H_i) \, P(H_i)}{\sum\limits_{i=1}^{n} \prod\limits_{j=1}^{m} P(D_j/H_i) \, P(H_i)} \tag{1}$$

Among the conditions for applying this equation, the most restrictive one is that all data D_j have to be conditionally
stochastically independent. If this assumption cannot be maintained, however, there are various modifications possible.
Mai and Hachmann (1977) and Victor (1973, 1976) have given
comprehensive descriptions of the different modifications of
Bayes theorem.

For practical diagnostic applications of Bayes theorem, one
must first arrive at numerical values for the probabilities
$P(H_i)$ and $P(D_j/H_i)$. In medical applications, this is most often
achieved by counting relative frequencies in more or less extensive samples of patients. Often, however, such samples are
not available, and the only possibility is to make as effective use as possible of expert knowledge. The use of subjective probabilities (Raiffa & Schlaifer, 1961; Edwards, 1962)
was suggested early for quantifying expert knowledge. Edwards

(1962) proposed a system of particular interest for processing probabilistic information like expert knowledge (PIP-system: probabilistic information processing). After having considered all information, $P(H_i/D_1, \ldots, D_m)$, the complex judgment on the probability of an hypothesis is decomposed into components of the form $P(D_j/H_i)$ and $P(H_i)$ that are easier to evaluate. The integration of the individual component judgments into the overall judgment can then be done mathematically according to Bayes theorem. Thus, this approach is just another variation of the fundamental idea of prescriptive decision theory. The evaluation of likelihoods $P(D_j/H_i)$ is much more simple than the direct evaluation of posterior probabilities, especially because, in the medical field, know-how is most often transmitted in the form of likelihoods. In medical text-books, however, information is given prevailingly in qualitative form as, for instance, in the following statements: in the case of disease H_i, symptom D_j is found "almost always", "occasionally", "frequently", "rarely". Such qualitative statements do not suffice for reckoning. They still need to be quantified. A method for further quantifying such statements with the help of experts is described in section 3.2.

3.1. Probabilistic information processing in medical diagnosis

The increasing specialization in medicine and the steadily growing number of diagnostic procedures and treatment possibilities confront the physician with an immense flood of information. There has as yet, however, been little progress made in developing techniques for processing this information. Attempts at introducing computers to support medical decision making have so far been rather disappointing.

Only very few authors have until now tried to construct decision aids that, besides diagnosis, also take therapy planning into consideration (cf. Gorry, Kassierer, Essig and Schwartz, 1973; Teather, Emerson and Hadley, 1974). The majority of the

existing studies focus on the application of probabilistic
allocation rules, based primarily on Bayes theorem, to problems
of differential diagnosis. A detailed literature survey (Mai &
Hachmann, 1977) on the application of Bayes theorem shows that,
even in this limited field, progress has only been slight.

Formal development of the models - for example, consideration
of dependencies (Bahadur, 1961) or reliabilities (Gettis &
Wilke, 1969) - have not yet been put into practice. The lack
of documentation on the data sources used, the prior probabilities or the operationalization makes the adaptation of a decision aid in many cases impossible. Mai and Hachmann analyzed
73 studies covering 42 different diagnostic issues, thus addressing only a negligible portion of the full range of relevant problems. Moreover, the issues were frequently selected
only on the basis of their relevance for verifying the Bayes
procedure and relatively rarely for their medical relevance.

The chief data base has been the counting of relative frequencies, with many authors being satisfied with very limited samples. Until now, subjective probabilities have been considered in only seven studies on likelihood evaluation. If one compares the elicitation method applied to subjective probabilities with the procedures known (cf. Schütt, 1976, Mai, 1975)
it is striking to see that only the simplest methods (simple
rating scales) have been used so far. No author makes any effort to train his "experts" in giving probability estimates.
They obviously presuppose that the experts can directly translate their medical knowledge into the "language" of probabilities, though in no case arguments or data in support of this
position are offered.

The extraordinary heterogeneity of the studies done so far on
the application of Bayes theorem prevents far-reaching generalizations on the method's validity. Comprehensive solutions
of medical diagnostic problems can hardly be expected in the
near future. For the moment, we must rest content with developing decision aids for relatively delimited problems. Never-

theless, the currently existing inventory of methods is still
far from being exhausted in practical applications. The following studies briefly describe two attempts made to develop practical decision aids in the medical context.

3.1.1. Setting indication for cerebral angiography

This study concerns a decision problem drawn from neurological
diagnostics. In the case of various space-demanding and vascular brain-processes, cerebral angiography almost always permits
one to state the correct diagnosis and to exclude specific
differential diagnoses. As in all tests using a contrast medium,
however, the large amount of diagnostic information provided
by the angiographical method is linked with a certain risk for
the patient, especially for those patients who have an already
damaged vascular system. A complication rate of about 1% mor-
tality and 4% morbidity is to be assumed when applying cerebral
angiography to patients suffering from cerebro-vascular diseases.

Given the possible complications, it is the neurologist's duty
to set the indication for angiography as exactly as possible.
Angiography examinations are, for instance, indispensible preconditions for surgical intervention. This applies equally to
other localized processes (e.g. introcranial hetoma) where it
is necessary to know the exact location before operating. On
the other hand, the indication for angiography on arterios
rotic patients, for instance, is limited to the exclusion of
possible alternative diagnoses.

The data available to the physician prior to angiography are
frequently very general in nature. The **physician** often comes to
know whether an angiography was appropriate or not only after
the angiography and after the patient had been exposed to the
risk of the examination. Therefore, our aim was to help the
physician by providing him/her with a means of arriving at a
probabilistic indication based on the data available before
angiographic examination.

In our studies, we differentiated between three alternative
hypotheses characteristic of the pre-angiographic decision
situation:

1) T: tumor, angiography indicated
2) VA: vascular brain process, angiography indicated
3) VAN: vascular brain process, angiography not indicated

A precise subdivision of the individual diseases included in
these hypotheses is given in Mai, Henrich, Cramon and Brinkman
(1977). From the literature and from expert discussion, a data
check list was compiled containing five personal characteristics concerning sex and age, 39 facts concerning previous diseases, six internal neurological signs, and the results of
four different laboratory analyses. On the basis of this check
list, the medical histories of 328 patients were analyzed. As
all these patients had undergone an angiography, a final evaluation of the actual angiography indication was possible. Relative frequency counts served as a basis for estimating the
likelihood matrix. Some of the estimates were subjectively modified by two experts. In a reclassification analysis, these
data were processed by Bayes theorem (equation 1). The classification results are displayed in table 4 (see page   ). The
mean success rate or diagnostic accuracy is about 70% when
three hypotheses are taken into consideration (T v. VAI v. VAN).
If only two hypotheses are considered (angiography indicated
(AI) vs. not indicated (AN)), we get a value of 78% (cf. Table
4b). In this second comparison, the group VAN is of special
interest, as the cases in this group are those in which the
performed angiography could subsequently be classified as
having been unnecessary. The reclassification shows that Bayes
theorem had allocated 70% of these cases correctly; i.e. in
70% of the cases, an unnecessary angiography could have been
avoided. This figure must, however, be seen in connection with
the program's overall performance. If decisions were made on
the basis of the program's suggestion, 16% of the indicated
angiographies in the group AI would not have been performed.

Table 4. Reclassification results. Comparison of the Bayes-
   diagnosis with the actual values*

a) Comparison for 3 diagnoses (T vs. VAI vs. VAN)

| | | Bayes-diagnosis | | | |
		T	VAI	VAN	Σ
actual state of the patient	T	108 68% 82%	6 11% 5%	17 15% 13%	131
	VAI	21 13% 27%	40 74% 51%	17 15% 22%	78
	VAN	31 19% 26%	8 15% 7%	80 70% 67%	119
	Σ	160	54	114	328

b) Comparison for 2 diagnoses (AI vs. AN)

| | | Bayes-diagnosis | | |
		AI	AN	Σ
actual state of the patient	AI	175 82% 84%	34 30% 16%	209
	AN	39 18% 33%	80 70% 67%	119
	Σ	214	114	328

----

*In addition to the absolute number of cases, the proportion
of persons in the respective column (upper) and row (lower
percentages) that is included in each cell is given.

The primary way of improving the classification results obtained so far appears to be improving the manner in which data are elicited from individual patients. In the present study, a great deal of otherwise relevant data could not be taken into account since they had been inaccurately elicited and hence were not reliable. On the other hand, the employed data list seems to be too extensive for routine usage. With methods drawn from information theory, we were however, able to reduce this list to the data that were most relevant diagnostically. This method is applied in the following investigation.

3.1.2. Classification of comatose states

The present study uses a Bayes program to determinate various comatose states on the basis of selected neurological signs and symptoms (Mai, Henrich & Cramon, 1978). Two 5-step GUTTMAN-scales, tested in previous investigations for evaluating aspects of susceptibility to stimulation and reactivity, served as criteria for assessing the comatose states. Besides being difficult to apply, the use of these GUTTMAN-scales is time consuming and requires special training of the examining physician. For this reason, we wanted to know whether the states defined by the GUTTMAN-scales were also accessible with sufficient accuracy by other neurological signs and symptoms that are easier to observe. Fourteen neurological signs and symptoms were selected and were found to be relatively reliable as predictors of "reactivity" (accuracy ratio: 95% in reclassification; 77% in new classification), whereas "susceptibility to stimulation" was not predicted with sufficient accuracy.

We will here cover only a part of this study concerning an attempt to further reduce the number of required examinations by a sequential selection of neurological signs.

A measure taken from information theory was used to determine the differential diagnostic importance of the individual signs. The notation for a single sign D_j is extended by the index k

($k = 1, 2, \ldots, 1$) standing for the possible subclasses of the datum. Thus, D_{jk} denotes one subclass, and D_j stands for a sign including all subclasses. The information content of a sign, $I(D_j)$, is defined as the difference between the mean uncertainty, H, of H_i before, $H(H_i)$, and after, $H(H_i/D_j)$, examination of D_j.

$$I(D_j) = H(H_i) - H(H_i/D_j) \tag{2}$$

The mean uncertainties $H(H_i)$ and $H(H_i/D_j)$ can be calculated as follows:

$$H(H_i) = - \sum_{i=1}^{n} P(H_i) \log_2 P(H_i) \tag{3}$$

$$H(H_i/D_j) = -\sum_{k=1}^{1} P(D_{jk}) \sum_{i=1}^{n} P(H_i/D_{jk}) \log_2 P(H_i/D_{jk}) \tag{4}$$

Using Bayes theorem, $P(H_i/D_{jk})$ in eq. (4) can be substituted by:

$$P(H_i/D_{jk}) = \frac{P(D_{jk}/H_i) \cdot P(H_i)}{P(D_{jk})} \tag{5}$$

Inserting (3), (4) and (5) into (2) and rearranging terms yields the following expression:

$$I(D_j) = \sum_{k=1}^{1} \sum_{j=1}^{n} P(D_{jk}/H_i) P(H_i) \log_2 P(D_{jk}/H_i) P(D_{jk}) \tag{6}$$

This information measure allows the easy formulation of heuristic rules for the sequential selection of data (cf. Taylor, 1970).

In the present example, this method led to a remarkable simplification of the diagnosis procedure. Figure 6 (see page 715) shows that only five of the 14 signs are needed in sequential applications, and each individual patient can even be assigned on the basis of at most three of these five signs to one of the coma levels.

Compared with the use of all 14 signs, the use of the decision tree illustrated in figure 6 led to no information loss in the patient samples examined (accuracy ratio: 95 % for reclassification, 88 % for new classifications). So far, the published

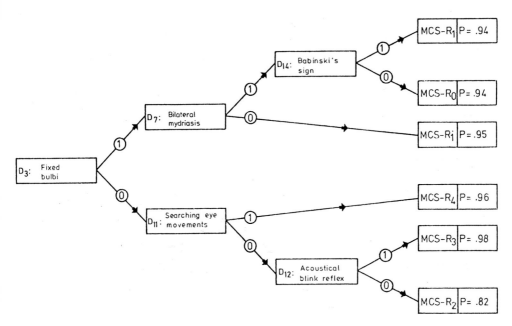

Figure 6. Decision tree for the classification of MCS-R.
A posteriori probabilities are given for the hypothesis
at each terminal point

results (Mai et al., 1978) are based on relatively small samples, but they are encouraging for further investigation with
this method.

3.2. Elicitation of subjective probability distributions

When a physician is asked how probable it is that a certain
symptom (D_j) will appear together with a certain disease (H_i),
one cannot simply expect that he will be able to indicate a
number between 0 and 1 that corresponds exactly to his intuitive judgment. Instead of an exact answer (e.g. 0.731), we
would expect instead a less specific statement such as, "it lies
between 0.60 and 0.80". This, however leads to the problem of
precisely determining what is meant by such an interval. Does
it mean that the "actual" value lies within the stated interval

with a high certainty degree; for instance, with 99% certainty,
or does the interval include the actual value with only 50%
certainty? Obviously it is necessary to come to a clear agreement with the consulted physician concerning the meaning of
each interval indicated.

Instead of explicitly determining the intervals, one could also
follow the following procedure: let us suppose that a physician
first answers a concrete question on $P(D_j/H_i)$ by .70. If asked
further whether a value of .75 or .85 would still be acceptable, the physician might give a positive answer. The further the
questioning is continued, however, the more likely it should
become that the physician would respond by saying no. Instead
of asking many such questions, we could also ask the physician
to state a second order probability distribution over the range of the "uncertain quantity" (i.e. the possible probabilities
$P(D_j/H_i)$). Such a distribution could look like the one in
Figure 7.

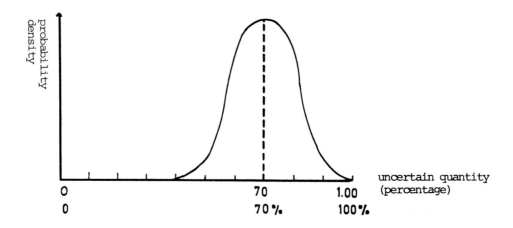

Figure 7.   An uncertainty distribution (probability
density function) for the uncertain
quantity $\tilde{p}$ (percentage)

The figure shows that 70% is considered the most probable value. The more the values of the uncertain quantity depart from 70%, the more improbable they become in the expert's eyes. The steeper the distribution is, the smaller is the range of values that the expert considers plausible.

Of course, such probability distributions (as well as exact numerical specifications) are not simply "present in the expert". Rather, one must try, with specific questioning techniques, to specify the distribution that best represents the expert's knowledge.

The questioning technique can be considerably simplified if some theoretical assumptions about the possible uncertainty distributions are made. If uncertainty distributions are to be determined for $P(D_j/H_i)$, the uncertain quantity P varies from 0 to 1.0 or from 0% to 100%. This already excludes uncertainty distributions from the family of the normal distribution, since the latter are defined for a range of values extending from $-\infty$ to $+\infty$. More appropriate is the family of Beta-distributions described by Raiffa and Schlaifer (1951) as "naturally conjugated distribution" of the binomial distribution. Mai (1975) gave a thorough justification for the use of Beta-distribution. Hogarth (1973) objected that it is unreasonable to assume that a judge or estimator follows a specific distributional form, however plausible this form may appear to the researcher. Actually however, it is not presupposed at all that a subjective uncertainty distribution follows a precise theoretical pattern. It is only assumed that a judge is able to specify certain aspects of his uncertainty rather than its exact distribution. If a theoretical distribution (e.g. a Beta-distribution) adequately describes these specific aspects, it is considered to be as well applicable for decision making as any other distribution that takes the same aspects into account (cf. Raiffa & Schlaifer, 1961, p. 59).

Once the Beta-distribution is accepted as a representation of the subjective probability distribution over P, the elicitation procedure can be conceived as the selection of one out of the various possible Beta-distributions. In practice one can start by provisionally specifying a convenient Beta-distribution, then analyze it with respect to its aspects of interest and make whatever modifications appear necessary. This approach, however, is only practicable if suitable mathematical aids and graphical and tabular illustrations of the various distributions are available.

A series of programs called "MANECON" (Schlaifer, 1971) was available for studying this elicitation procedure (Mai, 1975). This series consists of dialogue-programs that determine, inter alia, subjective probability distributions. Roughly, the function of the dialogue-program is characterized as follows:

(1) First, the program asks for an interval estimate of the uncertain quantity P; more specifically, it asks for the first and third quartile of the subjective uncertainty distribution. In other words, the judge is asked to specify an interval for P in such a way that he expects it to contain the actual value P with probability of 1/2. This interval estimate suffices for uniquely specifying one member of the Beta-distribution family. This Beta-distribution then represents the first evaluation.

(2) The program reports the median of the specified distribution and asks whether it agrees with the judge's knowledge or whether the previously stated interval has to be modified.

(3) Beyond that, the judge has various possibilities for further examining the distribution so far evaluated. The program can, inter alia, illustrate the distribution as a density function or as a cumulative distribution; for selected fractiles, it can calculate the corresponding P-values; also it is capable to analyze the impact of hypothetical, additional samples of cases on the specified distribution.

Thus, the program allows to formulate questions of considerably diverse significance for the same evaluation problem. The goal of the procedure is to obtain as high as possible agreement

between the various judgments (substantial statements) of the
expert and the distribution specified eventually.

The program was used with six experts in EEG-diagnosis in four
individual sessions to specify probability distributions for a
total of 70 uncertain quantities drawn from their immediate
working field. The physicians' performance could be evaluated
by comparing the resulting Beta-distributions with distributions
calculated from two extensive documentations of routinely used
EEG-marking sheets (Helmchen et al., 1968). One documentation
from a hospital in Berlin was based on 7199 patients; the other
one from the experts' own ward in a Hannover hospital described
1024 patients. As expected, the experts' estimates varied
strongly depending on the specific questions they were asked,
their complexity, and clinical relevance. In some cases, there
was also considerable divergence between the experts' subjective distributions and the ones calculated from the two documentations.

In general, however, these divergences were in the same range
as the divergence between the two documentations. Measured in
units of the probability scale, the average difference (over
70 magnitudes) between the two documentations is .142 whereas
the average difference between the medians of the subjective
distributions and the P-values calculated from the documentations amounts to .120. This means that the unreflected diagnostic application of statistics from one hospital would, on
the average, not yield better diagnoses in another hospital
than the use of sophisticated subjective estimates, even if the
statistics are calculated from samples of considerable size.

The experts judged the elicitation procedure itself as manageable and easy to understand. In the course of the study, experience brought a noticeable revision of the initial doubts
about the use of subjective probabilities. This could be particularly observed when comparing the subjective estimates with
the documentation findings, the divergences between the two
bringing the experts to place a major part of their doubt on

the documentation and not on their subjective probability estimates, even though one of the documentations was collected by
themselves. Consequently, even when likelihood estimates for
computer-assisted diagnoses are based on relative frequencies,
one should compare them with expert opinion. The theoretical
concepts of subjective probability, together with the practical elicitation techniques, offer various possibilities both
for establishing language rules and for building formal models
for combining subjective opinion and statistical results.

3.3. Motivational components in probability estimation

Another method frequently used for training probability assessors are the so-called scoring rules, first introduced by
Brier (1950) in meteorology. These rules determine a numerical
or monetary reward as a function of the probability estimate
and the actually occurring event. The expected value of the
function is maximal when the "true" probability is indicated
(cf. Murphy & Winkler, 1970). An example of such a rule is the
quadratic scoring rule that calculates the score as $S =
1-(E-P)^2$. P is the probability estimate of the event's occur-
rence. E=1, if the event that was to be predicted (e.g. rain)
actually occurs; otherwise, E=0. It can be proved that the better P is estimated, the higher is the expected value of S.
Such scoring rules are applied, for instance, to train meteoro-
logists in estimating the probability of the weather for the
next day (Staël von Holstein, 1971). The better the probability
estimates of a meteorologist reflect the uncertainty of the
weather, the more points he will accumulate in the long run.

Such scoring rules, however, have the same disadvantage as the
bidding procedures discussed in section 2.3.; that is, they
have a so-called flat maximum (cf. Winterfeld & Edwards, 1973).
In a broad area around the optimal estimate, the expected value decreases relatively little with the departure from the
true probability. Only large departures are appreciably penalized. In line with Wendt's (1975) argument that other motives

besides expectation maximation may play an important role in decision experiments, Aschenbrenner and Wendt (1976, 1978) tried to turn this disadvantage into an advantage by playing off judges' ambition against maximization of expectation. For this purpose, we had several subjects competitively estimate probabilities and then announced each subject's scoring rule reward in front of the others. Our hypothesis was that, because of the flat maximum, the numerical differences between the estimators' scores would remain small. We expected the less successful estimators to get the impression that they could easily reach the better ones by trying harder, while the latter would also increase their effort in order to avoid being caught up.

To test this hypothesis, we compared the flat quadratic scoring rule with Vlek's (1973) steeper, fair bet scoring rule in a probability learning experiment. Student subjects were asked to make 50 repeated estimates of the probability of picking a breadwinner when randomly drawing inhabitants of the Rheinland-Pfalz (West-Germany). After each estimate, a calculator stimulated such a sampling with the true probability of 0.379 and the estimators received their scores according to one of the scoring rules. Four subjects participated in each session, being paid according to the rank order of their cumulative scores. In addition, the information on the competitors' position was varied. Under both scoring rules, five groups of four (i.e. 20 estimators) received either:

a) full information about their competitors' scores and sums of scores after each estimate, or

b) only their own score and sum of scores and the rank order of the other subjects' sums of scores in their group, or

c) only their own score and sum of scores, or finally

d) only information about which event occurred.

Contrary to our hypothesis, the results showed no difference between the two scoring rules. However, full information about

the competitors' position proved to be a necessary condition
for both scoring rules to be effective. The subjects' estimates
improved only under full information, there being almost no
improvement under the three other conditions. Thus, scoring
rules lead to the desired result only if the estimators are
informed about the other estimators' scores, whereas the rules'
steepness plays no important role. This also accounted for the
contradictory results obtained by other studies on the effect
of scoring rules (cf. Beach, 1975, for a survey) in which information was not manipulated.

4. Risk perception and risk preference

When choosing among risky alternatives, people often show systematic departures from what one should expect on the basis
of the theory of expected utility (cf. Rapoport & Wallsten,
1972; Slovic et al., 1977). Coombs' portfolio theory (1969,
1975) is an attempt to explain this divergence accounting for
the preference for risky alternatives in terms of the two dimensions: expected value and perceived risk. In contrast to
normative theories, Coombs proposes that people to a certain
extent seek risk rather than have an aversion to it. Portfolio
theory assumes that for each expected value, an individual has
an ideal level of risk at which his/her preference is maximal.
Since positive or negative deviations from this ideal risk reduce preference, preferences over bets with equal expected value should be a single-peaked function of the bets' perceived
risk.

Coombs and his associates successfully tested portfolio theory
in a series of experiments without making specific assumptions
about the nature of the risk continuum (cf. Coombs, 1975). This
led to the question of what factors constitute the risk impression. Huang's theory of expected risk (1971a) provided the best
answer, describing risk as another kind of subjectively expected

value. She postulated that a risk value is assigned to each
outcome of a risky alternative. The perceived risk of the alternative is then the sum of these risk values weighted by
their respective probabilities.

Tests of Huang's (Huang, 1971b) and portfolio theory were, however, limited to the elicitation of preferences for alternatives in which the probability for winning or loosing was kept
constant. Since, however, probability plays an important role
in the formation of expectation, Aschenbrenner (1976b, 1978b)
tried to test both theories for alternatives with varying probability. For this purpose, two-outcome bets of the form (x,p,y)
were used, in which an amount x could be lost with probability
p and an amount y could be won with probability $1-p$. Aschenbrenner proved that subjective risk orders of such bets must
satisfy eight conditions from the system of polynomial conjoint
measurement (Krantz et al., 1971) in order to bear out the
theory of expected risk: weak order, sign dependence of probability and of each outcome, double cancellation of winning and
loss, a restricted form of double cancellation for winning or
loss, respectively, and probability, and distributive cancellation for probability.

These conditions were tested on 20 subjects who compared 31
such bets with respect to their perceived risk. Subsets of
these bets of equal expected value were further compared as to
their preferability in order to check the single-peakedness
assumption of portfolio theory.

Though the results support the theory of expected risk, almost
all subjects violated portfolio theory. If the judges are asked to estimate the risk of risky alternatives, they obviously
base their judgment on a kind of subjective expected value,
in contrast to their preferences. But this perceived risk does
not act on the preference in the way portfolio theory assumes.

In a further study on risk preference, Aschenbrenner (1978c)
investigated the reason why portfolio theory could so well ex-

plain preferences for risky alternatives with a constant probability while failing when probabilities are varied. A new theory by Coombs and Avrunin (1977a,b) was taken as explaining the
constitution of single-peaked preferences.This theory defines
characteristics that a set of multiattribute alternatives must
have in order for judges to show single-peaked preference patterns. The first condition is that the alternatives of such a
set, called an efficient set, are ordered in the same way on
each component attribute; for example, if a bet offers a higher
amount to win, it should also have a higher loss, etc.. The
second condition is that the attractive attributes, in this
case winning and probability of winning increase at a relatively slower rate than the unattractive ones, that is loss and
probability of losing. If a set of alternatives satisfies these
two conditions, then all preference functions pertaining to it,
should be single-peaked.

It is not possible, however, to construct such efficient sets
of two-outcome bets with varying probability simply because the
probability of winning is one minus the probability of losing;
instead of being ordered in the same way, these two components
are always ordered inversely. When the probability is held constant, however, sets of two-outcome bets with constant expected value are automatically efficient. This theory of single-
peakedness can thus explain both the single-peaked preferences reported by Coombs (1975) and the violations of single-
peakedness found by Aschenbrenner (1978b).

This possibility could be tested by using another way of presenting two-outcome bets that allowed the construction of efficient sets with varying probability. With this "stake presentation" mode, a player must pay in advance the possible loss,
x, as a stake. He can then win x+y, with probability p or nothing otherwise. In these new dimensions, one can, as Aschenbrenner (1978c) demonstrated, construct efficient sets with
constant expected value. If the bets of such a set are transformed into the usual form with final outcomes x and y and their
probabilities p and 1-p, the set is not efficient any more.

Aschenbrenner constructed three such sets with five gambles each. 30 subjects ordered these sets, as well as the corresponding ones presented in terms of final outcomes and their probabilities, according to preference. Indeed, the preference orders of almost all subjects (27) were single-peaked for all three stake sets. In the transformed final outcomes presentation, only half the subjects had single-peaked preferences for the same gambles.

Recently, Aschenbrenner (1980a,b) extended the single-peakedness theory to include other kinds of choice behavior than Coombs and Avrunin considered, especially the so-called heuristic choice strategies, and replicated the findings in two more experiments. To provide a stronger test, the efficient sets for these experiments were constructed in such a way that the gambles' expected values varied as single-dipped functions of the sets' orders, single-peakedness theory and expectation maximization thus leading to opposite predictions for subjects' preference orders. More than 90% of the 82 subjects satisfied single-peakedness theory, whereas no subject's preferences were consistent with expectation maximization.

Besides supporting Coombs and Avrunin's theory and Aschenbrenner's extension on the constitution of single-peaked preferences, these results show that preferences depend very strongly on formally irrelevant aspects of the presentation of the alternatives. By simply transforming the dimensions used for the presentation, it is possible to manipulate the decision makers' preferences in a predictable manner.

5. Contribution to the foundations of measurement

The following two sections present a concise survey of several resolution principles of the extension of classical utility models (e.g., Fishburn, 1970; Keeney & Raiffa, 1976). In section 5.1., we concern ourselves with problems of random error in algebraic measurement theory. In order to make clear the methodological distinctions between category theory, we follow a structural approach even though this means that our discussion, at times, becomes highly technical.

Section 5.2. focuses upon the special case of conditional expected utility and the problems that arise in the construction of a decision model for antihypertensive drug-therapy. Section 5.3. deals with the application of measurement theory to subjective probability, focusing especially on the development of a scaling procedure tested on horse-bettors

5.1. Non-standard model theory and the foundation of measurement

Looking at the concept of utility from a measurement theoretic point of view implies the following. Take a classical utility model $<A,R,F>$ with a binary preference relation R and a binary mid-value splitting operation F. Then A is your principal domain; that is, a finite or denumarable set of consequences whose utility is to be measured. $<R,F>$ the the structure imposed on A according to some specific ontological and/or structural assumptions; that is, axioms like connectedness, transitivity, monotonicity, etc.. Aside from the principal domain, one needs an auxiliary domain for $<A,R,F>$; that is, one needs a real-valued target structure $<Re,S,G>$, where Re is a nonempty set of real number and S and G numerical relations on Re. The basic task then consists in finding structure preserving maps (homomorphisms) of the sort $<A,R,F> \longrightarrow <Re,S,G>$ called utility scales.

This requires the solution of the following four problems:

Representation Problem: Suppose $<A,R,F>$ has been fixed for a particular domain of measurement. The problem is then to show that the numerical assignments by u preserve the postulated properties of R and F via S and G in Re.

Uniqueness Problem: Suppose $<A,R,F>$ and $<A',R,F>$ are two compatible structures of the same type and on the same universe of

discourse. There should then exist an automorphism $\delta: A \longrightarrow A'$
- called an indiscernability transformation - so that the numerical representation of <A,R,F> via u and the numerical representation of <A',R,F> via u' are unique under a permissible transformation $\psi: Re \longrightarrow Re'$, where ψ is called a scale-transform
from u to u'.

Meaningfulness Problem: The truth-value of any resulting numerical statement based upon appropriate statistical operations
should remain invariant under any admissible transformation of
the model's data.

Error Problem: Testing or fitting the model <A,R,F> to data,
error (random, not systematic) present a major difficulty. The
solution of this problem consists in showing that our model
<A,R,F> is empirically confirmed in the presence of random er-
ror if and only if its real-valued representation u is equivalent to the expectation E of its random-real-valued counterpart ξ; that is, that $u = E \cdot \xi$.

Let us focus our interest on the latter problem, since the former three problems have been sufficiently solved for a variety
of utility models (see Pfanzagl, 1971; Krantz et al., 1971;
Fishburn, 1970; Keeney & Raiffa, 1976). To begin with, there
are at least five different methods of approaching the problem
of random error. The first and weakest method amounts to the
introduction of probabilistic choice theory and families of
random variables (e.g., Davidson & Marschak, 1959; Pfanzagl,
1962; Falmagne, 1974, 1976, 1977), It is the weakest since it
centers exclusively on morphisms between purely numerical relation systems, thereby suppressing the delicate structure of
qualitative relations and operations, The second approach, derivable from Scott and Krauss' (1966) and Rusza's (1971) random model theory, is the most radical method from a logician's
point of view, but a nightmare to an experimental psychologist.
The third approach rests upon category theory (Arbib & Manes,
1975; Domotor, 1972; Egle, 1975; Hoehnke, 1974; Manes, 1976)
and centers on the randomization or fuzzification of founda-

tional concepts like orderings, monoids, groupoids, etc.. One of the central problems of applied category theory is this: Given a certain type of mathematical object, say a strict order, what are the corresponding morphisms that yield the representation of a stochastic order, or a fuzzy, or a proximitized order? Depending on the nature of the problem, a category formalizes the idea of an appropriate class of transformations in order to construct a new mathematical model from other (hopefully better) known mathematical models (cf. Domotor, 1975b, 1972; Manes, 1976 and, with respect to probabilistic orderings, Zaus, 1978).

The fourth method for treating foundation of random error applies Boolean-valued model theory to extend ordinary (two-valued) sets, relations, operation, and morphisms to their many-valued, viz. Boolean-valued, counterpart. The idea behind this is to use a complete, completely distributive Boolean algebra $\underline{B}$ (Halmos, 1963) as a system of generalized truth values; that is, 1 and 0 can still be identified with absolute truth and falsity, respectively, but with the addition of intermediate truth values as well. For example, let $R: A \times A \longrightarrow B$ be a Boolean-valued binary relation; then the value of R is defined by $R(a,b) =_{Df} [\![a \ R \ b]\!] \in B$. Hence $[\![a \ R \ b]\!]$ denotes the Boolean degree to which element $\underline{a}$ is R-related to element $\underline{b}$. The Boolean-valued framework serves for the clarification of the conditions that have to be imposed on random relations (e.g., completeness, cocompleteness, etc.) and random operations (Domotor, 1969, 1972, 1975a, 1976; Rutkowski, 1971; Scott, 1967; Scott & Solovay, 1967; Zaus, 1977, 1980).

Despite their importance, it is surprising how little has been done to extend classical relational systems $\langle A, R_1, \ldots, R_n \rangle$ to Boolean-valued relational systems $\langle A, B, \simeq, R_1, \ldots, R_n \rangle$. Another closely related approach is that of Kolmogorovian model theory, whereby a classical utility model $\langle A, R, F \rangle$ is superimposed on a probability space measure $\langle \Omega, \mathfrak{F}, P \rangle$ in order to analyze the probabilistic status of measurement axioms and morphisms between probabilistic relational systems (Kolmogorov, 1956; Domotor, 1969, 1972, 1975a, 1975b, 1976; Hildenbrand, 1971, Zaus, 1976, 1977, 1979, 1980). Superimposing a classical model on a probability space can be done in several different ways, depending upon which of the ingredients of the classical model are to be stochastisized. We can thus partially randomize the model $\langle A,R,F \rangle$, keeping some of its components classical (i.e., determinate). A partial stochastization is justified by the following observation. Establishing the probabilistic counterpart of $\langle A,R,F \rangle$ on a random set $\underline{A}$ would be drastic, since we would then have to consider random relations between random elements, or random operations on random elements. But it is entirely possible to consider random relations and operations on ordinary sets whose elements are definitely detectable. In fact this is presently under investigation with respect to three alternative probabilistic bisection structures, where axioms like transitivity, equal-spaciability, bisymmetry, monotonicity and commutativity are tested (Zaus, 1979, 1980). The general construction scheme for these bisection models is illustrated below.

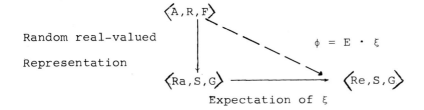

Random real-valued

Representation

Expectation of ξ

Thus, the qualitative side of the probabilistic counterpart concerns the model $\langle A,R,F \rangle$ over $\langle \Omega,\mathfrak{F},P \rangle$ while its quantitative side is grounded on a real-valued (viz. random-real-valued) homomorphism $\xi: \Omega \times A \longrightarrow Re$ or $\xi : A \longrightarrow Ra$. It is, however, too early to report all the details of this research project.

5.2. Non-standard model theory and conditional expected utility

The model-theoretic frame of reference discussed in section 5.1. is not limited to the probabilistic counterpart of fundamental measurement. It is applicable as well to the problem of conditional expected utility, to which we now turn. The decision problem to be considered concerns alternative antihypertensive therapies and may be characterized as follows.

Adequate treatment of hypertension requires that the physician understands the pharmacologic actions of antihypertensive drugs. Although none of the existing major drugs in use is without adverse reactions, it should be possible to choose a drug or a combination of drugs that can effectively lower blood pressure with a minimum of adverse side effects. Among the basic drugs, there are seven, that are used internationally (Diurectics, beta-blockers, reserpine, dihydralacine, clonidine, alpha-metyldopa, and guanethidine). This general pharmalogical effect consists of reducing the cardiac-output, the veinal back-flow, and the natrium- and water-level (which in turn serves to reduce the total peripheral resistance), the totality of these effects inducing a decrease in arterial blood pressure. Suppose now that a physician is forced to lower the blood pressure of some patient and that he considers drugs d_i, d_j, d_k, ... for possible use. It has been demonstrated (Zaus, 1977) that each such possible treatment involves certain risks, and that these risks may vary, at least partially, from one drug to another. In the corresponding conditional-expected utility model, each choice delimits the role of chance to choose events (occurrence of adverse side effects) peculiar to that mode of treatment and, in evaluating each conditional decision, one only needs to take the corresponding alternative's risks into account. According to this model, decisions are actions that, depend on how the state of nature is assessed in view of comparable events. A more detailed treatment of medical decision making and antihypertensive drug therapy, especially concern-

ing decision aids, is still in progress; for a specification
of the decision alternatives, facts about adverse side effects,
probability and utility consideration, see Zaus (1978).

It is perhaps convenient to close this section with a still
unresolved problem: Given a closed decision structure $\left\langle C^T, +, \underset{\sim}{\geq} \right\rangle$
over the probability space $\langle \Omega, \mathfrak{F}, P \rangle$, what are the necessary
and sufficient conditions on $+$ and $\overset{\geq}{\sim} : \mathfrak{F} \times C^T \times C^T \longrightarrow C^T$ such that
the following representation hold:

(1) $t_x(c_i) \underset{\sim}{\geq} t_y(c_j) \iff u(t_x(c_i)) \geq u) t_y(c_j))$

(2) $u(t_x(c_i) \underset{A}{+} t_y(c_j)) = P(A) u (t_x(c_i)) \oplus P(\bar{A} u (t_y(c_j))$,

where C^T is an indexed set of consequences over all points
in time from some initial time into future, t_x, $t_y \in T$, c_i,
$c_j \in C$, $u: C \longrightarrow Re$.

5.3. Scaling subjective probability from a measurement theo-
   retical point of view

Ksiensik (1978) shows the feasibility of an axiomatic approach
for the measurement of subjective probability. There are many
techniques for eliciting subjective probability estimates that
are not based on measurement theory (cf. section 3.2.). These
techniques rest on the assumption that subjective probability
is measurable but never in fact subject this assumption to a
critical test. One advantage of measurement theory is that its
axiomatic structure enables one to exhibit directly testable
sets of conditions (the axioms) necessary and sufficient to
guarantee the existence of a numerical representation. Testing
these conditions in the corresponding empirical domain thus
means testing the property of being measurable (Adams, 1966).

There are, however, several reasons why the axiomatic view of
measurement has not yet entered the daily life of the social
scientist. First, formally defining an empirical domain involves
axioms formulated in set-theoretical language that cannot be
operationalized for certain empirical fields. Secondly, some

The axioms and the representation theorem for measuring subjective probability:

Definition: Suppose that X is a nonempty set, the E is an algebra of sets on X, and that $\succsim$ is a binary relation on E. The triple $\langle X, E \succsim \rangle$ is a *structure of*
qualitative probability iff
for every A, B, C, D $\in$ E the following axioms
hold:

Axiom 1. $\langle E, \succsim \rangle$ is a weak order

Axiom 2. $X \succsim \emptyset$ and $A \succsim \emptyset$

Axiom 3.   Suppose that A ∩ B = A ∩ C = $\emptyset$. Then B $\succsim$ C $\leftrightarrow$
A ∪ B $\succsim$ A ∪ C

The structure is called Archimedean iff:

Axiom 4.   for every A $\succsim$ $\emptyset$ any standard sequence to A is
finite.

Axiom 5.   Suppose that $\langle X, E \succsim \rangle$ is a structure of qualitative probability. If A, B, C, D $\in$ E are such
that A ∩ B = $\emptyset$, A $\succsim$ C and B $\succsim$ D, then there exist
C', D', E', $\in$ E such that

i   E' $\sim$ A ∪ B   iii   E' $\supset$ C' ∪ D'

ii   C' ∩ D' = $\emptyset$ iv   C' $\sim$ C and D' $\sim$ D

Representation Theorem:

Suppose that $\langle X, E \succsim \rangle$ is an Archimedean structure
of qualitative probability for which Axiom 5 holds,
then there exists a unique order-preserving function P from E into the unit interval [0,1] such
that $\langle X, E, P \rangle$ is a finitely additive probability
space.

of these axioms cannot be operationalized at all. The well-known approaches by Pfanzagl (1968) and by Krantz, Luce, Suppes and Tversky (1971), for example, both contain untestable axioms (the "Continuity" and "Archimedean" axioms, respectively), a fact that, when looked at from the outside, constitutes a contradiction within axiomatic measurement theory per se. Finally, there remains the requirement of having, in most cases, to develop a scaling procedure that derives from the axioms. Though most of these difficulties can be resolved, such purely theoretical efforts do not provide much help when it comes to concrete measurement problems.

Starting from the general considerations of Suppes (1962) and Suppes and Zinnes (1963) concerning models of data, Ksiensik (1978) discusses the possibility of operationalizing Krantz et al.'s (1971) axioms for the representation of subjective probability. Krantz et al.'s formulation has several advantages when compared to other approaches to measure subjective probability: It does not combine subjective probability with utility (Fishburn, 1970; Pfanzagl, 1968) can do without conditional subjective probabilities (Koopman, 1940) and has explicitly formulated the representation theorem (Savage, 1954; Finetti, 1970).

Since the proof of the representation theorem involves reducing this structure of extensive measurement, the second difficulty mentioned above can be overcome: By means of their basic concept of "data equivalence", Adams, Fagot and Robinson (1972) show that certain axioms in the theory of extensive measurement are purely "technical" in the sense that a theory with these axioms is "data equivalent" to a theory without these axioms. Consequently, Axiom 4 can be neglected. The Axioms of Connectivity and Transitivity (Axiom 1) are easily operationalized, but frequently violated in the empirical fields. Therefore, either an explicit error theory is needed (see the pages above) or some means for replacing these axioms with equivalent axioms that better conform to the empirical field (van Acker,

1977). In most cases, Axiom 2 is trivial and need not be proven. Axiom 5 is almost never fulfilled in a finite set, but it can be replaced by the stronger version of Savage. The Concatenation Axiom (Axiom 3) is qualified for a scaling procedure, as will be described below with respect to horse bettors.

Application

For illustration, Ksiensik (1978) chose to operationalize measurement theory using the "Große Woche des internationalen Galopprennens Baden-Baden 1978"[1] as the empirical field. Horse betting is a classical empirical field for eliciting subjective probability (cf. de Finetti, 1972, 1974) and is well suited for exploring and testing measurement theories for subjective probability. Since the pairwise comparison of all elements of the power set of the set of horses in a run is nearly impossible, the actual betting system was used as a criterion for selecting subsets. The cancellation axiom was interpreted as the union of disjoint events. After obtaining the rank order for all horses, and then for a specific selected subset, the total metric information is acquired if transitivity and additivity hold. The metric information restricts the corresponding intervals. With Ordmet (Coombs, 1964; McClelland & Coombs, 1974) or linear programming, a solution may then be calculated (Ksiensik, 1979).

There are two limitations to such an approach. First, in a strict sense one can compute scale values only if all axioms are fulfilled, and even then the scaling procedure yields only relations between intervals and not point estimates. Though the uniqueness theorem enables one to choose specific solutions within these intervals this is not satisfactory for many practical problems.

The second limitation is independent of the validity of measurement theory, depending instead on assumptions concerning

---

[1] One of the most famous horse racing events.

the nature of subjective probability; that is, whether the
latter is seen as depending on a single person or on events
over all persons (cf. Winkler, 1972; Marschak et al., 1975).
For a large number of practical decision problems, it is important to obtain scale values for the object of interest that
are interindividually valid. A treatise of combining separate
subjective probabilities to a composite value is, however, outside the scope of the present discussion.

Chapter 19 Occupational Choice: Information Behavior and Decision Aids

S. Jeromin and E. Kroh-Püschel

1. Introduction

The main objective of this research project was to modify information behavior of persons who are in actual job decision situations. Our research was done with the cooperation of youths who were at the stage of occupational choice and involved observing the processes of information-gathering and information-processing that occurred before the final job decision was made. Besides gaining a clearer understanding of information-processing at job decisions, we wanted to indicate ways of introducing qualitative and quantitative improvements in people's informational behavior in job decision settings.

1.1. Conditions of occupational choice

Occupational choice and job realisation are influenced by psychological, socio-cultural, economic and historical determinants (Jaeger, 1973; Langenheder, 1975). Realisation of job aspirations are strongly restricted by demographic characteristics (e.g. sex, nationality and education), socio-economic variables (the number of suited jobs offered by the labor market) and political factors. Especially marked is the effect that the present shortage of apprenticeships has on the future career development of students who leave school with no higher than a primary school diploma. These young people's choice is severely restricted, and many start apprenticeships without any long-term job perspective. The problem of occupational training must thus also be seen as a structural problem of western industrial

societies, occupational choice being subject to market mechanisms and the interests prevalent in the market economy.

Besides these restrictive conditions, there is a great deal of
empirical proof that many of the individually as well as socio-
economically wrong career decisions made by primary school drop-
outs and apprentices are the result of the insufficiency, obscurity and inconsistency of the available, career-relevant
information (Pross, 1969; Heinen, Welbers & Windszus, 1972;
Infratest, 1973; Pross, 1973; Hille, 1974; Laatz, 1974; Quickstep, 1974; Schweikert, 1975; Petzold, 1976; Schoop, 1976). It
seems clear, however, that basic improvements in job decisions
can only be brought about by a thorough reform of occupational
training. In October 1973, 40 scientists demanded in a "mani-
festo to reform occupational training", the development of new
learning methods and the intensification of vocational counselling. In a resolution adopted by the Commission of European
Communities, the member states agreed to concentrate on policies of job preparation and develop measures aimed fundamental,
improving of their youths' occupational choices (Bulletin of
EEC, 1976).

After these general remarks on the situation in which occupational choice takes place, we like to orient the discussion
that follows around our research on two major problems:
- Modification of information behavior and thus improvement of
  decision-making by male and female school-leavers before
  deciding on a job.
- The development and assessment of suitable methods of information transfer.

The objective of accompanying measures to occupational choice
is to improve these abilities to choose the appropriate occupation. By this ('Berufswahlreife') we understand, according
to Steffens (1975), an acquired matrix of vocational choice
behavior, which enables the person to gather and process information in a specific way. It is possible to encourage adequate occupational choice behavior by the adoption of learning

principles. In order to do so the special situation of the
person looking for counsel must be analyzed in a behavior analyses and the learning objective must be defined in terms of
observable behavior. This comprises the kind and amount of
planning, information-seeking and decision-making behavior.

2. Theoretical framework

A basic assumption underlying our own research is that occupational choice is a process in which the youth becomes progressively tied to an occupational position, either by his own
initiative or as the result of socio-structural factors. In
talking of occupational choice of primary school drop-outs,
we refer to their decision about what kind of vocatical
training to follow immediately after finishing school. Currently there are several different research orientations to occupational choice (cf. Crites, 1972; Jepsen & Dilley, 1974;
Lange, 1975a; Langenheder, 1975; Scheller, 1976), each of
which concentrate on different aspects of the occupation-choice
complex. In our own research, we deal with information behavior just prior to the final job decision and are thus oriented primarily towards psychological theory and research on
decision-making.

The various approaches to decision-making differ as to their
assumptions about the decision-maker and his environment.
Hilton (1962), for example, assumes that the decision-maker
disposes of only a low level of information with respect to
the various decision alternatives. Kalkor and Zytowski (1969)
postulate,in contrast, a relatively unlimited knowledge about
the alternatives, their consequences and the related probabilities. Some theories feature assumptions concerning risk
in the decision-making process, others having decisions occur
under conditions of uncertainty. The former "risk" approaches
start from "objective" probabilities that derive from the ex-

perience of other persons (Katz, 1966), an approach by Gelatt
and Clarke (1967) even assuming that "objective" data are present that enable one to examine subjective probabilities for
biases. The latter, "uncertainty" approaches on the other hand,
proceed by treating "information" as being equivalent to
"facts" (Hilton, 1962).

The different theories vary also with respect to their assumptions concerning the strategies and rules of decision-making.
According to Vroom (1964), for example, the decision-maker
chooses the alternative, that he/she thinks yields maximum
utility, while Hilton (1962) has the decision-maker opting for
the first alternative which first encountered that lives up to
his/her minimum standards. Mitchell and Beach (1975) cite in
their summary of empirical studies of occupational choice
several experiments that, despite differences in theory, mathematics and methodology, all start from similar rational principles of gain maximization; the person being postulated to select those jobs that promise the greatest positive outcomes.

Due to the fact that occupational decisions are made with multiple objectives in mind, the decision maker has to process a
great amount of relevant information. Since, however, man is
limited in his information processing capacity (Miller, 1956),
there is little possibility of objective, rational behavior
in the sense of classical, ideal-normative decision theory.
Behavioral research on decision-making comes closer to reality
by taking into account the particular conditions the decision-
maker faces (making allowance, for example, for the subjective
probability of an event, identifying utility functions, value
hierarchies, aspiration level, dealing with achievement motivation and information-seeking: cf. Kirsch, 1970). In the
latter sense, rational decision making does not mean optimizing with respect to "objective" goals but rather is evaluated
with respect to subjective goals established by the decision-
maker his- or herself.

The more comprehensively and precisely the problem is defined, the more closely further information may be looked for. The level of information thus determines on the one hand precision and specifity of further information-seeking; it is responsible on the other hand for weighing one alternative against the other.

The quality of a decision depends upon the amount and the content of the information processed. The extent to which the decision-maker takes advantage of all the information available depends, in term, on a variety of factors, among which is the level of insecurity experienced with respect to the decision that has to be made. This insecurity is itself a function of the number, the relative strength and compatibility of the competing reaction tendencies (Berlyne, 1962; Lanzetta, 1969).

The degree to which the available information is exploited is also influenced by the importance of the decision, which in turn is determined by the outcomes expected from the varous alternatives. According to Lanzetta and Driscoll (1968), increasing decision importance increases experienced insecurity. The more strongly a person is effected by a decision-making situation, the more strongly he experiences the concomitant conflict.

Some experiments by Witte (1972) indicate that information-seeking is strongly influenced by the person's expectation of success; if the person does not expect to find any new information, his informational needs are only partially manifest. The search for information is, in addition, determined by various situational determinants (e.g. information costs or the possibility of revising the decision), but we will not discusss these in this paper.

How a person has been socialized plays an important part in determining how he/she goes about looking for information, people with different socialization history often preferring different information types, sources and media. Language, too,

leads to differences in information use among the social classes. A person's specific cognitive complexity guides his/her
search for and processing of information, and only if certain
cognitive categories are present can the person inform himself
conprehensively about special attributes of the various occupational alternatives.

Training in decision-making must focus on the complexity of
real-life situations and must allow the person to establish
his/her own goals and behavioral strategies (Steffens, 1973).
"It is not the objective reality but the subjective inner model,
which an individual creates, and underlies his problem-solving
process (Kirsch, 1970)."

3. Information behavior and decision-making during choice of occupation

In order to identify the information base that primary school
drop-outs use to make their occupational choice, we made a
survey sampling experts (occupational counsels, representatives of the labor office and primary school teachers), drop-
outs (240 male and female drop-outs from the 8th and 9th grades) and a group of thirty apprentices, the results of which
are presented in Jeromin and Kroh-Püschel (1977). In the following, we will briefly summarize the results of this survey,
supplementing our discussion whenever possible with the mention
of findings from other, related empirical work.

3.1. The phase before realisation of occupational choice

The results indicated that the pupils felt pressure by the
decision-making situation and that most had no clear concept
in mind when they arrived at individual counselling and the
employment service despite received prior occupational counselling in school. In the district of Ludwigshafen, for

example, more than one third of the pupils looking for counselling could not formulate precise wishes or could not give
any ideas of the job they wanted to take up. Consistent with
our findings Manstetten (1975) and Götz and Zimmer (1977) found
that people choosing occupations often found themselves pres-
sured by the complexity of the choice, and that insecurity concerning job realisation leads them to consider a thorough analysis of job alternatives as being useless (see also Kappeler,
1976; Götz & Zimmer, 1977). Difficulties in obtaining relevant
information pose another central problem for occupational
choice (Götz, 1973; Infratest, 1973; Götz & Zimmer, 1977; Saterdag & Jäger, 1977; Köditz, 1978).

Of the drop-outs interviewed, 102 had completed the 9th grade
and 138 the 8th grade. The main issues were questions about
the knowledge and determining the extent that they consulted
a variety of information sources. It should be noted though
that low scores with regard to some information sources do
not enable one to conclude as did Ries (1970) that drop-outs'
information behavior is insufficient, since it may be that
they simply prefer different sources. Rational decision-making
does not require that all available information be used.

*Information behavior: Information sources, the use they made
of and assessment.* In the phase before decision-making, the
youth is asked to define his/her individual occupational choice
by specifying the criteria that his/her future job should meet.
To do this, the youth must have some basic idea of the main
decision criteria as well as information about occupational
alternatives available.

Contrary to what we expected, the drop-outs interviewed were
quite familiar with the available information. Several examples may be cited.[1]

---

[1] In the following, we want to report the results of the interviews accomplished with the school-leavers of primary school,
because these pupils stood immediately before the realisation
of their job decision. The results for the 8th grade of primary school are outlined in Jeromin and Kroh-Püschel (1977).

All the drop-outs were acquainted with several brochures dealing with occupational choice that are annually published by
the German Labor Office. For example, 83% were familiar with
"Beruf aktuell", a booklet containing a description of all jobs
needing apprenticeship training, with 60% indicating that they
had read the book carefully and 52% (43% of the total sample)
that they found the brochure useful. "Mach's richtig", another
brochure for occupational choice, was known familiar to 40%
of the respondents, 43% of these (i.e. 17% of the total sample)
indicating that they found it useful. The exercise-book to
"Mach's richtig" (with exercises and problems to prepare people
for occupational choice) was familiar to 22%, 8% of whom found
it useful.

Approximately half of the interviewers had listened to *radio or
television programs* dealing with occupational choice. Of the
39% who could remember at least one special program, half of
them (18% of all those interviewed) indicated that the program
was useful. 67% of all those interviewed had *consulted* a labor
office, and 68% had talked with their teachers about occupational choice.

80% had *visited a factory,* while 64% had visited several factories. Of all those who visited at least one factory, half
indicated that their visit was useful.

These results show that even if the pupils did not make use of
all the information known to them, the conventional information
sources were used to a great degree. On the other hand, many
respondents judged this information to be of only low or moderate utility, saying often that they had expected much more
help or support than they received.

The respondents rated the benefits gained from their *own practical experiences* (e.g. practical courses, part-time work and
hobbies) as being highly valuable as a decision aid. 53% of
all thise interviewed had taken a practical course, 79% of whom
found it useful. 38% had gathered practical experience during
part-time work, 36% of these finding it useful. When asked for

the most important source of information, the respondents
named the practical courses second only to their parents.

Asked how they would describe their information-seeking, approximately half of the respondents indicated that they had
been looking for specific information themselves. 45% obtained
information mainly in school, and 27% said that they had obtained information by chance. 66% gave more than one information source when asked which sources they would recommend to
their friends.

Generating of alternatives. In order to arrive at satisfactory
solutions to career decision, it is necessary that the decision maker be sufficiently aware of the available alternatives.
Conversely, the number, homogeneity and inter-connectedness of
the alternatives determine the complexity of the decision-
making situation.

In our present survey most of the respondents indicated that
they had developed their interests in certain jobs as a result
of discussions with their families or friends. Written material,
films, radio and televion programs had inspired only approximately one third of the respondents, while factory visits and
practical courses were also named by one third each.

In a survey of apprentices by Heinen, Welbers and Windszus
(1972), one fourth of the respondents stated that they had not
considered any other alternatives when decising for their jobs,
while one third limited their consideration to jobs pertinent
to a specific trade. The early commitment to a single trade is
especially problematic when considered in light of the presently surcharged labor market.

Level of information. The more relevant information that a person has available, the more efficient he/she will be at reducing the initial set of job alternatives to those that are to
be considered more closely.

68% of the survey respondents had taken some sort of ability
test, 40% of these in the firm where they had applied for a job.

It should be remarked, however, that people are seldom informed of the results of such ability tests and thus gain little
information that could aid their own decision-making.

Asked if they know the requirements of the job for which they
had decided, 69% of the respondents answered in the affirma-
tive, though only 22% could name at least three requirements
for the job in question. When asked the same question concerning alternative jobs, 28% thought themselves informed about
the most important requirements, with only 9% being able to
give realistic answers.

Only 49% of the drop-outs surveyed could name at least three
activities involved in their future work. 13% beleived that
they were informed about the activities involved in alternative jobs, but only 5% could actually name the activities.

3.2. The decision-making phase

In making a decision, the anticipated consequences with respect
to job requirements and job training are considered in light
of the subject's goals, supposed abilities, and capacities for
further learning.

The drop-outs sampled gave the following list of characteristics for what they considered as a good job:
- good career possibilities
- good salary after apprenticeship training
- interesting activities
- provision of apprenticeship or training
- contact with other people
- offers much independence
- highly sought after

In a survey of students from a variety of different types of
schools, Lange (1975b) identified three, largely independent
complexes of occupational value orientation:

- an "individual utility-orientation" in which values like "income", "career" and "prestige" are stressed;

- a "socio-political value orientation" stressing values like "being useful to other people", "improving society", "having contact with other people";

- a "safety- and order-orientation" with values like "safety", "ordered activity" and "ordered working time".

Our own research turned up the following criteria as being central in the choice of an apprenticeship: good working climate, possibilities to stay employed after apprenticeship training, and salary during training (see also the apprentice survey by Heinen, Welbers & Windszus, 1972).

Towards the end of the school year, 68% of the 9th grade drop-outs had definitely decided on a job, while 67% of the 8th grade drop-outs had done so. In their interviews and compositions,. the drop-outs often stated that they would look for any kind of apprenticeship, even if they would not later be able to work at the job in question. Twelve percent of the drop-outs were prepared to take any job whatsoever, while 24% wanted jobs in only one special branch.

According to vocational counsellors, many of those looking for jobs show little flexibility in making their decisions; a high percentage of those pupils who had not found an apprenticeship post before the end of their school careers would have found one if they would not have stuck so long to aspiring towards jobs whose possibilities were limited (oral statements of vocational counsellors of the labor offices of Ludwigshafen and Mannheim, 1977; 1978).

The period immediately following the decision is characterized by feelings of regret since the benefit of alternatives not chosen have to be passed by and the negative aspects of the one chosen have to be tolerated. Dissonance theory's (Festinger, 1957) prediction that decision makers reduce dissonance by increasing the attractiveness of the chosen alternative

and/or decreasing that of the other alternatives has also been
confirmed in studies on occupational choice behavior. Vroom
(1966) found that subjects perceived a firm to which they committed themselves as being more suited for their personal goals
after the commitment than they had before. Vroom and Deci
(1971) found that, besides increasing this attractiveness of
the chosen firm, subjects decreased the judged attractiveness
of the firms that they had not chosen. Finally, Mann (1972)
reports that students preferred supportive information about
the college they had chosen to attend rather than information
that was critical of the college.

3.3. The post-decision phase

In the course of our interviews, it became clear that many
apprentices were discontented with their job and training
choice. In a study by Heinen, Welbers and Windszus (1972), one
fourth of the apprentices interviewed would not have chosen
their job if they had their decision to make over again. Similarly, Quickstep (1974) found with students at a vocational
school that 40% would have changed their decision regarding
training if they could have, while Schweikert (1975) reports
a 15% drop-out rate among male apprentices. The reasons given
by the youths for dropping out of training suggest that a considerable number of them were not sufficiently informed about
their jobs or apprenticeships before having made their decision (Schober-Gottwald, 1977).

Vroom and Deci (1971) show that, having worked for one year,
employees find their firm less suitable for realizing their
personal objectives than they did when they took up the job
(Vroom & Deci, 1971). The same authors found an even greater
discrepancy after 3 1/2 years of work experience. The depre-
ciation of an option commences, according to the authors, as
soon as the person acquires new knowledge about the job and
confronts the real conditions with his former expectations.

People who reduced post-decisional dissonance by revalorizing
the chosen firm later showed the greatest tendency for deva-
lorization. People, in contrast, who showed little post-decision dissonance reduction, later tended to judge the firm more
positively than did the others. Similar results were found by
Lawler, Kuleck & Rhode (1975).

3.4. Conclusions

We can conclude that the conventional information sources are
known and consulted by young job seekers. The relative ineffectiveness of information gathering in comparison with the expenditure of effort and the job seeker's aspirations has, in
our opinion, a number of different causes:

The information is being provided without taking the specific
needs of youth into account. According to Witte (1972), information, no matter how abundant, will lead to more efficient
decision making only if it is met by a preparedness and capacity for information processing. A lack of direct interaction
between the informant and the recipient adversely affects information content; in order to address all concerned, information is so general that it is no longer helpful in solving
specific decision problems.

Most conventional information sources use language as their
medium of communication. Most drop-outs, however, were from
working class families and rely to a much greater degree than
members of the middle and upper classes on non-verbal modes of
communicating (Koschorke, 1973, 1975). In analyzing the efficiency of the present information system, Schmidt-Hackenberg
(1975) concluded with respect to youths without training contracts that institutionalized vocational counselling, with its
preference for verbal communication, does an inadequate job at
reaching the audience to which it is addressed.

The respondents' positive assessment of information gained from
practical experience most likely indicates the superiorty of

action-oriented over verbal information transfer for audiences
of this level.

That the drop-outs were discontent and uninformed about the
available work options even though they made use of the standard information sources suggest that the latter are insufficient in informing people about many aspects concerning their
future job life. Our interviews show that youths tend to take
only particular aspects of jobs as criteria for assessing the
complete range of job-related activity. This undifferentiated
perception of working life results in incomplete information-
seeking on the part of the youths. They complain that the information offered by the labor offices does not mention the
negative aspects of jobs and training courses.

This discrepancy between source-use and job familiarity is
further aggravated by selective information-seeking, which can
in turn be attributed by certain value orientations adopted
through socialization and to the youths' efforts at reducing
post-decisional dissonance. With regard to their latter point,
Lange (1975b) empirically demonstrated that subjects find it
easier to decide on a job when they learn that lots of other
people are interested in it, this information supporting their
decision and reducing whatever dissonance they might experience (Frey, 1978; Jeromin, 1978; Jeromin & Kroh-Püschel, 1978;
Jeromin & Kroh-Püschel, 1978b).

4. Some aspects of information behavior and vocational decision making

Most studies concerned with the information behavior of young
people searching for an occupation assess information behavior
solely on the basis of quantitative criteria. These criteria
include the number of information sources used, the number
and comprehensiveness of the attributes considered, and the
number of alternatives compared. Such an approach, however,

neglects important qualitative aspects of information behavior
and decision-making, like how systematically information is
being gathered, or whether the gathering is being done in a
balanced fashion. Another point that is very often neglected
is that information behavior does not only consist of the active search and avoidance of information but also in the preparedness to accept and process information once it is obtained.

The studies reported below examine quantitative as well as qualitative aspects of information behavior and together give a
comprehensive picture of how untrained youths go about making
occupational choices.

4.1. Quantitative aspects of informational behavior and deci-
sion-making

Gerdts (1977) observed information behavior of male and female
primary school pupils in a simulated occupational choice setting, the pupils having to decide between several similarly
attractive apprenticeship posts. Gerdts found, among other
things, that his subjects used only 19% of the available information as a basis for their decision (see also Gerdts,
Aschenbrenner, Jeromin, Kroh-Püschel & Zaus, 1978a,b). Similar
findings are reported by Jeromin (1978), who had primary
school pupils seek information about the attributes of their
preferred job (see also Jeromin, Jeromin & Kroh-Püschel, 1978).
Jeromin and Kroh-Püschel (1978a) found that information behavior and decision-making differed between the primary school
and secondary school levels, but that subjects in either case
made insufficient use of the information offered.

These three experiments each use a different paradigm to show
that subjects faced with an occupational choice make relatively little use of the information available. These results are
especially striking when it is considered that the subjects -
as is too often not the case in real-life decision situations -
were informed of what information was available and that this

"meta-information" (Witte, 1972) probably increased information seeking to a considerable degree. Information seeking must
be expected substantially lower in real-life situations.

4.2. Qualitative aspects of information behavior and decision-making

Incomplete information seeking does not necessarily result in
inadequate decisions. For a decision to prove adequate, it suffices simply that the decision makers' needs are met to the
greatest extent possible; complete acquaintance with all decision-relevant information is not necessary (Kirsch, 1970). A
decision becomes inadequate or "irrational" only if vital concerns of the person are not taken into account, the decision
being based instead on needs less central to the person's
well-being.

Several of the above-mentioned studies (Gerdts, 1977; Gerdts
et al., 1978a,b; Jeromin & Kroh-Püschel, 1978a) are relevant
to this point. In each, subjects' "target" or "value orientation" was measured by presenting them with 35 attributes of
varying relevance to the determination of training position
quality which they were to rank according to importance. These
ratings were then compared with the actual priorities accorded
to the attributes during a subsequent simulated decision situation. In each case it was found that untrained primary school
students did not succeed in adapting their information behavior
to the objectives that they had previously rated as important.
Again, type of education was found to make a difference, with
students of secondary schools ('Realschüler') showing more
need-focused information behavior than students of primary
schools ('Hauptschüler') (Jeromin & Kroh-Püschel, 1978a).

Another important criteria for evaluating information behavior
arised from comparing the latter with the assumptions implicit
in formal models of decision-making. There two basic types
of decision-making models, both of which have been applied to

occupational choice. The first of these, the regression approach, begins by having subjects rank order a number of vocational alternatives as to their attractiveness and then, by
adjusting the parameters of various decision rules, seeks to
fit these rankings to general judgment patterns. The aim of
this approach is to identify the decision model that, if followed, would lead to the optimal decision being made.

Mitchell and Beach (1975) present a survey of this research,
while Gerdts (1977) offers a critique of its bearing on occupational choice, arguing that the attributes used are not representative of those that play a role in real-life and that
the judgments called for in the experiments are overly artificial. Most important for our present purposes, however, is the
fact that completely different cognitive processes can be represented by mathematically equivalent models. An accurate decision model does not, therefore, necessarily reflect the underlying cognitive processes of the decision-maker.

The second approach to analyzing decision-making (cf. Van Raaj,
1977 or Aschenbrenner, 1978, for a general survey) registers
the decision process itself by different recording techniques
and compares it with assumptions underlying various alternative decision models. Information processing is characterized
by various "transition types", these being regular patterns
of transition from one set of information to another. Type 1
represents a double search for information. Furthermore, a
decision maker could, for example, search for information concerning two different attributes for the same alternative
(type 2) or, alternatively, seek information on the same attribute for two different alternatives (type 3). Transition type
4 describes a change of alternatives and attributes. The number and kind of transitions observed during information-seeking
indicates the structure of the information-processing.

Such a process orientated method was applied by Gerdts (1977)
and Jeromin and Kroh-Püschel (1978a). In order to decide among
hypothetical training situations, the subjects (students from

secondary and primary schools) were offered information in the
form of an information board, the columns of which represented
the alternatives (there were 3 or 5) and the lines the attributes (35), each cell containing information about the characteristics of the given alternative on the specific attribute.
The pupils could select as much information as they wanted for
their decision-making and could sample the same information
more than once if they desired to. The sequence in which the
information was chosen reveals various qualitative and quantitative criteria of information behavior and decision-making.
Both experiments found that information behavior of subjects
without training in occupational decision-making seldom conforms to any decision model. How structured the subjects' information search was could be characterized by the proportion
of type 4 transitions - that is, simultaneous transitions with
respect to alternative *and* attribute -, the higher the proportion of these transitions, the less structured the information
behavior. Subjects drawn from primary schools showed type 4
transitions approximately 60% of the time, whereas those from
secondary schools did so only 40% (Jeromin & Kroh-Püschel,
1978a).

Other theories provide still other perspectives for approaching pre-decisional information seeking (see Grabitz & Grabitz-
Gniech, 1973). Festinger (1964), for example, distinguishes between pre- and post-decisional information seeking, pointing
out that while the latter may be biased as a way of reducing
dissonance, the former is always objective. It may often be
the case, however, that people's final decisions are preceded
by a number of preliminary decisions, each of which introduces
mild, dissonance-reductive biases in their information gathering. Frey (1978) showed in one of the few studies on pre-decisional information seeking that secondary school pupils prefer
information that supports their preliminary occupational decisions and avoid contradicting information. This bias occurs,
however, only when the two types of information come from sources of equal competence; subjects prefer dissonant information
when its source is more competent than the consonant informations.

Similarly, Jeromin (1978) found that students from primary schools show a considerable preference for information supporting their preliminary occupational decisions (see also Jeromin, Jeromin & Kroh-Püschel, 1978). Jeromin and Kroh-Püschel (1978b) obtained similar results both with respect to active information seeking and a more structured preference rating among a set of available booklets.

The various experimental analyses of youths' information behavior during occupational decision-making supports the conclusions of authors who, mainly on the basis of interviews, describe that decision-making (especially with respect to primary school students) as 'muddling through' (Jaide, 1966; Lange, 1975a, 1976; Ries, 1970). The insufficient use of available information is compounded by the tendency of prefer - variations in source competence aside - information that supports the subjects preliminary decision. Subjects have been found to prefer booklets whose titles suggest a positive outcome of their occupational decisions (Frey, 1978; Jeromin & Kroh-Püschel, 1978b) as well as that information which is consonant with their utility preferences with respect to certain attributes (Jeromin, 1978; Jeromin, Jeromin & Kroh-Püschel, 1978). In Jeromin and Kroh-Püschel (1978), this tendency toward information selection was also apparent by the fact that the subjects were unwilling to include dissonant information in the further decision processes. Such an insufficient consideration of dissonant information before deciding on an occupation makes unsatisfactory decisions highly probable (Janis & Mann, 1977).

Besides being biased and insufficiently comprehensive, information behavior generally shows little specific orientation towards the individual's goals. The selection of information concerning the attributes of the available alternatives rarely matches the subjects' own decision criteria. Students in primary schools especially seem to have difficulties in transforming their goals into decision behavior.

The information behavior of young decision makers must therefore be considered as being highly unstructured. Due to the
lack of processing strategies, only a small part of the selected information can be ordered, compared and integrated to a
conclusion. Despite highly structured and favorable information conditions in the experiments cited so far, the youths
showed inadequate information behavior and decision-making.
There seems to be a need for decision aids that support the
pupils in their search for information necessary for arriving
at satisfactory job decisions.

5. Measures to improve information behavior and decision-making with respect to occupational decisions

Learning-theoretical counselling, developed in the United
States during the 1960's, does not deal out counsel on adequate
alternatives or specific decision outcomes but rather proceeds
on the assumption that an appropriate decision depends on an
adequate choice behavior and that such behavior can be learned. A more or less comprehensive training in decision behavior
offers the additional advantage that the counselling aim becomes observable and controllable. The acquired behavior can
also be applied to further career decisions and to the solution
of other complex problems besides job choice. The various
techniques are presented by Hosford (1969), Myers (1971),
Krumboltz and Baker (1972), Campbell, Walz, Miller and Kriger
(1973) and Jeromin and Kroh-Püschel (1978c).

5.1. Methods for reinforcing information search

Most studies on behavioral counselling aim at increasing the
amount of information behavior. As a rule, the techniques are
based on principles of operant conditioning and observation
learning.

Krumboltz and his collaborators counducted a series of experiments between 1964 and 1968 on the effectiveness of reinforcement counselling and model reinforcement counselling. Based on the findings of verbal conditioning, this counselling method involves giving the client cues to utter certain verbal statements concerning planned or already conducted information behavior that are then reinforced by giving either verbal and/ or non-verbal approval. Such reinforcement is thought, in turn, to increase the frequency and variety of the information behavior itself (Krumboltz & Thoresen, 1964; Ryan & Krumboltz, 1964; Krumboltz & Schroeder, 1964; Meyer, Strowing & Hosford, 1970; Borman, 1972; Aiken & Johnston, 1973; Samaan & Parker, 1973). In some cases, this phase of conditioning is preceded by a phase of observation learning; via auditory or video tape, the youths observe a model who displays the desired behavior and gets reinforced by a model counsellor (Krumboltz & Thoresen, 1964; Krumboltz & Schroeder, 1964; Thoresen & Krumboltz, 1967; Thoresen, Krumboltz & Varenhorst, 1967; Thoresen & Krumboltz, 1968; Meyer, Strowing, & Hosford, 1970; Wachowiak, 1973).

Research findings show that both reinforcement techniques lead to a greater number and variety of statements concerning information behavior during the counselling session and that there is a positive correlation between these statements and subjects' subsequent, actual behavior as stated later on during interviews (Krumboltz & Schroeder, 1965; Thoresen & Krumboltz, 1967; Samaan & Parker, 1973).

Krumboltz and collaborators later examined the effectiveness of counselling based on behavioral learning in stimulating information search. They assumed that subjects perceived the usual printed information as being aversive, especially the underprivileged youths who do not, as a rule, have well-developed reading habits. Instead of presenting printed matter, Krumboltz and his colleagues worked together with specialists to develop characterizations of specific jobs which they then presented to their subjects either orally or in film scenarios.

Immediately after the presentation, subjects were reinforced according to the quality of their problem solving. The results of these studies show that these "job experience kits" are effective in generating immediately and short term interest, but that this interest is rarely transformed into actual increases in information seeking (Berland & Krumboltz, 1969; Krumboltz & Sheppard, 1969; Jones & Krumboltz, 1970; Krumboltz, 1970; Nelson & Krumboltz, 1970).

Some of the above mentioned studies must be criticized because of their restricted view of information behavior and decision-making, with "variety" being the only qualitative aspect of information behavior investigated. Also, with some exceptions, the subjects were youths who were already motivated and who looked for advice, thus possibly limiting validity of the findings. Finally, measures of information behavior were often based on interview or questionnaire responses rather than on direct observation. Even if these responses were highly reliable and valid (which has hardly been corroborated), they still would not offer insight on how objective, goal-directed and structured the information seeking is.

5.2. Measures for the qualitative improvement of information behavior and decision-making

Besides the techniques mentioned above, a number of other approaches exist that aim not only at activating information search but in improving information behavior and decision-making in a qualitative way. Most well known are various simulation games, especially the "Life Career Game" (Boocock, 1967, 1972; Boocock & Coleman, 1966; Varenhorst, 1968, 1969), where the subject plays the role of a decision maker in a hypothetical choice situation. The subjects are reinforced by means of chips that are administered according to the relative contentedness of the hypothetical person with the outcomes of the decision, this contentedness being deduced from matrices of experience ('Erfahrungstafeln') constructed from observations of analogous, real-life situations (see, for example, Yabroff, 1969). The uncritical use of correlation statistics as an indicator for the quality of an individual decision is, however, methodologically questionable. Also, this relevance on 'adequateness' judgments seems to represent a step back to a kind of occupational counselling that behavior-oriented counselling was supposed to have outmoded. Finally, what little evidence there is (e.g. Johnson & Euler, 1972) concerning the "Life Career Game" effectiveness is not very promising. Better results were achieved with special simulation tasks used in the training of educational decisions (Ryan, 1969; Lindblad, 1973; Quatrano & Bergland, 1974).

A number of programs based on structured group interaction have also been used to train people in decision-making. The starting point is the splitting of the occupational decision process into various phases (cf. Gelatt, 1962). Through instruction and observing models, subjects are taught the most effective responses to make at each phase (Gelatt & Varenhorst, 1968; Evans & Cody, 1969; Stegard, 1962; Hamilton & Bergland, 1971; Hamilton & Jones, 1971; Smith & Evans, 1973; Bergland, Quatrano & Lundquist, 1975).

Techniques are especially numerous that convey the knowledge necessary in order to sort out the decision problem and generate alternatives in a "self-exploration" program (Magoon, 1969; Ryan, 1969; Holland, 1970; Graff, Danisg & Austin, 1972; Krivatsy & Magoon, 1976). In the Federal Republic of Germany, there is a similar program[2] issued by the 'Bundesanstalt für Arbeit' (Labor Office) with which an individual's abilities and value orientations can be explored. Unfortunately, Selg's (1977) evaluation of this program does not examine how it actually affects students' decision-making.

---

[2] In Germany known as 'Systematisches Trainings- und Entscheidungsprogramm (STEP)'.

The occupational counselling approach offered by the Bundesanstalt für Arbeit relies primarily on information *booklets* to
help the pupils realize comprehensive job perceptions. Such
booklets are thought suitable to train students to differentiate job opportunities accoding to relevant job-attributes,
generate alternatives and outline the particular decision problem. Bodden and James (1976) found, however, that *engagement*
with such informative texts does not necessarily result in a
more differentiated *perception of occupations*, and results
from replications of this study using standard texts from the
'Bundesanstalt für Arbeit' will be presented in the following
chapter (Kratzmann, 1979; Kratzmann, Kroh-Püschel & Jeromin,
1979).

5.2.1. Our own contribution to improvement of occupational information behavior and decision-making

Our major concerns were the following: First, we wanted to develop a decision aid, mainly for drop-outs from primary school,
to support job or occupational decisions; second, we wanted
to directly monitor the impact of these decision aids by observing subjects' actual search for and processing of information. In two of the studies, a procedure was chosen that allowed the immediate and direct observation of the quantitative
and qualitative aspects of information behavior in simulated
training decisions (Gerdts, 1977; Gerdts et al., 1978a,b;
Gerdts, 1979; Jeromin & Kroh-Püschel, 1978a). Jeromin (1978),
on the other hand, aimed at determining whether decision-
makers' relative preference of consonant information could be
compensated for by a decision aid that reinforced the processing of dissonant information, the same decision aid being put
to a further test in a follow-up study by Jeromin and Kroh-
Püschel (1976b). Finally, several studies were done to test
the effect that an information booklet on occupation put out
by the Bundesanstalt für Arbeit had on cognitive complexity,
and whether further "perceptual" training would augment the

booklet's effect in yielding more differentiated job perception during information search (Kratzmann, 1979; Kratzmann,
Kroh-Püschel & Jeromin, 1979).

*Goal-directed information behavior by working out hierarchical
goal systems.* The following investigation was guided by the
idea that poorly made decisions by young occupational decision-
makers are not only the result of a lack of motivation but also
of the fact that the young people have only an inexact, general idea of the criteria important for their own decision. In
other words, they very often do not know what to ask for. They
need help in seeking and processing more goal directed information to base their choices upon.

The hierarchical goal system ('Zweck-Mittel-Analyse') can provide such help. Used mainly by experts in the solving complex
decision-problems (e.g. Miller III, 1970; Zangemeister, 1970),
the procedure involves the decision-maker listing all the relevant goals and then structuring the goals according to certain principles in a hierarchical system. For instance, the
general goal 'obtaining the best apprenticeship' is accomplished by a list of less general goals (for instance, 'quality of instruction' or 'desirability of the job situation').
These still relatively general goals are transformed into progressively more concrete aims until, at the lowest level, they
provide the decision-maker with an immediate alternative to
ask for. Table 1 (see following pages) presents a comprehensive decision tree generated by experts.

Gerdts (1977) used the hierarchical goal system with students
who at that time were searching for training positions (see
also Gerdts et al., 1978a,b and Gerdts, 1979). Each student
generated relevant characteristics which he thought the best
training place ought to have and arranged them by a step-wise
procedure into an individual goal hierarchy (Gerdts, 1977,
1979). When he had accomplished this, the student was presented a goal hierarchy generated by experts, it being possible
to integrate such attributes important to him into his indi-

vidual goal hierarchy. Table 2 (see following pages) presents the hierarchical goal system generated by one of the pupils.

This goal generation task was tested against the effect of a detailed written text about apprenticeship choice, the subjects in the latter control group having opportunity to come to know all the attributes that the students of the experimental group were confronted with. The written text appealed to readers to inform themselves in detail before reaching a decision.

The treatment is based on the assumption that structuring the decision problem by a hierarchical goal system facilitates the search and structuring of subordinated goals when structuring the decision problem. The complex decision process can be divided into a step-wise transparent judgment procedure by which the information search becomes more goal directed and structured. Such information behavior ought to enable the decision-maker to process even greater amounts of information.

These hypotheses were tested by the observation of information behavior at the information board. After the treatment the pupils were to decide for the best alternative out of a number of fictitious alternatives. They could select the necessary information from a matrix (realized by a wooden box with little compartments). Each column represented an apprenticeship place. The 35 attributes are randomly arranged in rows. In each cell there are cards with information on the characteristics of certain apprenticeship places on the various attributes. Content number as well as the rank order of the various attributes were fixed by experts. The construction of attributes had the aim to arrange as realistically as possible hypothetical apprenticeship posts. The decision problem was to appear not too simple. This was to lead the decision-maker to a careful search process and decision-making. The search procedure of the youth could be reconstructed from the order of selected and laid aside information cards.

Gerdts found that working out a hierarchical goal system has the expected effect: the information behavior of the experimental group was significantly better than that of the control group. The greater use of available information was accompanied by greater goal-directedness in subjects' information seeking. Furthermore, the information behavior of subjects in the experimental group was - as indicated by the proportion of type 4 transitions - much more structured.

In a further analysis of the decision structures Gerdts showed that trained subjects confronted with decision problems of low complexity (choice among three apprenticeship places) tended in contrast to the control group to follow decision processes close to those prescribed by Tversky's (1969) additive difference correspondence model or with elimination by aspects model (Tversky, 1972a,b). With more complex problems (choice among five alternatives), no difference between experimental and control group was found, neither group showing decision behavior conforming to either model. Table 3 (see next page) presents the original search pattern of a subject and Table 4 presents the appropriate reduction of this information process.

Gerdt's study marks the first attempt to identify the influence of this prescriptive decision aid on problem solving behavior. The hierarchical goal system proved extraordinarily useful compared with conventional support methods. The large number of goals (an average of 46) that the subjects used to construct their individual goal system proved that they were capable with support by this method to define their decision problem in a highly differentiated manner. This kind of differentiation offers direct insight to the individual goals and results in both qualitative and quantitative improvements of problem solving strategies.

Structured decision behavior in complex decision situations through cognitive learning by observation. This study (Jeromin & Kroh-Püschel, 1978a) tests whether the observation of a model-apart from merely activating information behavior leads to

(to be cont. on page 770)

Table 1. Expert goal hierarchy for evaluating and choosing apprenticeship offers

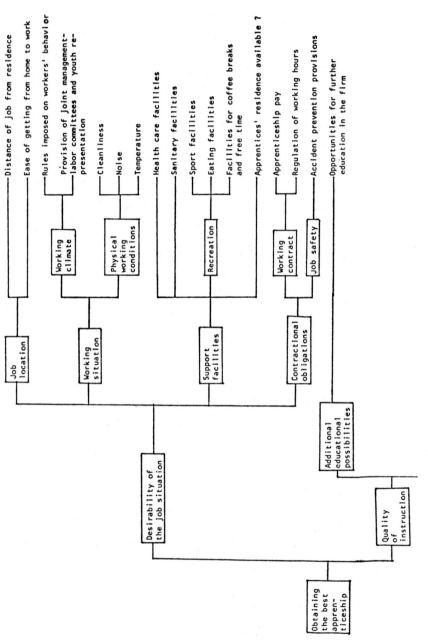

(cont. next page)

(Table 1 cont.)

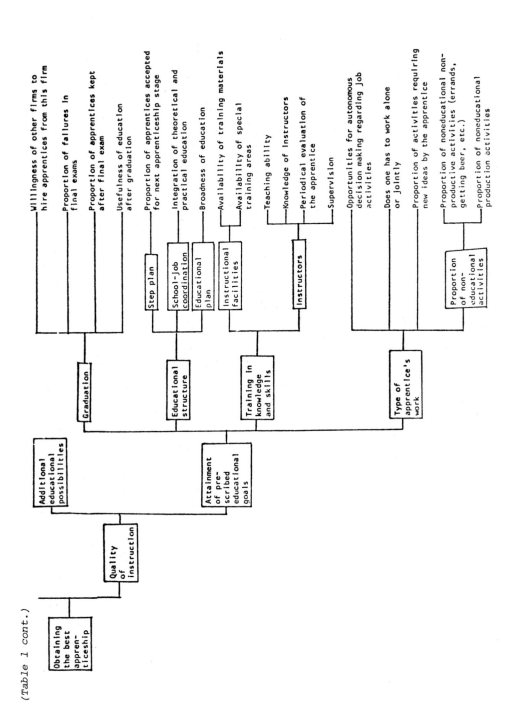

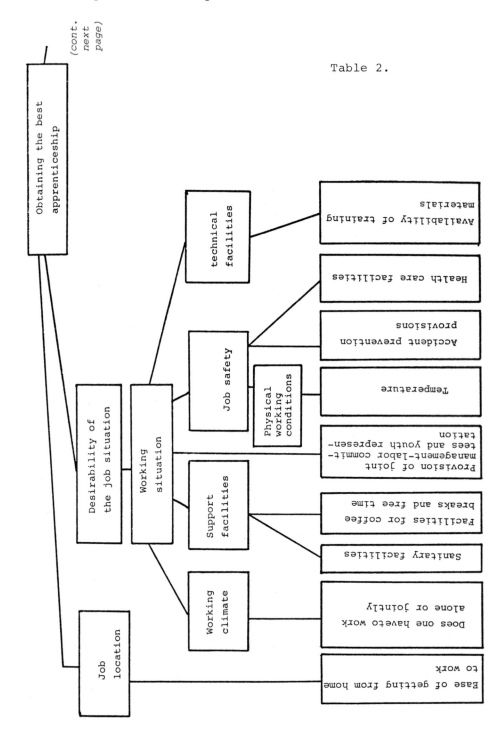

(cont. next page)

Table 2.

(Table 2 cont.)

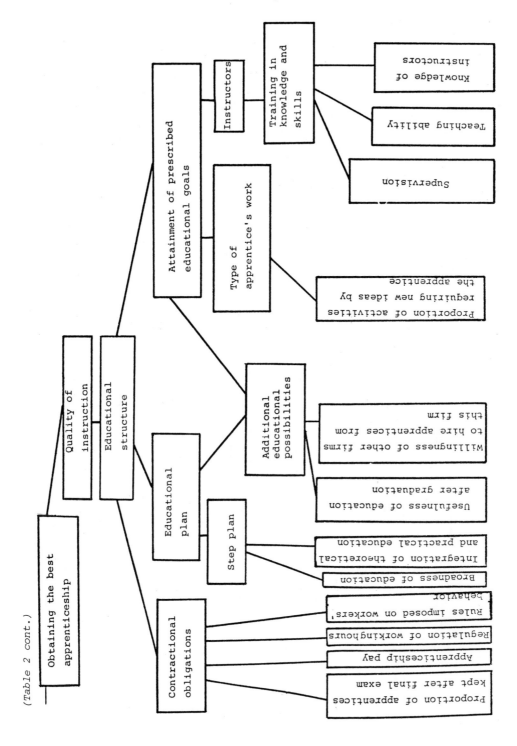

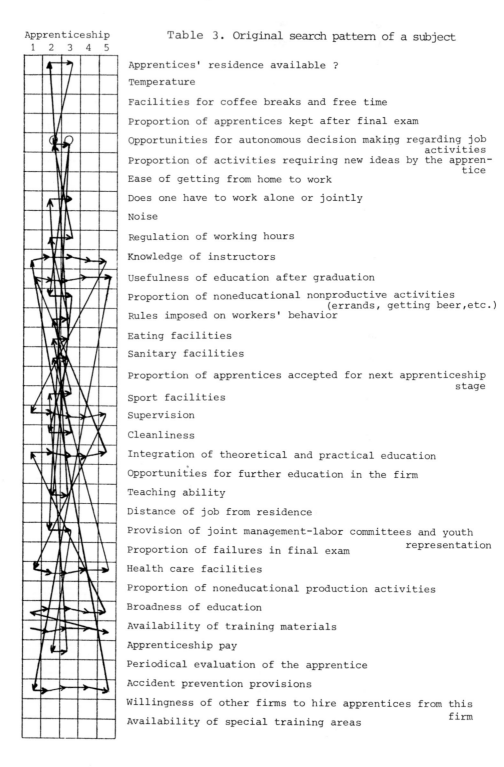

Apprenticeship
1 2 3 4 5

Table 3. Original search pattern of a subject

Apprentices' residence available ?

Temperature

Facilities for coffee breaks and free time

Proportion of apprentices kept after final exam

Opportunities for autonomous decision making regarding job activities

Proportion of activities requiring new ideas by the apprentice

Ease of getting from home to work

Does one have to work alone or jointly

Noise

Regulation of working hours

Knowledge of instructors

Usefulness of education after graduation

Proportion of noneducational nonproductive activities (errands, getting beer,etc.)

Rules imposed on workers' behavior

Eating facilities

Sanitary facilities

Proportion of apprentices accepted for next apprenticeship stage

Sport facilities

Supervision

Cleanliness

Integration of theoretical and practical education

Opportunities for further education in the firm

Teaching ability

Distance of job from residence

Provision of joint management-labor committees and youth representation

Proportion of failures in final exam

Health care facilities

Proportion of noneducational production activities

Broadness of education

Availability of training materials

Apprenticeship pay

Periodical evaluation of the apprentice

Accident prevention provisions

Willingness of other firms to hire apprentices from this firm

Availability of special training areas

Table 4.

Apprenticeship

```
1   2   3   4   5
```

Availability of training materials

Broadness of education

Integration of theoretical and practical education

Usefulness of education after graduation

Accident prevention provisions

Knowledge of instructors

Supervision

Health care facilities

Sanitary facilities

Cleanliness

Eating facilities

Apprentices' residence available ?

Opportunities for autonomous decision making regarding
                                        job activities
Provision of joint management-labor
                            committees and youth repres.
Apprenticeship pay

Sport facilities

Rules imposed on workers' behavior

Regulation of working hours

Proportion of noneducational nonproductive activities
                            (errands, getting beer, etc.)
Teaching ability

Does one have to work alone or jointly

qualitative improvements in decision behavior. In contrast to
previously cited studies on observation learning, this experiment is less concerned with a precise reproduction of model
behavior. Rather, the observers have to grasp rather the model's
underlying problem solving strategy and subsequently apply it
to their own decision problem.

The behavior of the model in this study was quantitatively as
well as qualitatively superior to that of the untrained
subjects (in the control group of the Gerdts (1977) study)
being characterized by an efficient use of available information and strong goal orientation. The model's decision behavior followed the elimination-by-aspects Model (Tversky,
1972a,b). This model approaches choice as an elimination process - the decision-maker chooses an important attribute in
terms of which he will compare all the decision alternatives,
those not possessing a minimum set of meaningful attributes
being eliminated. This procedure is carried through until a
single alternative emerges as the one that exceeded a minimum
criteria on the greatest number of attributes. Such an inter-
dimensional procedure seems, according to Gerdt's (1977) findings, to be easily coped with cognitively and is often adopted
intuitively in complex decision-making situations. Besides behaving in a way prescribed by elimination-by-aspects, the model verbalised the main principles underlying his strategy as
instructions given at the beginning of the session to both
the model and the subjects requested that they think aloud
during information-seeking. Observation of such self-instruction has already proved successful in behavior therapy (e.g.
Meichenbaum, 1971; Sarason, 1973).

The first stage of the procedure consisted of both the subject
and the model ranking the attributes according to their individual preferences. They then used the information board to
inform themselves of hypothetical apprenticeship places. In the
experimental condition, the subject first observed the model
during his information search, while in the control conditions,

the subject started with his decision process in the presence
of the model. Subjects were students from primary and secondary
schools who anticipated facing real apprenticeship choices in
the near future.

In the control condition, subjects from the secondary schools
showed a quantitative and qualitative superiority in the information behavior. Observing the model improved the decision
behavior of both groups considerably. The model's verbalising
the basic problem solving techniques (self-instruction) resulted in the subjects acquiring not only the form of the model's
behavior (i.e. its phenotype) but also the ability to apply
its basic principles in their own situations. This modelling
results in greater use of the available information, greater
goal directedness and more highly structured information behavior. As expected, the differences between both groups disappeared after exposure to the model.

Contrary to expectations, however, the experimenters positive
reinforcement of the model's behavior did not improve the observer's. There are some indications, though that reinforcement
did not, as intended, channel the observers' attention to problem solving mechanisms, but rather tended to center it upon
the behaviors phenotypic aspects. For example, the subjects
from the secondary schools showed less goal direction when the
model was reinforced, basing their information search to a
lesser degree on their own value hierarchies and imitating
surface characteristics of the model's behavior (e.g. choosing
of the same alternative).

In a final treatment (Jeromin & Kroh-Püschel, 1978a), it was
tested whether changing important characteristics of the model
leads to better learning by observers. Instead of a "Mastery
Model" (whose most important characteristic is his immediately
adequate problem solving behavior), we used a "Coping-Model"
(cf. Meichenbaum, 1971) who first verbalised certain problems
when presented with the task and then let the observer participate in the various steps of the solution process. On account

of the greater similarity between observer and model, the
latter's utterances should serve an additional, cue function
and hence result in greater learning. The findings, however,
indicate that subjects' qualitative and quantitative information behavior was the same under either a Mastery or Coping
model.

On the basis of these two studies, one can conclude that subjects were able to improve their information behavior and decision-making simply by observing a peer act in a similar de-
cision-situation and then applying what they observed to their
own individual problem solving situations. The improvement
lies not only in phenotypic reproduction but also on the acquisition of cognitive problem solving strategies than can be
applied to the individuals' own decision premises.

*Reduction of informational selectivity through use of a balance
sheet.* A good decision requires that the decision-maker shows
balanced information behavior; that is, he/she must search and
evaluate a sufficient amount of information on both positive
and negative aspects of the alternatives. The more complex the
choice situation, the more difficult it becomes to meet these
requirements.

Occupational choice and job decision represent a multi-attribute choice situation, and, as stated earlier, a large proportion of youths are discontent with their decision later on.
Besides the quantitatively insufficient, undirected and unstructured search for information (Gerdts, 1977, 1979; Gerdts
et al., 1978a,b; Jeromin & Kroh-Püschel, 1978a), another reason
for these poor decisions being made lies in the general tendency to prefer consonant over dissonant information before the
decision is finally made. The reformulated theory of cognitive
dissonance (see Frey, 1978), as well as the conflict theory
approach to decision making (Janis & Mann, 1977), state conditions - above all in the final stages of decision-making -
under which persons actively look for and prefer information
that supports their preliminary choice. As we have seen, these

claims have already been corroborated in the experiments by
Frey (1978), Jeromin (1978), Jeromin, Jeromin & Kroh-Püschel
(1978) on occupational choice discussed above.

A decision aid adequate for this problem has to stimulate cognitive processes that prepared the decision-maker to process
discrepant information and integrate it towards a solution to
the particular problem that he/she faces. Janis & Mann (1977)
showed in an analysis of pertinent literature that this can be
achieved by compelling the decision-maker to confront the
fears that he/she associates with the decision object.

In the 1950s, Janis & Mann developed a diagnostic device which
involves compelling subjects to generate lists of positive and
negative consequences anticipated as a result of a decision.
The subject given the task, and who afterwards evaluates the
consequences according to their "meaningfulness", will generally be able to take into account a great number of considerations during decision-making. This device was first tested by
Janis (1969) as a decision aid for students who faced educational and job decisions. Mann (1972) later tested it with
respect to decisions made by male and female high school students concerning which college to attend. In both these (as
well as other) studies, decision effectiveness was measured
in terms of *post*-decisional behavior like dissonance reduction,
it being assumed that a person is most strongly committed to
a decision (and will hence show the most dissonance reduction)
once he has considered carefully all expected positive and negative consequences (Janis & Mann, 1977).

The advantage of this procedure is that the decision-maker
can regard already gathered information on the alternatives
and, on the basis of their attributes, deduce the direction
and content of the outcomes that he anticipates from his choice.
The "balance sheet" provides eight categories under which the
generated outcomes can be ordered, thus compelling the decision-maker to direct his/her attention to additional considerations, thereby assuming a more comprehensive consideration

of the problem. Two of the categories consist of the instrumental utility which the decision-maker or significant others
connect with the alternative in question, while two other categories deal with the expected cost for the decision-maker
and others. There are categories pertaining to the evaluations
of important others - that is, their agreement or disagreement
with a decision on account of certain attributes - and to the
positive and negative reactions of the decision-maker himself
in response to each possible decision; for example, whether or
not the outcomes coincide with his/her self-concept? These
considerations, as a rule, are listed up on a sheet of paper
and can be applied to any number of alternatives.

After having listed all anticipated outcomes, they are each
assigned a rating between -5 and +5 depending upon their anticipated outlines or utility. By summing their ratings for each
alternative, the decision-maker can arrive at an idea of the
alternatives' relative utility. Table 5 (see following pages)
presented a typical subject's balance sheet.

In a study on the pre-decisional information behavior of primary school students (male and female), Jeromin (1978) assumed
that unused information concerning negative aspects of the
preferred alternative stimulates a cognitive state of conflict
that, under certain conditions, motivates the person to consider advantages and disadvantages of an alternative as objectively and comprehensively as possible (Janis & Mann, 1977).
Thus, if students who had already completed a balance sheet
are given credible, dissonance-arousning information, they
should tend to seek additional information that contradicts
their preliminary choice and should be more ready as well to
consider this information in further decision-making processes.

By thoroughly analyzing of the existent literature and consulting with experts, Jeromin came up with a comprehensive
set of attributes designed to aid information-seeking by providing a framework for describing all possible occupations.
Jeromin used this list at several points in his study. First,

Table 5. Balance sheet

what personel advantages would I have if I decided to become an electrician?

one has a wider range of work opportunities
often can work with others
you can construct something by yourself
you can specialize
you can start your own business
you can do some additional work on the side
I like working in big factories
I simply like that job
I know people in the factory
I need more dexterity and that's ok
diversified work
I could talk to my colleagues while working
chance to be re-engaged
regulated working time
my parents agree
economical independence
if I get a house, I will be able to do the electrical
work myself

*what personal disadvantages might I have if I decided
to become an electrician?*

I don't earn so much money
the work proves physically straining
the workshop is far away from my home and I've to
get up early in the morning
little free time
there are too many apprentices
I have only a few chances of finding a job
everything is prescribed
I don't have much time free for meals
I'm always dirty when I come home
I may be less preferable than others with higher education

long apprenticeship

tiring work

independent working

---

*what would the advantages be for other people that are
important to me if I decided to become an electrician?*

---

if they have something to repair I could do it

if someone of our family has a house, I could do the
electrical jobs

if I have a business, ma relatives could get things
cheaply

---

*what could the disadvantage be for other people that
are important to me if I decided to become an electrician?*

---

my mother would have to wash the dirty clothes

if I get married, I won't earn so much

I'll have only little time to spend with my friends

---

*how might my decision bring me into closer agreement
with people who are important to me?*

I would be able to do something better than my father
could; for example, repair a radio

I could repair things free of charge

---

*how might my decision bring me into disagreement with
other persons, who are important to me?*

---

my friends might say that anyone could do this job

my relatives might say that I should have studied more

---

how might my decision increase my self-respect?

---

if I could repair something my father could not

if I'm more skilled than the guys in the next stage
of apprenticeship

---

*how might my decision result in things that are con-
trary to my self-concept?*

---

it served as a basis for constructing a questionnaire for
assessing subjects' preliminary job aspirations and job perceptions, and thus indirectly to assess their familiarity and
agreement with the expert information that was to be presented later on. Secondly, the list served in the construction of
an "expert questionnaire" in which realistic information was
conveyed to subjects about the standing of various jobs they
had mentioned on the listed attributes.

In a second session, subjects in the experimental group accomplished a balance sheet for each of the occupations they liked
best at that time. Control group subjects, however, were told
to read a text that dealt with several aspects of occupational
choice and that asked them to intensify their information-
seeking and carefully evaluate what information they gathered.
After this, all subjects had the chance to consider expert information concerning their favored jobs. This was presented in
the form of a list of questions concerning the job's standing
on the 25 attributes from which subjects could select as many
questions as they wanted to be answered.

The balance sheet had, as expected, a highly significant influence on information seeking. Subjects in the experimental
group asked for more attributes and used the provided information much more. They also asked for a greater amount of dissonant information that the control subjects did, though the
two groups did not differ with respect to the amount of consonant information asked for. The decision aid also influenced
information processing, experimental group subjects making
greater use of the dissonant information they had asked for.

Subjects in the second session also rated the extent of their
decision security (0-100) as well as rating the attractiveness
of their preferred alternative at three different points of
time (before and after the balance sheet, and after the information phase). As expected, the subjects with low decision security asked for more attributes and more information than did
those with high security. Though Festinger (1964) hypothesizes

that insecure subjects should show greater selectivity in their
information seeking, the present findings indicate that such
selectivity occurs only with respect to the insecure subjects
showing a greater tendency to seek out consonant information;
that is, there was no effect for insecurity on the tendency to
avoid dissonant information. Decision security also had no influence on how the sought-after information was evaluated. The
perceived attractiveness of the job alternative had a considerable influence on information behavior, as subjects who aspiring towards jobs that they found relatively unattractive showed
greater information selectivity than those who perceived their
favored alternative as being attractive, though the combined
amounts of information sought by the two groups did not differ.
The failure of subjects with unattractive job alternatives to
show higher levels of information seeking might have over the
fact that no better alternative was available (see the Conflict
Theory approach by Janis & Mann, 1977). Due to the present scarcity of training places and the low awareness of occupation alternatives, a decision for another alternative is, indeed, often not possible. Young job seekers thus often have no other
strategy than to support their preliminary job decisions by
looking for consonant information and avoiding dissonant information. Whether the alternative was valued or not made no difference in how the sought-after information was evaluated.

Jeromin examined variations in decision security and attractiveness of the decision alternative during the balance sheet and
information phases. As expected, neither the balance sheet nor
reading the text produced changes in decision security and attractiveness of the alternative. After the information phase
which for the control group was above all characterized by adding consonant cognitions and for the experimental group by adding dissonant cognitions to occupational ideas the following
differences resulted as was assumed: decision security becomes
lower with pupils (male and female) of the experimental group,
whereas it rises with the control group. At that time both
groups differed significantly. No difference, however, between

the two groups is found as to the perceived attractiveness of the alternatives.

In a follow-up study, Jeromin and Kroh-Püschel (1978b) examined whether the impact of the balance sheet would be equally stable under less favorable conditions. Similar to real-life situations, information search followed the filling out of the balance sheet by a period of between three days and one month. The principles of the decision aid were transferred by a written instruction and by action orientated learning by means of a simulation game (accomplishment of the balance sheet for an imaginative primary school pupil) and third by observation of a film showing pupils (male and female) simulating the decision aid (peer models). Some of the subjects were given the opportunity after this transfer to accomplish a balance sheet for their own occupational choice situation aided by a self-help booklet (experimental group). The treatment as well as the later data gathering was done in group sessions; no individual help was given.

The hypothesis that the balance sheet would reduce selective exposure to information was put to a severe test by using a paradigm developed by Frey (1978). Subjects were presented with a file containing five consonant and five dissonant titles of information booklets referring to their preferred job alternative. First, they were asked to indicate three titles that they definitely wanted to read (limited active search for information) as well as three others that they definitely did not want to read (limited active avoidance of information). After this they were asked to indicate their interest in each title (unlimited indication of the wish to read) by rating it on ten-point scale. On a similar scale, they were finally asked to indicate the extent to which they agreed with the individual statements in the various titles of the information booklets (unlimited evaluation of information).

All three methods of transfer proved highly effective. Contrary to our expectations, no difference was found between "role

playing" observation learning and the written text. Despite the
more rigorous conditions under which it was tested, the balance
sheet again resulted in a reduction of selective exposure to
information. Our findings on the reduction of the selective
exposure to information can thus be summarized as follows: When
information seeking is restricted, there is no difference between experimental and control groups, both strongly preferring
consonant information; when, however, information seeking is
not limited (and choosing to see dissonant information does not
imply a passing up of consonant information), filling out a
balance sheet results in significantly less selectivity, the
subjects showing an interest in both consonant and dissonant
information.

*More differentiated perception of individual job opportunity
by combining information text and perception training.* Job decision demands different sorts of cognitive activity at different times in the decision-making process. During the early
phases, a high degree of cognitive complexity is required
(Bodden, 1970; Bodden & Klein, 1972; Lange, 1976): the more
complex the decision maker's cognitive structure with regard
to the relevant material, the greater the number of job alternatives he/she will be able to take into consideration and the
finer the differentiations he/she can draw between them.

Training for occupational choice issued by the Labor Office
consists primarily of handing out various information booklets
to students in the final grades of school. These booklets provide a first glimpse of the job and training opportunities and
on the basis for various measures taken by schools and the Bundesanstalt für Arbeit (Labor Office) to support occupational
choice. The question whether these booklets actually fulfill
their intended effect of progressively differentiating available decision alternatives was examined, however, only in a
single experiment by the Americans Bodden and James (1976), who
came to the conclusion that the booklets do not have the effect intended.

In light of some criticisms by Kratzmann (1979), we (Kratzmann,
Kroh-Püschel & Jeromin, 1979) have replicated Bodden and James'
experiment taking care to control for factors like subjects'
certainty in their decisions. We wanted to see whether reading
a text facilitates the differentiated use of occupational categories, improves the ability to differentiate and integrate
information concerning job characteristics, widens the range of
perceived job alternatives and increases interest in additional,
job-relevant information. It was further tested whether perceptual training would enhance the impact of information booklets on cognitive complexity, decision certainty and information seeking.

The subjects in the experiment were female primary school students in the seventh grade who, in response to a preliminary
questionnaire, indicated that they were already in the process
of generating alternatives for their occupational decisions.
The information booklet issued by the Bundesanstalt für Arbeit
(Labor Office), "Mach's richtig", was employed together with
some additional job descriptions. The perceptual training was
similar to that used in experiments by Sieber and Lanzetta
(1966) and Salomon and Sieber-Suppes (1972) and was based on a
Labor Office film showing the variety of activities demanded
from a window-dresser. The effects of information text and perception training were recorded some days later in order to provide realistic text conditions.

In contrast to Bodden and James' findings, we found that occupational information booklets were effective in enhancing decision makers' cognitive complexity; after having read the text,
our subjects showed more differentiated job perception and
greater ability to integrate relevant job information. This
greater complexity seemed to arise, however, more from the subjects generating their own job attributes then by adopting
those discussed in the booklet. The text had consequences also
for decision certainty, those having read it being less fixed
on a single job and entertaining a broader spectrum of possible

alternatives than those who had not read the text. Also, the quantitative and qualitative aspects of information seeking were affected by the text, in that those who read it asked for information concerning a greater range of attributes for jobs from a greater number of different trades.

The perception training, too, increased subjects' ability to differentiate and integrate, thus affecting as well decision certainty. The training also influenced the qualitative aspects of subjects' information seeking by heightening their "problem awareness."

Giving perception training prior exposure to the written text increased subjects' ability to identify and name job charac- teristics and thus enhanced their ability to generate dimen- sions along which jobs could be differentiated. Our findings, thus support Salomon and Sieber-Suppes (1972), who argue that the effects of such training rests in increasing subjects' awareness of problem-relevant information and thereby facili- tating the finding of effective solution strategies.

6. Integration decision aids into job preparation programs in the Federal Republic of Germany

The various decision aids we tested are not in competition with each other, but may be implemented either singly or in combina- tion. Training people to become aware of occupational decision criteria, for example, can be done by providing occupational information in booklet form and hence improve as well their ability to generate decision alternatives. The hierarchical goal system proves to be especially effective in aiding the in- dividual to define the decision problem but can also be of use in the later stages of the decision process when the alterna- tives are evaluated against the formulated goals. Observation learning may prove more effective than reinforcement counsel- ing in influencing both the quantitative and qualitative aspects

of information behavior. Especially in highly complex decision
problems, observation learning represents an economic form of
communicating the best-suited solution strategies. Finally, the
balance sheet helps people in the ordering and evaluation of
alternatives and results as well in more balanced information
behavior during the final stages of decision-making. This latter effect generally leads to a higher satisfaction with the
final decision.

Until now, only the balance sheet has been tested under rigorous conditions, but its effects on information behavior have
proven to be stable. This decision aid as well as the others
ought, however, to be tested in real-life settings. In contrast
to experiments conducted in the USA where the subjects consisted, as a rule, of people looking for counsel and who had special decision problems, our experiments were conducted with
pupils participating on their own wish and who were extraordinarily secure in their decisions. The findings to this point,
however, indicate that these procedures can be implemented in
non-controlled settings (e.g. in employment "workshops" or job
preparation lessons) and that their effectiveness is not restricted to special populations. A model test, partly financed
by the European Community and planned and conducted by the
School Psychological Service of Ludwigshafen, will apply the
hierarchical goal system and balance sheet to aid occupational
choices in some primary school classes and it is planned as
well to integrate these decision aids into employment workshops. The results of an evaluation study of this model test
should be ready by about 1982.

It was not long ago that preparation for job decision consisted
entirely of booklets distributed by the Bundesanstalt für Arbeit (Labor Office), lecture, and above all, individual counseling (for reference to vocational counselling in the Federal
Republic and in other countries see Eichner, Harmann, Lohmann
& Wagner, 1976). More recently, however, schools and labor offices have collaborated in the development of employment work-

shops that are obligatory in all primary schools. In Baden-Württemberg, for instance, a lesson in "trade orientation" was tested (Hartmann, 1975) and, beginning with school year 1978/79, will be given in each of the eight classes in the State primary schools.

It should at this point be noted that West Germany still has only short term job preparation courses, a fact inconsistent with the now prevalent view that occupational choice is a developmental process that lasts for years (a survey on long term programs in the USA is given, for instance, by Campbell et al., 1973). An essential part of such programs should be the communication of decision techniques applicable long after the student has left school and in a variety of complex decision-making situations. A step in this direction is now being undertaken by the School Psychology Service of Ludwigshafen which has developed occupational choice lessons that are administered to students in the last three grades of primary school and which enable them to progressively sharpen their perceptions of their decision making situations as their experience and knowledge increase.

An essential problem with respect to occupational choice is that the working life of present-day adults is more or less separate from the world of the children. One consequence is that, as our experiments have shown, youths facing occupational choice are able neither to formulate their goals with regard to their future job activity nor evaluate the consequences in case they obtain information or certain characteristics of a job. Information-seeking which is quantitatively as well as qualitatively limited is thus linked with a limited possibility to evaluate the obtained information reliably and validly. Also, the Vierte Jugendbericht (1978) der Bundesrepublik Deutschland (4th report on youth in the Federal Republic of Germany) criticized the fact that the youths are little prepared for working life when leaving school. The Expert Commission (1978) subsequently formulated recommendations to the ef-

fect that comprehensive information on working life, job activities et cetera should be communicated in the job preparation
lessons. It is, however, difficult to meet this recommendation
when the number of practical courses given by firms are few
in number despite the generally positive evaluations they
elicit from students.

The model project in Ludwigshafen provides the students with
two practical courses supplemented by preliminary and follow-
up procedures which, it is hoped, will augment the courses'
effectiveness. Before the courses start, students complete
goal hierarchy that enables them to more clearly differentiate
between various job and training alternatives. The criteria
that emerge in doing this goal hierarchy are subsequently used
to evaluate students' experiences during the course itself.
Also, these preliminary hierarchies enable the students to modify their goals and adapt their ideas more closely to occupational realities.

There have been some private undertakings that demonstrate how,
despite a scarcity of practical courses, ideas of job conditions and working life can be provided to young people. The
magazine 'Stern', for example, reports of an employer who orga-
nizes periodic visits for the children of his employees to
various sections of his enterprise, the children, in addition,
being allowed to visit the factory themselves in order to fa-
miliarize themselves with their parents work place (Wingert,
1978).

One example of a comprehensive program for preparing people for
job decisions is the cooperative youth consultation office,
integrated into a youth center in Munich (Sowade, von Ahnen,
Babiel & Eichner, 1975a, b). The vocational counselling there
consists of three phases. First, a number of "occupational
information dyads" are arranged, in which, for example,
apprentices come to inform the students. This kind of counselling having the advantage that the counsellors - in contrast to the usual practice - are near the same level as

those looking for counsel and are thus able to give more concrete information. The students themselves generate additional
job information by forming study groups that visit apprentices
at their work places and record their experiences using film
or slides that are then shown to the others. Some preliminary
structuring of students' goal hierarchies could enhance the
effectiveness of these information days by resulting in more
organized information gathering. Besides the information days,
weekend workshops dealing with occupational expectation and
reality are given. Though students' balance sheets show that
the number and diversity of consequences listed suffers from
the lack of familiarity with jobs and working life (Jeromin,
1978), a combined approach using the balance sheet together
with group discussion contributes to enlarging students' ideas
and evaluating them more realistically. In the last of the
three phases the associates of the counselling institution
help the students during their search for a suitable training
post.

The experiments on information behavior and occupational decision-making lead to several conclusions on how to improve
information processing. Experiments by Witte (1972) have demonstrated that necessary information about the contents of
further information serves to stimulate information seeking
considerably. Especially since young people today are not provided with practical experiences about relevant job decision
criteria, it would be advisable to inform the students before
the counselling sessions about how to use the available most
effectively. This could be done by means of a list of questions
as in our own experiments.

Frey (1978), Jeromin (1978) and Jeromin and Kroh-Püschel
(1978b) found out that subjects under certain conditions are
interested in dissonant information about their preliminary
choice. In reality, however, it is extraordinarily difficult
to get such information, the available information usually
describing aspects of activities and jobs which the students,

since they lack experience, can only judge with great difficulty. Disadvantages of a job are rarely described. The students themselves are conscious of this information problem
(Jeromin & Kroh-Püschel, 1977).

Another problem is that the direct comparison of occupational
alternatives on various attributes is seldom possible, even
though such comparisons are the favored strategy of students
for solving complex decision problems (Gerdts, 1977). The official information issued by Labor Office makes such an interdi-
mensional approach impossible, since readers have to go through
great amounts of uninteresting information before arriving at
the relevant attributes, if he/she finds them at all. Direct
access, which would lower the cost of information search considerably, is not possible. In Berlin, the Labor Office has
opened a modern information centre in which the youths have
access to various information media. When furnishing such centres, it would be worth considering whether the pupils should
not be offered the opportunity to compare various jobs on relevant attributes directly, one with the other.

Work in the United States has shown, however, that diversity
and effective presentation of available information are not
alone sufficient to enable young people to arrive at an appropriate decision-making base. The use of decision aids in such
information centres could help decision-makers develop more
comprehensive and balanced information behavior and thus provide a better basis for occupational choices, high in long-term
satisfaction.

References

Abelson, R.P. Script processing in attitude formation and decision making. In J.S. Carroll & J.W. Payne (Eds.), Cognition and social behavior. Hillsdale, N.J.: Erlbaum, 1976.

Acker, van, P. Models for intransitive choice. Profschrift Universitaet Nijmegen, 1977.

Adams, E. On the nature and purpose of measurement. Synthese, 1966, 16, 125-169.

Adams, E., Fagot, R.F. & Robinson, R.E. on the empirical status of axioms in theories of fundamental measurement. Journal of Mathematical Psychology, 1970, 7, 379-409.

Adams, J.S. Toward an understanding of inequity. Journal of Abnormal and Social Psychology, 1963, 67, 422-436.

Adams, J.S. Inequity in social change. In L. Berkowitz (Ed.), Advances in experimental social psychology. New York: Academic Press, 1965, 2, 267-299.

Adams, J.S. Behavior in organization boundary roles. Unpublished manuscript, University of North Carolina at Chapel Hill, 1969.

Adams, J.S. The structure and dynamics in behavior in organization boundray roles. In M.D. Dunnette (Ed.), Handbook of industrial and organizational psychology. Chicago: Rand McNally, 1976.

Adams, J.S. & Freedman, S. Equity theory revisited: Comments and annotated bibliography. In L. Berkowitz & E. Walster (Eds.), Advances in experimental social psychology. New York: Academic Press, 1976.

Ahmavaara, Y. The mathematical theory of factorial invariance under selection, 1954, 19, 27-38.

Ahnen, H., Babiel, U. & Eichner, A. Kooperative Jugendberatung Quiddenstraße. I: Zur Konzeption einer informativen Freizeitpädagogik. Deutsche Jugend, 1975a, 23, 349-358. II: Neue Vermittlungsformen in der Jugendberatung. Deutsche Jugend, 1975b, 23, 417-427.

Aiken, J. & Johnston, J.P. Promoting career information seeking in college students. Journal of Vocational Behavior, 1973, 3, 81-87.

Akamatsu, J.L. & Thelen, M.H. A review of the literature on observer characteristics and initiation. Developmental Psychology, 1974, 10, 38-47.

Albert, H. Traktat über kritische Vernunft. Tübingen: Mohr, 1968.

Albert, H. Aufklärung und Steuerung. Hamburg: Hoffmann und Campe, 1976.

Alderman, M.K. Relations between origin-pawn disposition, situational elements of freedom and constraint, origin-pawn feelings, and perceptions of success and satisfaction. Dissertation Abstracts International, 1976, 37, (4-A), 2065-2066.

Alexander, R.S., Cross, J.S. & Hill, R.M. Industrial marketing. Homewood, 1956; 3. Aufl., 1967.

Allen, M.K. & Liebert, R.M. Effects of live and symbolic deviant-modeling cues on adoption of a previously learned standard. Journal of Personality and Social Psychology, 1969, 11, 253-260.

Allen, W. Situational factors in conformity. In L. Berkowitz (Ed.), Advances in experimental social psychology. New York: Academic Press, 1965.

Allport, F.H. Social psychology. Cambridge, Mass.: Riverside Press, 1924.

Allport, F.H. Theories of perception and the concept of structure. New York: Wiley, 1955.

Allport, G.W. & Kramer, B.M. Some roots of prejudice. Journal of Psychology, 1946, 22, 9-39.

Alper, T.G. & Korchin, S.J. Memory for socially relevant material. Journal of Abnormal and Social Psychology, 1952, 47, 25-37.

Anderson, N.H. Averaging versus adding as a stimulus combination rule in impression formation. Journal of Experimental Psychology, 1965, 70, 394-400.

Anderson, N.H. Component ratings in impression formation. Psychological Science, 1966, 6, 2, 279-280.

Anderson, N.H. Averaging model analysis of set-size effect in impression formation. Journal of Experimental Psychology, 1967, 75, 158-165.

Anderson, N.H. Likeableness ratings of 555 personality trait words. Journal of Social Psychology, 1968, 9, 272-280.

Anderson, N.H. Two more tests against change of meaning in adjective combinations. Journal of Verbal Learning and Verbal Behavior, 1971, 10, 75-85.

Anderson, N.H. Information integration theory: A brief survey. Technical Report CHIP 24, Center for Human Information Processing. University of California, San Diego, 1972.

Anderson, N.H. Cognitive algebra: Integration theory applied to social attribution. In L. Berkowitz (Ed.), Advances in experimental social psychology, vol. 7, New York: Academic Press, 1974.

Anderson, N.H. & Jacobson, A. Effect of stimulus inconsistency and discounting instructions in personality impression formation. Journal of Personality and Social Psychology, 1965, 2, 531-539.

Andrews, F.M. & Withey, S.B. Social indicators of well-being. Americans' perception of life quality. New York, 1976.

Antonoff, R. Industrielle Werbung und Öffentlichkeitsarbeit. Düsseldorf, 1970.

Apfelbaum, E. On conflicts and bargaining. In L. Berkowitz (Ed.), Advances in experimental social psychology, Vol. 7, New York: Academic Press, 1974.

Arbib, M.A. & Manes, E.G. A category-theoretic approach to systems in a fuzzy world. Synthese, 1975, 30, 381-406.

Aronfreed, J. The concept of internalization. In D.A. Goslin (Ed.), Handbook of socialisation, theory and research. New York: Rand McNally, 1968, 263-323.

Aronfreed, J. The problem of imitation. Advances in Child Development & Behavior, 1969, 4, 209-319.

Asch, S.E. Forming impressions of personality. Journal of Abnormal and Social Psychology, 1946, 41, 258-290.

Asch, S.E. Effects of group pressure upon the modification and distortion of judgements. In H. Guetzkow (Ed.), Groups, Leadership and Men. New York: Russell and Russell, 1963.

Atkinson, J.W. An introduction to motivation. New York: Van Nostrand, 1964.

Atkinson, T. Is satisfaction a good measure of the perceived quality of life? Paper presented at the Meeting of the American Statistical Association, 1977.

Atteslander, P. Quality of life: Objective or subjective? In M. Pfaff & F. Gehrmann (Eds.), Means for information and steering for a higher level of quality of life in urban areas. Göttingen, 1976, 122-136 (in German).

Ausubel, D.P. Educational psychology: A cognitive view. New York: Holt, Rinehart & Winston, 1968.

Backhaus, K. Direktvertrieb in der Investitionsgüterindustrie. Eine Marketingentscheidung. Wiesbaden: Gabler, 1974.

Bahadur, R.R. A representation of the joint distribution of responses to n dichotomous items. In H. Solomon (Ed.), Studies in item analysis and prediction. Stanford, Calif.: Stanford University Press, 1961.

Baker, M.J. Marketing new industrial products. Bristol, 1975.

Bandura, A. Principles of behavior modification. New York: Rinehart & Winston, 1969.

Bandura, A. Vicarious- and self-reinforcement processes. In R. Glaser (Ed.), The nature of reinforcement. New York: Academic Press, 1971a, 1-55.

Bandura, A. Modeling theory: Some traditions, trends, and disputes. In R.D. Parke (Ed.), Recent trends in social learning theory. New York: Academic Press, 1972, 35-61.

Bandura, A. Behavior theory and the models of man. American Psychologist, 1974, 29, 859-869.

Bandura, A. Social learning theory. Englewood Cliffs, N.J.: Prentice Hall, 1977.

Bandura, A. & Barab, P.G. Conditions governing nonreinforced imitation. Developmental Psychology, 1971, 5, 244-255.

Bandura, A. & McDonald F.J. The influence of social reinforcement and the behavior of models in shaping children's moral judgement. Journal of Abnormal and Social Psychology, 1963, 67, 274-281.

Bandura, A. & Mischel, W. Modification of self-imposed delay of reward through exposure to live and symbolic models. Journal of Personality and Social Psychology, 1965, 2, 689-705.

Bandura, A., Ross, D. & Ross, S.A. Transmission of aggression through imitation of aggressor models. Journal of Abnormal and Social Psychology, 1961, 63, 575-582.

Bandura, A., Ross, D. & Ross, S.A. Vicarious reinforcement and imitation learning. Journal of Abnormal and Social Psychology, 1963, 67-601-607.

Banks, W.P. Signal detection theory and human memory. Psychological Bulletin, 1970, 74, 81-99.

Bannister, D. & Fransella, F. Inquiring man: The theory of personal constructs. Harmondsworth, 1971.

Barndt, R.J. & Johnson, D.M. Time orientation in delinquents. Journal of Abnormal and Social Psychology, 1955, 51, 343-345.

Baron, R.A. Exposure to an aggressive model and apparent probability of retaliation from the victim as determinants of adult aggressive behavior. Journal of Experimental Social Psychology, 1971, 7, 343-355.

Bartlett, F.C. Remembering: A study in experimental and social psychology. London: Cambridge University Press, 1932.

Bauer, R.A. Consumer behavior as risk taking. In R.S. Hancock (Ed.), Dynamic marketing in a changing world. Chicago, 1960, 289 ff.

Bauer, R.A. Risk handling in drug adoption: The role of Company preference. In D.F. Cox (Ed.), Risk taking and information handling in consumer behavior. Boston, 1967.

Bauer, V., Gebert, A. & Meise, J. Evaluation in urban planning. Report, Batelle Institut e.V., Frankfurt/M., 1973.

Beach, B.H. Expert judgment about uncertainty: Bayesian decision making in realistic settings. Organizational Behavior and Human Performance, 1975, 14, 10-59.

Beals, R., Krantz, D.H. & Tversky, A. Foundations of multidimensional scaling. Psychological Review, 1968, 75, 127-143.

Becker, G.M., DeGroot, M.H. & Marschak, J. Measuring utility by a single response sequential method. Behavioral Science, 1964, 9, 226-233.

Beckman, L. Effects of students' performance on teachers' and observers' attributions of causality. Journal of Educational Psychology, 1970, 61, 75-82.

Beckwith, N.E. & Lehman, R. The importance of differential weights in multiple attribute models of consumer attitude. Journal of Marketing Research, 1973, 10, 141-145.

Belcher, T.L. Effect of different test situations on creativity scores. Psychological Reports, 1975a, 36, 511-514.

Belcher, T.L. Modeling original divergent responses. An initial investigation. Journal of Educational Psychology, 1975b, 67, 351-358.

Bem, D.J. An experimental analysis of self-persuasion. Journal of Experimental Social Psychology, 1965, 1, 199-218.

Bem, D.J. Inducing belief in false confessions. Journal of Personality and Social Psychology, 1966, 3, 706-707.

Benton, A.A. Accountability and negotiations between group representatives. Proceedings of the 80th Annual Convention of the American Psychological Association, 1972, 227-228.

Benton, A.A. & Druckman, D. Salient solutions and the bargaining behavior of representatives and non-representatives. International Journal of Group Tensions, 1973, 3, 28-39.

Benton, A.A. & Druckman, D. Constituent's bargaining orientation and intergroup negotiations. Journal of Applied Social Psychology, 1974, 4, 141-150.

Benton, A.A., Kelley, H.H. & Liebling, B. Effects of extremity of offers and concessing rate on the outcome of bargaining. Journal of Personality and Social Psychology, 1972, 24, 73-83.

Berekoven, L. Die Werbung für Investitions- und Produktionsgüter. GfK-Schriften Nr. 16, Nürnberg, 1961.

Berelson, B. & Steiner, G.A. Menschliches Verhalten. Vol. II, Soziale Aspekte. Weinheim, 1972.

Bergland, B.W. & Krumboltz, J.D. An optimal grade level for career exploration. Vocational Guidance Quarterly, 1969, 18, 29-33.

794   References

Bergland, B.W., Quatrono, L.A. & Lundquist, G.W. Group social
    models and structured interaction in teaching decision making;
    Vocational Guidance Quarterly, 1975, 24, 28-36.

Berkowitz, L. Resistance to improper dependency relationships.
    Journal of Experimental Social Psychology, 1969, 5, 283-294.

Berkowitz, L. The self, selfishness, and altruism. In J. Macau-
    lay & L. Berkowitz (Eds.), Altruism and helping behavior.
    New York: Academic Press, 1970.

Berlyne, D.E. Uncertainty and epistemic curiosity. British
    Journal of Psychology, 1962, 53, 27-34.

Bermant, G. & Starr, M. On selling people what they are likely
    to do: Three experiments. Proceedings of the Annual Conven-
    tion of the APA, 1972, 7, 171-172.

Bettman, J.R. Perceived risk and its components. A model and
    empirical test. Journal of Marketing Research, 1973, 10,
    184-190.

Bieri, J. et al. Clinical and social judgment: The discrimina-
    tion of behavioral information. New York, 1966.

Bills, R., Vance, E. & McLean, O. An index of adjustment and
    values. Journal of Consulting Psychology, 1951, 15, 257-261.

Bingemer, K. Gastarbeiter in Krisen. In K. Bingemer et al.
    (Eds.), Leben als Gastarbeiter. Köln-Opladen, 1970, 152-153.

Black, W. & Gregson, R. Time perspective, purpose in life, ex-
    traversion and neuroticism in New Zealand prisoners. British
    Journal of Social and Clinical Psychology, 1973, 12, 50-60.

Blalock, H.J., Jr. Causal inferences, closed publications and
    measures of association. In H.M. Blalock (Ed.), Causal models
    in the social sciences. Chicago, 1971, 139 ff.

Blickenstorfer, H.U. Die Stellung der Werbung im Marketing der
    Produktionsgüterindustrie. Zürich, 1970.

Bock, H.H. Automatische Klassifikation. Göttingen, 1974.

Bodden, J.L. Cognitive complexity as a factor in appropriate
    vocational choice. Journal of Counseling Psychology, 1970,
    17, 364-368.

Bodden, J.L. & James, L.E. Influence of occupational informa-
    tion giving on cognitive complexity. Journal of Counseling
    Psychology, 1976, 23, 280-282.

Bodden, J.L. & Klein, G. Cognitive complexity and appropriate
    vocational choice: Another look. Journal of Counseling Psy-
    chology, 1972, 19, 257-258.

Böcker, F. Die Bestimmung der Kaufverbundenheit von Produkten.
    Berlin, 1978.

Böhler, H. Methoden und Modelle der Marktsegmentierung.
    Stuttgart, 1977.

Börsig, C. Entscheidungskriterien und Werbeinhalte beim Absatz von Standard-Anwendungssoftware. Unpublished manuscript, Munich, 1976.

Bonarius, J. Research in the personal construct theory of G.A. Kelly. In B. Maher (Ed.), Progress in experimental personality research, 1965, 2, 1-46.

Boocock, S.S. The life career game. Personnel and Guidance Journal, 1967, 46, 328-334.

Boocock, S.S. The life career game. In M. Inbar & C.S. Stoll (Eds.), Simulation and gaming in social sciences. New York: Free Press, 1972, 22, 256-286.

Boocock, S.S. & Coleman, J.S. Games with simulated environment in learning. Sociology of Education, 1969, 39, 215-236.

Bousfield, A. K. & Bousfield, W. Measurement of clustering and sequential constancies in repeated free recall. Psychological Reports, 1966, 19, 935-942.

Bousfield, W.A. The occurrence of clustering in the recall of randomly arranged associates. Journal of General Psychology, 1953, 49, 229-240.

Bousfield, W.A. & Sedgewick, H.W. An analysis of sequences of restricted associative responses. Journal of General Psychology, 1944, 30, 149-165.

Borman, C. Effects of reinforcement style of counseling on information seeking behavior. Journal of Vocational Behavior, 1972, 2, 255-259.

Bormuth, J.R. On the theory of achievement test items. Chicago-London, 1970.

Borris, M. Ausländische Arbeitnehmer in einer Großstadt. Frankfurt/M., 1973.

Bossert, R. Promotionen im Marketing von Investitionsgütern. Dissertation, Mannheim, 1975.

Bowersox, D.J. Changing channels in the physical distribution of finished goods. In D.J. Bowersox, B.J. Lalonde & E.W. Smykay (Eds.), Readings in physical distribution management. London, 1969, 94 ff.

Bowman, E.H. Consistency and optimality in managerial decision making. Management Science, 1963, 9, 310-321.

Boyd, H.W. & Davis, R.T. (Eds.), Readings in sales management. Homewood, Ill., 1970.

Brandt, U. & Köhler, B. Norm und Konformität. In C.F. Graumann (Ed.), Handbuch der Psychologie, Vol. 7, Sozialpsychologie (2. Halband). Göttingen: Hogrefe, 1972, 1710-1789.

Bransford, J.D. & Johnson, M.K. Contextual prerequisites for understanding: Some investigations of comprehension and recall. Journal of Verbal Learning and Verbal Behavior, 1972, 61, 717-726.

Bransford, J.D. & McCarrel, N.S. A sketch of a cognitive approach to comprehension: Some thoughts about understanding what it means to comprehend. In W. B. Weimer & D.S. Palermo (Eds.), Cognition and the symbolic processes. Hillsdale, N. J.: Lawrence Erlbaum, 1974.

Braver, S.L. & Rohrer, V. Superiority of vicarious over direct experience in interpersonal conflict resolution. Journal of Conflict Resolution, 1978, 1, 143-155.

Brehm, J.W. Postdecision changes in the desirability of alternatives. Journal of Abnormal and Social Psychology, 1956, 52, 384-389.

Brehm, J.W. A theory of psychological reactance. New York, London: Academic Press, 1966.

Brehm, J.W. Attitude change from threat to attitudinal freedom. In A.G. Greenwald, T.C. Brock & T.M. Ostrom (Eds.), Psychological foundations of attitudes. New York: Academic Press, 1968.

Brehm, J.W. Responses to loss of freedom. A theory of psychological reactance. Morristown, N.J.: General Learning Press, 1972.

Brehm, J.W. & Cole, A.H. Effect of a favor which reduces freedom. Journal of Personality and Social Psychology, 1966, 3, 420-426.

Brehm, J.W. & Mann, M. Effect to importance of freedom and attraction to group members on influence produced by group pressure. Journal of Personality and Social Psychology, 1975, 31, 816-824.

Brehm, J.W. & Rosen, E. Attractiveness of old alternatives when a new, attractive alternative is introduced. Journal of Personality and Social Psychology, 1971, 20, 261-266.

Brehm, J.W. & Sensenig, J. Social influence as a function of attempted and implied usurpation of choice. Journal of Personality and Social Psychology, 1966, 4, 703-707.

Brehm, J.W. & Wicklund, R.A. Regret and dissonance reduction as a function of post decision salience of dissonant information. Journal of Personality and Social Psychology, 1970, 14, 1-7.

Brehm, S.S. The application of social psychology to clinical practice. New York: Wiley, 1976.

Brehm, S.S. & Weinraub, M. Physical barriers and psychological reactance: 2-year olds' responses to threats to freedom. Journal of Personality and Social Psychology, 1977, 11, 830-836.

Breyer, R.F. Some observations on structural formation and the growth of marketing channels. In R. Cox, W. Alderson & S.J. Shapiro (Eds.), Theory in marketing. Homewood, Ill, 1964, 163 ff.

Brickenkamp, R. Handbuch psychologischer und pädagogischer Tests. Göttingen, 1975.

Brier, G.W. Verification of forecasts expressed in terms of probability. Monthly Weather Review, 1950, 75, 1-3.

Brigham, J.C. & Cook, S.W. The influence of attitude on the recall of controversial material: A failure to confirm. Journal of Experimental Social Psychology, 1969, 5, 240-243.

Brim, Jr., O.G., Glass, D.C., Lavin, D.E. & Goodman, N. Personality and decision processes. Stanford, Calif.: Stanford University Press, 1962.

Brock, T.C. Implications of commodity theory for value change. In A.G. Greenwald, T.C. Brock & T.M. Ostrom (Eds.), Psychological foundations of attitudes. New York: Academic Press, 1968.

Brody, N. The effect of commitment to correct and incorrect decisions on confidence in a sequential decision task. American Journal of Psychology, 1965, 78, 251-256.

Brown, R. Social psychology. New York: Free Press of Glencoe, 1965.

Bruggemann, A., Groskurth, P. & Ulich, E. Arbeitszufriedenheit. Bern, 1975.

Bruner, J.C. & Goodman, C.C. Value and need as organizing factors in perception. Journal of Social Psychology, 1947, 42, 33-44.

Bruner, J.C. & Postman, L. Symbolic values as an organizing factor in perception. Journal of Social Psychology, 1948, 27, 203-208.

Bruner, J.C. & Postman, L. Tension and tension release as organizing factors in perception. Journal of Personality, 1947, 15, 300-308.

Bruner, J.C. & Postman, L. On the perception of incongruity: A paradigm. Journal of Personality, 1949a, 18, 206-223.

Bruner, J.C. & Rodriguez, J.S. Some determinants of apparent size. Journal of Abnormal and Social Psychology, 1953, 48, 17-24.

Bruner, J.S., Postman, L. & Rodriguez, J. Expectation and the perception of color. American Journal of Psychology, 1951, 64, 216-227.

Bruner, J.S. & Potter, M.C. Interference in visual recognition. Science, 1964, 144, 424-425.

Brunswik, E. Perception and the representative design of experiments. Berkeley: University of California Press, 1956.

Bucklin, L.P. Research, role enactment and marketing efficiency. The Journal of Business, 1949, 42, 416-438.

Bunge, M. Scientific research II - The search for truth. New York: Springer, 1967.

Bunz, A.R., Jansen, R. & Schacht, K. Qualität des Arbeitslebens. Soziale Kennziffern zu Arbeitszufriedenheit und Berufschancen. Bonn, 1974.

Bulletin of EEC. Von der Schule ins Berufsleben. Bericht des Ausschusses für Bildungsfragen, 1976, 12.

Caesar, B. Autorität in der Familie. Reinbeck: Rowohlt, 1972.

Campbell, A., Converse, P. & Rodgers, W. The quality of American life. Perceptions, evaluation and satisfactions. New York, 1976.

Campbell, D.T. Stereotypes and the perception of group differences. American Psychologist, 1967, 22, 817-829.

Campbell, R.E., Walz, G.R., Miller, J.V. & Kriger, S.T. Career guidance: A handbook of methods. Columbus: Merrill, 1973.

Cantor, N. & Mischel, W. Traits as prototypes: Effects on recognition memory. Journal of Personality and Social Psychology, 1977, 35, 35-48.

Cantor, N. & Mischel, W. Prototypes in person perception. In L. Berkowitz (Ed.), Advances in experimental social psychology, Vol. 12, New York: Academic Press, 1979.

Cantril, H. The pattern of human concerns. New Brunswick, New Jersey: Rutgers University Press, 1965.

Caplovitz, D. The poor pay more. New York, 1967.

Carroll, J.D. Individual differences and multidimensional scaling. In R.N. Shepard, A.K. Romney & S.R. Nerlove (Eds.), Multidimensional scaling. Theory and applications in the behavioral sciences. New York, 1972.

Carroll, J.D. & Chang, J.J. MDPREF Program. Bell telephone laboratories. Murray Hill, 1969.

Carroll, J.S. & Payne, J.W. (Eds.), Cognition and social behavior. Hillsdale, N.J.: Erlbaum, 1976.

Carter, L. & Schooler, K. Value, need and other factors in perception. Psychological Review, 1949, 56, 200-208.

Cartwright, D. The nature of group cohesiveness. In D. Cartwright & A. Zander (Eds.), Group dynamics: Research and theory. New York: Harper & Row, 1968.

Cartwright, D. & Zander, A. (Eds.), Group dynamics: Research and theory. New York: Harper & Row, 1968.

Carver, C.S., Glass, D.C., Snyder, M.L. & Katz, I. Favorable evaluations of stigmatized others. Personality and Social Psychology Bulletin, 1977, 3, 232-235.

Cattell, R.B. Psychological measurement: Normative, ipsative, interactive. Psychological Review, 1944, 9, 267-283.

Charms, R. de. Personal causation. New York: Academic Press, 1968.

Charms, R. de & Shea, D.J. Beyond attribution theory. The human conception of motivation and causality. In L.H. Strickland, F.E. Aboud & K.J. Gergen (Eds.), Social psychology in transition. New York: Plenum Press, 1976.

Chestnut, R.W. & Jacoby, J. Consumer information processing: Emerging theory and findings. Purdue paper in consumer psychology Nr. 158, West Lafayette, Indiana, 1976.

Chisnall, P.M. Marketing research: Analysis and measurement. London, 1973.

Christensen, P.R., Guilford, J.P. & Wilson, R.C. Relations of creative responses to working time and instructions. Journal of Experimental Psychology, 1957, 53, 82-88.

Clark, R.D. & Sechrest, L.B. The mandate phenomenon. Journal of Personality and Social Psychology, 1976, 34, 1057-1061.

Codol, J.-P. On the so-called "superior conformity to the self" behavior: Twenty experimental investigations. European Journal of Social Psychology, 1976, 5, 457-501.

Cohen, A.R. Some implications of self-esteem for social influence. In C.I. Hovland & I.L. Janis (Eds.), Personality and Personability. New Haven: Yale University Press, 1959.

Cohen, J.L. & Davis, J.H. Effects of audience status, evaluation, and time of action on performance with hidden-word problems. Journal of Personality and Social Psychology, 1973, 27, 74-85.

Cohen, R. Eine Untersuchung zur diagnostischen Verarbeitung widersprüchlicher Informationen. Psychologische Forschung, 1967, 30, 211-225.

Cohen, R. Systematische Tendenzen bei Persönlichkeitsbeurteilungen. Bern: Huber, 1969.

Cohen, R. & Schümer, R. Eine Untersuchung zur sozialen Eindrucksbildung. I: Die Verarbeitung von Informationen unterschiedlicher Konsonanz. Archiv für die gesamte Psychologie, 1968, 120, 151-179.

Cohen, R. & Schümer, R. Die diagnostische Verarbeitung widersprüchlicher Informationen in Abhängigkeit vom Ausmaß des Widerspruchs. Diagnostica, 1969, 15, 3-13.

Cohen, R.L. Mastery and justice in laboratory dyads: A revision and extension of equity theory. Journal of Personality and Social Psychology, 1974, 29, 464-474.

Collaros, P. & Anderson, L.R. Effect of perceived expertness upon creativity of members of brainstorming groups. Journal of Applied Psychology, 1969, 53, 159-163.

Collins, B.E. & Hoyt, M.F. Personal responsibility-for-consequences: An integration and extension of the "forced compliance" literature. Journal of Experimental Social Psychology, 1972, 8, 558-593.

Conrath, D.W. Experience as a factor in experimental gaming behavior. Journal of Conflict Resolution, 1970, 14, 195-202.

Coombs, C.H. Theory of data. New York: Wiley, 1964.

Coombs, C.H. Portfolio theory: A theory of risky decision making. La Décision, Paris, 1969.

Coombs, C.H. Portfolio theory and the measurement of risk. In M.F. Kaplan & S. Schwartz (Eds.), Human judgment and decision processes. New York: Academic Press, 1975.

Coombs, C.H. & Avrunin, G.S. A theorem on single-peaked preference functions in one dimension. Journal of Mathematical Psychology, 1977b, 16, 261-266.

Coombs, C.H. & Avrunin, G.S. Single-peaked functions and the theory of preference. Psychological Review, 1977a, 84, 216-231.

Coombs, C.H., Dawes, R.M. & Tversky, A. Mathematische Psychologie. Weinheim: Beltz, 1975.

Cooper, J. & Zanna, M.P. Dissonance and the attribution process. In J.H. Harvey, W.J. Ickes & R.F. Kidd (Eds.), New directions in attribution research. Hillsdale, N.J.: Erlbaum, 1976.

Coram, T. & Hill, R. New ideas in industrial marketing. London, 1970.

Corey, R.E. Industrial marketing, cases and concepts. New York: Englewood Cliffs, 1962.

Cottrell, N.B. Performance in the presence of other human beings: More presence, audiance and affiliation effects. In E.C. Simmel, R.A. Hoppe & G.A. Milton (Eds.), Social facilitation and imitative behavior. Boston: Harcourt, 1968.

Cowan, P.A., Langer, J., Heavenrich, J. & Nathanson, M. Social learning and Piaget's cognitive theory of moral development. Journal of Personality and Social Psychology, 1969, 11, 262-274.

Cox, D.F. Risk taking and information handling in cosumer behavior. Boston, 1967.

Cox, R.C. & Vargas, J.S. Ein Vergleich von Itemauswahltechniken für normbezogene und kriterienbezogene Tests. In P. Strittmatter (Ed.), Lernzielorientierte Leistungsmessung. Weinheim-Basel, 1973.

Crites, J.O. Career counseling: A review of major approaches. Counseling Psychologist, 1974, 4, 3-23.

Cronbach, L. Testvalidation. In R.L. Thomdike (Ed.), Educational measurement. American council on education. One Dupont Circle, 1971.

Crowne, D.P. & Marlowe, D. The approval motive: Studies in evaluative dependence. New York: Wiley, 1964.

Crumbaugh, J. Cross-validation of purpose-in-life-test based on
Frankl's concepts. Journal of Individual Psychology, 1968,
24, 74-81.

Cunningham, M.T. & White, J.G. The determinants of choice of
supplier. European Journal of Marketing, 1974, 189 ff.

Cunningham, S.M. The major dimensions of perceived risk. In D.
Cox (Ed.), Risk taking and information handling in consumer
behavior. Boston, Mass., 1967.

Cyert, R.M. & March, J.G. A behavioral theory of the firm.
Englewood Cliffs, 1963.

Dabbs, J.M. Physical closeness and negative feelings. Psychonomic Science, 1971, 23, 141-143.

Dabrunz, M. Rechtsvorschriften zum Thema "Stadtplanung, Verbraucher und Einzelhandel". Hamburg: Co-Op-Verlag, 1975,
59-96.

Dailey, C.A. The effects of premature conclusion upon the acquisition of understanding of a person. Journal of Psychology,
1952, 33, 133-152.

Davidson, D. & Marschak, J. Experimental tests of a stochastic
decision theory. In C.W. Churchman & P. Ratoosh (Eds.), Measurement: Definitions & theories. New York: Wiley, 1959,
233-269.

Davis, H.L. Decision making within the household. Journal of
Consumer Research, 1976, 2, 241-260.

Davis, W.L. & Davis. D.E. Internal - external control and attribution of responsibility for success and failure. Journal of
Personality, 1972, 40, 123-136.

Dawes, R.M. Grundlagen der Einstellungsmessung. Weinheim:
Beltz, 1977.

Dawes, R.M. & Corrigan, B. Linear models in decision making.
Psychological Bulletin, 1974, 81, 95-106.

Debus, R. Effects of brief observation of model behavior on
conceptual tempo of impulsive children. Developmental Psy-
choly, 1970, 2, 22-32.

Deci, E.L. Intrinsic motivation. New York: Plenum Press, 1975.

Delgado, M.J. Die Gastarbeiter in der Presse. Köln-Opladen,
1972.

Deutsch, M. Trust and suspicion. Journal of Conflict Resolution, 1958, 2, 265-279.

Deutsch, M. The resolution of conflict. New Haven: Yale University Press, 1973.

Deutsch, M. Equity, equality, and need: What determines which value will be used as the basis of distributive justice? Journal of Social Issues, 1975, 31, 137-149.

Deutsch, M. & Krauss, R.M. The effect of threat upon interpersonal bargaining. Journal of Abnormal and Social Psychology, 1960, 61, 181-189.

Deutsch, M. & Krauss,R.M. Studies of interpersonal bargaining. Journal of Conflict Resolution, 1962, 6, 52-76.

Deutsch, M. & Solomon, L. Reactions to evaluations by others as influenced by self evaluation. Sociometry, 1959, 22, 92-113.

Devolder, M. Time orientation: A review. Psychological Reports, No. 9, University of Leuven, 1978.

Dodge, H.R. Industrial marketing. New York, 1970.

Doise, W. Intergroup relations and polarization of individual and collective judgments. Journal of Personality and Social Psychology, 1969, 12, 136-143.

Domotor, Z. Probabilistic relational structures and their applications. Technical Report No. 144, Institute for Math. Studies in the Social Sciences, Stanford University, Stanford, 1969.

Domotor, Z. Species of measurement structures. Theoria, 1972, 1-2, 64-81.

Domotor, Z. Inductive structures: Lecture notes in probability, decision, and gaming. Unpublished, University of Pennsylvania, 1975a.

Domotor, Z. The probability structure of quantum mechanical systems. Synthese, 1975b, 29, 155-185.

Domotor, Z. Random relations and their measurement. Unpublished manuscript. Institute for Math. Studies in the Social Sciences, Stanford University, Stanford, California, 1976.

Doob, A. & Zabrack, M. The effect of freedom-threatening instructions and monetary inducement on compliance. Canadian Journal of Behavioral Science, 1971, 3, 408-412.

Dornseif, F. Der deutsche Wortschatz nach Sachgruppen. Berlin, 1954[4].

Dorr, D. & Fey, S. Relative power of symbolic adult and peer models in the modification of children's moral choice behavior. Journal of Personality and Social Psychology, 1974, 29, 335-341.

Downing, G.D. Sales management. New York, 1969.

Drever, J. & Fröhlich, W.D. dtv Wörterbuch der Psychologie. München: Deutscher Taschenbuchverlag, 1972.

Drews, J.L. Some determinants of favor acceptance. Dissertation Abstracts International, 1970, 30 (7-A), 3094.

Druckman, D. Prenegotiation experience and dyadic conflict resolution in a bargaining situation. Journal of Experimental Social Psychology, 1968, 4, 367-383.

Druckman, D. The influence of the situation in interparty conflict. Journal of Conflict Resolution, 1971, 15, 523-534.

Druckman, D. Negotiations. New York, 1977.

Druckman, D., Solomon, D. & Zechmeister, K. Effects of representational role obligations on the process of children's distribution of resources. Sociometry, 1972, 35, 387-410.

Dweck, C.S. The role of expectations and attributions in the alleviation of learned helplessness. Journal of Personality and Social Psychology, 1975, 31, 674-685.

Ebbesen, E.B., Cohen, C. E. & Lane, J.L. Encoding and construction processes in person perception. Paper presented at APA Convention Chicago, 1975.

Edney, J.J. Territoriality and control: A field experiment. Journal of Personality and Social Psychology, 1975, 31, 1108-1115.

Edwards, A.L. The retention of affective experiences: A criticism and restatement of the problem. Psychological Review, 1942, 49, 43-53.

Edward, W. Dynamic decision theory and probabilistic information processing. IEEE Transactions on Human Factors in Electronics, 1962, 4, 59-73.

Edwards, W. Probabilistic information processing system for diagnosis and action selection. In J. Spiegel & D.E. Walker (Eds.), Second Congress on the Information Sciences. Washington, D.C.: Spartan Books, 1965, 141-155.

Edwards, W. Social utilities. Engineering Economics Summer Symposium Series, 1971, 6.

Egle, K. Entscheidungstheorie: Eine strukturelle Darstellung. Basel: Birkhäuser Verlag, 1975.

Eichholz, G. Der Markt als Erkenntnisobjekt der empirischen Wirtschafts- und Sozialforschung. Beiträge zu ihrer Interpretation. Bern, 1968.

Eichner, H., Hartmann, J., Lohmann, U. & Wagner, U. Berufsberatung und Berufslenkung. Göttingen: Otto Schwarz & Co., 1976.

Einhorn, J. The use of nonlinear noncompensatory models in decision making. Psychological Bulletin, 1970, 71, 221-230.

Eiser, J.R. & Stroebe, W. Categorization and social judgment. London, 1972.

El-Gazzar, M.E., Saleh, S.D. & Conrath, D.W. Situational and individual difference variables in chance-determined activities. Journal of Personality and Social Psychology, 1976, 34, 951-959.

Elms, A.C. Role playing, incentive, and dissonance. Psychological Bulletin, 1967, 68, 132-148.

Emerson, R.M. Power-dependence relations. American Sociological Review, 1962, 31 ff.

Englert, G. Marketing von Standard-Anwendungs-Software. Dissertation, München, 1977.

Epstein, S. The self-concept revisited, or: A theory on a theory. American Psychologist, 1973, 28, 404-415.

Erdelyi, M.H. A new look at the new look: Perceptual defense and vigilance. Psychological Review, 1974, 81, 1-25.

Esser, J.K. & Komorita, S.S. Reciprocity and concession making in bargaining. Journal of Personality and Social Psychology, 1975, 31, 864-872.

Evan, W.M. Toward a theory of inter-organizational relations. Management-Science, 1965, B-217 ff.

Evans, F.B. Selling as a dyadic relationship. American Behavioral Scientist, 1963, 76 ff.

Evans, J.R. & Cody, J.J. Transfer of decision making skills learned in a counseling-like setting·to similar and dissimilar situations. Journal of Counseling Psychology, 1969, 16, 427-432.

Fahrenberg, J. & Selg, H. Das Freiburger Persönlichkeitsinventar - FPI. Göttingen: Hogrefe, 1970.

Falmagne, J.-C. Grundlagen der Fechnerschen Psychophysik. In L. Eckensberger & U. Eckensberger (Eds.), 28. Kongreß der DGfP Saarbrücken, 1972, Bd. 2 Psychologische Methodik und Mathematische Psychologie. Göttingen: Hogrefe, 1974.

Falmagne, J.-C. Random conjoint measurement and loudness summation. Psychological Review, 1976, 83, 1, 65-79.

Farkas, A. & Anderson, N.H. Input summation and equity summation in multi-cue equity judgements. Technical Report CHIP 47). San Diego: University of California, December 1974.

Feather, N.T. Attribution of responsibility and valence of success and failure in relation to initial confidence and task performance. Journal of Personality and Social Psychology, 1969, 13, 129-144.

Feger, H. Die Erfassung individueller Einstellungsstrukturen. Zeitschrift für Sozialpsychologie, 1974, 5, 242-254.

Feldmann, S.P. Some dyadic relationships associated with consumer choice. In R.M. Haas (Ed.), Science, technology and Marketing. Chicago, 1966, 758-775.

Ferguson, G.A. On learning and human ability. Canadian Journal of Psychology, 1954, 8, 95-112.

Ferguson, G.A. On transfer and the ability of man. Canadian Journal of Psychology, 1956, 10, 121-131.

Festinger, L. A theory of social comparison processes. Human Relations, 1954, 7, 117-140.

Festinger, L. A theory of cognitive dissonance. Stanford, Calif.: Stanford University Press, 1957.

Festinger, L. The motivating effect of cognitive dissonance. In G. Lindzey (Ed.), Assessment of human motives. New York: Rinehart, 1958, 65-86.

Festinger, L. Conflict, decision, and dissonance. Stanford, Calif.: Stanford University Press, 1964.

Finetti, B. de, Probability, induction and statistics. New York: Wiley, 1972.

Finetti, B. de, Theory of probability, Vol. 1, New York: Wiley & Sons, 1974.

Fischer, C.S. The effect of threats in an incomplete information game. Sociometry, 1969, 32, 301-314.

Fischer, G.W. Four methods for assessing multiattribute utilities: An experimental validation. Pd. D. dissertation. The University of Michigan, 1972.

Fischer, G.W. Experimental application on multiattribute utility models. In D. Wendt & C. Vlek (Eds.), Utility, probability, and human decision making. Dordrecht: Reidel, 1975.

Fishbein, M. An investigation of the relationship between beliefs about an object and the attitude toward that object. Human Relations, 1963, 16, 233-239.

Fishbein, M. The prediction of behavior from attitudinal variables. In C.D. Mortensen & K.K. Sereno (Eds.), Advances in communication research. New York, 1972.

Fishbein, M. & Hunter, R. Summation versus balance in attitude organization and change. Journal of Abnormal and Social Psychology, 1964 (a), 69, 505-510.

Fishbein, M. & Hunter, R. Summation versus balance: A replication and extension. Paper read at Western Psychological Association, Portland, Oregon, April, 1964 (b).

Fishburn, P.C. Methods of estimating additive utilities. Management Science, 1967, 13, 435-453.

Fishburn, P.C. Utility theory for decision making. New York: Wiley, 1970.

Fisher, L. Industrial marketing: An analytical approach to planning and execution. London, 1969.

Fitch, G. Effects of self-esteem, perceived performance and change on causal attributions. Journal of Personality and Social Psychology, 1970, 16, 311-315.

Flanders, J.P. Effects of vicarious reinforcement, verbalization and number of stimulus dimensions upon imitation in an observational learning experiment. Dissertation Abstracts, 1968, 29, 1186-1187.

Fontaine, G. Social comparison and some determinants of expected performance in a novel task situation. Journal of Personality and Social Psychology, 1974, 29, 487-496.

Franzen, G. Marktforschung für Investitionsgüter. In Marketing Enzyklopädie, Bd. I. München, 1974, 723 ff.

Freedman, J.L. & Sears, D.O. Selective exposure. In L. Berkowitz (Ed.), Advances in experimental social psychology, Vol. 2. New York: Academic Press, 1965, 57-97.

French, W.A. & Barksdale, H.C. Food labeling regulations: Efforts toward full disclosure. Journal of Marketing, 1974, 38, 14-19.

Frender, R. & Doubilet, P. More on measures of category clustering in free recall - although probably not the last word. Psychological Bulletin, 1974, 81, 64-66.

Frey, D. (Ed.), Kognitive Theorien der Sozialpsychologie. Bern: Huber, 1978.

Frieze, I. & Weiner, B. Cue utilization and attributional judgments for success and failure. Journal of Personality, 1971, 39, 591-605.

Fryrear, J.L. & Thelen, M.H. Effect of sex of model and sex of observer on the imitation of the affectionate behavior. Developmental Psychology, 1969, 1, 298.

Gallo, P.S. The effect of differential motivational orientations in a mixed-motive game. Unpublished doctoral dissertation, University of California, Los Angeles, 1963.

Gallo, P.S. Effects of increased incentives upon the use of threat in bargaining. Journal of Personality and Social Psychology, 1966, 4, 14-20.

Garber, R.B. Influence of cognitive and affective factors in learning and retaining attitudinal materials. Journal of Abnormal and Social Psychology, 1955, 51, 387-389.

Gassner, B. Imitation in Abhängigkeit von der Verstärkungsart des Models und der Sozialschicht des Beobachters. Unpublished diploma thesis, University of Mannheim, 1973.

Gatting-Stiller, I., Stiller, K. & Voss, B. Die Änderung der Kausalattribuierung und des Ausdauerverhaltens in Leistungssituationen bei Mißerfolgsmotivierten durch Modellernen. Unpublished diploma thesis, Technical University of Braunschweig, 1978a.

Gatting-Stiller, I., Stiller, K., Voss, B. & Wender I. Änderung der Kausalattribuierung und des Ausdauerverhaltens bei mißerfolgsmotivierten Kindern durch Modellernen. Unpublished manuscript, Technical University of Braunschweig, 1978b.

Gatting-Stiller, J., Gerling, M., Stiller, K., Voss, B. & Wender, I. Änderung der Kausalattribuierung und des Ausdauerverhaltens bei mißerfolgsmotivierten Kindern durch Modellernen. Zeitschrift für Entwicklungspsychologie, 1979, 11, 1001-1013.

Geiselberger, S. Schwarzbuch: Ausländische Arbeiter. Hrsg. i.A. des Bundesvorstandes der Jungsozialisten, Frankfurt am Main, 1972.

Geisser, H.O. Marktforschung in der schweizerischen Produktionsgüterindustrie. Freiburg/Schweiz, 1961.

Gelatt, H.B. Decision making: A conceptual frame of reference for counseling. Journal of Counseling Psychology, 1962, 9, 240-245.

Gelatt, H.B. & Clarke, R.B. Role of subjective probabilities in the decision process. Journal of Counseling Psychology, 1967, 14, 332-341.

Gelatt, H.B. & Varenhorst, B.A. A decision making approach to guidance. The Bulletin of the National Association of Secondary School Principals, 1968, 52, 88-109.

Geller, E.S. & Pitz, G.F. Confidence and decision speed in the revision of opinion. Organizational Behavior and Human Performance, 1968, 3, 190-201.

Gerard, H.B. Compliance, expectation of reward, and opinion change. Journal of Personality and Social Psychology, 1967, 6, 360-364.

Gergen, K.J., Ellsworth, Ph., Maslach, C. & Seipel, M. Obligation, donor resources and reactions to aid in three cultures. Journal of Personality and Social Psychology, 1975, 31, 390-400.

Gettys, C.F. & Willke, T.A. The application of Bayes' theorem when the true data state is uncertain. Organizational Behavior and Human Performance, 1969, 4, 125-141.

Gewirtz, J.L. The roles of overt responding and extrinsic reinforcement in "self-" and "vicarious"-reinforcement phenomena and in "observational learning" and imitation. In R. Glaser (Ed.), The nature of reinforcement. New York: Academic Press, 1971, 279-309.

Gewirtz, J.L. & Baer, D.M. The effect of brief social deprivation on behaviors for a social reinforcer. Journal of Abnormal and Social Psychology, 1958a, 56, 49-56.

Gewirtz, J.L. & Baer, D.M. Deprivation and satiation of social reinforcers as drive conditions. Journal of Abnormal and Social Psychology, 1958b, 57, 165-172.

Glass, D.C. & Singer, J.E. Urban stress. Experiments on noise and social stressors. New York: Academic Press, 1972.

Götz, J. Studien- und Berufswahl. Eine empirische Untersuchung an saarländischen Oberschülern. Vervielfältigte Arbeitsberichte, Saarbrücken, Arbeitsgruppe für empirische Sozialforschung, 1973.

Götz, J. & Zimmer, H. Das gestufte Informations- und Entscheidungsprogramm. Arbeitsgruppe für empirische Studienforschung der Universität des Saarlandes, Saarbrücker Studien zur Hochschulentwicklung, 1977, Bd. 29.

Goldberger, A. & Duncan, O.D. (Eds.), Structural equation models in the social sciences. New York, 1973.

Gollin, E.S. Forming impressions of personality. Journal of Personality, 1954, 23, 65-76.

Goodman, L.A. & Kruskal, W.H. Measures of Association for Cross-Classifications. Journal of American Statistical Association, 1954, 49, 732-764.

Gorry, G.A., Kassierer, J.P., Essig, A. & Schwartz, W.J. Decision analysis as the basis for computer-aided management of acute renal failure. American Journal of Medicine, 1973, 55, 473-484.

Graumann, C.F. Interaktion und Kommunikation. In C.F. Graumann (Ed.), Handbuch der Psychologie, Band 7, Sozialpsychologie. Göttingen: Hogrefe, 1972.

Greeno, J.G. The structure of memory and the process of solving problems. In R.L. Solso (Ed.), Contemporary issues in cognitive psychology: The Loyola symposium. Washington, D.C.: Winston, 1973.

Greenwald, A.G. & Sakamura, J.S. Attitude and selective learning: Where are the phenomena of yesterday? Journal of Personality and Social Psychology, 1967, 7, 387-397.

Greif, S. Gruppenintelligenztests. Bern: Lang, 1972.

Groffmann, K.-J. Persönlichkeitsformende Lernvorgänge. In K.-J. Groffmann & K.H. Wewetzer (Eds.), Person als Prozeß. Bern: Huber, 1968, 83-113.

Groffmann, K.-J. & Schmidtke, A. Persönlichkeitspsychologische Grundlagen. In L.J. Pongratz & K.H. Wewetzer (Eds.), Handbuch der Psychologie in 12 Bänden (Bd. 8, 1. Halbband). Göttingen: Hogrefe, 1977, 664-714.

Groffmann, K.-J., Zschintzsch, A., Köster, W. & Messer, J. Bericht über das Mannheimer Prüfungsangstprojekt. In L.H. Eckensberger (Ed.), Bericht über den 31. Kongreß der Deutschen Gesellschaft für Psychologie in Mannheim, 1978 (Bd. 2). Göttingen: Hogrefe, 1979, 362-370.

Grusec, J.E. Power and the internalization of self-denial. Child Development, 1971, 42, 93-105.

Grusec, J.E. & Skubiski, S.L. Model nurturance, demand characteristics of the modeling experiment, and altruism. Journal of Personality and Social Psychology, 1970, 14, 352-358.

Guernsey, M. Eine genetische Studie über Nachahmung. Zeitschrift für Psychologie, 1928, 107, 105-178.

Guilford, J.P. Psychometric Methods. New York: McGraw-Hill, 1954.

Guilford, J.P. Three faces of intellect. American Psychologist, 1959a, 14, 969-979.

Guilford, J.P. Traits of creativity. In H.H. Anderson (Ed.), Creativity and its cultivation. New York: Harper, 1959b, 142-161.

Guilford, J.P. The nature of human intelligence. New York: McGraw Hill, 1967.

Guilford, J.P. & Hoepfner, R. The analysis of intelligence. New York: McGraw Hill, 1971.

Guth, E. Die Probleme der Erfolgskontrolle der Werbung für Konsumgüter in absatzpolitischer Sicht. ZfbF, 1968, 20.

Guth, E. Betriebswirtschaftliche Absatz- und Marktforschung. Wiesbaden: Gabler, 1970.

Guydosh, R.M. Overcompliance as a response model to psychological reactance. Dissertation Abstracts International, 1974, 34 (10-A), 6745.

Haas, R.W. Industrial marketing management. New York, 1976.

Haeberle, J. Beiträge zur Bilanzierung von Pensionskassenverpflichtungen. 1970.

Haire, M. & Grunes, W.F. Perceptual defense: Processes protecting an organized perception of another personality. Human Relations, 1950, 3, 403-412.

Hakansson, H. & Östberg, C. Industrial Marketing: An organizational problem? Industrial Marketing Management, 1975, 4, 113 ff.

Hakansson, H. & Wootz, B. Supplier selection in an international environment. Journal of Marketing Research, 1975, 46 ff.

Halmos, P. Lectures on Boolean algebras. New York: Van Nostrand, 1963.

Hamilton, D.L. Responses to cognitive inconsistencies: Personality, discrepancy level, and response stability. Journal of Personality and Social Psychology, 1969, 11, 351-362.

Hamilton, D.L. & Katz, L.B. A process-oriented approach to the study of impressions. Paper presented at APA Convention, Chicago, 1975.

Hamilton, J.A. & Bergland, B.W. Interactive relationship among students characteristics and group counseling methods. Psychology in the Schools, 1971, 50-55.

Hamilton, J.A. & Jones, G.B. Individualizing educational and vocational guidance designing a prototype program. Vocational Guidance Quarterly, 1971, 19, 293-299.

Hamilton, M.L. Vicarious reinforcement effects on extinction. Journal of Experimental Child Psychology, 1970, 9, 108-114.

Hamner, C.W. & Harnett, D.L. The effects of information and aspiration level on bargaining behavior. Journal of Experimental and Social Psychology, 1975, 11, 329-342.

Hannah, T.E., Hannah, R. & Wattie, B. Arousal of psychological reactance as a consequence of predicting and individual's behavior. Psychological Reports, 1975, 37, 411-420.

Harford, T. & Solomon, L. "Reformed sinner and "lapsed saint" strategies in the prisoner's dilemma game. Journal of Conflict Resolution, 1967, 11, 104-109.

Hargreaves, D.J. & Bolton, N. Selecting creativity test for use in research. British Journal of Psychology, 1972, 63, 451-462.

Harris, M.B. & Meyer, F.W. Dependency, threat and helping. Journal of Social Psychology, 1973, 90, 239-242.

Harris, R.J. Handling negative inputs: On the plausible equity formulae. Journal of Experimental So al Psychology, 1976, 194-209.

Harrison, A.A. & McClintock, C.G. Precious experience within the dyad and cooperative game behavior. Journal of Personality and Social Psychology, 1965, 1, 671-675.

Hartkopf, M. Berufswahlvorbereitung als gemeinsame Aufgabe von Schule and Berufsberatung. Arbeit und Beruf, 1975, II, 361-363.

Hartup, W.W. & Coates, B. The role of imitation in childhood socialization. In R.A. Hoppe, G.A. Milton & E.L. Simmel (Eds.), Social Psychology. New York: Academic Press, 1970, 109-142.

Hartup, W.W. & Lougee, M.D. Peers as models. School Psychology Digest, 1975, 4, 11-21.

Harvey, J.H., Ickes, W.J. & Kidd, R.F. (Eds.), New directions in attribution research, Vol. I, New York: Wiley, 1976.

Harvey, O.J. et al. Conceptual systems and personality organization. New Yor-, 1961.

Harvey, O.J., Hoffmeister, J., Coates, C.& White, J.B. A partual evaluation of Torrance's tests of creativity. American Educational Research Journal, 1970, 7, 359-372.

Hastorf, A.H., Schneider, D.J. & Polefka, J. Person perception. Reading, Mass., 1970.

Hays, W.L. Statistics for Psychologists. London: Holt, 1963.

Heckhausen, H. Hoffnung und Furcht in der Leistungsmotivation. Meisenheim am Glan: Hain, 1963.

Heckhausen, H. Attribuierungswandel bei erwartungswidrigem Verlauf. Unpublished manuscript, Wassenaar, 1972.

Heckhausen, H. Motivation: Kognitionspsychologische Aufspaltung eines summarischen Konstrukts. Psychologische Rundschau, 1977, 28, 175-189.

Heckhausen, H. Achievement motivation and its constructs: A cognitive model. Motivation and Emotion, 1977, 1, 283-329.

Heider, F. Social perception and phenomenal causality. Psychological Review, 1944, 51, 358-374.

Heider, F. The psychology of interpersonal relations. New York: Wiley, 1958.

Heilmann, M.E. Oppositional behavior as a function of influence attempt intensity and retaliation threat. Journal of Personality and Social Psychology, 1976, 33, 5, 574-578.

Heilmann, M.E. & Toffler, B.L. Reacting to reactance: An interpersonal interpretation of the need of freedom. Journal of Experimental Social Psychology, 1976, 12, 519-529.

Heinen, J., Welbers, G. & Windszus, B. Lehrlingsausbildung. Erwartung und Wirklichkeit. Eine empirische Studie zur Situation der beruflichen Bildung in Schule und Betrieb. Mainz: v. Hase & Koehler, 1972.

Heller, J.F., Pallak, M. & Picek, J.M. The interactive effects of intent and threat on boomerang attitude change. Journal of Personality and Social Psychology, 1973, 26, 273-279.

Helmchen, H., Künkel, H., Oberhofer, A. & Penin, H. EEG-Befund Dokumentation mit optischem Markierungsleser. Nervenarzt, 1968, 39, 408-413.

Helmke, A. & Wender, I. Zum Einfluß habitueller Leistungsangst und unterschiedlicher Instruktionen auf Imitationsverhalten und auf die Leistung. Unveröffentlichtes Manuskript, Technische Universität Braunschweig, 1979.

Herbig, M. Verfahren zur experimentellen Validierung lehrzielorientierter Tests. Unveröffentlichtes Manuskript, Braunschweig, 1975.

Herzberg, F.H. Work and the nature of man. Cleveland, 1966.

Heskett, J.L., Stern, L.W. & Beiler, F.J. Bases and uses of power in interorganization relations. In L.P. Bucklin, (Ed.), Vertical marketing systems. Glenview, Ill., 1970, 75 ff.

Hicks, D.J. Imitation and retention of film-mediated aggressive peer and adult models. Journal of Personality and Social Psychology, 1965, 2, 97-106.

Higgins, E.T. & Rholes, W.S. Impression formation and role fulfillment: A "holistic reference" approach. Journal of Experimental Psychology, 1976, 12, 422-435.

Higgins, E.T., Rholes, W.S. & Jones, C.R. Category accessibility and impression formation. Journal of Experimental Social Psychology, 1977, 13, 141-154.

Hildenbrand, W. Random preferences and equilibrum analysis. Journal of Economic Theory, 1971, 3, 414-429.

Hilgard, E.R. & Bower, G.H. Theorien des Lernens, Vol. 1. Stuttgart, 1975[4].

Hill, R.W. Marketing technological products to industry. Oxford/New York, 1973.

Hille, B. Berufs- und Lebenspläne sechzehnjähriger Schülerinnen. Eine empirische Studie in Realschulen, Gymnasien und Hauptschulen. Dissertation, Technische Universität Braunschweig, 1973.

Hilton, T.L. Career decision making. Journal of Counseling Psychology, 1962, 19, 291-298.

Hirschman, A.O. Abwanderung und Widerspruch. Tübingen, 1974.

Hoehnke, H.J. Existence of nontrivial stochastic monoids. Semigroup Forum, 1974, 9, 102-108.

Hoffmann, M.L. Personality and social development. Annual Review of Psychology, 1977, 28, 295-321.

Hoffmann, J. Neue Produkte. Marketing Journal, 1970, 3, 146-149.

Hofstätter, P.R. Einführung in die Sozialpsychologie. Stuttgart, 1963[3].

Hogarth, R.M. Cognitive processes and the assessment of subjective probability distributions. Journal of the American Statistical Association, 1975, 70, 271-289.

Holland, J.L. The self-directed search: A guide to educational and vocational planning. Palo Alto: Consulting Psychologists Press, 1970.

Holmes, J.G. Agents of conflict: Defensive and adaptive reactions of representatives in intergroup conflict. Unpublished manuscript, University of Waterloo, 1976.

Holmes, J.G. & Lamm, H. Boundary roles and the maintenance of conflict. In W. Austin & S. Worchel (Eds.), The social psychology of intergroup relations. Belmont, Calif.: Brooks/Cole, 1979.

Holzkamp, K. Das Problem der "Akzentuierung" in der sozialen Wahrnehmung. Zeitschrift für experimentelle und angewandte Psychologie, 1965, 12, 86-97.

Holzkamp, K. Soziale Kognition. In C.F. Graumann (Ed.), Handbuch der Psychologie, Bd. 7, 2. Halbband. Göttingen: Hogrefe, 1972, 1263-1341.

Holzkamp, K. & Keiler, P. Seriale und dimensionale Bedingungen des Lernens der Größenakzentuierung: Eine experimentelle Studie zur sozialen Wahrnehmung. Zeitschrift für experimentelle und angewandte Psychologie, 1967, 14, 407-441.

Holzkamp, K. & Perlwitz, E. Absolute oder relative Größenakzentuierung? Eine experimentelle Studie zur sozialen Wahrnehmung. Zeitschrift für experimentelle und angewandte Psychologie, 1966, 13, 390-405.

Holzkamp, K., Keiler, P. & Perlwitz, E. Die Umkehrung der Akzentuierungsrichtung unter serialen Lernbedingungen: Theoretische und experimentelle Beiträge zum Problem der sozialen Wahrnehmung. Psychologische Forschung, 1968, 32, 64-88.

Homans, G.C. Human behavior as exchange. American Journal of Sociology, 1958, 63, 597-606.

Homans, G.C. Social behavior. New York, 1961.

Homans, G.C. Elementarformen menschlichen Verhaltens. Köln-Opladen, 1968.

Horai, J. & Tedeschi, J.T. Compliance and the use of threats and promises after power reversal. Behavioral Science, 1975, 20, 177-224.

Horn, J.L. On subjectivity in factor analysis. Educational and Psychological Measurement, 1967, 27, 811-820.

Horn, J.L. The structure of intellect: Primary abilities. In R.M. Preyer (Ed.), Multivariate personality research: Contributions to the understanding of personality in honor of Raymond B. Cottrell. Baton Rouge: University Press, 1972.

Horn, J.L. & Knapp, J.R. Thirty wrongs do not make a right. Psychological Bulletin, 1974, 81, 502-504.

Horowitz, H. The relationship of confidence to competence and initation behavior. The Journal of Psychology, 1966, 63, 235-247.

Hosford, R.E. Behavioral counseling - A temporary overview. The Counseling Psychologist, 1969, 1, 1-33.

Hovland, C.J. & Sherif, M. Judgmental phenomena and scales of attitude measurement: Item displacement in Thurstone scales. Journal of Abnormal and Social Psychology, 1952, 47, 822-832.

Howard, J.A. & Sheth, J.N. The theory of buyer behavior. New York, 1969.

Huang, L.C. The expected risk function. Michigan Mathematical Psychology Program, 71-6 Ann Arbor, University of Michigan, 1971a.

Huang, L.C. Experiments on the measurement of risk. Michigan Mathematical Psychology Program 71-7, Ann Arbor, University of Michigan, 1971b.

Huber, G.P., Daneshgar, R. & Ford, D.L. An empirical comparison of five utility models for predicting job preferences. Organizational Behavior and Human Performance, 1971, 6, 267-282.

Hubert, L.J. & Levin, J.R. A general statistical framework for assessing categorial clustering in free recall. Psychological Bulletin, 1976, 83, 1072-1080.

Hubert, L.J. & Levin, J.R. Inference models for categorial clustering. Psychological Bulletin, 1977, 84, 878-887.

Hull, C.L. Principles of behavior. New York: Appleton, 1943.

Ihde, G.B. Größenersparnisse der Distribution. Wiesbaden, 1976.

Infratest. Ausbildungs- und Berufswahl bei Hauptschülern in der Bundesrepublik und in West-Berlin. Ergebnisse einer schriftlichen Befragung von Adressaten der Broschüre "Verschenke doch keine Chance". München: Infratest, 1973.

Inglehart, R. The silent revolution: Changing values and political styles among western publics. Princeton, 1977.

Irle, M. Entstehung und Änderung von sozialen Einstellungen (Attitüden). In F. Merz (Ed.), Bericht über den 25. Kongreß der DGfP. Göttingen: Hogrefe, 1967, 194-221.

Irle, M. Macht und Entscheidungen in Organisationen. Frankfurt/M.: Akademische Verlagsgesellschaft, 1971.

Irle, M. Lehrbuch der Sozialpsychologie. Göttingen: Hogrefe, 1975.

Irle, M. Is aircraft noise harming people? In M. Deutsch & H.A. Hornstein (Eds.), Applying social psychology. Hillsdale, N.J.: Erlbaum, 1975.

Irle, M. The state of psychology in the Federal Republic of Germany. The German Journal of Psychology, 1977, 1, 3-12.

Irle, M. (Ed.), Kursus der Sozialpsychologie, Teil I. Angewandte sozialpsychologische Forschung und ethische Probleme der Anwendung. Darmstadt, Neuwied: Luchterhand, 1978.

Irwin, F.W. & Smith, W.A.S. Wert, Kosten und Information als Determinanten der Entscheidung. In H. Thomae (Ed.), Die Motivation menschlichen Handelns. Köln, Berlin, 1975[6], 398-404.

Jacob, W. Industriebetriebslehre in programmierter Form. Wiesbaden, 1972.

Jacoby, J., Chestnut, R.W., Weigl, K. & Fisher, W. Pre-purchase information acquisition: Description of a process methodology, research paradigma, and pilot investigation. Purdue Paper in Consumer Psychology, No. 151, Purdue University, West-Lafayette, Indiana, 1975.

Jacoby, J. & Kaplan, L.B. The components of perceived risk. Purdue Paper in Consumer Psychology, No. 118, West-Lafayette, Indiana, 1972.

Jacoby, J., Kohn, C.A. & Speller, D.E. Time spent acquiring product information as a function of information load and organization. Proceedings of the American Psychological Association's 81st Annual Convention, 1973, 813-814.

Jacoby, J., Speller, D.E. & Kohn, C.A. Brand choice behavior as a function of information load. Journal of Marketing Research, 1974, 11, 63-69.

Jacoby, J., Szybillo, G.H. & Busato-Schlach, J. Information acquisition behavior in brand choice situations. Journal of Consumer Research, 1977, 3, 200-206.

Jacoby, J., Szybillo, G.H. & Kaplan, L.B. The varieties of perceived risk: A cross-validation. Purdue Paper in Consumer Psychology No. 129, West-Lafayette, Indiana, 1973.

Jaeger, A. Jugendliche in der Berufsentscheidung. Eine Analyse der Verhaltensweisen von Jugendlichen bei der Berufswahl nach Abschluß der Hauptschule. Weinheim: Beltz, 1973.

Jaeger, A.O. Dimensionen der Intelligenz. Göttingen: Hogrefe, 1967.

Jaide, W. Die Berufswahl. Eine Untersuchung über die Voraussetzungen und Motive der Berufswahl bei Jugendlichen von heute. München: Juventa, 1961.

Janis, I.L. Pilot studies on a balance-sheet procedure and other interventions for improving personal decision making. Unpublished manuscript, 1969. (Reprinted in I.L. Janis & L. Mann (Eds.), Decision making. London: Collier MacMillan, 1977).

Janis, I.L. Victims of groupthink. Boston: Houghton Mifflin, 1972.

Janis, I.L. & Mann, L. (Eds.), Decision making. London: Collier MacMillan, 1977.

Jellison, J.M. & Ickes, W.J. The power of glance: Desire to see and be seen in cooperative and competitive situations. Journal of Experimental Social Psychology, 1974, 10, 444-450.

Jepsen, D.A. & Lilley, J.S. Vocational decision making models: A review and comparative analysis. Review of Educational Research, 1974, 44, 331-349.

Joereskog, K.G. Statistical estimation in factor analysis. Stockholm, 1963.

Johnson, H.H. Some effects of discrepancy level on responses to negative information about one's self. Sociometry, 1966, 29, 52-66.

Johnson, R.H. & Euler, D.E. Effect of the life career game on learning and retention of educational-occupational information. The School Counselor, 1972, 19, 155-159.

Johnson, T.J., Feigenbaum, R. & Weibey, M. Some determinants and consequences of the teacher's perception of causation. Journal of Educational Psychology, 1964, 55, 237-246.

Jones, E.E. & Aneshansel, J. The learning and utilization of contravaluant material. Journal of Abnormal and Social Psychology, 1956, 53, 27-33.

Jones, E.E. & Davis, K.E. From acts to dispositions - the attribution process in person perception. In L. Berkowitz (Ed.), Advances in experimental social psychology (Vol. 2). New York: Academic Press, 1965.

Jones, E.E. & Gerard, H.B. Foundations of social psychology. New York: Wiley, 1967.

Jones, E.E., Kanouse, D.E., Kelley, H.H., Nisbett, R.E., Valins, S. & Weiner, B. Attribution: Perceiving the causes of behavior. Morristown, New Jersey: General Learning Press, 1972.

Jones, E.E. & Kohler, R. The effects of plausibility on the learning of controversial statements. Journal of Abnormal and Social Psychology, 1958, 57, 315-320.

Jones, G.B. & Krumboltz, J.D. Simulating vocational exploration through film-mediated problems. Journal of Counseling Psychology, 1970, 17, 107-114.

Jones, R.A. Volunteering to help: The effects of choice, dependence, and anticipated dependence. Journal of Personality and Social Psychology, 1970, 14, 121-129.

Jones, R.A. Choice, degree of dependence, and possibility of future dependence as determinants of helping behavior. Proceedings of the 77th Annual Convention of the APA, 1969, 4, 381-382.

Jones, R.A. Self-fulfilling prophecies. Hillsdale, N.J.: Erlbaum, 1977.

Jones, R.A. & Brehm, J.W. Persuasiveness of one- and two-sides communications as a function of awareness there are two sides. Journal of Experimental Social Psychology, 1970, 6, 47-56.

Judson, A.I. & Cofer, C.N. Reasoning as an associative process: I. "Direction" in a simple verbal problem. Psychological Reports, 1956, 2, 469-476.

Kahn, A. & Tice, T.E. Returning a favor and retaliating harm: The effects of stated intentions and actual behavior. Journal of Experimental Social Psychology, 1973, 9, 43-56.

Kaldor, D.R. & Zylowski, D.G.A. A maximizing model of occupational decision making. Personnel and Guidance Journal, 1969, 47, 781-788.

Kanein, W. Das Ausländergesetz und die westlichen fremdrechtlichen Vorschriften. München-Berlin, 1966.

Kanouse, D.E. & Hanson, L.R. Jr. Negativity in evaluations. In E.E. Jones et al. (Eds.), Attributions: Perceiving the causes of behavior. Morristown: General Learning Press, 1972.

Kanungo, R.N. & Das, J.P. Differential learning and forgetting as a function of the social frame of reference. Journal of Abnormal and Social Psychology, 1960, 61, 82-86.

Kanungo, R.N. & Dutta, S. Retention of affective material: Frame of reference or intensity? Journal of Personality and Social Psychology, 1966, 4, 27-35.

Kaplan, L.B., Szybillo, G.J. & Jacoby, J. Components of perceived risk in product purchase: A cross-validation. Journal of Applied Psychology, 59, 1974, 287-291.

Kaplan, M.F. Context effects in impression formation: The weighted average versus the meaning change formulation. Journal of Personality and Social Psychology, 1971, 19, 92-99.

Kappeler, M. Isolierung und Kriminalisierung oder Unterstützung positiver Erfahrungsmöglichkeiten. In H.J. Petzold (Ed.), Jugend ohne Berufsperspektiven. Weinheim: Beltz, 1976.

Kassner, E. Die Werbung für Maschinen. Aus der Praxis erfolgreicher Absatzvorbereitung. München: Hauser, 1959.

Kastenbaum, A. An experimental study of the formation of impressions of personality. Unpublished master's thesis, New School for Social Research, 1951. (Cited in: Stotland, E. & Canon, L.K. Social psychology. A cognitive approach. Philadelphia: Saunders, 1972.)

Kastenbaum, R. The dimensions of future time perspective: An experimental analysis. Journal of General Psychology, 1961, 65, 203-218.

Katona, G. & Mueller, E. A study of purchase decisions. In L.H. Clark (Ed.), Consumer behavior, Vol. I: The dynamics of consumer reactions. New York, 1955.

Katz, M.M., Cole, J.O. & Lowery, H.A. Studies of the diagnostic process: The influence of symptom perception, past experience, and ethnic background on diagnostic decisions. American Journal of Psychiatry, 1969, 125, 937-947.

Katz, M.R. A model of guidance for career decision making. Vocational Guidance Quarterly, 1966, 12, 2-10.

Kawlath, A. Theoretische Grundlagen der Qualitätspolitik. Wiesbaden, 1969.

Keeney, R.L. & Raiffa, H. Decisions with multiple objectives: Preferences and value trade offs. New York: Wiley, 1976.

Kelley, H.H. The warm - cold variable in first impressions of persons. Journal of Personality, 1950, 18, 431-439.

Kelley, H.H. Attribution theory in social psychology. In Nebraska Symposium on Motivation. Lincoln: University of Nebraska Press, 192-238, 1967.

Kelley, H.H. Attribution in social interaction. In E.E. Jones, D.E. Kanouse, H.H. Kelley, R.E. Nisbett, S. Valins & B. Weiner (Eds.), Attribution: Perceiving the causes of behavior. Morristown, N.J.: General Learning Press, 1971.

Kelley, H.H. Causal schemata and the attribution process. New York: General Learning Press, 1972.

Kelley, H.H., Beckmann, L.L. & Fischer, C.S. Negotiating the division of a reward under incomplete information. Journal of Experimental Social Psychology, 1967, 3, 361-398.

Kelley, H.H., Deutsch, M., Lanzetta, J.T. Nuttin, J.M., Jr., Shure, G.H., Faucheux, C., Moscovici, S. Rabbiet, J.M. & Thibaut, J.W. A comparative experimental study of negotiation behavior. Journal of Social Psychology, 1970, 16, 411-438.

Kelley, H.H. & Stahelski, A.J. Errors in perception of intentions in a mixed-motive game. Journal of Experimental Social Psychology, 1970, 6, 379-400.

Kelley, H.H. & Thibaut, J.W. Group problem solving. In G. Lindzey & E. Aronson (Eds.), Handbook of social psychology, Vol. 4, Cambridge, Mass.: Addison-Wesley, 1969[2].

Kelley, H.H. & Thibaut, J.W. Interpersonal relations. New York: Wiley, 1978.

Kelley, H.H., Thibaut, J.W., Radloff, R. & Mundy, D. The development of cooperation in the "minimal social situation". Psychological Monographs, 1962, 76, No. 19 (whole No. 538).

Kelly, G.A. The psychology of personal constructs. New York: Norton, 1955.

Kendler, H.H. & D'Amato, M.F.A. A comparison of reversal and nonreversal shifts in human concept formation behavior. Journal of Experimental Psychology, 1955, 49, 165-174.

Kendler, H.H. & Kendler, T.S. Vertical and horizontal processes in problem solving. Psychological Review, 1962, 69, 1-16.

Kendler, H.H. & Kendler, T.S. From discrimination learning to cognitive development: A neobehavioristic odyssey. In W.K. Estes (Ed.), Handbook of learning and cognitive processes, Vol. 1. Hillsdale, N.J.: Erlbaum, 1975.

Kiesler, C.A. & Corbin, L.H. Commitment, attraction and conformity. Journal of Personality and Social Psychology, 1965, 2, 890-895.

Kiesler, C.A. & Munson, P.A. Attitudes and Opinions. Annual Review of Psychology, 1975, 26, 415-456.

Kiesler, C.A. & Pallak, M.S. Arousal properties of dissonance manipulations. Psychological Bulletin, 1976, 83, 6, 1014-1025.

Kießler-Hauschildt, K. & Scholl, W. Partizipation und Macht in aufgabenorientierten Gruppen. Frankfurt am Main, 1976.

Killias, L. Marktforschung in der Werkzeugmaschinenindustrie. ifb-Schrift, Heft 14. Bern, 1961.

Kirsch, W. Entscheidungsprozesse, Vol. 1: Verhaltenswissenschaftliche Ansätze der Entscheidungstheorie. Wiesbaden: Gabler, 1970.

Kirsch, W., Börsig, C., Englert, G. & Gabele, E. Der Einsatz von standardisierten Anwendungsprogrammen in der industriellen Praxis - Verwenderbericht. München, 1975.

Kirsch, W., Englert, G., Börsig, C. & Gabele, E. Marketing von Standard-Anwendersoftware - Herstellerbericht. München, 1975.

Kirsch, W., Huppertsberg, B. & Kutschker, M. Beschaffungsentscheidungen auf Investitionsgütermärkten. Kriterien der Auswahlentscheidung beim Kauf von Investitionsgütern. München, 1977.

Kirsch, W., Kutschker, M. & Lutschewitz, H. Ansätze und Entwicklungstendenzen im Investitionsgütermarketing. Stuttgart, 1980.

Klein, G.S., Schlesinger, H. & Meister, D.E. The effect of personal values on perception: An experimental critique. Psychological Review, 1951, 58, 96-112.

Klemm, H.W. Die Grundlagen des deutschen Investitionsgüter-Exportes und die Möglichkeiten zur Mitarbeit von deutschen-beratenden Ingenieurfirmen. In K. Mellerowics & O. (Eds.), 7. Bd. "Betriebswirtschaftliche Forschungen". Berlin, 1957.

Klineberg, S.L. Changes in outlook on the future between childhood and adolescence. Journal of Personality and Social Psychology, 1967, 7, 185-193.

Knüvener, H.B. Die Problematik der Absatzmarktforschung für Produktivgüter. Dissertation, Münster, 1967.

Köditz, V. Berufswahlverhalten und berufliche Motivation Jugendlicher in den Ländern der Europäischen Gemeinschaft. Veröffentlichung der Arbeitsgruppe für empirische Bildungsforschung e.V., Heidelberg, 1978.

Kogan, N., Lamm, H. & Trommsdorff, G. Negotiation constraints in the risk-taking domain: Effects of being observed by partners of higher or lower status. Journal of Personality and Social Psychology, 1972, 23, 143-156.

Kogan, N. & Wallach, M.A. Risk-taking: A study in cognition and personality. New York: Holt, Rinehart & Winston, 1964.

Kogan, N. & Wallach, M.A. Modification of a judgmental style through group interaction. Journal of Personality and Social Psychology, 1966, 4, 165-174.

Kogan, N. & Wallach, M.A. Risk-taking as a function of the situation, the person and the group. In G. Maudler, P. Mussen, N. Kogan & M.A. Wallach (Eds.), New directions in psychology III, New York: Holt, Rinehart & Winston, 1967.

Kohlberg, L. Early education: A cognitive-developmental view. Child Development, 1968, 39, 1013-1062.

Kohlberg, L. Stage and sequence: The cognitive-developmental approach to socialization - theory and research. In D.A. Goslin (Ed.), Handbook of socialization - theory and research. Chicago: Rand McNally, 1969, 347-480.

Kolmogorov, A.N. Foundations of the theory of probability. New York: Chelsea Publications Co., 1956.

Komorita, S.S. & Brenner, A.R. Bargaining and concession making under bilateral monopoly. Journal of Personality and Social Psychology, 1968, 9, 15-20.

Komorita, S.S. & Esser, J.K. Frequency of reciprocated concessions of bargaining. Journal of Personality and Social Psychology, 1975, 32, 699-705.

Koopman, B.O. The axioms and algebra of intuitive probability. Annals of Mathematics, 1940, 41, 269-292.

Koopman, B.O. The bases of probability. Bulletin of the American Mathematical Society, 1940, 46, 763-774.

Kornberg, A., Linder, D. & Cooper, J. Understanding political behavior: The relevance of reactance theory. Midwest Journal of Political Science, 1970, 14, 131-138.

Koschoske, M. Unterschichten und Beratung. Wege zum Menschen, 1973, 25, 129-163.

Koschoske, M. Zur Praxis der Unterschichtberatung. Wege zum Menschen, 1975, 27, 315-331.

Kotler, P. & Cox, K.K. (Eds.), Readings in marketing management. Englewood Cliffs, 1972.

Kozielecki, J. Investigation of the strategy of thinking in different probabilistic situations. Psychologia Wychowawcza (Educational Psychology), 1961, 4, 458-459.

Kozielecki, J. Mechanism Samopotwierdzania Hipotezy W Sytuacji Probabilistycznej. Unpublished doctoral dissertation, University of Warsaw, 1964.

Kozielecki, J. The mechanism of self-confirmation of hypothesis in a probabilistic situation. In Symposium 25: Heuristic processes in thinking. International Congress of Psychology, Moscow, 1966, 86-95.

Kozielecki, J. Psychologia procesów przeddecyzyzjnych. (The psychology of predecisional processes). Warsaw: PWN Polish Scientific Publishers, 1969.

Kozielecki, J. Diagnosis and decision. Polish Psychological Bulletin, 1971, 2, 91-98.

Kozielecki, J. A model for diagnostic problem solving. Acta Psychologica, 1972, 36, 370-380.

Krantz, D.H., David, H., Luce, R.D., Duncan R., Suppes, P. & Tversky, A. Foundations of measurement, Vol. I: Additive and Polynomial Representations. New York: Academic Press, 1971.

Kraus, R.M. & Deutsch, M. Communication in interpersonal bargaining. Journal of Personality and Social Psychology, 1966, 4, 572-577.

Krechevsky, D. "Hypothesis" versus "chance" in the pre-solution period in sensory discrimination learning. University of California Publications in Psychology: University of California at Berkeley, 1932, 6, 27-44.

Kreutz, H. Soziologie der empirischen Sozialforschung. Stuttgart, 1972.

Krivatsy, W.E. & Magoon, T.M. Differential effects of three vocational counseling treatments. Journal of Counseling Psychology, 1976, 23, 112-118.

Kroeber-Riehl, W. Konsumentenverhalten. München: Vahlen, 1975.

Kroeber-Riehl, W. Werbung als beeinflussende Kommunikation. In W. Kroeber-Riehl (Ed.), Konsumentenverhalten und Marketing. Opladen: Westdeutscher Verlag, 1973.

Kruglanski, A.W., Schwartz, J.M. Maides, S. & Hamel, I.Z. Covariation, discounting, and augmentation: Towards a clarification of attributional principles. Journal of Personality, 1978, 46, 176-189.

Krumboltz, J.D. Job experience kits. Personnel and Guidance Journal, 1970, 2, 233.

Krumboltz, J.D. & Baker, R.D. Behavior counseling for vocational decisions. In H. Borow (Ed.), Career guidance for a new age. Boston: Houghton-Mifflin, 1973, 235 ff.

Krumboltz, J.D. & Schroeder, W.W. Promoting career planning through reinforcement. Personnel and Guidance Journal, 1965, 44, 19-26.

Krumboltz, J.D. & Sheppard, L.E. Vocational problem-solving experiences. In J.D. Krumboltz & C.E. Thoresen (Eds.), Behavioral counseling: Cases and techniques. New York: Holt, Rinehart & Winston, 1969, 293-306.

Krumboltz, J.D. & Thoresen, C.E. The effect of behavior counseling in group and individual settings on uniformation-seeking behavior. Journal of Counseling Psychology, 1964, 11, 324-333.

Kruse, L. Gruppen und Gruppenzugehörigkeit. In C.F. Graumann (Ed.), Handbuch der Psychologie, Bd. 7 Sozialpsychologie, 2. Halbband. Göttingen: Hogrefe, 1972, 1539-1593.

Kruskal, J.B. Multidimensional scaling by optimizing goodness of fit to a nonmetric hypothesis. Psychometrika, 1964, 29, 1-27.

Kruskal, J.B. Multidimensional scaling: A numerical method. Psychometrika, 1964, 29, 115-119.

Kuhl, J. & Blankenship, V. The dynamic theory of achievement motivation: From episodic to dynamic thinking. Psychological Review, 1979, 86, 141-151.

Kuhlmann, E. Das Informationsverhalten des Konsumenten. Freiburg, 1970.

Kuhn, D. Imitative theory and research from a cognitive perspective. Human Development, 1973, 16, 157-180.

Kupsch, P., Hufschmied, P., Mathes, D. & Schöler, K. Die Struktur von Qualitätsurteilen und das Informationsverhalten von Konsumenten beim Kauf langlebiger Gebrauchsgüter. Opladen, 1978.

Kutschker, M. Ansätze und Entwicklungstendenzen im Investitionsgütermarketing. Stuttgart: Poeschel, 1980.

Kutschker, M. & Kirsch, W. Das Marketing von Investitionsgütern: Theoretische und empirische Perspektiven eines Interaktionsansatzes. Wiesbaden: Gabler, 1978.

Laatz, W. Berufswahl und Berufszufriedenheit der Lehrlinge. München: Verlag Deutsches Jugendinstitut, 1974.

Labbie, S. Primacy-recency effects in impression formation and congruity-incongruity of stimulus material. Perceptual and Motor Skills, 1973, 37, 275-278.

Landau, S.F. Future time perspective of delinquents and non-delinquents: The effect of institutionalization. Criminal Justice and Behavior, 1975, 2, 22-36.

Lane, I.M. & Coon, R.C. Reward allocation in preschool children. Child Development, 1972, 43, 1382-1389.

Lange, E. Berufswahl als Entscheidungsprozeß. In E. Lange & M. Büschges (Eds.), Aspekte der Berufswahl in der modernen Gesellschaft. Frankfurt: Aspekte, 1975a.

Lange, E. Du glaubst zu schieben und Du wirst geschoben . In E. Lange & G. Büschges (Eds.), Aspekte der Berufswahl in der modernen Gesellschaft, Frankfurt: Aspekte, 1975b.

Lange E. Berufswahl als Interaktionsprozeß - Theoretische Überlegungen für ein empirisches Projekt. Kölner Zeitschrift für Soziologie und Sozialpsychologie, 1976, 28, 479-505.

Lange, L. Unkontrollierte sozialpsychologische Faktoren in der Versuchssituation als Beeinträchtigungsmöglichkeiten für die Validität psychologischer Experimente. Probleme und Ergebnisse der Psychologie, 1972, 42, 5-23.

Langenheder, W. Determinanten der Berufswahl - Versuche einer integrierenden Theorie. Habilitationsschrift, Universität Erlangen-Nürnberg, 1975.

Langer, J., Kuhn, D. & Turiel, E. Cognitive variables in imitation experiments. Unpublished manuscript, University of California, 1972.

Lanzetta, J.T. Response uncertainty, importance and information search in decision making - Symposium "Decision making", XIX Internationaler Kongreß für Psychologie, London, 1969.

Laucken, U. Naive Verhaltenstheorie. Stuttgart: Klett, 1974.

Lautmann, R. Justiz. Die stille Gewalt. Frankfurt: Athenäum, 1972.

Lawler, E.E. Motivation in Work Organizations. Belmont, 1973.

Lawler, E.E., Kuleck, W.J. Jr. & Rhode, J.G. Job choice and post-decision dissonance. Organizational Behavior and Human Performance, 1975, 13, 133-145.

Lee, W. Decision theory and human behavior. New York: Wiley, 1971.

Lehmann, M.A. & Cardozo, R.N. Product or Industrial Advertisements? Journal of Advertising Research, April 1973.

Lehr, U. Das Problem der Sozialisation geschlechtsspezifischer Verhaltensweisen. In C.F. Graumann (Ed.), Handbuch der Psychologie, Vol. 7,2, Sozialpsychologie. Göttingen: Hogrefe, 1972.

Lepsius, R.M. Soziale Ungleichheit und Klassenstrukturen in der Bundesrepublik Deutschland. Lebenslagen, Interessenvermittlung und Wertorientierungen. In H.-U. Wehler (Ed.), Klassen in der Europäischen Sozialgeschichte. Göttingen: Vandenhoeck & Ruprecht, 1979, 166-209.

Lerner, M. The justice motive: 'Equity' and 'partity' among children. Journal of Personality and Social Psychology, 1974, 29, 539-550.

Lerner, M.J. The justice motive in social behavior: Introduction. Journal of Social Issues, 1975, 31, 1-19.

Lerner, M.J. The justice motive: Some hypotheses as to its origins and forms. Journal of Personality, 1977, 45, 1-52.

Lerner, M., Miller, D.T. & Holmes, J.G. Deserving and the emergence of forms of justice. In L. Berkowitz & E. Walster (Eds.), Advances in Experimental Social Psychology, Vol. 9. New York: Academic Press, 1976, 133-162.

LeShan, L.L. Time orientation and social class. Journal of Abnormal and Social Psychology, 1952, 47, 589-592.

Lessing, E.E. Extension of personal future time perspective, age, and life satisfaction of children and adolescents. Developmental Psychology, 1972, 6, 457-468.

Leventhal, G.S. The distribution of rewards and resources in groups and organizations. In L. Berkowitz & E. Walster (Eds.), Advances in experimental social psychology (Vol. o). New York: Academic Press, 1976a.

Leventhal, G.S. Fairness in social relationships. In J. Thibaut, J.T. Spence & R.C. Carson (Eds.), Contemporary topics in social psychology. Morristown: General Learning Press, 1976b.

Leventhal, G.S. & Michaels, J.W. Locus of cause and equity motivation as determinants of reward allocation. Journal of Personality and Social Psychology, 1971, 17, 229-235.

Leventhal, G.S. & Whiteside, H.D. Equity and the use of reward to elicit high performance. Journal of Personality and Social Psychology, 1973, 25, 75-83.

Levine, J.M. & Murphy, G. The learning and forgetting of controversial material. Journal of Abnormal and Social Psychology, 1943, 38, 507-515.

Levine, M. Hypothesis behavior by humans during discrimination learning. Journal of Experimental Psychology, 1966, 71, 331-338.

Levine, J. & White, P.E. Exchange as a conceptual framework for the study of interorganizational relationships. Administrative Science Quarterly, 1961, 583 ff.

Levinger, G. & Schneider, D.J. Test of the "risk is a value" hypothesis. Journal of Personality and Social Psychology, 1969, 11, 165-170.

Levy, L.H. Group variance and group attractiveness. Journal of Abnormal and Social Psychology, 1964, 68, 661-664.

Levy, L.H. The effects of value, variance, and sample size on judgmental confidence and variance in social perception. Paper presented at MPA Meeting, Chicago, 1965.

Lewin, K. The conceptual representation and the measurement of psychological forces. Durham, N.C.: Duke University Press, 1938.

Lewin, K. Time perspective and morale. In K. Lewin (Ed.), Resolving social conflicts. New York: Harper, 1948.

Lewin, K. Feldtheorie in den Sozialwissenschaften. Ausgewählte theoretische Schriften. Bern und Stuttgart, 1963.

Lichtenstein, S., Fischhoff, B. & Baruch & Phillips, L.D. Calibration of probabilities: The state of the art. In H. Jungermann & G. de Zeeuw (Eds.), Utility, probability, and human decision making. Dordrecht: Reidel, 1977.

Liebert, R.M. & Fernandez, L.E. Effects of vicarious consequences on imitative performance. Child Development, 1970, 41, 847-852.

Lindblad, S. Simulation and guidance: Teaching career decision making skills in the Swedish compulsory school. Simulation and Games, 1973, 4, 429-439.

Linder, D.E. & Crane, K.A. Reactance theory analysis of predecisional cognitive processes. Journal of Personality and Social Psychology, 1970, 15, 258-264.

Linder, D.E., Wortman, C.B. & Brehm, J.W. Temporal changes in predecision preferences among choice alternatives. Journal of Personality and Social Psychology, 1971, 19, 282-284.

Linder, P. Die Auslandswerbung für Investitionsgüter auf der Grundlage systematischer Marktuntersuchung. Vertriebswirtschaftliche Abhandlungen. Berlin: Duncker & Humblot, 1966, Heft 10.

Lindzey, G. & Rogolsky, S. Prejudice and identification of minority group membership. Journal of Abnormal and Social Psychology, 1950, 45, 37-53.

Lingle, J.H., Geva, N. & Ostrom, T.M. Cognitive processes in person perception. Paper presented at APA Convention, Chicago, 1975.

Lingle, J.H. & Ostrom, T.M. Principles of memory and cognition in attitude formation. In R.E. Petty, T.M. Ostrom & T.C. Brock (Eds.), Cognitive responses in persuasive communications. A text in attitude change. New York: McGraw Hill, in press.

Lingoes, J.C. & Roskam, E.E. A mathematical and empirical study of two multidimensional scaling algorithms. Psychometrika, 1973, Monogr. 19, 38, 4. Pt.2.

Litwak, E. & Hylton, L.F. Interorganizational analysis: A hypothesis on coordinating agencies. Administrative Science Quarterly, 1962, 395 ff.

Lorenz, C. Forschungslehre der Statistik, Bd. 3: Angewandte Sozialstatistik. Berlin: Duncker & Humblot, 1964.

Lowin, A. Further evidence for an approach-avoidance interpretation of selective exposure. Journal of Experimental Social Psychology, 1969, 5, 265-271.

Luce, R.D. & Raiffa, H. Games and decisions. New York: Wiley, 1957.

Luce, R.D. & Suppes, P. Preference, utility, and subjective probability. In R.D. Luce, R.R. Bush & E. Galanter (Eds.), Handbook of mathematical psychology, Vol. 3. New York: Wiley, 1965.

Lueck, H.E. Soziale Aktivierung. Köln: Kiepenheuer & Witsch, 1969.

Lutschewitz, H. & Kutschker, M. Ansätze und Entwicklungstendenzen im Investitionsgütermarketing. München, 1977.

MacGrimmon, K.R. & Messick, D.M. A framework for social motives. Behavioral Science, 1976, 21, 86-100.

MacNeill, L.W. Cognitive complexity: A brief synthesis of theoretical approaches and a concept attainment task analogue to cognitive structure. Psychological Reports, 1974, 34, 3-11.

Madaras, G.R. & Bem, D.J. Risk and conservation in group decision making. Journal of Experimental Social Psychology, 1968, 4, 350-365.

Maddox, R.N. Measuring consumer satisfaction. Dissertation, Ohio State University, 1976.

Magoon, T.M. Developing skills for educational and vocational problems. In J.D. Krumboltz & C.E. Thoresen (Eds.), Behavioral Counseling: Cases and techniques. New York: Holt, Rinehart & Winston, 1969, 393-396.

Mahrer, A.R. The role of expectancy in delayed reinforcement. Journal of Experimental Psychology, 1956, 52, 101-105.

Mai, N. Bestimmung subjektiver Wahrscheinlichkeiten. Training von Wahrscheinlichkeitsschätzern in der medizinischen Diagnostik. Unveröffentlichte Dissertation, Universität Hamburg, 1975.

Mai, N. & Hachmann, E. Anwendung des Bayes-Theorems in der medizinischen Diagnostik - Eine Literaturübersicht. Metamed, 1977, 1, 161-205.

Mai, N., Hachmann, E., Henrich, G., von Cramon, D. & Brinkmann R. Indikationsstellung für die zerebrale Angiographie. Entwicklung eines Bayes-Programms zur Entscheidungshilfe. Methods of Information in Medizine, 1977, 16, 45-51.

Mai, N., Henrich, G. & von Cramon, D. Application of a Bayes Program for classification of Coma. Methods of Information in Medizine, 1978, 17, 41-46.

Malpass, R.S. Effects of attitude on learning and memory: The influence of instruction induced set. Journal of Experimental Sqcial Psychology, 1969, 5, 441-453.

Maltzman, I. Thinking: From a behavioristic point of view. Psychological Review, 1955, 62, 275-286.

Manderscheid, R.W. A theory of spatial effects. In R. Trappl & F.R. Pichler (Eds.), Progress in cybernetics and systems research: Volume I. Washington, D.C.: Hemisphere, 1975.

Manes, E.G. Algebraic theories. New York, Heidelberg: Springer, 1976.

Manis, M., Gleason, T.C. & Dawes, R.M. The evaluation of complex social stimuli, Journal of Personality and Social Psychology, 1966, 3, 404-419.

Mann, L. Use of a "balance-sheet" procedure to improve the quality of personal decision making: A field experiment with college applicants. Journal of Vocational Behavior, 1972, 2, 291-300.

Manstetten, R. Das Berufsberatungsgespräch. Trier: Spee-Verlag, 1975.

March, J.G. & Olson, J.P. Ambiguity and choice in organisations. Bergen/Norway: Universitetsforlaget, 1976.

Markefka, M. Vorurteile, Minderheiten, Diskriminierung. Neuwied-Berlin, 1974.

Markowitz, H. Portfolio selection. Journal of Finance, 1952, 7, 77-91.

Markowitz, H. Portfolio selection: Efficient diversification of investments. New York: Wiley, 1959.

Markus, H. Self-schemata and processing information about the self. Journal of Personality and Social Psychology, 1977, 35, 63-78.

Marschak, J. et al. Personal probabilities of probabilities. Theory and Decision, 6, 2, 1975, 121-123.

Martialla, J.A. Word-of-month communication in the industrial adoption process. Journal of Marketing Research, 1971, 8, 173 ff.

Maslow, A.H. Motivation and personality. New York, 1954.

Mayer, R.E. Different problem-solving competencies established in learning computer programming with and without meaningful models. Journal of Educational Psychology, 1975, 67, 725-734.

Mayer, R.E. Thinking and problem solving: An introduction to human cognition and learning. Glenview, Ill.: Scott, Foresman and Comp., 1977.

Mazis, M.B. Antipollution measures and psychological reactance theory: A field experiment. Journal of Personality and Social Psychology, 1975, 31, 654-660.

Mazis, M.B., Settle, R.B. & Leslie, D.C. Elimination of phosphate detergents and psychological reactance. Journal of Marketing Research, 1973, 10, 390-395.

McClelland, D.C. The achieving society. Princeton, 1961.

McClelland, G. & Coombs, C. Ordmet: A general algorithms for constructing all numerical solutions to ordered metric structures. Michigan Mathematical Psychology Program, MMPP, 1974-10.

McClintock, C.G. Social motivation - A set of propositions. Behavioral Science, 1972, 17, 438-454.

McClintock, C.G. & Avermael, E.V. The effects of manipulating feedback upon children's motives and performance: A propositive statement and empirical evaluation. Behavioral Science, 1975, 20, 101-116.

McClintock, C.G., Messick, D.M., Kuhlmann, D.M. & Compos, F.T. Motivational bases of choice in three-choice decomposed games. Journal of Experimental Social Psychology, 1973, 9, 572-590.

McCurdy, F.G. Coin perception studies and the concept of schemata. Psychological Review, 1956, 63, 160-168.

McGillis, D.B. & Brehm, J.W. Compliance as a function of inducements that threaten freedom and freedom restoration - A field experiment. Unpublished manuscript, Duke University, 1973.

McGrath, J.E. A social psychological approach to the study of negotiation. In R.V. Bowers (Ed.), Studies on behavior in organizations: A research symposium. Athens, Ga.: University of Georgia Press, 1966.

McGuire, W.J. A syllogistic analysis of cognitive relationships. In M.J. Rosenberg, C.I. Hovland, W.J. McGuire, R.P. Abelson & J.W. Brehm (Eds.), Attitude organization and change. New Haven: Yale University Press, 1960.

McGuire, W.J. Résumé and responses from the consistency theory viewpoint. In R.P. Abelson et al. (Eds.), Theories of cognitive consistency: A sourcebook, Chicago: Rand McNally, 1968, 275-297.

McMains, M.J. & Liebert, R.M. Influence of discrepancies between successively modeled self-reward criteria on the adoption of a self-imposed standard. Journal of Personality and Social Psychology, 1968, 8, 166-171.

Meffert, H. Produktivgüter - Marktforschung im System des Marketing. Der Marktforscher, 1974, 1, 6ff.

Mehrländer, U. Soziale Aspekte der Ausländerbeschäftigung. Bonn-Bad Godesberg, 1974.

Meichenbaum, D.H. Examination of model characteristics in reducing avoidance behavior. Journal of Personality and Social Psychology, 1971, 17, 298-307.

Mertens, W. Sozialpsychologie des Experiments. Das Experiment als soziale Interaktion. Hamburg: Hoffmann & Campe, 1975.

Merton, R.K. Social theory and social structure. New York: The Free Press, 1957.

Messé, L.A. Equity in bilateral bargaining. Journal of Personality and Social Psychology, 1971, 17, 287-291.

Messick, D.M. & McClintock, C.G. Motivational bases of choice in experimental games. Journal of Experimental Social Psychology, 1968, 4, 1-25.

Meyer, J.B., Strowing, W. & Hosford, R.E. Behavioral reinforcement counseling with rural high school youth. Journal of Counseling Psychology, 1970, 17, 127-132.

Mikes, P.S. & Hulin, C.L. Use of importance as a weighting component of job satisfaction. Journal of Applied Psychology, 1968, 52, 394-398.

Mikula, G. Die Entwicklung des Gewinnaufteilungsverhaltens bei Kindern und Jugendlichen. Eine Untersuchung an 5-, 7-, 9- und 11jährigen. Zeitschrift für Entwicklungspsychologie und pädagogische Psychologie, 1972, 4, 151-164.

Mikula, G. Considerations of justice in allocation decisions. Berichte aus dem Institut für Psychologie der Universität Graz, 1977.

Mikula, G. On the role of justice in allocation decisions. In G. Mikula (Ed.), Justice and interaction. New York: Huber, 1980.

Mikula, G. & Uray, H. Die Vernachlässigung individueller Leistungen bei der Lohnaufteilung in Sozialsituationen. Zeitschrift für Sozialpsychologie, 1973, 4, 136-144.

Miller, D.T. & Ross, M. Self-serving bias in the attribution of causality: Fact or fiction? Psychological Bulletin, 1975, 82, 213-225.

Miller, G.A. The magical number seven, plus or minus two: Some limits on our capacity for processing information. Psychological Review, 1956, 63, 81-87.

Miller, J.R. Professional decision-making. A procedure for evaluating complex alternatives. New York: Praeger Publishers, 1970, Parts I, III (1-112; 302-353).

Miller, L.W., Kaplan, R.J. & Edwards, W. Judge: A value-judgment-based tactical command system. Organizational Behavior and Human Performance, 1967, 2, 329-374.

Miller, N. As time goes by. In R.P. Abelson et al. (Eds.), Theories of cognitive consistency: A sourcebook. Chicago: Rand McNally, 1968.

Miller, N.E. & Dollard, J. Social learning and imitation. New Haven: Yale University Press, 1941.

Mischel, T. Human action. New York: Academic Press, 1969.

Mischel, W. Theory and research on the antecedents of self-imposed delay of reward. In B.A. Maher (Ed.), Progress in experimental personality research, Vol. 3. New York: Academic Press, 1966.

Mischel, W. Toward a cognitive social learning reconceptualisation of personality. Psychological Review, 1973, 80, 252-283.

Mischel, W. Processes in delay of gratification. In L. Berkowitz (Ed.), Advances in Experimental Social Psychology, Vol. 7. New York: Academic Press, 1974.

Mischel, W. & Grusec, J. Waiting for rewards and punishments: Effects of time and probability on choice. Journal of Personality and Social Psychology, 1967, 5, 24-31.

Mischel, W., Zeiss, R. & Zeiss, A.R. Internal/external control and persistence. Validation and implications of the Stanford I. E. Scales (SCIES). Journal of Personality and Social Psychology, 1974, 29, 265-278.

Mitchell, T.R. & Beach, L.R. Expectancy theory, decision theory and occupational preference and choice. Technical Report, University of Washington, Seattle, Department of Psychology, Ni-25, 1975.

Moll, K. Erwartungsprofile des österreichischen Konsumenten in bezug auf den Lebensmitteleinzelhandel. Dissertation, Vienna, 1978.

Montada, L. & Setter to Bulte, U. Strafwirkung als Funktion der Strafbewertung. Zeitschrift für Entwicklungspsychologie und Pädagogische Psychologie, 1974, 6, 75-89.

Moore, F.C.T. The psychology of Maine deBiran. Oxford: Clarendon Press, 1970.

Morgan, W.R. & Sawyer, J. Bargaining, expectations, and the preference for equality over equity. Journal of Personality and Social Psychology, 1967, 6, 139-149.

Morley, I.E. & Stephenson, G.M. Interpersonal and interparty exchange: A laboratory simulation of an industrial negotiation at the plant level. British Journal of Psychology, 1969, 60, 543-545.

Morley, I.E. & Stephenson, G.M. The social psychology of bargaining. London: Aldey, 1977.

Moscovici, S. Social influence and social change. London/New York: Academic Press, 1976.

Moscovici, S., Doise, W. & Dulong, R. Studies in group decision II: Differences of positions, differences of opinion and group polarization. European Journal of Social Psychology, 1972, 2, 385-399.

Moscovici, S. & Lecuyer, R. Studies in group decision I: Social space, patterns of communication and group consensus. European Journal of Social Psychology, 1972, 2, 221-244.

Moscovici, S. & Zavalloni, M. The group as a polarizer of attitudes. Journal of Personality and Social Psychology, 1969, 12, 125-135.

Murphy, A.H. & Winkler, R.L. Scoring rules in probability assessment and evaluation. Acta Psychologica, 1970, 34, 273-286.

Myers, D.G. Summary and bibliography of experiments on group-induced response shift. Catalog of Selected Documents in Psychology, 1973, 3, 123.

Myers, D.G. & Kaplan, M.F. Group-induced polarization in simulated juries. Personality and Social Psychology Bulletin, 1976, 2, 63-66.

Myers, R.A. Research on educational and vocational counseling. In A.E. Bergin & S.L. Grasfield (Eds.), Handbook of psychotherapy and behavior change. New York: Wiley, 1971.

Naatz, T. & Dieckhoff, U. Zur empirischen Bewährung der kognitiven Akzentuierungstheorie: Eine experimentelle Entscheidung zwischen der allgemein qualitativen Konzeption Ertels und dem Berliner habituell kognitiven Ansatz. Zeitschrift für Sozialpsychologie, 1975, 6, 150-159.

Naatz, T. & Hümmelink, W. Zur Realisation einer kognitiven Akzentuierungstheorie: Eine experimentelle Entscheidung zwischen dem serialen Ansatz (Tajfel) und dem modifizierten absoluten Ansatz (Holzkamp) bei serialer Stimuluskonstellation. Zeitschrift für Sozialpsychologie, 1971, 2, 361-373.

Nardin, T. Communication and the effect of threats in stratetic interaction. Papers of the International Peace Research Society, 1968, 9, 69-86.

Nelson, D.E. & Krumboltz, J.D. Encouraging career exploration through 'simulated work' and 'vocational detective' experiences. Journal of Employment Counseling, 1970, 7, 58-65.

Nemeth, C. A critical analysis of research utilizing the prisoner's dilemma paradigm for the study of bargaining. In L. Berkowitz (Ed.), Advances in experimental social psychology (Vol. 6). New York: Academic Press, 1972.

Neubeck-Fischer, H. Gastarbeiter - eine neue gesellschaftliche Minderheit. Dissertation, München, 1972.

Neuberger, O. Theorien der Arbeitszufriedenheit. Stuttgart, 1974a.

Neuberger, O. Messung der Arbeitszufriedenheit. Stuttgart, 1974b.

Newman, J.W. & Staelin, R. Prepurchase information seeking for new cars and major household appliances. Journal of Marketing Research, 1972, 9, 249-257.

Nuttin, J.R. The future time perspective in human motivation and learning. Proceedings of the 17th International Congress of Psychology. Amsterdam: North-Holland Publ. Co., 1964.

Nuttin, J.M. The illusion of attitude change: Towards a response contagion theory of persuasion. New York: Academic Press, 1975.

Nuttin, J.R. & Grommen, R. Zukunftsperspektive bei Erwachsenen und älteren Menschen aus drei sozioökonomischen Gruppen. In U. Lehr & F.E. Weinert (Eds.), Entwicklung und Persönlichkeit. Stuttgart: Kohlhammer, 1975.

Opp, K.D. & Schmidt, P. Einführung in die Mehrvariablenanalyse. Reinbek, 1976.

Organ, D.W. Social exchange and psychological reactance in a simulated superior-subordin te relationship. Organizational Behavior and Human Performance, 1974, 12, 132-142.

Osgood, C.E. An alternative of war or surrender. Urbana, Ill.: University of Illinois Press, 1962.

Osgood, C.E. & Tannenbaum, P.H. The principle of congruity in the prediction of attitude change. Psychological Review, 1955, 62, 42-55.

Pallak, M.S. & Heller, J.F. Interactive effects of commitment to future interaction and threat to attitudinal freedom. Journal of Personality and Social Psychology, 1971, 17, 325-331.

Pallak, M.S., Sogin, S.R. & van Zante, A. Bad decisions: Effect of volition, locus of causality, and negative consequences on attitude change. Journal of Personality and Social Psychology, 1974, 30, 217-227.

Panne, F. Das Risiko im Kaufentscheidungsprozeß des Konsumenten. Die Beiträge risikotheoretischer Ansätze zur Erklärung des Kaufentscheidungsverhaltens des Konsumenten. Frankfurt am Main, 1977.

Parsons, T. Equality and inequality in modern society, or social stratification revisited. In E.O. Laumann (Ed.), Social stratification: Research and theory for the 1970s. New York: Bob Merrill, 1970.

Parton, D.A. Imitation as a subset of no-practical learning and the role of intrinsic reinforcement. Paper presented at the biennial meeting of the Society of Research in Child Development, Minneapolis, 1971.

Parton, D.A. & Geshuri, Y. Learning of aggression as a function of presence of a human model - intensity and target of the response. Journal of Experimental Child Psychology, 1971, 11, 491-504.

Parton, D.A. & Siebold, J.R. Nurturance and imitation: The mediating role of abstraction. Developmental Psychology, 1975, 11, 859-860.

Partsch, D. Daseinsgrundfunktionen. Handwörterbuch der Raumforschung und Raumordnung. Hannover, 1970.

Pawlik, K. Dimensionen des Verhaltens. Bern: Huber, 1968.

Pearlin, L.I. & Kohn, M.L. Social class, occupation and parental values: A cross-national study. American Sociological Review, 1966, 31, 466-479.

Pepitone, A. & Hayden, R.G. Some evidence for conflict resolution in impression formation. Journal of Abnormal and Social Psychology, 1955, 51, 302-307.

Peres, K.-H. Marktforschung für Spezialmaschinen. Dissertation, Universität Mannheim, 1952.

Peters, A. Die Bundesrepublik Deutschland als Beschäftigungsland für ausländische Arbeitnehmer. In K. Bolte (Ed.), Mitteilungen aus der Arbeitsmarkt und Berufsforschung. Stuttgart, 1972, 5.

Peterson, C.R. & DuCharme, W.M. A primacy effect in subjective probability revision. Journal of Experimental Psychology, 1967, 73, 61-65.

Peterson, C.R., Schneider, R.J. & Miller, A.J. Sample size and the revision of subjective probabilities. Journal of Experimental Psychology, 1965, 69, 522-527.

Petzold, H.-J. (Ed.), Jugend ohne Berufsperspektive. Weinheim: Beltz, 1976.

Pfaff, M. Who decides what is good for whom? Zeitschrift für Verbraucherpolitik, 1977, 1, 138-142.

Pfanzagl, J. Über die stochastische Fundierung des psychophysischen Gesetzes. Biometrische Zeitschrift, 1962, 4, 1-14.

Pfanzagl, J. Theory of measurement. Würzburg-Wien: Physica
Verlag, 1968, 1971^2.

Pfeiffer, W. Absatzpolitik bei Investitionsgütern der Einzel-
fertigung. Stuttgart, 1965.

Philipps, A. A theory of interfirm organization. Quarterly Journal of Economics, 1960, 602 ff.

Piaget, J. Play, dreams and imitation in childhood. Melbourne:
Heinemann, 1951.

Piaget, J. Das moralische Urteil beim Kinde. Zürich: Rascher,
1954.

Pitz, G.F. An inertia effect (resistance to change) in the revision of opinion. Canadian Journal of Psychology, 1969, 23,
24-33.

Pitz, G.F., Downing, L. & Reinhold, H. Sequential effects in
the revision of subjective probabilities. Canadian Journal
of Psychology, 1967, 21, 381-393.

Plass, H., Michael, J.H. & Michael, W.B. The factorial validity
of the Torrance tests of creative thinking for a sample of
111 sixth-grade children. Educational and Psychological Mea-
ment, 1974, 34, 413-414.

Platt, J.E. & Eisenman, R. Internal/external control of reinforcement, time perspective, adjustment, and anxiety. Journal of General Psychology, 1968, 79, 121-128.

Podell, H.A. & Podell, J.E. Quantitative connotation of a concept. Journal of Abnormal and Social Psychology, 1963, 67,
509-513.

Polanyi, M. Personal knowledge. Chicago: University of Chicago
Press, 1958.

Popitz, H., Bahrdt, H.P., Jüres, E.A. & Kesting, H. Das Ge-
sellschaftsbild des Arbeiters. Tübingen: Mohr, 1967^3.

Popper, K.R. Logik der Forschung. Wien: J. Springer, 1935.

Porter, L.W. & Lawler, E.E. Managerial attitudes and performance. Homewood, 1968.

Postman, L. Perception and learning. In S. Koch (Ed.), Psychology - A study of science, Vol. 5. New York: McGraw Hill,
1963.

Preis, H. Merkmale des Modellverhaltens als motivationale Bedingungen der Imitationsbereitschaft. Dissertation, Universität Mannheim, 1978.

Prinz, H. Einkaufsgewohnheiten und Verbrauchereinstellungen.
BAG-Nachrichten, 1977, 8, 11-15.

Pross, H. Über die Bildungschancen von Mädchen in der BRD.
Frankfurt: Suhrkamp, 1969.

Pross, H. Gleichberechtigung im Beruf. Frankfurt: Fischer Athenäum, 1973.

Pruitt, D.G. Informational requirements in making decisions. American Journal of Psychology, 1961, 74, 433-439.

Pruitt, D.G. Choice shifts in group discussion: An introductory review. Journal of Personality and Social Psychology, 1971, 20, 339-360 (a).

Pruitt, D.G. Conclusions: Toward an understanding of choice shifts in group discussion. Journal of Personality and Social Psychology, 1971, 20, 495-510 (b).

Pruitt, D. Methods for resolving differences of interest: A theoretical analysis. Journal of Social Issues, 1972, 28, 133-154.

Pruitt, D.G. & Lewis, S.A. Development of integrative solutions in bilateral negotiations. Journal of Personality and Social Psychology, 1975, 31, 621-633.

Quatrono, L.A. & Bergland, B.W. Group experiences in building planning strategies. Elementary School Guidance and Counseling, 1974, 8, 173-181.

Quickstep. Informationsschrift für Hauptschulabgänger. Nürnberg: Bundesanstalt für Arbeit, 1974.

Raaig, W.F. van. Techniques for process tracing in decision making. Tilburg Papers on consumer evaluation processes, No. 16. Paper presented at the 6th Research Conference on Subjective Probability, Utility and Decision Making. Warsaw, Poland, 1977.

Raffée, H. Konsumenteninformation und Beschaffungsentscheidung des privaten Haushalts. Stuttgart, 1969.

Raiffa, H. Arbitration schemes for generalized two-person games. In H.W. Kuhn & A.W. Tucker (Eds.), Contributions to the theory of games, II. Annals of mathematics studies, 28. Princeton: Princeton University Press, 1953.

Raiffa, H. Preferences for multi-attributed alternatives. Memorandum RM-5868-DOT/RC, Santa Monica: The Rand Corporation, 1969.

Raiffa, H. & Schlaifer, R. Applied statistical decision theory. Boston: Division of research, Harvard Business School, 1961.

Rapoport, A. & Wallsten, T.S. Individual decision behavior. Annual Review of Psychology, 1972, 23, 131-176.

Raven, B.H. & Kruglanski, A.W. Conflict and power. In P. Swingle (Ed.), The structure of conflict. New York: Academic Press, 1970.

Raynor, J.O. Future orientation in the study of achievement motivation. In J.W. Atkinson & J.O. Raynor (Eds.), Motivation and achievement. New York: Wiley, 1974.

Regan, D.T. Effects of a favor and liking on compliance. Journal of Experimental Social Psychology, 1971, 7, 627-639.

Regan, D.T., Straus, E. & Fazio, R. Liking and the attribution process. Journal of Experimental Social Psychology, 1974, 10, 385-397.

Rice, M.E. The development of responsiveness to vicarious reinforcement. Developmental Psychology, 1976, 12, 540-545.

Ries, H. Berufswahl in der modernen Industriegesellschaft. Beitrag zu einer Theorie der Berufswahl mit einer empirischen Untersuchung bei 320 Berufswahlschülern. Bern: Huber, 1970.

Roberts, A.H. & Greene, J.E. A cross-cultural study of relationships among four dimensions of time perspective. Perceptual and Motor Skills, 1971, 33, 163-173.

Robinson, P.J., Faris, C.W. & Wind, Y. Industrial buying and creative marketing. Boston, 1967.

Rodrigues, A. Motivational forces of cognitive dissonance and psychological reactance. International Journal of Psychology, 1970, 5, 89-98.

Roos, P. & Albers, R. Performance of alcoholics and normals on a measure of temporal orientation. Journal of Clinical Psychology, 1965, 21, 34-36.

Roselius, T.L. An exploratory investigation of buyer attitude toward eleven methods of relieving. Buyer's perception of five kinds of buying risk. Dissertation, University of Colorado, 1969.

Rosenbaum, M.E. & Tucker, I.F. Competence of the model and the learning of initation and non-initation. Journal of Experimental Psychology, 1962, 63, 183-190.

Rosenberg, M.J. Cognitive structure and attitudinal affect. Journal of Abnormal Social Psychology, 1956, 53, 367-372.

Rosenberg, M.J. When dissonance fails: On eliminating evaluation apprehension from attitude measurement. Journal of Personality and Social Psychology, 1965, 1, 28-42.

Rosenstiel, L. von. Messung der Arbeitszufriedenheit. In H.-C. Pfohl & B. Rürup (Eds.), Wirtschaftliche Meßprobleme. Köln, 1977, 109-127.

Rosenthal, A.M. Thirty-eight witnesses. New York: McGraw Hill, 1964.

Rosenthal, R. & Rosnow, R.L. The volunteer subject. New York: Wiley, 1975.

Rosenthal, T.L. & Zimmermann, B.J. Social learning and cognition. New York: Academic Press, 1978.

Roskam, E.E. & Lingoes, J.C. MINISSA. MDS (X) Programs. Cardiff, 1970.

Ross, L. The intuitive psychologist and his shortcomings: Distortions in the attribution process. In L. Berkowitz (Ed.), Advances in experimental social psychology. New York: Academic Press, 1977.

Ross, L., Lepper, M. & Hubbard, M. Perseverance in self perception and social perception: Biased attributional processes in the debriefing paradigm. Journal of Personality and Social Psychology, 1975, 32, 880-892.

Ross, L., Lepper, M.R., Strack, F. & Steinmetz, J. Social explanation and social expectation: Effects of real and hypothetical explanations on subjective likelihood. Journal of Personality and Social Psychology, 1977, 35, 817-829.

Rotter, J.B. Generalized expectancies for internal control of reinforcement. Psychological Monographs, 1966, 80, whole no. 609.

Rotter, R.B., Chance, J.E. & Phares, J.E. Applications of a social learning theory of personality. New York: Holt, 1972.

Rubin, Z. Measurement of romantic love. Journal of Personality and Social Psychology, 1970, 16, 265-273.

Rubin, Z. & Brown, B.D. The social psychology of bargaining and negotiation. New York: Academic Press, 1975.

Ruiz, R.A., Reivich, R.S. & Krauss, H. Tests of temporal perspective: Do they measure the same construct? Psychological Reports, 1967, 21, 849-852.

Rule, S.J., Curtis, D.W. & Markley, R.P. Input and output transformations from magnitude estimation. Journal of Experimental Psychology, 1970, 86, 343-349.

Rusza, I. Random models of logical systems, Part I. Studia Scientiarum Mathematicarum Hungarica, 1971, 1, 195-208.

Rutkowski, A. Some remarks about boolean-valued models. Bulletin de l'academie polonaise des sciences, 1971, 19, 87-93.

Ryan, M.J. & Bonfield, E.H. The Fishbein extended model and consumer behavior. Journal of Consumer Research, 1975, 2, 118-136.

Ryan, T.A. Reinforcement techniques and simulation materials for counseling clients with decision making problems. Proceedings of the 77th Annual Convention of the APA, 1969, 4, 693-694.

Ryan, T.A. & Krumboltz, J.D. Effects of planned reinforcement counseling on client decision making behavior. Journal of Counseling Psychology, 1964, 11, 315-323.

Salomon, G. & Sieber-Suppes, J. Learning to generate subjective uncertainty: Effects of training verbal ability and stimulus structure. Journal of Personality and Social Psychology, 1975, 23, 163-174.

Samaan, M.K. & Parker, C.A. Effects of behavioral (reinforcement) and advice giving counseling on information-seeking behavior. Journal of Counseling Psychology, 1973, 20, 193-201.

Sampson, E.E. On justice as equality. Journal of Social Issues,
1975, 31, 45-64.

Samuel, W. Suggested amendments to "new directions in equity
research". Personality and Social Psychological Bulletin,
1976, 2, 36-39.

Sarason, I.G. Test anxiety and cognitive modeling. Journal of
Personality and Social Psychology, 1973, 28, 58-61.

Sarason, I.G., Test anxiety and the self-disclosing copying
model. Journal of Consulting and Clinical Psychology, 1975,
43, 148-153.

Saterdag, H. & Jäger, U. Modellversuch 'Orientierung in Berufs-
feldern' - Ergebnisse einer Erfolgskontrolle. Lehren und
lernen, 1977, 5, 25-28.

Savage, L.J. The foundations of statistics. New York: Dover,
1972^2.

Savitz, L.D. & Tomasson, R.F. The identifiability of Jews.
American Journal of Sociology, 1959, 64, 468-475.

Sawyer, J. & Guetzkow, H. Bargaining and negotiation in international relations. In H.C. Kelman (Ed.), International behavior. New York: Holt, Rinehart and Winston, 1965.

Schank, R.C. & Abelson, R.P. Scripts, plans, goals, and understanding. Hillsdale, N.J.: Erlbaum, 1977.

Schanz, G. Grundlagen der verhaltenstheoretischen Betriebswirtschaftslehre. Tübingen, 1977.

Scheller, R. Psychologie der Berufswahl und der beruflichen Entwicklung. Stuttgart: Kohlhammer, 1976.

Schelling, T.C. The strategy of conflict. Cambridge, Mass.:
Harvard University Press, 1960.

Scheuch, F. Entscheidungen im Marketing. Fälle, Probleme, Methoden. Opladen: Westdeutscher Verlag, 1974.

Scheuch, F. Investitionsgütermarketing. Opladen: Westdeutscher
Verlag, 1975.

Schiffmann, L.G. Sources of information for the elderly.
Journal of Marketing Research, 1971, 11, 33-37.

Schlaifer, R. Computer programs for elementary decision analysis. Graduate School of Business Administration, Harvard
University, 1971.

Schmalt, H.-D. Entwicklung und Validierung einer neuen Technik
zur Messung verschiedener Aspekte des Leistungsmotivs:
Das LM-Gitter. Dissertation, Universität Bochum, 1974.

Schmidt-Hackenberg, D. Die Einflüsse des Informations- und Ver-
mittlungssystems. In K. Schweikert (Ed.), Jugendliche ohne
Berufsausbildung: Ihre Herkunft, ihre Zukunft. Schriften zur
Berufsbildungsforschung, Bd. 30. Hannover: Herrmann Schwoe-
del, 1975.

Schneider, D.J. Tactical self-presentation after success and
failure. Journal of Personality and Social Psychology, 1969,
13, 262-268.

Schneider, D.J., Hastorf, A.H. & Ellsworth, P.C. Person perception. Reading, Mass., 1979.

Schober-Gottwald, K. Der Weg in die Arbeitslosigkeit: Berufliche und soziale Herkunft von jugendlichen Arbeitslosen. Mitteilungen aus der Arbeitsmarkt- und Berufsforschung, 1977,
10, 143-165.

Schoch, R. Der Verkaufsvorgang als sozialer Interaktionsprozess.
Winterthur, 1969.

Schoop, R. (Ed.), Was soll man machen? Reinbek: Rowohlt Taschen-
buch Verlag, 1976.

Schopler, J. & Matthews, M. The influence of the perceived causal locus of partner's dependency on the use of interpersonal power. Journal of Personality and Social Psychology,
1965, 2, 609-612.

Schoppe, K.-J. Verbaler Kreativitätstest (V-K-T), Handanweisung.
Göttingen: Hogrefe, 1977.

Schroder, H.M., Driver, M. & Streufert, S. Human information
processing. New York, 1967.

Schroder, H.M. & Suedfeld, P. (Eds.), Personality theory and
information processing. New York, 1971.

Schütt, K.-P. Unterstützung der Schätzung subjektiver Wahr-
scheinlichkeiten durch formale Prozesse. Manuskripte aus dem
Institut für Betriebswirtschaftslehre der Christian-Albrechts-
Universität, Nr. 34. Kiel, 1976.

Schum, D.A. & DuCharme, W.M. Comments on the relationship between the impact and the reliability of evidence. Organizational Behavior and Human Performance, 1971, 6, 111-131.

Schwartz, S.H. Awareness of interpersonal consequences, responsibility denial, and volunteering. Journal of Personality
and Social Psychology, 1974, 30, 57-63.

Schwartz, S.H. Elicitation of moral obligation and self-sacri-
ficing behavior: An experimental study of volunteering to a
bone marrow donar. Journal of Personality and Social Psychology, 1970, 15, 283-293.

Schweiger, G., Mazanec, J. & Wiegele, O. Das Modell des "er-
lebten Risikos" ("perceived risk"): Struktur und Operationa-
lisierungskonzepte. Der Markt, 1976, 93-102.

Schweikert, K. (Ed.), Jugendliche ohne Berufsausbildung, ihre Herkunft, ihre Zukunft. Schriften zur Berufsbildungsforschung, Bd. 30. Hannover: Herrmann Schroedel, 1975.

Schwinger, T. Zur Entwicklung gruppenspezifischer Normen der Gewinnaufteilung. Unpublished doctoral dissertation, Universität Graz, 1976.

Scodel, A. & Austrin, H. The perception of Jewish photographs by non-Jews and Jews. Journal of Abnormal and Social Psychology, 1957, 54, 278-280.

Scott, D. Boolean models and nonstandard analysis. In W.A.J. Luxemburg (Ed.), Application of model theory to algebra, analysis, and probability. New York: Holt, Rinehart & Winston, 1969.

Scott, D. & Krauss, P. Assigning probabilities to logical fomulas. In J. Hintikka, & P. Suppes (Eds.), Aspects of inductive logic. Amsterdam: North-Holland, 1966.

Scott, D. & Solovay, R. Lectures on Boolean-valued models for set theory. Lecture notes prepared in connection with the Summer Institute on axiomatic set theory. Los Angeles: University of California, 1967.

Seaver, D.A. How groups can assess uncertainty: Human interactions versus mathematical models. Paper at the IEEE International Conference on Cybernetics and Society, Washington, D.C., 1977.

Seaver, D.A. Assessing uncertainty with multiple persons. Unpublished doctoral dissertation, 1978.

Seiffge-Krenke, I. Probleme und Ergebnisse der Kreativitätsforschung. Bern: Huber, 1974.

Selg, R. Das Selbsterkundungsprogramm STEP für Hauptschüler. Ergebnisse aus Feld-, Labor- und Kontrollversuch, einschließlich qualitativ-theoretischer Analyse. Unveröffentlichtes Papier. Mannheim: Transmedia, im Auftrag der Bundesanstalt für Arbeit, 1977.

Seligman, M.E.P. Helplessness: On depression, development, and death. San Francisco: Freeman, 1975.

Selz, O. Zur Psychologie des produktiven Denkens und des Irrtums. Bonn: Cohen, 1922.

Sensenig, J. & Brehm, J.W. Attitude change from an implied threat to attitudinal freedom. Journal of Personality and Social Psychology, 1968, 8, 324-330.

Sharpe, W.F. A simplified model for portfolio analysis. Management Science, 1963, 9, 277-293.

Shaver, K.G. An introduction to attribution processes. Cambridge, Mass.: Winthrop Publ., 1975.

Shaw, M.E. A comparison of individuals and small groups in the rational solution of complex problems. American Journal of Psychology, 1932, 44, 491-504.

Shepard, R.N. On subjectively optimum selection among multi-attribute alternatives. In M.W. Shelly & G.L. Bryan (Eds.), Human judgment and optimality. New York: Wiley, 1964.

Shepard R.N. & Carroll, J.D. Parametric representation of non-linear data structures. In P.R. Krishnaiah (Ed.), Multivariate analysis. New York, 1966, 561-592.

Shepard, R.N., Romney, A.K. & Nerlove, S.B. Multidimensional scaling, Vol. 1. New York, 1972.

Sherif, M. & Hovland, C.J. Social judgment - assimilation and contrast effects in communications and attitude change. New Haven, 1961.

Sherrod, D.R., Hage, J.N., Halpern, P.L. & Moore, B.S. Effects of personal causation and perceived control on responses to an aversive environment: The more control, the better. Journal of Experimental Social Psychology, 1977, 13, 14-27.

Sheth, J.N. A model of industrial buyer behavior. Journal of Marketing, 1973, 73, 50 ff.

Sieber, J.E. & Lanzetta, J.T. Conflict and conceptual structure as determinants of decision making behavior. Journal of Personality, 1964, 4, 627-641.

Siegel, S. Level of aspiration and decision making. Psychological Review, 1957, 64, 253-262.

Siegel, S. & Fouraker, L.E. Bargaining and group decision making: Experiments in bilateral monopoly. New York: McGraw-Hill, 1960.

Silberer, G. Warentest, Informationsmarketing, Verbraucherverhalten. Berlin, 1979.

Singer, J.E. Consistency as a stimulus processing mechanism. In R.P. Abelson et al. (Eds.), Theories of cognitiv consistency: A sourcebook. Chicago: Rand McNally, 1968.

Slovic, P., Fishhoff, B. & Lichtenstein, S. Behavioral decision theory. Annual Review of Psychology, 1977, 28, 1-39.

Slovic, P. & Lichtenstein, S. Comparison of Bayesian and regression approaches to the study of information processing in judgment. Organizational Behavior and Human Performance, 1971, 6, 649-744.

Smith, P.C., Kendall, L.M. & Hulin, C.L. The measurement of satisfaction in work and retirement. A strategy for the study of attitudes. Chicago, 1969.

Smith, R.D. & Evans, J.R. Comparison of experimental group guidance and individual counseling as facilitators of vocational development. Journal of Counseling Psychology, 1973, 20, 202-208.

Smith, W.P. & Anderson, A.J. Threats, communication, and bargaining. Journal of Personality and Social Psychology, 1975, 32, 76-82.

Snyder, M., Stephan, W.G. & Rosenfield, D. Egotism and attribution. Journal of Personality and Social Psychology, 1976, 33, 435-441.

Sonnek, J. Marketing-Politik in der Investitionsgüterindustrie. Dissertation, Berlin, 1962.

DeSoto, C.B. Learning a social structure. Journal of Abnormal Psychology, 1960, 60, 417-421.

DeSoto, C.B. & Kuethe, J.L. Subjective probabilities of interpersonal relationships. Journal of Abnormal Psychology, 1959, 59, 290-294.

Spence, J.T. Do material rewards enhance the performance of lower-class children? Child Development, 1971, 42, 1461-1470.

Spence, K.W. Behavior theory and conditioning. New Haven: Yale University Press, 1956.

Springer, W. Kriminalitätstheorien und ihr Realitätsgehalt. Stuttgart: Enke, 1973.

Srull, T.K. & Wyer, R.S. The role of category accessibility in the interpretation of information about persons: Some determinants and implications. Journal of Personality and Social Psychology, 1979, 37, 1660-1672.

Stael von Holstein, C.-A. An experiment in probabilistic weather forecasting. Journal of Applied Meteorology, 1971, 10, 635-645.

Stapf, K.H., Herrmann, Th., Stapf, A. & Stäcker, K.H. Psychologie des elterlichen Erziehungsstils. Bern: Huber-Klett, 1972.

Steffenhagen, H. Konflikt und Kooperation in Absatzkanälen. Wiesbaden, 1975.

Steffens, H. Berufswahl und Berufswahlvorbereitung zur Theorie und Praxis eines Aufgabenbereiches der Arbeits- und Wirtschaftslehre. Ravensburg: Otto Maier, 1975.

Stein, A.H. Imitation and resistance to temptation. Child Development, 1967, 38, 157-169.

Steiner, J.D. Group process and productivity. New York: Academic Press, 1972.

Stelltitz, G., Edrichs, H. & Cook, S.W. Ratings on favorableness of statements about a social group as an indicator of attitude towards the group. Journal of Personality and Social Psychology, 1965, 2, 408-415.

Stephan, C., Presser, N.R., Kennedy, J.C. & Aronson, E. Attributions to success and failure after cooperative or competitive interaction. European Journal of Social Psychology, 1978, 8, 269-274.

Stern, L.W. Channel-control and inter-organization management. In D.G. Bowersox et al. (Eds.), Readings in physical distribution management. The Logistics of Marketing, London, 1969a, 85 ff.

Stern, L.W. (Ed.), Distribution channels: Behavioral dimensions. Boston, 1969b.

Stern, M.E. Marketing Planung. Eine Systemanalyse. Berlin: Berlin Verlag, 1968.

Stokols, D. A social psychological model of human crowding phenomena. Journal of the American Institute of Planners, 1972, 38, 72-83.

Stoner, J.A.F. A comparison of individual and group decisions involving risk. Unpublished master's thesis. Massachussets Institute of Technology. School of Industrial Management, 1961.

Stotland, E. & Canon, L.K. Social psychology. A cognitive approach. Philadelphia: Saunders, 1972.

Streufert, S. Complexity and complex decision making: Convergences between differentiation and integration approaches to the prediction of task performance. Journal of Experimental Social Psychology, 1970, 6, 494-509.

Streufert, S. & Driver, M. Conceptual structure, information load and perceptual complexity. Psychonomic Science, 1965, 3, 249-250.

Strickland, B.R. Delay of gratification and internal locus of control in children. Journal of Consulting and Clinical Psychology, 1973, 40, 338.

Stroebe, W. & Fraser, C. Riskiness and confidence in choice dilemma decisions. European Journal of Social Psychology, 1971, 1, 519-526.

Strothmann, K.H. Produktionsgüter: Verkauf als Informationsproblem. Marketing Journal, 1968, Heft 1.

Suppes, P. Introduction to logic. Princeton: Van Nostrand, 1957.

Suppes, P. Studies in the methodology and foundations of Science. Dordrecht: Reidel, 1969.

Suppes, P. & Zinnes, J.L. Basic measurement theory. In R.D. Luce, R.R. Bush & E. Galanter (Eds.), Handbook of mathematical psychology, Vol. 1. New York: Wiley, 1963.

Sutcliffe, J.P. A general method of analysis of frequency data for multiple classification designs. Psychological Bulletin, 1957, 54, 134-137.

Taffel, C. Anxiety and the conditioning of verbal behavior. Journal of Abnormal and Social Psychology, 1955, 51, 496-501.

Taft, R. Selective recall and memory distortion of favorable and unfavorable material. Journal of Abnormal and Social Psychology, 1954, 49, 23-28.

Tajfel, H. Value and the perceptual judgment of magnitude. Psychological Review, 1957, 64, 192-204.

Tajfel, H. Quantitative judgment in social perception. British Journal of Psychology, 1959, 50, 16-29.

Tajfel, H. Stereotypes. Race, 1963, 5, 3-14.

Tajfel, H. Cognitive aspects of prejudice. Journal of Social Issues, 1969, 25, 79-97.

Tajfel, H., Sheikh, A.A. & Gardner, R.C. Content of stereotypes and the inference of similarity between members of stereotyped groups. Acta Psychologica, 1964, 22, 191-201.

Tajfel, H. & Wilkes, A.L. Classification and quantitative judgment. British Journal of Psychology, 1963, 54, 101-114.

Tausch, R. & Tausch, A.-M. Erziehungspsychologie. Göttingen: Hogrefe, 1963.

Taylor, I., Walton, P. & Young, J. The new criminology. For a social theory of deviance. London: Routledge & Kegan Paul, 1973.

Taylor, T.R. Computer guided diagnosis. Journal of the Royal College of Physics, 1970, 4, 188-195.

Teather, D., Emerson, P.A. & Hadley, A.J. Decision theory applied to the treatment of deep vein thrombosis. Methods of Information in Medicine, 1974, 13, 92-97.

Tedeschi, J.T., Schlenker, B.R. & Bonoma, T.V. Cognitive dissonance: Private ratiocination of public spectacle? American Psychologist, 1971, 26, 685-695.

Teger, A.I. The effect of early cooperation on the escalation of conflict. Journal of Experimental Psychology, 1970, 6, 187-204.

Tesmar, H. von. Zahlungsbedingungen als Mittel des Wettbewerbs im Großanlagengeschäft. Berlin: Schmidt, 1964.

Thelen, M.H. & Rennie, D.L. The effect of vicarious reinforcement on imitation: A review of the literature. In B.H. Maher (Ed.), Progress in experimental personality research, Vol. 6, New York: Academic Press, 1972, 83-108.

Thibaut, J.W. & Kelley, H.H. The social psychology of groups. New York: Wiley, 1959.

Thibaut, J.W. & Riecken, H.W. Some determinants and consequences of the perception of social causality. Journal of Personality, 1955, 24, 113-133.

Thurstone, L.L. The indifference function. Journal of Social Psychology, 1931, 2, 139-167.

Tietz, R. Der Anspruchsausgleich in experimentellen Zwei-Personen-Verhandlungen mit verbaler Kommunikation. In H. Brandstaetter & H. Schuler (Eds.), Entscheidungsprozesse in Gruppen. Beiheft 2 der Zeitschrift für Sozialpsychologie, Bern: Huber, 1976.

Toda, M. A computational procedure for obtaining additive utility functions from observed indifference curves. Hokkaido Report of Psychology, Sapporo, Japan: Hokkaido University, 1974.

Tolman, E.C. & Krechevsky, I. Means-and-readiness and hypothesis - a contribution to comparative psychology. Psychological Review, 1933, 40, 60-70.

Torrance, P.E. Torrance tests of creative thinking. Norms-technial Manual. Princeton, 1966.

Tosi, H.L. The effects of expectation levels and role consensus on the buyer-seller-dyad. The Journal of Business, 1966, 39, No. 4.

Triandis, H.C. Einstellungen und Einstellungsänderungen. Weinheim, 1975.

Tulving, E. Subjective organization in free recall. Psychological Review, 1962, 69, 344-354.

Turiel, E. An experimental test of the sequentiality of development stages in a child's moral judgements. Journal of Personality and Social Psychology, 1966, 3, 611-618.

Tversky, A. Intransitivity of preference. Psychological Review, 1969, 76, 31-48.

Tversky, A. Choice by elimination. Journal of Mathematical Psychology, 1972a, 9, 341-367.

Tversky, A. Elimination by aspects: A theory of choice. Psychological Review, 1972b, 79, 281-299.

Tversky, A. & Kahnemann, D. Judgment under uncertainty: Heuristics and biases. Science, 1974, 165, 1124-1131.

Tversky, A. & Kahneman, D. Causal schemata in judgments under uncertainty. In M. Fishbein (Ed.), Progress in social psychology. Hillsdale, N.J.: Erlbaum, 1977.

Überla, K. Faktorenanalyse. Berlin, 1971.

Ullrich, L. Verkaufsförderung für Investitionsgüter. Wiesbaden: Gabler, 1972.

Upshaw, H.S. Own attitude as an anchor in equal-appearing intervals. Journal of Abnormal and Social Psychology, 1962, 64, 85-96.

Upshaw, H.S. The personal reference scale: An approach to social judgement. In L. Berkowitz (Ed.), Advances in Experimental Social Psychology, Vol. 4, New York: Academic Press, 1969.

Upshaw, H.S. Judgement and decision processes in the formation and change of social attitudes. In M.F. Kaplan & S. Schwartz (Eds.), Human judgement and decision processes. New York: Academic Press, 1975.

Uray, H. Leistungsverursachung, Verantwortungszuschreibung und Gewinnaufteilung. Zeitschrift für Sozialpsychologie, 1976, 7, 69-80.

Valins, S. Cognitive effects of false heart-rate feedback. Journal of Personality and Social Psychology, 1966, 4, 400-408.

Valins, S. Persistent effects of information about internal reactions: Ineffectiveness of debriefing. In H. London & R. E. Nisbett (Eds.), Thought and feeling: Cognitive modification of feeling states. Chicago: Aldine, 1974.

Varenhorst, B. Innovative tool for group counseling: The life career game. School Counselor, 1968, 15, 357-362.

Varenhorst, B. Learning the consequences of life's decision. In J.D. Krumboltz & C.E. Thoresen (Eds,), Behavioral counseling: Cases and techniques. New York: Holt, 1969.

Victor, N. Probabilistische Zuordnungsverfahren. Methods of Information in Medicine, 1973, 12, 238-244.

Victor, N. Probleme der Auswahl geeigneter Zuordnungsregeln bei unvollständiger Information, insbesondere für kategoriale Daten. Biometrics, 1976, 32, 571-585.

Vidmar, N. Effects of representational roles and mediators on negotiation effectiveness. Journal of Personality and Social Psychology, 1971, 17, 48-58.

Vierter Jugendbericht der Bundesrepublik Deutschland, Bonn, 1978.

Vinacke, W.E. Variables in experimental games: Toward a field theory. Psychological Bulletin, 1969, 71, 293-318.

Vinokur, A. & Burnstein, E. Effects of partially shared persuasive arguments on group-induced shifts: A grou-problem-solving approach. Journal of Personality and Social Psychology, 1974, 29, 305-315.

Vinokur, A. & Burnstein, E. Novel argumentation and attitude change: The case of polarization following group discussion. European Journal of Social Psychology, 1978, 8, 335-348.

Vinokur, A., Trope, Y. & Burnstein, E. A decision making analysis of persuasive argumentation and the choice-shift effect. Journal of Experimental Social Psychology, 1975, 11, 127-148.

Vlek, Ch.A.J. The fair betting game as an admissible procedure for assessment of subjective probabilities. British Journal of Mathematical and Statistical Psychology, 1973, 26, 18-30.

Vroom, V.H. Work and motivation. New York, 1964.

Vroom, V.H. Organizational choice: A study of pre- and post-decision processes. Organizational Behavior and Human Performance, 1966, 11, 212-225.

Vroom, V.H. & Deci, E.L. The stability of post-decision dissonance: A follow-up study of the job attitudes of business school graduates. Organizational Behavior and Human Performance, 1971, 6, 36-49.

Waagenaar, W.A. & Padmos, P. Quantitative interpretation of stress in Kruskal's multidimensional scaling techniques. British Journal of Mathematical and Statistical Psychology, 1971, 24, 101-110.

Wachowiak, D.G. Personality correlates of vocational counseling outcome. Journal of Counseling Psychology, 1973, 20, 567-568.

Walde, H. & Berlinghoff, G. Das Auslandsgeschäft mit Industrieanlagen. Anbahnen, projektieren, finanzieren, abwickeln. München: Verlag Moderne Industrie, 1967.

Wallace, M. Future time perspective in schizophrenia. Journal of Abnormal and Social Psychology, 1956, 52, 240-245.

Wallach, M.A. & Kogan, N. Modes of thinking in young children. New York: Holt, Rinehart & Winston, 1965.

Waller, M. Soziales Lernen und Interaktionskompetenz. Stuttgart: Klett-Cotta, 1978.

Waller, M. & Preis, H. Entwicklungspsychologische Bedingungen im Motivationseinfluß auf das Imitationsverhalten. Eine Überprüfung des Kohlbergschen Erklärungsansatzes. Zeitschrift für Entwicklungspsychologie und Pädagogische Psychologie, 1975, 7, 73-87.

Waller, M. & Preis, H. Kompetenz und Interessantheit des Modellverhaltens als Anregungsbedingungen der Imitationsbereitschaft. Zeitschrift für Sozialpsychologie, 1977, 8, 256-264.

Walster, E. The temporal sequence of post decision processes. In L. Festinger (Ed.), Conflict, decision and dissonance. Stanford: Stanford University Press, 1964.

Walster, E. & Berscheid, E. The effect of time on cognitive consistency. In R.P. Abelson et al. (Eds.), Theories of cognitive consistency: A sourcebook. Chicago: Rand McNally, 1968.

Walster, E., Berscheid, E., Abrahams, D. & Aronson, V. Effectiveness of debriefing following deception experiments. Journal of Personality and Social Psychology, 1967, 6, 371-380.

Walster, E., Berscheid, E. & Walster, G.W. New directions in equity research. Journal of Personality and Social Psychology, 1973, 25, 151-176.

Walster, E., Berscheid, E. & Walster, G.W. New directions in equity research. In L. Berkowitz & E. Walster (Eds.), Advances in experimental social psychology. New York: Academic Press, 1976.

Walster, E., Utne, M.K. & Traupman, J. Equity-Theorie und intime Sozialbeziehungen. In G. Mikula & W. Stroebe (Eds.), Sympathie, Freundschaft und Ehe: Psychologische Grundlagen zwischenmenschlicher Beziehungen. Bern: Huber, 1977.

Walster, E. & Walster, G.W. Equity and social justice. Journal of Social Issues, 1975, 31, 21-43.

Walster, E., Walster, G.W. & Berscheid, E. Equity: Theory and research. Boston: Allyn & Bacon, 1978.

Walster, E., Walster, G.W., Piliavin, J. & Schmidt, L. "Playing hard to get": Understanding an elusivephenomenon. Journal of Personality and Social Psychology, 1973, 26, 113-121.

Walster, G.W. The Walster et al. (1973) equity formula: A correction. Representative Research in Social Psychology, 1975, 6, 65-67.

Walster, G.W. Reply to Dr. William Samuel: Suggested amendments to new directions in equity research. Personality and Social Psychology Bulletin, 1976, 1, 40-44.

Walster, G.W. & Walster, E. Choice between negative alternatives: Dissonance reduction or regret? Psychological Reports, 1970, 26, 995-1005.

Walter, H. & Lorenz, W. Handbuch der Auslandswerbung für Investitionsgüter und das Entwicklungsgeschäft. Berlin: Berlin-Verlag, 1970.

Waly, P. & Cook, S.W. Attitude as a determinant of learning and memory: A failure to confirm. Journal of Personality and Social Psychology, 1966, 4, 280-288.

Ward, J.H. Hierarchical grouping to optimize an objective foundation. Journal of the American Statistical Association, 1963, 58, 236.

Warren, R.L. Interorganizational field as a focus of investigation. Administrative Science Quarterly, 1967, 396 ff.

Weber, A.B. Die Theorie der kognitiven Dissonanz in ihrer Relevanz für Kaufentscheidungen von Konsumenten und für die Gestaltung der Marketing-Kommunikation. Zürich, 1978.

Weber, P. Die Organisationsstruktur des Absatzbereiches in Unternehmungen der Maschinenindustrie. Winterthur, 1967.

Webster, F.E. Modelling the industrial buying process. Journal of Marketing Research- 1965, 370 ff.

Webster, F.E. New product adoption in industrial markets: A framework for analysis. Journal of Marketing, 1969, 33, 35 ff.

Webster, F.E. Informal communication in industrial markets. Journal of Marketing Research, 1970, 7, 186 ff.

Webster, F.E. Communication and diffusion process in industrial markets. Presented at: The American Marketing Association Workshop on Industrial Buying Behavior, Berkeley, California, 1971.

Webster, F.E. & Wind, Y. Organizational buying behavior. Englewood Cliffs, N.J., 1972.

Weede, E. Zur Methodik der kausalen Abhängigkeitsanalyse (Pfadanalyse) in der nicht-experimentellen Forschung. Kölner Zeitschrift für Soziologie und Sozialpsychologie, 1970, 22, 532 ff.

Weede, E. Zur Pfadanalyse. Neuere Entwicklungen, Verbesserungen, Ergänzungen. Kölner Zeitschrift für Soziologie und Sozialpsychologie, 1972, 24, 101 ff.

Wegner, D.M. & Vallacher, R.R. Implicit psychology. An introduction to social cognition. New York: Oxford University Press, 1977.

Weiner, B. Wirkung von Erfolg und Mißerfolg auf die Leistung. Bern, Stuttgart: Klett, Huber, 1975.

Weiner, B. Theorien der Motivation. Stuttgart: Klett, 1976.

Weiner-Regan, J. & Brehm, J.W. Konsequenzen eingeschränkter Entscheidungsfreiheit am Beispiel des Kaufverhaltens. In J.-J. Koch (Ed.), Sozialer Einfluß und Konformität. (Das Feldexperiment in der Sozialpsychologie). Weinheim: Beltz, 1977.

Wendt, D. Some criticism of stochastic models generally used in decision making experiments. Theory and Decision, 1975, 6, 197-212.

Wendt, D. & Zaus, M. Gutachten über die Durchführbarkeit einer empirischen Untersuchung zur Bewertung von Freizeitgebieten. Unveröffentlichtes Manuskript. Psychologisches Institut II, Universität Hamburg, 1975.

Wenzel, W. Die Gestaltungselemente der Verkaufswerbepolitik für Investitionsgüter, unter besonderer Berücksichtigung des Faktors Erklärungsbedürftigkeit. Berlin: Duncker & Humblot, 1964.

Werner, W. Comparative psychology of mental development. New York, 1957.

West, St.G. Increasing the attractiveness of college cafeteria food: A reactance theory perspective. Journal of Applied Psychology, 1975, 60, 656-658.

Wettschurek, G. Indikatoren und Skalen in der demoskopischen Forschung. In C. Behrens (Ed.), Handbuch der Marktforschung. Wiesbaden, 1974, 285-324.

White, R.W. Motivation reconsidered: The concept of competence. Psychological Review, 1959, 66, 317-330.

Wichman, H. Effects of isolation and communication on cooperation in a two-person game. Journal of Personality and Social Psychology, 1970, 16, 114-120.

Wicklund, R.A. Freedom and reactance. New York: Academic Press, 1974.

Wicklund, R.A. & Brehm, J.W. Attitude change as a function of feld competence and threat to attitudinal freedom. Journal of Experimental Social Psychology, 1968, 4, 64-75.

Wicklund, R.A. & Brehm, J.W. Perspectives on cognitive dissonance. Hillsdale, N.J.: Erlbaum, 1976.

Wicklund, R.A. & Ogden, J. The effects of unavailability on liking for the opposite sex. In R.A. Wicklund, Freedom and reactance. New York: Wiley, 1974.

Wicklund, R.A., Slattum, V. & Solomon, E. Effects of implied pressure toward commitment on ratings of choice alternatives. Journal of Experimental Social Psychology, 1970, 6, 449-457.

Wieczerkowski, W., Nickel, H., Janowski, A., Fittkau, B. & Rauer, W. Angstfragebogen für Schüler (AFS). Braunschweig: Westermann, 1974.

Wilkie, W.L. & Pessemier, E.A. Issues in marketing's use of multiattributive attitude models. Journal of Marketing Research, 1973, 10, 428-441.

Williamson, O.E. The economics of discretionary behavior. Managerial objectives in a theory of the firm. Ford Foundation, Diss., 1963.

Willis, R.H. Stimulus pooling and social perception. Journal of Abnormal and Social Psychology, 1960, 60, 365-373.

Wilson, A. The marketing of industrial products. London: Hutchinson, 1968.

Wingert, H. Im Büro spielen die Kinder. Stern, 1978, 27, 66-68.

Winkler, R.L. The assessment of prior distributions in Bayesian analysis. Journal of the American Statistical Association, 1967, 62, 776-800.

Winkler, R.L. Introduction to bayesian inference and decision. New York: Holt, Rinehart & Winston, 1972.

Winnubst, J.A.M. Hed Westerse tijdssyndroom. Conceptuele integratie en eerste aanzet tot construct validatie van een reeks molaire tijdsvariabelen in de psychologie. Amsterdam: Sweets & Zeitlinger, 1975.

Winterfeldt, D. von & Edwards, W. Costs and payoffs in perpetual research. Technical Report No. 11313-1-T, Ann Arbor: Engineering Psychology Laboratory, University of Michigan, 1973.

Wiswede, G. Reaktanz (zur Anwendung einer sozialwissenschaftlichen Theorie auf Probleme der Werbung und des Verkaufs.) Jahrbuch der Absatz- und Verbrauchsforschung, 1979, 25, 81-110.

Wiswede, G. Soziologie des Verbraucherverhaltens. Stuttgart, 1972.

Witte, E. Phasen-Theorem und Organisation komplexer Entscheidungsverläufe. Schmalenbachs Zeitschrift für betriebswirtschaftliche Forschung, 1968, 20, 625-547.

Witte, E. (Ed.), Das Informationsverhalten in Entscheidungsprozessen. Tübingen: Mohr, 1972.

Wolosin, R.J., Sherman, S.J. & Till, A. Effects of cooperation and competition on responsibility attribution after success and failure. Journal of Experimental Social Psychology, 1973, 9, 220-235.

Worchel, S. The effects of films on the importance of behavioral freedoms. Journal of Personality, 1972, 40, 417-435.

Worchel, S. & Arnold, S.E. The effects of consorship and attractiveness of the censor on attitude change. Journal of Experimental Social Psychology, 1973, 9, 365-377.

Worchel, S. & Brehm, J.W. Direct and implied social restoration of freedom. Journal of Personality and Social Psychology, 1971, 18, 294-304.

Worchel, S., Lee, J. & Adewole, A. Effects of supply and demand on ratings of object value. Journal of Personality and Social Psychology, 1975, 32, 906-914.

Wortman, C.B. & Brehm, J.W. Responses to uncontrollable outcomes: An integration of reactance theory and the learned helplessness model. In L.E. Berkowitz (Ed.), Advances in experimental social psychology, Vol. 8., New York: Academic Press, 1975.

Wyer, R.S., Jr. Cognitive organization and change: An information processing approach. New York, 1974.

Wyer, R.S., Jr. & Carlston, D.E. Social cognition, inference and attribution. Hillsdale, N.J.: Erlbaum, 1979.

Wyer, R.S., Jr. & Watson, S.F. Context effects in impression formation. Journal of Personality and Social Psychology, 1969, 12, 22-33.

Yabroff, W. Learning decision making. In J.D. Krumboltz & C.E. Thoreson (Eds.), Behavioral Counseling: Cases and techniques. New York: Holt, 1969.

Yarrow, M.R. & Scott, P.M. Imitation of nurturant and non-nurturant models. Journal of Personality and Social Psychology, 1972, 23, 259-270.

Yntema, D.B. & Torgerson, W.S. Man-computer cooperation in decisions requiring common sense. IRE-Transactions on Human Factors in Electronics, 1961, HFE-2, 20-26.

Young, F.W. Nonmetric multidimensional scaling: Recovery of metric information. Psychometrika, 1970, 35, 455-473.

Yukl, G.A. Effects of situational variables and opponent concessions on a bargainer's perception, aspiration, and concessions. Journal of Personality and Social Psychology, 1974, 29, 227-236.

Zajonc, R.B. The process of cognitive tuning in communication. Journal of Abnormal Psychology, 1960, 61, 159-167.

Zajonc, R.B. Social facilitation. Science, 1965, 149, 269-274.

Zajonc, R.B. Die verblüffende Beziehung zwischen Intelligenz und Geburtsposition. In L.H. Eckensberger (Ed.), Bericht über den 31. Kongreß der Deutschen Gesellschaft für Psychologie in Mannheim, 1978, Vol. 1, Göttingen: Hogrefe, 1979, 25-45.

Zajonc, R.B. & Burnstein, E. The learning of balanced and unbalanced social structures. Journal of Personality, 1965, 33, 153-163.

Zangemeister, C. Grundsätze zur Aufstellung eines Zielsystems. Industrielle Organisation, 1970, 39, 293-297.

Zanna, M.P. & Cooper, J. Dissonance and the pill: An attribution approach to studying the arousal properties of dissonance. Journal of Personality and Social Psychology, 1974, 29, 703-709.

Zaus, M. Die Skalierung multiattributer Eignungsfunktionen als Bewertungsgrundlage der Infrastruktur städtischer Grün- und Freiflächen. Unveröffentlichte Diplomarbeit, Universität Hamburg, 1975.

Zaus, M. Über die Verwackelung experimentell realisierbarer Gruppoide in der psychologischen Meßtheorie. Forschungsbericht aus dem Fach Psychologie der Universität Oldenburg. Vorgetragen anläßlich der 21. Tagung experimentell arbeitender Psychologen, Universität Heidelberg, 1979.

Zaus, M. Stochastic measurement structures: An application of Boolean-valued model theory to the probabilistic counterpart of fundamental measurement. Dissertation, in prep.

Zavalloni, M. & Cook, S.W. Influence of judges' attitudes on ratings of favorableness of statements about a social group. Journal of Personality and Social Psychology, 1965, 1, 43-64.

Zieris, E. So wohnen unsere ausländischen Mitbürger. Ministerium für Arbeit, Gesundheit und Soziales des Landes Nordrhein-Westfalen, Düsseldorf, 1972.

Zigler, E. & Balla, D. Developmental course of responsiveness to social reinforcement in normal children and institutionalized retarded children. Developmental Psychology, 1972, 6, 66-73.

Zimmermann, B.J. & Dialessi, F. Modeling influences on childrens's creative behavior. Journal of Educational Psychology, 1973, 65, 127-134.

Zimmermann, B.J. & Rosenthal, T.L. Concept attainment, transfer and retention through observation and rule-precision. Journal of Experimental Child Psychology, 1972, 14, 139-150.

Zimmermann, B.J. & Rosenthal, T.L. Observational learning of rule-governed behavior by children. Psychological Bulletin, 1974, 81, 29-42.

Zumkley-Münkel, C. Imitationslernen. Düsseldorf: Schwann, 1976.

Publications originating from studies conducted in the SFB 24, University of Mannheim

Andritzky, K. Know-how für segmentierte Investitionsgütermärkte. Absatzwirtschaft, 1974, 10.

Andritzky, K. & Finck, G. Who offers more? An investigation on the image of various store-types. Lebensmittel-Zeitung, 1977, 4, XL-XLII. (in German)

Aschenbrenner, K.-M. Eine empirische Überprüfung der Theorie vom erwarteten Risiko. Unpublished manuscript, SFB 24, University of Mannheim, 1976a.

Aschenbrenner, K.-M. Flat maxima in bidding procedures for utility estimation. Unpublished manuscript, SFB 24, University of Mannheim, 1976b.

Aschenbrenner, K.-M. Influence of attribute formulation on the evaluation of apartments by multiattribute utility procedures. In H. Jungermann & G. de Zeeuw (Eds.), Decision making and change in human affairs. Dortrecht: Reidel, 1977a.

Aschenbrenner, K.-M. Komplexes Wahlverhalten: Entscheidungen zwischen multiattributen Alternativen. In K.D. Hartmann & K. Koeppler (Eds.), Fortschritte der Marktpsychologie, Vol. 1. Frankfurt: Fachbuchhandlung für Psychologie, 1977b.

Aschenbrenner, K.-M. Komplexes Wahlverhalten als Problem der Informationsverarbeitung. In H. Ueckert & D. Rhenius (Eds.), Komplexe menschliche Informationsverarbeitung. Bern: Huber, 1978a.

Aschenbrenner, K.-M. Expected risks and single-peaked preferences. Acta Psychologica, 1978b, 42, 343-356.

Aschenbrenner, K.-M. Single-peaked risk preferences and their dependability on the gambles' presentation mode. Journal of Experimental Psychology: Human Perception and Performance, 1978c, 4, 513-520.

Aschenbrenner, K.-M. Single-peaked preferences over efficient sets of gambles with varying expected value. Unpublished manuscript, SFB 24, University of Mannheim, 1978d.

Aschenbrenner, K.-M., Borcherding, K., Kasubek, W., Schaefer, R., Schümer, R. & Schümer-Kohrs, A. Eine empirische Untersuchung zur Bewertung von Forschungsprojekten. Unpublished manuscript, SFB 24, University of Mannheim, 1975.

Aschenbrenner, K.-M. & Kasubek, W. Convergence of multiattribute evaluations when different sets of attributes are used. Unpublished manuscript, SFB 24, University of Mannheim, 1975.

Aschenbrenner, K.-M. & Kasubek, W. Challenging the cushing syndrome: Multiattribute evaluation of cortisone drugs. Organizational Behavior and Human Performance, 1978a.

Aschenbrenner, K.-M. & Kasubek, W. Effect of training and group work on utility estimation by lottery methods. Unpublished manuscript, SFB 24, University of Mannheim, 1978b.

Aschenbrenner, K.-M. & Wendt, D. Erwartungsmaximierung versus Wettbewerbsmotivation beim Wahrscheinlichkeitsschätzen. Unpublished manuscript, SFB 24, University of Mannheim, 1976.

Aschenbrenner, K.-M. & Wendt, D. Expectation maximization versus ambition motivation in probability estimation. Organizational Behavior and Human Performance, 1978, 21, 160-170.

Aufsattler, W. Die Quantifizierung stochastischer Abhängigkeiten bei kategorialen Daten durch log-lineare Datenstrukturmodelle. Talk given at the 20. Tagung experimentell arbeitender Psychologen, Marburg, 1978.

Aufsattler, W. & Schaefer, R.E. Der Einfluß der Komplexität auf die Güte probabilistischer Informationsverarbeitung. Archiv für Psychologie, 1978, 130, 139-155.

Balzer, H.G., Schümer-Kohrs, A. & Schümer, R. Kontexteffekte bei der Eindrucksbildung. Zeitschrift für experimentelle und angewandte Psychologie, 1974, 21, 25-38.

Bandilla, W., Klump, H. & Volkert, M. Der Einfluß der Struktur impliziter Bezugsskalen auf die Beurteilung physikalisch bzw. sozial definierter Reize. Unpublished manuscript, SFB 24, University of Mannheim, 1978.

Bandilla, W., Krolage, J. & Lilli, W. Urteilsverzerrungen bei der Einschätzung von Gemälden. Unpublished manuscript, SFB 24, University of Mannheim, 1978.

Beeskow, W. Classification and representation of time series. In E. Dichtl & R. Schobert (Eds.), Multidimensional scaling. München, 1979, 147-158 (in German).

Beeskow, W. & Finck, G. Ein empfängerorientierter Ansatz zur Bestimmung der Versorgungsqualität - dargestellt für den Bereich der Waren des täglichen Bedarfs. Unpublished manuscript, SFB 24, University of Mannheim, 1979.

Bollinger, G. Strukturanalysen von Verfahren zur Messung kreativer Fähigkeiten. Unpublished doctoral dissertation, University of Mannheim, 1978.

Bollinger-Hellingrath, C. Resonanz bei der Einfallsproduktion in Gruppen. Unpublished doctoral dissertation, University of Mannheim, 1978.

Borcherding, K. Calibration of probabilistic estimates as a function of objective difficulty, subjective difficulty, and misinformation. Paper presented at the Sixth Research Conference on Subjective Probability, Utility and Decision Making, Warsaw, 1977.

Borcherding, K. Subjektive Bestimmung der Erträge von Aktien für Entscheidungshilfe bei der Portfolio Selektion. Theoretischer Bezugsrahmen und eine experimentelle Überprüfung. Unpublished doctoral dissertation, University of Mannheim, 1978.

Borcherding, K. & Schaefer, R.E. Konsensus bei Entscheidungen. In H. Brandstaetter & H. Schuler (Eds.), Entscheidungsprozesse in Gruppen. Zeitschrift für Sozialpsychologie, 1976, Beiheft 2, 47-61.

Bülles, U. & Borcherding, K. Wahrscheinlichkeiten und Wahrscheinlichkeitsverteilungen bei produktspezifischen Konfidenzen. Ein empirischer Methodenvergleich. Technical report, Sonderforschungsbereich 24, University of Mannheim, (in preparation).

Burger, C. Soziale und kognitive Determinanten der Zukunftsorientierung. Unpublished diploma thesis, University of Mannheim, 1975.

Busz, M., Cohen, R., Poser, U., Schümer-Kohrs, A., Schümer, R. & Sonnenfeld, C. Die soziale Bewertung von 880 Eigenschaftsbegriffen sowie die Analyse der Ähnlichkeit zwischen 60 dieser Begriffe. Zeitschrift für experimentelle und angewandte Psychologie, 1972a, 19, 282-308.

Busz, M., Schümer-Kohrs, A. & Schümer, R. Zum Einfluß von Informationsmenge und -homogenität auf die Prägnanz des Eindrucks. Unpublished manuscript, SFB 24, University of Mannheim, 1972b.

Cohen, R. & Schümer, R. Kontexteffekte bei der Eindrucksbildung - eine experimentelle Untersuchung. Zeitschrift für Sozialpsychology, 1972, 3, 313-328.

Crott, H.W. Experimentelle Untersuchung zum Zusammenhang von Gewinnerwartungen und Gewinnen in asymmetrischen Verhandlungssituationen. Unpublished manuscript, SFB 24, University of Mannheim, 1971a.

Crott, H.W. Experimentelle Untersuchung zum Verhandlungsverhalten in kooperativen Spielen. Zeitschrift für Sozialpsychologie, 1971 b, 2, 61-74.

Crott, H.W. Der Einfluß struktureller und situativer Merkmale auf das Verhalten in Verhandlungssituationen, Teil I. Zeitschrift für Sozialpsychologie, 1972a, 3, 134-158.

Crott, H.W. Der Einfluß struktureller und situativer Merkmale auf das Verhalten in Verhandlungssituationen, Teil II. Zeitschrift für Sozialpsychologie, 1972b, 3, 227-244.

Crott, H.W., Kayser, E. & Lamm, H. The effects of information exchange and communication in an asymmetrical negotiation situation. European Journal of Social Psychology, 1980, 10, 149-163.

Crott, H.W., Kutschker, M. & Lamm, H. Verhandlungen I: Individuen und Gruppen als Konfliktparteien. Stuttgart: Kohlhammer, 1977a.

Crott, H.W., Kutschker, M. & Lamm, H. Verhandlungen II: Organisationen und Nationen als Konfliktparteien. Stuttgart: Kohlhammer, 1977b.

Crott, H.W., Lumpp, R.P. & Wildermuth, R. Der Einsatz von Be-
strafungen und Belohnungen in einer Verhandlungssituation.
In H. Brandstaetter & H. Schuler (Eds.), Entscheidungsprozesse in Gruppen. Zeitschrift für Sozialpsychologie, Beiheft 2,
Bern: Huber, 1976.

Crott, H.W. & Möntmann, V. Der Effekt der Information über die
Verhandlungsmöglichkeiten des Gegeners auf das Ergebnis einer
Verhandlung. Zeitschrift für Sozialpsychologie, 1973, 3, 209-
219.

Crott, H.W., Möntmann, V. & Wender, I. Der Einfluß sozialer
Normen auf die Attraktivität von Entscheidungsalternativen
in Gruppensituationen. In M. Irle (Ed.), Wirtschafts- und
Sozialpsychologie. Hamburg: Hoffmann & Campe, 1978.

Crott, H.W. & Müller, G.F. Der Einfluß des Anspruchsniveaus
und der Erfahrung auf Ergebnis und Verlauf dyadischer Verhandlungen bei vollständiger Information über die Gewinnmög-
lichkeiten. Zeitschrift für experimentelle und angewandte
Psychologie, 1976, 23, 548-568.

Crott, H.W. & Müller, G.F. Interessenkonflikte und ihre Lösung
durch Verhandlung. In H.W. Crott & G.F. Müller (Eds.), Wirt-
schafts- und Sozialpsychologie. Hamburg: Hoffmann & Campe,
1978.

Crott, H.W. & Müller, G.F. Entscheidungen in einem Gewinnspiel.
(In preparation).

Crott, H.W., Müller, G.F. & Hamel, P. The influence of persons'
aspiration level for the process and outcome in a dyadic
bargaining situation with different information and bargaining experience conditions. In H. Sauermann (Ed.), Contributions to experimental economics. Tübingen: Mohn, 1978.

Crott, H.W., Müller, G.F. & Maus, E. Der Einfluß der Partner-
strategie auf das Bestrafungsverhalten von Personen in dyadischen Verhandlungen. Archiv für Psychologie, 1978, 39-42.

Crott, H.W., Scholz, R.W. & Michels, B. The effect of bargaining experiences on information exchange and cheating in an
asymmetrical bargaining situation. Unpublished manuscript,
SFB 24, University of Mannheim, 1978.

Crott, H.W., Simon, K. & Yelin, M. Der Einfluß des Anspruchsniveaus auf den Verlauf und das Ergebnis von Verhandlungen.
Zeitschrift für Sozialpsychologie, 1974, 5, 300-314.

Crott, H., Wender, I., Oldigs, I. & Reihl, D. Modifikation des
Aufteilungsverhaltens bei Jungen in der dritten Grundschul-
klasse. Zeitschrift für Entwicklungspsychologie und Pädagogische Psychologie, 1975, 11, 144-152.

Dichtl, E. Grundzüge der Binnenhandelspolitik. Stuttgart, 1979.

Dichtl, E., Bauer, H.H. & Funck, G. Die Versorgung der Bevöl-
kerung mit Waren des täglichen Bedarfs - ein meßtheoretischer
Problemaufriß. In R. Bratschitsch & E. Heinen (Eds.), Absatz-

wirtschaft-Marketing: Betriebswirtschaftliche Probleme und gesellschaftlicher Bezug. Wien, 1978a, 91-112.

Dichtl, E., Bauer, H.H. & Funck, G. Die Versorgung mit Gütern des täglichen Bedarfs im Urteil von Verbrauchern. "Die Betriebswirtschaft", 1978b, 38, 219-230.

Dichtl, E., Beeskow, W. & Funck, G. Versorgungsprobleme von Verbrauchern. Ein empirischer Stadt-Land-Vergleich. In Forschungsstelle für den Handel e.V. (Ed.), Handelsforschung heute. Berlin, 1979a, 179-191.

Dichtl, E., Beeskow, W. & Finck, G. Versorgung der Überfluß-Gesellschaft. "Wirtschaftswoche", 1979b, 9, 94-98.

Dickenberger, D. Ein neues Konzept der Wichtigkeit von Freiheit. Konsequenzen für die Thorie der Psychologischen Reaktanz. Weinheim: Beltz, 1979 (Beltz Forschungsberichte).

Dickenberger, D. & Bender, B. Auswirkungen von Erfahrungen mit erfolgreichem bzw. nicht erfolgreichem Reaktanzverhalten auf die Häufigkeit des Auftretens von Reaktanz (in preparation).

Dickenberger, D. & Grabitz-Gniech, G. Restrictive conditions for the occurrence of psychological reactance: Interpersonal attraction, need for social approval, and a dealy factor. European Journal of Social Psychology, 1972, 2, 177-198.

Dickenberger, D., Holtz, S. & Gniech, G. Bedürfnis nach sozialer Anerkennung: Validierung der "Marlow-Crowne Social Desirability Scale" über ein Konzept individuell relevanter Gruppen. Diagnostica, 1978, 24, 24-38.

Dickenberger, D. & van Kaick, G. Der Abbau von Reaktanz durch die Effekte (in preparation).

Dickenberger, D. & Link, R. Antizipierte Reaktanz in Partnerschaften (in preparation).

Dickenberger, D. & Papastefanou, G. Direkter und indirekter Widerstand gegen persuasive Kommunikation (in preparation).

Ebert, U., Grabitz, H.-J. & Haisch, J. Alternativensteuerung und Validität der "cues" beim "multiple-cue" Lernen. Technical Report, SFB 24, University of Mannheim, 1977.

Etzel, G. Akzentuierung als Zwei-Stufen Prozeß: Eine Sekundäranalyse der Daten von Upmeyer & Cleary (1975). Unpublished manuscript, University of Mannheim, 1977a.

Etzel, G. Stereotype Wahrnehmung: Eine alternative Interpretation klassifikatorischer Urteile. Zeitschrift für Sozialpsychologie, 1977b, 8, 234-241.

Etzel, G. Kognitiv induzierte Verzerrungen in der stereotypen Urteilsbildung. Unpublished doctoral dissertation, University of Mannheim, 1978.

Faust, E., Helmke, A. & Wender, I. Der Einfluß von Modellverhalten und Leistungsangst auf das Leistungs- und Imitationsverhalten von 9-10jährigen Schulkindern. Zeitschrift für Empirische Pädagogik, 1979, 3, 285-296.

Finck, G. & Müller, D. Die Auswirkungen eines Verbrauchermark-
tes auf den örtlichen Einzelhandel. Lebensmittel-Zeitung,
1978, 26, F26-F32.

Finck, G. & Niedetzky, H.-M. Beschaffungskosten der Landbevöl-
kerung für Waren des täglichen Bedarfs. Jahrbuch der Absatz-
und Verbrauchsforschung, 1979, 25.

Frey, D. Der augenblickliche Stand der "forced compliance"
Forschung. Zeitschrift für Sozialpsychologie, 1971, 2, 323-
342.

Frey, D. Dissonanzreduktion nach tatsächlichem und antizipier-
tem attitüdendiskrepantem Verhalten. Archiv für Psychologie,
1975a, 127, 23-34.

Frey, D. Zum Problem der Reduktion kognitiver Dissonanz in Öf-
fentlichkeitssituationen. Zeitschrift für experimentelle und
angewandte Psychologie, 1975b, 22, 561-572.

Frey, D. A new provocation for dissonance theory? European
Journal of Social Psychology, 1976, 6 (3), 387-399.

Frey, D. Social psychology and decision making processes. The
Interdisciplinary Research Institute of SFB 24 at the University of Mannheim. The German Journal of Psychology, 1977,
1, 147-164.

Frey, D. Die Theorie der kognitiven Dissonanz. In D. Frey (Ed.),
Kognitive Theorien der Sozialpsychologie. Bern: Huber, 1978a.

Frey, D. Reactions to success and failure in public and in private conditions. Journal of Experimental Social Psychology,
1978b, 14, 172-179.

Frey, D. Konsistenztheorien und Einstellungsänderung. In H.
Crott & F.G. Müller (Eds.), Sozial- und Wirtschaftspsycholo-
gie. Hoffmann & Campe, 1978c.

Frey. D. Experimentelle Untersuchungen zur selektiven Suche und
Vermeidung von Informationen vor Entscheidungen. Eine Über-
prüfung der Thesen der Theorie der kognitiven Dissonanz.
Unpublished Habilitatia, University of Mannheim, 1978d.

Frey, D. Dissonanztheoretische Forschung: Ein Überblick. In S.
Hormuth (Ed.), Sozialpsychologie der Einstellungsänderung.
Königstein/Ts.: Athenäum-Hain, 1979, 30-49.

Frey, D. Einstellungsforschung: Neuere Ergebnisse der Forschung
über Einstellungsänderungen. Marketing, Zeitschrift für Forschung und Praxis, 1979b, 31-45.

Frey, D. The effect of negative feedback about oneself and cost
of information on preferences for information about the source of this feedback. Journal of Experimental Social Psychology, 1980a.

Frey, D.Postdecisional preferences for decision-relevant information as a function of the competence of its source and
the degree of familiarity with this information. Journal of
Experimental Social Psychology, 1980b.

Frey, D. Experimental investigations to selective exposure to information and some speculations about the transfer to political issues. In H. Moser (Ed.), Perspectives in Political Psychology (in press).

Frey, D. Experimentelle Untersuchungen zur selektiven Suche und Vermeidung von Informationen. Bern: Huber (in press).

Frey, D. & Gniech, G. Negative Attitüdenänderung als Folge von freiheitseinengendem Einfluß. Unpublished manuscript, SFB 24, University of Mannheim, 1976.

Frey, D., Götz, J. & Götz-Marchand, B. Selbstdarstellung unter öffentlichen oder anonymen Bedingungen bei erwartetem oder nicht erwartetem feedback. Unpublished manuscript, SFB 24, University of Mannheim, 1975.

Frey, D., Götz, J. & Marchand, B. War die Landtagswahl 1972 in Baden-Württemberg eine Testwahl? Eine Untersuchung zum Urteil der Wähler. Unpublished manuscript, SFB 24, University of Mannheim, 1972.

Frey, D. & Irle, M. Some conditions to produce a dissonance and an incentive effect in a "forced-compliance" situation. European Journal of Social Psychology, 1972, 2, 45-54.

Frey, D., Irle, M. & Hochgürtel, G. Performance of an unpleasant task: Effects of over- vs underpayment as perception of adequacy of rewards and attractiveness of the task. Journal of Experimental Social Psychology, 1979, 15, 275-284.

Frey, D., Irle, M. & Kumpf, M. Attribution oder Reduktion kognitiver Dissonanz? Zeitschrift für Sozialpsychologie, 1973, 4, 366-377.

Frey, D., Irle, M. & Kumpf, M. Hypothesen in kognitiver Dissonanz, 1974. In M. Irle (Ed.), Lehrbuch der Sozialpsychologie. Göttingen: Hogrefe, 1975, 343-346.

Frey, D., Irle, M., Kumpf, M., Ochsmann, R. & Sauer, C. Der Einfluß von 5 unterschiedlichen Belohnungsstufen auf Attitüdenänderungen bei attitüdendiskrepantem und -kongruentem Verhalten. Bericht über den 29. Kongreß der Deutschen Gesellschaft für Psychologie, Salzburg, 1974.

Frey, D. & Kumpf, M. Reaktionen auf kognitive Dissonanz in Abhängigkeit von sozialer Angst und öffentlicher bzw. anonymer Übermittlung diskrepanter Informationen. Unpublished manuscript, SFB 24, University of Mannheim, 1973.

Frey, D., Kumpf, M., Raffée, H., Sauter, B. & Silberer, G. Informationskosten und Reversibilität des Entschlusses als Determinanten der Informationsnachfrage von Entscheidungen. Zeitschrift für experimentelle und angewandte Psychologie, 1976, 23, 569-585.

Frey, D. & Wicklund, R.A. The impact of choice in selective exposure. Journal of Experimental Social Psychology, 1978, 14, 132-139.

Fries, A. & Frey, D. Misattribution of arousal and self-threatening information. Journal of Experimental Social Psychology, 1980.

Fries, A., Frey, D. & Pongratz, L. Ängstlichkeit, Selbsteinschätzung und kognitive Dissonanz. Archiv für Psychologie, 1977, 129, 83-98.

Fritz, W. Informationsbedarf und Informationsbeschaffung des Konsumenten bei rezeptfreien Medikamenten - Eine empirische Untersuchung, dargestellt anhand einer Stichprobe alter Menschen. Unpublished diploma thesis, University of Mannheim, 1977.

Füchsle, T. Soziale und situative Determinanten des Aufschubverhaltens und der Selbst- vs. Außendetermination zukünftiger Ereignisse. Unpublished diploma thesis, University of Mannheim, 1975.

Füchsle, T. & Trommsdorff, G. Eine Längsschnittstudie zur Entwicklung von Zukunftsorientierung und Aufschubverhalten bei Unter- und Mittelschichtkindern. Paper presented at the Tagung Entwicklungspsychologie, Berlin, 1979.

Füchsle, T., Trommsdorff, G. & Burger, C. Entwicklung eines Meßinstrumentes zur Erfassung kognitiver und affektiver Komponenten der Zukunftsorientierung. Unpublished manuscript, SFB 24, University of Mannheim, 1979.

Gerdts, U. Entscheidungshilfe für Hauptschüler bei der Wahl einer Ausbildungsstelle. Unpublished diploma thesis, University of Mannheim, 1977.

Gerdts, U. Entscheidungshilfe für Hauptschüler bei der Wahl einer Ausbildungsstelle. Technical Report, SFB 24, University of Mannheim, 1979.

Gerdt, U., Aschenbrenner, K.-M., Jeromin, S., Kroh-Püschel, E. & Zaus, M. Problemorientiertes Entscheidungsverhalten mit mehrfacher Zielsetzung. In D. Rhenius & H.P. Ueckert (Eds.), Komplexe menschlicher Informationsverarbeitung. Bern: Huber, 1979a.

Gerdts, U., Aschenbrenner, K.-M., Jeromin, S., Kroh-Püschel, E. & Zaus, M. Problemorientiertes Entscheidungsverhalten mit mehrfacher Zielsetzung. In L.H. Eckensberger (Ed.), Bericht über den 31. Kongreß der deutschen Gesellschaft für Psychologie in Mannheim (Bd. 2). Göttingen: Hogrefe, 1979b.

Götz-Marchand, B., Götz, J. & Irle, M. Preference of dissonance reduction modes as a function of their order, familiarity and reversibility. European Journal of Social Psychology, 1974, 4, 201-228.

Gniech, G. Störeffekte in psychologischen Experimenten. Stuttgart: Kohlhammer, 1976.

Gniech, G. Experimenteller Bias (dargestellt am Beispiel der Attitüdenforschung). In F. Petermann & S. Hormuth (Eds.),

Sozialpsychologie der Einstellungsänderung. Köln: Kiepenheuer & Witsch, 1977.

Gniech, G. & Grabitz, H.-J. Freiheitseinengung und psychologische Reaktanz. In D. Frey (Ed.), Theorien der Sozialpsychologie. Bern: Huber, 1978.

Gniech, G., Gumbel, H. & Dickenberger, D. Ist der Reaktanzeffekt ein Artefakt? (in preparation).

Gniech, G., Schmidt, B. & Dickenberger, D. Antizipierte Reaktanz: Welche Reaktionen auf Freiheitseinengungen erwarten andere? Unpublished manuscript, SFB 24, University of Mannheim, 1976.

Grabicke, K. Das Zustandekommen stereotyper Urteile über komplexe Sachverhalte. Unpublished diploma thesis, University of Mannheim, 1972.

Grabicke, K. & Hilger, H. Informationsbedarf und Informationsbeschaffung jugendlicher Konsumenten beim Kauf langlebiger Güter. In K.D. Hartmann & K. Koeppler (Eds.), Fortschritte der Marktspychologie, Vol. 2. Frankfurt/M., 1980.

Grabicke, K., Raffée, H., Schätzle, T. & Schöler, M. Die Veränderung des Informationsstandes und ihre Auswirkungen auf den Kaufentscheidungsprozeß privater Haushalte - eine Paneluntersuchung. In K.D. Hartmann & K. Koeppler (Eds.), Fortschritte der Marktpsychologie, Vol. 2. Frankfurt/M., 1980.

Grabicke, K., Schätzle, T. & Schöler, M. Die kriterienbezogene Messung als Mittel der Marktpsychologie - Entwicklung eines Tests zur Ermittlung des produktbezogenen Informationsstandes. In K.D. Hartmann & K. Koeppler (Eds.), Fortschritte der Marktpsychologie, Vol. 1. Frankfurt/M. 1977, 145-167.

Grabitz, H.-J. Experimentelle Untersuchungen zur Bewertung von Information vor Entscheidungen. Unpublished doctoral dissertation, University of Mannheim, 1969.

Grabitz, H.-J. Zur Beziehung von Inertia Effekt und sequentieller Position widersprechender Ereignisse bei der Revision subjektiver Wahrscheinlichkeiten. Psychologische Forschung, 1971, 85, 35-45.

Grabitz, H.-J. & Grabitz-Gniech, G. Der Inertia Effekt in Abhängigkeit vom diagnostischen Wert einer Information. Zeitschrift für experimentelle und angewandte Psychologie, 1972a, 19, 364-375.

Grabitz, H.-J. & Grabitz-Gniech, G. Konsistenz als Mechanismus bei sequentieller Informationsverarbeitung. Archiv für Psychologie, 1972b, 124, 39-49.

Grabitz, H.-J. & Grabitz-Gniech, G. Der kognitive Prozess vor Entscheidungen: Theoretische Ansätze und experimentelle Untersuchungen. Psychologische Beiträge, 1973, 15, 522-549.

Grabitz, H.-J. & Haisch, J. Umbewertung von unterstützender und widersprechender Information vor Entscheidungen. Archiv für Psychologie, 1972, 124, 133-144.

Grabitz, H.-J. & Haisch, J. Motivationale Aspekte diagnosti-
scher Probleme. Unpublished manuscript, University of Düsseldorf, 1976.

Grabitz, H.-J. & Haisch, J. Der Prozeß des Datentestens bei Diagnoseproblemen als Funktion von "Steuerung" und Reliabilität der Information. Diagnostica, 1980.

Grabitz, H.-J., Haisch, J. & Kozielecki, J. Die Rolle der Alternativensteuerung und Ereignisklassifikation bei der Verifi-
zierung von Entscheidungspräferenzen. Unpublished manuscript,
SFB 24, University of Mannheim, 1974.

Grabitz, H.-J., Haisch, J. & Wolfshörndl, P. Alternativenspezi-
fikation und Kontrolle durch Beobachter bei Diagnoseproblemen.
Manuscript submitted for publication, 1980.

Grabitz, H.-J. & Klump, H. Konsistenzmechanismus und Kontrolle
bei der Bewertung von verläßlicher Information. Archiv für
Psychologie, 1973, 125, 39-49.

Grabitz-Gniech, G. Some restrictive conditions for the occurrence of psychological reactance. Journal of Personality and Social Psychology, 1971, 19, 188-196.

Grabitz-Gniech, G. Bericht über eine Analyse von sieben Persön-
lichkeitsfragebögen. Unpublished manuscript, SFB 24, University of Mannheim, 1972.

Grabitz-Gniech, G., Auslitz, K. & Grabitz, H.-J. Die Stärke des
Reaktanz-Effektes als Funktion der absoluten Größe und der
relativen Reduktion des Freiheitsspielraumes. Zeitschrift
für Sozialpsychologie, 1975, 6, 122-128.

Grabitz-Gniech, G. & Benad, A. Hilfeverhalten nach einem vor-
herigen Gefallen - Eine Untersuchung zur Reaktanztheorie
mit den Variablen moralischer Druck, Wichtigkeit der Situation und Geschlecht des Helfers. Unpublished manuscript,
SFB 24, University of Mannheim, 1972.

Grabitz-Gniech, G. & Dickenberger, M. Opposition bei Versuchspersonen im psychologischen Experiment, hervorgerufen durch
Hypothesenkenntnis, Argwohn gegenüber Täuschung sowie errun-
gene Teilnahme. Psychologische Beiträge, 1975, 17, 392-405.

Grabitz-Gniech, G. & Grabitz, H.-J. Psychologische Reaktanz:
Theoretisches Konzept und experimentelle Untersuchungen.
Zeitschrift für Sozialpsychologie, 1973a, 4, 19-35.

Grabitz-Gniech, G. & Grabitz, H.-J. Der Einfluß von Freiheitseinengung und Freiheitswiederherstellung auf den Reaktanzeffekt. Zeitschrift für Sozialpsychologie, 1973b, 4, 361-365.

Grabitz-Gniech, G. & Niketta, R. Soziale Macht und Ich-Beteili-
gung als bedingende Variablen im sozialen Einflußversuch:
Konformität oder Opposition? Unpublished manuscript, SFB 24,
University of Mannheim, 1971.

Grabitz-Gniech, G. & Schmidt, B. Der Einfluß von freiheitsein-
engenden Instruktionen eines psychologischen Experiments auf

das Versuchspersonenverhalten. Archiv für Psychologie, 1973, 125, 153-165.

Grabitz-Gniech, G. & Zeisel, B. Bedingungen für Widerstandsverhalten in psychologischen Experimenten: Ton der Instruktion sowie Einstellung zum Forschungsgegenstand und Studienfach der Versuchsperson. Zeitschrift für Soziologie, 1974, 3, 138-148.

Groffmann, K.-J. & Wender, I. Experiments on learning from models. Proceedings of the Second International Conference on Psychology Solving. Prague: Czechoslovak Academy of Sciences, 1975, 435-438.

Haefele, J. Der Einfluß unterschiedlich zahlreicher Verankerungen von Kognitionen mit Dritt-Kognitionen auf kognitive und affektive Änderungen von Attitüden. Unpublished diploma thesis, University of Mannheim, 1978.

Haisch, J. & Grabitz, H.-J. Der Einfluß der Reliabilität der Information und der Spezifikation der Lösungsalternativen auf die Bearbeitung von Diagnoseproblemen. Archiv für Psychologie, 1979, 132, 41-48.

Haisch, J., Grabitz, H.-J. & Prester, H.-G. Effekte von Arbeitshypothesen und "Steuerung" auf den Lösungsprozeß bei Diagnoseproblemen. Psychologische Beiträge, 1979, 21, 237-248.

Haisch, J., Grabitz, H.-J. & Trommsdorff, G. Reliabilität von "cues" und Situationspräferenz. Unpublished manuscript, SFB 24, University of Mannheim, 1975.

Hefner, M. Der Gastarbeiter als Konsument. Göttingen, 1978.

Hellingrath, C. & Bollinger, G. Imitierendes Verhalten in einfallsproduzierenden Gruppen. Unpublished manuscript, SFB 24, University of Mannheim, 1976.

Hellingrath, C., Werling, F. & Bollinger, G. Anwesenheitseffekte in einfallsproduzierenden Gruppen. Unpublished manuscript, SFB 24, University of Mannheim, 1976.

Hilger, H. Informationsbedarf und Informationsbeschaffung des Konsumenten bei langlebigen Gütern - eine empirische Untersuchung, dargestellt anhand einer Stichprobe berufstätiger Jugendlicher. Unpublished diploma thesis, University of Mannheim, 1977.

Hormuth, S., Lamm, H., Michelitsch, I., Scheuermann, H., Trommsdorff, G. & Vögele, I. Impulskontrolle und einige Persönlichkeitscharakteristika bei delinquenten und nichtdelinquenten Jugendlichen. Psychologische Beiträge, 1977, 19, 340-354.

Hormuth, S. Michelitsch, I., Scheuermann, H. & Vögele, I. Zeitwahrnehmung, Zukunftsperspektive und Impulskontrolle bei jungen Strafgefangenen. Unpublished diploma thesis, University of Heidelberg, 1975.

Huppertsberg, B. Verhandlungsspiele. als Instrument exploratorischer Forschung. Unpublished manuscript, SFB 24, University of Mannheim, 1972.

Huppertsberg, B. Verhandlungsspiele im Investitionsgütermarketing - Methodologische Probleme exploratorischer Simulation.
Unpublished doctoral dissertation, University of Mannheim,
1975.

Huppertsberg, B. & Kirsch, W. Beschaffungsentscheidungen auf
Investitionsgütermärkten. München, 1977.

Huppertsberg, B., Roth, K. & Schneider, J. Empirische Untersuchung zum Investitionsgütermarketing. Unpublished manuscript, SFB 24, University of Mannheim, 1974.

Ickert, C., Schümer-Kohrs, A. & Schümer, R. Einige Daten zum
Rep-Test. Unpublished manuscript, SFB 24, University of
Mannheim, 1972.

Ickert, C., Schümer-Kohrs, A., Schümer, R. & Sonnenfeld, C.
Kurzbericht über eine Untersuchung zum Einfluß von Informationsmenge und -homogenität auf die Suche nach weiteren Informationen. Unpublished manuscript, SFB 24, University of
Mannheim, 1972.

Irle, M., Gniech, G., Frey, D. & Kumpf, M. Die Umbewertung der
Attraktivität von Alternativen nach Entscheidungen.
(in preparation).

Irle, M. & Krolage, J. Kognitive Konsequenzen irrtümlicher
Selbsteinschätzung. Zeitschrift für Sozialpsychologie, 1973,
4, 36-50.

Irle, M. & Möntmann, V. Die Theorie der kognitiven Dissonanz:
Ein Resumee ihrer theoretischen Entwicklung und empirischen
Ergebnisse 1957-1976. In M. Irle, L. Festinger & V. Möntmann (Eds.), Theorie der kognitiven Dissonanz. Bern: Huber,
1978.

Iseler, A. Einige Intensitätsmodelle für stochastisch abhängi-
ge Ereignisse in kontinuierlicher Zeit. Unpublished manuscript, SFB 24, University of Mannheim, 1973.

Iseler, A. Methoden der Bestimmung des Clustering bei freier
Reproduktion. Paper presented at the 20th Tagung experimentell arbeitender Psychologen. Marburg, 1978.

Jeromin, F. Entscheidungshilfe für Hauptschüler bei der Wahl
eines Berufes. Unpublished diploma thesis, University of
Mannheim, 1978.

Jeromin, S. & Kroh-Püschel, E. Informationsverhalten von Haupt-
schülern und Hauptschülerinnen vor ihrer Berufsentscheidung.
Eine Befragung Ludwigshafener und Mannheimer Jugendlicher.
Unpublished manuscript, SFB 24, University of Mannheim, 1977.

Jeromin, S. & Kroh-Püschel, E. Training vor Entscheidungsverhalten durch kognitives Beobachtungslernen. Unpublished manuscript, SFB 24, University of Mannheim, 1978a.

Jeromin, S. & Kroh-Püschel, E. Der Einfluß einer Entscheidungs-
hilfe auf die Höhe der Informationsselektion vor komplexen
Entscheidungen. Unpublished manuscript, SFB 24, University of
Mannheim, 1978b.

Jeromin, S. & Kroh-Püschel, E. Methoden der verhaltensorientier-
ten Berufsberatung: Eine Übersicht. Unpublished manuscript,
SFB 24, University of Mannheim, 1978c.

Jeromin, S. & Kroh-Püschel, E. Informations- und Entscheidungs-
verhalten bei der Berufs- und Stellenwahl und Maßnahmen der
Verbesserung. Unpublished manuscript, SFB 25, University of
Mannheim, 1979.

Kasubek, W. & Aschenbrenner, K.-M. Multiattribute Einschätzung
der Gefährlichkeit von Cortisonpräparaten bei der Langzeit-
therapie. Unpublished manuscript, SFB 24, University of Mannheim, 1977.

Kasubek, W. & Aschenbrenner, K.-M. Optimierung subjektiver Urteile: Anwendung der multiattributen Nutzentheorie bei medizinischen Therapieentscheidungen. Zeitschrift für experimentelle und angewandte Psychologie, 1978, 25, 594-616.

Kayser, E. Experimentelle Untersuchung zu Wirkungen und Beziehung von Informationsaustausch und Kommunikation in einer
asymmetrischen Verhandlungssituation. Unpublished diploma
thesis, University of Mannheim, 1974.

Kayser, E. "Kognitive Algebra" bei Aufteilungsentscheidungen.
Zeitschrift für Sozialpsychologie, 1979, 10, 134-142.

Kayser, E. & Lamm, H. Causal explanation of performance in
high-attraction dyads and allocation behavior. Unpublished
manuscript, SFB 24, University of Mannheim, 1979.

Kayser, E. & Lamm, H. Input integration and input weighting in
allocations of gains and losses. European Journal of Social
Psychology, 1980, 10, 1-15.

Kirsch, W. & Huppertsberg, B. Verhandlungsspiele als "Simulation" von Verkaufsprozessen. Mannheimer Berichte, 1972, 141 ff.

Kistner, K. Computerunterstützte Diagnose: Anwendung des Bayes
Theorems bei der Diagnose psychiatrischer Krankheiten.
Unpublished diploma thesis, University of Mannheim, 1980.

Klump, H. & Bandilla, W. Wertkonnotationen der Skalenbenennung
und ihr Einfluß auf Extremisierungseffekte bei der Beurteilung von Attitüdenitems. Zeitschrift für Sozialpsychologie,
1978, 9, 142-151.

Kratzmann, M. Einfluß von beruflicher Information auf die
Differenziertheit der Berufswahrnehmung und auf die Informa-
tionssuche von Hauptschülerinnen. Unpublished diploma thesis,
University of Mannheim, 1978.

Kreft, W. Der Einfluß des elterlichen Erziehungsstils auf das
divergente Denken als Teilaspekt der Kreativität. Unpublished diploma thesis, University of Mannheim, 1976.

Kroh-Püschel, E., Rennert, M. & Wender, I. Imitation bei Reduktion der Modellkomponenten. Psychologische Beiträge, 1976, 18, 297-311.

Kroh-Püschel, E., Rennert, M. & Silberer, G. Soziale Beeinflussung und Informationskosten als Determinanten der Informationsnachfrage vor Entscheidungen. Zeitschrift für experimentelle und angewandte Psychologie, 1978, 25, 617-630.

Kroh-Püschel, E. & Wender, I. Modification der Bereitschaft zum Belohnungsaufschub durch Lernen an multiplen Modellen. Zeitschrift für Entwicklungspsychologie und Pädagogische Psychologie, 1978, 10, 305-314.

Kroh-Püschel, E. & Wender, I. Die Messung der Aufschuborientierung bei Kindern. Zeitschrift für Erziehungswissenschaftliche Forschung, 1979, 13, 103-117.

Ksiensik, M.I. Some problems in the application of Krantz, Luce, Suppes and Tversky's Axioms of measuring subjective probability. Unpublished manuscript, SFB 24, University of Mannheim, 1978.

Ksiensik, M.I. Scaling subjective probability under a measurement theoretical point of view. Unpublished manuscript, SFB 24, University of Mannheim, 1979.

Kumpf, M. Kognitive und Verhaltenskonsequenzen von Passivität bei Notfällen. Unpublished doctoral dissertation, University of Mannheim, 1978.

Kumpf, M. & Götz-Marchand, B. Reduction of cognitive dissonance as a function of magnitude of dissonance, differentiation, and self-esteem. European Journal of Social Psychology, 1973, 3, 255-270.

Kutschker, M. Empirische Untersuchung zum Investitionsgütermarketing. Unpublished manuscript, SFB 24, University of Mannheim, 1974.

Kutschker, M. Rationalität und Entscheidungskriterien komplexer Investitionsentscheidungen - ein empirischer Bericht. Unpublished manuscript, SFB 24, University of Mannheim, 1975.

Kutschker, M. & Roth, K. Das Informationsverhalten vor industriellen Beschaffungsentscheidungen. Unpublished manuscript, SFB 24, University of Mannheim, 1975.

Lamm, H. Intragroup effects of intergroup negotiation. European Journal of Social Psychology, 1973, 3, 179-192.

Lamm, H. Analyse des Verhandelns: Ergebnisse der sozialpsychologischen Forschung. Stuttgart: Enke, 1975.

Lamm, H. Negotiation in symmetric dyads as affected by information and costliness of bidding. European Journal of Social Psychology, 1976a, 6, 99-103.

Lamm, H. Dyadic negotiations under asymmetric conditions: Comparing the performance of the uninformed and of the informed party. European Journal of Social Psychology, 1976b, 6, 255-259.

Lamm, H. Group-related influences on negotiation behavior: Two-person negotiation as a function of representation and election. In H. Sauermann (Ed.), Contributions to experimental economics (Vol. 1). Tübingen: Mohr, 1978a.

Lamm, H. Intragruppen-Effekte auf Intergruppen-Verhandlungen. In M. Irle (Ed.), Kursus der Sozialpsychologie. Darmstadt: Luchterhand, 1978b.

Lamm, H. & Kayser, E. Verhandlungsvorbereitung und Verhandlungs-verhalten bei verschiedenen Kommunikations- und visuellen Kontaktmöglichkeiten. Zeitschrift für Sozialpsychologie, 1976, 7, 279-285.

Lamm, H. & Kayser, E. The allocation of monetary gain and loss following dyadic performance: The weight given to effort and ability under conditions of low and high intra-dyadic attraction. European Journal of Social Psychology, 1978a, 8, 275-278.

Lamm, H. & Kayser, E. An analysis of negotiation concerning the allocation of jointly produced profit or loss: The roles of justice norms, politeness, profit maximation, and tactics. International Journal of Group Tensions, 1978b, 8, 64-80.

Lamm, H. & Kayser, E. The effects of anticipation of future interaction on negotiation behavior (in preparation).

Lamm, H., Kayser, E. & Schanz, V. Allocation of monetary gain or loss produced by team work: An attributional analysis of the role of differences in members' ability and effort. Unpublished manuscript, SFB 24, University of Mannheim, 1978.

Lamm, H. & Kogan, N. Risk taking in the context of intergroup negotiation. Journal of Experimental Social Psychology, 1970, 6, 351-363.

Lamm, H. & Meyers, D.G. Group-induced polarization of attitudes and behavior. In L. Berkowitz (Ed.), Advances in experimental social psychology (Vol. 11). New York: Academic Press, 1978.

Lamm, H. & Rosch, E. Information and competitiveness of incentive structure as factors in two-person negotiation. European Journal of Social Psychology, 1972, 2, 459-462.

Lamm, H., Rost-Schaude, E. & Trommsdorf, G. Der Einfluß von Gruppendiskussion auf die Attraktivitätsbeurteilung bei riskanten Entscheidungen. In M. Irle (Ed.), Attraktivität von Entscheidungsalternativen und Urteilssicherheit. Zeitschrift für Sozialpsychologie, Beiheft 4. Bern: Huber, 1978.

Lamm, H. & Sauer, C. Discussion-induced shift toward higher demands in negotiation. European Journal of Social Psychology, 1974, 4, 85-88.

Lamm, H., Schaude, E. & Trommsdorff, G. Risky shift as a function of group members' value of risk and need for approval. Journal of Personality and Social Psychology, 1971, 20, 430-435.

Lamm, H., Schmidt, R.W. & Trommsdorff, G. Sex and social class as determinants of future orientation (time perspective) in adolescents. Journal of Personality and Social Psychology, 1976, 34, 317-326.

Lamm, H. & Schwinger, T. Die Größe individueller Bedürfnisse und Beiträge und die Art der Soziabeziehung zwischen den Empfängern als Determinanten der Bedürfnisberücksichtigung bei Aufteilungen. Unpublished manuscript, SFB 24, University of Mannheim, 1979.

Lamm, H. & Schwinger, T. Norms concerning distributive justice: Are needs taken into consideration in allocation decisions? Social Psychology Quarterly, 1980, 43, 425-429.

Lamm, H. & Schwinger, T. Höhe des Anreizes und Risiko des Scheiterns als Determinanten des Verhandlungsverhaltens von Repräsentanten und Nicht-Repräsentanten. In preparation (a).

Lamm, H. & Schwinger, T. Verhandlungen zwischen Repräsentanten und Nicht-Repräsentanten: Kognitive, emotionale und behaviorale Reaktionen des Nicht-Repräsentanten. In preparation (b).

Lamm, H. & Trommsdorff, G. Group versus individual performance on tasks requiring ideational proficiency: A review. European Journal of Social Psychology, 1973, 3, 361-388.

Lamm, H. & Trommsdorff, G. Group influences on probability judgments concerning social and political change. Psychological Reports, 1974, 35, 987-996.

Lamm, H., Trommsdorff, G., Burger, C. & Füchsle, T. Group influences on success expectancies regarding social influence attempts. Human Relations, 1980, 10, 673-685.

Lamm, H., Trommsdorff, G. & Kogan, N. Pessimism-optimism and risk taking in individual and group contexts. Journal of Personality and Social Psychology, 1970, 15, 366-374.

Lamm, H., Trommsdorff, G. & Rost-Schaude, E. Self image, perception of peers' risk acceptance, and risky shift. European Journal of Social Psychology, 1972, 2, 255-272.

Lamm, H., Trommsdorff, G. & Rost-Schaude, E. Group-induced extremization: A review of the evidence and a minority-change explanation. Psychological Reports, 1973, 33, 471-484.

Lang, S. Identifikationsleistung und Antwortpräferenzen von Personen mit unterschiedlichem beruflichem Status bei der Identifikation von Gastarbeitern. Unpublished diploma thesis, University of Mannheim, 1976.

Lilli, W. Das Zustandekommen von Stereotypen über einfache und komplexe Sachverhalte. Experimente zum klassifizierenden Urteil. Zeitschrift für Sozialpsychologie, 1970, 1, 57-79.

Lilli, W. Relative Akzentuierung und kategoriale Urteilsbildung: Kritische Bemerkungen zur absoluten Akzentuierungstheorie. Zeitschrift für Sozialpsychologie, 1972, 3, 287-296.

Lilli, W. Aktive und passive Bevorzugung von komplexen Stimuli in Abhängigkeit von kognitiver Urteilsdifferenziertheit. Psychologische Beiträge, 1973, 15, 291-300.

Lilli, W. Zur Konvergenz der absoluten und relativen Akzentuierungstheorie. Zeitschrift für Sozialpsychologie, 1975a, 6, 189-201.

Lilli, W. Soziale Akzentuierung. Stuttgart, 1975b.

Lilli, W. & Krolage, J. Zur Wirkung kognitiver Schemata bei der Beurteilung von Gesichtern. Unpublished manuscript, SFB 24, University of Mannheim, 1975.

Lilli, W. & Krolage, J. The functioning of a cognitive schema in the judgment of faces. European Journal of Social Psychology, 1976, 6, 491-494.

Lilli, W. & Krolage, J. Zur Stereotypisierung sozialer Reize. Zeitschrift für Sozialpsychologie, 1977, 8, 156-166.

Lilli, W., Krolage, J: & Rosch, E. Die Veränderung der Einschätzung von CDU und SPD und ihrer Kanzlerkandidaten im Bundestagswahlkampf 1976. Unpublished manuscript, SFB 24, University of Mannheim, 1977.

Lilli, W., Krolage, J. & Rosch, E. Stereotyping in a natural setting: Classification effects in the judgments of political parties and politicians during a German parliamentary election. Unpublished manuscript, University of Mannheim, 1978.

Lilli, W. & Lehner, F. Stereotype Wahrnehmung: Eine Weiterentwicklung der Theorie Tajfels. Zeitschrift für Sozialpsychologie, 1971, 2, 285-294.

Lilli, W. & Lehner, F. Akzentuierung und klassifikatorische Wahrnehmung. Zeitschrift für experimentelle und angewandte Psychologie, 1972, 19, 109-121.

Lilli, W. & Rosch, E. Der Einfluß von kognitiver Komplexität auf die Beurteilung sozialer Sachverhalte bei zwei verschiedenen Informationsmengen. Psychologische Beiträge, 1977, 19, 250-255.

Lilli, W. & Winkler, E. Accentuation under serial and non-seriel conditions: Further evidence in favour of the relative concept. European Journal of Social Psychology, 1973, 3, 209-212.

Marchand, B. Auswirkung einer emotional wertvollen und emotional neutralen Klassifikation auf die Schätzung einer Stimulusserie. Zeitschrift für Sozialpsychologie, 1970, 1, 264-274.

Mikula, G. & Schwinger, T. Inter-member relations and reward allocation: Theoretical considerations of affects. In H. Brandstätter, J.H. Davis & H. Schuler (Eds.), Dynamics of group decisions. Beverly-Hills: Sage, 1978.

Möntmann, V. & Irle, E. Bibliographie der wichtigen seit 1956 erschienenen Arbeiten zur Theorie der kognitiven Dissonanz. In M. Irle & V. Möntmann (Eds.), L. Festinger, Theorie der kognitiven Dissonanz. Bern: Huber 1978.

Möntmann, V., Katz, L. & Irle, M. Subjektive Hypothesen - Antezedensbedingungen für kognitive Dissonanz. In L. Eckensberger (Ed.), Bericht über den 31. Kongreß der Deutschen Gesellschaft für Psychologie in Mannheim 1978. Göttingen: Hogrefe, 1979, 366-368.

Müller, G.F. Interpersonales Konfliktverhalten: Eine experimentelle Untersuchung zum Einfluß des Geldanreizes und der Erfahrung auf den Konfliktlöseprozeß in einer dyadischen Verhandlungssituation. Unpublished doctoral dissertation, University of Mannheim, 1976.

Müller, G.F. Orientierungsdominanz in Verhandlungssituationen. Psychologie und Praxis, 1979, 2, 51-58.

Müller, G.F. Interpersonales Konfliktverhalten: Ein Test zweier Erklärungsmodelle. Unpublished manuscript, SFB 24, University of Mannheim, 1980a.

Müller, G.F. Machtzentriertes Verhalten bei der Konfliktregelung in Zwei-Personen-Gruppen (in preparation, 1980b).

Müller, G.F. & Crott, H.W. Gerechtigkeit in sozialen Beziehungen: Die Equity-Theorie. In D. Frey (Ed.), Sozialpsychologische Theorien. Bern: Huber, 1978a.

Müller, G.F. & Crott, H.W. Behavior orientation in bargaining. The dynamics of dyads. In H. Brandstätter, J.H. Davis & H. Schuler (Eds.), Dynamics of group decisions. Beverly-Hills: Sage, 1978b.

Müller, G.F. & Crott, H.W. Soziale Austauschprozesse und ihr ökonomischer Bezug: Die Equity-Theorie. In H.W. Crott & G. F. Müller (Eds.), Wirtschafts- und Sozialpsychologie. Hamburg: Hoffmann & Campe, 1978c.

Müller, G.F. & Crott, H.W. Der Einfluß der Verhandlungspraxis in gemischt erfahrenen Gruppen. In W. Albers, G. Bamberger & R. Selten (Eds.), Mathematical systems in economics, Nr. 45: Entscheidungen in kleinen Gruppen. Königstein: Hain, 1979.

Myers, D.G. & Lamm, H. The group polarization phenomenon. Psychological Bulletin, 1976, 83, 602-627.

Ochsmann, R. Revision kognitiver Urteile als Konsequenz von Entscheidungen: Ein Test der reformulierten Theorie der kognitiven Dissonanz. Unpublished doctoral dissertation, University of Mannheim, 1979.

Ochsmann, R. & Frey, D. Attraktivitätsänderungen der Entscheidungsalternativen als Möglichkeit der Reduktion kognitiver Dissonanz. In M. Irle (Ed.), Attraktivität von Entscheidungsalternativen und Urteilssicherheit. Zeitschrift für Sozialpsychologie, Beiheft 4, 1978, 88-100.

Raffée, H., Hefner, M., Schöler, M., Grabicke, K. & Jacoby, J. Informationsverhalten und Markenwahl. Die Unternehmung, Schweizerische Zeitschrift für Betriebswirtschaft. Bern-Stuttgart 1976, 2, 95-107.

Raffée, H., Sauter, B. & Silberer, G. Theorie der kognitiven Dissonanz und Konsumgüter-Marketing, Wiesbaden: Gabler, 1973.

Raffée, H., Schöler, M. & Grabicke, K. Informationsbedarf und Informationsbeschaffungsaktivitäten des privaten Haushalts. Unpublished manuscript, SFB 24, University of Mannheim, 1975.

Raffée, H. & Silberer, G. Ein Grundkonzept für die Erfassung und Erklärung des subjektiven Informationsbedarfs bei Kauf-entscheidungen des Konsumenten. Unpublished manuscript, SFB 24, University of Mannheim, 1975.

Rennert, M. Der Einfluß der Versuchssituation bei Imitations-experimenten. Archiv für Psychologie, 1975, 127, 70-77.

Rennert, M. & Wender, I. Verhaltensmodifikation bei auditiver und visueller Modelldarstellung sowie bei Instruktionen. Zeitschrift für experimentelle und angewandte Psychologie, 1975, 127, 499-513.

Rosch, E. Theoretische und meßtechnische Probleme bei der Er-fassung kognitiver Komplexität mit dem Role Construct Re-pertory-Text (Rep-Test). Unpublished manuscript, SFB 24, University of Mannheim, 1975.

Rosch, E. Zur Angemessenheit von Integrationsmodellen in der sozialen Eindrucksbildung. Zeitschrift für Sozialpsychologie, 1977, 8, 247-255.

Rosch, E. & Klump, H. Der Einfluß von Gruppenzugehörigkeit und Sympathiegrad physiognomisch beschriebener Gesichter auf die Zuschreibung von Persönlichkeitseigenschaften. Unpublished manuscript, SFB 24, University of Mannheim, 1975.

Rosch, E. & Müller, S. Klassifikatorisches Urteil - Randbedin-gungen zur Erklärung von Stereotypen. Zeitschrift für Sozial-psychologie, 1978, 9, 246-256.

Rosch, E., Spindler, H. & Klump, H. Der Einfluß unterschiedli-cher Zusatzinformationen auf die Personenbeurteilung. Un-published manuscript, SFB 24, University of Mannheim, 1976.

Rosch, M. Kognitive Steuerungsfunktion und Urteilsverhalten: Untersuchungen zur relativen und absoluten Akzentuierung. Unpublished diploma thesis, University of Mannheim, 1975.

Rost-Schaude, E. Attitüdenänderung durch Kommunikation in Klein-gruppen. Ein Experiment zur These der gruppeninduzierten Ex-tremisierung. Unpublished doctoral dissertation, University of Mannheim, 1975.

Roth, K. Informationsbeschaffung von Organisationen. Unpublish-ed doctoral dissertation, University of Mannheim, 1976.

Roth, K., Huppertsberg, B. & Schneider, J. Empirische Untersuchungen zum Investitionsgütermarketing - Verwenderbericht.
Unpublished manuscript, SFB 24, University of Mannheim.

Rühle, H. Informationsfunktion des Modells und Einfluß auf die
Informationsnachfrage von Beobachtern vor Entscheidungen.
Unpublished diploma thesis, University of Mannheim, 1975.

Sauer, C., Bauer, W., Ochsmann, R., Kumpf, M. & Frey, D. Eine
kognitive Erklärung von Alkoholismus. Eine Feldstudie. Unpublished manuscript, SFB 24, University of Mannheim, 1976.

Sauer, C., Frey, D., Irle, M., Kumpf, M. & Ochsmann, R.
Kognitive Konsequenzen der Wahl eines Verlierers. Zeitschrift
für Soziologie, 1977, 3, 297-301.

Sauter, B. Objektiver Informationsbedarf und Problemverein-
fachungsbeitrag von Informationen bei Kaufentscheidungen des
Konsumenten. Unpublished manuscript, SFB 24, University of
Mannheim, 1974.

Sauter, B. & Raffée, H. Informationswünsche als Indikatoren
für den Informationsbedarf und die Bereitschaft des Konsumenten zur Informationssuche. Unpublished manuscript, SFB 24,
University of Mannheim, 1973.

Schaefer, R.E. Diskussion spezieller Auszahlungsfunktionen zur
Bewertung subjektiver Wahrscheinlichkeitsschätzungen. Unpublished diploma thesis, University of Mannheim, 1969.

Schaefer, R.E. Entscheidungshilfe bei der Projektbewertung am
Beispiel eines Sonderforschungsbereiches. Unpublished manuscript, SFB 24, University of Mannheim, 1973.

Schaefer, R.E. Das Bayes Theorem als Spezialfall probabilisti-
scher Inferenz und das Basisproblem. In W. Tack (Ed.),
Bericht über den 29. Kongreß der Deutschen Gesellschaft für
Psychologie. Göttingen: Hogrefe, 1975, 417-419.

Schaefer, R.E. Probabilistische Informationsverarbeitung:
Theorie, Methoden und ein Experiment. Bern: Huber, 1976a.

Schaefer, R.E. The evaluation of individual and aggregated
subjective probability distributions. Organizational Behavior and Human Performance, 1976b, 15, 199-210.

Schaefer, R.E. Empirische Überprüfung eines Markoff Modells
zur Entscheidungsbildung in Gruppen. In W. Tack (Ed.), Bericht über den 30. Kongreß der Deutschen Gesellschaft für
Psychologie. Göttingen: Hogrefe, 1977, 265-267.

Schaefer, R.E. Urteile über Wahrscheinlichkeit, Sicherheit und
Nutzen: Komponenten für Entscheidungshilfen. Unpublished
habilitation, University of Mannheim, 1978a.

Schaefer, R.E. Eine entscheidungstheoretische Analyse des risky
shift Phänomens. Unpublished manuscript, SFB 24, University
of Mannheim, 1978b.

Schaefer, R.E. & Borcherding, K. The assessment of subjective probability distributions: A training experiment. Acta Psychologica, 1973a, 37, 117-129.

Schaefer, R.E. & Borcherding, K. A note on the consistency between two approaches to incorporate data from unreliable sources in Bayesian analysis. Organizational Behavior and Human Performance, 1973b, 9, 504-508.

Schaefer, R.E. & Borcherding, K. Wirkung von Feedback auf die Abgabe von Sicherheitsurteilen. In M. Irle (Ed.), Attraktivität von Entscheidungsalternativen und Entscheidungssicherheit. Zeitschrift für Sozialpsychologie 1978a, Beiheft 4, 147-155.

Schaefer, R.E. & Borcherding, K. Probleme bei der Messung von subjektiver Sicherheit. In M. Irle (Ed.), Attraktivität von Entscheidungsalternativen und Urteilssicherheit. Zeitschrift für Sozialpsychologie, 1978b, Beiheft 4, 133-146.

Schaefer, R.E., Borcherding, K., Grabicke, K., Raffée, H. & Schöler, M. Multi-attributive Bewertung von Produkten: Eine experimentelle Untersuchung. Unpublished manuscript, SFB 24, University of Mannheim, 1975.

Schaefer, R.E., Borcherding, K. & Laemmerhold, C. Consistency of future event assessments. In H. Jungermann & G. de Zeeuw (Eds.), Decision making and change in human affaires, Dordrecht: Reidel, 1977, 331-345.

Schätzle, T. & Grabicke, K. Paneluntersuchungen und ihre mögliche Anwendungsproblematik - Eine Erhebungsmethode zur Erforschung des Ablaufs tatsächlicher Entscheidungsprozesse. In H. Meffert, H. Steffenhagen & H. Freter (Eds.), Konsumentenverhalten und Information. Wiesbaden, 1979.

Schellhammer, E. Reizanalyse und Antwortverhalten bei der Verarbeitung attitüdenrelevanter Informationen. Unpublished diploma thesis, University of Mannheim, 1977.

Schifferer-Kornfeld, U. & Wender, I. Aufgabenrelevantes und aufgabenirrelevantes Imitieren in Abhängigkeit von der Art der Interaktion zwischen Modell und Beobachter, der Leistungsmotivation des Beobachters und des Verstärkungsmodus des Modells. In L.H. Eckensberger & K.S. Eckensberger (Eds.), Bericht des 28. Kongresses der Deutschen Gesellschaft für Psychologie in Saarbrücken 1972, Bd. 3. Göttingen: Hogrefe, 1974, 109-120.

Schleicher, G. Informationsbedarf und Informationsbeschaffung des Konsumenten bei Lebensmitteln - eine empirische Untersuchung, dargestellt anhand einer Stichprobe alter Menschen. Unpublished diploma thesis, University of Mannheim, 1978.

Schmidt, B., Dickenberger, D. & Gniech, G. Die Veränderung der Attraktivität von Alternativen durch Einengung der Wahlmöglichkeiten. In M. Irle (Ed.), Attraktivität von Entscheidungsalternativen und Urteilssicherheit. Zeitschrift für Sozialpsychologie, Beiheft 4, Bern: Huber, 1978.

Schmidt, R.W., Lamm, H. & Trommsdorff, G. Social class and sex
   as determinants of future orientation (time perspective) in
   adults. European Journal of Social Psychology, 1978, 8, 71-90.

Scholz, R.W. & Fleischer, A. Die Prognosegüte von Anspruchsni-
   veauvorhersagemodellen in einer realitätsnahen Verhandlungssituation (in preparation).

Schümer, R. Eine experimentelle Untersuchung zur sozialen Eindrucksbildung. Zeitschrift für Sozialpsychologie, 1971, 2,
   92-108.

Schümer, R. Kontexteffekte bei der Eindrucksbildung in Abhängigkeit von der Mehrdeutigkeit der Informationen. Unpublished
   manuscript, SFB 24, University of Mannheim, 1973a.

Schümer, R. Context effects in impression formation as a function of the ambiguity of test traits. European Journal of
   Social Psychology, 1973b, 3, 333-338.

Schümer, R. Untersuchungen zur Eindrucks- und Urteilsbildung.
   Unpublished manuscript, SFB 24, University of Mannheim, 1976.

Schwarz, N., Frey, D. & Kumpf, M. Interactive effects of writing and reading a persuasive essay on attitude change and
   selective exposure. Journal of Experimental Social Psychology, 1980, 16, 1-17.

Schwinger, T. Just allocations of goods: Decisions among three
   principles. In G. Mikula (Ed.), Justice and interaction.
   New York: Huber, 1980.

Semin, G.R., Rosch, E. & Chassein, J. A comparison of the common-sense and 'scientific' conceptions of extraversion-intro-
   version. European Journal of Social Psychology, 1980, 10.

Silberer, G. The cost-benefit model of the consumers search for
   information. Unpublished manuscript, SFB 24, University of
   Mannheim, 1975.

Trommsdorff, G. Intra- und Intergruppenprozesse beim Verhan-
   deln. Zeitschrift für Sozialpsychologie, 1971, 2, 75-91.

Trommsdorff, G. Veränderung zukunftsbezogener Urteile unter
   sozialen und nicht-sozialen Bedingungen. Unpublished habilitation, University of Mannheim, 1975.

Trommsdorff, G. Gruppeneinflüsse auf Zukunftsbeurteilungen.
   Meisenheim am Glan: Hain, 1978a.

Trommsdorff, G. Some social conditions of future orientation.
   Paper for European Association of Social Psychology, March,
   1978b.

Trommsdorff, G. Zukunftsorientierung delinquenter Jugendlicher.
   Paper for Sektionstagung Familien- und Jugendsoziologie der
   Deutschen Gesellschaft für Soziologie, April, 1978c.

Trommsdorff, G. Gesellschaftliche Probleme der Zukunftsorientierung von Jugendlichen. Kultur und Politik, 1979, 4, 57-
   66.

Trommsdorff, G., Burger, C., Füchsle, T. & Lamm, H. Erziehung für die Zukunft. Düsseldorf: Schwann, 1978.

Trommsdorff, G., Haag, C. & List, R. Zukunftsorientierung und Belohnungsaufschub bei weiblichen Delinquenten. Kölner Zeitschrift für Soziologie und Sozialpsychologie, 1979, 4, 732-745.

Trommsdorff, G. & Lamm, H. Cognitive and social influences on judgments concerning uncertain future events. XX. International Congress of Psychology, Tokyo, Abstract Guide, 1972, 643.

Trommsdorff, G. & Lamm, H. An analysis of future orientation and some of its social determinants. In J.T. Fraser & N.M. Lawrence (Eds.), The study of time, Vol. II. Heidelberg, New York: Springer, 1975.

Trommsdorff, G. & Lamm, H. Fragebogen zur Erfassung von Zukunftsorientierung. Unpublished manuscript, SFB 24, University of Mannheim, 1976.

Trommsdorff, G. & Lamm, H. Future orientation of institutionalized delinquents and nondelinquents. European Journal of Social Psychology, 1980, 10, 247-278.

Trommsdorff, G., Lamm, H. & Schmidt, R.W. A longitudinal study of adolescents' future orientation (future time perspective). Journal of Youth and Adolescence, 1979, 8, 131-147.

Trommsdorff, G. & Schmidt-Rinke, M. Situations- und Persönlichkeitsfaktoren als Bedingungen des Belohnungsaufschubes. Unpublished manuscript, SFB 24, University of Mannheim, 1979.

Upmeyer, A. Social perception and signal detectability theory: Group influence on discrimination and usage of scale. Psychologische Forschung, 1971, 34, 283-294.

Upmeyer, A. Ethnische Identifikation. Zeitschrift für Sozialpsychologie, 1976, 7, 143-153.

Upmeyer, A. & Cleary, P.D. Coin estimation as a two-stage process. Unpublished manuscript, SFB 24, University of Mannheim, 1975.

Upmeyer, A., Krolage, J., Etzel, G., Lilli, W. & Klump, H. Accentuation of information in real competing groups. European Journal of Social Psychology, 1976, 6, 95-97.

Upmeyer, A. & Layer, H. Effects of inferiority and superiority in groups on recognition memory and confidence. Psychologische Forschung, 1972, 35, 277-290.

Upmeyer, A. & Layer, H. Attitüden und Gedächtnis bei sozialer Urteilsbildung. Zeitschrift für Sozialpsychologie, 1973, 4, 181-194.

Upmeyer, A. & Layer, H. Accentuation and attitude in social judgment. European Journal of Social Psychology, 1974, 4, 469-488.

Upmeyer, A., Layer, H. & Schreiber, W.K. Über Verarbeitung ste-
reotypisierter Eigenschaften fremder Völker. Psychologische
Beiträge, 1972, 14, 521-540.

Upmeyer, A. & Schreiber, W. Effects of agreement and disagreement in groups on recognition memory performance and confidence. European Journal of Social Psychology, 1972, 2, 109-
128.

Wender, I., Neu-Weissenfeld, R. & Groffmann, K.-J. Der Einfluß
von Sozialstatus des Beobachters und der Verstärkungsart des
Modells auf Imitationsverhalten. Zeitschrift für Soziapsycho-
logie, 1974, 5, 292-299.

Winkler, E., Rosch, E. & Lilli, W. Faktorenanalyse der Rep-Test
Daten 110 weiblicher Versuchspersonen. Unpublished manuscript,
SFB 24, University of Mannheim, 1973.

Zaus, M. Elementary concepts for the probabilistic counterpart
of the foundations of measurement. Technical Report, University of California, Berkeley, Group in Logic and Methodology
of Science, 1976.

Zaus, M. & Wendt, D. A case of study in the design and assessment of hierarchical goal structures in applied multiattribute utility analysis. Proceedings of the 6th Research Conference on subjective probability, utility and decision making,
Warschau, 1977.

Author Index

Subject Index

Management Under Differing Value Systems

Political, Social, and Economical Perspectives in a Changing World
Edited by Günter Dlugos and Klaus Weiermair in Collaboration with Wolfgang Dorow
1981. 17 x 24 cm. XIV, 866 pp. Hardcover. DM 148,–; approx. US $67.50 ISBN 3 11 008553 4

This informative volume is concerned with value research and its use in explaining the fundamental exchange relationships inherent in the workplace. This collection of readings stems from the 1980 Toronto conference on "Management Under Differing Value Systems," combining a cross-section of authors from several industrialized nations.

Opening with a discussion on the role and concept of values in the social sciences in general, the book moves on to deal with topics such as perspectives on value change, values

and the employment relationship, values and the management process, and industrial democracy. The collection concludes with a number of comparative empirical studies on organizational structures and management processes.

These articles represent one of the most complete collections in the emerging field of value systems and management, combining a social science outlook with a business-oriented perspective. It will be an invaluable resource for managers, labor researchers, and social scientists alike.

Table of Contents

Walter de Gruyter · Berlin · New York

Verlag Walter de Gruyter & Co. · Genthiner Straße 13 · D-1000 Berlin 30 · Telefon (030) 2 60 05-0
Walter de Gruyter Inc. · 200 Saw Mill River Road · Hawthorne N. Y. 10532 · Telephone (914) 747-0110

DM prices are definite; $ prices are approximate and subject to fluctuation in the exchange rates.